The Different Forms of Abuse of Law and Process in the European Union

THE DIFFERENT FORMS OF ABUSE OF LAW AND PROCESS IN THE EUROPEAN UNION

BY DIMITRIS LIAKOPOULOS[1]

1 Full Professor of European Union Law at the Fletcher School-Tufts University (MA in international law and MA of Arts in Law and diplomacy). Full Professor of International and European Criminal and Procedural Law at the De Haagse Hogenschool-The Hague. Attorney at Law a New York and Bruxelles. ORCID ID: 0000-0002-1048-6468. The present work is updated until February 2019.

THE DIFFERENT FORMS OF ABUSE OF LAW AND PROCESS IN THE EUROPEAN UNION

Dimitris Liakopoulos

Published by:

Vandeplas Publishing, LLC – April 2019

801 International Parkway, 5th Floor
Lake Mary, FL. 32746
USA

www.vandeplaspublishing.com

ISBN 978-1-60042-308-6

Table of Contents

CHAPTER 1

CHAPTER 2

PART A

PART B

CHAPTER 4

CHAPTER 5

Dedicated to Sofia and Irini

CHAPTER 1

Methodological premise and introductory notions

RESEARCH OBJECTIVES AND SURVEY PERSPECTIVES

The present study/research aims to understand the functioning of prohibition on the abuse of law in the EU, as a "legal technique"[2] to deny the exercise of the right or exclude the application of EU law[3] where an abusive behavior by the private is found. Such an analysis is indeed the starting point for understanding more deeply the legal meaning of this prohibition, also by relating to other protection techniques that the Union system disposes[4]. More specifically, through a

2 R. IONESCU, L'abus de droit en droit de l'Union européenne, in C. KESSEDJIAN, Autonomie en droit européen Stratégie des citoyens, des entreprises et des Etats, LGDG, Paris, 2013, pp. 210ss.

3 It is now clear that the objective is not to illustrate the notion of abuse of law developed in the various areas of EU legal order. It can be considered that the analysis of "European Union" jurisprudence with the objective of verifying whether the EU legal system knows the notion of abuse of rights constitutes a prospect of investigation now outdated: the existence of such a notion, in fact, at present cannot be questioned.

4 See ex multis: D. ANDERSON, Abuse of rights, in Judicial Review, 11, 2006, pp. 348ss. L. CERIONI, The "abuse of rights" in EU company law and EU tax law: A re-reading of the ECJ case law and the quest for a unitary notion, in European Business Law Review, 21 (4), 2010 pp. 783ss. A. DE GRAAF, M. EVERS, Limiting benefit shopping: Use and abuse of EC law, in EC Tax Review, 18, 2009, pp. 4ss; R. DE LA FERIA, Prohibition of abuse of (European Union law): The creation of a new general principle of EC law through Tax, in Common Market Law Review, 45, 2008, pp. 396ss. R. DE LA FERIA, S. VOGENAUER, Prohibition of abuse of law: a new general principle of EU law?, Oxford University Press, Oxford, 2011. V. EDWARDS, P. FARMER, The concept of abuse in the freedom of establishment of companies: A case of double standards?, in F.G. JACOBS (a cura di), Continuity and change in EU law: Essays in Honour of Sir Francis Jacobs, Oxford University Press, Oxford, 2007, p. 205 ss. A. KJELLGREN, On the border of abuse: The jurisprudence of the European CJEU on circumvention, fraud and other misuses of European Union law, in European Business Law Review, 11 (1), 2000, pp. 180ss. R. IONESCU, L'abus de droit en droit de l'Union européenne, cit; F. LAGONDET, L'abus de droit dans la jurisprudence communautaire, in Journal des Tribunaux Droit Européen, 95, 2003, pp. 9ss. A. LENAERTS, The general principle of the prohibition of abuse of rights: a critical position on its role in a codified European contract law, in European Review of Private Law, 18, 2010, pp. 1122ss. L. NEVILLE BROWN, Is there a general principle of abuse of rights in European European Union law?, in D. CURTIN et al. (a cura di), Institutional dynamics of European integration: Essays in Honour of Henry G. Schermers, Martinus Nijhoff Publishers, Leiden, 1994, pp. 512ss. A. SAYDÉ, Abuse of EU law and regulation of the internal market, Oxford University Press, Oxford, 2014. P. SCHAMMO, Arbitrage and abuse of rights in the EC legal system, in European Law Journal, 14, 2008,

comparison with the use of alternative techniques, the aim of the research is to define whether this prohibition can be considered as an effective technique in EU law, that is to say concretely applicable to the fight against abuse.

It must be stated that the use of this prohibition proves to be undoubtedly problematic within the Union, both for structural and ideological reasons. An example of this problem is the growing attention that the doctrine has shown in recent years. The concept of abuse in EU is a recent figure that is still slowly developing in practice with special acknowledgment to the contribution (also of reflection and in-depth study) of the Court of Justice of the European Union (CJEU). The face of various indications is not always unambiguous on the part of the jurisprudence, doctrine, institutions of the Union, as well as the variety of situations in which the abuse is invoked and the multiple meanings it assumes from time to time. Thus, it is not always simple for the interpreter to establish the nature and function of the prohibition in question.

Precisely, in order to understand whether an interpretative scheme can be found that makes it possible to clarify the scope of the prohibition on the abuse of the right[5], the first part of the research will be devoted to a critical analysis of CJEU jurisprudence. This analysis will help reconstruct what circumstances may be considered an abuse of law from the European Union's viewpoint and if the related prohibition can operate in such cases.

However, the prohibition in question does not exhaust the cases in which EU law allows member states and institutions to sanction abuse, and the use of other and different legal instruments is found in law. First, we will analyze the alternative mechanisms employed by CJEU to counteract abusive behavior, such

pp. 352ss. D. SIMON, A. RIGAUX, La technique de la consécration d'un nouveau principe général du droit communautaire: l'exemple de l'abus de droit, in M. BLANQUET (a cura di) Mélanges en hommage à Guy Isaac: 50 ans de droit communautaire, Presse de l'università de Toulouse, Toulouse, 2004, pp. 560ss. K. SØRENSEN, Abuse of rights in European Union law: A principle of substance or merely rhetoric?, in Common Market Law Review, 43, 2006, pp. 423ss. D. TRIANTAFYLLOU, L'interdiction des abus de droit en tant que principe général du droit communautaire, in Cahiers de Droit Européen, 38, 2002 pp. 612ss. S. VRELLIS, Abus et fraude dans la jurisprudence de la Cour de Justice des Communautés Européennes, in H. GAUDEMET-TALLON, J.P. LANCET (a cura di), Vers de nouveaux equilibres entre ordres juridiques: Liber Amicorum H. Gaudemet-Tallon, ed. Dalloz, Paris, 2008, pp. 634ss. D. WAELBROECK, La notion d'abus de droit dans l'ordre juridique communautaire, in Mélanges en hommages à J.V. Louis, ed. Bruylant, Bruxelles, 2003, vol. I, p. 595 ss.

5 It's affirmed that: "(...) this primacy of iurisdictio over the legislative power is due to the fact that statutory tools are inadequate to contrast abuse phenomenon" (P. PIANTAVIGNA, Tax abuse in European Union law: A theory, in EC Tax Review, 20, 2011, pp. 135). If this statement is valid in principle with reference to abuse in internal law, the present research aims to demonstrate how, in reality, with reference to abuse of law involving several systems and jurisprudential instruments to prove inadequate.

as restrictive interpretation of the scope of EU rules and acceptance of the invocation by member states to override reasons of general interest to fight against abusive practices. In this regard, the study of the possible interrelations between the various evoked "palliatives" and the consequences of using one rather than the other is worthy of further study. Lastly, attention will be paid to the consequences of CJEU's attitude toward national legislation, focusing on the role that the national and Union legislators can play in the fight against abuse.

ABUSE OF LAW: A FIRST GENERAL DEFINITION IN ORDER TO UNDERSTAND THE RATIONALE OF THE PROHIBITION

The abuse of law is one of the most controversial elaborations within the national legal systems that is, still today, subject to a lively and not over-dated doctrinal and jurisprudential debate regarding its configurability. The notion in question is configured as "polymorphous" in relation to the various (national and supranational) areas in which it is emphasized, so that it is almost impossible to provide a single, confined definition[6].

Nevertheless, it is considered necessary to establish some fixed points in this construction, albeit in general terms, in order to understand the rationale of prohibition.

The difficulty of providing a definition of the abuse is already at the national level. Indeed, civil law systems have also generally accepted the theory of abuse of law but do not offer a unitary notion of abuse, since the relative modalities diverge, sometimes even sensibly, if this is generally sanctioned. Moreover, it cannot be underestimated that at the national level, as supranational, an important contribution to the elaboration of this principle comes from the jurisprudence. Yet, the latter is an aspect that brings with it further difficulties of a practical nature, starting from the relief that "the judge must be daily invested with a variegated series that allows the progressive clarification of the limits to the exercise of the right"[7].

6 L. NEVILLE BROWN, Is there a general principle of abuse of rights in European European Union law?, op. cit., pp. 513-515.

7 Suffice it to recall that traditionally two different conceptions of abuse have been elaborated, which can also be combined with each other: according to subjective theory an abuse can be found in the formally correct use of a right with the intention to damage third parties. An abuse is found when the owner of the right contradicts the social function assigned to the rule used. R. IONESCU, L'abus

Without wishing to dwell on the debate[8] concerning the delimitation of the concept of abuse and the criteria of application in national laws, the abuse can be defined as a juridical category referring to the anomalous exercise of or beyond the limits of a right by its owner. In fact, the anomaly is found in this: the right is formally exercised in accordance with the conditions laid down by the law that gives the right, but the result that is achieved is contrary to the objective of the standard.

Analyzed in the words that compose it, the formula is presented, at first impression, as intimately contradictory, approaching a sort of "oxymoron". On one hand, if the term "law" refers to a subjective legal situation of advantage attributed by a law to a subject towards other subjects, the possibility of abuse leads inevitably to the idea that the exercise of a right, in itself a lawful act, is a source of responsibility. The judge is therefore left with the right to judge ex post facto, an act that prima facie presented itself in the capacity to exercise the right. The contradiction inherent in this figure is well understood by referring to the well-known brocardo qui iure sua utitur neminem laedit.

On the other hand, we cannot neglect that, in cohabitation with other rights and positions of advantage, every right is subject to multiple limits, including those that can be deduced from the social regulatory system as a whole. The contradiction that has just been highlighted proves to be more apparent than real, on the condition of distinguishing a static moment of the story by a dynamic moment. This split, due to the necessary existence of an indeterminate space between the norm and the case of life, is substantiated in the concrete exercise of the same by its owner[9].

It is clear in each case is that the notion in question, to an extent not clearly defined, nor easily definable, brings with it, and is substantiated in, a limitation to the exercise of the right, and therefore, as such, cannot that is exceptional, as well as justified.

---

de droit en droit de l'Union européenne, in C. KESSEDJIAN, Autonomie en droit européen Stratégie des citoyens, des entreprises et des Etats, op. cit., pp. 208-211, which distinguishes between subjective, subjective temperate and objective conception.

8 A. ZALASINSKI, Some basic aspects of the concept of abuse in the tax case law of the European CJEU of Justice, in Intertax, 2008, pp. 160ss.

9 V. KARAYANNIS, L'abus de droits découlant de l'ordre juridique communautaire. A propos de l'arret C-367/96 Alexandros Kefalas e.a./Elliniko Dimosio (Etat hellenique), in Cahiers de Droit Européen, 36, 1999, pp. 521ss.

What justification then exists to the prohibition of abuse? In general, the principle finds its rationale in the common sense, in an idea of substantial justice that makes up for the failure of necessarily abstract and general legislation. Therefore, it is unable to prevent a priori the possibility of distortion in the concrete case by the owner of formal law[10]. What is at stake is the tension between the rigid application of the norm and its "spirit". In such situations, the prohibition of abuse of law functions in the same way as a corrective mechanism. Through which, the abusive exercise of the legal situation of advantage conferred by that rule to normal use will be reduced, reconnecting it to principles that act as a standard behavior, such as good faith, morality, justice, and respect for the purpose of the norm.

There is therefore a close correlation between the principle we are discussing and the rationale of the juridical rules abused from time to time. Far from being considered as values in themselves, these rules are nothing but products of certain causes and at the service of certain objectives, which co-determine their interpretation, leading in some cases to a distancing, even notable, from the literal text. Only referring to the objective of the rule, we can determine whether its invocation or application is in conformity with its "spirit". Looking at the will of the historical legislator and the circumstances of the moment, the use made of a rule can be considered as normal or not, whereby an abuse is only found in the latter case, according to the brocardo abusus non tollit usum.

Also, at the EU level, the problem of abuse arises essentially with regard to those legal situations of advantage deriving from directly applicable "European" rules, which attribute, in a more or less detailed manner, prima facie a precise legal protection to the agent. It can be said that even in the EU legal system, as well as in national law, abuse of rights must be conceived, in general terms, as a limit to the exercise of a right[11]. The private, benefiting from a right descending by EU law, exercises it in conditions that exceed the threshold of normality implicit in the rule in question: abuse is a prohibitive concept, and its purpose consists not so much in defining the content of law, as in setting its limits[12].

10 D. TRIANTAFYLLOU, L'interdition des abus de droit, op. cit., pp. 612ss.

11 C. JOSSERAND, Essais de téléologie juridique, I,-De l'esprit des droits et de leur relativité, Théorie dite de l'abus de droit, ed. Dalloz, Paris, 1939, pp. 245ss, which is defined the abuse as: "celui qui, accompli en vertu d'un droit subjectif dont les limites ont été respectées, est cependant contraire au droit envisagé dans son ensemble et en tant que juridicité (...)".

12 D. SIMON, A. RIGAUX, La technique de la consécration d'un nouveau principe général du droit communautaire, op. cit., pp. 564.

In this regard, the famous definition formulated by the French civilian Planio[13] according to which "le droit cesse là où l'abus commence" remains current. This clearly shows how the issue of abuse ultimately resolves to define the substantial content of the subjective situation. Moreover, the scope of the faculties recognizes to the subject who is the owner. In other words, assessing whether the concrete exercise of a right is abusive, or not, does not mean that it delimits the scope of the right on a substantive level.

Abuse, however, takes on an original connotation in the context of EU law. Understood as synonymous with circumvention, it goes beyond the classical theme concerning the subjective rights, without excluding it altogether, to invest in the complex relations between EU and national laws. Particular reference is made to connection techniques that allow retreating to the normative discipline applicable to subjective legal situations of private subjects[14].

In fact, alongside the just delineated meaning of abuse, which recurs first of all in the law of national legal systems, a different and broader scope can be set up, which operates both in inter and vertical relations between citizens, states, and the European Union. Here, the term abuse is synonymous with circumvention, and the relative prohibition prevents a subject from exploiting a benefit derived from the formal respect of a rule, but whose use goes beyond the objectives of the standard itself[15]. On the other, the notion of abuse just described is also known in most legal systems of member states. It is therefore not surprising that the case law of the Union was naturally brought to bear on abusive behavior, both through the transmigration of national concepts, thanks to the numerous questions submitted by national judges, and because, as a rule of reason, abuse is also a necessary limitation to EU law[16].

13 M. PLANIOL, Traité Élémentaire de Droit Civil-Tome II, LGDJ, Paris, 1939, par. 871.

14 T. TRIDIMAS, Abuse of right in EU law, op. cit., pp. 1-2.

15 We take, for example, in consideration: art. 35 of Directive 2004/38/EC of the European Parliament and Council of 29 April 2004 on the right of Union citizens and their family members to move and reside freely within the territory of member states, amending Regulation (EEC) 1612/68 and repealing Directives 64/221/EEC, 68/360/EEC, 72/194/EEC, 73/148/EEC, 75/34/EEC, 75/35/EEC, 90/364/EEC, 90/365/EEC and 93/96/EEC (OJ, L 158, pag. 77); and art. 11 of Council Directive 90/434/EEC of 23 July 1990 on the common system of taxation applicable to mergers, divisions, transfers of assets and exchanges of shares concerning companies of different member states (OJ, L 225, pp. 1).

16 Precisely the stability of the market constitutes the objective of protecting legal certainty. The identification of the legal value of legal certainty. What was controversial was the coordination of the same principle with respect to the other norms of primary law. The identification of proportionality, as a criterion for applying legal certainty, as a general principle of European Union law, has led to the identification of the concrete forms of protection of the stability of the legal and economic

framework. Consequently, the same legal treatment of protection against foreign investors, whose investment risks being frustrated by unforeseen and/or unpredictable interventions by Member States, must now be recognized also by companies that only operate within the national territory. In any case, it will be fundamental to balance the aforementioned legal certainty with the additional general requirements that underlie the adoption of the authoritative measures: the suitability to achieve the public goal and the impossibility of adopting less invasive measures. They constitute the two parameters of detail that allow respect of proportionality and, therefore, consideration of legitimate intervention of the State in the market. On the contrary, the certainty of the law is different in relation to the phase of execution of economic activities. If, in fact, the competition law seems to guarantee the freedom of companies also by the undue intrusion of public administrations, as well as by abuses, the same rules discount certain differences in the jurisprudential application that oscillate between the definition of the strict prohibition of conduct and agreements between companies up to the evaluation of the reasonableness of the same with respect to the further objectives of a public nature. Also in this case, the CJEU, even if it has never recognized a complete application of the US rule of reason, has led to the application of a sort of proportionality adapted to the requirements of protection of competition. In this way, agreements are justified between companies, concerted practices or abuses of a dominant position that result in the benefiting of consumers or of better protection of further publicity needs that must be balanced with free competition. In any case, whether it is access to the market or protection of competition, legal certainty remains an absolute prerogative for companies that needs constant balancing with the further provisions of the Treaties. The national judges are called to the material exercise of reconciliation, which, through the examined procedural instruments, can directly apply the principles set out in the body of work and provide an effective protection to companies whose rights have suffered a compression. There remains, however, a large limit to the effectiveness of legal certainty: its european source means that its direct application can only be invoked in matters falling within the scope of European Union law. In the EU, although there has recently been a greater acceptance that article 101, article 102 TFUE and merger analysis should converge around a single analytical framework based on uniform concepts, it has been seen that the system governing agreement in fact continues to rely much more heavily on presumptions of both illegality and legality than in the US and in the EU's own dominance and merger frameworks. In consequence, few agreement cases exist in which a balancing of actual or likely restrictions on parameters of competition against efficiencies is actually required. Our analysis proposes that EU decision-takers should become more willing to analyse whether theory, experience and especially context justifies a finding that an agreement is restrictive by object. Up until now, they have been more disposed to have regard to experience and context as a mechanism for expanding the by object category than as a means of narrowing it. To ensure that the object category is not overinclusive, it is essential that it be confined to agreements demonstrating a high likelihood of anticompetitive effects (capability, potential or likelihood of anticompetitive is insufficient) and that it should not be applied in cases where the restraint on competition is not obvious. If the breadth of the object category is more realistically limited, a claimant will more frequently be required to demonstrate restrictive effects (actual or likely) before the parties can be required to provide a robust justification of the efficiencies within article 101(3) TFUE. The EU administrative framework provides a flexible forum for the competing effects of agreements to be scrutinised and balanced. If the EC were to bring more effect cases, resources could be concentrated on developing the article 101 framework (rather than the limits of the by object category) and clarifying important issues such as the role of the EU ancillary restraints and objective necessity principles. Although these doctrines may have made sense in the pre-modernized era (and when getting an article 101(3) TFUE exemption for an agreement was frequently impractical) and make sense as characterization mechanisms, they are harder to rationalise within a modernized framework which requires economic analysis at both the article 101(1) and article 101(3) TFUE stage of the assessment. Not only do the cases seem to miss some important steps in competition analysis but they appear to demand inquiries under article 101(1) TFUE which duplicate or overlap with analysis required in the process of applying article 101(3) TFUE. We see a larger purpose for courts and antitrust enforcement agencies in the EU and the US to focus additional attention upon the framework

In the last forty years[17], the problem of abuse and the related ban has seen an exponential development in the EU regulatory system as an independent legal system both in international and member states law.

The expression "le droit cesse ou l'abus commence"[18] has been used to summarize that particular situation of abuse of law that is revealed in the limit outside the exercise, potentially full and absolute, of a subjective right whose recognition implies attribution of a certain freedom. The subtle line that characterizes this institution is clear: what is defined in terms of freedom or law can

---

for assessing restrictive agreements. Intense discussions about disparities in how the two jurisdictions treat unilateral conduct seem to eclipse important differences in the evolution of the essential tools for assessing concerted action. Mutual reflection on the different evolutionary paths could deepen understanding about possible doctrinal options and inform improvements in both regimes. This also could be the occasion for a broader examination of how experience across all of the shared areas of competition law-agreements, dominant firm conduct, and mergers-could guide the establishment of a unified analytical framework that ensures that the assessment of all forms of antitrust-relevant conduct is liberated from the need to place behaviour in certain historical categories and instead concentrates upon core concepts involving the presence of actual or likely anticompetitive effects and the existence of valid business justifications. t may become clear at a subsequent stage that a standard-based approach more accurately captures the nature and the likely effects of the practice in question. This fact does not mean, however, that legal change is easy, even in the absence of a formal doctrine of stare decisis. By the same token, the fact that CJEU (and national Courts, too) stick to a particular line of case law cannot in any way be interpreted as meaning that judges are not familiar with contemporary debates. If there is something that stems from the analysis above, it is that EU courts have a very solid grasp of mainstream economics and have regularly displayed remarkable intuition about the logic behind corporate strategies. Adherence to a well-established precedent simply reveals that there are typically other factors at play when the convenience of overruling it is considered. The question is, as a result, far more complex in practice. Judges, regardless of the discipline, are routinely asked to rule in instances in which previous judgments sit at odds with each other. Refining doctrines and addressing contradictions between individual cases are essential tasks fulfilled by courts. Much could be gained-more, it is submitted, than what would be gained by sticking to precedent-if the two lines of CJEU jurisprudence converged into the approach (standard-based) that is now known to be more appropriate and that has decidedly been endorsed by the CJUE in future. For further analysis see: D. LIAKOPOULOS, The regulation of transnational mergers in international and european law, Brill/Martinus Nijhoff Publishers, The Hague, 2010. D. LIAKOPOULOS, The regulatory autonomy in the EU and WTO after Lisbon Treaty and the need of reform of the EU Institutions for the commercial disputes, op. cit.

17 CJEU, C-26/62, Van Gend & Loos of 5 February 1963, ECLI:EU:C:1963:1, ECR 00003, CJEU concludes that "the European Union constitutes a new kind of legal system in the field of international law, in favor of which states have renounced, even if in limited sectors, their sovereign powers, an order that recognizes as subjects not only member states but also their citizens (...)". In this sense, also judgment C-6/64, Costa v. ENEL of 15 July 1964, ECLI:EU:C:1964:66, ECR 01141 states that "(...) unlike the common international treaties, the EEC Treaty has established its own legal order integrated into the legal system of member states to the entry into force of the Treaty and that national courts are bound to observe. "In fact, according to the court states "have limited their sovereign powers, albeit in circumscribed fields, and thus created a complex of law binding for their citizens and for themselves (...)".

18 M. PLANIOL, Traitè élémentaire de droit civil, op. cit., pp. 269ss.

integrate an abusive practice when an action, although positively admitted and recognized, is in contrast with the ultimate economic and social goals of the norm, or better, of the reference system. Abuse and law are two complementary aspects, where the former is a borderline for the exercise of the second.

From a purely theoretical point of view, the abuse finds its origin in the tension between the freedom to act and the personal goals underlying this action. The clash between the aforementioned elements constitutes the fertile ground on which it is grafted and grows. In fact, the subjective right is articulated in the (legitimate) possibility to assume a behavior foreseen by the norm and, therefore, to be able to act to satisfy an interest worthy of protection at the legislative level. Since this, understood as a license, is a "positive" faculty, the legal system cannot tolerate the pursuit of objectives not contemplated by the normative ratio, which presents itself as the very negation of a corpus iuris. Configuring itself in terms of faculty not subject to any rule, it stands in open contrast with the principle of systematicity and consistency that characterizes a system of rules. Here, the case of abuse arises from the continuous and inexorable commitment by the legal system to provide individuals, whether natural or legal persons, an area for the pursuit of "personal" interests worthy of protection by the order, without this being able to encroach on an action without a legal basis.

THE SAME ETYMOLOGICAL ROOT OF THE TERM LEADS TO REFLECTION

The abuse derives from the term ab-uti, which alludes to an improper or unusual use of the subjective right, such as to make the behavior of the individual exceeding the sphere of the actual exercisable prerogatives[19]. To be able to configure a hypothesis of abuse, it is necessary to ascertain whether the act carried out by the subject is attributable to the content of the right itself or emerges in such a way as to represent abuse as an excess of law. Precisely on the problem of the juridical autonomy of such an institute, the doctrine did not express itself in a uniform way. A part of it, with different arguments, denied autonomous legal dignity to the case in point. On one hand, it can be said that the abuse of law is not attributable to the sphere of lawfulness, because the abusive act is not

19 In Latin, the verb abutor is used in the sense of not only benefiting but also of "misusing something" (and therefore abusing), as well as consuming something completely and squandering.

allowed, and the order sanctions its behavior. Nor does is the abuse ascribed to the sphere of the illicit behavior because the abusive act it is not punctually prohibited by a specific regulation, where the only thing that contravenes a ban is illegal. On the other hand, the idea of abuse has been supported as the result of a gap in the rule of law, such that an attentive lawmaker carefully calibrates the normative case, circumscribes it, and takes away space from the category of abuse. This is because every hypothesis of misleading normative follows the paradigm: and it will not be necessary, to underline its illegality, in order to resort the category of abuse[20].

On the contrary, the orientation that supported the independence of the institution in question with respect to the category of excess of law is more shareable. Since the latter involves a trespassing of the permitted business, the abuse cannot be considered a substitute because it has a peculiarity that justifies its construction as an independent category: the apparent conformity of the subject's behavior to the content of his right. The essence of abuse of law is precisely the conduct of behavior apparently consistent with the content of a subjective legal position attributed by the legal system, but in reality, it contrasts the substantial reasons underlying this attribution. Another element of distinction between the categories in question is the fact that, while in the case of excess, the encroachment from the content of the right is immediately detectable as the act going beyond the limits set to the subject's prerogatives and falls outside the normative dictate in the case of abuse. On the other, the encroachment is not immediately perceived because the act, abstractly compatible with the content of law, is consistent with the scheme outlined by the case in point. In other words, the abuse of right is detectable only on the basis of an assessment activity carried out retrospectively of the interest concretely pursued by the subject. From a purely pro-European point of view, the abuse has been placed and posed as the synthesis of the binomial freedom of action or choice versus the ultimate goal of the action or choice. While the founding EU treaties grant fundamental rights to subjects in a legal space without frontiers, this raises the problem of containing all those phenomena in which the formal exercise of the right attributed is completely incoherent with the objective of law, giving rise to possible forms of contrast between what has been granted and, therefore, what has actually been achieved.

20 M. PLANIOL, Traitè élémentaire de droit civil, op. cit.

The interest in the topic in question stems from the fact that, especially in case law, the principle has been repeatedly stated that it is not possible to abuse European law in an abusive or fraudulent manner.

There are two considerations that can be drawn from this formula. Firstly, that the individual can "exploit" the freedoms attributed to him to his advantage. Therefore, the individual has the concrete possibility of obtaining results that are in contrast with the ultimate goal of the system, although the behavior is formally conferring with the letter of the provision authorizing that action. Secondly, analyzing the aforementioned expression according to a literal interpretation, CJEU seems to want to identify a general principle/category that characterizes the entire EU legal system. Indeed, this seems to stand up to a safeguard clause to protect a system that, due to its complexity, could be the subject of improper use.

Naturally, the abuse in the European context is shown differently from that at the national level. Although the goal is the same, i.e. the consistency of the system, the ways to operate are, octus oculi, different. If from an internal point of view, it is a matter of exploiting the small incongruities or flaws that may exist within a specific field of law. From a supranational vision, it is based on identifying and, therefore, choosing the legal system that be more favorable to the interests of the individual, through the legitimate exercise of EU fundamental freedoms.

From the point of view of competition between the legal systems and, thus, of the circulation of regulatory models, the possibility of using European law for purposes that are not consistent with the legislative provision is realized. As you know, one of the objectives of EU law is to achieve a greater degree of harmonization and approximation of national laws and not to replace oneself different national rights. The plurality of legislation, an intrinsic characteristic of the Union itself, places the European subject in the best conditions for tracing the most favorable national law, thus obtaining results that are difficult to reach if their freedom of action emerges only within the legal system of belonging. In light of this, there is the need to define what is the abuse of law according to the European legislation and how the article prohibits the illegal or fraudulent use of EU law.

It is important to anticipate that the abuse occurs differently depending on whether the analysis is carried out on the normative level or on the jurisprudential one.

It may be possible at a "legislative" level to identify a particular form of reluctance to define what should be understood by abuse, from the point of view of living law. Instead, CJEU, through a series of important rulings that we will analyze in the next paragraphs, sought as much as possible to trace the characteristic elements of the question under study with the intent (so it transpires!) to elaborate a true theory.

The legal framework is complicated by the fact that the reference to the notion inevitably invests the problem of relationship between European and national law regarding the division of tasks between the internal judges and the European court when an illegal practice is revealed. Therefore, there is a need to combat such circumstances. To this must be added the problem of the exact identification of the boundaries of the burden of proof in the procedural field: it will be necessary to clarify which evidence will be indispensable in litigation to avoid that the action taken is considered abusive and, thus, not consistent with the objectives of the European Union.

Because of the many critical issues, this study will have as its ultimate objective not only to attempt a reconstruction of the abuse of EU law but above all to check whether the simultaneous prohibition can be elevated to the general principle of the European system .Hence, this study will not be limited only and exclusively to certain sectors or areas, such as tax, as a mere interpretive canon that should characterize the same European provisions. Therefore, such offense would not worthy of autonomous legal status of cornerstone of EU law, as an expression of the principle of good faith or of consistency system.

PROHIBITION OF ABUSE OF LAW: A TRANSVERSAL PROBLEM TO THE EUROPEAN LEGAL SYSTEM

The prohibition of abuse of law is a principle of civil origin that has always aroused great attention on the part of doctrine and jurisprudence both for its controversial configurability and for its disruptive scope.

Introducing the concept of "abuse of law" for the purposes of reflection on its relevance in criminal law is a complex matter, since such a research object requires, for its treatment, to move continuously between the different plans and sectors of the sources of law positive. This serves as a means to operate raids in the philosophy of law, and to consider lackluster legislative data, both as as a colorful jurisprudential panorama and a careful doctrinal elaboration.

The discourse on the abuse of rights is, in fact, a discourse on the limits of subjective legal positions, on the gradualness of the concepts of lawful and illicit behavior, but also on the interpretation of rules, the discretion of the deciding bodies and the contact points between law and reasons external to law, such as justice or morality. Wishing to accept, for the purposes of our reflection, the notion that currently gathers around itself the greatest number of consents, we can affirm that it is an improper exercise of a right the exercise of the latter with purposes other than the purpose for which it was attributed by the law, that is to say the realization of a certain interest of its owner.

This reconstruction considers elements constituting the abuse of right: a) the ownership of a right by a subject; b) the possibility that the concrete exercise of the right can be carried out according to a plurality of methods that are not rigidly predetermined; c) the fact that this exercise was actually carried out according to methods that, although formally respectful of the law, are open to criticism regarding a legal or extra-juridical criterion; and d) the fact that, due to this mode of operation, there is an unjustified disproportion between the benefit obtained by the right holder and the sacrifice imposed on the counterparty.

The institute, in its modern form, was born as a doctrinal and jurisprudential creation within the French system between the nineteenth and twentieth centuries, with the aim of acting as a corrective to the dogmas of legal formalism and the absolutism of rights (first of all, the right to property) characterizing the Napoleonic system. The ability to cope with the distortions produced by the formal application of the rules, at the time crossed by the myth of the law and the legislator, is the characteristic trait and raison d'être of the category. Thus, it is confirmed by the fact that the same category had not found complete elaboration in different legal systems, which are not characterized by the centrality of the law.

The theory of abuse of law does not find an enunciation in Roman jurisprudence, although it has categories such as the emulative acts or the exceptio doli, to which, as we shall see, the abuse is traced back to the doctrine that deals with it in modern times. This is because the creative force of Roman jurisprudence, which is allowed to adapt the right to the concrete situation and participate in its evolution, paralyzing the claims of the civil jus that appear unfair or protecting new claims leads to absorb the reason for the abuse in the elastic operate from various Roman sources. In intermediate law, attention focuses on the concept of abnormal use of a right, which circumvents the rationale of law and, in so doing, produces the result of incurring iniquatates. In this era, the notion of abuse of law, elaborated by glossators and jurists of common law, serves as a link between the sphere of law and of morality. In particular, elaborating the Christian doctrine, the category of the abuse of law concerns the problem of morality of law, of the moral legitimacy to make use of one's own right. However, even in this system characterized by legal pluralism, judicial practice and doctrine concur to adapt the right to reality, also through the instrument of aequitas, and therefore, the practical result offered by the abuse of law does not need its conceptual systematization. Coming to the present day, it should be noted that in common law countries, there is no autonomous elaboration of the theory of abuse of law.

The origin of the category within the French positivist experience, as a reaction to the rigidity of the jus positum, immediately imprints on the principle characters that will be highlighted by the following commentators. An extralegal tool with uncertain contours, the institute proves to be so capable of offering solutions, as to reintroduce those elements of arbitrariness and complexity that the codification hoped to have handed over to the past. In any case, it offers an answer to the rigidity of the legislative data in the encounter with things, correcting dysfunctions that cannot be resolved in terms of strict legality.

In particular, since its origin, the prohibition of abuse of law is fully among the respiratory organs of the law that allow the jurisprudential evolution of law, without contradicting the primacy of law in the system of sources, but bringing to the surface what in the work of the legislator has remained latent. It is not by chance that the abuse of law is referred to in the more elaborate experience of German codification, aware of the need to provide the judge with a means to remedy the inequalities of the system. For example, through the Verwirkung institute of §242 BGB, on which, through good faith, the concept of inadmissible exercise of the right, and by §226 BGB[21], prohibits emulation. The theoretical nature of debate on the category has been encouraged by the fact that, in Italy, unlike other systems (such as, Germany, Spain and Switzerland)[22], the prohibition of abuse of law has not received a codification.

21 N. JANSEN, R. ZIMMERMANN, Commentaries on European contract laws, Oxford University Press, Oxford, 2018.

22 With reference to par. 226 of the German BGB, already mentioned in the text, in art. 334 of the Civil Code of Portugal, in art. 7 c.3 of the Spanish Codigo Civil, in art. 13 of the Civil Code of the Netherlands, in art. 248 of the Greek Civil Code, art. 2 of the Swiss Civil Code.

Juridical science has divided between positions, where the one is aimed at recognizing the existence of a prohibition on the abuse of law in national law, considered a modernizing valve through which to adapt the rigidity of the legislative data. The second position has looked with suspicion to the category in question, considering it capable of undermining legal certainty and introducing excessive judicial discretion on the legal relationships of individuals.

The divergence of opinions is clear and is recorded in the first instance on what is undoubtedly the preliminary problem of the whole speech: to admit, first on the logical level and then on the legal one, that a right can be abused.

The comparison between supporters and detractors of configurability of abuse of rights has in fact re-proposed the nature and scope of the subjective right, particularly between the Enlightenment, individualistic, liberal, and solidaristic conceptions of the twentieth century (of catholic or socialist inspiration) for which the subjective right is in a not absolute position, but placed within a dense network of social relations to be protected.

The debate on the abuse of law is a battleground for the different conceptions of law, so that the reflection around the category is influenced by the sensibilities of the jurists participating in it. In fact, on the background of reflection around the abuse of law, the traditional civil division is between the subjective and objective theories, compared to the point of subjective rights and legal transactions. I note that in the secular debate around the foundation of subjective law, two main theories have contested the field: the will or power of choice (will or choice theory) and the interest theory. According to the theory of will, the justification for the attribution of a right is to assure its owner of a protected individual choice, in recognizing the possibility of making independent decisions, such as exercising or not the right, or to act or not for its protection. The subjective right, which is Willensherrschaft in the elaboration accomplished by Savigny in the treatment of the juridical store, then taken by the German Pandettists[23] also in the formula of WillensMacht, (lordship of the will), coincides with the sphere in which the will of right is sovereign[24].

---

23 F. C. SAVIGNY, System des heutigen Römischen Rechts (new edition of the Berlin Deit, 1840-1856), Aalen, Berlin, 1981, pp. 331ss. F. G. PUCHTA, Pandekten, Leipzig, 1838, par. 21.

24 P. GROSSI, L'Europa del diritto, ed. Laterza, Roma, 2016. J. VAN DER WALT, The horizontal effect

As it is easy to perceive, the theory of will produces as a corollary that of considering unquestionable the individual conduct adopted in the action of the exercise of a right.

The theory of will contrasts with the theory of interest, which was coined by Jhering[25] and has become prevalent, for which the subjective right is a juridically protected interest. Therefore, the justification of the right consists in assuring a form of protection to an interest of the owner, the attribution of a right takes place to ensure protection against a certain interest. It is the theory of interest that opens the space to the possibility of abuse of law, because it frames the latter in a teleological perspective, which overcomes the individual in the perspective of an objectivized function of law, that of protecting a certain interest.

As well emphasized by the doctrine, and as we will find for many institutes, the twentieth century civil law is crossed by a tendency towards objectification which is found not only for the foundation of the subjective right, but also in matters of contract. One thinks, for example, of the objective notion of the cause, and of other elements, such as the prevalence of will evidenced in theories of entrustment and self-responsibility, or in the discipline of malice, for which the cancellation aims, to repair the damage of his interest, or, again, the objective notion of good faith operating in the formation, interpretation and execution of the contract.

ABUSED RIGHTS: RATIONES OF RIGHTS AND EVALUATION PARAMETERS OF THEIR EXERCISE

Once the cultural matrix of abuse of law has been clarified and the debate about its admissibility is presented, let's move on to deepen its elements. To this end, it may be useful to recall the definition given at the beginning of the speech, whereby the right is abused when it is exercised by choosing, among a plurality of possible ways, a mode that appears censurable and that produces a result in

revolution and the question of sovereignthy, De Gruyter, Hamburg, 2014. L.J. WINTGENS, Legisprudence: Practical reason in legislation, Ashgate Publishing, London, 2013, pp. 341ss. M.J. FALLON Y TELLA, A three-dimensional theory of law, Martinus Nijhoff Publishers, Leiden, Boston, 2010, pp. 328ss. N. HORN, Einführung in die Rechtswissenshaft und Rechtsphilosophie, C.F. Müller, Heidelberg, 2011, pp. 106ss.

25 R. JHERING, Der geist des römischen Rechts lauf den verschiedenen Stufen seiner Entwicklung, II, Leipzig, 1869.

which benefits obtained from right holder and sacrifices imposed on others are disproportionate. As can be easily understood, each of the elements referred to hides, behind its postulation, a universe of problems that has held, and still holds, engaged the minds of theoretical and practical law.

Who can say which and how many are the means by which to exercise a right, when it is devoid of a discipline that binds its exercise, and presents itself in what in criminal law would be called a "free form"? What are, and above all, where are the parameters in the light of which we can unify an exercise of the law resulting conforming to the norm? What are the rights that can be abused? How is the balance between the advantages obtained and the sacrifices imposed through the exercise of the right? The organ discretion deciding on these aspects still flows between reasonableness embankments balances or comes out with the risk of subjective evaluations, capricious or even liberticide?

To answer these questions, there is no other way to elaborate on the elements of the institute outlined above. At this point, the first problem to be faced is that of identifying the criterion in the light of which a use of law can be defined as abusive. We have seen how, in the reflection on the abuse of law, references to the underlying interest are the abused subjective right, the subjective function of the subjective position, good faith, and proportion, which are strong but at the same time elusive concepts.

Before addressing the problem of identifying the underlying interest of law, and hence of the function of this, we must acknowledge how, in addition to the reconstruction of the abuse of law as an exercise that betrays the interest posed by law its foundation, other reconstructions are possible. In fact, on the subject of the union of the exercise of the law, different types of criteria or parameters have been identified in the light of which to carry out the evaluation, which can be distinguished between: a) intentional-subjective, b) economic, c) moral, and d) teleological criteria[26].

These are, first of all, the economic criteria, offering a judgment on the exercise of the right inspired by a criterion of Pareto efficiency cost-benefit calculation. The starting point of this reasoning is that the reduction of the benefit of the person who suffers the exercise of the right by its owner, it will pay a benefit increase for him. In other words, the exercise of its right, property or credit, is legitimate exercise of its prerogatives as long as it derives an advantage from it, but it is no longer an advantage when it does not achieve an efficient market

26 P. GROSSI, L'Europa del diritto, op. cit.

condition. It has been noted, however, that these criteria, although apparently objective, since they are linked to verifiable values in the calculation of costs and benefits of an economic operation, are not revealed to a more detailed analysis. They present the disadvantage of depending on the choice of the items entering the calculation itself, so as to be rejected because of the tendency to reduce the discourse on the exercise of the right to a sterile evaluation of the usefulness it derives from it.

The possibility of resorting to the criterion of social morality has been affirmed, admitting that the abuse of the right can be assessed in the same way as the criteria in force in the environment and in the group in which the act is framed. The choice of resorting to the "judge-sociologist", however, brings with it many problems, summarized in doubt on the judge's ability to know and identify the moral of a given community in a given historical moment. Above all, this occurs without replacing the moral of the its internal forum, and, in doubt, on the very possibility of determining whether there is indeed a univocal social morality in complex and pluralist societies.

We, thus, arrive at those that, as we have anticipated, are the criteria most recalled in recent literature and jurisprudence on the abuse of rights. The teleological criteria refer to the purpose for which the subjective right is attributed to its owner, as the right places a power, a liberty and a force on the part of its holder that are in connection with the protected individual interest, an objective not to be understood in a subjective sense, but objective, as a function of law. If we accept the idea that law is properly exercised when it pursues its purpose, the problem becomes determining what the purpose of the right is, the ratio of the attribution rule, or, in other words, the interest protected by it, since even this assessment is not exempt from a certain degree of discretion. It has been affirmed that in the current constitutional system, the purpose of law can be identified with reference to the sectoral or general principles, also of a constitutional nature, which means to consider it legitimate to exercise the right that falls within the shadow cone offered by the principle that concerns it.

Clearly, this choice also requires further questions to be addressed, since the same right can bring into play several principles. At the same time, it is possible that the legitimate exercise of a right, as justified by a principle, interferes with another's right, respondent to another principle, with the consequent need to proceed to a balance between conflicting principles (aspect, this, on which we will return).

It is also argued that the purpose for which a right is recognized cannot be determined only in the abstract, in the link with a principle from which it is derived, but must also be assessed in relation to the concrete fact to be decided.

In any case, the recourse to juridical principles, to delineate the function of law, guarantees an answer to the problem of abuse within the legal system, not exposed, at least in theory, to overt encroachments in the fields of ethics or politics. In fact, the review of the criteria, in the light of which it is possible to speak of an abuse of law, is divisible into two families. One is that of criteria outside the legal system, inspired by values that lie outside the juridical system. The other is that of the criteria within the legal system, which assume as parameters values that have a juridical capacity, as they are assumed to principles of the legal system or placed in constitutional texts. The main post-war doctrinal productions on the abuse of law have reconstructed the category as an instrument of expression of a logic proper to the legal system (therefore as an instrument of self-integration of the system) and not of a mixture of this with moralizing or socializing elements external to the law (therefore as an instrument of hetero integration of the system).

The abuse of law would operate as an instrument of self-observation and self-correction of the legal system, of a rethinking of the law on itself and evolution.

Through the search for a positive foundation of the prohibition of abuse of law, it was intended to demonstrate that it is not aimed at superimposing norms on an external moral or solidary order, but on the unfolding of a more complete and balanced order, which is already given, not fully explained and implemented, in the order of the rules.

The abuse of law would therefore be a tool for developing the system, which lends itself to the jurisprudential adaptation of the law, affecting the individual case, without requiring legislative changes to the provision. It has been pointed out how to use the abuse of law as a tool for self-integration of the legal system, through systematic and adaptive interpretation, is certainly more reassuring than considering the abuse of rights as an instrument of ethical-social, or functional control of the law, but ends up reducing the institution to a re-proposal of the techniques of balancing and reasoning on principles, and therefore to something superfluous.

Recourse to the instrument of good faith in contractual relations and to its nucleus of proportion, and to the distorted use of its right are frequent in the aforementioned recent jurisprudence on the subject of abuse of rights. The review of the principle of good faith under the new light of the prohibition of abusive behavior has led in this way to affirm that not so much legal positivism. Although, a reading of it based on legal formalism, contrasted with the admissibility of the abuse of rights. By explaining the abuse of law with good faith, it cannot hide how the risk is that of falling into a "tautological spiral" in which two indeterminate concepts are used, with wide discretion, to clarify the other.

CONTRARY TO NORMS, RULES AND PRINCIPLES

Having admitted that we can find a prop in the written right for the abuse of right, the basic problem is to give an answer to the question of whether to abuse the right means to transgress the norm.

To this end, it is necessary to dwell on the different concepts of illicit behavior, abuse, and excess. It is then known that the offense is resolved in a violation of law. The legal system knows various types of offenses, for example, the unlawful act and the contractual violation, different manifestations of the tort, and then the criminal and the administrative offense. All these behaviors are accumulated by their being contra jus. Abuse, on the other hand, is an abnormal use and, according to the prevailing opinion, teleologically distorted by law. In abuse, there is a conduct that appears secundum legem in comparison with only one of the rules that come into play in the concrete situation, precisely that attributing the law, but which, by widening the field of investigation and placing the right and its owner in reality articulated of the legal traffics, it reveals its contrast with other norms and principles. The offense involves the transgression of the specific discipline of law, while abuse involves the violation of the purpose for which the law itself is recognized. It has been observed that illicit behavior and abuse are based on different legal restrictions, which are characterized by the presence of external limits. The violation of such limits produces an illicit, which are given by legal or conventional constraints or by the presence of minor competing rights and internal limits, the overcoming of which results in an abuse, given by the interest placed at the foundation of the law.

Alongside these two categories, the different concepts of excess of law also operate. With this last phrase, in civil law, reference is made to the exercise of a power absent or beyond the limits of a present power; the limits are the external borders of law, the overcoming of which implies an assessment of unlawfulness. In the excess of law, the illicit nature of the act is easily perceivable, since there is no record of that appearance of conformity with the norm that characterizes the abuse of law. It therefore seems possible, in terms of the description and at least in the abstract, discriminate against the abusive and illicit behavior tout court.

The real dilemma, which afflicts the abuse of law, arises on the level of the evaluation of the abusive behavior and of the situation generated by it, which is clearly disapproved by the legal system. On closer inspection, while the illicit value of the offense is already perceived at the time of conduct, that of the abuse embraces the effects produced by the conduct, and, only moving from them, is then reflected on the latter, giving it a negative connotation. In other words, it is the result of the conduct, which appears to be disapprovable, to act as a spy for the improper exercise of law and to make people look back (to the agent's behavior), by judging that abusive conduct. The result from abusive behavior, although not itself the object of a direct prohibition, is an undue result and, therefore, objectively not justified.

The problem is, then, to frame the situation that arises from abuse. Upstream it is not expected to be illicit, descending from a possible exercise of law, but, downstream, we cannot say that it is lawful, being disapproved by the law. In this regard, it was written that the abusive exercise of a right cannot be described as "illicit" as it does not conflict with any legal or contractual rule. In contrast, it cannot be called "lawful", since the abuse is something that arises contra jus, although with an opposition to the law that expresses itself as an opposition to its purpose, which generates advantages that are considered unjust.

In an attempt to solve the problem of the lawfulness of abusive behavior, there were those who stated that the abuse of rights can only be considered a lawful act, in the sense of valid and admissible on the basis of comparison with the law, but not worthy of protection. Faced with this rigid alternative between licit and illicit nature, reflection on the abuse of rights ends up enveloping itself without giving results. Back then, the warning that accompanies the category of abuse of right from the cradle is: the droit cesse où l'abus commence[27].

To overcome this stalemate, several reconstructions have attempted to move the problem to a different level. A first attempt to solve the problem referred to the concept of legitimacy. It has been observed that the road to solving the problem of the judgment on abusive behavior would be that which places the

27 A. LUNEL, L'abus de droit et la redèfinition des rapports juridiques entre patrons et ouvries en droit français, in Revue Historique de Droit Français et Étranger, 87 (4), 2009, pp. 580ss.

prohibition of abuse on a different legal assessment plan, one designated by the term "lawfulness" and that the way out could be to move the discourse on the level of legitimacy.

According to this approach, there would be a first level of lawfulness and a second of judgment (legitimacy). Speaking of legitimacy, rather than lawfulness, it was noted that the abuse is an illegitimate "all considered" use, that is, a use of the formally correct law, which according to the strict law, is legitimate but substantially becomes illegitimate according to the true right.

An interesting proposal can be found in the category of atypical offenses. The doctrine, which accepts this category, refers to treaties of "atypical wrongdoing" to illicit things that would be characterized to express the opposition to principles rather than to rules. The premise of the speech on atypical offenses is the finding of a process of constitutionalisation of the law, which, following the transition from the legislative to the constitutional state of law, has made the systems of law positive pervaded and conformed by the principles. Being in contrast with principles, rather than rules, is, according to the theory under examination, the common trait of the figures of abuse of law, of fraud to the law, and of misuse of power, which are called atypical offenses. According to this reconstruction, the illicit is an (active or omission) act contrary to a rule that governs a command, or that orders or forbids something. Since the commands can be expressed as much by rules as by principles, the offense can occur because of opposition to the former and the latter and, in this last case, there are atypical offenses.

The atypical offenses can be the result of the analogical extension of the unlawfulness established in rules (analogia legis) or of a weighting between the relevant principles of the system (analogia iuris), or they can be illicit that reverse the sense of a rule. The abuse of law is part of this second group, characterized by the existence of a rule that allows a certain conduct, which turns into illicit by reason of its opposition to a principle. Unlawfulness by analogy would work when the concrete case, which does not appear prima facie subsumed under any rule and, therefore, is theoretically permitted, as not expressly prohibited, becomes illicit as a result of the application of the rule of a different case or a certain principle. The inversion of the rule, instead, operates in cases, such as the abuse of law, in which the behavior is initially foreseen by a permissive rule, but modifies its deontic status following a more in-depth evaluation, which reveals how the rule is over-including and incorporates cases that it should not include.

The theory of atypical offenses, however intriguing, has been subjected to harsh criticism, in particular that of not sufficiently highlighting the discretion of the interpretive activities when the principles are used. It has also been observed that it may be a priori to believe that it is the violation of principles to identify atypical offenses and that the contrary does not happen. That is, a circulation of elements of the system is activated starting from the abuse of the law that allows reconstruction of principles and rules in the light of the concrete case.

In any case, for the purposes that interest us, the theory in question is functional to clarify, if it were still needed, that the abuse of law is an unacceptable behavior, punishable by its discrepancy with a parameter of judgment that can be derived not so much from punctual rules as from the principles of the legal system.

The difficulty in recognizing that this opposition to the principles is resolved in an unlawful tout court affects the identification of the consequences of the abuse, which is not necessarily the instruments of civil unlawfulness, or compensation for damage or invalidity. Rather, from time to time, those instruments are better able to protect the interests affected by the individual abuse, such as the ineffectiveness, inappropriateness, and exceptibility of the exceptio doli.

(FOLLOWS) ABUSE OF LAW AND EXCEPTIO DOLI GENERALIS

The exception of general fraud has a history that is much more evident than that of the abuse of rights, instead intimately connected and dependent on the affirmation of the subjective right. Yet, similarly to the latter, it now appears to be the object of a renewed and close interest in similar to what happened in relation to the abuse of law. As far as the exception of general fraud is concerned, it can be observed that the essential and qualifying nucleus of this institute consists in the protection mechanism that it places at the disposal of the agent subject of the juridical relationship. The exceptio doli finds its autonomy and its characteristic configuration in proposing to the subject and presenting in the context of the legal order a legally relevant initiative of reaction to a claim of others who, abstractly, arising from a position of law, it reveals, in reality, unauthorized side. The intended reaction, governed by the rule of the exceptio doli, is aimed at paralyzing the effectiveness of that claim, invoking for it the use of legal protection.

It seems, therefore, to be able to affirm that the exceptio doli has a sure physiognomy, regarding the reconstructive and proactive profile in its sanctioning content. On the other hand, its descriptive profile, necessary to define the situations to which it is applicable and the conditions of abusiveness, must face the same cognitive and definitive problems affecting the figure of the abuse of law (but also of the fraud to the law), of the prohibition to come contra factum proprium, etc., and among these find their place. Indicative of this logical debt of the exceptio doli towards both a more comprehensive category capable of qualifying the abuse of behavior, as well as more specific categories representative of particular modes of behavior not worthy of protection, are the most significant definitions that have been provided.

The most extensive, and among the most recent, speaks of the exception of general fraud as a possibility, granted by the law, to oppose another's claim or exception, where the claim must have the characteristics of an exercise of the malicious or incorrect right, specifically materialized in the realization of interests deemed not deserving of protection by the same order.

Therefore, the same elements that are discussed for the configuration of an abusive situation contribute to defining the figure. These include the conduct of exercising a right, the subjective element given by the "malicious" attitude, and the objective element consisting in the suitability of the aforementioned exercise to put in place "interests not worthy of protection". All this with the need to specify that the exceptio doli includes and responds to two other more specific rules, implicit in the law, and aimed at the same instance of "fairness": the prohibition to come contra factum proprium, or to maintain a juridical disposition not consistent with one's previous material behavior, and the prohibition of taking advantage of one's own curse.

The true proprium of the exceptio doli is, in reality, represented by the legal effect that it legitimizes: the result that comes with the recourse to the exceptio doli consists in the disregard of positive norms that have allowed the illegitimate exercise of the right. Characterizing elements of the institute, in its present conformation, are the strict pertinence to the field of juridical rules and the rigidity of the remedy, which is substantiated, precisely, in the application of the illicitly invoked norm and in the consequent rejection of the question incorrectly or fraudulently proposed. And so, it was at the very origins of the institute, where dolus pointed out as a criterion of imputation of responsibility, at the foundation of the actio de dolo, and as a vice of consent, presupposition of the exceptio (or specialis) doli praeteriti. But above all, it was to indicate behaviors in violation of the duties of correctness protected, in the context of the iudicia bonae fidei, in action, in the iudicia stricti iuris by way of exception, precisely through the exceptio doli praesentis (or generalis). Unlike the bona fides, the exceptio doli therefore operates only in negative, allowing the correction of the civil ius through the complete rejection of the application, and therefore with prevalency and defensive purposes. In fact, it has been effectively pointed out that the same application and this same essential mechanism constitute the justification of various rules, which in particular govern the system of obligations and contracts. The formal refusal to the remedy of exceptio doli has provoked the proliferation, in jurisprudential arguments, of the mechanisms that are nothing other than tacit applications of general fraud and the prohibition to come contra factum proprium.

Now, the mentioned reappearance of the institute of the exceptio doli generalis in the formulas and applications of jurisprudence proposes again the problem of identifying its systematic foundation, function and collocation. The pivot of this investigation is resolved in the description of the mutual relations between exceptio doli and abuse of the law. This is probably the most problematic and able to qualify the institute, since the element that is undoubtedly recognized as representative of the autonomy of the exceptio doli is substantiated in allowing the disregard of the norm that protects the qualified position, where used "mischievously", that is to say, the remedy. Much more pronounced, however, is the uncertainty, the difficulty of taking a position, beyond the typed hypotheses, on the conditions that legitimize the appeal to the exceptio doli. It seems that it is difficult to deny that the assumptions are given by a case in which a right is exercised with intent and in a direct, abusive way. In the light of this, priority could be given to the commitment to deepen the reflection and abuse of law, on its identification and assessment parameters, and then discuss the exception of malice as a peculiar among the possible sanctions of abusive behavior.

The definition of this relationship is both problematic and potentially qualifying of the figure of the exceptio doli, especially for the fact that this figure, as well as that of abuse of rights, has undeniably returned in vogue in the wake of enormous fortune and acquired flexibility meaning of the principle of objective good faith.

Both institutions are sensu due to the canon of objective good faith, even if with many discussions whether as a systematic foundation or, more simply, as a canon, consecration of a substantial rule to be used as a parameter of interpretation and evaluation of the concrete situation. The consolidated orientation that tends to lead these institutions to the sphere of good faith has in fact stimulated, in support of the autonomous importance of the exception itself, some systematic clarifications of considerable importance, above all on the procedural regime to which the exception is subject. In this perspective, the more or less stringent link of the exception of malice with the rule of good faith, accompanied by the fact that the latter presides over the conduct of any binding relationship, have allowed the prevailing doctrine and jurisprudence to affirm that the exceptio doli same "rises to rule of substantive law". The recurrence of whose violation, du nque, is detectable ex officio by the judge. Although developed essentially in reference to the obligatory relationships, the reconciliation of the exceptio doli to the good faith has caused many authors to question whether the remedy can actually be spoken only in the context and in the force of a binding relationship. Faced with the positions of traditional doctrine, there is no shortage of voices that observe how the exceptio doli, while resorting as its natural seat to preside over the conduct of mandatory and contractual cases, actually embodies a ratio and provides a remedy valid for the whole field of private law; nor are there any voices that even consider the restriction of the exceptio to the case of the execution of contractual relations to be unsatisfactory, at least insofar as it is exclusively made to coincide with the rule of good faith. Above all, however, the theorization of the link between the principle of good faith and the abuse of law, but also the exception of general fraud, marked the reconstructive moment of this last figure, and has more than significantly affected identification of its premises.

In particular, it has led to the reconstruction of the subjective element of the exceptio doli, leading to the abandonment of the requirement of malice or to behavior, giving instead full centrality to the importance of concrete and objective unfairness. Consequently, what today legitimizes the recourse to the exception of general malice is the confirmation of a conduct to exercise a right, which aims to put in place a set of interests that damages the negotiating counterpart or that, however, it is not that set of interests that the regulatory provision set out to protect.

It is therefore proposed that the close link between the principle of objective good faith, on the one hand, and the abuse of right and the exceptio doli generalis, on the other, is proposed as a fact acquired with full awareness of the doctrinal and jurisprudential elaborations. Consciousness can also be considered that both these two figures frame the same vast and elastic category of behaviors that qualify for their abusive character or of abnormality, which can be revealed both in the presence of fraudulent or the exclusive intent to harm others. Above all is the reason for its protection legislative by the confirmation of an objective, unjustified, discrepancy, in the procedure or result, between the exercise of the right and its legal scheme.

What varies and, therefore, differentiates the abuse and exception of malice, are essentially accidental and practical aspects. The structure of a particular case makes the figure of the exceptio doli more effective and useful, and, as the only significant reaction of the order, the remedy that it can provide.

All this detracts from the fact that, although the exceptio can have an independent and detailed definition and configuration, the only category with legal and conceptual relevance is that of abuse. In this sense, we can consider the vast doctrinal and jurisprudential opinion that frames the exceptio doli, with its peculiarities and dynamic characteristics, as one of the typical effects of the recurrence of an abuse of law. This does not in the least affect the specific conditions of its value and applicability, but at the same time, firmly affirms the logical priority of the abuse of rights. Where there is an abuse of law, and certain circumstances of fact occur (claim put forward in judgment, intersubjective relationship, and others) may prove useful. However, it has historically proven useful to follow the recognition of the abuse the disregard of the standard invoked, rectius the proposals of the European legislator.

SUBJECTIVE ABUSABLE POSITIONS

The abuse of law is a concept within the legal system that allows the integration of the positive data while remaining within the legal system, which can be assessed on the basis of an objective-teleological criterion, whose content (the function covered by law, the interest for which the right has been attributed) can be identified through the use of principles. It is now appropriate to point out and review the abusive subjective positions, or, in other words, the subjective legal situations which, by undergoing a distorted exercise by their owner, may damage goods or interests of others or of the company, in such a way as to give place of a hypothesis of "abuse of rights". This is because, in the criminal reflection on the abuse of law, the presence of these positions in the criminal case or their interference with it can be a sign of a possible importance, even in that location, of their abuse. We therefore try to outline, at least briefly, the figure of the abused right.

THE ABUSE OF LAW AS A MORAL IMPERATIVE HISTORICAL PROBLEM

A first order of theories takes on the historical-sociological perspective (the analytical opinion is implicit or hinted). The most radical positions reject the abuse of law in pre-juridical terrain. Abusiveness is a qualification that operates in the antechamber of law, which denounces, from the irrelevant ground of ethical and moral judgments, the dissimilarity of the letter of law from the feeling of social conscience. Its logical possibility is given by the incessant evolution of social and economic relations, and the phenomenon constitutes a reaction of the collective consciousness to the inadequacy of the current order. The prohibition of abuse of law is resolved in the pre-juridical warning, in a moral imperative, which denounces the divergence of law and the effective needs of protection of a given community, running out in the eminently political-sociological dimension. Reformulating the famous phrase of De Vareilles-Sommière, in which the abus commence le droit cesse[28], Rotondi affirms that the droit commence l'abus cesse[29], to imply that we can no longer speak of abuse when the conduct is legally relevant, from which one can speak lawful or illicit, legal or anti-juridical, but not of abuse. Abuse of law and excess from the law are logically autonomous, but that is a pre-legal concept, so that as a rule, the licit conduct will be abusive but rejected by the social conscience. There are no qualifications of behavior other than the lawful (in accordance with the law) and the unlawful (contrary to law). From a historical-sociological point of view, the abuse of law denotes this divergence of legal reality and collective consciousness, and from an analytical point of view, the interpretation of the case attributing the right and the delimitation of the faculties attributed to the owner can only give rise to figure of excess from law.

---

28 See, P. DE VAREILLES-SOMMIÉRES, Forum shopping in the European judicial area, Hart Publishing, Oxford & Oregon, Portland, 2007, pp. 58ss.

29 C. MINGAM, A. DUVAL, L'abus de droit, ètat du droit positif, in Revue Juridique de l'Quest, 4, 1998, pp. 547ss.

The idea of divisibility of ownership and exercise rests on the rethinking of the subjective right, (exceptionally) limited to guaranteed power in view of an interest protected by law. It postulates the existence of an abstract and "objectified" interest in the subjective right, the result of the choice of the legislator regarding the socially prevalent interest. Considered an abstract interest, justifying reason for power, it is possible to concretely predict the deviation and to qualify the concrete, conforming interest, which is different or contrasting with the typical interest. The abuse identifies the teleological deviation with respect to the interest for whose pursuit the power has been attributed. In other words, it allows us to conceive of a gap between "individual and concrete" interest pursued by the owner and "objective and abstract" for whose prosecution the right is granted. Note that the French version of the abus des droits isolates from the scope of the abuse theory and the control over the normality or abuse of the conduct the whole category of discretionary or unmotivated or acausal rights. That is to say, at least in Josserand's mind, there is a vast category of subjective, insurmountable syndic rights on the reasons and methods of exercise: it is the category of potential rights, such "by law" or "by their nature". The finalistic theories use the image, of immediate effectiveness, of the deviation of the concrete from the typical purpose. On closer inspection, the results of these theories can be reformulated in an analytical perspective, since they clearly define the applicative extension of the source in consideration of the typical purpose. The list of facts attributable to the offense of the subjective right is reduced by virtue of an endogenous criterion: the ratio legis of the disposition conferring power. The reasoning will be clearer through the thought of the authors who criticize the divisibility of ownership and the exercise of law. Reformulation of the results of teleological theories in an analytical key. The abuse as a problem of interpretation. Endogenous criteria for reducing the case in point are: ratio legis and social function of law.

The critique of the divisibility of ownership and the exercise of law is contained in the tight unfolding of Rodolfo Sacco's thought: law and lawfulness-relevance of the act are the same thing, seen with different glasses. There is no right, with its own autonomous content with respect to the lawfulness of the act. There is no exercise, independent of the intrinsic structure of law". The conduct of man is in itself mute and waits to be qualified by a juridical norm, which allows to say the acts of exercising a right. The formula is nothing else from the result of the juridical qualification of a fact: "we see that in many cases the objective law regulates an act to assure legal legitimacy and effectiveness, and the jurist likes to call this act, the exercise of law. In these cases, the whole normative phenomenon will be exhausted in the norm that regulates the act; all the subjective legal situation will be exhausted in the lawful nature of the act, or in the eventual relevance and effectiveness of the act"[30].

From the point of view of legal qualifications, the abusive act is resolved as a phenomenon of irrelevance: it does not take the form of an act of exercising the right, because exceeding the limit made by the agent places the deed outside the scope of law which attributes the faculty of power. This does not exclude that the conduct can be compared with a different rule and, therefore, be relevant to other cases (so the effective conduct could be noted for the case that requires the duty to behave according to loyalty and fairness. It is the phenomenon of double qualification, on which we will soon return, and where the conduct is irrelevant as an act of exercising the right, it is not able to rise to an act of impediment of the responsibility of illicit fact).

These observations seem to suggest that the abuse of law is a moment of interpretation: the criteria of abuse of conduct (normality, morality, teleological deviation) guide the interpreter in defining the content of law, i.e. of the category of conduct that can be added to the case attributable to law.

In this sense, the theories that root the distinction between abuse and excess from law in the apparent legitimacy of conduct, which actually comes out of the limits of law while appearing to remain within the limits of the imperfect definition of law itself, indicate a logical intermediate stage of interpretive moment. Far from identifying a different outcome from the one leading to excess by law, they would seem to warn the interpreter of the inadequacy of an "imperfect interpretation" of the provision. The admonition to the correct and rigorous execution of the interpretative activity does not introduce an autonomous element in the table of the legal qualifications, which are exhausted in the qualification of permission "you can" or prohibition "you cannot" (except, it is right to reiterate, that other norm place a status deontico of "must" or "must not", with the typical consequences of the violation of the obligation). The hermeneutical process will be more or less immediate, and it is necessary to isolate the criteria for determining the extent to which the source is applied. The views are fragmented into a plurality of opinions, which radically diverge on the extent of the interpreter's

30 P. GROSSI, L'Europa del diritto, op. cit.

discretion in the assignment of meaning to the rule of law and to the extent of the admission of extra-juridical criteria in the classification of conduct. We will try to group them according to the criteria for reducing the number of pipelines.

EXOGENOUS CRITERIA. THE THEORY OF ATYPICAL OFFENSES. FROM TELEOLOGICAL INTERPRETATION TO ANALOGY

A metatheoretical investigation describes the abuse of law (in teleological theories) as a phenomenon of "over-inclusiveness" of a rule. The case attributable to the right includes a case, where regard to the justification of the right, should not fall within its scope. So, the result of the interpretation according to the rationale of the norm determines the reversal of the deontological status of the conduct from permission to forbidden.

If in the classical version of the teleological theories the rationale of the disposition of law is in the system of economic-social purpose of power, the ratio of attribution of law can be expressed by a principle, potentially in contrast with the permissive rule. The case attributing the right is restricted on the basis of an exogenous criterion, moving from another positive datum (the principle). It is the theory of atypical crimes by Manuel Atienza and J. Ruiz Manero[31], which presupposes a positive order composed of rules and principles, each of which is able to express a preceptive content. Conduct would be permitted by a rule but prohibited in the light of a justifying principle (rectius; since every permissive rule is governed by a justifying principle, the inversion of deontic status is the result of the balance between the justifying principle of the rule and the other prevalent principle)[32].

The fact permitted by the rule but prohibited by the prevailing principle is an atypical wrong, of which the abuse of law is a species. The permissive rule covers the corresponding conduct; the subsumption under this rule is inconsistent with the balance between the system principles applicable to the case. Since the justification of the principle prevails over that of the rule, a new rule arises, consistent with the principle, which prohibits behavior in the concrete case. On closer inspection, the theory concerns the delicate relationship between sources

31 For further details see: M. ATIENZA, J. RUIZ MANERO, A theory of legal sentences, ed. Springer, New York, 1998.

32 See, C. JAAP, D. VON DER PFORDTEN, Concepts in law, ed. Springer, New York, 2009, pp. 17ss.

of law. It is not just a matter of reconstructing the meaning of provision attributing the right according to its ratio, but to resolve an antinomy between rationes legum: one expressed by the rule of law; the other from the prevailing principle among those relevant to the solution of the case.

Critics of the theory of atypical wrongdoing have concerned, on the one hand, the coherence of a theory that ultimately ends up depriving the rules of compulsory force and utility. If it is true that the judge must disapplicate them every time they fight with an underlying principle, the qualification of lawfulness/illicitness of the conduct exclusively to the principles is entrusted: "for the purposes of the legal qualification of a behavior as lawful or illicit, the rules are irrelevant"[33]. On the other, it has been observed that recognizing a generalized judicial power to disregard the law is not coherent with our current positive legal system, nor is it a desirable objective de iure condendo.

With the mechanism of disregarding the permissive rule and applying another rule in its place, we pass from the teleological to the analogy interpretation. For this to happen, it is necessary to assume the configurability of axiological gaps, which express exactly the difference between what law is and what should be. Is the axiological gap identified or created? At this point, the discrimine becomes really labile from the interpreter through the argument of dissociation. In the case of the provision envisaged two subclasses are distinguished, it states that the provision only applies to one of these subclasses, leaving the other without qualification, in which the abusive conduct re-enters.

Here lies the perplexity of entrusting the axiological choice to an organ of the state that would seem different from the one appointed and the need to examine the compatibility of the argument of the abuse with the lawfulness method. The latter authorizes the overcoming of the literal tenor of the disposition, favoring the meaning that it has according to its ratio (teleological interpretation), making it possible to apply to an unregulated case a provision that regulates similar cases or similar matters. Perhaps, it does not tolerate the removal of a case from its rule and its reconditioning to another case. The interpreter seems to take the place of the legislator in his fundamental work to choose which rule is appropriate for the case. Keeping the argument with respect to the minimum conditions of a positive method is entrusted to the element of the axiological gap, which can hardly be said to be found and not created by the interpreter,

33 C. JAAP, D. VON DER PFORDTEN, Concepts in law, op. cit.

thereby severing the thread that links this way of arguing to the principle of legality.

ABUSE OF LAW AND GOOD FAITH. THE REDIAL THEORIES

A central junction of the theory of abuse of law is the relationship between this figure and good faith, which the most recent jurisprudence in civil matters tends to overlap. The abuse of law is a social type, a phenomenon of the violation of the obligation of good faith, of which, although with a variety of nuances and with authoritative voices of dissent, it is affirming an applicative scope further than the only mandatory relationships.

A variant of teleological theories constructs the prohibition of abuse of law as a function of good faith in an evaluative key: "the diversion from the interest reveals a violation of good faith because it is the result of ways of exercising the subjective situations to be countered. Good faith is the precept, even if indeterminate, and the prohibition of abuse of law one of the functions"[34]. The reduction in a number of behaviors is carried out through an exogenous criterion (the rules on good faith) and with a two-stage reasoning (lawfulness/legitimacy). In adherence to the evaluative conception of good faith, reasoning postulates a duplicity of plans of qualification of conduct, one of lawfulness, the other of legitimacy. The first island in the abstract is the ratio of the norm attributing the law, but does not exhaust the interpreter's task. Even if licit, the conduct is illegitimate when its modalities are censurable in the light of an evaluative canon expressing less merit or justice. Legitimacy should be understood as intrinsic congruence with respect to the "overall sense" of the rule, which would be grasped not by an a priori but only by an ex post evaluation of the protection needs expressed by the specific case. To the lawful but illegitimate conduct, the right would reconnect the general opposability of the exceptio doli generalis. It is thus argued that "the concept of abuse of law presupposes a rule that outlines a certain set of interests involved and takes shape when the way in which the rule is deployed does not present itself as an infringement. The rule unfolds as a sequence of acts or activities contrary to the order engraved on it, but the betrayal doesn't change the meaning, substance, and therefore the composition of interests it prefigured. The overall sense of the rule is not obtained

34 C. JAAP, D. VON DER PFORDTEN, Concepts in law, op. cit.

only from the abstract ratio but from putting into contact the abstract ratio and the hypothesized normative effects that represent the epiphany, with the case to be decided. A judgment of legitimacy of the lawful conduct (according to the evaluative conception of the good faith) seems to introduce in the decision a judgment according to criteria not predetermined, whose opportunity is debatable. In concrete, for the possibilities of action that the legal situation confers that are defined in the light of the need for protection, the substantial relativity of the subjective legal situation seems to exist, which does not exist before the fact from which protection needs arise. This way of arguing finds comfort in the dogmatics of the general clauses as open-ended norms, which would empower the judge to construct the rule of the individual case; it is also placed in the wake of the sensibility shown towards a construction of the remediation order. On the basis of the system of community origin, whose legislative technique undoubtedly proceeds for protection objectives and reasons in terms of remedies for protection needs rather than patterns of conduct and of effects, the same conceptual category has been seriously questioned of the subjective right and the opportunity to proceed with legal reasoning in this case. The perspective explains a certain suggestion but raises the doubt that the legislator of the Union is a normative technique imposed by the contingent diversity of the dogmatic categories of the legal systems of member states, which is only quantitatively distinguished from the legislative technique of the analytic case.

Reaffirming the need for the pre-existing criterion of judgment to be decided does not mean excluding appreciation of circumstantial elements from the hermeneutical operation, which cannot be isolated from the document or from the conduct structurally corresponding to the case attributable to the law. There is nothing to prevent law from providing an appreciation of the conduct having as its object the concrete result pursued, broadening the judgment of lawfulness of elements of the fact that otherwise they would remain extraneous to it. This adds a logical moment of hermeneutics, which continues to take place according to legal rules of lawfulness with the exclusion of metagiuridic criteria of "justice" or "merit" or "preferability" of the result achieved. For the right reason, there is no just and unjust result if not comparing it with the sensitivity (indeed unpredictable) of the interpreter. We tried to show that the decision according to justice escapes the criteria of rational verifiability.

The need to keep good faith in its ability to direct the conduct (obviously, only possible when the criterion of pre-trial judgment to be judged) is felt by the precepts of good faith, which build it as a source of supplementary obligations of the contractual regulation and, according to some, as an intrinsic limit to the exercise of the claim (limit-control theory). Unlike evaluative theories, the criterion of judgment according to good faith is defined a priori; it is not determined but can be determined according to objective evaluation standards.

(FOLLOWS) ANALYTICAL THEORIES

The study of the relationship between good faith and abuse of law suggests to investigate the measure of relevance of the circumstances and the modalities of conduct in determining the deontic status of the latter (permitted/prohibited). The circumstances burst into the interpretive activity, gaining a place of absolute centrality. For analytical theorists, however, it is always a dialogue with the source[35], whose validity, but also the scope of extension, must be ascertained. It is then necessary to establish whether behavior contrary to good faith can qualify as an impediment to the exercise of the right, or if one can imagine a double qualification of behavior. Since conduct is also relevant as an act of exercising the right because it can be added to the source, it is also a source of obligation to compensate, as referable to the case described by another provision. The theme moves from the union of the reasons for withdrawal to nutum, i.e. the idea that the same historical event can be multiple legal facts, because the legal relevance of the historical fact depends on the point of view (or/and of the norm) from which it is observed. Thus, the executive behavior must be considered from a double angle: under the profile of the negotiating source and according to the criterion of good faith. Each of the two perspectives presupposes its own context of reference, which can give rise, as happens in the use of the common language, to a different legal meaning.

The behavior contrary to good faith would be able to reduce the scope of extension of the (valid) source, excluding the relevance of facts and statements otherwise capable of determining the production of effects. In analytical terms, good faith places a burden on the holder of the right of withdrawal: the general clause would have the function of determining a "different logical configuration of the case" attributing the right, which we could then reformulate: If A + has a contrary behavior to B, then A is not B.

---

35 C. JAAP, D. VON DER PFORDTEN, Concepts in law, op. cit.

In this case, there would be a fragment of norm, constituted by a general clause (the good faith) that in the concrete case could deprive the conduct for the remainder structurally conforming to the case. The configuration of good faith as a burden (in the particular duty of coherence, but potentially of the most diverse content), does not encounter logical obstacles, but perhaps needs to overcome some of them systematically.

It is coherent with the system on the condition that the dogmatic construction (which as such is certainly susceptible to refutation) traces a diversity of rules of structure and rules of conduct and links to their violation or disability/irrelevance respectively and the obligation to compensate. The dual qualification theory is based precisely on the distinction between the validity of the source and the discipline of behavior. Faced with the source attributive to the law, there is another relevance and effectiveness, according to a different and equally applicable formal scheme. However, the opposition to good faith puts a head, never a phenomenon of irrelevance of behavior, that is ineffective due to differences from the source of attribution, but to the hypothetical violation of an obligation. Dealing with obligations of execution, the rule on good faith does not affect autonomous space (i.e. it cannot be converted into the logical scheme of "you cannot") and implies a further qualification of dutifulness (you must not). But if the act of exercising the right, also effective, complements the non-fulfillment of the obligation of good faith, it generates the obligation to compensate the damage. At the outcome of the review of these doctrinal positions, the idea seems that the abuse of law is resolved in determining the scope of extension of the source of power, and that the interpreter is indicated to consider (if and) how the methods of conduct and the actual interest pursued are held to be relevant to the law. It is therefore appropriate to move to the analysis of the legislative provisions that regulate this two-fold aspect of human action. In their light, the scope of the source can be determined, which, to remain in the example of the recession ad nutum, assumed as a paradigm of a potestative right, could lead us to consider the limited owner's powers and the reasons for the exercise of the right not all unquestionable.

TYPES OF SUBJECTIVE POSITIONS

Speaking of "abuse of law", we speak in reality of a "relevant abuse for the law", given that, in the history of Western legal thought, numerous forms of abuse of law that have different objects can be enumerated. The doctrine has pointed out how the abuse can have a subjective right as its object, a juridical power expressed by a procedural or/and de facto power (like economic power), a freedom, in particular economics. In these cases, the abuse is realized in the accomplishment of a conscious and voluntary act, structurally conforming to the behavior model allowed by the power giving norm, functionally in contrast with imperative rules or principles, to which they achieve negative effects, sanctions.

Furthermore, the notion of abuse can also include the abuse of interpretation of objective law, and that of legal forms and legal types (mostly in contractual matters). In these cases, abuse is an ideal behavior, given from the attribution of senses to norms or acts. Therefore, in the prohibition of abuse of law, the term "right" should be understood in a broad sense: the object of abuse is to be able to make legal, or, more simply, a legal power, a legal position of advantage. The main criterion to be used to identify an abusable right is to assess whether it can be exercised in ways that are not predetermined, such as to assume abusive methods alongside physiological methods of exercise.

This happens without doubt in the presence of absolute rights, such as the right to property, for which the owner is faced with a wide range of possibilities of exercise, including that of emulation. Plurime modalities of exercise are hypothetical also for the relative rights that are resolved in the claim to another behavior, as evidenced, for example, by the jurisprudence in the matter of abuse of the process and fractioning of the credit. In these cases, in fact, although the number is reduced for the possible ways of exercising the right, there are those among them that are subject to a different purpose from the order and those that are extremely damaging to the interests of others. The same is also true for the rights of withdrawal, where, as we have seen, the choice to exercise the right can take arbitrary and capricious forms, considered abusive by CJEU jurisprudence.

EUROPEAN UNION BETWEEN HARMONIZATION AND NATIONAL PLURALITY

Internal market, regulatory harmonization, and national plurality represent the rails along which the process of European integration has been articulated, from the birth of the community to the changes introduced by the Lisbon Treaty.

It is important to clarify, first of all, an interpretative problem.

Given that the concept of market has central importance in treaties, this definition lacks a legal definition, nor is it possible to refer to similar cases or legislative "external" interventions to the European sphere. To this, it is added that for a long time two meanings of the market have coexisted: the common one and the internal one. In fact, the Single European Act, in art. 14[36], had enucleated the concept of internal market in terms of space without frontiers, in which the freedom of movement of goods, persons, services, and capital was ensured. Despite the introduction of this expression, no definition was provided in this regard, and the relationship between the two notions of "market" was also not clarified. Furthermore, the new legislation did not remove the reference to common market by the treaties. In this regard, CJEU has come to the rescue, which has clarified the relationship between the two cases, stating that the notion of common market aims to eliminate any obstacle to intra-Union trade in order to merge national markets into a single one, as long as possible similar to a real internal market[37]. The passage in question uses three distinct terms. In particular, those of the common and of the single market are treated as if they were completely equivalent, while the engraved internal market is used as a term of comparison, in which the internal adjective seems to allude to the reality of a market national. Although the various underlying linguistic variants of the market term have been widely discussed, every doubt has been dispelled by the Lisbon Treaty[38].

In view of this, it is important to note that the realization, or rather the consolidation of the internal market, has emerged not only in the existence of

36 A. HARTKAMP, C. SIBURGH, W. DEVROE, Cases, materials and text on European Union law and private law, Hart Publishing, Oxford & Oregon, Portland, 2017, pp. 282ss. K. LENAERTS, I. MASELIS, K. GUTMAN, European Union procedural law, Oxford University Press, Oxford, 2014, pp. 133ss.

37 CJEU, C-15/81, Schulz of 5 May 1982, ECLI:EU:C:1982:135, I-01409. C-270/80, Polydor and others v. Herlequin and others of 9 February 1982, ECLI:EU:C:1982:43, I-00329.

38 It is important to note how, in practice, the use of the term "single market" is very widespread in relation to the problem of European integration and is still very often used in official documents drawn up by the institutions or on their behalf. This is evident from the Report that Mario Monti has prepared for the President of the European Commission, José Manuel Barroso, of May 9, 2010, entitled "A new strategy for the single market". In the aforementioned document, in addition to highlighting how, from a conceptual and communicative point of view, the term "single market" is the most correct to be used, it is stated that "the solidity of the single market is an essential factor for the general health of EU, precisely because it is the very foundation of the integration project". This is directly confirmed in the Communication that the European Commission sent to the European Parliament, the Council, the Economic and Social Committee and the Committee of the Regions, on 13 April 2011 (COM/2011/0206 final) and entitled Act for the European single market: twelve levers to stimulate growth and strengthen confidence-together for new growth (...)".

a customs union but, in particular, in the possibility of exercising fundamental freedoms. Such freedoms allow individuals, whether they are natural or legal persons, to be able to circulate, establish themselves, and express their "economic self", as if all this happened within the same territory.

This result was initially pursued through a process of exogenous integration between the different national economic realities characterized by the imposition of specific prohibitions on member states in order to eliminate any internal barriers that could have hindered the effective realization of such a reality target. The measures adopted in this direction were aimed at preventing national measures and acts from conflicting with the process of market integration. The activity of the legislator, therefore, was focused on harmonizing and standardizing the internal regulatory systems in the belief that effective integration could be guaranteed, only by imposing from outside the simultaneous presence of rules of identical content in member states. The strong momentum towards the completion of internal market has mainly materialized along two guidelines: the approximation of national laws and the elimination of technical, fiscal and physical barriers, with the ultimate aim of smoothing out regulatory differences of potential obstacle to unification of local markets. Since the goal was to build a common system of rules, the process of regulatory harmonization was implemented through the massive use of the EU directive. This act, unlike the Regulation, allowed (and allows) each state to preserve its national legislation, while at the same time imposing harmonization. Through the legal basis of art. 94 TEC (now article 115 TFEU), the Council was vested with power (article 144 TFEU)[39] to adopt specific directives aimed at bringing national legislation closer together that had a direct impact on the establishment or functioning of the common market. This modus operandi, however, had to deal with two orders of problems.

First, the excessive proliferation of European acts, aimed at obtaining an obligation of result, has clearly weighed down the integration process. States have had to cope with a growing regulatory burden that most often lead to considerable delays in transposing directives. Second, the affirmation of the principles of

39 F. MARTUCCI, Droit de l'Union europèenne, LGDG, Paris, 2017.

subsidiarity[40] and proportionality[41] strongly limited Union action. Respectively, if the latter should stop if the regulatory power of a state proves capable of achieving the objectives set in a complete manner, and if the European action cannot exceed what is necessary to achieve the aforementioned purposes, then alternative ways have been sought for the realization of the EU market, meeting at the same time, the national needs.

The legal context has been the fertile ground in which mutual recognition has taken root as a principle of pretoria matrix, used above all in the field of free movement of goods. Subsequently, it has been crystallized as a positive rule whose scope has concerned both the freedom of establishment[42] and the free movement of services[43]. If the role of the legislator has been preponderant (starting from the 80s, CJEU[44]) in a first phase of the integration process, it has played a role of absolute importance in the aforementioned process. CJEU's thought is clear: the legislation of a member state concerning the technical requirements of products can only be applied to goods imported from other member state if

40 CJEU, C-491/01, The Queen v. Secretary of State for Health, ex parte: Britsh American Tobacco Investments Ltd e Imperial Tobacco of 10 December 2002, ECLI:EU:C:2002:741, I-11453. C-377/98, Kingdom of The Netherlands v. European Parliament and Council of 9 October 2001, ECLI:EU:C:2001:523, I-07079. C-233/94, Germany v. European Parliament and Council of 13 May 1997, ECLI:EU:C:1997:231, I-02405. More details and analysis see: K. GUTMAN, The constitutional foundations of European contract law: A comparative analysis, Oxford University Press, Oxford, 2014, pp. 332ss. N. LANG, Procedural rules in tax law in the context of European Union and domestic law, Wolters Kluwer, The Hague, 2010, pp. 359ss.

41 CJEU, C-210/00, Kaiserei Ghampignon Hofmeister of 11 July 2002, ECLI:EU:C:2002:440, I-06453. C-137/85, Maizena v. BALM of 18 November 1987, ECLI:EU:C:1987:493, I-04587. C-84/94, United Kingdom v. Council of 12 November 1996, ECLI:EU:C:1984:431, I-05755. For further details see: E. CANNIZZARO, N. EMILIOU, The principle of proportionality in European law, Kluwer Law International, London, The Hague, Boston, 1996. V. TOMLJENOVIĆ, N. BODIROG-VUKOBRAT, V. BUTORAC MALNAR, European Union competition and State aid rules: Public and private enforcement, ed. Springer, Berlin, 2017. E. HERLIN-KARNELL, The constitutional dimension of European criminal law, Hart Publishing, Oxford & Oregon, Portland, 2012, pp. 17ss.

42 CJEU, C-149/7, Bastei Lübbe of 19 October 2017, ECLI:EU:C:2017:790, published in the electronic Reports of the cases.

43 D. LIAKOPOULOS, Services publics dans le droit communautaire après le traité de Lisbonne, in International and European Union Legal Matters-working paper series, 2011.

44 CJEU, C-788/79, Gilli of 26 June 1980, ECLI:EU:C:1980:171, ECR 02071; C-27/80, Fietje of 16 December 1980, ECLI:EU:C:1980:293, I-03839; C-281/83, Commission v. Italy of 15 October 1985, ECLI:EU:C:1985:407, I-03397; joined cases C-60 and 61/84, Cinéthèque of 11 July 1985, ECLI:EU:C:1985:329, ECR 02605; C-240/83, Procureur de la Rèpublique v. ADBHU of 7 February 1985, ECLI:EU:C:1985:59, ECR 00531; C-178/84, Commission v. Germany of 12 March 1987, ECLI:EU:C:1987:126, I-01227; C-298/87, Smanor of 14 July 1988, ECLI:EU:C:1988:415, I-04489. For further details see: M. ANDENAS, T. BEKKEDAL, L. PANTALEO, The reach of free movement, Asser Press & Springer, The Hague, 2017, pp. 135ss.

such legislation is justified by imperative general requirements. On the contrary, if the national legislation is not legitimated by one of the reasons mentioned above or by reasons of the same nature, it is not possible to require compliance by products from other countries[45].

By virtue of this ruling, a general obligation has been created for member states to overcome obstacles due to differences in their own regulations. Mutual recognition[46], therefore, based on the logic of the legal equivalence of the various

45 It must be emphasized that a member state wishing to impose its technical regulations on imported products cannot simply find the rationale in one or more mandatory requirements, but must demonstrate certain conditions: i) the legislation in question applies indiscriminately to imported as to the corresponding domestic products; ii) there should be no EU provisions such as to make national legislation superfluous; iii) the legislation in question must be necessary for the pursuit of the prefixed purpose and no other less restrictive means must exist to achieve the same result; iv) the state will have to assess whether the technical legislation which the product conforms to in the state of production does not offer guarantees equivalent to those required by the legislation in force in the state of importation: if so, this state cannot impose respect on the product also of its technical legislation. See also: M. ANDENAS, T. BEKKEDAL, L. PANTALEO, The reach of free movement, op. cit.

46 CJEU, opinion of 18 December 2014, P-2/13. L. HALLESKOV STORGAARD, European Union law autonomy versus European fundamental rights protection. On opinion 2/13 on EU accession to ECHR, in Human Rights Law Review, 15 (3), 2015, pp. 487ss. On the one hand, art. 53 does not oblige states to guarantee a higher level of protection than that of ECHR, on the other the same CFREU must guarantee the same level of protection of ECHR so that there is no conflict between the two provisions. Moreover, CJEU has evoked the specificity of Union's control system on respect for fundamental rights, in particular the principle of mutual trust in the areas of civil and criminal judicial cooperation, visa, asylum and immigration, namely the area of freedom, security and justice that obliges each member state to presume respect for fundamental rights by the other member states and the absence of their jurisdictional powers in the field of foreign and security policy. See also in case: C-168/13 PPU, Jeremy F. of 30 May 2013, ECLI:EU:C:2013:358, published in the electronic Reports of the cases. The CJEU affirmed that: "(...) the absence of the necessary provisions of the Framework it frameworks, it must be that the framework for the implementation of the objectives of the framework to a European Arrest Warrant (...)". In the same spirit see also. CJEU, C-399/11, Stefano Melloni of 26 February 2013, ECLI:EU:C:2013:107; C-396/11, Ministerul Public-Parchetul de pe lângă Curtea de Apel Constanţa v. Radu of 29 January 2013, ECLI:EU:C:2013:39, both of them published in the electronic Reports of the cases. F.M.W. BILLING, The right to silence in transnational criminal proceedings. Comparative law perspectives, ed. Springer, Berlin, 2016, pp. 323ss. C. JANSSENS, The principle of mutual recognition in European Union law, Oxford University Press, Oxford, 2013, pp. 208ss. F. KORENICA, The EU accession to the ECHR: Between Luxembourg's search for autonomy and Strasbourg's credibility on human rights protection, ed. Springer, Berlin, 2015, pp. 282ss. S. MORANO-FOADI, L. VICKERS (eds.), Fundamental Rights in the EU-A matter for two Courts, Oxford University Press, Oxford, 2015. T. LOCK, The future of EU accession to the ECHR after Opinion 2/13: Is it still possible and is it still desirable?, in Edinburgh School of Law Research Paper Series, 2015. F. PICOD, La Cour de justice a dit non à l'adhésion de l'Union européenne à la Convention EDH, in La Semaine Juridique, Édition Générale, 2015, pp. 230, 234. J.P. JACQUÉ, The accession of the European Union to the European Convention on Human Rights and Fundamental Freedoms, in Common Market Law Review, 48 (4), 2011, pp. 995, 1005. S. PEERS, The EU's Accession to the ECHR: The dream becomes a nightmare, in German Law Journal, 16, 2015, pp. 213, 222. E. SPAVENTA, A very fearful Court? The protection of fundamental rights in the European Union after Opinion 2/13, in Maastricht Journal of European and Comparative Law, 22, 2015, pp.

national legislations, places these on the same level, recognizing them as functional equivalents though they are different from one another. It is reconstructed as an expression of the principle of mutual trust that states, precisely because inspired by different logics, must nourish each other. This absolute value finds its justification in that cornerstone of European law that influences both vertical and horizontal relationships, i.e. loyal cooperation[47]. Thus, CJEU postulates the

51ss. M. KUIJER, The accession of the European Union to the ECHR: A gift for ECHR's 60th anniversary or an unwelcome intruder at the party?, in Amsterdam Law Forum, 4 (3), 2011, pp. 17-32. C. LADENBURGER, Vers l'adhésion de l'Union européenne à la Convention européenne des droits de l'homme, in Revue Trimestrielle de Droit Européen, 47 (1), 2011, pp. 20-26. T. LOCK, The ECJ and the ECtHR: The Future Relationship between the Two European Courts, in The Law and Practice of International Courts and Tribunals, 8, 2010, pp. 375-398. D. ASHIAGBOR, N. COUNTOURIS, I. LIANOS, The European Union after the Treaty of Lisbon, Cambridge University Press, Cambridge, 2012, pp. 109-135. N. O'MEARA, A more secure Europe of rights? The European Court of Human Rights, the Court of Justice of the European Union and EU Accession to the ECHR, in German Law Journal, 12, 2011, pp. 1813-1832. J. POLAKIEWICZ, EU law and the ECHR: Will the European Union's accession square the circle?, in European Human Rights Law Review, 6, 2013, pp. 592-605. A. POTTEAU, Quelle adhésion de l'Union Européenne à la CEDH pour quel niveau de protection des droits et de l'autonomie de l'ordre juridique de l'UE?, in Revue Générale Droit International Public, 115, 2011, pp. 77-111. A. TORRES PEREZ, Too many voices? The prior involvement of the Court of Justice of the European Union? in European Journal of Human Rights, 40, 2013, pp. 565-583. L. BESSELINK, M. CLAES, J.H. REESTMAN, A Constitutional moment: Acceding to the ECHR (or not), in European Constitutional Law Review, 11, 2015, pp. 2ss. D. HABELSTAM, It's autonomy stupid. A modest defense of Opinion 2/13 on EU accession to the ECHR, and a way forward, in Michigan Law Paper 105, 2015. L.H. HALLESKOV STORGAARD, European Union law autonomy versus European fundamental rights protection-On Opinion 2/13 on EU accession to the ECHR, op. cit., pp. 485. J.P. JACQUÉ, CJUE-CEDH: 2-0, in Revue Trimestrielle de Droit Européen, 40 (4), 2014 pp. 823ss. C. KRENN, Autonomy and effectiveness as common concerns: A path to ECHR accession after Opinion 2/13, in German Law Journal, 16 (1), 2015, pp. 147ss. S. LAMBRECHT, The sting is in the Tail: CJEU Opinion 2/13 objects to draft agreement on accession of the EU to the European Convention on Human Rights, in European Human Rights Law Review, 15 (1), 2015, pp. 185ss. M. PETITE, The battle over Strasbourg: The protection of human rights across Europe has suffered a setback, thanks to the Court of Justice of the European Union, in Competition Law Insight, 2015, pp. 10ss. R.A. WESSEL, A. ŁAZOWSKI, When Caveats Turn into Locks: Opinion 2/13 on Accession of the European Union to the ECHR, in German Law Journal, 16, 2015, pp. 179ss. B. DE WITTE, Article 53, in S. PEERS et al. (eds.), The EU Charter of Fundamental Rights, A Commentary, Hart Publishing, Oxford & Oregon, Portland, 2014, pp. 1523-1538. J. MEYER (ed.), Charta der Grundrechte der Europäischen Union, ed. Nomos, Baden-Baden, 2014, pp. 813-826. J.P. JACQUÉ, La Cour de Justice de l'Union et l'application de la Charte dans les Etats membres: "Mehr Licht", in European Yearbook on Human Rights, 14, 2014 pp. 125-147. T.WISHMEYER, Generating trust through law? Judicial cooperation in the European Union and the "principle of mutual trust", in German Law Journal, 17, 2016, pp. 342ss. M. WELLER, Mutual trust in search of the future of European Union private international law, in Journal of Private International Law, 11 (1), 2015, pp. 66ss. M. ZILINSKY, Mutual trust and cross-border enforcement of judgments in civil matters in the European Union. Does the step-by-step approach work?, in Netherlands International Law Review, 64 (1), 2017, pp. 117ss. A. BAKARDJIEVA ENGELBREKT, N. BREMBER, A. MICHALSKI, Trust in the European Union in challenges time. Interdisciplinary European studies, Palgrave Macmillan, London, 2018, pp. 179ss.

47 A. VON BOGDANDY, M. IOANNIDIS, Systemic deficiency in the rule of law: What is this, what has been done, what can we done, in Common Market Law Review, 51, 2014, pp. 64ss. A. JAKAB, D.

full acceptance of the normative differences existing between the state regulatory systems, provided that these do not conflict with the ultimate goals and the principles of European matrix. In light of this, national plurality represents, inter alia, another important value on which the Union is founded. Although the European system is characterized by a strong tension towards unity and the perfect harmonization of the parts that compose it, at the same time, we cannot overlook the fact that this normative order contemplates not only a plurality of minorities, but above all a set of regulatory systems whose diversity is clearly recognized, admitted, and, therefore, protected.

What has been said is derived not only by the jurisprudence, but also by the institution of European citizenship, the foundation of the single market in which it is possible to exercise the fundamental freedoms provided for by the EU law. Analyzing the status of a European citizen, both with reference to the possibilities that could arise from the possession of this legal status (so-called external dimension) and to the methods of assigning this status (internal dimension), it is possible to argue that the plurality of legislation is at the foundation of the single market in which unity and plurality are not only intertwined but are functional to each other. As is known, in the European system, the ownership of certain rights is not generalized but is subject to possession of the citizenship of one of member states, i.e. EU citizenship.

COMPETITION BETWEEN EU LEGAL SYSTEMS

The Union recognizes and presupposes domestic regulatory differences, which are accepted by virtue of their functional equality. If this is true, the circumstance that European subjects are recognized the possibility of choosing any EU regulatory system that, at that particular moment in history, is more suited to their needs or intentions will be undisputed.

This is reflected by the fact that the project of European integration included something more than the creation of a free trade zone or customs union. The Charter of Nice included the need for an economic union in which the free circulation of all economic factors was realized, involving the coordination of

KOCHENOV, The enforcement of EU laws and values. Ensuring member states compliance, Oxford University Press, Oxford, 2017.C. KLAMMERT, The principle of loyalty in European Union law, Oxford University Press, Oxford, 2014. S. MORANO-FOADI, J. NELLER, Fairhurst's law of the European Union, op. cit.

monetary and fiscal policies, as well as the adoption of common objectives, such as employment or economic growth. This design, to tell the truth, had wider objectives: by eliminating national barriers, we wanted not only to guarantee the free movement of goods, people, services and capital[48], but also the same national rules and legal models on which these were based. Therefore, the need has emerged to construct the European integration and proceed at the same time on different political, technical, legal, and economic levels, ensuring that the free movement of goods, services, and persons could also be guaranteed by the free circulation of legal models.

Precisely, this particular fungibility of the different but equivalent regulatory systems has pushed and pushes every order to offer to the individual the most advantageous conditions compared to those of the "neighbor", in order to attract in their territory economic factors that allow a faster growth in the national economy of one member state over the others.

We are creating a particular phenomenon of legal competition between national laws that responds to the needs of that single market that has been and will always be at the center of the interest of the EU institutions. In this regard, the competition between legal systems has been strongly criticized for the obvious contrast and ambiguity that is revealed when these two elements are approached. Whereas the expression "system" includes a system of binding and exclusive rules, instead, the reference to "competition" presupposes the classification of the alternative within a different order criterion, allowing users a choice between alternative disciplines applicable to same relationship. This conceptual forcing exists at the moment in which the aforementioned element is linked to the dimension of a national legal system. But when the statistic dimension of law is exceeded, reference is made to a concept of a state-based legal system, such as the European one, where the legal system in question is made up of as many systems of rules as the member states of the Union, then that juridical-conceptual friction fails. Where the individual has the right to choose the rules intended to regulate the situations to which he or she wants to give life, this is placed within a system that inevitably ensures the choice of rules intended to regulate certain relationships, that is to say, functionally equivalent legal systems[49]. In fact, competition between jurisdictions is the foundation of

48 CJEU, C-550/07 P, Akzo Nobel Chemicals and Akcros Chemicals v. Commission of 29 April 2010, ECLI:EU:C:2010:229, I-08301.

49 J. FINNIS, Revolution and continuity of law, in A.W.B. SIMPSON (edited by) Oxford essays in juris-

the internal market itself. The latter requires that the economic operator should be free to move away from its headquarters or secondary offices, to provide its services, or simply to circulate in the country of which it appreciates more the benefits that are given by the relative order. It also demands that the consumer is free to choose the product or service of the state or in the territory whose rules bring him or her more advantages. In light of what has been outlined, it is possible to identify the elements that characterize competition between legal systems. First of all, the plurality of the legal systems is postulated when there is a set of legal systems that coexist, totally or partially, thanks to a set of rules that guarantee their coexistence.

The second assumption is that there is a difference, even if minimal, between the systems being compared. Only in this way, the individual is able to sift the opportunities that they make available and, therefore, choose accordingly. The third element is represented by the freedom, or ease, of the movement of production factors between different geographical areas and by the different attractiveness, for investors and residents, of the rules and regulations in force in these areas. The aforementioned elements, as envisaged, seem to exist within the Union, which is configured as an integrated juridical-economic space, composed of a plurality of national laws that coexist on the basis of a subtle balance between unity and diversity. Although the European legal system has always shown itself to be a unitary corpus iuris, at the same time, it has never pretended to carry out a reductio ad unum because the plurality of peoples and states on which it is founded does not allow this process. This circumstance means that the Union is based on coexistence between the legal systems, which is guaranteed and supported by a series of instruments, such as mutual recognition and harmonization, which do nothing but make continuous contact and comparison of national laws. Without, however, nullifying the differences between legislation, the EU has well-founded the element of competition between legal models.

What has been said has found its consecration also on the jurisprudential level. In C-212/97, Centros sentence of 9 March 1999, it was stated that in the absence of harmonization, competition between legal systems must be given free play, since only in this way can the free economic initiative of individual operators be guaranteed[50]. Having established that the European Union presents

---

prudence, Second Series, Oxford University Press, Oxford, 1973, pp. 64ss.

50 CJEU, C-212/97, Centros v. Ltyd v. Erberevs-og Selskabsstyrelsen of 9 March 1999, ECLI:EU:C:1999:126, I-01459.

itself as an integrated system in which different national legal realities coexist, it is inevitable that the subjects have the right to identify and, therefore, to choose a member state whose rules are less severe or more attractive than those of the regulatory system of origin. If, in light of the differences between internal legal systems, the operator is free to express his economic self in the country in which he or she appreciates the order for the benefits he brings, the systems are put in competition with each other in order to favor the use of their right within the European market.

On the basis of the aforementioned passage, it would seem, however, that competition between the legal systems can exist only when there is no harmonization of that particular sector in which it operates. As if to say: where there is harmonization, there is no competition, and where there is competition, there is no harmonization. This conclusion is not acceptable because, by supporting this "legal equation", the existence of the same Union would be denied, since the latter is based on both national plurality and the harmonization of state legislations. It should be noted that competition between legal systems does not fail when the harmonization process occurs in an invasive way. Although in the sectors of major legislative production, the national legal differences have been annulled, making the path of competition of the legal systems impractical. It cannot be ignored that the sectors where the legislator of the Union has widely legislated (i.e. pharmaceutical, food, means of locomotion and company) has, however, left space, albeit minimal, to the state competence. In particular, intervening in this sense, we have created the minimum inequality that has allowed national laws to compete with each other and, therefore, to offer different solutions for the same sector, leaving the individual faculty of choice.

Furthermore, it is not possible to claim that regulatory competition is merely a transitory phenomenon and destined to die when a standardization process is implemented within the Union. This can hardly happen. Firstly, the European system has always developed in the tension between unity and plurality, and its ultimate goal has never been to "flatten" the legal landscape within the European space. On the contrary, it was precisely that of nurturing local differences in order to guarantee to the EU subjects a multiplicity of solutions to be adopted in a harmonized system. Secondly, it seems very difficult to conceive competition between legal systems as a "comet star" because, in compliance with the principles of subsidiarity and proportionality, the EU legislator's intervention is foreseen in residual terms compared to that of member states. Therefore, there is ample space for national legislators who can and must intervene to meet internal needs, always with a view to European harmonization.

Precisely from these elements, we can see that harmonization and competition are not mutually exclusive, but are linked by a relationship of direct proportionality[51]: the more one grows, the other tends to decrease, without the complete suppression of an element for the other. On the contrary, to define the relationship better, harmonization is the boundary within which competition can develop, without going beyond the limits imposed by the first. The latter will be more vague in the sectors of minor legislative intervention, while they will be more marked in those matters most affected by the choices made in Brussels. If this is true, it is undeniable that competition between legal systems exceeds its potential due to minimal harmonization. Leaving space for national legislators will offer a variety of solutions that the private entity can adopt to meet their needs.

THE FACULTY OF CHOICE AMONG THE VARIOUS REGULATORY SYSTEMS AS AN INTRINSIC ESSENCE OF EU LAW

The first consequence derives from the competition between the legal systems within the European Union the right to choose national law. This expression means the possibility offered to the individual to be able to use the rules of another national legal system, part of the European area, as an alternative to the provisions of the legal order to which they could govern the same case. With the birth of EU law and with the creation of a common juridical-economic space, free from barriers and obstacles, the paradigm of law as a given, in the sense of ius positum, has been superseded to law as a choice, in terms of ius inventum. EU law is very different from that of a national system. When a subject operates in a closed system of rules, such as that of a state, the case in question will be governed by one or more provisions that characterize a particular legal framework. Although it is possible to exploit, as very often happens, gaps or flaws in the system and, therefore, to obtain small benefits resulting from regulatory oversights by the national legislator, it is not permissible to choose different or alternative provisions with respect to that prescribed for that situation in fact

51 For further analysis see: A. HARTKAMP, C. SIEBURGH, W. DEVROE, Cases, materials and text on European law and private law, op. cit., pp. 287ss.

it has been integrated. Contrarily, when we move on to the European level, the perspective changes radically. It is no longer a question of applying the related legislative provision envisaged by the legislator to that particular case. Instead, it is possible to choose a legal system among all those available within the Union and, once chosen, to be able to promptly identify the provision that best fits the specific case. The possibility of choice is twofold. It is not only in a position to opt for a system of rules different from that of origin, but even to decide which norm of the order so chosen to apply. This consequence is the result of that functional equivalence that characterizes national laws within the EU, which, by placing themselves in the same way as a res that can satisfy the interests of a subject, may be the subject of choice without any type of legal or territorial limit. Therefore, the possibility of expressing one's preference in terms of a legal system is an element characterizing EU law. In the absence of this condition, fundamental freedoms would have no reason to exist because there would be no space without frontiers called the internal market within which to use them. In fact, if the subject, being both physical and juridical persons, was not able to opt for a valid alternative to their state of belonging, then it would mean denying the existence of the European system.

THE CHOICE OF THE MOST FAVORABLE ARRANGEMENT. MULTIPLE NORMATIVE EXAMPLES CONFIRM THIS REFLECTION

The inevitable consequence of the right of choice is that individuals use to their advantage the national legal diversity that the EU system recognizes. In this way, each individual can choose the most appropriate legislation for his or her purpose. A subject is not bound by the discipline of his or her own state, but rather by virtue of that called functional equivalence between legal systems, as well as the existence of a European legal area characterized by circulation of legal models, and can freely choose the country that guarantees greater advantages than the one to which it belongs.

First of all, it is inevitably the external dimension of EU citizenship, i.e. the right "to move and reside freely within the territory of member states" to Union citizens (article 21 TFEU)[52]. The aforesaid statement, clearly recalling an

52 R. GEIGER, D.E. KHAN, M. KOTZUR, EUV/AEUV, C.H. Beck, München, 2016. M. DECHEVA, Recht der europäischen Union, ed. Nomos, Baden-Baden, 2018. C. BARNARD, S. PEERS, European Union law, Oxford University Press, Oxford, 2017, pp. 586ss.

immediately tangible implication of the attribution of European citizenship, postulates the particular condition of the individual who, once this status is recognized, is free to choose where to go and where to settle, as it circulates and stays in the state of destination assumes the same value of moving and staying in the country of origin. Precipitated by this principle is the free movement of workers, as governed by art. 45 TFEU[53]. The letter of the provision sets out in the first paragraph, as a general rule, only the possibility to move freely within the Union[54]. This, however, must be read together with the regulations contained in the third paragraph, which, in listing a series of rights that belong to the worker, includes the right not only to respond to actual job offers but also to move freely to that end in the territory of member states. As it is possible to notice from such normative discipline, to the worker or to the person who is seeking employment, the faculty is given the right to reply to actual work proposals, where it is necessary to understand the concrete and real ones and, above all, the advantageous ones for themselves. To guarantee this, we attribute the possibility to move freely in the common space, or rather to identify that country in which the working conditions are more advantageous than the state of belonging. This derives, first of all, from the same aims of the Union, as well defined in art. 2, TCE[55]. When one of the objectives is to ensure the improvement of the standard and quality of life within the Union, this cannot be separated from the possibility of seeking and finding a job offer that is more advantageous for one's own being. Only through work and, therefore, economic support, it is possible to improve the quality of life itself. Therefore, the individual cannot be denied the right to choose the national system that can guarantee the achievement of this goal, in line with the ultimate objectives of the Union. This is confirmed also in the words of CJEU[56], which to explain the words "effective job offers", stated that, in the light of the article, third paragraph of TFEU, nationals of member states have the right to move freely on territory of other states to take

53 A. HATJE, J.P. TERHECHTE, P.C. MÜLLER-GRAFF, Europarechtswissenschaft, op. cit.

54 R. GEIGER, D.E. KHAN, M. KOTZUR, EUV/AEUV, op. cit. M. DECHEVA, Recht der europäischen Union, op. cit., C. BARNARD, S. PEERS, European Union law, op. cit.

55 R. GEIGER, D.E. KHAN, M. KOTZUR, EUV/AEUV, op. cit.

56 CJEU, C-292/89, Antonissen of 26 February 1991, ECLI:EU:C:1991:80, I-00745. C-344/95, Commission of the European Communities v. Kingdom of Belgium of 20 February 1997, ECLI:EU:C:1997:81, I-01035. In the same spirit see also: C-484/14, MCFADDEN of 15 September 2016, ECLI:EU:C:2016:689, published in the electronic Reports of the cases.

up residence in order to look for a job, id est to choose the country that can offer work offers more advantageous for their personal situation[57].

The same can be said about freedom of establishment. Treaties recognize the individual's ability to pursue an autonomous economic activity in a member state in which he was not previously established. From the combined provisions of the first and second paragraphs of article 49 TFEU[58], it is possible to grasp the essence of the primary right of establishment, that is to say, the opportunity of choice which is the foundation of this freedom.

This responds to the logic underlying this freedom, namely that of putting any EU person in a position to pursue, in a stable and continuous manner, a professional activity in another member state, which he or she considers most appropriate to his or her needs as a business or activity. This is confirmed, a fortiori, when the right of secondary establishment[59] is added to the freedom of primary establishment. In this way, it allows the subject established in an EU state to open and manage, in another member country, a second activity center, i.e. agency, branches, and subsidiaries, without having to renounce establishment in the first country (article 49, first paragraph, second sentence)[60]. In particular, by attributing to the already established subject the so-called right to open a branch, the latter is totally free to identify the state in which to settle with its business, thus being able to exploit the advantages of another national system to offer. In this regard, CJEU also postulated the right to choose the most favorable national law as an intrinsic element of the freedom of establishment, or the

57 CJEU, C-197/84, Steinhauser v. Ville de Biaritz of 18 June 1985, ECLI:EU:C:1985:260, I-01819. The aforementioned principle can also be considered violated in the case of indirect or covert discrimination, which is found when the legislation of a member state, while applying on the basis of criteria independent of nationality, effectively discriminates against the citizens of other member states, since it is more difficult for the latter to satisfy the requirements for the application of rule that is not for national citizens (in this sense see: C-279/89, Commission of the European Communities v. United Kingdom of 17 November 1992, ECLI:EU:C:1992:439, I-05785. C-111/91, Commission of the European Communities v. Grand Duchy of Luxembourg of 10 March 1993, ECLI:EU:C:1993:92, I-00817). Finally, the principle of national treatment is violated when an internal rule is applicable both to national citizens as well as those of other member states and the latter, precisely because they are treated like the former, are in fact unfavorable (material discrimination). In this sense see: C-451/03, Servizi Ausiliari Dottori Commercialisti v. Giuseppe Calafiori of 30 March 2006, ECLI:EU:C:2006:208, I-02941.

58 R. GEIGER, D.E. KHAN, M. KOTZUR, EUV/AEUV, op. cit.

59 CJEU, C-14/17 VAR and ATM of 12 July 2018, ECLI:EU:C:2018:568, published in the electronic Reports of the cases.

60 R. GEIGER, D.E. KHAN, M. KOTZUR, EUV/AEUV, op. cit.

whole European system[61] last of the freedom of establishment. On this point, CJEU establishes that the possibility of opening up to new markets by rooting them with branches or agencies is a fully recognized freedom for the citizens of the Union. It further ascertains that this right cannot be limited in any way by virtue of the underlying the action, even if the choice of the order in which to exercise this right recognizes a more favorable tax regime than that of the state of belonging.

The same considerations can also be formulated for the free movement of services[62]. Although this freedom differs from that of establishment in a substantial manner, inasmuch as it does not imply the possibility for a European citizen to participate in a stable and continuous manner in the economic life of a state other than his own but only to exercise his activity therein temporary[63]. The treaty recognizes an intrinsic and particular right to the choice of national law and, therefore, is presumed to be the most favorable for one's own activity. Article 57 TFEU, in addition to defining what is meant by service and listing what activities are included in the aforesaid concept, establishes that the provider, for the execution of his service, is free to settle on a temporary basis, in the member state where the service is provided. It is therefore clear that the lender will be able to choose where to temporarily settle for the performance and, in doing so, try to exploit the benefits that can be obtained from a national system rather than another.

From such arguments, it emerges that the right to choose the most favorable legal order is nothing other than a constituent element of freedom of movement, be it workers, establishment, or services and the same EU citizenship, which is the foundation of such freedom[64]. It is the inevitable consequence of the process of realization of the single market that, when considering the legal systems of member states, admits and protects the right of individuals to prefer one

61 P. BEHRENS, Centros and the proper law of companies, in J. FERRARINI, K.J. HOPT, E. WYEMMERSCH, Capital markets in the age of the euro, Kluwer Law International, The Hague, 2002, pp. 503ss. E. WYMEERSCH, Centros: A landmark decision in European company law, in T. BAUMS, K.J. HOPT, N. HORN (a cura di), Corporations, capital markets and business in the law. Liber Amicorum Richard M. Buxbaum, Wolters Kluwer, London, 2000, pp. 629ss.

62 CJEU, C-52/09, Telia Sonera Sverige of 02 September 2010, ECLI:EU:C:2010:483, I-00527.

63 CJEU, C-215/01, Schnitzer of 11 December 2003, ECLI:EU:C:2003:662, I-14847.

64 CJEU, C-106/16, Polbub-Wykonawstwo of 25 October 2017, ECLI:EU:C:2017:804, published in the electronic Reports of the cases. See also for further comments: S. RAMMELOO, Cross-border company migration in the EU: transfer of registered office (conversion)-the last piece of the puzzle? Case C-106/16 Polbub, in Maastricht Journal of European and Comparative Law, 25 (1), 2018, pp. 89ss.

system of rules over another because there is no substantial difference between them. The right to choose is none other than the maximum expression of that peculiar liberalizing ratio, which has always distinguished fundamental freedoms within the Union. Such freedoms could not be defined in this sense if they were not accompanied by the possibility given to the individual to express themselves freely through the choice of the most adequate and favorable legal system for one's own life model, always respecting the objectives and limits set by the treaty. It is precisely the notion of circulation that postulates the right of choice. "Circular" indicates the action of the individual who moves freely in a circumscribed space in order to achieve a legitimate objective, and such activity subsists only if at the base of the latter the freedom to choose the place or the objective to be achieved is postulated. If this were not the case, we could not speak of freedom or right of circulation because the legal assumption on which it is based would be lacking, i.e. the choice. Now, since the right of preference is at the foundation of the internal market and, therefore, of fundamental freedoms, it is also necessary to understand the exact scope of this "value" in order to comprehend the limits that characterize it.

THE POSITIVE LIMITS TO THE CHOICE OF THE MOST FAVORABLE ARRANGEMENT

The need to identify the boundaries of the right of choice stems from the assumption that the subjects, or rather the protagonists of the EU legal system, are not only individuals but also states, in the absence of which the European Union would not have reason to exist. Although the latter, by limiting their sovereignty and thus recognizing European law, comply with the obligations and ensure legal positions of supranational origin, they are bearers of national interests, which cannot be neglected.

If this is true, the right to choose national law cannot be assessed only in the perspective of individuals who "circulate" in the Union. The state dimension must also be taken into consideration because the aforementioned right is expressed in that European area called the "internal market" made up of the territories of the member states of the Union. In the moment in which an individual exercises, through fundamental freedoms, the faculty to choose the order more favorable to him, not coinciding with that of origin, for the latter, it will integrate a situation of subtraction of the individual from his own sovereignty.

For the state of belonging, the right of choice of the individual consists, therefore, in the subtraction of its internal regulation. A state that is helpless to this phenomenon results from the establishment of the internal market and the free circulation that characterizes the European space, as well as that granitic orientation jurisprudence according to which the national laws, although different, are substantially equivalent.

The foregoing must be assessed, however, in the light of the circumstance that the freedom of movement, and therefore the right of choice to this underlying, are not absolute. The European system, at the primary level, provides substantial limitations to oppose if the behavior of the individual is potentially suitable to harm the national system. Here is the prospect of the possibility of compressing a supranational freedom through a national need, provided that this finds reason to exist thanks to a European provision. The reference can only concern the power of member states to adopt national measures aimed at restricting fundamental freedoms for reasons of public policy, security, and health. When one of these three situations is deemed to have been integrated, the individual's ability to move, and therefore to freely choose the most favorable regulatory system, is clearly limited. If the choice of the individual were to be revealed in a concrete prejudice of the aforementioned national parameters, the state would be entitled to limit this freedom, being able to recognize full internal supremacy over the European legislative order. In addition to the aforementioned provisions, national measures are also required to protect national coherence, which, although apparently discriminatory, are designed to protect imperative requirements linked to a general interest, provided they are proportional to the intended purpose. These measures are effective above all in terms of freedom of establishment and free movement of services[65], so that they must:

65 CJEU, C-67/98, Zenatti of 21 October 1999, ECLI:EU:C:1999:514, I-07289. C-232/01, Hans Van Lent of 2 October 2003, ECLI:EU:C:2003:535, I-11525. C-243/01, Gambelli and others of 6 November 2003, ECLI:EU:C:2003:597, I-13031, relating to the Italian legislation which reserved the organization of games of chance and betting on sporting events to certain institutions; joined cases C-49/98, C-50/98, C-52/98 to C-54/98 and C-68/98 to C-71/98, Finalarte and others of 25 October 2001, ECLI:EU:C:2001:564, I-07831, relating to the German legislation requiring construction companies established in another member state to apply the provisions of this law to workers employed in work carried out in German territory paid holiday. For freedom of establishment see: CJEU, C-19/92, Kraus of 31 March 1993, ECLI:EU:C:1993:125, I-01663 on the German legislation which authorized the possibility of using specialization diplomas issued by foreign universities and the case C-108/96, Mac Queen and others of 1st February 2011, ECLI:EU:C:2011:67, I-00837, on the reserve in favor of ophthalmic graduates with the right to perform special eye tests and, C-294/00, Gräbner of 11 July 2002, ECLI:EU:C:2002:442, I-06515, concerning the reserve for doctors of heilpraktiker activities. For further details and analysis of the above sentences see: P. SYRPIS, N. NIC SHVIBHNE, P. SYRPIS,

a) apply in a non-discriminatory way; b) be justified on grounds of general interest; c) be suitable to guarantee what is necessary to achieve the aim pursued; and d) must not go beyond what is necessary to achieve the established objectives. However, it is important to underline that the aforementioned measures have limited scope. Although the principle of free movement, precisely because of the central role it occupies in the overall economy of the European system, has had a very broad reading. On the contrary, the retained competences of member states, even in areas of a typically state nature such as the public order, public security and health, have always been interpreted and applied rigorously and restrictively[66].

In this regard, the case law has, in particular, specified the limits that member states must comply with in defining the aforementioned national requirements underlying the derogations in question. First of all, the application of the restrictive measure cannot have economic aims, or in any case not connected to the requirements of public order normally recognized in a democratic society[67]. To this must be added that the restrictive requirements placed on the basis of national provisions limiting fundamental freedoms do not necessarily have the same territorial scope of the law, which is limited and, more generally, must be always appreciated taking into account the principle of proportionality according to which it is possible to limit only what is necessary to achieve the aim[68].

Exceptions from European Union free movement law: Derogation, justification and proportionality, Hart Publishing, Oxford & Oregon, Portland, 2016. P. CARO DE SOUZA, The European fundamentral freedoms: A contextual approach, Oxford University Press, Oxford, 2015.

66 CJEU, C-357/98, Yiadom of 9 November 2000, ECLI:EU:C:2000:604, I-09265. C-36/75, Rutili of 28 October 1975, ECLI:EU:C:1975:137, I-01219. C-41/74, Van Duyn v. Home Office of 4 December 1974, ECLI:EU:C:1974:133, I-01337. C-348/96, Calfa of 19 January 1999, ECLI:EU:C:1999:6, I-00011. joined cases C-482/01 to 493/01, Orfanopoulos and Oliveri of 29 April 2004, ECLI:EU:C:2004:262, I-05257. For further analysis see: P. CARO DE SOUZA, The European fundamental freedoms: A contextual approach, op. cit.

67 CJEU, joined cases C-115 and 116/81, R. Adoui v. Belgian State and City of Liège of 18 May 1982, ECLI:EU:C:1982:183, I-01665. joined cases C-65/95 and C-111/95, Shingara of 17 June 1997, ECLI:EU:C:1997:300, I-03343. C-98/79, Pecastaing of 5 March 1980, ECLI:EU:C:1980:69, I-00691. C-131/79, Santillo of 22 May 1980, ECLI:EU:C:1980:131, I-01585.

68 CJEU, C-131/85, Gül of 7 May 1986, ECLI:EU:C:1986:200, I-01573 in which, with reference to the principle of proportionality and to public health reasons, CJEU has established that the right of member states to restrict the free movement of persons for reasons of public health is not intended to remove an economic sector from application of fundamental freedoms, but to make it possible to refuse access to or stay in the territory to persons whose access would constitute a danger to public health. For further details see: C. BERNERI, Family reunification in the European Union. The movement and residence rights of the third country national family members of European Union citizens, Hart Publishing, Oxford & Oregon, Portland, 2017, pp. 74ss.

Similar arguments also apply to restrictions justified by imperative requirements. Assuming that the category of overriding reasons of public interest must be interpreted in a rigorous and restrictive manner, it must be emphasized that the interest in question is protected by the rules to which the European subject is already subject in the member state in which he is established or it belongs. Thus, national measures cannot be drawn up in this sense because the guarantees provided by the state of origin cancel the exceptions of the state in which the subject establishes or exercises (temporarily) his activity. The aforementioned exceptions have a very limited and well-circumscribed scope.

THE LIMITATION OF NOT ABUSING OR FRAUDULENTLY EXPLOITING EU LAW

The concern that EU law could be used beyond what is permitted, or constitute a legitimate legal basis to justify the improper removal of a European subject from its own state, has prompted CJEU judges to enucleate the second sentence that EU law cannot be used illegally or fraudulently.

According to the writer, this must be justified in light of that need to identify a general clause suitable to fill the possible gaps of a particularly complex system, such as the European one. Given the limited scope of internal measures aimed at protecting national legal systems, CJEU, with the aforementioned reference, wanted to "create" an instrument capable of both preserving the coherence of the European system from possible improper use of the same and also to avoid that through this, phenomena of circumvention or fraud of the national discipline were born. The abuse has been identified whenever individuals have used the rights of European matrix for purposes not allowed by the regulatory provisions that attributed these rights. Furthermore, it was considered legitimate for member states to refrain from recognizing the case integrated by the individual, inasmuch as it was carried out in clear violation of the sovereignty of national laws, i.e. the state of origin. In doing so, the exercise of European provisions, possibly endowed with direct effect, is paralyzed, with the consequent recognition of the binding force of the improperly circumvented national standard.

From the copious European jurisprudence, it emerges that the real problem of abuse arises when we are faced with individual behaviors that correspond to cases of exercise of legal situations, determined by a positive rule in a more or less detailed way, but in each a case such as to give, prima facie, a precise protection to the agent. It is precisely in such situations that one creates the appearance of legitimacy of individual behavior, in accordance with the abstract case of exercising a right covered by the rule, which generally does not correspond to the ultimate rationale of the provision and, therefore, of the European legal system. The aforementioned formula, and the cases in which it has been used, make it clear that the notion of abuse (as well as that of fraud!) and the related prohibition are linked precisely to the exercise of the faculties related to fundamental freedoms, particularly when considering situations in which there is a difference in the regulation of certain situations between national laws. Abuse and fraud constitute the improper use, id est beyond the limits, of the faculty offered by the European legal system to choose among several alternatives in the exercise of fundamental freedoms. Furthermore, we cannot overlook the fact that in many cases the reference to the notion of abuse was done very quickly, without specifying anything about what should be considered abuse and, therefore, what are the peculiar characteristics of this institution.

From this succinct preamble, a series of doubts emerges that the following pages will try to clarify. It will be necessary to understand whether the concept of abuse is only and exclusively an institution of a pre-trial origin or whether it is possible to trace it also on the legislative level. If the latter is so, it will be important to highlight the points of contact between "positive" and "jurisprudential" nature. Of course, this will have as its objective not only that of outlining the characteristics of the institution in question, but also that of verifying if the latter can be considered superimposable to the category of fraud to the law, as appears to appear from the words used by the Luxembourg judges. All this is in order to understand if the prohibition of the abuse of the right can be considered, to all intents and purposes, a general principle of EU law.

The orientation that denies autonomous importance to the notion of abuse of law and its contextual prohibition, tracing the problem back to a simple question of interpretation, is based on the need not to excessively burden the European legal system. In this sense, significant is the thought of a part of the doctrine which, precisely on the subject in question, has argued as the prohibition of abuse of right "(...) is a principle of interpretation that must be considered in conjunction with other well established concepts of EU law, such as legal certainty and fiscal neutrality (...)[69].

69 L. DE BROE, International tax planning and prevention and prevention of abuse. A study under do-

From this point of view, it appears evident that there is no need whatsoever to raise the abuse at the beginning or in the autonomous category of the EU when the remedy to the problem of improper behavior is found on the interpretative level. The attempt to misuse a legal position, with the ultimate aim of obtaining an undue advantage, can be "paralyzed" through a restrictive interpretation of the reference provision, in compliance with the principles of the useful effect, systematic proportionality and consistency[70]. Precisely, a teleological interpretation of the provisions subject to improper exercise would restrict the scope for the abuse and, at the same time, guarantee the maximum effectiveness of the well-crystallized principles on which the European Union is based, such as the supremacy and the effectiveness of European law, as well as legal certainty (Rechtssicherheit) and legitimate expectations. The impossibility of reconstructing the prohibition of abuse of law as an autonomous general principle of EU law would also be confirmed by the discipline that permeates the EU contract sector, where the abuse and the related prohibition assume legal relevance only as an expression of the most significant principle of good faith. Starting from the assumption that good faith must characterize every legal transaction both in the pre-contractual and in the implementation phase, the prohibition is a peculiar interpretative tool aimed at ensuring that the actions carried out in accordance with the contract and are suitable for fully realizing the interest of the parties involved. In fact, if this last circumstance were not identified, in the sense that one part prevails over the other, an abusive practice would be integrated, or rather a behavior detrimental to the absolute value of good faith, and the irrelevance of the prohibition of abuse as an autonomous category was important because it was already subsumed in the notion of good faith, a cornerstone of both national and European rights.

---

mestic tax law, tax Treaties and EC law in relation to conduit and base company, in IBFD, Leidend, 2007, pp. 765ss.

70 P. SYRPIS, N. NIC SHVIBHNE, P. SYRPIS, Exceptions from European Union free movement law: Derogation, justification and proportionality, op. cit.

THE ABUSE OF LAW AS A GENERAL PRINCIPLE OF EU'S LEGAL SYSTEM

The reconstruction of the abuse of law and of the simultaneous prohibition in terms of a mere interpretive canon has been challenged by the orientation that is found in the aforementioned category, a general principle of the European legal system.

Firstly, it has been emphasized that the formula for individuals cannot abusively or fraudulently exploit Union law has progressively expanded into EU jurisprudence, so as to allow its almost constant application in the various sectors that make up the supranational system. In particular, CJEU, in reiterating strongly that the application of the European provisions cannot be extended to admit abusive practices, i.e. behaviors that, although apparently conforming to the normative dictate, are aimed at achieving a benefit not due, it has not only made a growing reference to its precedents in the matter but has tried to underline, where possible, the constitutive elements in the presence of which a case in point abusive can be considered integrated. This approach seems to find its justification in that need to effectively protect the European legal system but, above all, to prevent the latter from being a "victim" of that first principle on which it is founded: freedom of choice. It is precisely from the necessity of achieving this objective that the obligation for national authorities to apply in a balanced manner, the aforementioned European as well as the final objectives, which characterize the European provisions that are circumvented or abused would result.

Those who support the nature of the general EU principle of the prohibition of the abuse of law base some of their theory on the basis of which the European CJEU would have well clarified how the abuse and its prohibition are to all effects an absolute European value. The starting point is traced in those sentences in which it is pointed out that the supranational provisions, although they attribute to individuals the right to act, cannot at the same time recognize as legitimate the conduct that results in contrast with the rationale of those same rules attributive to the subjective legal position. Moreover, those decisions are taken into consideration in which the requirements are outlined, in a general and abstract manner, in the light of which the individual actions can be assessed, and, if they are integrated, the conduct thus realized can be dismissed as groundless. In particular, the attention is focused on the sentence of the C-110/99, Emsland-Stärke case of 14 December 2000[71] in which the European supreme judges see the causal factor altering the main characteristic that would attribute to the prohibition of the abuse of a right that generality typical of the principles of EU law, which reveal their nature as an "open" standard suitable to be used in every regulatory field[72].

Starting from the moment that, as CJEU highlights, this norm is nothing but a simple form of codification, or rather "reflection", of a general principle that permeates European law. Then, this absolute value would exert its effects in any sector of the European legal system, regardless of the existence or otherwise of specific rules that reiterate, perhaps even unnecessarily, the principle according to which EU law cannot be the subject of abusive practices. Precisely, the fact that this institution appears, to all effects, deviated from any form of legal crystallization, would support the thesis that identifies in the prohibition of abuse of EU law a general principle of the Union. That is, an absolute security clause suitable to contain all those behaviors that, in one way or another, exceed the limits of what is legally permissible, at the same time damaging both European and national legal systems.

THE SUB-CATEGORIES OF THE GENUS OF ABUSE OF LAW

Although there is still no uniformity of views on the issue in question, both the legislative and jurisprudential analysis revealed the importance assumed by the conceptual category of the abuse of right and of the related prohibition in the EU legal system. It appears that no area of EU law is exempt from the effects of the aforementioned situation that revolves around the alteration of the causal factor, i.e. the divergence between behavior apparently in conformity with the normative dictate and the ratio of the norm on which the action is based. The keystone to ascertain the abusive nature of a behavior is represented, therefore, from the ultimate objective that we want to protect, that is from that peculiar a judgment of congruity between the behavior actually performed and the model behavior expected to reach that peculiarity result contemplated by the standard reference.

71 CJEU, C-110/99, Emsland-Stärke of 14 December 2000, ECLI:EU:C:2000:695, I-11569.

72 In the same spirit see also: GC, T-325/09, Adjemian and Others v. European Commission of 21 September 2011, ECLI:EU:C:2011:506, I-06515, in which paragraph 59 states, incidenter tantum, that "(...) the prohibition of abuse of right by which no one can abusing juridical norms, it is part of the general principles of the right of which the judge guarantees the respect (...)".

When the concrete purpose is manifestly extraneous or contrary to the institutionally contemplated purpose, it is possible to consider an operation that can be defined as abusive if it is abnormal or exceptional compared to the objective contemplated by the reference standard. If by "ordinary" action, it is customary to indicate the behavior that an individual should take to achieve a goal relevant to the legal system in which he operates, so that his action conforms to the normative dictate that legitimizes his conduct, when this action diverges from that normally contemplated, then an improper exercise of a legally recognized and protected position could be integrated an abusive case, whose direct consequence is the fruition of an unfair advantage.

On the basis of this assumption, it could be seen that the abusive exercise of a juridical position could manifest itself differently depending on whether national or European legislation is affected. This distinction is of utmost importance since the abuse of law includes a plurality of situations, which, although united by the improper exercise of a right or a freedom, are different from one another, going to constitute autonomous sub-categories of the same genus.

A first aspect to be clarified concerns the relationship that exists between the concept of abuse and that of fraud against the law. From the copious jurisprudence taken into consideration and in the light of what has been found on the normative level, it has been possible to see how the two categories in question have been flanked with a view to full fungibility. In fact, more than in such terms, it is possible to argue that fraud to the law constitutes a peculiar species of the abuse of EU law. This is what emerges from the way in which fraud occurred in the supranational order. Under the principles of direct effectiveness and the primacy of European law, individuals invoke a specific subjective situation recognized at the EU level to escape the application of a certain internal regulation and, therefore, to obtain an undue advantage. Here, if on the subtraction or scam of national discipline under EU law appears from a statist point of view as a phenomenon of fraud to national law on the supranational level, it could constitute the exercise improper of the European discipline, that is a behavior conforming to the normative dictates but contrary to the final purpose that informs the aforesaid norm.

It is important to underline how the abuse of law includes all the cases in which the behavior of the individual is not simply aimed at circumventing the national legislation of belonging, but to deceive the same European discipline, giving rise to a phenomenon of fraud to the European law or avoidance of supranational regulation. In such species must be counted all the behaviors although formally correct, are put in place in an artificial way in order to take advantage of the application of EU rules. Therefore, the requirements for the application of an EU provision are met, but these have been pre-established in order to obtain advantages resulting from the application of this provision.

Finally, another expression of the abuse must be considered. This refers to the sub-category of abuse of law in the strict sense that manifests itself every time the exercise of a right, based on a normative provision or fundamental EU principle, goes beyond what is allowed by the underlying European legal basis. In fact, the action carried out, not being consistent with the ultimate purpose that informs the disposition or the principle to which it is still, negatively affects an equivalent legal position attributed to a third party, creating a phenomenon of compression or even legal cancellation.

THE CONSTITUENT ELEMENTS OF ABUSE: THE OBJECTIVE DIMENSION

In order to rationalize the category of abuse, it is necessary to examine the constituent elements as they emerged from the analysis of legislation as well as EU jurisprudence.

In order for an abusive practice to be considered integrated, it is first of all necessary to verify the existence of the so-called objective dimension. With this circumstance, we wanted to indicate that particular behavior that, apparently, complies with the normative dictate to which this is still done. In this regard, it has been possible to point out the extreme variety with which abusive practices have gradually manifested themselves in phenomenal reality, differentiating themselves according to the type of regulatory sector or freedom involved.

A first mode of improper exercise of fundamental freedoms is realized in that action of the individual who, in order to escape the restrictive legislation of the country of origin, is rooted in another state, more favorable legislation, and from this directs completely or in its main activity is towards the first, giving rise to a U or boomerang effect. Through a phenomenon of temporal and territorial dissociation between the activity carried out and the sending and/or destination state, the subject has the possibility to circumvent a national discipline inappropriately by means of European law, benefiting from advantages that could hardly have been obtained in the absence of the structure referred to above[73].

In such situations of use of EU law to the detriment of the national law, all those transactions whose abusiveness is subordinated to the type of advantage achieved must be included. These are behaviors that, although conforming to European and national legislation that transposes the latter, guarantee the achievement of that one benefit, which, if placed exclusively at the foundation of the action, transforms the latter from legitimate to abusive. The peculiarity of this circumstance is based on the fact that the inadequacy of the action exists only if from the set of objective conditions, there is evidence of the tension of the individual to reach that particular objective capable of creating a legal dystonia. The most striking example, in this sense, is that taken into consideration in the field of European tax law.

Another modality of objective expression of the improper use of EU law is represented by the action that does not damage national laws, but the same European law. When the subject acts beyond the limits contemplated by the law that allows the latter to realize his own interest, a phenomenon of compression or even the cancellation of a legal position of a third party that results injured is generated. In this sense, consider the situations of abuse contemplated in the field of private international law of the European Union, with particular reference to conflicts of jurisdiction in contractual obligations. The abuse of EU law is not substantiated only when a person engages in a national constitution by means of European law, but also when a legal position of supranational derivation is exerted beyond measure in order to restrict or limit a freedom or a right of equal nature. This is confirmed by the "normative" wording contained in art. 54 of the Charter of the Fundamental Rights of the European Union (CFREU)[74]

73 This problem has been dealt with the context of free movement of services. In particular, in the sectors related to cross-border television, banking and credit, as well as the secondment of personnel abroad, there were situations in which the typical effect of abusive exercise of this fundamental freedom was identified: the so-called U-shaped or boomerang effect.

74 For further details and analysis see: X. GROUSSOT, G.T. PETURSSON, The EU Charter of the Fundamental Rights five years on. The emergence of a new constitutional framework?, in S. DE VRIES, U. BERNITS, S. WEATHERILL, The EU Charter of Fundamental Rights as a binding instrument. Five years old and growing, Oxford University Press, Oxford, 2015. S.I. SÁNCHEZ, The Court and the Charter: The impact of the entry into force of the Lisbon Treaty on the ECJ's approach to fundamental Right, in Common Market Law Review, 49 (5), 2012, pp. 1566ss. T. TRIDIMAS, Fundamental rights, general principles of EU law and the Charter, in Cambridge Yearbook of European Legal Studies, 16 (3), 2014, pp. 364ss. H. VON DER GROEBEN, J. SCHWARZE, A. HATJE, Europäisches

pursuant to which no provision of the Charter has to be interpreted in the sense of entailing the right to exercise an activity or to perform an act aimed at the destruction of the rights or the freedoms recognized in this CFREU or to impose more extensive restrictions on these rights and freedoms than those laid down by the CFREU. The exercise of a subjective legal position cannot, therefore, materialize in a disproportionate action. If the exercise of a right exceeds the boundaries of the same, that is beyond the finality to this subtended, a hiatus is created between the ratio of the legitimately recognized subjective position and the related modes of extrinsication.

The objective plan is also integrated, when the conduct of a subject is grounded in an artificial construction in order to obtain, at least formally, a European "coverage" and, therefore, allow the subject to abuse the reference discipline abusively. This category includes all those actions whose ultimate aim is not to avoid the discipline of a member state, exploiting what is recognized at supranational level, but to take advantage of the benefits provided for by the national regulation for a relevant situation at EU level.

Individual's action, in violation of the national law of belonging, produces its effects in another EU state on the basis of a distorted use of a fundamental principle or freedom. In this sense, consider the case of circulation of national judgments if they were pronounced in violation of the procedural law of the state of origin. The principle of mutual recognition guarantees the effectiveness of an act that, as a result of its origin, exerts its effects in another EU state, jeopardizing the coherence of the European judicial area[75].

Unionsrecht, ed. Nomos, Baden-Baden, 2015, pp. 820ss. K. STERN, M. SACHS, Europäische Grundrecht Charta, ed. C.H. Beck, München, 2016, pp. 756ss. S. PEERS et al. (eds.), The EU Charter of Fundamental Rights, A Commentary, Hart Publishing, Oxford & Oregon, Portland, 2014, pp. 1523-1538. J. MEYER (ed.), Charta der Grundrechte der Europäischen Union, op. cit., pp. 813-826. J.P. JACQUÉ, La Cour de Justice de l'Union et l'application de la Charte dans les Etats membres: "Mehr Licht", in European Yearbook on Human Rights, 14, 2014 pp. 125-147. T. KERIKMÄE, Protecting human rights in the EU. Controversies and challenges of the Charter of Fundamental Rights, ed. Springer, Berlin/Heidelberg, 2014, pp. 80ss. K. LENAERTS, Exploring the limits of the EU Charter of Fundamental Rights, in European Constitutional Law Review, 2012, pp. 375ss. N. LAZZERINI, (Some of) the fundamental rights granted by the Charter may be a source of obligations for private parties: AMS, in Common Market Law Review, 51 (4), 2014, pp. 908ss. J. KROMMENDIJK, Principled silence or mere silence on principles? The role of the EU Charter's principles in the case law of the court of Justice, in European Constitutional Law Review, 11 (2), 2015, pp. 322ss. F. HOFFMEISTER, Enforcing the EU Charter of Fundamental Rights in member States: How far are Rome, Budapest and Bucharest from Brussels, in A. VON BOGDANDY, P. SONNEVAND, Constitutional crisis in the European constitutional area, theory, law and politics in Hungary and Romania, Hart Publishing/Nomos, Oxford, Baden-Baden, 2015, pp. 126ss.

75 CJEU, C-394/07, Gambazzi of 2 April 2009, ECLI:EU:C:2009:219, I-02563. For further analysis see: J.

THE CONSTITUENT ELEMENTS OF ABUSE: THE SUBJECTIVE DIMENSION

In order to speak of an abusive exercise of EU law, it is necessary that the action results in antithesis with the rationale underlying the rule or the principle on which the same action is based. At the same time, however, the abuse does not end with the objective dimension alone but also includes the subjective dimension, that is the intention of the individual to act in such a way as to reach an undue advantage or benefit through an improper use of the legal position recognized to him. In this regard, we have seen a wavering orientation. On the one hand, there has been no lack of legal and jurisprudential references, precise references to the need to evaluate abusive behavior based only on objective elements. Moreover, we have seen the need to reconstruct the improper exploitation of a right or of a liberty in an exhaustive way has prompted CJEU to attribute the proper relevance to the subjective element. In fact, the interpreter will have to evaluate and prove the will that has characterized the action taken because in the absence of this, it will be difficult to consider a hypothesis of integrated abuse. In particular, in order to make the assessment of the requirement of intentionality less haphazard, CJEU has anchored the assessment of the subjective element to data of an objective nature, enhancing the factual circumstances that may have relevance in order to reconstruct the intent of a person. Starting from the assumption that the abusive exercise of a right can be considered integrated if, on the basis of precise, objective and concordant elements, the intention to obtain an advantage contrary to the disposition that authorized the subject to act is clear, the Europeans judges have explicitly admitted the need to investigate the precise desire to unjustifiably benefit from what has been made available by EU law, in close connection with the objective dimension. The sentence of the C-110/99, and the Emsland-Stärke case of 14 December 2000 clarifies that the abuse takes the form of a misuse of the objective pursued by the legislation, which can be detected by a set of circumstances, such as damage to third parties, the interposition of artificial constructions, the undue benefit, which results, in compliance with the conditions laid down by the same, whether the objective pursued by the same legislation has not been achieved is the desire to obtain an advantage deriving from the supranational legislation in question.

HILL, A. CHONG, International commercial disputes: Commercial conflict of laws in english courts, Hart Publishing, Oxford & Oregon, Portland, 2014.

Regarding the consequences deriving from the abusive conduct of the individual, the need emerged to prevent and to remove the advantages obtained unduly by this behavior. The aim is to ensure the correct application of the reference legislation according to the aims and objectives of the same, as well as to protect the overall order from actions that can undermine the consistency on which this is based.

This question has its own connotation according to whether the contrast to such phenomena takes place ex ante or ex post, that is, if the measures adopted have the purpose of preventing or canceling the effects of the improper exercise of a subjective legal position.

With reference to measures of a preventive nature, it is possible to note the tension, or rather, the concern of the European legislator in creating a normative system suitable to contrast, according to the type of sector, possible phenomena of abuse of law, understood both in the sense of improper exercise of European law to the detriment of the state system that damages the same EU law. First of all, it is not possible to ignore those normative references postulating the power of member states to adopt measures to prevent the use of advantages deriving from the abusive use of EU rules. In particular, consider what is expected in the banking and credit sector, by Directives n. 2000/12/EC1[76] and 2006/48/EC[77], which precisely with reference to national preventive measures, establish how the principles of mutual renaissance and supervision exercised by the member state of origin require that the competent authorities of each member state do not authorize or revoke the authorization. Elements of such authorization, including the activity program, the location of activities, or activities actually carried out show clearly that the credit institution has chosen the legal system of a member state in order to avoid the most in force in another member state in whose territory it carries out or intends to carry out most of its activities. All of this is immediately confirmed by the regulation contained in the sixth VAT

76 Directive 2000/12/EC of the European Parliament and of the Council of 20 March 2000 relating to the taking up and pursuit of the business of credit institutions, OJ L 126, 26.5.2000, p. 1-59, no longer in force from 19 July 2006.

77 Directive 2006/48/EC of the European Parliament and of the Council of 14 June 2006 relating to the taking up and pursuit of the business of credit institutions (recast), OJ L 177, 30.6.2006, p. 1-200, no longer in force from 31 December 2013. J. KILPONEN, Sovereign risk European crisis-resolution policies and bond spreads, in International Journal of Central Banking, 11 (2), 2015, pp. 287ss.

Directive, in which a reinforced procedure is contemplated precisely to allow states to introduce in tax systems specific internal measures aimed at preventing phenomena of abuse of the law in terms of tax evasion. CJEU has also expressed itself in this regard. Called to assess the conformity of these internal provisions with European law, it has endorsed national measures by setting a series of conditions which are essential for their application. In accordance with the principles of proportionality and adequacy[78], internal measures must be appropriate to avoid the misuse of EU law, since it cannot, at the same time, restrict the legitimate exercise of what is offered by the EU law. It should be emphasized that the legitimacy of national measures will only be considered integrated if the national legislation does not go beyond what is necessary to ensure the objective pursued. In fact, in order for the national legislation to be admissible, it is necessary that it pursues an interest deemed worthy of protection, such as the fight against tax evasion or media pluralism and that it imposes the limitations strictly necessary for the application of EU law.

The question concerning the ex post contrast of abusive behavior is extremely interesting. In giving national courts, the power to counteract the improper exercise of a legal position, CJEU assigns to the state courts the task of preserving the systematic coherence that characterizes European law. At the moment when a subject, by improperly exploiting the general principles or fundamental freedoms of EU, takes action to obtain an undue benefit, the national courts can (and must!) prevent the realization of the effects resulting from the legal situation exercised abusively. It is the duty of the judge to sanction, in an appropriate and proportionate manner, this behavior, whose power may be expressed either in sanctioning the nullity of the operation carried out or in disregarding the benefits achieved or in providing an obligation to return what has been improperly obtained. However, it should be noted that CJEU has set limits within which the national court can operate. In fact, the latter can classify the behavior as abusive only in the presence of serious and sufficient indications and this inevitably entails an adaptive interpretation of the internal regulations where the latter does not provide for application assumptions that conform to those reported above.

Furthermore, when ascertaining an abuse, it must bear in mind the ultimate objectives that inform the European provisions inappropriately used in order to

78 See in argument: A. HARTKAMP, C. SIEBURGH, W. DEVROE, Cases, materials and text on European law and private law, op. cit.

assess the correspondence between what has actually been achieved and what is legally granted. This is because the activity of the judge must be aimed at achieving a precise balance between the need to ensure the correct application of EU law and that of repressing abusive behavior that are a real threat to the uniform application of EU law and its full effect.

THE BURDEN OF PROOF AND ABUSIVE CONDUCT

The issue of the abuse of EU law also exerts its effects with reference to the procedures for ascertaining the improper exercise of a legal position. Both the CJEU and the European Commission (EC) have argued that the abuse of right includes, inter alia[79], a procedural element which is essentially a commercial transaction in the obligation to prove the conduct considered to be unlawful. This obligation is incumbent on the person who is affected by such conduct, therefore, not only the private parties but also and above all member states by means of the respective administrative articulations.

In this regard, it should be stressed that this question must be assessed in the light of the principle of procedural autonomy, which characterizes member states in whose view the national authorities are under an obligation to ensure the judicial protection of the rights of individuals by virtue of rules of European law, within their respective competences. In the absence of a common discipline on the matter, it is therefore up to the legal system of each state not only to designate the competent judges but, above all, to establish the procedural arrangements for the protection of the positions of European origin to be guaranteed[80].

79 CJEU, C-312/93, Peterbroeck, Van Campenhout & Cie SCS v. Belgian State of 14 December 1995, ECLI:EU:C:1995:437, I-04599. C-432/05, Unibet of 13 March 2007, ECLI:EU:C:2007:163, I-02271. C-99/16, Lahorgue of 18 May 2017, ECLI:EU:C:2017:391, published in the electronic Reports of the cases. For further details see: P. GILIKER, The Europeanisation of english tort law, Hart Publishing, Oxford & Oregon, Portland, 2014.

80 See in argument from the CJEU the next cases: joined cases C-205/82 to C-215/82, Deutsche Milchkontor GmbH and others of 21 September 1983, ECLI:EU:C:1983:233, I-02633. C-222/84, Johnston of 15 May 1986, ECLI:EU:C:1986:206, I-01651. C-212/94, FMC and others of 8 February 1996, ECLI:EU:C:1996:40, I-00389. joined cases C-418/97 and C-419/97, ARCO Chemie Nederland and others, of 15 June 2000, ECLI:EU:C:2000:318, I-04475. C-453/99, Courage and Crehan of 20 September 2001, ECLI:EU:C:2001:465, I-06297. C-13/01, Safalero of 11 September 2003, ECLI:EU:C:2003:447, I-08679. For further details see: B. THORSON, Individual rights in European Union law, ed. Springer, 2016, pp. 181ss. C. BERRY, M.J. HOMEWOOD, B. BOGUSZ, Complete European Union law: Text, cases and materials, Oxford University Press, Oxford, 2013.

In light of this, the ascertainment of an abusive operation of European law rests on those who believe they are suffering the effects of such conduct, having to provide timely proof before the state courts of the improper use of a right or a freedom what is, as a consequence, the undue fruition of an unjustified benefit. The national courts, in accordance with the principle of proportionality and non-discrimination, must apply all the guarantees provided for the verification of the violation of provisions of a purely national nature. This verification cannot rest on absolute presumption: the verification of the abusive exercise of a legal position must be based on objective and concrete elements. In particular, it will be necessary to demonstrate, on the one hand, the existence of all those objective circumstances which show that, despite the formal compliance with the conditions laid down by the European legislation, the objective pursued by the aforementioned provision has been improperly achieved. On the other hand, it is also necessary to reveal the desire to obtain an advantage deriving from EU legislation through or the artificial creation of the necessary conditions for obtaining or subtracting it from the national framework by virtue of that right of choice contemplated at European level.

Starting from the assumption that it is up to the referring court to verify, on the basis of what is shown by those acting as active legitimates and in accordance with national rules, the existence of an abusive case, the European supreme judges say that in the most serious cases of abuse would also be possible a principle of proof which leads eventually to an inversion of the burden of proof. This incident seems to postulate, therefore, a probation reversal on the part of the individual operator who has used the right inappropriately and, at the same time, the possibility for the other party to use absolute presumptions in cases where the abuse of law is of extremely relevance for EU law. The boundary between a behavior that tends to legitimately exploit the advantages offered by EU law is also weak through competition between the various laws in force in the legal systems of member states and the one put in place in order to improperly enjoy a benefit through an instrumental use of Union rules. Precisely for this reason, according to the writer, it is not possible to subordinate the reversal of the burden of proof and, therefore, the use of absolute presumptions to any possible circumstance of abuse of right, not even those allegedly considered more serious. This is due to, without the exact identification of an interpretative tool suitable to assess the greater or lesser severity of an action taken, the reference to the abuse of right could be used in a pretentious way. All the hypotheses of abuse must be considered of equal negative relevance because what is at stake is the coherence of the European system understood as a consistency that is continually threatened when trying to use a legitimately assigned right to reach objectives in contrast to the law itself. However, the statement that the most serious cases of abuse postulate the existence and use of absolute presumptions cannot be shared also because, in the absence of timely explanations and being a sporadic assertion that has not been re-proposed by the organs of European jurisdiction, appears to have no practical scope.

THE ABUSE OF LAW AND THE OTHER INTERESTS AT STAKE: PRIVATE AUTONOMY

The freedom of individuals, be natural or legal persons, in the choice of the most appropriate ways to carry out their activity is absolutely linked to the concept of private autonomy protected both at national and European level. In particular, the right to act, making use of what is legitimately provided by the law in which it operates, constitutes a declination of the more general freedom of economic initiative, understood as a voluntary behavior aimed at the realization of interests of the person acting. At the same time, this autonomy of choice is subordinated to the legitimate possibilities contemplated by the legal system of reference, not being able to admit all those actions that are not consistent with the purposes that permeate that ordering. Precisely in this sense, then, the abuse of law and the prohibition related to it can be assessed. When we support the impossibility of using EU law illegally, we want to indirectly define the range of choices that the European legal system considers compatible with the objectives to which it tends, in compliance with the principles of legal certainty[81] and the legitimate expectations of individuals.

81 Among these the most relevant, i.e. those that have found greater application in CJEU jurisprudence, are: a) the prohibition of retroactivity of rules (CJEU, 98/78, A. Racke v. Hauptzollamt Mainz of 25 January 1979, ECLI:EU:C:1979:211, ECR 00069; 99/78, Weingut Gustav Decker KG v. Hauptzollamt Landau of 25 January 1979, ECLI:EU:C:1979:15, ECR 00101; C-34/92, GruSa Fleisch GmbH & Co KG v. Hauptzollamt Hamburg-Jonas of 15 July 1993, ECLI:EU:C:1993:317, 1-4147; joined cases C-74 and 75/00, P Falck SpA and Acciaierie di Bolzano SpA v. Commission of 24 September 2002, ECLI:EU:C:2002:2002:524, 1-7869; C-376/02, Stichting 'Goed Wonen v. Staatssecretaris van Financien of 26 April 2004, ECLI:EU:C:1004:251, 1-3445; C-459/02, Willy Gerekens et Association Agricole pour la Promotion de la Commercialisation Laitiere Procola v. Luxembourg of 15 July 2004, ECLI:EU:C:2004:454, 1-7315; C-161/06, Skoma-Lux sro v. Celni feditelstvi Olomouc of 12 May 2011, ECLI:EU:C:2011:773, 1-10841); b) the need to enact clear and specific law (C-63/93, Duff and others v. Minister for Agriculture and Food and Attorney General of 15 February 1996, ECLI:EU:C:1996:51, I-00569; 169/80, Gondrand Frères of 9 July 1981, ECLI:EU:C:1981:181, ECR 01931; joined cases 92

By virtue of this, the prohibition on the abusive exercise of European law must be interpreted in such a way as not to jeopardize legitimate conduct or operations. The scope of this prohibition is clear: the right invoked by a subject is excluded when the activity carried out has no other explanation than that of improperly reaching a benefit that collides with the aims and results admitted and protected by the provisions of a determined branch of law. Such operations do not deserve to be protected because they manifest themselves in their tension to subvert the purpose of the same legal system in which they are placed. The prohibition of abuse of rights, therefore, constitutes a limitation to the freedom of initiative of individuals who operates when the exercise of a right takes the form of a situation that, although it complies with the conditions set by law for the application of the positive discipline, arises in contrast with the objectives pursued by it, and at the same time, it lacks valid motivations to justify it.

Private autonomy, which includes the freedom to choose the legal forms through which to achieve its objectives, does not therefore constitute an absolute dogma. In the internal market, this cannot be considered an intangible value as it is founded and limit in the values and principles that permeate the European system. In light of this, it is possible to grasp the precarious balance that characterizes private autonomy within the Union. The protection of this freedom does not include those actions whose purpose is represented by the attainment of an advantage through artificial and/or misleading behaviors, lacking adequate motivations that can legitimize such conduct. On the other hand, where such autonomy and, therefore, the underlying freedom of initiative were not adequately guaranteed, the same objectives as the European legal system tends to be compromised, namely the creation and consolidation of an area without frontiers in which freedom of choice and the equivalence between the legal systems constitutes its essence. Here, then, the need to interpret the actions taken in light of the ultimate purpose they tend because only in this way it is possible to ascertain the abusive nature of the conduct and, alternatively, to leave unaffected the legitimate behavior resulting from that freedom of choice founded on the basis of private autonomy and the same European order.

---

and 93/87, Commission v. France and United Kingdom of 22 February 1989, ECLI:EU:C:1989:77, ECR 00405); c) the protection of legitimate expectations (C-120/86, Mulder v. Minister van Landbouw en Visserijof 28 April 1988, ECLI:EU:C:1988:213, ECR 02321; C-333/08, European Commission v. Republic of France of 28 January 2010, ECLI:EU:C:2010:44, I-00757).

ABUSE OF LAW AND OTHER INTERESTS AT STAKE. PROPORTIONALITY, EFFECTIVENESS AND UNIFORM APPLICATION OF EU LAW

On several occasions, CJEU made the legitimacy of national anti-abuse provisions subject to two basic requirements: their effectiveness and proportionality. The internal measures, in addition to being suitable to combat abusive conduct, must be based on the principle of proportionality[82], i.e. they cannot exceed what is necessary to achieve the aforementioned purpose. They must also ensure that the verification of the abusive nature of an action-verification that must be carried out on a case-by-case basis is subject to the screening of a third party, i.e. the national judge.

Having said that, the category of abuse of rights and the related prohibition tend to intersect with the principles of effectiveness and uniform application of European law, to which the proportionality one is linked[83], when attention is focused on national anti-abuse measures whose implementation must be carried out according to the indications provided, sector by sector, by CJEU. Precisely, with regard to the relationship between the principles in question and the aforementioned prohibition, it is necessary to take into consideration the orientation that has emerged in the triad of Greek judgments on the application of the Greek legislation concerning the extraordinary administration procedure of companies in economic crisis. In the aforementioned decisions, the question of whether the national provision which crystallized the prohibition of abuse of rights had the ultimate effect of disapplying the European legislation which was the subject of abusive use by some economic operators, was raised by the European Court. CJEU, initially supporting the pre-eminence of the principles of effectiveness and uniform application of EU law on national rules on the abuse of rights, proceeded to verify the compatibility with the mentioned principles of internal anti-abuse provisions, attributing to the national court such delicate task based on specific interpretative parameters. It is important to underline how the logical-legal procedure underlying the aforementioned judgments, CJEU seems to raise the prohibition on the abuse of European law in the general category on which

82 A. HARTKAMP, C. SIEBURGH, W. DEVROE, Cases, materials and text on European law and private law, op. cit.

83 L.N. BROWN, Is there a general principle of abuse of rights in European European Union law?, in D. CURTIN, T. HEUKELS (eds.), Institutional dynamics of European integration: Essays in Honor of Henry G. Schermers, Martinus Nijhoff Publishers, Leiden, 1994.

the EU order is placed. Intended as an expression of the principle of proportionality, this is the tool for evaluating that particular action which, in contrast with the ultimate aim of the European standard to which it is still infringing the systematic coherence of the European legal system, violates the principles of effectiveness and uniform application around which the latter rotates.

CJEU, by the C-441/93, Panagis Pafitis and others v. Trapeza Kentrikis Ellados A.E. and others sentence of 12 March 1996[84], highlights how a national anti-abuse rule, as a general system clause aimed at protecting the coherence of one's own system and, therefore, at sanctioning the illicit nature of abusive acts. That is, those acts conducted that clearly exceed the limits imposed by the reference standard or those imposed by good faith, morality, as well as the social or economic purpose of this right, do not affect the uniform application and effectiveness of European standards in the regulations of individual member states. According to the European supreme judges, when the provisions result in an abusive exercise of rights, the basis of which is to be found in European provisions, effective protection must be guaranteed only at EU level, as they are legal situations of European and not national nature. Although national courts can apply a rule of national law to assess whether or not a right deriving from a Union provision has been exercised, they cannot change the content of the latter provision nor, at the very least, compromise the achievement of the objectives of this subtended.

Finally, in C-373/97, Diamantis sentence of 23 March 2000[85], the European courts, in reiterating the relationship between the jurisdiction of the national court and that of CJEU in case of compatibility between an internal provision and EU law, support the absolute legitimacy of the prohibition of abuse of the law at European level, being based on a principle of proportionality: it would not have any restrictive effect on the absolute values of uniform application and effectiveness of supranational law. On the contrary, it is precisely the application of this "clause", aimed at eliminating the negative effects that would result from the distinction between what was actually pursued and the ultimate objective that permeates the European provision exerted, that would protect not only the national law in which the action in question is implemented but also and above all European law. In fact, evaluating the exercise of an EU law in the light

---

84 CJEU, C-441/93, Panagis Pafitis and others v. Trapeza Kentrikis Ellados A.E. and others of 12 March 1996, ECLI:EU:C:1996:92, I-01347.

85 CJEU, C-373/97, Diamantis of 23 March 2000, ECLI:EU:C:2000:150, I-01705.

of a national provision on the basis of specific parameters established by CJEU would not be detrimental to the rationale of the provision on which the use of the supranational legal position is based. In reality, it would constitute a safeguard clause from the abusive exercise of Union law.

As emerges from the reconstruction made by CJEU, the aforementioned warning, in countering all those actions characterized by the divergence between what is achieved and what is normatively admitted, presupposes a judgment of proportionality by virtue of which it can protect, in the last instance, the European law. Only in this way is it possible to evaluate the existence or not of that indispensable requirement in the presence of which to consider integrated a situation of abuse of EU law: the alteration of the causal factor and, therefore, the non-compliance of the benefit obtained with respect to the ratio of supranational arrangement.

ABUSE OF LAW AND OTHER INTERESTS AT STAKE: LEGAL CERTAINTY AND LEGITIMATE EXPECTATIONS

By virtue of these values, the European provisions must be characterized by a very precise normative content so that their application is predictable to the interested parties. This requirement of legal certainty responds to the need to guarantee individuals an adequate degree of knowledge of the obligations to which they are subject, so as to identify the most appropriate action to be carried out in relation to the objectives to be achieved. It is important to underline how the prohibition of abuse of rights, if correctly applied, appears to be an instrument aimed at strengthening the certainty of EU law. Given that the application of the rules in complete divergence with the purposes they pursue generates situations of abuse of law that, de facto, threaten the "foundation" of the legal system, the aforementioned warning is a valid instrument to protect the legal system in its entirety. At the same time, however, it is important to underline the accuracy with which this legal device should be used. Keeping in mind the objectives of the law object of the abusive exercise, the interpreter must guarantee the correct reconciliation with the general principles that are at the foundation of the legal system in which the improper exercise of a right is realized.

The link, which characterizes the values at stake, was taken into consideration in C-321/05, Kofoed v. Skateministeriet sentence of 5 July 2007[86]. In the present case, CJEU was asked about the legality of national measures taken by the administrative authority to combat abusive practices, even though the state legislature did not transpose Directive 90/434/EEC[87], concerning extraordinary operations, that, in art. 11, n. 1, lett. a) provides for the right of member states to withdraw the inherent benefits of transactions covered by the European act, if it appears that they have been implemented only to achieve undue tax savings, i.e. an abuse of law. Starting from the assumption that in the case in question it was possible to find the details of an abusive conduct, CJEU, while considering the existence of the faculty of the state concerned to apply the principle crystallized in the letter of art. 11[88], denies the application of this rule in the absence of its punctual transposition. European judges, in order to reconcile the values of legal certainty and legitimate expectations with the principle of direct effectiveness of European law, show how directives cannot create, in themselves, obligations on the part of individuals, let alone, as such, they can be relied on by the member state against individuals.

If the authorities of a state, when applying national law, are still obliged to interpret it in the light of the letter and the purpose of European law, that obligation of consistent interpretation cannot reach the point that a directive, independently of a national law of transposition, create obligations for individuals or determine or exacerbate the criminal liability of those who transgress its provisions. However, the state may oppose a consistent interpretation of the law with respect to individuals, if there is a provision or principle in the national legislation on which to anchor the aforementioned prohibition on the abuse of

86 C-321/05, Kofoed v. Skatteministeriet of 5 July 2007, ECLI:EU:C:2007:408, I-05795.

87 Council Directive 90/434/EEC of 23 July 1990 on the common system of taxation applicable to mergers, divisions, transfers of assets and exchanges of shares concerning companies of different member states, OJ L 225, 20.8.1990, p. 1–5, no longer in force from 14 December 2009. For further details see: P. MÄNTYSAARI, The law of corporate finance. General principles and European Union law, ed. Springer, Berlin, 2020, pp. 256ss. D. LIAKOPOULOS, The regulation of transnational mergers in international and European law, ed. Brill/Nijhoff, Leiden, Boston, 2010. D. LIAKOPOULOS, A comparative analysis of EU and US transnational mergers regulation, Grin Verlag, II edition, München, 2017.

88 CJEU, C-14/86, Pretore di Salò v. X of 11 June 1987, ECLI:EU:C:1987:275, I-02545, par. 19 and 20. C-80/86, Kolpinghuis Nijmegen of 8 october 1987, ECLI:EU:C:1987:431, I-03969, par. 9 and 13. C-168/95, Arcaro of 26 September 1996, ECLI:EU:C:1996:363, I-04705, parr. 36 and 37. joined cases C-387/02, C-391/02 and C-403/02, Berlusconi and others of 3 May 2005, ECLI:EU:C:2005:2005:270, I-03565, parr. 73 and 74.

European law or other provisions to combat all those circumstances fraud or unlawful tax evasion, provisions that can be interpreted in accordance with the provisions of the directive. In the light of this, according to what was established by CJEU, there would be no breach of legal certainty since the aforementioned interpretation and application of the directive would be such as to guarantee the legitimate expectation of the individual, namely awareness of the effects that could arise from his own action in clear contrast with the ratio of the European act.

It is important to underline how the application of the prohibition of the abuse of rights finds a particular "limit" in the protection of legal certainty and legitimate expectations. CJEU, in balancing the interests at stake, has defined inadequate a regulatory change, adopted under the European legislation, aimed at excluding a right legitimately acquired by an economic operator when, as a result of the aforementioned legislative novelty, the behavior established in being intact an alleged misuse of the aforementioned legal position. The principles of the protection of legitimate expectations and legal certainty form part of the European legal system, therefore, must be respected by both the EU institutions and the member states in the exercise of the powers conferred on them by European acts. On the basis of this, if an operator acquires the possibility of exercising a right that guarantees him an economic benefit of absolute importance, this advantageous situation cannot be considered the result of an abusive exercise if, following a new law, the aforementioned exercise does not is allowed and, on the basis of what is conferred at European level, is abusive.

According to the European courts, under the principles of legal certainty and legitimate expectations, there would be no risk of abuse that could justify a redevelopment of the case in regard. The disowning of a position of advantage cannot find its justification in the European legal acts that allow states to introduce measures to avoid phenomena of abuse of the law as the action of the individual has been realized before the legal order of reference that power was recognized. Therefore, for the legislation of the time, that particular behavior was considered legitimate and conforms to both national and European law. Here, then, according to the reasoning of CJEU, it is not possible to accept an assessment in terms of abusiveness of an action taken without taking into account that this qualification could substantially affect both the legal certainty and legitimate expectations of the individual who operates in the internal market[89].

89 CJEU, joined cases C-487/01 and C-7/02, Gemeente Leusden and Holin Groep BV v. Staatssecretaris

In particular, if this were the case, a review of a finding contained in a court decision that acquired the effectiveness of a judgment could not be carried out. From this, it follows that if the decision is based on an incorrect interpretation of the European standard aimed at protecting the legal system from abusive practices, the incorrect application of these rules would also occur over time, without the possibility of any remedy. In the light of CJEU's findings, obstacles such as those referred to in the above ruling on the application of European rules providing for anti-abuse measures cannot be justified either because of the principle of res judicata or because, if that were the case, such measures are harmed principles of legal certainty and legitimate expectations to which the aforementioned prohibition still applies.

ABUSE OF LAW AS A RIGHT SYNTHESIS BETWEEN THE INTERPRETATIVE PRINCIPLE AND THE GENERAL CATEGORY OF EUROPEAN LAW: STATE OF ART AND PERSPECTIVES

The analysis carried out in the course of the work on the nature, the scope and the effects connected to the notion of abuse of law detects the peculiar connotation of the underlying prohibition, which, according to the writer, manifests itself in the general category dimension of European law as much as an interpretative canon of EU law. Although, it is rather reductive to classify the aforementioned warning in one or the other category. In fact, by doing so, one would risk neglecting the hybrid nature of this prohibition, which, in addition to being a guarantee of the European legal system, is an effective tool for assessing the conduct of European Union under the provisions of this regulation. It is

van Financiën of 29 April 2004, ECLI:EU:C:2004:263, I-05337. In particular, the Dutch legislation had abolished the option for taxation of real estate leases. By virtue of this amendment, the financial administration saw the need to rectify VAT deduction relating to contracts concluded before the entry into force of the aforementioned regulatory change. CJEU emphasizes that it would be contrary to the objectives of combating abusive practices pertaining to VAT legislation to suppress the right to opt for the imposition of special real estate leases, if the state was aware of the fact that the right of option was exercised in the scope of tax avoidance mechanism. CJEU concludes that a taxable person cannot legitimately rely on the circumstance that a legal system exists which, even indirectly, admits fraudulent or abusive behavior; nor the overturning of the regulatory framework of which a taxable person has benefited, without however abusing it, could violate the legitimate expectation of European law. Therefore, where a member state suppresses the right to opt for the leasing of buildings, it must necessarily take into account the legitimate expectations of taxable persons in the choice of methods of application of the legislative ex novo (which in the aforementioned case had occurred). See parr. 57 and 81 of the aforementioned judgment.

emphasized that the use of the term "category" and not "principle" is the result of a conscious choice, although CJEU has incidentally designated it as a general or sectoral in fiscal discipline European principle. It seems still premature to assimilate it to the EU hinge principle, given its distinctive elements, which vary from sector to sector, as well as its effects. Without forgetting the fact, manifestly abusive situations were not always defined in such terms.

The dual characteristic on which to reconstruct the prohibition in question in terms of the Union category is the generality as well as the changeability of the same. The copious jurisprudential and normative material examined has shown that the aforementioned warning, in the absence of a precise normative crystallization, can find application in the various EU regulatory sectors but assuming a different connotation in relation to each single branch of the European regulatory system in which operates. Assuming that is necessary, as an unavoidable condition, to integrate an abusive conduct, the alteration of the causal factor of the provision on which the action taken is based requires an assessment for the conduct of those acting under European law.

In fact, the objective dimension can take on the most diverse forms depending on the area in which it operates. What is decisive, however, is the divergence between the conduct of the individual and the result obtained in contrast with the normatively prefigured one. This malleability and elasticity makes the prohibition from being a "legal-normative category" of guarantee on which the European legal system is based in its complexity, whose effectiveness, however, is subordinated to a careful evaluation by the interpreter. In fact, an incorrect application could affect not only the illegitimate but also those that are entirely legitimate.

Another aspect to consider is the application on multiple levels. If, as seen, the notion of abuse of EU law includes the behaviors that are expressed: a) in the wandering of state norms through the instrumental use of European prerogatives; b) in the fictitious or artificial preconstitution of the conditions required by supranational legislation for the purposes of ownership of a legal situation of advantage; and c) in the improper exercise of an EU law so as to limit an equivalent supranational legal position attributed to a third party. Then, the prohibition, in striking such cases, arises to protect the systematic coherence that permeates the European Union. This feature further confirms the nature of "proposition/legal clause"[90] of the prohibition in question. In particular, the end

90 S. VOGENAUER, The prohibition of abuse of law: An emerging general principle of EU law, in R. DE

to which the latter tends does not present any kind of political, moral or social connotation, but only and exclusively legal-economic: we want to avoid that the system can be deprived of foundation through the distorted employment of those positions of legal provisions that it recognizes, attributes and protects. In light of this, a particular cascade effect is created which inevitably invests both those who use the law and those who must guarantee its correct application. When it is affirmed that the European Union does not recognize the abusive exercise of its own right, the use of legal situations governed by EU law does not integrate conduct that, on balance, are contrary to the rationes of the attributive provisions. In fact, the prohibition arises to protect the autonomy of acting (legitimately) as well as the right of choice in the absence of which the European legal system would have a short duration. To this must also be added the power granted to the national courts, which, thanks to the aforementioned prohibition, are put in a position to disregard the benefits obtained improperly, being able to correctly redevelop the operations carried out. In this direction, the internal courts, by virtue of the ultimate aims that permeate the provisions subject to abuse and in the light of it, are a guarantee of the uniform application of EU law, which could not legitimize the conduct that, although found in the European legal system, they are antithetical to the latter.

Finally, it is not possible to ignore the normative background on which this prohibition is grafted, as well as the incessant activity of CJEU, which has assumed a primary role on the issue in question. It is important to underline that the notion of abuse of law and the prohibition of carrying out abusive conduct are well rooted in national laws as sectoral categories. At the same time, however, albeit with the proper differences of civil law systems as well as those of common law, the element in common with the two types of systems is that conduct is abusive when the latter exceeds the limits of the provision by virtue of which it was acted. Having said that, from the analysis of the copious EU jurisprudence, it is noted that CJEU has taken a cue from the experiences of member states. In particular, it has identified in the alteration of the causal factor that requirement of absolute importance that is common to any improper behavior, regardless of the regulatory sector in which it operates. Precisely, the alteration of the causal factor is none other than that excess behaviorally contemplated at the national level that definitively sanctions the illegitimacy of an action.

LA FERIA, S. VOGENAUER (eds), Prohibition of abuse of law. A new general principle of EU law?, Oxford University Press, Oxford 2011, pp. 520ss.

Given the suggested nature of the general category of the European Union, it is important to stress that the prohibition of abuse of law has unveiled its own hermeneutic canonical habit, a connotation that is added and does not exclude the aforementioned one. As we have seen, on several occasions, the notion of abuse has been denied independent relevance and the related prohibition has been defined as a mere hermeneutic canon, as a direct precipitate of the principle of objective good faith. This vision is certainly consistent with the reality of the facts. First of all, the aforementioned prohibition postulates for the individual who exercises the legal position assigned to him the task of acting in compliance with the rationale underlying the reference standard, under penalty of disowning what has been obtained. This is linked to the obligation of national courts to carry out an overall assessment of the concrete circumstances that characterized the action of the individual, having to restrictly interpret the provision in question in the event of abuse. If the assertion that the EU law is not used abusively is clearly defined at the interpretative level, this does not mean that its general scope can be excluded. To tell the truth, only recognizing the dual role it is possible not to diminish the importance of the role covered by this warning. In fact, the prohibition not to abuse illegally the European law, in its general category, arises as an absolute safeguard clause of system: resting on the characteristics of each single sector, prevents supranational provisions from legitimizing actions that, although at a priori and abstract comply with the content of a subjective legal situation of supranational origin, allow the achievement of results that a simple formal application of the rule would guarantee. There are two consequences that stem from connotation as an interpretive canon. Firstly, it is intended that the individual who operates under a European provision correctly interprets the content of the norm, and therefore, that acts in such a way that his behavior is consistent with the ultimate purpose of this subtended. Secondly, that the national courts, as substantial recipients of the obligation to ensure the uniform application of EU law, carefully evaluate the cases that are submitted to their attention and, where appropriate, to disregard the improperly achieved benefits.

Precisely, by combining the dual role of a hermeneutic canon as well as the general category of EU law, the prohibition of abuse is shown in its capacity as a corrective to the regulatory gaps of the supranational legal system. It fulfills the function of resolving regulatory conflicts, protecting common spaces and ensuring the continuous adaptation of European law to the transformation of society. Its functional stability binds, then, to an intrinsic operational dynamism, tended to preclude the improper exercise of the rights attributed by the law and also to protect the systematic coherence of the latter. The prohibition in question lends itself to be a malleable corrective to the unpredictable abusive phenomenologies, of extreme importance for the national court whose task is to preserve its own legal system and, therefore, also the European one. This aspect should not be underestimated. The prohibition operates in the cases not properly typified. It could not be otherwise because one could not speak of abuse in cases where a conduct results ex if already prohibited according to a specific regulatory provision. In other words, the prohibition fills the gaps of the legal system, assigning the judge the task of first reconstructing the case in the light of the circumvented rule, then identifying, in the specific case, the related limit to the freedom of the individual to improperly use the legal situations attributed and, eventually, if necessary, repress the censurable behaviors for the material result that they allow.

In light of this, the prohibition on the abuse of European law, given the nature that distinguishes it, turns out to be that peculiar evolutionary remedy that can be considered in the category of anti-formal methodologies that allows effective protection from the substantive side. Here is the right combination between the principle of construction that characterizes the correct interpretation of European law and a general category of system that informs the EU. In fact, article 54, CFREU could be the starting point from which CJEU could intervene in order to reduce, or better to say, to eliminate any margin of uncertainty that characterizes the topic under study. To date, no jurisprudential decisions have been made in this sense, and this is certainly due to the recent entry into force of the Lisbon Treaty and the new legal role assumed by CFREU.

THE ROLE OF CJEU: REAL OR APPARENT CONTRADICTION?

Although codified in various texts of secondary legislation[91], the prohibition on the abuse of EU law is characterized by being an institution of pre-trial origin. In fact, the principle according to which private individuals "cannot abusively

91 CJEU, C-373/97, Diamantis of 23 March 2000, op. cit., par. 33. C-321/05, Kofoed v. Skatteministeriet of 5 July 2007, op. cit. par. 38. C-251/16, Cussnes and others of 22 November 2017, ECLI:EU:C:2017:618, published in the electronic reports of the cases. For further details see: M. LANG, P. PISTONE, J. SCHUCH, Introduction to European tax law on direct taxation, Linde Verlag, Wien, 2015. M. HELMINEN, EU tax law: Direct taxation, IBFD, Leidend, 2011, pp. 21ss.

or fraudulently use European law is rooted in the jurisprudence of the Union judge"[92]. Similarly, the assertion that a member state "has the right to take measures to prevent, thanks to the possibilities offered by the treaty, some of its citizens from escaping the empire of its national laws" is constant in CJEU jurisprudence. Because it is a notion shared between the legal systems[93], at least in the ratio, the definition of the abuse in the "European Union" jurisprudence has been shaped mainly thanks to the dialogue of CJEU with national courts, through the instrument of preliminary reference.

The cases in which CJEU has for the first time referred to the abuse of rights now count for more than forty years[94]. Over time, there has been a considerable increase in the sentences in which at least an evocation of the term "abuse" is[95], even if only by the referring court, in relation to the most disparate sectors, from freedom of establishment to family reunification and right of residence[96], from incentives to export agricultural products to television services, from company to the tributary law, so that today the rulings on abuse cover "the whole spectrum" of EU law[97].

92 CJEU, C-212/97, Centros v. Ltyd v. Erberevs-og Selskabsstyrelsen of 9 March 1999, ECLI:EU:C:1999:126, I-01459, par. 24; C-33/74, Van Binsbergen v. Bestuur van de Bedrijfsvereniging voor de Metaalnijverheid of 3 December 1974, ECLI:EU:C:1974:131, ECR 01299, par. 13. C-148/91, Veronica Omroep Organisatie v. Commissariaat voor de Media of 3 February 1993 Veronica of 3 February 1993, ECLI:EU:C:1993:45, I-00487, par. 12. C-23/93, TV10 of 5 October 1994, ECLI:EU:C:1994:362, I-04795, par. 21. C-61/89, Bouchoucha of 3 October 1990, ECLI:EU:C:1990:343, I-03551, par. 14. C-39/86, Lair v. Universität Hannover of 21 June 1988, ECLI:EU:C:1988:322, I-03161, par. 43. C-115/78, Knoors v. Staatssecretaris van Economische Zaken of 7 February 1979, ECLI:EU:C:1979:31, I-00399, par. 25. For further analysis and details see: L.J. CONANT, Justice contained: Law and politics in the European Union, Cornell University Press, U.S, 2018, pp. 46ss. C. JANSSENS, The principle of mutual recognition in European Union law, op. cit., pp. 63ss. T. STOREY, A. PIMOR, Unlocking European Union law, ed. Routledge, London & New York, 2018, pp. 296ss.

93 T. TRIDIMAS, Abuse of rights in EU law, op. cit., pp. 2, which is affirmed that: "(...) in European Union law, the doctrine of abuse was a latecomer".

94 A. SAYDÉ, Abuses of European law, regulatory mobility and the law of the internal market, CELS paper, 2011, pp. 2ss, has defined the phenomenon as: "impressive". In particular, the author pointed out that, during the period 2000-2009, the term "abuse", or a derivative thereof, had been used by CJEU once every ten judgments, and by the Advocates General almost once every five conclusions. The author speaks of a "frivolous use of the terminology", which would lead to the definition of the concept of EU law abuse to become a "crucial enterprise".

95 The expression is to P. SCHAMMO, Arbitrage and abuse of rights in EC legal system, op. cit., pp. 35ss, which is stated that: "the case-law on abuse of rights now cuts across the entire spectrum of EC law (...)".

96 CJEU, C-23/16, MA.TI Sud of 28 February 2018, ECLI:EU:C:2018:122, published in the electronic Reports of the cases.

97 T. TRIDIMAS, Abuse of rights in EU law, op. cit.

The copious jurisprudence on the matter is primarily a reflection of the heightened awareness of the potential of the freedom of movement regime acquired both by individuals, who have begun to invoke EU law, as a legal "weapon" to be used against those national measures considered to be too severe, and by the member states, which have identified a "shield" in the prohibition of abuse to react in situations where freedom of movement is invoked in a pretense. Secondly, the evolution of abuse doctrine can be explained by the proliferation of EU legislation in areas such as indirect taxation and subsidies, which inevitably have increased opportunities for misuse of the benefits conferred by EU law[98].

Starting from the new millennium, CJEU then specified the conditions under which abusive behavior can be ascertained, requiring the presence of two elements. First is "a set of objective circumstances showing that, despite the formal respect of conditions laid down by the European legislation, the objective pursued by the said legislation has not been reached". Second is "a subjective element consisting in the desire to obtain an advantage deriving from community legislation by artificially creating the conditions necessary for obtaining it"[99].

Although the EU judicature has repeatedly invoked the prohibition of abuse in principle, while also preparing a general test which can help the national court to verify the existence of an abuse of law, it must be noted that CJEU that has then concretely applied or delegated to the national court to apply the prohibition in question. Even in the presence of manifestly abusive situations, at least according to the perspective of member states[100], such cases are far from numerous[101]. In other words, the abuse of right has been defined by the "European

98 A. ILIOPOULOU-PENOT, Liberté de circulation et abus de droit, in E. DUBOUT, A. MAITROT DE LA MOTTE (a cura di), L'unité des libertés de circulation: in varietate concordia?, ed. Bruylant, Bruxelles, 2013, pp. 185ss.

99 T. TRIDIMAS, Abuse of rights in EU law, op. cit., pp. 2ss.

100 CJEU, C-110/99, Emsland-Stärke of 14 December 2000, ECLI:EU:C:2000:695, I-11569, parr. 52 and 53.

101 A. SAYDÉ, Abuse of EU law and regulation of the internal market, op. cit., pp. 47. The author called by CJEU the next cases in the abuse of right: C-110/99, Emsland-Stärke of 14 December 2000, op. cit. C-255/02, Halifax and others of 21 February 2006, ECLI:EU:C:2006:121, I-01609. C-456/04, Agip Petroli of 6 April 2006, ECLI:EU:C:2006:241, I-0241. C-196/04, Cadbury Schweppes and Cadbury Schweppes Overseas of 12 September 2006, ECLI:EU:C:2006:544, I-07995. C-279/05, Vonk Dairy Products of 11 January 2007, ECLI:EU:C:2007:18, I-00239. C-524/04, Test Claimants in the Thin Cap Group Litigation of 13 March 2007, ECLI:EU:C:2007:161, I-02107. C-425/06, Part Service of 21 February 2008, ECLI:EU:C:2008:108, I-00897. For further details see: N. NIC SCHUIBHNE, The coherence of European Union free movement law: Constitutional responsibility and the Court of Justice, Oxford University Press, Oxford, 2013, pp. 88ss. K. DZIURDZ, C. MARHGRABER, Non discrimination in European and tax treaty law. Open issues and recent challenges, Linde Verlag, Wien, 2015.

Union" jurisprudence mainly in negative terms: CJEU, in fact, usually comes to believe that the situations of fact submitted to its judgment cannot be considered unfair from the point of view of the Union law.

So much premised as to the attitude that shows to adopt CJEU, it is then necessary to wonder about what may be the reasons for its foundation.

First of all, the difficulty in finding CJEU when exceptions relating to the abusive use of rights arising from Union's order have been raised, could be justified by the lack of a definition of abuse universally accepted in the internal legal systems of member states[102]. In this sense, we find again a problematic in the already mentioned lack of precision in the analysis of the concept by the Union judge, as well as in the fragmentary and sometimes contradictory nature of the jurisprudence in this area.

The selective and restricted use that CJEU has made of the ban in question could find an explanation in the leading role that assumes the national judge. This is because the CJEU, when ruling for a preliminary ruling, should confine itself to providing the interpretation of the Union's rules, and also because the assessment of the abuse inevitably requires an assessment of the actual situation and facts that characterize it[103]. In fact, it follows from the jurisprudence that the principle according to which it is for the national court to verify the existence of circumstances that indicate the presence of an abuse, an assessment which must be carried out according to the procedural rules in force in member state[104]. Thus, when CJEU ascertains in a preliminary ruling whether an abuse of law is configurable, it sometimes assigns the task of verification to the national court, providing indications that sometimes appear vague, sometimes detailed, about the interpretation to be given in that Union context. It must not be forgotten, however, that in many cases CJEU expressed itself clearly on the existence or on of the abuse, without leaving any margin of appreciation to the referring court.

The above arguments, although, cannot be considered sufficient to justify the apparent aporia that characterize the concrete applications of the prohibition of abuse by jurisprudence, applications that present themselves not only very

---

102 N. N. SHUIBHNE, The coherence of EU free movement law, constitutional responsibility and the Court of Justice, Oxford University Press, Oxford 2013, pp. 85ss. B. HOFSTOFFER, A cascade of rights, or who shall care for little Caterine?, in European Law Review, 34, 2009, pp. 548, has defined the abuse as: "a frequently tested but ineffective argument".

103 See the conclusions of the AG Tesauro presented in case C- 367/96, Kefalas and others of 12 May 1998, ECLI:EU:C:1998:41, I-02843, parr. 25ss.

104 CJEU, C-110/99, Emsland-Stärke of 14 December 2000, op. cit., par. 54.

limited, but also differentiated, and which testify to the "structural" difficulties that CJEU encounters in applying the logical scheme itself.

It is therefore necessary to seek a more exhaustive explanation of the attitude of extreme caution adopted by the EU judge, who prefers to rigorously reconstruct the limits relating to the actual content of "European" freedoms, to highlight the need for such freedoms to be exercised bona fide, to clarify the circumstances in which states can legitimately set limits to the exercise of these freedoms, or to interpret specific European legislation according to restrictive criteria[105]. To this end and in this context, although it should be taken into account that, what is called a case by case analysis plays an undeniable role, and that, on the other hand, the prohibition of abuse, as long as there is a general and unwritten clause, it cannot be considered ex if as an exactly predefined concept. Otherwise, the elasticity that is functional to it will vanish[106], an attempt to systemize the matter is not without utility.

The need for an in-depth study of case law studies in order to understand whether an interpretative scheme can be found that makes it possible to clarify in what circumstances one is in the presence of abusive behavior, after all, assumes a relevant practical scope. This takes into account the serious consequences they refer to the use of the prohibition on abuse, i.e. the non-application of EU law in the internal legal system or, in another perspective, the non-attribution of the right[107]. More precisely, if an abuse is established, the right to avail

105 It must be noted that the prohibition of abuse of law operates casually, depending on the circumstances of each legal and factual situation and, above all, always presupposes a value judgment, which is not totally unrelated to an assessment linked to equity or moral order. This particular feature of a legal standard is inherent in the nature and function of the notion of abuse: judgment must be made in terms of normality rather than normativity. In other words, if the identification of an abusive behavior could be the object of a preventive regulatory framework, the concept itself would become useless. This is precisely the reason why the concept of abuse refers to a meta-judicial evaluation that operates as a "valve" to legal formalism, like other general clauses, such as good faith or fairness.

106 It is, moreover, a functional operation also to guarantee legal certainty, one of the legal values in continuous tension with the prohibition of abuse.

107 See AG Mengozzi's opinion in case C-83/13, Fonnship and Svelnska Transportarbetarförbundet of 1st April 2014, ECLI:EU:C:2014:201, published in the electronic Reports, parr. 65 to 67, points out that "CJEU in its case-law does not seem to have firmly opted for one or the other of these qualifications of abuse of rights. In that sense, it stated that according to settled case-law, the application of Union Regulations cannot extend to the protection of abusive practices of economic operators, suggesting, therefore, that the concept of abuse (of law) constitutes a rule delimiting the scope of EU law provisions, whereas, on the contrary, it has found that any abuse of rights granted by the legal order (of the Union) under the provisions relating to the freedom of movement for workers presupposes that the person concerned falls within the scope ratione personae of that Treaty, fulfilling the conditions for qualifying as a "worker", and has also examined the fight against abusive practices on the

a fundamental freedom set out in the treaty may be denied to a natural or legal person. From this point of view, the use of a prohibition in question allows member states to significantly affect the choice of the law applicable to their conduct which the Union system assigns to private individuals as a consequence of the exercise of freedom of movement, so that it becomes a fundamental question to define whether and to what extent the EU system allows member states to take measures to prevent the evasion of domestic legislation by their citizens, through an instrumental reference to EU law[108].

THE RESEARCH METHOD: DISTINCTION BETWEEN INTERNAL AND CROSS BORDER ABUSE OF LAW

As stated by the Advocate General (AG) La Pergola in its opinion in C-212/97, Centros case of 9 March 1999: "the principle that data subjects cannot abusing or fraudulently use European Union law is constant in the case-law of this college and is included among the general principles of European law. It is, however, far from easy to specify the exact contours"[109].

Indeed, in pursuing this objective, the doctrine has traditionally classified behaviors considered abusive on the basis of the legal result pursued through undeserving behavior of protection, so as to distinguish two types of abuse[110], i.e.

grounds of general interest which may justify restrictions on the freedom of movement, which also presupposes that the situations of they are certainly within the scope of these freedoms. For my part, I would be inclined to favor the latter view of CJEU, rather than conceive the notion of abuse of rights as a principle of delimitation of the scope of EU law provisions (...)". For further analysis see: D. PATTERSON, A. SÖDERSTEN, A companion to European Union law and international law, J. Wiley & Sons, New York, 2016.

108 Conclusions of AG La Pergola in case C-212/97, Centros of 9 March 1999, ECLI:EU:C:1999:380, I-01459, par. 20.

109 Conclusions of AG La Pergola in case C-212/97, Centros of 9 March 1999, op. cit. For further details see: D. ANDERSON, Abuse of rights, op. cit. pp. 348-350. P. KOUTRAKOS, The Emsland-Stärke abuse of law test in the law of agriculture and free movement of goods, in R. DE LA FERIA, S. VOGENAUER, Prohibition of abuse of law: A new general principle of EU law?, op. cit. pp. 204ss. S.VOGENAUER, The prohibition of abuse of law: An emerging general principle of EU law, in R. DE LA FERIA, S. VOGENAUER (a cura di), Prohibition of abuse of law, op. cit., pp. 522 ss. S. VRELLIS, Abus et fraude, dans la jurisprudence de la Cour de Justice des Communautés Européennes, in H. GAUDEMET-TALLON, J.P. LANCET (a cura di), Vers de nouveaux equilibres entre ordres juridiques: Liber Amicorum H. Gaudemet-Tallon, op. cit., pp. 633ss.

110 D. SIMON, A. RIGAUX, La technique de la consécration d'un nouveau principe général du droit communautaire: l'exemple de l'abus de droit, in M. BLANQUET (a cura di) Mélanges en hommage à Guy Isaac: 50 ans de droit communautaire, op. cit., p. 568, they synthetically define this category as

the abuse of EU law[111] and the circumvention of national law. Jurisprudence also seems to know this distinction[112].

The first hypothesis occurs in cases of fictitious pre-establishment of the conditions prescribed by the European rules, in order to derive an improper advantage, in conflict with the aims and objectives of the same provisions. The private person here intends to invoke a rule of EU law, in order to enjoy its benefits, using constructions of "U" or "Y"[113].

The second hypothesis consists in circumventing the stricter national rules (e.g. law avoidance), through the instrumental or artificial use of prerogatives deriving from EU law[114].

The two cases are inextricably linked to the degree of harmonization achieved in the different areas in which the abuse occurred. In one case, with reference to the first hypothesis, it is precisely the invocation, even if formally correct, of rights contained in the rules of EU law, the result of harmonization, which produces undesired or unfair results, in the case of circumvention of the most stringent national legislation, instead, a central role by the cross-border

"fraud on EU law". It should be noted here that this phrase refers to the "fraud to law", which must be kept separate from the fraud in proper sense.

111 Which can be added the abuse of law in the strict sense, which is realized when the exercise of a right based on a EU provision is to be considered in practice not in accordance with its purposes. Article 54 refers to such an abuse of the Charter of Fundamental Rights of the European Union.

112 See the conclusions of AG Poiares Maduro presented in case: C-419/02, BUPA Hospitals Ltd and University of Huddersfield Higher Education Corporation v. Commissioners of Customs and Excise of 21 February 2006, ECLI:EU:C:2006:122, I-01685, par. 63. C-223/03, C-255/02, Halifax and others of 21 February 2006, op. cit., there are "two main contexts in which CJEU has analyzed the notion of abuse, when EU law provisions are invoked to evade national legislation and when to obtain facilitations in a manner that contrasts with the aims and purposes of those same provisions (...)". See, by the same, the conclusion of AG Tesauro in case: C- 367/96, Kefalas and others of 12 May 1998, op. cit., par. 24. This distinction is made by CJEU itself, C-196/04, Cadbury Schweppes and Cadbury Schweppes Overseas of 12 September 2006, op. cit.

113 See the conclusions of AG Maciej Szpunar presented in case: C-202/13, Sean Ambrose McCarthy of 18 December 2014, ECLI:EU:C:2014:2450, published in the electronic Reports, par. 111, where it reads: "as far as EU law is concerned, since this concept only appears sporadically in secondary legislation, reference should be made to CJEU case-law for the purposes of its examination. On the one hand, the latter sees a principle of national law in the context of which a legal person asserts Union law "for the sole purpose of avoiding the application of national law" and, secondly, a principle of Union law, in the context of which a legal person "fraudulently or excessively uses a right conferred on him by EU law (...)". For analysis see also: A. ROSAS, L. ARMATI, European Union constitutional law. An introduction, Hart Publishing, Oxford & Oregon, Portland, 2018.

114 CJEU, C-110/99, Emsland-Stärke of 14 December 2000, op. cit., C-8/92, General Milk Products v. Hauptzollamt Hamburg-Jonas of 3 March 1993, ECLI:EU:C:1993:82, I-00779. See also: T. LYONS, European Union customs, Oxford University Press, Oxford, 2018.

element, which allows the private sector to benefit from the regulatory differences between legal systems is assumed.

From a different angle, the circumvention of national law has also been qualified as "arbitrage type of behavior"[115]. In this case, the ultimate purpose of the legal or physical person is not so much to circumvent certain national provisions, but in benefiting from the most permissive or efficient provisions of another member state, invoking for this purpose the Union's rules. The escape from the less convenient legal system would thus typically be combined with a "flight into" the legal regime of another member state, which provides for minor legal burdens for the activities pursued by the person, such as, for example, lower taxation, immigration rules or less stringent labor rights or lower initial capital to create a company[116]. This would result in a triangulation between the norms of the national laws and those of the legal system of the Union, which allows "the acquisition" of the norms of another internal legal system, avoiding the application of the discipline of the legal system of origin[117].

In the case of misuse of EU law, a right conferred by Union rules will not be recognized because the conditions that determine its allocation do not exist or were created artificially. In the second hypothesis, the defined one of circumvention, a formally correct application of Union law, may meet a limitation in the requirement that the exercise of this right does not frustrate the application of the internal rules that regulate (in accordance with the law of Union) conducting an economic activity.

As already mentioned, the cases object of attention by CJEU in which a potential abuse was discussed, have traditionally been traced back to one or the other category respectively. Yet, even if this distinction is made, it is not clear at all, if not following a purely casuistic approach, for which reasons, having to judge cases falling within the same paradigm, the judge in some sentences has recognized an abuse and in others, on the contrary, have denied it, showing, at least in appearance, an inconsistent attitude.

It may, therefore, prove useful to favor a visual angle that only partially coincides with the aforementioned bipartition between abuse of EU law and circumvention of national legislation, starting from the consideration that this

115 CJEU, C-81/87, Daily Mail of 27 September 1988, ECLI:EU:C:1988:456, I-05483 and C-196/04, Cadbury Schweppes and Cadbury Schweppes Overseas of 12 September 2006, op. cit.

116 CJEU, C-212/97, Centros of 9 March 1999, op. cit.

117 A. SAYDÉ, Abuse of EU law, op. cit., pp. 48ss.

distinction can be better defined by the two cases of internal and cross-border abuse of law. In the first hypothesis, the abusive behavior, like what happens for the abuse at the national level, is put in place within an order, that of the European Union, which contains two or more alternative rules that regulate the same case. In the second case, the abusive construction involves, or rather it is based on, several separate legal systems, the national and the Union, where there are channels of connection between them, so that the owner of the right is in the condition to use the norms of a different instead of those of the order of belonging[118].

This is a distinction that is not without consequences for practical applications. In this regard, we immediately point out the greater problematic nature of the second hypothesis, completely extraneous to the abuse of rights as known in the state system.

(FOLLOWS) ILLUSTRATION OF THE METHOD

Starting from this distinction, with the aim of identifying a common thread of CJEU jurisprudence that could explain the exceedingly "differentiated" operation of the prohibition of abuse, it seems appropriate to classify the cases having regard to their national or "European Union" provenance, is the norm that represents the means to realize the abusive behavior, both by the expected advantage that is derived and the number of systems involved in the illegal operation. In this regard, it must be borne in mind that the advantageous situation which the objective of obtaining through abusive conduct may derive from the application of a provision of the European Union, be it contained in the Treaty or provisions of secondary law, as far as legislation of a member state other than the one of origin is available, invoked as a result of Union law. Alternatively, the means used to obtain such an advantage, that is to say the abused rule, can also be identified in a national or Union law. In addition, one or more legal systems may be involved in the abusive operation. Combining the elements already exposed, it is possible to elaborate different categories, which will be studied in depth, in order to verify the coherence of CJEU judgment regarding the choice to apply or not the prohibition of abuse of rights, with all the implications that derive from

118 With reference to internal abuse of law, in fact, jurisprudence has not failed to specify the conditions under which the presence of abusive behavior can be found, coordinating a test to verify the abuse, applied several times (or sometimes only recalled) in other harmonized areas.

it. The casuistry related to the hypothesis in which only the supranational order is involved in the illegal operation will be analyzed. As will be shown, this is the area in which the prohibition of abuse not only finds a generalized application, but has also been forged in its current characteristics. The hypothesis in which the "triangulation" between the systems mentioned above was carried out is different. In this regard, the cases in which individuals, through the exercise of freedom of movement, pre-establish the conditions for circumventing the legislation of the member state to which they belong and to apply other national legislation most favorable to them, will be studied first. It is anticipated here that the jurisprudence on the matter shows how, in relation to such cases, CJEU has not shown itself inclined to apply the prohibition under discussion, but has mostly admitted as a palliative the appeal by the member state concerned from abuse to imperative reasons of general interest.

Furthermore, the jurisprudence which has been able to rule on the invocation of the freedoms of movement by private individuals in order to circumvent the otherwise applicable national legislation and at the same time seek the application of the secondary legislation of the European Union will be taken into consideration. The hypotheses in which the private individual, claiming a particular status descending from the exercise of the freedoms of movement, wants to apply the national legislation of a certain member state which gives him an advantage. The latter hypothesis involves only two legal systems, that of the European Union and that of the host member state, since the private has completely severed the links with the state of origin, so that it cannot be considered subsisting, if not in a reflex element of the avoidance of less favorable national legislation. However, it is considered that the same can be analyzed in conjunction with the triggered triangulation in order to obtain a benefit from EU law, since even in these cases the advantage invoked deriving from a status assigned by the EU law by virtue of exercise of freedom of movement and the principle of non-discrimination. Moreover, when confronted with the last two categories cited above, CJEU showed a certain propensity for the restrictive interpretation of the Union's rules, in place of the application of the abuse doctrine[119].

In the opinion of the writer, what has just been described is a particularly interesting angle from which to evaluate the effectiveness of the prohibition on abuse and other techniques designed to protect the European Union and

119 A. ROSAS, L. ARMATI, European Union constitutional law. An introduction, op. cit., R. DE LA FERIA, S. VOGENAUER, Prohibition of abuse of law: A new general principle of EU law? op. cit., A. LENAERTS, The general principle, op. cit.

member states' legal systems from behavior that tends to purposes other than those for which the law gives the right. This does not mean that we are dealing with the best method, but only with a road that has not yet been broken, which seems worthy of being traveled.

The doctrine has already provided several readings of the phenomenon underway, using as many methodologies and criteria to try to bring to unity the jurisprudence of CJEU and its codifications, which, however, with a view to understanding the effectiveness of the prohibition of abuse in its concrete applications, have limitations. In particular, an evolutionary view of the abuse doctrine is often presented, observing how the latter has matured an increasing importance in recent years. This significant change has been attributed to several factors, including the increase in the volume of free circulation in the internal market, the enlargements in 2004 and 2007, as well as the development by CJEU of an abuse test and its subsequent implementation on tax matters[120].

This time perspective certainly has the merit of highlighting the initial opening of the Union system to the recognition of sanctioning hypotheses of abuse and a subsequent narrowing of the scope of the prohibition in the name of the ratio of the European norm, starting from the known C-212/97, Centros sentence of 9 March 1999, which established the legitimacy of an enterprise's use of EU law in order to choose the most convenient solution from a corporate point of view[121]. As will be better pointed out below, however, the temporal criterion risks not adequately highlighting the fundamental distinction in terms of practical implications between internal and cross border abuse of law. Indeed, the underlying idea is that the prohibition of abuse, although intended in a more limited sense, operates as a general principle even in cases of circumvention of national legislation. On the contrary, as it will be possible to explain funditus, the jurisprudence of CJEU does not seem to leave room, beyond the affirmations of principle, to a use in this sense.

Similarly, the methodology that suggests a difference in approach by CJEU towards the abuse in cases concerning legal entities compared to those in which natural persons are involved[122] does not seem to be successful. At first glance, a

120 R. DE LA FERIA, S. VOGENAUER, Prohibition of abuse of law: A new general principle of EU law? op. cit., pp. 398ss.

121 A. LENAERTS, The general principle, op. cit., pp. 1122ss.

122 The principle of abuse was used by CJEU to restrict the exercise of economic freedoms, while with regard to the free movement of persons and the right to citizenship, judges proved to be more sensitive to integration values and welfare policies. It is noted that in the area of free movement of

clear tendency of CJEU jurisprudence would seem to have been aimed at excluding, or at least reducing, the use of the abuse of the right when it comes to applying the principles and rules relating to the free movement of individuals. Although in the presence of entirely peculiar circumstances, it is apparently artificial and specifically adopted to be able to obtain the advantages deriving from these regulations, and to use it frequently, however, when it is necessary to verify the legitimacy of the exercise of freedom of circulation with regard to its effects on the law of economics or business. This criterion of distinction, to a more careful analysis of the jurisprudence, does not always seem useful to arrive at coherent solutions. It is true that in recent years the Union judge has significantly increased the protection of the fundamental rights of persons and in particular the rights deriving from their status as citizens of the Union. However, even in business law, CJEU, while recognizing the possibility for a member state to react to the abuse, denies the existence of an abusive practice, even in the paradigmatic case of the ghost company, contrived by definition. Therefore, from a pragmatic point of view, it is clear that it is not sufficient to affirm in principle a prohibition against abusing one's rights by the jurisprudence to establish a concrete use of the prohibition of abuse in business law. On the contrary, ruling in principle and concrete application are concepts that must remain distinct.

It was also decided to discard an approach by purely matter[123], since, although it allows for an orderly and complete classification, it is linked to an outdated type of study. It is now well established that the case law has (at least) affirmed the principle in question in various areas of EU law. Useful for descriptive purposes, this distinction cannot therefore alone make sense to CJEU indications.

The objective of this study, as we have seen, is indeed another, that of defining not only the established conditions of prohibition of abuse but also the alternative protection techniques employed from time to time.

The abuse of law presents itself as a polysemantic concept, susceptible to assume the most disparate meanings in the different jurisdictions that recognize the prohibition, as well as, specifically, an original and polymorphous

persons CJEU is animated by a shareable self-restraint that leads it not to apply the prohibition of abuse of the right to promote integration. In this spirit see: B. HOFSTOTTER, A cascade of rights, or who shall carefor little catherine? Some reflections on the Chen case, in European Law Review, 30, 2005, pp. 558ss. J. SNELL, And then there were two: Products and citizens in European Union law, in T. TRIDIMAS, P. NEBBIA (a cura di), European Union Law for the twenty-first century, vol. II, Oxford University Press, Oxford, 2004, pp. 62ss.

123 R. IONESCU, L'abus de droit en droit de l'Union européenne, op. cit.

physiognomy in EU law. In this context, it is therefore necessary to precisely delimit the research field of research, specifying right away which of the innumerable facets of the abuse of rights will not be the object of our analysis. First of all, the case of fraud in the proper sense must be kept separate from the concept of abuse of rights. If it is true, in fact, that CJEU, stating that the interested parties cannot abusively or fraudulently use Union law makes reference to the two concepts, the fraud differs from the abuse as described in the previous paragraphs, as it consists of a behavior that already formally, without needing to examine the substance, is not correct, as false documents or information are presented, in an attempt to obtain the rights deriving from EU law. This element, which precisely characterizes the figure in question[124], also makes it more easily frameable by the interpreter. In the moment in which there is a fraud, in fact, it is indisputable that the person who put in place the operation cannot benefit from "European" rights, so that member states can deny the rights to those who commit fraud, without having to prove that it was an attempt to circumvent national law or otherwise act contrary to the purpose of EU rule[125]. Having said this and referring now to the abuse, it was considered appropriate to focus attention on the most problematic problem of abuse in the European Union, that is to say what has been described as cross-border abuse of law. This figure is more characteristic of the EU legal system as a supranational order intrinsically linked

124 Various examples in the case series with regard to the presentation of false information to obtain the right of residence, see case: C-285/95, Suat Kol v. Land Berlin, of 6 March 1997, ECLI:EU:C:1997:280, I-03069, on which CJEU excluded "that an occupation carried out on the basis of a residence permit issued following fraudulent behavior (declaration false that he and his wife were living a family life in common in the marital home in order to obtain a residence permit) could give rise to (residence) rights for the benefit of the Turkish worker (...)" (par. 28). See also the case: C-235/99, Kondova of 27 September 2001, ECLI:EU:C:2001:489, I-06427 where we read, in paragraph 80, that "a Bulgarian citizen who, intending to start work as an employee or autonomous in a member state, evades the relevant controls of national authorities, falsely declaring to travel to that state for the purpose of seasonal work, falls outside the sphere of protection granted to him under the association agreement (...)". For further details see: M. MENDOZ, The legal effects of European Union agreement, Oxford University Press, Oxford, 2013, pp. 130ss.

125 It is also recalled, with regard to the presentation of false employee certificates of workers, in case: C-206/94, Brennet AG v. V. Paletta of 2 May 1996, ECLI:EU:C:1996:182, I-02357, CJEU has admitted, in par. 28, that "the interpretation of art. 18, nos. 1-5 of the Regulation n. 574/72 does not imply that it is forbidden for the employer to provide evidence that will allow, if necessary, national CJEU to ascertain the existence of abusive or fraudulent behavior resulting from the fact that the worker, despite declaring incapacity to work proven in accordance with the aforementioned art. 18, he was not sick (...)". See also judgment: C-130/88, Van de Bijl of 27 September 1989, ECLI:EU:C:1989:349, I-03039, concerning a certificate attesting to professional training, which contains a manifest inaccuracy "and case: C-347/93, Belgian State v. Boterluc SPRL of 9 August 1994, ECLI:EU:C:1994:314, I-03933, with reference to reimportation of some goods in a EU country with false documents.

to the national legal systems that are part of it, and it is absolutely linked to the functioning of the internal market and the policies developed within it.

First of all, ratione materiae should be excluded from a deepening of the abuse of rights in other areas of EU law, such as contract law, international private law[126], and competition law[127].

More generally, for the reasons set out below, the abuse of rights in the strict sense will not be examined, in which the abuse of process[128], a concept that

126 Under private international law, it may be noted that the rule of prohibiting the abuse of rights is expressed by the "law fraud" theory, defined as the abusive use of a conflict rule in order to escape the application of a provision imperative of the law of the forum. See in argument: V. KARAYANNIS, L'abus de droits découlant de l'ordre juridique communautaire, op. cit. pp. 527ss.

127 With regard to art. 102 TFEU which prohibits "the abuse of a dominant position", it should be noted here that this is at least a technical use of the term "abuse" as described above. However, it should be noted that, more recently, the Italian national authorities have reconnected the concept of "abuse of rights" in art. 102 concerning patents in the well-known Pfizer case. In particular, with the sentence dated 12 February 2014 n. 693, the Council of State noted that "the abuse of a dominant position, ascribed to Pfizer, is nothing but the specification of the broader category of abuse of rights, which presupposes the existence of a right, of the what is an instrumental use, not consistent with the purpose for which the system recognizes it in this case, the exclusion from the market of competitors. As has already been pointed out, elements constituting the abuse of rights are, in fact, precisely the ownership of a subjective right by a subject; the possibility that the concrete exercise of that right can be carried out according to a plurality of methods that are not rigidly predetermined; the fact that such a concrete exercise, even if formally respectful of the frame attributable to that right, is carried out according to censurable methods with respect to an evaluation criterion, legal or extra-juridical; the fact that, due to such a mode of operation, there is an unjustified disproportion between the benefit of the right holder and the sacrifice to which the counterpart is subject; consequently, the abuse of law, far from assuming a violation in the formal sense, involves the altered use of the formal scheme of law, aimed at achieving further and different objectives than those indicated by the legislator. For further details and analysis in argument see also: L. LOVDAHL GORMSEN, A principled approach to abuse of dominance in European competition law, Cambridge University Press, Cambridge, 2010. R. NAZZINI, The foundations of European Union competition law: The objective and principles of article 102, Oxford University Press, Oxford, 2011. R. O'DONOGHUE, J. PADILLA, The law and economics of article 102 TFEU, Hart Publishing, Oxford & Oregon, Portland, 2013. P. NIHOUL, The ruling of the General Court in intel: Towards the end of an effect-based approach in European competition law?, in Journal of European Competition Law & Practice, 5, 2014, pp. 52ss. J. BOURGEOIS, D. WAELBROECK (eds), Ten years of effects-based approach in EU competition law: State of play and perspectives, ed. Bruylant, Bruxelles, 2012. J. DREXL, W. KERBER, R. PODSZUN (eds), Competition policy and the economic approach: Foundations and limitations, Edward Elgar Publishers, Cheltenham, 2011. L. LOVDAHL GORMSEN, Are anti-competitive effects necessary for an analysis under article 102 TFEU?, in World Competition, 36, 2013, pp. 224ss.

128 M. TARUFFO (a cura di), Abuse of procedural rights: Comparative standards of procedural fairness, Kluwer, London, Boston, 1999. With reference to international perspective, on the other hand, it should be noted that the figure has attracted the attention of CJEU: in particular, any behavior manifestly contrary to the right of appeal established by the Convention and constituting an obstacle to the proper functioning of CJEU or to the proper conduct of the procedure before it. The existence of an independent category of abuse of the process in EU was then highlighted by D. SIMON, A. RIGAUX, F. LAGONDET, La technique de la consécration d'un nouveau principe général du droit communautaire: l'exemple de l'abus de droit, in M. BLANQUET (a cura di) Mélanges

deserves a brief mention here, in order to highlight the differentiating aspects with the different notion of abuse intended as circumvention of the law, as sketched in the preceding paragraphs.

While the abuse of law in the strict sense is substantiated in the exercise of a right in an "excessive" and unreasonable way, so as to cause a disproportionate damage to others, the abuse that interests us is manifested in the form of improper use of the norm to obtain certain advantages.

Although both concepts have elements in common, they differ in reality in many ways. The first, which finds its roots not by chance in civil law, has the objective to limit the exercise of a right naturally attributed by the legal system, in the light of social objectives and, ultimately, to curb the excesses of individualism, while the latter comes into play when a person puts himself in a specific juridical situation, with the main intention to evade mandatory provisions otherwise applicable or to obtain advantages that otherwise would not be the case. The abuse in this second meaning therefore recalls a behavior conforming to the letter of law, but is in reality artificial. As can be seen, therefore, the abuse in the latter meaning does not necessarily have as its objective or effect of causing damage to others, but rather, it is elusive.

The two concepts must remain distinct, since only the abuse described above implies a circumvention of the law to obtain an illicit advantage, an element which, on the contrary, would be absent in the case of abuse of rights in the strict sense[129].

Even if the abuse of law in the strict sense was born and found fertile ground in the national legal systems, in the European Union's system, some traces are presented. In particular, on the basis of the distinction just drawn, it is considered useful to bring two examples with the aim of making some clarifications about the emergence of such a figure in Union law and, all in all, referring to the encoded law of the European jurisprudence.

---

en hommage à Guy Isaac: 50 ans de droit communautaire, op. cit. see in argument the next cases: C-338/82, Albertini and Montagnani v. Commission of the European Communities of 17 May 1984, ECLI:EU:C:1984:181, ECR 02123, parr. 51-52. C-243/78, Simmenthal SpA v. Commission of the European Communities of 5 March 1980, ECLI:EU:C:1980:65, I-00593, parr. 10-11). For details see: G. BECK, The legal reasoning of the Court of justice of the European Union, Hart Publishing, Oxford & Oregon, Portland, 2013.

129 T. TRIDIMAS, Abuse of right on EU law, op. cit., pp. 12ss.

THE EXAMPLE IN CODIFIED LAW: ART. 54 OF CHARTER OF THE FUNDAMENTAL RIGHTS OF EUROPEAN UNION

Frequent is the statement that the abuse of law now finds an explicit legislative recognition in art. 54 CFREU signed in Nice on 7 December 2000[130], which, as is known, following the entry into force of the Lisbon Treaty, has acquired the same legal value as the Treaties. The aforementioned article, entitled "prohibition of the abuse of rights", states that "no provision of this CFREU must be interpreted as the right to exercise an activity or perform an act aimed at the destruction of rights and freedoms recognized in this CFREU or to impose more extensive restrictions on these rights and freedoms than those laid down in this Charter"[131]. It should not be overlooked that the provision in question actually reproduces the content of art. 17 of the European Convention of Human Rights (ECHR). This statement is justified not only by the almost absolute coincidence of the content of the two provisions, but also by the accompanying report to the CFREU.

From this it follows that, in interpreting it, the historical significance of art. 17 ECHR, which in turn requires to be understood as a defensive guarantee of the European order, having the general function of safeguarding the rights that the Convention enumerates for the protection of the free functioning of democratic institutions. This prevents groups or individuals from exploiting they benefit the principles set by the convention in order to harm the rights and freedoms of others, in short, as a provision to prevent democratic freedoms from being invoked to pursue anti-democratic purposes, cannot be ignored.

The rule then places a prohibition on groups and individuals to exercise their recognized rights for acts or destructive activities of others' freedoms, and on

130 J. MAURY, L'éviction de la loi normalement competente in l'ordre pubblic et la fraude à la loi, University of Valladolid, 1952, pp. 163ss.

131 For further details and analysis see: X. GROUSSOT, G.T. PETURSSON, The EU Charter of the Fundamental Rights five years on. The emergence of a new constitutional framework?, in S. DE VRIES, U. BERNITS, S. WEATHERILL, The EU Charter of Fundamental Rights as a binding instrument. Five years old and growing, op. cit., S.I. SÁNCHEZ, The Court and the Charter: The impact of the entry into force of the Lisbon Treaty on the ECJ's approach to fundamental Right, op. cit., T. TRIDIMAS, Fundamental rights, general principles of EU law and the Charter, op. cit., H. VON DER GROEBEN, J. SCHWARZE, A. HATJE, Europäisches Unionsrecht, op. cit., K. STERN, M. SACHS, Europäische Grundrecht Charta, op. cit., pp. 756ss. S. PEERS et al. (eds.), The EU Charter of Fundamental Rights, A Commentary, op. cit., pp. 1523-1538. J. MEYER (ed.), Charta der Grundrechte der Europäischen Union, op. cit., pp. 813-826. J.P. JACQUÉ, La Cour de Justice de 'Union et application de la Charte dans les Etats membres: "Mehr Licht", op. cit., pp. 125-147. T. KERIKMÄE, Protecting human rights in the EU. Controversies and challenges of the Charter of Fundamental Rights, op. cit., pp. 80ss.

the other imposes on states not to take liberticide measures and limitations of rights further to those conventional. The two precepts, in apparent contradiction between them, reveal the tension between the need to defend democracy and the definition of intervention limits to protect it. The jurisprudence of the European Court of Human Rights (ECtHR) has clearly defined the rationale of art. 17, stating that it is a norm invoked by a member state in order to defend the values underlying the convention. This can be deduced from the relevant preamble (Garaudy v. France, 24 June 2003); to "prevent that groups of totalitarian matrix use in their own interest the principles enunciated by the convention", (Lawless v. Ireland, 1st July 1961). It is also invokable by any subject when it considers that the state has availed itself of its power of interference in the enjoyment of individual rights for purposes and in ways that go beyond what is established by the ECHR. It is precisely from the application of the rule, that one can derive the scope of this prohibition of abuse of law. Historically the first application of art. 17 ECHR is given by the German communist party v. Germany sentence of 20 July 1975, which is characterized by a broad reading of the ban. In this case, the Commission considers compatible with the ECHR, pursuant to art. 17, the dissolution of the German communist party, which proposed the end of the dictatorship of the proletariat, a situation incompatible with the democratic values embraced by the ECHR.

The application of art. 17 therefore ends up not involving a simple limitation, but the total ablation of the whole system of rights guaranteed by the ECHR. Moreover, the fact that the law was invoked to affirm the inadmissibility of the appeal precluded any judgment of merit on the effective exercise of rights.

The subsequent Lawless v. Ireland sentence of 1st July 1961 witnesses the first attempt to limit the scope of prohibition of abuse and the launch of a guaranteed trend in the interpretation of the law. The ECtHR called upon to rule on the legality of an administrative measure of detention issued by the Irish government against a member of I.R.A., circumscribes the scope of art. 17 ECHR seeking to identify the rights that, if invoked to protect the exercise of deeds or liberticide activities, can put at risk the rights and the liberties conventionally guaranteed (liberticide rights). Among them, for example, the freedom of expression (article 10 ECHR) and the freedom of association (article 11 ECHR) would fall, but not the personal freedom (article 5 ECHR) and the right to fair trial (art. 6 ECHR)[132].

132 D. LIAKOPOULOS, Die Rechte des Verurteilten Strafrecht: Kritische und vergleichende, in Interna-

Subsequently, with the De Becker v. Belgium sentence of 27 March 1962, further limits have been placed on art. 17 ECHR, establishing that it should be interpreted restrictively and applied as an extrema ratio. In the De Becker case, the applicant was a Belgian journalist deprived of civil and political rights, in application of a provision of the criminal code, on the basis of his collaboration with the German authorities during World War II. On this occasion, the judges of Strasbourg excluded to be able to apply art. 17 ECHR, stating that this rule could come into play only against those who threaten the democratic structure of the contracting states and in proportion to the severity and duration of the threat itself. Furthermore, starting from the Kuhnen v. Federal Republic of Germany sentence of 12 May 1988, on the foundation of an organization aimed at restoring the national socialist party, the prohibition of abuse of rights was not used to affirm the mere inadmissibility of the appeal, but as an instrument of interpretation and examination of the merits of the applicant's complaint.

It can be observed, with reference, that the cases involved in the prohibition of abuse of law can be traced to two broad categories. One includes the cases of incitement to hatred, of denialism, of the apology of nazism, in which art. 17 ECHR excludes the operation of art. 10 ECHR, and the second applies to the cases of dissolution of parties, groups and associations with anti-democratic purposes, in which art. 17 excludes art. 11 ECHR. The requirement of the existence of "acts and activities" is interpreted in a rather flexible manner, including heterogeneous facts (such as the drafting of a private letter, the diffusion of a book, the carrying out of political activity), focusing instead the attention on the liberticidal aims pursued. We can also note how the ECtHR jurisprudence also insists on a threat severity threshold to conventional values, so that where the applicant's behavior is not serious enough to constitute a real threat to democratic values, the prohibition of abuse of right does not find application.

Turning the attention towards the Union, the prohibition of abuse of law is foreseen in art. 54 CFREU. Alternatively, art. 52 par. 3, provides that where the CFREU contains rights corresponding to those guaranteed by the European Convention for the Protection of Human Rights and Fundamental Freedoms, the meaning and scope of these should be determined by relationem, and could also apply to the prohibition of abuse of law.

It has been observed in doctrine that an operation of translation of the contents of art. 17 ECHR on art. 54 in question, however correct, is still incomplete.

---

tional and European Union Legal Matters-working paper series, 2015.

According to our opinion, if we accept the notion of abuse of law as a misleading exercise of the prejudicial right to the interests of others, it can also be hypothesized for fundamental rights, with the same problems already dealt with on the general plan. In regards to the aspect of instrumentalization of the right for purposes that are averse to it, the general right is valid for the subjective one: it is also conferred on the legal system to protect an interest, strictly and immediately linked to person's prerogatives, of primary rank in the legal system. However, any case potentially subjected to its holder for other purposes, on the other hand, precisely the jurisprudence on the misuse of the law that developed by articles 17 ECHR and 54 CFREU. In this respect, therefore, as for any abuse of law, the problem is the identification of the parameter in the light of which to unify the removal from the orderly end.

Also, the aspect of the intolerable sacrifice imposed on other goods and interests, produced as a consequence of this diversion of interest, can be assessed through the recourse to a balancing with what happens in case of abuse of other rights.

As for other rights, even with reference to fundamental rights, the abuse must be confronted with the exact identification of the content of law, often difficult to establish, especially with regard to the suburban areas far from its essential core (think, to example, to the right to life, peacefully recognized, and to the problems of rights connected with the end of life and the assisted origin of life).

These issues, however, are only the re-proposal on a larger and more articulated scale of those difficulties in identifying the ratio of the law and the parameters that have been posed, in general, for the abuse of law.

Rather, with reference to the abuse of fundamental rights, the most critical aspect is given by the repetition of the same problem that also afflicts the conflict between fundamental rights. It seems that these doubts, which grip the problem of the border between fundamental rights or the external limit (problem of conflict) are substantially the same ones that arise when one goes in search of their "internal limit" (problem of abuse).

As for the profile of who is responsible to resolve the conflicts between fundamental rights is the task of the judge or the legislator. One wonders who is responsible for the decision on the content (and therefore the limits) of individual rights, their hierarchical ordination and their mutual succumbence, whether it is for the parliament or a judge. In this second case, which judge, if to constitutional courts or ordinary judges. In doctrine, it has been pointed out how the question of relations between rights cannot be solved only in abstract by the intervention of the legislator, since in practice the conflict between rights inevitably manifests itself in a particular way and, therefore, necessarily requires an assessment of the individual case, of the way in which rights pose in it, which is the task of the judge. On the other hand, however, it must be noted how in such a political matter, such as that of fundamental rights, it cannot resort to a purely technical and legal balancing, but rather a criterion of negotiation, stipulation and agreement between rights emerges, which led to the belief that, in matters of fundamental rights, there is a politicization of the judge and the legalization of politics. As for the parameter with which to resolve the conflict between fundamental rights, the doubts derive from the fact that, as regards fundamental rights, the interpreter does not have any legal or conventional limitations to establish the boundary between them, being rights not governed by punctual rules (for which it is easy to identify the methods of exercise according to descriptive parameters), but of rights established by principles, where valuation parameters also operate. In fact, this aspect, as we said, reveals an inevitable political element in the legal substance of fundamental rights, which returns to present itself in every discourse on them, including that on their abuse.

Due to the abuse of fundamental rights, the uncertainties afflicting, in general, the abuse of law do not seem to be a good reason to exclude its configurability, for these rights once the category is accepted.

As was mentioned, the even greater difficulties encountered in answering questions as for what interest of man is conferred a human right, or when exercising a constitutional freedom imposes an unbearable sacrifice to others. They are proportionate to the greater rank and to the greater legal amplitude, as well as to the general problematic of the category, which causes problems concerning the abuse of law to intervene on an elusive matter.

However, it is necessary to clarify the configurability of the abuse of right for fundamental rights. It must be assessed whether all fundamental rights can be abused. In the literature, a negative answer was given and it was highlighted that the criterion for selecting fundamental rights that are abusive seems to be the possibility that the right can be exercised in a number of ways that are not predetermined, which is not surprising given that it is a question of the prerequisites for configurability of the abuse of rights.

Thus, the category of abuse of right can be applied to the rights of liberty, such as freedom of expression, association and strike, because their indefinite content makes it possible to use misguided or disproportionate, which ends up prejudicing or overwhelming a right of others (think of reputation, to the image, to the honor in the case of freedom of expression).

This does not apply to rights in the strict sense, such as the case of the right not to be tortured. The right not to be subjected to torture is satisfied not by an act of exercise of its holder, but by the abstention of the other consociated by torture. The same could be said for the right of habeas corpus. Also, in this case, for the fundamental right that applies to the subjective right: for it to be abused it is necessary that the exercise of the right can be carried out in ways disapproved by the law for the purposes they pursue and the results they achieve.

In this sense, the elaboration of the prohibition of abuse of law in CFREU, although art. 54 is more extensive and flexible than art. 17 ECHR, must be read with a view to preventing the instrumental use of subjective positions concerning economic rights and freedoms that attack the market. In this regard, if it cannot be doubted that according to the editors of the Nice Charter, because a catalog of rights was complete, it was necessary to insert an explicit provision for the prohibition of abuse, the central question requiring clarification concerns, the relationship that binds this codification of the jurisprudence on abuse of rights.

However, it must be recognized that in the formulation of CFREU the objective element given by the alteration of the causal factor, common to the notion of abuse of Union or national law, is easily identifiable. In the event that the exercise of a specific right recognized by the CFREU determines the elimination of other rights guaranteed by the same, the purpose for which this right has been practically exercised can only be structurally different from that for which the right itself is attributed[133]. However, you are faced with the exercise of a right that must be able, on the one hand, or to determine the destruction of the rights and freedoms provided in CFREU catalog, or in any case to circumscribe the scope. Article 54 CFREU, in other words, refers to an abuse for relationem, against a different right that is compressed by this abusive exercise[134]. It is inter-

133 As we can see in case: C-206/94 of 2 May 1996, ECLI:EU:C.1996:182, I-02357, par. 25. From this CJEU deduced that it is for the national authorities and national courts to deny the benefit of that right if it is shown in the light of objective factors that the latter is invoked fraudulently or illegally according to the next cases by CJEU, C-439/04 and C-440/04, Kittel and Recolta recycling of 6 July 2006, ECLI:EU:C:2006:446, I-06161, par. 55 and C-285/11, Bonik of 6 December 2012, ECLI:EU:C:2012:69, published in the electronic Reports, par. 26. For further details see also: D. PATTERSON, A. SÖDERSTEN, A companion to European Union law and international law, op. cit.

134 R. IONESCU, L'abus de droit en droit de l'Union européenne, op. cit. pp. 16-17, according to which the abuse described in art. 54, which is manifested in the restrictions on fundamental rights, would

esting to note that the alteration of the causal factor is an element that unites the abuse of right to misuse of power, also known to the legal order of the Union. Indeed, it is the distorted use of a power expressly recognized and attributed by a norm of the order. However, while the abuse of the right when the abusive behavior is put in place by the owner of the right is misuse of power when the same conduct is put in place by the holder of public authority.

In light of the aforementioned considerations regarding the historical ratio of the provision, as well as its formulation in the sense of requiring the compression of the rights and freedoms provided by CFREU, it must be considered that art. 54 make reference to the notion of abuse of law in the strict sense.

Given this, although consciously in disagreement with some of the literature, it is believed that art. 54 cannot be elected as a codification standard of the previous jurisprudence of CJEU on the abuse that will be analyzed in the following paragraphs, since no structural analogy can be found with the elements constituting the figure of the abuse of EU law, as elaborated by CJEU jurisprudence[135].

Moreover, the interpretation that considers to assimilate the two notions of abuse seems to stifle a further consideration. That is, starting from its topographic location and forbidding any interpretation that aims at the destruction of rights or imposing more extensive limitations on them than those provided by CFREU, the provision in question would be awarded the function of a wide-ranging, not already preceptive, interpretation rule, a reading that could also explain the absence, in the provision, of the express provision of loss of the right[136]. In conclusion, for the reasons set out above, it cannot therefore be said

---

be a legal category that does not present common elements with the abuse of law which is occupied by EU jurisprudence, since, taking exactly ECHR provisions of art. 17, i.e. forbidding a member state to impose more extensive restrictions on a protected right than those provided for by the Charter, would reflect a publicist need: that of giving democracy the chance to defend itself, lacking the versatility and flexibility of the notion of abuse that is found in the provisions of some civil codes and distinguishes EU jurisprudence contra D. TRIANTAFYLLOU, L'interdiction des abus de droit en tant que principe général du droit communautaire, op. cit. pp. 630. According to which, precisely the decision to include such an article in a catalog of rights demonstrates that EU law, without any doubt, has the sole objective of establishing a single market in which everything circulates freely, in contrast to the invocation of abuse, has reached a degree of maturity such as to have the opportunity to recognize, without hesitation, beyond the protection of public finances, the prohibition of abuse of law as a general principle at EU level and no longer national.

135 CJEU, C-441/93, Panagis Pafitis and others v. Trapeza Kentrikis Ellados A.E. and others of 12 March 1996, op. cit. C-367/96, Kefalas and others of 12 May 1998, ECLI:EU:C:1998:222, I-02843. C-373/97, Diamantis of 23 March 2000, op. cit.

136 Article 8 of the Greek law n. 1386/1983 provided for this possibility. This law, more in detail, provided that companies in serious difficulty were placed under the management of a new public company called OAE (Organization for the reorganization of companies), following a request or a ministerial

that art. 54 CFREU[137] constitutes a solid basis for the codification of the institution as a general principle, at least if not understood in the sense of abuse of law in the strict sense.

THE DUAL FUNCTION OF THE RULE: INTERPRETATIVE PARADIGM AND CLAUSE OF INADMISSIBILITY OF THE APPEALS

There is no doubt that the letter of art. 17 ECHR together with its genesis, leads to its classification in terms of limit clause. As mentioned, the need to preserve democratic society and its key principles leads to insert an explicit prohibition on the arbitrary exercise of conventional freedoms that has as effect that of canceling or unduly compressing the contents of those same freedoms that, as mentioned, establish the cultural and democratic substratum common to member states.

Political genesis, it was said: and this aspect was fully confirmed by the applications that the Commission (at that time, body established to ensure compliance with the international agreement, then replaced for this function by the ECtHR) made of art. 17 ECHR since the early years of European ECHR[138]: conceived as an instrument to prevent subversive groups from taking hold in Europe, leading to the establishment of new dictatorial regimes. It was a perfect tool for the rejection of appeals complaining of the injury of an "abused" prerogative, i.e. directed to subvert the principles underlying it.

The same practical declination of art. 17 is essentially originally, therefore, in terms of "political" affirmation, moving within a more ideological and cultural

---

decision. This provision openly violated art. 25 of the Second Company Directive, according to which the decision to increase the capital is the exclusive competence of shareholders' meeting. Precisely for this art. 8 was subsequently amended in accordance with the directive. The new 1882/1990 law, however, did not provide for a specific sanction for the infringement of EU rights of former shareholders, who had lost the value of their shares because of the capital increases by administrative means and the unwillingness to exercise their right of first refusal. Only in 1999 was adopted the Greek law n° 2685/1999, which provided for the possibility for former shareholders to file an appeal for damages against the Greek State as a remedy for the violation of article 25 of the Second Directive.

137 K. LENAERTS, Exploring the limits of the EU Charter of Fundamental Rights, op. cit., pp. 375ss. N. LAZZERINI, (Some of) the fundamental rights granted by the Charter may be a source of obligations for private parties: AMS, op. cit., pp. 908ss. J. KROMMENDIJK, Principled silence or mere silence on principles? The role of the EU Charter's principles in the case law of the court of Justice, op. cit., pp. 322ss.

138 ECtHR12 June 2012 (dec.), Hizb Ut-Tahrir and others v. Germany of 12 June 2012.

ideological direction tout court. However, this refers to further meanings[139] or rather: the construction of the same as a broad clause, as well as the openings left by the normative dictate in a reaction-remedy point (aspect on which the ECHR is silent), would in reality allow a configuration under different hermeneutical and practical keys.

It would not be at stake, so it would seem, the simple denial against the individual of conventional protection in the hypothesis of abuse of the freedoms stated; no one (state or individual or group) can abuse those guarantees: the prohibition is formulated in such lapidary terms that no exception is allowed. It is universal, thus instilling the idea of a specific obligation on the part of the contracting state to prevent or repress the abuse of rights covered by the ECHR, even if it were implemented by the authority. In any case, leaving aside this aspect for the moment, we will concentrate on the interpretation and application profiles of art. 17 ECHR according to the declinations concretely offered in practice[140].

Always in relation to the primitive practical modulations, we can say that art. 17 ECHRs have traditionally been offered two application methods. In the first place, the standard under analysis was used to stop the birth of those germs of xenophobic and pro-nazi ideology that continued to meander in Europe[141]. Secondly, the provision has been used as a tool for implementing the proportionality parameter which (as already mentioned) innervates the entire conventional fabric: the concrete events raised the question of the limits inherent in the interference of public authority (the state) in exercise by the individual freedom of expression of thought (in this case: in the electoral). Three conditions are necessary for the authoritarian meddling in the exercise of conventional freedoms to be justified. This limitation must be provided for by law, must aim to implement legitimate purposes, and lastly, must be necessary in a democratic society for the attainment of said goals. What else does not mean that the need

139 ECtHR, Féret v. Belgium of 16 July 2009, par. 52.

140 A. BUYSE, M. HAMILTON (eds.), Transitional jurisprudence and the European Convention on Human Rights. Justice, politics and rights, Cambridge University Press, Cambridge, 2011, pp. 155-156.

141 ECtHR, Orban and others v. France of 15 January 2009; Garaudy v. France of 24 June 2003, concerning the publication of contributions inspired by denialism, or the Jersild judgment (Jersild v. Denmark of 23 September 1994), in relation to the competition of a journalist in the dissemination of racist ideas advocated by a group of extremists. For further analysis see: E. FRONZA, Memory and punishment: Historical denialism, free speech and the limits of criminal law, ed. Springer, Berlin, 2018.

for a proportional relationship between the public interest justifying the interference of the state and the essential legal good of the individual who comes to counterpart.

In general terms, some (more or less sensitive) diversifications of the interpretative and applicative modules of art. 17 ECHR are found, particularly depending on the subject responsible for the abusive conduct[142].

Let's start (so to speak) from above: quid iuris whether to abuse the law is the member state. For greater conceptual rigor, when it comes to the abuse of law by the state, it is more appropriate to speak about the abuse of the conventional limitations of the rights and freedoms sanctioned. On a principle level, in fact, the guarantees covered by the text of international law refer to the individual, in favor of which they are expressly prepared (except to introduce, when necessary, the possibility that they are subject to limitation or balancing with opposing interests of public relevance). Logically, therefore, the "conventional" abuse by the state would materialize in the abuse of limitations that the ECHR provides for the freedoms (both as regards the restrictions obtainable from the normative text, and those that can be deduced from the relevant jurisprudence rulings).

Given this premise, the reference immediately runs to art. 15ECHR. In speciem, the rule (entitled: "derogation in case of emergency status") gives the contracting state the possibility to introduce limitations on the guarantees established by the European ECHR, particularly, in the case of war or other public danger at risk the life of the nation, if the situation makes it necessary, and if such restrictions do not conflict with other obligations of international law. We must understand limitations (amplitude and severity apart) different from those already specifically permitted by the ECHR (or recognized legitimate by the European ECtHR in the interpretation). In any case, it is not possible to derogate in relation to certain rights explicitly provided for by art. 15, par. 2 (there is talk of absolute guarantees such as the right to life, the prohibition of torture or enslavement, or the non-retroactivity of criminal law). In any case, if the state intends to apply some limitation to them, it should promptly inform the General Secretary of the Council of Europe, both on the content of these limitations and on the reasons that would have determined them.

On some occasions, the ECtHR in Strasbourg has recognized the violation by the state party of art. 15 ECHR. Given that it is up to the supranational judge to

142 ECtHR, Vejdeland and others v. Sweden of 9 February 2012, par. 8.

assess whether the conduct of the state falls within the limits set by the provision referred (through the evaluation of parameters such as the extent of the right touched by the restriction, the temporal extent of the limitation, the discretion that may have exercised the state in making such a limitation), the conceptual nucleus that can be derived from the rulings on the matter would be summarized in the exclusion of the possibility that the state has an indiscriminate power in the matter of limitations of ECHR guarantees. Otherwise, the risk would be incurred, where the boundaries of the operation of art. 15, of the disappearance of the overall effectiveness of the conventional regulatory apparatus[143].

It should be emphasized that, in these hypotheses, the abusive behavior of the state manifests itself as excess in the exercise of the authoritative power. In other words, if art. 15 ECHR expressly empowers, under the exceptional conditions laid down therein, the public authority to impose restrictions on the exercise of liberties established by the ECHR, we could then more properly speak in this case of excess power, as distinct from the abuse of right[144].

In such cases, the concrete state conduct overflows the power exerted by the "spatial" borders imposed on the normative level (emergency situation), as well as by the equally expressed purpose (to remedy the danger for the life of the nation).

In this sense, art. 15 ECHR is only very close to the substantial idea of abuse of law (as well as of abuse of process), elaborated in the internal system: in this last perspective, in fact, separate sociological matrix, the prohibition moves from the necessity (repeats) of maintain the consistency and rationality of the system and, last but not least, to "moralize" the exercise of recognized rights.

Article 15, otherwise, admits a further restriction of liberties due to exceptional events, which precisely confirm the "plasticity" of guarantees: an urgency, in short, there is or is not; the risk here, through the abuse, is the direct annulment of liberties by the state, not the use of a power deviating from its purpose and which indirectly compresses a freedom. Systemic rationality and moralizing needs, in essence, have something to do with it: the factual respect of fundamental rights counts, safeguarding them from an "abuse of urgency", not from a surreptitious use.

---

143 ECtHR, Ireland v. United Kingdom of 18 January 1978. Brannigan and McBride v. United Kingdom of 26 May 1993. Aksoy v. Turkey of 18 December 2006. For details see: B. RAINEY, W. WICKS, C. OVEY, Jacbos, White and Ovey: The European Convention on Human Rights, Oxford University Press, Oxford, 2017.

144 For further details see: A. SAYDÉ, Defining the concept of abuse of Union law, in Yearbook of European Law, 33 (1), 2014, pp. 140ss.

In this way, the meaning that within art. 15 would come to have any state abuse is that of overflowing or excess of the power of derogation. The observations carried out immediately lead to a point. In short, art. 15ECHR does not inherently pertain to the genus abuse of the law, limiting itself to authorizing the restrictions on liberties in an exceptional way by authoritative means. Article 17, otherwise, constitutes the pivotal disposition, also in relation to the authority, in the matter of abuse[145]. Far from being a special norm with respect to the latter, art. 15 ECHR is a structurally different norm, aimed at safeguarding the minimum connotations of legal civilization and respect for human rights even in exasperated situations such as war or other serious public danger[146]. Therefore, it does not overlap with art. 17 ECHR, not even limiting its application or even integrating it.

The question to this point with reference to the authority is: what is the function covered by art. 17 ECHR?

To exemplify, art. 10 ECHR[147] sanctions the freedom of expression of the individual, but at the same time providing that this right does not prevent a state

145 ECtHR, Vona v. Hungary of 9 July 2013, par. 10, which it is affirmed that: "(...) the government that the applicant expressed contempt for the victims of a totalitarian regime (...) or belonged to a group with totalitarian ambitions (...) the application does not constitute an abuse of right of petition for the purposes of article 17 of the Convention (...)".

146 E. BREMS, J. ERARDS (eds.), Shaping rights in the ECHR. The role of the European Court of Human Rights in determining the scope of human rights, Cambridge University Press, Cambridge, 2014, pp. 188ss.

147 ECtHR, Fatullayev v. Azerbaijan of 22 April 2010, par. 81. The applicant was in fact merely "supporting one of the conflicting opinions in the debate concerning the existence of an escape corridor for the refugees and, based on that, expressing the view that some Azerbaijani fighters might have also borne a share of the responsibility for the massacre. By doing so, however, he did not seek to exonerate those who were commonly accepted to be the culprits of this massacre, to mitigate their respective responsibility or to otherwise approve of their actions (...)". Perinçek v. Switzerland of 15 October 2015, par. 26. It subsequently held that: "(...) in cases concerning the right to freedom of expression in article 10 ECHR means that it should only be resorted to if it is immediately clear that the impugned statements sought to deflect this article from its real purpose by employing the right to freedom of expression for ends clearly contrary to Convention values (...) made a detailed evaluation of all the relevant aspects of the case and eventually concluded (...) that taking into account all the elements (...) that the applicant's statements bore on a matter of public interest and did not amount to a call for hatred or intolerance, that the context in which they were made was not marked by heightened tensions or special historical overtones in Switzerland, that the statements cannot be regarded as affecting the dignity of Armenian community's members to the point of requiring a criminal law response in Switzerland, that there is no international law obligation for Switzerland to criminalise such statements, that the Swiss courts appear to have censured the applicant for voicing an opinion that diverged from the established ones in Switzerland, and that the interference took the serious form of a criminal conviction (...) in a democratic society, to subject the applicant to a criminal penalty in order to protect the rights of the Armenian community at stake in the present case (...) there has therefore been a breach of article 10 of the Convention (...)".

from subjecting the exercise of broadcasting, film and television companies to a licensing regime[148]. However, any abuse of this power of restriction, outside the limits imposed by the law (as well as the interpretation of the same offered by ECtHR), would not be an abuse/excess falling within art. 15 ECHR, since the latter refers to "measures derogating from the obligations envisaged by the ECHR", susceptible to adoption in the presence of specific historical-factual contexts (war or danger for the life of the nation), but more properly in the riverbed very different from art. 17 ECHR: in the present case, it would prohibit the contracting state from interpreting and applying the power conferred on it by the law in order to annul factually contained (substantial abolition of freedom of expression)[149].

The conclusion about the relationships between articles 15 and 17 ECHR could be summarized as follows: the former limits exceptions to the obligations set out by the ECHR, so that any abuse of any restrictions (in the public interest) that the ECHR puts forward in individually regulating a right or a freedom would be prohibited according to the second. To this end, the letter of the same also explicitly forbids the application distortions of guarantees, even by the member states (although we speak of "right" and not of power, but the terminological aspect does not seem to be a decisive obstacle).

That said, we can move on to the abuses committed by the individual.

With regard to this aspect, art. 35, par. 3, lett. a) ECHR: the ECtHR has the power to declare an appeal inadmissible, submitted pursuant to art. 34 ECHR, if this is incompatible with the provisions of ECHR (or its Protocols), manifestly unfounded or abusive. The applicative barricum of the norm must be

148 As we can see in the case: Pavel Ivanov v. Russia of 20 February 2007, par. 1. and Soulas and others v. France of 10 July 2008. The prohibition of abuse of rights was considered as a consequence of the examination of the merit of the inapplicable complaint on the assumption that the statements contained in the text were not serious enough to justify the application of art. 17. In the same spirit Feret v. Belgium case of 10 December 2009, par. 77, where ECtHR has declared that: "(...) political discourse that incites to the podium based on religious, ethnic or cultural prejudices represents a danger for the social peace and for the political stability of democratic states (...)".

149 ECtHR, Fáber v. Hungary of 24 July 2012. CJEU stressed that: "(...) when the right to freedom of expression is exercised in the context of political speech through the use of symbols, utmost care must be observed in applying any restrictions, especially if the case involves symbols which have multiple meanings (...) it is only by a careful examination of the context (...) that one can draw a meaningful distinction between shocking and offensive language which is protected by article 10 and that which forfeits its right to tolerance in a democratic society (...)". For further details in argument see: H. CANNIE, D. VOORHOOF, The abuse clause and freedom of expression in the European Human Rights Convention: An added value for democracy and human rights protection?, in Netherlands Quarterly of Human Rights, 29 (1), 2011, pp. 59ss.

individuated rather than in the act or activity in itself considered in the liberticidal end which attracts of them, groups or individuals pursue. If an individual questions the values underlying the ECHR that can be deduced from the related preamble and intimately linked to the concept of democracy[150], the system withdraws and deprives it of its protection. This is through the adoption of decisions of inadmissibility pursuant to art. 35, par. 3 ECHR or through the union of the question of applicability of art. 17 to examine the merits of the dispute. A diachronic reading does not allow to account for this duplicity of application penalties by alternating the Strasbourg judge with one another. While taking due account of the strictly case-by-case approach followed by the ECtHR, both the declaratory claims of inadmissibility and the appraisals of the applicability of the prohibition of abuse of rights combined with merit seems to be not consistently consistent[151].

As we immediately understand, we are faced with a provision that specifies how much in general expressed by art. 17 ECHR: however, it does not share the ratio[152]. If, in fact, the latter moves from the political need to contain the risks of authoritarian and anti-democratic drift in member states, art. 35, par. 3, lett. a) logically acts as a mechanism aimed at introducing a filter with respect to those appeals, which show a clear distortion of the right of the private party to appeal in accordance with the preceding article. If we wanted to "translate" it according to the categories and the nomenclature related to the domestic jurist, we could say that it performs a function quite similar to the interest to challenge.

We are here, therefore, at a function of the abuse of law that is profoundly different from the one highlighted in art. 17 ECHR, i.e. state abuse (article 15ECHR). To the reported political and interpretive director together with art. 17 ECHR, in fact, is added a connotation of the abuse of the right (seen in the perspective of the abusive exercise of the right to appeal by the private) as an instrument for the selection of eligible applications[153]. An "economic" function, therefore, aimed at avoiding the flooding of the jurisdictional machine, as well as ensuring the

150 J. ZAND, The concept of democracy and the European Convention on Human Rights, in University of Baltimore Journal of International Law, 5 (2) 2017.

151 In argument see the case from the ECtHR: Dimitriyev et Abramov v. Russia of 18 September 2018.

152 ECtHR, Kasymakhunov and Saybatalov v. Russia of 14 March 2013.

153 S.G. HINGHOFER-SZALKAY, Extreme Meinungen und Meinungsäußerungsfreiheit: Die Schranke des Artikel 17 EMRK. Die Straßburger Rechtsprechung und ihre Struktur, in Journal für Rechtspolitik, 20 (2), 2012, pp. 106-114.

distinction between the actual injuries of guarantees from the minimal ones or even only apparent (or non-existent).

On the other hand, unlik art. 17, art. 35 par. 3 lett. a) ECHR expressly mentions the "abuse" lemma (more correctly: the adjective "abusive"), asking the problem to identify its meaning.

In this sense, the answer that derives from the jurisprudence of ECtHR is quite similar to that found in the internal system. Referring to the elements of the general theory of law, the connotation that is given is based on the concept of purpose of the act: id est, fulfillment of an act for a purpose other than that established by the law or in any case by that for which the right is recognized[154].

In any case, we are faced with a measure of an exceptional nature (suggesting that, except for the manifest abusiveness, there would be as a presumption of admissibility of the appeal of the private).

In general, the situations in which the supranational judges generally had recourse to the category in question were two.

In the first place, the intrinsically abusive nature of the appeal characterized by false allegations, capable of generating an erroneous representation of the reality of the facts in the ECtHR was to be recognized[155]. Thus, the appeal must be declared inadmissible with the production of falsified documents; equally inadmissible will be the appeal of the private individual in which the clarification of pre-existing circumstances to the sentence is omitted, which are necessary for the decision of the case. Not least, the hypothesis of non-disclosure of circumstances that occurred when the appeal was filed and that, like those mentioned above, are decisive for the examination of the ECtHR in Strasbourg (article 47, paragraph 6 of the ECtHR)[156].

---

154 ECtHR, Petrovic v. Serbia of 18 October 2011. On the other hand, the meaning of the term "abuse", as outlined by the court, had already been preceded in the same terms reconstructed in the light of general rules of interpretation on the right of treaties laid down by the Vienna Convention to articles 31 and 33, where it is stated (art. 31, par. 1) that the normative text should be attributed the ordinary sense derived from the context within which they are inserted, as well as from the content and purpose of the provision (ECtHR, Mirolubovs and others v. Serbia of 15 September 2009). J.P. COSTA, La Cour europèenne des droits de l'homme. Des juges pour la libertè, ed. Dalloz, Paris, 2017.

155 ECtHR, Jian v. Romania of 30 March 2004. F. TIMMERMANS, Fundamental rights protection in Europe before and after accession of the European Union to the European Convention on Human Rights, in Liber amicorum Pieter Van Dijk, M. Van Roosmalen and others (eds.), Intersentia, Antwerp, Oxford, 2013, pp. 225ss.

156 ECtHR, Verbanov v. Bulgaria of 27 June 1996. Kérétchachvili v. Georgia of 2 May 2006. Hadrabovà and others v. Republic Czech of 25 September 2007. Furthermore, the applicant's intention to mislead the ECtHR must be proven in case: Nold v. Germany of 29 June 2006.

The second category of cases in which the ECtHR has used the clause of art. 35, par. 3, lett. a) ECHR: the use of expressions grossly outrageous and offensive towards the state involved in the dispute, exorbitant from the limits of a logical, lively but at the same time measured and civil criticism in the linguistic register[157].

In any case, the two orders of situations summarized above do not exhaust the possibility of an abusive appeal, since they must be identified further in the hypothesis of the "media" appeal. We refer, in essence, to the case of the private who has recourse to the only (or, in any case, prevalent) purpose of carrying out political propaganda, exceeds in the statements before the mass media (such as television or the press), manifesting a behavior unjustifiably devoid of seriousness and demeanor or disrespectful towards the role and procedure of ECtHR[158].

Faced with this hypothesis, the reference to what we saw in the previous paragraph cannot be run with regard to the second pole of operation of the abuse of process doctrine in the Anglo-Saxon system. It is not simply a question of distorting the aims of the process of the European ECtHR (purely propagandistic purposes), but also of a conduct which, due to its ethical reprisals, leads to throw an intolerable discredit on the image of moral integrity of the supranational judge. In short, the point of contact between the setting of the ECtHR of Strasbourg and the reconstruction of common law is evident, even if does not seem wrong to hypothesize an influence of the second on the hermeneutical address of the first.

For the sake of completeness, therefore, the hypothesis of the repeated proposition of appeals, which are manifestly unfounded or, in any case, similar in the content to another declared inadmissible by the judges of Strasbourg must be indicated. Here, too, we are faced with a mechanism for selecting appeals based on those evidently specious, returning to mind the filter-clause which, in the national procedural system, is constituted by foreclosure[159].

157 ECtHR, Di Salvo v. Italy of 11 January 2007. It must also be stated that, in any case, the applicant cannot be declared inadmissible if, following a warning from the court on the basis of threatening abusive expressions contained in the application, he has taken steps to eliminate or rectify them (Tchernitsine v. Russia of 6 April 2006).

158 ECtHR, Unified Communist Party v. Georgia of 22 May 2007.

159 Commission, decision of 15 October 1987, M. v. United Kingdom.

(FOLLOWS) A MEANING OF "ABUSE" IN ITS OWN RIGHT: THE CONCEPT OF "DISPROPORTION"

The concept of abuse, in itself, evokes the idea of proportion: regardless of the terms of comparison on which the judgment of proportionality is poured out, the image of an abusive conduct immediately leads to that of a surpassing of limits. In essence, any selfish interest (concept within which the subjective right can be fairly approximated) always entails a more or less significant sacrifice of a public interest which, comes to tolerate the "costs" that the exercise of that right entails. To abuse a right, therefore, means to induce an unjustifiable squeeze or cancellation of that opposing (public) interest. Proportionality, therefore, would serve to ensure an appropriate congruence of the aims of the subjective right, guaranteeing the economic "sustainability" of public interest.

In reconstructing the concept of "disproportion" of the appeal, thus referring to the wider category of abuse, the ECtHR has constantly moved in the comparison of two substantial parameters: of the injury complained of by the applicant (and eventually suffered) and of the practical result targeted by the individual (for example: the measure of indemnity assigned to recast the prejudice suffered).

Even in this case, the ECtHR approach is eminently substantial, being able to even define itself as "practical". If, in fact, the injury suffered owing to the proposition of the appeal come less (as, by hypothesis, object of repair by the respondent state) and this circumstance was silenced by the plaintiff (article 47 paragraph 6 of the ECtHR Regulation), the abuse of appeal should not be doubted, as the reiteration of the request would be manifestly disproportionate to the actual factual situation or even completely without reason for circumstances that have occurred.

In any case, the judgment of proportionality inherent in the proposition of abusive recourse (article 35, paragraph 3 letter a) ECHR) must be kept clearly distinct from the hypothesis described in par. 3, lett. b) of art. 35, which regards the inadmissibility of the appeal due to the absence of significant prejudice on the part of the private individual[160].

Of course, in practice, it will often be difficult to discern the case in which there is total absence of injury (where, therefore, there will be rejection of the appeal pursuant to the last provision referred) from the one in which it subsists

160 ECtHR, Miroļubovs and other v. Latvia of 15 September 2009, par. 62-65.

but, for facts occurring omitted by the appellant, it appeared less or at least minimal compared to the final requests (to be considered manifestly incongruous). From the conceptual point of view, there is a line of distinction between the two hypotheses. On one side, the appeal would be abusive due to disproportion when the vice of incongruity between petitum and injury suffered (not simply complained, but in fact non-existent ab origin) it is due to circumstances following the submission of application. The other side, however, concerns the original deficiency of injury to the private individual and, therefore, of substantial violation by the member state.

The practical sense suggests to be faced with an application of the notion of abuse to two situations which, although at different times (ab origine and ex post), also show a distortion of the right to appeal. Change the terms, to showdown, to diagnose the abuse: the disproportion, in one case; the defect of an essential element of the appeal (suffered injury, original effective interest in the formulation of the introductory act), in the other.

In conclusion, in relation to the abuse by the private individual of the right recognized by art. 34, ECHR can be drawn into two macro-categories of abusive manifestations: abuse of appeal and of procedure[161].

The second, evidently, will occur in the context of the abuse due to "disproportion", when an appeal, originally (let's say so to summarize), is founded, due to events that have occurred and ceases to be so. Here, the single abuse of the conventional procedure, distorting some procedural instruments or, in any case, failing to comply with some obligations (look at those of communication imposed by the ECtHR Regulation).

Otherwise, we will have abuse of the appeal in the other hypotheses: if we want to evoke a conceptual parallelism, here we have abused the action or, if we want, substitute the introductory act.

161 In this sense see the next cases: Basileo v. Italy of 23 August 2011. Cretella v. Italy of 11 October 2011. Di Gennaro v. Italy of 12 October 2011. Bock v. Germany of 19 January 2010. Dudek v. Germany of 23 November 2010. For further analysis see: D. HARRIS, M. O'BOYLE, C. WARBRICK, Law of the European Convention on Human rights, Oxford University Press, Oxford, 2014, pp. 372ss. A. ZRVANDYAN, Casebook on European fair trial standards in administrative justice, Council of Europe, Strasbourg, 2016, pp. 108ss. F. DE LONDRAS, K. DZECHTSIAROV, Great debates on the European Convention on Human Rights, ed. Macmillan, London, 2018.

ARTICLE 17 OF THE EUROPEAN COURT OF HUMAN RIGHTS AS A STANDARD SYSTEM AND A FUNDAMENTAL RIGHT?

We can now go back to the central question. It has been said that art. 17 ECHR is born with a mainly political intent, that is to avoid the rebirth in Europe of totalitarianism. It has been joined by that of measuring instrument (so to speak) of the merit of protection of the injury complained of by the individual, when the same in reality constituted a reaction of the national system to the use of a guarantee in freedom.

The possibility of a different reconstructive option was also highlighted, namely that of a further function of the provision in comment. Using the same as a concrete tool for the repression of state abuses committed at the expense of the individual, there is an effective right of the private party to appeal in cases of abuse of power by the member state and, in a special way, the jurisdiction of the European ECtHR. In essence, the reconstructive key to which we would aim is that art. 17 ECHR would, like the previous articles that identify the catalog of the inalienable rights of the human person, directly invoked by the individual before the international jurisdiction.

If one can say this, a precipitate immediately comes about: the setting in comment, in fact, would lead to one (if we want to call it) heterogenesis of the ends of art. 17 ECHR because, if such a function were to be admitted, which is added to that traditionally associated with it and which originates from its very genesis, one should further recognize its nature as a prescriptive and sanctioning norm at the same time (or, better said, provided with specific protection). With greater clarity: if the standard in question joins those of Title I ECHR, thereby fulfilling the function of a genuine guarantee provision that speculates to those other governing a fundamental right or freedom, which is banned from being refolded freedom, should be given full jurisdiction in EctHR under articles 34 et seq., or to ascertain any violations deriving from state abuses falling within the scope of operation of art. 17 ECHR and, consequently, to impose an adjustment pursuant to art. 46 ECHR.

The idea would be suggestive, at first glance. Nevertheless, on one hand, it does not exempt itself from a fundamental analysis aimed at evaluating the actual added value that would derive from its configuration in the aforesaid terms. On the other, if the proposed approach would lead to the verification of an intolerable interpretative distortion of the disposition, thus "distorting" its aims and main ratios, if not even proposing a mechanism in total antithesis with the will of the conventional legislator.

Now, with regard to the first pole of reflection introduced, there should be no doubt about the added value that would derive from an approach of art. 17 ECHR in the manner envisaged. In these terms, the provision fulfills the function that, in national law, would be covered by the clause of the abuse of rights, thus acting as a "valve" for opening and closing the system, at the same time with respect to the provisions that primarily establish the content of a guarantee. In essence, the function that would be obtained would be that of extending and completing the freedoms enunciated, avoiding a possible misuse, in the present perspective, by an authoritative way.

Conventional liberties would receive protection in the face of a violation (so to speak) directly and not, instead (certainly no less insidious hypothesis), than an indirect or surreptitious lesion, that is, through state's limitation of agreements to exercise guarantees.

With regard to the second aspect, on the other hand, if this approach is irreducible in contrast to the spirit of ECHR, this doubt should reasonably be excluded. It is true that the reconstruction in comment exceeds the original purpose of the provision in question. However, it does not seem that a possible functional "integration" in the terms illustrated above could lead to a phase shift or a distortion of the overall conventional apparatus, contributing to a strengthening of its effectiveness and raising the standard of protection. In short, the "practical" function of art. 17 ECHR, in the proposed configuration, is summarized in the following terms. In principle, every freedom sanctioned by the European ECHR provides operating limits which, in essence, correspond to collective interests with which the subjective guarantee is counterbalanced and faced with the which, under certain conditions, could in fact yield. Article 17ECHR in the advanced approach, would prevent the abuse of the prevalence of those collective or publicistic interests on individual freedom, sanctioning the protection of the individual from such application distortion.

Certainly, a (albeit brief) historical excursus about the interpretative evolutions succeeding within the jurisprudence of Strasbourg could make the problems underlying the analysis of art. 17 ECHR. A look at the pronunciations in which the ECtHR, directly or indirectly, had to deal with the clause in this exhibition, under a first profile, a certain caution (if not reluctance) to the invocation of the same as an instrument to stigmatize behaviors concretizing an abuse of the exercise of certain individual guarantees. Alternatively, we perceive "in filigrana", in the text of some pronunciations, the will of supranational judges to overcome the traditional collocation of the norm in the "political" dimension repeatedly highlighted, to try to bring it back to the more meaningful one of disposition autonomously with substantial protection (from abuse of rights) and jurisdiction.

To summarize the terms of the interpretative querelle that concerned the judgments in comment, the scenario that has emerged has fluctuated from the denial of the occurrence of the abuse due to the non-existence of the requirements set out in the point under art. 17 ECHR[162]. It has extended to the omitted evaluation of the violation of the abuse of right (proposed in the appeal)[163], until the irrelevance of the clause was affirmed, because, more properly, the case here indicated a manifest overflow by the individual of the limits established by a specific freedom and, therefore, a direct violation of art. 17 ECHR[164].

The case-law referred to has therefore shown an express or implicit use, no matter-of the provision under analysis as a possible instrument, invoked by the respondent state, to deny the private protection afforded by a freedom of ECHR, if the latter had exceeded the limits of the correct exercise of a right within a democratic society.

Certainly, from the textual point of view, this hermeneutical modulation is permitted by art. 17 ECHR, which bans the abuse of law both by the state, a group or an individual. It is also, evidently, a limited interpretative use, which could receive a wider practical implementation.

In fact, the text of art. 17 ECHR reveals a basic ambiguity, which, when well looked at, is expressed in an internal contradiction. On the one hand, in fact, it prohibits all acts of individuals or groups resolving in liberticidal actions, that is contrary to the spirit of the liberties of the ECHR and, therefore, in open antithesis with the unattainable substratum of the values of a democratic society. On the other, it reveals the intent to prohibit state conduct capable of unduly

162 In this sense see: Lehideux and Isorni v. France of 23 September 1998. For analysis see: S. LOYTOMAKI, Law and the politics of memory: confronting the past, ed. Routledge, London & New York, 2014.

163 ECtHR, Glasenapp v. Federal Republic of Germany of 28 August 1986. Kosiek v. Federal Republic of Germany of 28 August 1986. Vogt v. Germany of 26 September 1995. For further details see: P. COPPEL, Information rights: Law and practice, Hart Publishing, Oxford & Oregon, Portland, 2014. F. DORSSEMONT, K. LÖRCHER, I. SCHÖMANN, The European Convention on Human Rights and the employment relation, Hart Publishing, Oxford & Oregon, Portland, 2013.

164 ECtHR, Jersild v. Denmark of 23 September 1994 and in the same spirit see also: Orban and others v. France of 15 January 2009.

compressing the areas of operation of the guarantees covered by the supranational text, such as (for example, hypothesis that it does not exhaust the possibilities of demonstration in practice) the legislation introducing restrictions beyond the limits (expressed or obtained by way of interpretation) set by the conventional rules.

Now, the idea of stopping at a reading of the disposition according to an exclusively political key or, in any case, solely set as a barrier to the action of subversive individuals or groups (reading to which there would in truth be subtended a declaration of impotence towards the opponent, far more powerful than the private, of democratic liberties, i.e. public authority), would be "heuristically" poor operation, which would deprive the provision of concrete and useful effect.

As it would seem correct, the use of art. 17 ECHR in a single direction, given by the contrast of those behaviors of the private that result in an attack on democratic freedoms of which the same complaints the violation and, therefore, as an instrument in the hands of the resistant government to oppose the appeals of the applicant, not only constitutes "amputated" application of art. 17 ECHR (which, it is repeated, also refers to the behavior of the state), but is in contrast with the basic spirit of the European ECHR, aimed at conceiving a nucleus of minimum and indispensable guarantees for the single, insurgent of aggression, direct or indirect, by the authority.

In no uncertain terms, one could say that ECHR is born for the "weak", not for the "strong". It is not by chance, in fact, that the danger of compression of fundamental freedoms is, by definition, linked to the acts of authority[165].

The same literal tenor of the norm would push towards such a setting, having to remind the prohibition on interpreting ECHR in the sense of entailing the right of a state to impose restrictions on these rights and liberties wider than those foreseen by ECHR itself. Not to mention, then, that a hermeneutical approach, limited to the above represented direction, would risk subverting the well-known relationship between freedom (rule) and limitations of the same (exception) of which the conventional text becomes the primary spokesperson. In fact, the connectable connotations to the defense of the principles of a

165 S. VAN DROOGHENBROECK, La proportionnalité dans le droit de la Convention européenne des droits de l'homme, Facultè St Louis, 2001, pp. 396ss. S. VAN DROOGHENBROECK, Le droit international et europèen des droits de l'homme devant le juge national, ed. Larcier, Bruxelles, 2014. A. FØLLESDAL, N. PETERS, G. ULFSTEIN, Constituting Europe: The European Court of Human Rights in a national, European and global context, Cambridge University Press, Cambridge, 2013.

democratic society are excessively elastic and broad, risking to deliver to the governments of member states an easy ploy to justify undue compressions of protected guarantees.

In short, if you really want to extend the discussion, you could perhaps come to hypothesize the substantial uselessness or, in any case, the misleading nature of the prohibition of abuse imposed by art. 17 ECHR to the individual. If, in fact, the individual provisions governing liberties provide, at the same time, limitations on the exercise of the same, other do not introduce specularly if not a power to the state party to restrict those freedoms, precisely in order to protect those advertising interests that crystallize in the need to preserve the democratic "statute". The canonization of the prohibition on the abuse of the individual would risk, if we look, to legitimize a (though unexpected) insidious interpretive reconstruction: that of allowing the state to restrict the greater liberties or, in any case, different from those established by the individual provisions. In fact, there have been attempts by ECtHR to reconnect to art. 17 ECHR the meaning of prohibition of state abuse[166].

To the showdown, then, what would be the effective use of an interpretive reconstruction for which art. 17 ECHR was not limited to a purely "political" scope, nor would it prohibit the conduct of private individuals aimed at a subversion of the fundamental values of a democratic society, but also those of abuse of authority that goes beyond the limits (so to say) logical or ontological of ECHR guarantees.

To all evidence, the concrete function of such an approach should be to legitimize, when not even impose within the national laws, in consideration of the cogency of the liberties sanctioned by supranational legislation, a general prohibition of abuse of the limitations inherent to the exercise of conventional guarantees. Thus, the interpretative operation would be rationally legitimated by the provision in question would be that in the same way that the individual is prevented from carrying out acts that result in an attack on democratic liberties protected by ECHR. The state would be prohibited from imposing restrictions on

166 For a first fundamental ruling to that effect, although rejection of applicant's direct application against the defendant state see article 17, ECtHR, Golder v. United Kingdom of 21 February 1975. Here, the ECtHR rejects appellant's grievance, according to which the state had exceeded the limitations on the right to fair trial arising from art. 6, on the basis of the fact that this last provision does not explicitly consecrate (as instead proposed by the applicant) a right of access to justice, not due to the obvious inference of art. 17 invoked. Say, then, that it would be followed in the subsequent: Ireland v. United Kingdom of 18 January 1978. Campbell and Fell v. United Kingdom of 28 June 1984. Garaudy v. France, op. cit. B. EMMERSON, A. ASHWORTH, A. MACDONALD, Human rights and criminal justice, Sweet & Maxwell, London, 2012.

the freedoms of CFREU wider than those expressly provided for or carrying out acts which, although formally integrating the exercise of a power granted by the supranational legislator, in fact result in a misuse of the aforementioned restrictions, hence in an abuse. Basically, function of art. 17 ECHR would be to allow the introduction into national law of a general prohibition of abuse by the state when it exercised its interference in the enjoyment of individual rights according to modalities or in any case beyond what was legitimized by the ECHR.

The terms of the reasoning do not change at all if in any case the concept of the necessary garrison of liberal democracy is recalled. It is true that art. 17 ECHR is a general principle of ECHR and so also that democracy is a fundamental requirement of the European public order[167]. Yet, how could one hypothesize the protection of a system of values, such as that of a liberal-democratic society, where the prohibition of abuse did not apply primarily to the person (state-authority) who is most able to produce the authoritarian drifts as well as the compressions of fundamental freedoms? Not by chance, it would seem to be able to add, the same Preamble to the European Human Rights ECHR, with regard to the necessity to create the essential conditions for the respect of ECHR rights, makes primary and exclusive reference to European states, as determined to take the first steps to ensure the collective guarantee of some of the rights set out in the universal declaration. This, in good approximation, would translate in practical terms what would be the intimate essence of the abuse of the right: the ability to highlight the overflow achieved by the government in adopting the single measure of compression of freedom[168], which, in any event, would also result in a functional misuse of the state power to apply restrictions to conventional guarantees. We would still be outside the coverage area of art. 18 ECHR, which, as is known, prohibits the imposition of restrictions on conventional freedoms for purposes other than those for which they are provided for in the legislative text.

Poor application of the separate provision, we are faced with a prohibition requiring the contracting state to maintain the compressions of ECHR rights in the scope of the objectives explicitly allowed by the individual rules conferring

167 ECtHR, Zdanoka v. Latvia of 16 March 2006.

168 D.I. GOMIEN, D. HARRIS, L. ZWAAK, Law and practice of the European Convention on Human Rights and the European Social Charter, Strasbourg, 1996, pp. 526. Moreover, it is repeated, the provision has received almost no application, settling-even at the jurisprudence emerged on the subject-more as an "ancillary" prediction than the provisions of the individual liberties, as well as a statement of principle (ECtHR, Kamma v. The Netherlands of 14 July 1974).

guarantees[169]. Therefore, as correctly observed, the forecast in question it would not be suitable to found a garrison, let alone a right or a freedom, having a non-autonomous supplementary character. Moreover, the teleological constraint prescribed by art. 18 ECHR refers to the practical modalities through which the rights of ECHR will be implemented in member states. Practical modalities, as we can see, are extremely variable due to the specificity of the chosen national system and, again, to be concretely identified and defined in their scope. On the other hand, misuse of the ends (if we want to call it) is very different from the much wider and more meaningful term of the abuse of the right (article 17 ECHR). Given that, even in this last expression, as known conceptually, the prohibition of "distraction of an institution from its own ends" would be conceived (in this, perhaps, further emphasizing the pleonastic character of article 18), it is necessary to further highlight the greater extent of the prohibition imposed by the first provision and, therefore, the markedly greater practical capacity of the command contained therein. If, in fact, art. 18 ECHR would appear to be more like an ethical directive to member states, faced with any restrictions on the rights allowed by art. 17 ECHR otherwise prescribes a clear and explicit prohibition of acts or behavior: a provision of ECHR cannot be interpreted or applied in such a way as to entail greater compressions to the freedoms of those expressly permitted.

THE EQUITY DOGMA (ARTICLE 6 ECHR) CHANNELED BY SUPRANATIONAL PRESSURES: RELATIONS WITH ART. 17 ECHR?

The conceptual preconditions above lead us to directly address the core of this work: if indeed European ECHR (article 17 ECHR) imposes a prohibition on abuse of law and in terms that this prohibition also applies to member states, is a prohibition of abuse of process specularly imposed? In fact, given that the abuse of right governed by art. 17 ECHR should be understood, inasmuch as it refers to the authority, more correctly as an abuse of a power, so in the procedural context we would be faced with the idea of an abuse, in the broadest sense, of the power of criminal persecution.

169 D. XENOS (ed.), The positive obligations of the State under the European Convention on Human Rights, ed. Routledge, London & New York, 2012.

This cannot be clearly the place to dwell on the analysis of what constitutes the "decalogue" or the "statute" of the fair trial contained in the European Human Rights ECHR (article 6): here is the broad outline for which the rule regulates a body of fundamental guarantees valid for the process in general (paragraph 1), then for the criminal trial in particular (paragraphs 2 and 3)[170].

As is known, the prediction in word enunciate is repeated, a catalog of essential guarantees within the criminal procedure, while at the same time explaining (thanks also to the hermeneutic integration carried out by the ECtHR) the possible limits to which they are subject.

One aspect must first be clarified: in the context of a reconstructive operation carried out within the conventional apparatus, the dimension within which it would be possible to elaborate a broad clause of procedural abuse (prohibition) would be of a guarantee type.

Reasons not at all different, in fact, from those previously represented with regard to art. 17 ECHR, focusing on the predominant "abusive" capacity of the authority with respect to that possessed by the individual, lead to converge in this direction; indeed, in front of art. 6 ECHR this dimension is imposed by its own structure (as well as by the letter), not to mention the systematic approach that characterizes the European ECHR: we refer expressly to the accused, in fact, as the recipient of the guarantees thickened in the provision of reference. So, an eventual reading of art. 6 "in combination" with art. 17 ECHR, aiming at the possibility of reconstructing a general prohibition of procedural abuse, would entail in the member state the obligation to obtain, to put it in general terms, appropriate tools (legislative and/or interpretative) to remedy its violation. In essence, if the hypothesis of a prohibition of abuse of process according to the aforementioned paradigm should be founded, the clause could only have as its recipient the state authority: id est, the prosecution body.

Some points of contact, so to speak, between the general category of the abuse of process doctrine and the "decalogue" of fairness established by art. 6 ECHR were highlighted in the previous paragraphs: example, in this sense, is the case of entrapment, where the instigating conduct of the undercover agent, when he determined someone to commit a crime that he would not otherwise have committed, entails an intolerable compression of the rights of the accused, producing a significant imbalance of the procedural antagonism, so that the

170 D. LIAKOPOULOS, Parità di armi nella giustizia penale internazionale, vol. 1, ed. Libellula, Puglia, 2018.

original probabilities of condemnation outweigh those of acquittal. But, it is a matter of course that can very well extend to the problem of the reasonable duration of the procedure (article 6, paragraph 1 ECHR): clearly, the tools for reacting to this systemic dysfunctionality are different according to national law and the abuse of process discretion is only one of the possible usable remedies. To summarize: the Anglo-Saxon doctrine, object of analysis in the previous paragraph, constitutes a substantial answer to the problem of the keeping of procedural fairness.

In short, this would be the point of contact: abuse of process (according to the reconstruction made in the Anglo-Welsh system) and equity (article 6 ECHR) are intimately linked, being clear that the part conduct, where characterized by the surreptitious use of a procedural authority, or even of the process itself, is capable of altering the underlying equilibrium that should ideally preside over the celebration of a fair criminal trial. Therefore, we would be outside of a tendentially ethical line, already the object of previous considerations, aimed at imposing a moralizing instance of criminal justice and recovering an ethical orthodoxy of judicial operators. The "meter" for measuring the fairness of criminal trial, even if dropped in the perspective of abuse, would be given by the guarantees laid down by art. 6 ECHR which, on closer inspection, are resolved in the minimum and inalienable conditions to which the defendant is able to carry out an effective defense in his/her process, therefore: on conditions of substantial parity with the accusation.

Thus, the excessive delay in the exercise of the prosecution can result in the loss of probative contributions, which otherwise, would have led with reasonable probability to the acquittal of the accused; the entrapment (to "brutally" synthesize) starts a process that otherwise would not have taken place, and so on. Nor can we stop at such exemplary hypotheses, being, as we have said repeatedly, insurmountable to exhaust the manifestations of procedural abuse in a closed number.

On balance, then, the real question should be another: does art. 6 ECHR together with art. 17 ECHR involves a general prohibition of abuse of process, independently of the conduct in which the individual it occurs?

The consequence of a possible affirmative answer would have repercussions of undoubted importance. In this case, in fact, we would no longer be faced with the assessment of the possibility of operating a legal "transfer" from a court order (Anglo-Welsh) to another (Italian). It would be a matter of identifying a precise obligation of protection for the member states with a supranational matrix that would, therefore, produce the duty of internal adjustment. The nerve point, in fact, would rest on the idea of drawing from articles 6 and 17ECHR a prohibition of procedural abuse, committed against the defendant who, for the consequent effect, could legitimize the appeal and the judicial protection before the ECtHR. It is a syllogistic scheme that could be summarized as follows: the prohibition of abuse of the trial as a fundamental right of the individual, which would be violated in the circumstance in which the authority exceeds the limits set by art. 6 ECHR, would come to give an application or an interpretation manifestly contrary to its spirit or, in any case, leading to the cancellation or compression of the guarantees below the minimum standard set.

This would certainly be a daring reconstruction, if only for the consequences in the national legal systems which it would be pregnant with; in any case, it would not even seem completely out of the box.

The logical and practical necessity of the "process abuse" tool (better: the prohibition) has already been widely said; regardless of the obstacles to which the category in question can be found. Firstly (consider procedural legality), it manifests with palpable evidence how the practice, both for the protection of system requirements and guarantee, tends to overcome the rigor of abstract forms.

They are needs, on closer inspection, to which the conventional apparatus is not withdrawn. Placed in front of the need to ensure a right balance between the collective interest in criminal persecution and subjective guarantees, the abuse of process would perform the function (it seems inevitable) to offer a "conventional" protection to the individual for those situations of authority abuse in the trial, aimed at diverting the criminal trial from the equitable fee. In short, even here, the function of the clause would not be different from that already hypothesized earlier with regard to the internal system: closing the system, ensuring the maintenance of procedural fairness beyond the written "potential" non-exhaustive "plots" of European ECHR.

Indeed, it is an operation that should not surprise so much, since the overpowering entry of supranational regulations (European and conventional in the first place) has at least for some years accustomed us to (so to call them) "broken schemes", as well as leading to the modification of the internal system by legislative means, to an amendment of the usual hermeneutical modules, also by questioning systemic postulates previously considered intangible (and the internal jurisprudential paths in matters of resolution and keeping of the criminal paradigmatic). At the reckoning, it is repeated, the practice surpasses the theory.

It does not seem, therefore, to be able to logically exclude the possibility of inferring a prohibition on the abuse of process within art. 6 and 17 ECHR, whose function, in addition to any abstract conjecture, should be to guarantee a steadfast and more effective holding of the principle of fairness established by ECHR.

The content in art. 54 CFREU, would be derived by relationem, i.e. referring to other rights or freedoms contained in the normative text in question. In substance, the clause in question would avoid the surreptitious exercise of a freedom, materializing a restriction of the same or other sanctioned by CFREU beyond the limits expressly permitted.

In this sense, art. 54 CFREU would be a system standard with horizontal effectiveness, or rather a "legitimate defense" clause in the face of the possible "antisystem" use of rights and freedoms", acting as a true principle of self-preservation of CFREU itself. In short, it would constitute a rule of interpretation aimed at avoiding the implosion of recognized fundamental rights. However, the degree and the cogency of human rights, likely to be drawn both from an individual's and authority's aspect, would rationally pose the problem of a far more meaningful efficacy than the clause in analysis. Remembering appropriately, it points out, not only the apical value of protected guarantees, but also the very rank of CFREU. In short, even in the silence of the normative text, which does not speak of sanctioning the abuse of rights but is limited to a general prohibition, it would not be wrong to envisage a sort of direct effect of art. 54 CFREU, involving the non-recognition of protection of the "abused" right or, specularly, the disregard of the internal norm which, formally implementing the supranational provision, indirectly legitimizes the fulfillment of acts capable of compressing the operational space of a CFREU freedom.

Otherwise, a clear short circuit would follow. In principle, the elevation of CFREU to the same level of Treaties, would sanction a direct operation (article 51, Charter of Nice and article 6, TEU) within member states, with an equally direct "viability" before the EctHR. Or else, the possible confinement of art. 54 CFREU for horizontal effectiveness, that is to say purely interpretative and for this reason incapable of directly generating a prohibition obligation and at the same time an individual's right, like the other provisions of the legislative text, would substantially reduce the effectiveness of value and content of recognized upstream freedoms.

Here, in fact, rationally speaking, we would play the real game of the Charter of Nice and, in particular, the sanctioned abuse of right. It is a norm, according to its letter, without an explicit sanction; but it does not seem to be a forgetfulness.

The Treaty of Lisbon itself gave a patent of hierarchical super ordination to the national law, elevating it to the juridical value of the Treaties. The sanction, therefore, in case of violation, should already be in nuce.

Among other things, ECHR too, following the final accession of the European Union to the Council of Europe, should receive the same legal treatment as CFREU, because of a need for rationality system (given the clear correspondence of contents and ethical and cultural principles underlying the two supranational texts) and of opportune osmosis between the two courts (European and Justice).

The question, at this point, is whether the clause contained in art. 54 Charter of Nice, like what has already been proposed previously with reference to art. 17 ECHR funds a real obligation on member states to suppress the abuse of law and, thus shifting the discussion to the theme of this work, if you fund a similar prohibition in the process.

Here, of course, in the event of a positive response, the impact would certainly be stronger for the internal legal system than that which the same would suffer from the European ECHR system. The reconstruction of a prohibition of procedural abuse by articles 6 and 17 ECHR could not in fact lead, at least to the current historical moment, i.e. to a direct disregard of the internal norm involving an abuse of conventional freedom. A characteristic connotation of EU law is the principle of primacy, which finds its maximum expression in the effect of disregarding the internal norm contrasting with the superordinate one (clearly, in relation to the supranational provisions provided with such efficacy).

Basically, admitting to be able to lean for a reconstructive hypothesis similar to that previously formulated with regard to the European ECHR of human rights, a possible act of the authority, carried out in violation of art. 54 CFREU which, surreptitiously, involves a compression of the fundamental procedural guarantees established by the Charter of Nice (article 47)[171].

It is undoubted, in fact, that the different legal effectiveness of which CFREU is provided with respect to the ECHR, leads the interpreter immediately to confront the problem of sanction. On the contrary, it would be at least contradictory to assume an obligation on member states to preparation of instruments

171 M.SAFFIAN, D. DÜSTERHAU, A Union of effective judicial protection: Addressing a multi-level challenge through the lens of article 47 CFREU, in Yearbook of European Law, 33 (1), 2014, pp. 3ss. C. MAK, Rights and remedies: Article 47 EUCFR and effective judicial protection in European private law matters, in Amsterdam Law School Research Paper No. 2012-88. Centre for the Study of European Contract Law Working Paper Series No. 2012-11. G. LEBRUN, De l'utilitè de l'article 47 de la Charte des droits fondamentaux de l'union europèenne, in Revue Trimestrielle des Droits de l'Homme, 106, 2016, pp. 433ss.

against the abuse of the trial and, at the same time, not provide any remedies following verification, awaiting the right of the individual to an effective appeal against any act giving rise to an infringement of the rights protected by the Union (article 47 para 1).

Now, it is clear that art. 47 CFREU does not mark a "decalogue" of the fairness of the proceedings with contents comparable to art. 6 ECHR. The principle in question, in fact, at the time when the CFREU was approved, did not (in a broad sense) constitute a priority within the fundamental objectives of the supranational system. However, it does not seem to be facing an irremediable gap, in view of the fact that the mechanism of increasingly opportune and fruitful dialogue between the courts ECtHR and CJEU, should rigorously avoid the danger of a systemic misalignment, which would be moreover to look at it with disdain, given the long-awaited endorsement of European Union to the Council of Europe.

In addition to this, we need to recognize the sharpened awareness of European Union regarding the fair trial, the relevance of this principle in judicial cooperation and the relationship of mutual trust between member states. This is borne out by the most recent regulatory products in terms of judicial cooperation and, in particular, the rights of the accused in the criminal procedure[172], which exemplify the (perhaps) slow but progressive and irreversible attitude.

If this is so, without necessarily penetrating, because of the prematurity of the times, on the aspect concerning the specific implementation of prohibition of abuse, which would derive from art. 54 CFREU, within the national legal systems, one can reasonably conclude in one sense that the European Union, through the above-mentioned provision, expressly conceives a prohibition on the abuse of right, which would correspond diametrically to that of species of abuse of process. A prohibition which, in any case, should entail the obligation of member states to provide for any protection and expediency intended to prevent their verification or to sanction their completion.

172 Specific reference is made to: Directive 2010/64/EU on the right to interpretation and translation in criminal proceedings; to Directive 2012/13/EU on the right to information in criminal proceedings; Directive 2103/48/EU (concerning the right to make use of a lawyer, or to inform a third party at the moment of deprivation of personal liberty and to communicate with third parties and consular authorities); Directive 2016/343/EU on the strengthening of certain aspects of the presumption of innocence and the right to be present at trial in criminal proceedings; Directive 2016/1919/EU, with which the European institutions aim to guarantee the effectiveness of the "fair trial" objective within the Union, as a starting point for any cooperation policy on justice between States. See for further details in argument: K. AMBOS, Treatise on international criminal law. Foundations and general part, Oxford University Press, Oxford, 2013.

The main critical aspects of abuse of law will be clear when the more acute the greater the difficulty of establishing the content of abused right would be. It is important to understand if and how this, explicitly or implicitly, works in a subject, in which neither the concept of abuse nor the role of rights are a discriminating function, and to understand if and how the criminal law may be affected by a general prohibition of abuse of rights, or may include within it particular abusive modes of use of rights.

The main reasoning of the abuse of right in criminal law is given by the difficulty of reconciling the interpretative discretion connected to the abuse of right with the typicality and punishment of the criminal offense, i.e. the characteristics that determine, for the crime, a very precise connotation in the category of offenses.

As we said, the detractors of abuse of right emphasize the poor predictability of the applicative outcomes of the category, and therefore the danger that it represents for the certain application of the right, calling into question the discretion, according to some too wide, of the interpreter in evaluating the elements reporting the presence of an abuse.

More precisely, and recapitulating what has been said so far, various moments are identified in which, in the abuse of law, a component of autonomy of the judge in the decisions is emphasized. A first aspect, delegated to the discretion of the judge, concerns the ascertainment of the purposes of the exercise of the right and of the interest it protects. The deciding body, in fact, must provide both the ascertainment of the purpose of the real action of its owner in the matter submitted for trial, and the ascertainment of the ideal purpose, rectius regulated directions of the right, that is the purpose of protection for which the ratio legis, the objective function of law, has been recognized in the legal system.

In criminal law, however, the scenario is very different. The criminal justice system, also by adhering to the most modern readings of the principles of legality and certainty, is structured around cases in which both the facts and the legal effects (sanctions) are legislatively determined and, above all, intelligible and predictable. In order to ensure a great deal, interpretative techniques admitted in other branches of the legal system, such as the analogical procedure, are forbidden in criminal law, and caution is required when the judge has to compare the concrete case with principles and rationes leges.

Precisely for this reason, before going into the analysis of this problem, we need to further investigate the aspect of the interpretative techniques underlying the recognition of abuse of law, recognized by the doctrine, precisely, in analogy with the application of principles and balancing of interests.

ABUSE OF LAW AND INTERPRETATION: ANALOGY, RULES OF PRINCIPLE AND BALANCING OF INTERESTS

Analogy, reasoning for principles and balancing of interests are techniques that allow us to better understand what the judge does when he recognizes an abuse of law. The correlation between interpretative techniques and abuse of law is so strong as to make doubted the same substance of category, as an argument or institute. In this regard, careful civil doctrine tends to deny the relevance of the abuse of law as an institute, in favor of its consecration as an argument of legal reasoning or as a reasoning scheme. According to these approaches, the abuse of law would be the instrument through which, respectively, subtract the concrete case from a permissive abstract case and subject it to a different rule, repressive, or through which to resolve a conflict between insistent principles on the concrete case.

On the other hand, the abuse of law would not be a stand-alone case, since it would not explain the structure of the fact (which I use?) Nor the legal effect (regulated as?).

Differently oriented, in the sense of reconstruction of the prohibition of abuse of law as an autonomous principle and therefore as an institute, given the existence of a prohibition, in which a subsumption is possible, and from the production of effects, although very general, is the civil jurisprudence of the last years. Within this debate of general theory, although without anticipating discourses to be held later, it seems useful to clarify immediately how cannot be given a univocal status (as a case or as an argument) of the abuse of law in criminal law. As anticipated, the abuse of right is mainly explained as the application result of three mechanisms: the analogy, the direct application of the principles and the balancing of interests. Moving from the first of these, it has been argued in doctrine that the reasoning followed by the interpreter in the affirmation of the abuse of law follows the pattern of analogy, ending up by extending a sensu sanctioning norm to a hypothesis not included in it. In particular, by examining the moments in which the abuse of law is ascertained, it is noted that it consists of two phases:

a first phase of subsumption, in which the correspondence between the concrete behavior under observation and the permissive case attributable to power is assessed, and a second evaluation phase, in which the law is applied according to the ratio legis. This second phase, on closer inspection, is not resolved, however, in a simple teleological interpretation according to the intention of the legislator or in the sole overcoming of the literal interpretation in the light of a principle. With respect to such interpretations, there would be something more, consisting in the disregard of the permissive disposition in the concrete case, in the subtraction, in the permissive norm individuated, of the prima facie case included in it, and in the application, in its place, of another rule, of a repressive type. As is well known, the application of a rule to a case not included in it, is the typical result of the analogical procedure, from which the reasoning in question differs, in fact, due to the presence, originally, rather than a gap from fill, a rule to be reduced.

This difference is however exceeded by noting that the rule not to be applied is the result of a supra-inclusive provision, which presents an axiological gap because it does not give due importance to a relevant element in light of the ratio of the permissive rule, which can give to this specific case a different regulation.

Thus, in civil law, the identification of the analogical method underlying the abuse of right allows the doctrine in question to affirm the compatibility of abuse of law with the lawful method, distinguishing a practicable analogy in conditions of correctness, that is in actual presence of a recognizable axiological gap, an interpretation that goes back to general clauses such as good faith. Already here we could make room for observations on the feasibility of this analogical method, even in the presence of an axiological gap, in criminal law, but we prefer to make other surveys first, which will be useful in the reasoning to follow.

Now, if one admits the existence of a general principle of prohibition of abuse of law, from the point of view of the effects it does not change much between the direct application of the prohibition-principle and the analogical of the prohibition-rule symptomatic of that principle.

The discourse on analogy is not so distant from the discourse on principles, since the norms that can be traced back to a principle can be extended by analogy, while the norms that enunciate a principle are susceptible of direct application. The principle can have an immediate qualifying value with respect to the situation to be regulated if it is applied directly to it, or it can have mediated qualifying value if it is applied through a subordinate provision. The choice between mediated application, typical of analogy, or immediate principle, typical of the use of principles, depends on the content of the situation to be qualified, on whether it is more similar to the fact hypothesized in the subordinate rule or to the fact hypothesized in the principle. The reasoning of similarity underlying the analogy would therefore be the reasoning in the research and application of the principle underlying the rule.

It is different if the existence of a general prohibition of abuse of law is not accepted as the underlying principle of the rule to be applied analogically. However, it is believed that through the argument of the abuse, rules can be applied as expression of other principles that would be been improperly waived by the law, for example those relating to civil liability.

This particular analogy, aimed at extending the scope of the negative (with effects of disavowal of protections, of ineffectiveness of the act, of responsibility, and so on) to the detriment of the permissive norm, responds to that sense of proportionality underlying the analogical procedure that makes it possible to establish a case of liability than a case of exercising the right, for example the presence of significant damage to third parties.

If therefore the abuse would be the argument to which the task of restricting the scope of a rule is left, leaving a space empty on which another analogically applied standard would be extended, it seems almost obvious to conclude that the norm intended to be applied analogically in the sanctioning key cannot be a criminal law, stating the prohibition of analogy in force on the matter.

The assessment of similarity presupposes in fact the opinions of the interpreter, on the common elements between the disciplined and unregulated case, which require a screening of interests and relevant interests very similar to the one placed at the base of typing choices reserved, in criminal law, to the legislative one. Thus, for example, an element of similarity traced to damage third parties may be a reason to apply the rules on civil liability, while the finding of a common offense to the asset does not allow analogously to apply the law that provides for a crime against property.

Otherwise, there would be an assimilation of offenses that contradicts the fragmentary nature of criminal law.

The internal repercussions of the choice to trace the foundation of the prohibition of analogy in the prohibition of abuse of EU law are not few. Firstly, there are no obstacles to the internal judge being able to directly apply the EU law on the abuse of rights, even to limit the application of EU law. Secondly, both in order to avoid differentiated applications of abuses and European rights, and in accordance with the principle of prevailing of EU law on domestic law, an intense frequency of references to the European court on the scope of the rights and abuse of law it should develop, resulting in a crushing of the notion of abuse of domestic law with that of the Union. Finally, the prohibition of abuse of right of art. 54 CFREU could be considered as an interposed parameter of constitutionality for direct violation of relevant articles on the subject in national law.

So, the problem would be not so much to concretize the general principle of prohibition of abuse of law, but to concretize and relate to each other the various principles that are overlooked by the normative data and come into play in the concrete case. Examples include constitutional principles that inspire the norms that place the individual rights, the duty of social solidarity, from which derives the principle of good faith, the so-called general principles, like the neminem laedere of the emulative acts, that accompanies the institute from its beginnings. The idea of solving conflicts between principles through reciprocal sizing calls, in fact, to the balancing technique. According to a traditional opinion, the method of application of balancing is what characterizes the rules of principle with respect to the rules. The application of principles requires a balancing of interests that allows to assess the weight that the principle has from time to time with respect to the case to be decided, in comparison with other principles[173]. The balance, therefore, expresses a weighting, a composition of conflicting interests.

In the literature, there were those who pointed out that the abuse of right would allow the judges to carry out what is overseas called an ad hoc balancing, i.e. a balancing case by case, aimed at resolving the concrete conflict and not to define the respective scope of the principles and to affirm a stable rule that can be repeated in the future.

There were also those who stressed that this tendency to resolve controversies through the use of principles and their concrete weighting, even by correcting and profoundly modifying literal interpretations, would be one of the consequences of the "new constitutionalism". This judicial activism in the application of the principles, currently strong in civil law, meets different resistances by penetrating the criminal field, where things are very different.

173 See the analysis of R. DWORKIN, Taking rights seriously, Harvard University Press, Cambridge, US, 1977, which is referred that: "(...) we make a case for a principle, and for its weight, by appealing to an amalgam of practice and other principles in which the implications of legislative and judicial history figure along with appeals to European practices and understandings (...) (p. 36); "applicable in all-or-nothing fashion (...)" (pp. 24ss).

Even without adopting a legalistic position, and trying to place itself in the perspective of the "law plus judge" rather than that of the "law versus judge", it will not be difficult to see how the possibilities assured to the interpreter by resorting to principles and balances are circumscribed in criminal law with respect to the other sectors of legal system.

First of all, the numerous, various, heterogeneous principles that balance the abuse of rights (for example, those that affirm the freedom of economic initiative, or the obligation to contribute, or the duties of parents towards their children, etc.) in criminal law to the extent that they affect the facts presided by punishment.

The latter concern, on pain of their unreasonableness, a situation of imbalance between principles. However, not every possible imbalance between principles, abstractly detectable through the scheme of abuse, must be criminally relevant. Precisely in this lies the fragmentary nature of criminal law: in the ability to select punishable facts avoiding all-pervasive protection. Criminal law, unlike civil law, does not raise the problem of resolving controversies or finding solutions to regulate legal trafficking, but that of preparing and managing the penalty, where necessary, for the protection of legal assets. In other words, criminal law is a reactive instrument with no training, promotional or development purpose. In the matter, therefore, there is always, inevitably, a first and main balance of interests, that between goods protected by the precept versus goods sacrificed by the use of penalty, which circumscribes the imbalances of the system that are criminally relevant. The relevance of the principles in criminal law is therefore registered, within the horizon of respect for the principles relevant to criminal law (for example: legality, certainty, non-retroactivity and retroactivity, in national and conventional forms, guilt), which, even in their more modern readings, could prevent recognition of criminal relevance to the situation of disequilibrium concretely considered. At the end of these quick observations on axiological gaps, reference to principles and concretization of the latter through balancing, it should be emphasized how these interpretative tools can be traced back to a unitary phenomenon, namely the shifting of the criteria of judicial decision above the law and the rise from the right to values. The abuse of law demonstrates precisely this capacity, overcoming the mechanism of syllogism and subsumption, of placing the concrete case face to face with the relevant value.

This new horizon, in which judicial protection, in the exercise of values, cannot be considered, in its ancient and customary way, application of law, but remains the decision of the conflict that can be evaluated more or less positively in extra-criminal law. In criminal law, however, the critical issues represented by a judgment that becomes more evaluation than application, are greater, to the point that admitting an interpretation that goes beyond the boundaries of the normative formulation would require, even, to review the structure of the matter.

It seems to us, however, that it may be useful to make a first distinction, depending on whether the abuse (and adjoining assessment) detects inside or outside the case. If the abuse of law is a discourse on the assessment of a fact, the major problems arise where it concerns the criminal case from the inside, that is when it presents a textual reference to the abuse of a private power, or when, and still moreover, the abuse of right is referred to as the rationale of the indictment. In identifying the criminally relevant facts, the value judgment (rectius, of disvalue) is recognized by the judge. However, it should be performed upstream by the legislator, who chooses which facts to sanction after making a balancing judgment, in the awareness that the more extensive it will be the criminal protection of an asset, the more limited will be other conflicting interests. If the civil disciplines tend not to express preferences for the interests that come into play (for example in the contract between peers, both interests are abstractly worthy of protection), the criminal law, instead, expresses a disapproval, and therefore an assessment of the behaviors that he goes to consider.

The abuse of law, however, may also concern a profile external to the prediction of the crime, which involves the problem of justification, independent of the criminal case. If in the first case, between the conflicts of principles underlying the abuses and the interpreter, there are cases in point, in the justification the abused rights come into play directly, and it is the judge to assess the interests at stake. So, let's start our reflection on the criminal relevance of the abuse of rights moving from this last field, and placing ourselves in that sector of matter in which the balancing of interests has a fundamental efficacy: the anti-juridicality.

(FOLLOWS) THE EXAMPLE DRAWN FROM THE JURISPRUDENCE: THE "GREEK CHALLENGE"

By shifting attention to "European" jurisprudence, it should be noted that CJEU had the opportunity to rule on the abuse of right in the strict sense in the "Greek lawsuits"[174]. It is considered appropriate here to clarify, taking into account not only the well-known statements referred to in relation to the relationship between national law and the European Union, but also and above all the meaning that normally is attributed by the traditional doctrine. As is well known, the Luxembourg court in the early 1990s received a series of preliminary questions from the Greek courts, which were called upon to settle disputes arising, all in general on the same question, namely the request by former shareholders to recognize the invalidity of the capital increases decided by the directors of some joint-stock companies that were experiencing a period of financial difficulty and envisaged by art. 8 of the Greek law n. 1386/1983[175], provision that stood in open contrast with art. 25 of the second Company Directive[176], pursuant to which a capital increase must be decided by the general meeting of shareholders. What is relevant here is that, in C-441/93, Panagis Pafitis and others v. Trapeza Kentrikis

174 Second Council Directive of 13 December 1976, 77/91/EEC, aimed at coordinating, to make them equivalent, the guarantees which are required in member states for the companies referred to in article 58, second paragraph, of the treaty, to protect the interests of shareholders and third parties with regard to the establishment of the joint-stock company, as well as the safeguarding and modification of company's share capital (OJ, L 26, p.1). According to art. 25, n. 1 "the capital increases are decided by the assembly. This decision and implementation of the subscribed capital increase shall be advertised in accordance with the procedures laid down by the legislation of each member state (...) but the articles of association or shareholders' meeting whose decision must be the subject of publicity (...) may authorize the increase in subscribed capital up to a maximum amount provided for by law. Within the limits established, the company body authorized for this purpose, if necessary, to increase the subscribed capital. The powers of the latter cannot exceed five years and can be renewed one or more times by the assembly for a period that, each time, cannot exceed five years (...)".

175 CJEU, joined cases C-19/90 and C-20/90, Karella and others of 30 May 1991, ECLI:EU:C:1991:229, I-02691, affirmed without hesitation that direct effect and supremacy article 25 of the Second Directive could not have encountered any exception, even for reasons of general interest. This strict line regarding the supremacy of European law was also followed in subsequent judgments: C-398/95, Syndesmos ton en elladi touristikon kai taxidiotikon grafeion v. Ypourgos Ergasias of 5 June 1997, ECLI:EU:C:1997:282, I-03091, and joined cases C-134/91 and C-135/91, Kerafina-Keramische-und Finanz Holding AG and Vioktimatiki AEVE v. Hellenic Republic and Organismos Oikonomiskis Anasygkrotissis Epicherisseon AE of 12 November 1992, ECLI:EU:C:1992:434, I-05699, until the Greek State invoked before CJEUs the exception of abuse of rights by former shareholders.

176 Directive 2012/30/EU of the European Parliament and of the Council of 25 October 2012 on coordination of safeguards which, for the protection of the interests of members and others, are required by member states of companies within the meaning of the second paragraph of article 54 of the Treaty on EU functioning, in respect of the formation of public limited liability companies and the maintenance and alteration of their capital, with a view to making such safeguards equivalent Text with EEA relevance, OJ, L 315, 14.11.2012, p. 74-97. For further details see: D. LIAKOPOULOS, The regulation of transnational mergers in international and European law, op. cit. D. LIAKOPOULOS, A comparative analysis of EU and US transnational mergers regulation, op. cit.

Ellados A.E. and others case[177] onwards, "which would be, to say the least, paradoxical"[178]. The AG does not hide that, indeed, the possibility of an abuse could potentially arise in some specific hypotheses. An instance of this is the case in which the shareholders "had paradoxically requested the capital increase in an administrative way, to then challenge the related decision in jurisdictional seat"[179], but then discarded this eventuality in the case in question, believing that the increase of capital by administrative means was decided against the will of the recurring shareholders. CJEU also does not hesitate, before arriving at the final decision, to cut out a small space-four points-to the question of the abuse of rights, stating that "the application of such a rule could not however jeopardize the full effectiveness and the uniform application of the community provisions in member states"[180]. Further, this would happen" in this case if one considers that a shareholder who makes use of art. 25 of the second Directive abuses its right by the mere fact that it is a minority shareholder of a company subject to

177 In case: C-441/93, Panagis Pafitis and others v. Trapeza Kentrikis Ellados A.E. and others, op. cit.,. what is striking in the first place is the fact that CJEU, as well as AG Tesauro, have dealt with the issue of abuse of office, without being asked in this regard a question for a preliminary ruling by the quo, accomplice, in all probability, the feeling that the national judge considered to be the only competent to decide ex art. 281 of the Greek civil code if the provisions of the directive had been invoked abusively, as had happened in joined cases: C-134/91 and C-135/91, Kerafina-Keramische- und Finanz Holding AG and Vioktimatiki AEVE v. Hellenic Republic and Organismos Oikonomiskis Anasygkrotissis Epicherisseon AE of 12 November 1992 in which, as AG Tesauro recalls in his Opinion (par. 27), the judge, following the postponement, had declared in law the exception of defendants based on the Greek civil code and had prepared preliminary investigations to verify its validity in fact (see CJEU of Appeal of Athens, sentence No. 9337/1992). In particular, the AG Tesauro motivates the long period (see par. 26 et seq.) highlighting that the question of the possible abuse of EU rights arising from secondary legislation "risks to decisively condition the outcome of the procedure" and that "at stake is ultimately the primacy of EU over internal law, as well as the useful effect of judgments pronounced by CJEU for a preliminary ruling (...)". He then goes on to say that "the mere exercise by shareholders of the right conferred by the European Directive (can not) be qualified by the national CJEU as abusive, without emptying the rule itself of its content", since the Second Directive aims to protect all shareholders indistinctly and independently of the outcome of a possible reorganization procedure and therefore to deny this protection would be tantamount to condemning not the abusive exercise of the right, but simply, its exercise, main cause (in this case a bank, later the Greek State itself), began to invoke, on the other, an exception based on art. 281 of the Greek Civil Code, according to which "the exercise of a right is forbidden, if it clearly exceeds the limits imposed by the good faith or morality or the social or economic purpose of such right", asserting that the shareholders had abusively invoking European law, having no interest in acting for the annulment of the act, which would not have caused them any harm and from which, on the contrary, they would have undoubtedly benefited, benefiting from the financial recovery followed.

178 C-441/93, Panagis Pafitis and others v. Trapeza Kentrikis Ellados A.E. and others, op. cit.

179 N. DE LUCA, European company law: Text, cases and materials, Cambridge University Press, Cambridge, 2017, pp. 302ss.

180 C-441/93, Panagis Pafitis and others v. Trapeza Kentrikis Ellados A.E. and others, op. cit.

a reorganization discipline or which would have benefited from the reorganization of the company"[181]. Furthermore, the centrality of its role in verifying the adequacy of judicial protection provided for by national legal systems is not lacking when rights claimed by the individual on the basis of European provisions are at stake.

The question submitted to CJEU was therefore essentially whether the national court had the possibility of rendering inoperative a right conferred by a "European" rule by virtue of the provisions of domestic law which prohibit the abuse of right[182].

For the purposes herein, we need to highlight how the "Greek causes", repeatedly cited by the doctrine as a real turning point in the definition of abuse, CJEU has not actually recognized the existence of an abuse of EU law in the above defined internal abuse of law, since it was rather a case of abuse of rights in the strict sense. Indeed, if cross-border abuse of law is certainly not to be ruled out, and a cross-border element is completely missing, the existence of an abuse of EU law, understood as artificial construction in order to derive an unfair advantage from EU law[183].

In all of these cases, in fact, private individuals had already been given a certain right, albeit from a European source, and were told that they had been used in an emulating way, with the aim of causing damage to third parties. Indeed, CJEU, in recognizing finally the possibility for the Greek court to declare abusive, according to domestic law, the exercise of a right recognized at Union level, has first emphasized, in the pronunciation of C-367/96, Kefalas and others case of 12 May 1998, as is possible where the judge, on the basis of sufficiently

181 C-441/93, Panagis Pafitis and others v. Trapeza Kentrikis Ellados A.E. and others, op. cit.

182 Only in case: C- 367/96, Kefalas and others of 12 May 1998, the national CJEU submits to CJEU the question whether the national CJEU can be granted the possibility of applying a provision of national law (article 281 of the Civil Code), in order to assess whether a right conferred by the European provisions in question in the present case is exercised by the party who owns it abusively, or if there are other principles of law or consolidated in European law, and which are founding. This presupposes the further question if, when the subjective situation that is assumed to be abusively exercised is of European origin, the regulation of abuse must be found in European law or within the implicit national law, the latter solution, which seems preferred by CJEU in these rulings.

183 More specifically, paragraph 28 reads "EU law does not however prevent CJEU from checking, in the presence of serious and sufficient evidence, whether the shareholder, availing himself of article 25, n. 1 of the Second Directive, has filed an action for declaration of invalidity of the capital increase in order to obtain, to the detriment of the company [emphasis added], unlawful and obviously extraneous to the purpose of this provision, which consists in shareholders that the decision to increase the share capital and, consequently, to alter the shares of shareholders is not taken without their participation in the exercise of the decision-making power of the company (...)".

convincing evidence, verifies that the shareholder is trying to derive, to the detriment of the company, illicit advantages and clearly contrary to the objective of this provision. Similarly, in C-373/97, Diamantis sentence of 23 March 2000 stated that there is a presumption of abuse of rights if the shareholder opts for a remedy "productive of a damage so serious to the legitimate interests of others that they are manifestly disproportionatem (...)"[184].

This highlights how the Union judge in these rulings funds the abuse not so much on the misuse of the purpose of the European rule, as on the prejudice caused to the rights of third parties[185], according to a subjective theory oriented to believe that the choice between the different remedies make presume the existence of a certain intention to harm. We therefore find the use of a notion of abuse stricto sensu understood, which cannot be superimposed on the notion of abuse as outlined in the preceding paragraphs, since there is no determination to artificially satisfy the conditions of a certain national standard.

In conclusion, therefore, the Greek challenge, far from indicating a changed approach of jurisprudence and from bringing elements of novelty with respect to the previous conception of the abuse of rights[186], must on the contrary be understood as an event untied from CJEU's path of abuse intended as abuse of law in the sense specified above, nor, a fortiori, can be considered the first step

---

184 D. TRIANTAFYLLOU, L'interdiction des abus de droit en tant que principe général du droit communautaire, op. cit., pp. 623-624, according to which CJEU, with this clarification, could have, in fact, tried to make the application of the principle of abuse by national CJEU only a procedural exception, concerning the remedies which can be operated, remaining in the hands of EU judicature, seit maître the definition of content and objective of EU rules, its true material scope.

185 The idea, in a nutshell, is that on the occasion of greek challenge EU judges have had the opportunity to draw a double limit on the right of individual member states to apply national provisions prohibiting abuse. Respect for the uniform application and full effect of EU law in applying internal rules to prevent abuse can be considered a guarantee of supremacy of Union law, See, D. ANAGNOSTOPOULOU, Do Francovich and the principle of proportionality weaken Simmenthal (II) and confirm abuse of rights?, in Common Market Law Review, 38, 2001, pp. 772-774. V. KARAYANNIS, L'abus des droits découlant de l'ordre juridique, op. cit., pp. 532ss. M. SCHMIDT-KESSEL, Rechtsmissbrauch im Gemeinschaftsprivatrecht. Folgerungen aus den Rechtssachen Kefalas und Diamantis, in Prinzipien des Privatrechts und Rechtsvereinheitlichung, Jahrbuch Junger Zivilrechtswissenschaftler, 2000, pp. 75ss. D. TRIANTAFYLLOU, L'interdiction des abus de droit en tant que principe général du droit communautaire, op. cit., pp. 159.

186 D. ANAGNOSTOPOULOU, Do Francovich and the principle of proportionality weaken Simmenthal (II) and confirm abuse of rights?, op. cit., pp. 771ss, which points out that in these cases CJEU did not fail to define itself the purpose of the right conferred by EU law and to re-elaborate the basis for the existence of an abuse of rights, determining, in substance, the content rights and, to this end, looking at the objective pursued by EU legislation.

towards the creation of a concept of abuse of the Union's own law, with its own conditions of application[187].

If therefore the judgments in question deserve to be remembered in terms of the relationship that has been outlined between the prohibition of abuse and primacy of Union law[188], an issue that certainly influences the use of palliatives to the ban by CJEU, nevertheless does not seem useful to replace these rulings in the line of jurisprudence regarding abuse[189].

Thus specifying the boundaries of research in the sense of excluding fraud in the proper sense, as well as abuse in the strict sense, it remains only to examine in depth the jurisprudence of CJEU with regard to artificial or fictitious constructions put in place in order to obtain improper advantages, constructions that can involve a single system, the EU (internal abuse of law), or more national and EU laws (cross-border abuse of law). The choice is not accidental. In fact, we wanted to clear the field from any possible overlap or link between concepts that, in the opinion of the writer, must be kept separate and, in doing so, focus attention only on the most problematic hypotheses of abuse, on which CJEU

187 In fact, it is possible to recognize to national CJEUs the power to apply the rules or principles of domestic law aimed at preventing the abuse of right, even when these rights have been conferred under EU law, provided that this power is subject to compliance certain conditions, namely that the anti-abuse provisions do not jeopardize the full effectiveness, uniform application of EU law, or alter the scope of provisions of EU law in question, or jeopardize their objectives prosecuted. Regarding the possible consequences on the primacy of EU law of an application by national CJEU of internal rules that allow to derogate from the uniform implementation of EU law on the basis of abuse. See in argument: D. TRIANTAFYLLOU, L'interdiction des abus de droit en tant que principe général du droit communautaire, op. cit.

188 For further details see: A. HARTKAMP, C. SIBURGH, W. DEVROE, Cases, materials and text on European Union law and private law, op. cit., pp. 282ss. K. LENAERTS, I. MASELIS, K. GUTMAN, European Union procedural law, op. cit., pp. 133ss. M. WIERZBOWSKI, A. GUBRYNOWICZ, International investment law for the 21st century, Oxford University Press, Oxford, 2015. A.H. TÜRK, Judicial review in European Union law, Edward Elgar Publishers, Cheltenham, 2010. L. WOODS, P. WATSON, M. COSTA, Steiner & Woods European Union law, Oxford University Press, Oxford, 2017, pp. 37ss C. BARNARD, S. PEERS, European Union law, op. cit., pp. 788ss. E. BERRY, M.Y. HOMEWOOD, B. BOGUSZ, Complete European Union law. Texts, cases and materials, op. cit., G. CONWAY, European Union law, ed. Routledge, London & New York, 2015. F. NICOLA, B. DAVIES, European Union law stories, Cambridge University Press, Cambridge, 2017. J. USHERWOOD, S. PINDER, The European Union. A very short introduction, Oxford University Press, Oxford, 2018. J.L. DA CRUZ VILAÇA, European Union law and integration. Twenty years of judicial application of European Union law, Hart Publishing, Oxford & Oregon, Portland, 2014. T.H. FOLSOM, Principles of European Union law, including Brexit, West Academic, Minnesota, 2017, pp. 278ss.

189 Contra, V. KARAYANNIS, L'abus des droits découlant de l'ordre juridique, op. cit., pp. 531ss, underlining how CJEU adds to the case-law Van Binsbergen-TV10 a teleological clarification. In this regard it should be noted that, while it is true that where it is an abuse, the scope of rule, be it "European" or national, marks the border between the use and abuse of law. The abuse remains a distinct hypothesis.

is more frequently pronounced and that the doctrine does not always frame correctly.

CONCLUDING REMARKS

Regardless, the concrete implications (direct or indirect) on the internal practice of prohibition of the abuse enshrined by both the European Human Rights ECHR and CFREU. It seems reasonable to argue that, in the same way the abuse integrates the supranational cultural and legal scenario establishing, thus, its relevance from a pragmatic point of view for the overall stability of the system, requiring the latter a timely implementation in the internal legislation level. In fact, it seems a problem linked to the general coherence of (domestic and supranational) systems. It is difficult to conceive, in short, an "upstream" order that clearly states a prohibition (of abuse), without "downstream" an effective implementation of the same, during the (internal legislative or interpretive) implementation.

In any case, what would not be possible to question is the essentiality of the prohibition clause (in our case). You do not appreciate it, in terms of supranational law, solely because of the peculiarities of the systems in question, i.e. the prohibition of abuse. The latter is not justified solely in European Union because of the need to resort to operational and interpretative tools, tending to recreate independently the forms through which the rights will be applied within national laws, a general convergence towards the objectives pursued. The prohibition in question is, additionally, justified within a supranational system, aimed at the circulation of freedoms within heterogeneous legal spaces (the national ones), for which the requirement of legal assistance clauses in the criminal proceedings, requesting, in particular, member countries to provide for the right to avail of a state paid defense lawyer, and Directive 2016/800/EU, on procedural safeguards for children suspected or accused in criminal proceedings[190].

190 Directive (EU) 2016/800 of the European Parliament and of the Council of 11 May 2016 on procedural safeguards for children who are suspects or accused persons in criminal proceedings, OJ L 132, 21.5.2016, p. 1–20. For further details and analysis see: M. JIMENO BULNES, Towards common standards on rights of suspected and accused persons in criminal proceedings in the EU, in Centre for European Policy Studies, 2010, pp. 1-20. V. FAGGIANI, Hacia la constitucionalización de los derechos del justiciable en el ELSJ, in Revista General de Derecho Procesal, 36, 2015, pp. 6ss. A. KLIP, European criminal law. An Integrative approach, ed. Intersentia, Cambridge-Antwerp-Portland, 2012, pp. 24ss. C. ARANGÜENA FANEGO, El derecho a la asistencia letrada en la directiva 2013/48/UE, in Revista General de Derecho Europeo, 32, 2014, pp. 8ss. D.L.F DE VOCHT, M. PANZAVOLTA,

Therefore, it is not a mere practical opportunity, i.e. direct to provide flexible tools through which to ensure a more efficient application of European law. There is need for different thickness: that of assuring the self-defense of the system and, at the same time, of "integrating" the effectiveness of the liberties undoubtedly enshrined. The expression of an upstream ban (of supranational matrix) that did not correspond to a speculative downstream prohibition and a specific obligation of repression for member states would certainly come to rest.

The reasoning, if valid with reference to the abuse of right (as it is generally referred to by the normative texts referred to), could reasonably be related to its different procedural projection.

There is no doubt about the specific function that the abuse of process has over the abuse of law. However, if the directness of the trial is an inviolable right of the individual, and if the trial abuse beyond to the efficiency of the judicial machine is able to draw and compromise the overall fairness of the procedure, it could not be doubted the necessity of a state obligation of prevention and sanction of the abuse of process.

This, then, will be valid within EU law. A systemic misalignment would arise if the direct effectiveness of CFREU forecasts on fundamental rights did not correspond to an equally direct effect of prohibition of abuse. In essence, there would be an irrational deficit of effectiveness of CFREU if the guarantees contained therein could be directly applied and, on the contrary, the former was not directly capable of self-protection.

M. VAN OOSTERHOUT, M. VAN & VANDERHALLEN, Procedural safeguards for juvenile suspects in interrogations: A look at the Commission proposal in light of an EU comparative study, in New Journal of European Criminal Law, 2014, 5 (4), pp. 486ss.

CHAPTER 2

ABUSE OF LAW IN A SINGLE LEGAL SYSTEM. THE FLYWHEEL OF HARMONIZATION

A SHORT INTRODUCTION

Taking into account the distinction between the abuse of EU law and the circumvention of national legislation[191], we have already noted that, on the one, the abused rule can be national or of the European Union. On the other hand is the advantageous situation that the private it wants to get abusively can come from the legal order of the European Union, as a national law that is involved as a result of EU law.

Focusing for the moment on the abuse of EU law, it should be remembered that such construction involves only the supranational order. In fact, it is achieved not through the abusive use of freedom of movement, but by creating an artificial situation for the sole purpose of formally meeting the conditions laid down by European Union legislation and, thus, benefiting from the advantages descend. It is therefore understandable that in this case only one regulation is highlighted: the latter is abused to obtain the advantage envisaged by the same. Evidently, this is a type of abuse that can only be achieved if there is a complete discipline that reconciles certain advantages to certain situations, that is, in areas where there is an advanced degree of harmonization.

It is anticipated here that, in this context, the prohibition of abuse can certainly be applied. Exactly for this reason, harmonization can be considered the "flywheel" of the prohibition of abuse, understood as an autonomous concept. In support of this affirmation, in the following sections, the jurisprudence which has pronounced itself on the case of "carousel" traffic or "deviated" goods in the matter of refunds and compensatory amounts on import and export will be taken as an example (section before), as well as the rulings made with reference

191 D. SIMON, A. RIGAUX, La technique de la consécration d'un nouveau principe général du droit communautaire: l'exemple de l'abus de droit, op. cit., pp. 568.

to the abuse in tax matters in the presence of a harmonized framework (second section).

Investigated by national judges of issues concerning the presence of abuse in the indicated contexts, in fact, the CJEU over time defined, albeit the hesitations and physiological oscillations in the praetorian law, uniform conditions in the presence of which can be found abusive behavior, coining the known Emsland-Stärke (C-110/99, Emsland-Stärke of 14 December 2000) test. This test was subsequently applied in the tax field with the cases: C-255/02, Halifax and others of 21 February 2006 and C-321/05, Kofoed v. Skateministeriet of 5 July 2007, a pronunciation in which the general scope of the principle was recognized. Fiscal matter represents a definitive turning point in the affirmation of the prohibition of abuse of rights, proving still today full of ideas.

Abuse of EU law in Common Agricultural Policy

The Common Agricultural Policy (CAP) is one of the privileged points of analysis of behaviors that are based on an abuse of Union law[192]. This is because, in the first place, the abuse of law in its objective and subjective constituent elements has been completely defined. Secondly, it must be considered that CJEU had to deal with the issue of "carousel" traffic or "deviated" goods in the field of refunds and compensatory amounts for imports and exports-abusive practices so frequent that the AG Alber called them "a latent danger for the financial compensation system"[193].

With regard to this chronological indication, a first notation is required: the most prominent pronunciations made in this sector, in fact, are coeval with those that first occupied themselves with the abuse of the perpetrated right by making use of the freedoms of movement[194]. This is a fact that is not without relevance since, as will be explained shortly, the jurisprudence, which has been able to decide on abusive transactions in CAP between the end of the seventies and the first half of the nineties already sketched the distinctive traits of the so-called abuse test. Then, it is elaborated completely for a period of twenty years, application reference is made, in particular, to the failure to achieve the objectives of secondary legislation, to the artificial nature of the operations carried

192 Conclusions of the AG Alber presented in case: C-110/99, Emsland-Stärke of 14 December 2000, ECLI:EU:C:2000:252, I-11569, par. 67.

193 C-110/99, Emsland-Stärke of 14 December 2000, op. cit.

194 V. P. KOUTRAKOS, The Emsland-Starke abuse of law test in the law of agriculture and free movement of goods, in R. DE LA FERIA, S. VOGENAUER, Prohibition of abuse of law: A new general principle of EU law?, op. cit., pp. 208ss.

out with the sole purpose of obtaining an advantage, and to the role of national authorities in judging application of the secondary legislation of the Union[195].

Well, it is anticipated here that such indications, on the contrary, have not been implemented with reference to the circumvention of the national discipline.

Before paying attention to C-110/99, Emsland-Stärke sentence of 14 December 2000 and to the clarifications made by the jurisprudence on the CAP[196], it is therefore useful to analyze, briefly, what CJEU has stated in the earlier cases, in order to make a comparison between the results achieved in this area and what was established in the first cases on the abuse of freedom of movement, which is analyzed in the next paragraphs.

The first indications of the jurisprudence on the abuse of law concerning compensatory amounts are the cases: C-250/80, Schumacher of 27 October 1981[197] and C-8/92, General Milk Products v. Hauptzollamt Hamburg-Jonas of 3 March 1993.

In the cases which will be analyzed, the Luxembourg court has dealt with the artificial export and import operations carried out for the sole purpose of formally fulfilling the conditions imposed by the Union legislation to benefit from the related financial advantages, in contrast with the aim pursued by the law conferring the right. In particular, in these cases the abusive construction consisted in exporting the goods to a new state of accession, with the sole purpose of obtaining compensatory amounts, and then re-exported it immediately to the true destination state, where the product was marketed.

Since the rationale for the adoption of regulations governing those years in which compensatory amounts were allocated, it was evidently to encourage the movement of goods respectively between two member states, one

195 As stated in the case C-250/80, Schumacher of 27 October 1981: "(...) at the time of the first enlargement of European Union in 1973 there were significant differences between the prices in force in the original member states and those applied in the new one. However, these differences were only gradually eliminated during the five years of the transitional period provided for in the Act of Accession. In the meantime, accession compensatory amounts were set up in order to avoid distorting conditions under which a product from one member state could be marketed in the territory of another (...)". The gradual rapprochement between the prices set for each new member state and the common ones has therefore led to a parallel reduction of these amounts, until their definitive disappearance with the expiry of the transitional period. Thus, with the implementation of the single market in 1993, a progressive automatic dismantling regime for MCAs was introduced, which consequently disappeared.

196 V. P. KOUTRAKOS, The Emsland-Starke abuse of law test in the law of agriculture and free movement of goods, in R. DE LA FERIA, S. VOGENAUER, Prohibition of abuse of law: A new general principle of EU law?, op. cit.

197 CJEU, C-250/80, Schumacher of 27 October 1981, ECLI:EU:C:1981:246, ECR 02465.

originating and one with a new accession, where there were considerable differences in prices between agricultural products[198]. It was a matter of understanding whether the exporter could benefit from the right to payment of the compensatory amounts governed by EU law even if the product had not been marketed in the country of new accession.

In answering this question, CJEU, in C-250/80 Schumacher case of 27 October 1981[199], first ascertains whether the purpose of the provision relied on by the private sector to obtain the compensatory amounts has been respected. On this point, CJEU observes that "in the event that a product from a new member state, or from the Union in its original composition, has remained in the territory of the member state designated as importer solely for the purpose and for the duration of customs formalities and has been, without being marketed in that state, immediately re-exported for marketing in a third member state, the aim of offsetting a price difference is not achieved", so that "one of the essential conditions for the application of a compensatory amount"[200].

Such considerations lead CJEU to conclude, ultimately, that "the exporter who sends agricultural products from another member state with higher prices to a new member state cannot claim payment of compensatory amounts if the completion of the customs formalities in the member state that has been declared to the competent authorities of the exporting member state as the state

---

198 C. BLUMANN (a cura di) Politique agricole commune, ed. Litec, Paris, 1996. W. GRANT, The Common Agricultural Policy, ed. MacMillan, London, 1997. A. MATTHEWS, The CAP and development in M. CARDWELL, J. MCMAHON (eds.), Research handbook on the Common Agricultural Policy, Edward Elgar Publishers, Cheltenham, 2014.

199 CJEU, C-250/80, Schumacher of 27 October 1981, op. cit. The referring CJEU asked CJEU to rule on the question whether a company which had exported wheat from Denmark to United Kingdom (State of new adhesion), applying for the "accession" compensatory amounts, and subsequently re-exporting the same product to Germany, was entitled to payment of the aforementioned amounts, as required by art. 5 of the Commission Regulation of 31 January 1973, n. 269 on the procedure for applying the system of accession compensatory amounts (OJ, L 30, pag. 73).

200 As AG Sharpston explains in his Opinion in C-279/05, Vonk Dairy Products of 11 January 2007, export refunds can be of two types: variable (or "differentiated") and fixed (or "do not differentiate"). The system of export differentiated refunds is intended to open or keep the markets of the third countries concerned open to EU exports, while the variability of the refund has been established to take account of the specific characteristics of each import market on which EU intends to be present. In par. 35, it is specified that: "(...) there are important differences, in economic terms, between differentiated export refunds and fixed ones. In the absence of effective controls, if the transport and other operational costs are sufficiently low and the difference between the two differentiated refund rates for two third countries is sufficiently high and an economic operator can profit by declaring that the goods are intended for export to country A (with a differentiated export refund rate the variability of the refund was established to take account of the specific characteristics of each import market on which the Union intended to be present (...))".

of destination does not follow the actual placing of those products on the market of that state"[201]. The EU judge therefore precludes that, in the absence of an actual operation, he may be entitled to payment of the compensatory amount.

As we can see, CJEU does not use the term abuse, nor does it refer to the possibility of invoking the related ban but, in denying the right to obtain payment of compensatory amounts to the exporter. It already looks to the aims of the discipline, as well as to the concept of effectiveness of the operation.

In the sense that CJEU wanted to sanction the abuse, they also lay the conclusions of the AG, which deal more fully with this aspect. The AG, in fact, in arriving at the same results as CJEU highlights how the contested operation should aim to achieve only an abusive purpose[202], an element that is related to the purely speculative nature of the operation[203]. On another account, the AG is clear in distinguishing the mere knowledge of the beneficiary exporter of the compensatory amounts of the subsequent steps to other member states of the goods he exports, which he does not take into account, from the intention of benefiting from technical defects of the aid system that "undoubtedly violates the general principle of good faith and results in an illegitimate abuse"[204]. In this passage, therefore, the subjective element of the abuse seems to already take shape, defined here as an intention to derive an unjust profit, an element that joins the artificiality of the operation.

The fact that the only objective pursued was that of obtaining benefits from the legislation of the Union, together with the illegality of the operation aimed at obtaining them, is found, even after a decade, also in C-8/92, General Milk Products v. Hauptzollamt Hamburg-Jonas of 3 March 1993 sentence concerning the application of monetary compensatory amounts for the export of a particular type of cheese covered by the European rules[205]. CJEU recalls that, in

201 "(...) in a case like this, there is an obvious abuse: for a Danish wheat supply to Germany, the exporter set a stop in England for the sole purpose of collecting the compensatory amount" (AG Sharpston's opinion in case: C-279/05, Vonk Dairy Products of 11 January 2007, op. cit.).

202 In general terms, there is no doubt that a purely speculative operation carried out by the exporter constitutes abuse, in which the placing in free trade of the member state where the goods are stopped is reduced to the formality of the customs clearance".

203 In this last regard, it may be interesting to note how, in this first embryonic application of a technique aimed at prohibiting the abuse of law, the latter is expressly linked to the violation of the general principle of good faith, a combination reminiscent of national traditions.

204 CJEU, C-8/92, General Milk Products v. Hauptzollamt Hamburg-Jonas of 3 March 1993, op. cit.

205 CJEU, C-8/92, General Milk Products v. Hauptzollamt Hamburg-Jonas of 3 March 1993, op. cit. The case concerned the monetary compensatory amounts ("ICM") for export of cheddar cheese import-

order to benefit from such advantages, the importation and re-export of these cheeses must be made in the context of normal commercial operations, and not only to unlawfully benefit from the granting of MCAs. In other words, as was pointed out in the same case the AG Darmon, the fictitious importation and for the sole purpose of benefiting from the compensatory amounts could take place if "the goods were imported into the first member state only to be immediately re-exported to another member state, without effective marketing in the first state"[206]. To this end, "the de facto assessments necessary to verify the real nature of these operations" are delegated by CJEU to the national court[207].

(FOLLOWS) IN MATTERS OF EXPORT REFUNDS: C-125/76, PETER CREMER V. BUNDESANSTALT FÜR LANDWIRTSCHAFTLICHE MARKTORDNUNG CASE OF 11 OCTOBER 1977

A similar approach was followed by CJEU also in the first rulings on export refunds. This is not surprising, given that the ratio of promoting the movement of goods and ultimately supporting the export of the product, making it more competitive, also underlies the provision of export refunds. The benefit is granted to exporters of agricultural products in order to compensate the difference between the costs of production and the prices of certain goods produced in the European Union but intended to be exported to third countries, and the costs or prices prevailing on the world market. In such a context, the "speculative" transaction consists of carrying out a provisional exportation to a new member state or to a third country. Such is done with the simultaneous completion of

ed from New Zealand to Germany and then exported to other member states. Whereas, according to the agreement between the then EU and New Zealand, cheese imports into a member state did not offer the possibility of being reimbursed, otherwise it was the case where the re-exportation took place in other member states, as well as envisaged by the Commission Regulations of 31 March 1984, n. 900, which fixes the monetary compensatory amounts, as well as certain coefficients and rates necessary for their application (OJ, L 92, p.2) and Commission Regulation (EEC) 19 May 1981, n. 1371, laying down procedures for the administrative application of monetary compensatory amounts (OJ, L 138, p.1). The question that was brought to the attention of CJEU was whether ICM positives could be applied to the export of imported cheese without application of a minimum price system, or of negative MCAs on imports.

206 Opinion of AG Darmon, brought on 19 January 1993, in the case C-8/92, General Milk Products v. Hauptzollamt Hamburg-Jonas of 3 March 1993, ECLI:EU:C:1993:18, I-00779, parr. 44 and 46.

207 C-8/92, General Milk Products v. Hauptzollamt Hamburg-Jonas of 3 March 1993, op. cit.

customs clearance operations, followed by immediate re-importation into the state of destination of the product, without the product in question ever being placed on the market of the first state of destination, in order to obtain financial advantages, which otherwise would not have been obtained.

Also in this context, we find an attitude of disfavor on the part of CJEU compared to "abnormal" operations, not unlike the one just highlighted with regard to the attribution of compensatory amounts, which takes the form, primarily of the attention shown in examining the objectives to which the schemes provided for by the secondary law rules from time to time invoked.

The C-125/76, Peter Cremer v. Bundesanstalt für landwirtschaftliche Marktordnungsentence of 11 October 1977[208], is a good example. The referring court wondered, inter alia, whether an exporter was entitled to the full export refund of a compound feeding stuff provided for in European legislation, even when the food in question contained only a very small part (in this case, the %) a single product (tapioca flour) among those governed by the legislation that gave the right to return[209].

The AG noted that, since the regulation in question did not establish any minimum content of products in the cereals sector, the addition of 2% of tapioca flour was sufficient to justify the return in favor of the exported product. Likewise, he had not failed to underline how the European discipline did not contain elements that would allow to maintain that the addition, for possible controls and to avoid abuses, should reach a minimum percentage. Moreover, "if the community legislature wished to dispose of this, it would have fixed a certain percentage in the framework (...)"[210].

---

208 CJEU, C-125/76, Peter Cremer v. Bundesanstalt für landwirtschaftliche Marktordnung of 11 October 1977, ECLI:EU:C:1977:148, I-01593. The question referred concerns the interpretation of Council Regulation of 30 October 1964, n. 166, concerning the regime to be applied to certain categories of compound feeding stuffs (OJ, p. 277) and of the Commission Regulation of 30 October 1964, n. 171 which establishes, on the basis of the previous regulation, the conditions for granting export refunds in third countries for certain categories of compound feeding stuffs.

209 Even the federal agency for the organization of the agricultural market, the defendant in the main proceedings, while admitting the flat and largely theoretical nature of the calculation methods laid down by regulations, nevertheless observed that the application of those provisions could not extend to abusive, that is, to requests for export refunds of compound feeding stuffs containing only minimum percentages of a product governed by the European legal order relating to the cereals market.

210 Opinion of AG Reischl presentend in case: C-125/76, Peter Cremer v. Bundesanstalt für landwirtschaftliche Marktordnung of 11 October 1977, op. cit.

On the contrary, CJEU considers in any case "unquestionable that a compound food, which, among the components includes, but only to a negligible extent, a single product governed by Regulation n. 19, cannot be returned"[211]. This is because, otherwise, the ratio of the regime governing export refunds to third countries would not be respected, which is to compensate the impact on the price of food composed of the discipline that governs the components used.

From these considerations, CJEU draws the conclusion that "the application of the Regulation in question, together with the Regulation no. 171/64 of the European Commission (EC), could not in any case be extended to include abusive practices of economic operators, thanks to the forfeit assessments used for the calculation of refunds, especially since at that time it was not to put into force a complete but a basic discipline, in which the national authorities should have carried out, under their own responsibility, the market management of the products in question"[212].

THE FUNDAMENTAL TURNING POINT OF C-110/99, EMSLAND-STÄRKE CASE OF 14 DECEMBER 2000. DEFINITION OF THE PARAMETERS IN WHOSE PRESENCE THE PROHIBITION OF ABUSE IS TRIGGERED

The first indications deriving from the jurisprudence concerning refunds and compensatory amounts have been accepted and deepened in the pronunciation in C-110/99, Emsland-Stärke case of 14 December 2000[213]. The latter is still of central importance in the elaboration of the doctrine of abuse of rights, also taking into account that it was made in the grand section. In fact, if the possibility of penalizing the abusive manifestations of the individuals had already been made explicit in the rulings just examined, an independent prohibition of abuse had not yet been theorized.

211 C-125/76, Peter Cremer v. Bundesanstalt für landwirtschaftliche Marktordnung of 11 October 1977, op. cit.

212 Par. 21. This is what was stated by CJEU in response to the doubts of national CJEU on the validity of Regulation no. 166/64 "as the latter could result in the granting of illicit advantages, since it does not distinguish, for the calculation of export refunds, depending on whether the components of a compound food are or are not governed by EU agricultural regulations (...)".

213 CJEU, C-110/99, Emsland-Stärke of 14 December 2000, op. cit.

The case, well known, concerned one of the numerous operations purely artificial and without economic logic implemented in those years in order to obtain export refunds: a German company exported potatoes to Switzerland and then immediately reimport them into the European customs area, more specifically in Italy, through the same means of transport used for their exportation, thus benefiting from the export benefits provided for by Regulation 2730/79[214].

This was evidently an operation aimed at obtaining an export refund by creating artificial conditions relating to a fictitious export, contrary to the Union objectives, which is why the German customs authority requested that the benefit already achieved be returned. When a dispute arose, the national courts asked CJEU whether the regulation in question prevented the exporter's right to pay the refund in case of immediate re-importation of the products.

The context was indeed mature enough to proceed to a definition of the parameters with which to assess the existence of an abuse of law: not only, as we have just observed and as will be seen below, there were now many cases in which CJEU she was faced with such questions. There was no single and repeatable notion of abuse of rights, but the EC itself, in its written observations, invited the European judges to do a work of clarification.

The weight of the written observations of the EC in this case cannot be overlooked. It is interesting to note in this regard that the questions referred did not properly refer to such a problem[215]. Nevertheless, the attention given by the European Institution to the definition of the notion of abuse presumably started a virtuous circle such that the AG Alber first. Then, consequently, CJEU considered it necessary to deepen the structural characteristics of the abuse, looking to respond to a growing need for clarity regarding a principle applied more and more frequently, also and above all by national judges, called to correctly assess the presence of an abuse in the concrete case.

Starting from the considerations of the EC[216], the AG Alber reiterates that in order to determine the presence of an abuse, it is necessary first to verify

214 Regulation n. Commission Regulation (EC) No 2730/79 of 29 November 1979 laying down common detailed rules for the application of the system of export refunds on agricultural products (OJ L 75, 32).

215 AG Alber immediately notes this in his assessments. "It is true that the referring CJEU specifically asks for the interpretation of art. 10 of the regulation, however, the Commission rightly points out that the applicability of the provision to a case such as that in the main proceedings must first be clarified (...)" (par. 48).

216 The Commission identified in the written observations of the case three elements constituting an abuse of rights. First of all, what defines an objective element, "namely the proof that the conditions

the objective element of reimportation. This would nullify the purpose of the refunds, that of compensating the difference between the prices of the products in the European and the quotations in the international commerce, since "the criterion of the legality of concrete transactions of import and export is therefore the end of the dispositions from time to time applicable"[217]. The AG states, however, that "the objective fact that a reimportation took place is not yet sufficient in itself to make the purpose not be achieved"[218]. It is also necessary to verify the existence of the subjective element, constituted by the "intention to claim refunds export for a purpose other than that foreseen by the advantaged exporter"[219], which excludes, consequently, its bona fide[220].

In the opinion of the AG, therefore, in order to consider the purpose of the rule as undamaged, it would not suffice to integrate the only objective element, constituted by reimportation, but also the presence of a subjective element. However, the test drawn up by the AG would seem to focus solely on achieving the aim of European legislation, moving closer to the technique of restrictive interpretation, which demonstrates the subtle boundary line and the contiguity between the techniques used to protect the legal EU system from the abuses of private individuals.

---

for the granting of a service have been artificially created, i.e. the commercial operation does not pursue any economic purpose, but has been concluded exclusively for obtaining subsidies, to be charged to the European budget, which accompany this commercial operation (...)". This element must be complemented by a subjective element, "that is, the fact that the commercial transaction in question was accomplished primarily in order to obtain a financial advantage contrary to the purpose of European legislation". Finally, the need for both the competent national administration to take charge of proof of abusive behavior, except in cases of more extreme abuse, in which a test for simple presumption would be conceivable, which may lead to an inversion of the burden, is affirmed probative. Although the Commission considers that the verification of the presence of these elements is a matter for the national CJEU. The Commission points out that a significant financial gain, determined by the difference between the amount of the refund and that of the import duties, and the time very short between the export and reintroduction of products and the use of the same means of transport, can be considered symptomatic indices of the presence of the objective element of abuse (see parr. 42 and 43 of the conclusions).

217 CJEU, C-110/99, Emsland-Stärke of 14 December 2000, op. cit.

218 CJEU, C-110/99, Emsland-Stärke of 14 December 2000, op. cit.

219 Precisely, at good faith the attorney general refers to par. 80, where he states that "the subject of law that acts by abusing the law loses for this the protection guaranteed by the legal system to an economic operator acting in good faith".

220 In fact, the goods satisfied the condition of having left the European geographical territory, as per art. 9, n. 1. As for the other conditions foreseen by art. 10. n. 1, of the Regulation n. 2730/79, they could have been imposed only before the granting of the refund" (parr. 47 and 48).

The grand section, on the other hand, takes into consideration the purpose of the European standard only in defining the objective element of the test, reserving the right to evaluate at a later time, once it is established that the purpose has not been met, the intentions of the agent. It, thus, finds confirmation of a fundamental principle in the matter, namely that, when the purpose of the norm has been observed, the reasons that push the subject to act are not relevant. So, the judges, after having found that the operations examined satisfied all the conditions for the granting of export refunds provided for by the regulation, make an extremely clear distinction between the failure to achieve the objective of the reference legislation, understood as a necessary condition but not sufficient, and the subjective element of the intention.

The finding that it is an abusive practice requires, on the one hand, "a set of objective circumstances from which it appears that, despite the formal compliance with the conditions laid down by the European legislation, the objective pursued by that legislation has not been achieved (...)"[221]. On the other hand, "the desire to obtain an advantage deriving from European legislation by artificially creating the necessary conditions for obtaining it"[222], the existence of which can be demonstrated, in particular, by evidence of a collusion between the exporter of the Union, beneficiary of the refunds, and the importer of the goods in the third country.

Lastly, the EU judge defines the role of the national court, who will also be responsible, in accordance with the principle of loyal cooperation, for establishing the existence of those two elements. The evidence of which can be provided in accordance with the rules of national law, provided that this does not prejudice the effectiveness of European Union law[223].

In the present case, CJEU does not, however, fail to provide certain precise indications to the national court, specifying that the sale of a product by the purchaser established in the third country concerned, to a company with him personally and economically connected, also established in the same country, "is

221 CJEU, C-110/99, Emsland-Stärke of 14 December 2000, op. cit.

222 CJEU, C-110/99, Emsland-Stärke of 14 December 2000, op. cit.

223 On the basis of indications the Union judge who made the reference for a preliminary ruling repressed the decision of Finanzgericht, which ordered the repayment of the reimbursement for failure to comply with the conditions set out in art. 10 n. 1 of Regulation (EEC) no 2736/79, although, under the regulation, these conditions could be verified only before the reimbursement was granted, instead requiring them to check the existence of the subjective element in support of the existence of an abuse (Bundesfinanzhof, Urteil vom del 24 April 2001, VII R 5/98).

part of the factual elements that can be taken into consideration by the national court to assess whether the operation in question is artificial (...)"[224].

Lastly, it should be noted that in this case, as in C-250/80, Schumacher of 27 October 1981, the company, in response to the EC's observations on the abuse of rights, claimed that it required repayment of the export refund or to subsequently withdraw the benefit obtained would have violated the principle of legality. The general principle of abuse of rights does not constitute a clear and unequivocal legal basis on which to base the adoption of such a measure. In this regard, the grand section replies that, in this case, the reimbursement does not constitute a sanction but merely represents the consequence of the fact that the conditions required for obtaining the advantage deriving from the European rules were artificially created, an assertion, which draws inspiration from art. 4 n. 4 of Regulation 2988/95[225].

SOME NOTATIONS ON THE EMSLAND-STÄRKE (C-110/99, EMSLAND-STÄRKE OF 14 DECEMBER 2000) TEST.

The general scope of the Emsland-Stärke test, of extreme importance not only with reference to the subject directly concerned, the CAP. This is especially in the sense of an autonomous elaboration of the European doctrine of abuse, precisely because the pronunciation appears integrally extensible to other sectors of EU law, has been highlighted since the first comments[226]. Moreover, the presumable amplitude of the scope of the pronunciation derives, in turn, from the versatility of the test conceived therein, susceptible of application, as formulated, in the most disparate breakers[227].

224 CJEU, C-110/99, Emsland-Stärke of 14 December 2000, op. cit.

225 Council Regulation (EC, Euratom) No 2988/95 of 18 December 1995 on the protection of the European Communities financial interests, OJ L 312, 23.12.1995, p. 1-4. see in argument also: J. ÖBERG, Limits to European Union powers: A case study of European Union regulatory criminal law, Hart Publishing, Oxford & Oregon, Portland, 2017, pp. 124ss.

226 D. WEBER, Abuse of law, European CJEU of Justice, 14 December 2000, Case C-110/99, Emsland-Stärke, in Legal Issues of Economic Integration, 31, 2004, pp. 43.

227 At most, the specialty of the sector in which the sentence was pronounced may be taken in another way. The most complete reflections on behaviors capable of integrating an abuse of rights, in fact, have been made with reference to issues that directly affected financial interests of the then Union, which CJEU, on many occasions, has shown itself particularly attentive to protect. He finds it, among others, P. KOUTRAKOS, The Emsland-Stärke abuse of law test, op. cit., pp. 208ss.

The finding, which cannot be revoked in doubt, of the potentially wide-ranging applicability of a test made requires some clarifications as to its constituent elements, which show somewhat uncertain boundaries in followed by a more careful reconstruction while appearing extremely linear to a fleeting reading.

If the objective element could pose some problems with regard to its predictability, with consequent harm to the principle of legal certainty, in the event that the purpose for which the legal system assigns a right is disputed or is not completely clear[228], is however, the subjective element that inevitably presents the greatest critical points.

In fact, the full insertion of animus in the test was considered one of the most controversial aspects of the decision in question, originating reservations first of all about its usefulness in identifying an abusive situation, so that the reference to the same by the European judges has even been called "improvident"[229]. The subjective criterion, in particular, is considered problematic not so much because of the specific characteristics of legal persons, incapable of any subjective will, but rather because of the intrinsically indeterminate nature of a test that evaluates whether this condition is satisfied or not. The problem arises precisely when the judge is asked to verify the intention of private individuals, where the latter do not openly admit their design aimed at obtaining an improper advantage from Union law[230].

---

228 It is also pointed out that the test, as far as general application is concerned, does not appear in this first part which can be concretely extended to all the recognized macro-categories of abuse in EU law. In fact, the aim to which some rights tend is the right itself, for example in the case of human rights, where the underlying idea is to guarantee a protected sphere and not to achieve a certain social objective. In this case, as is clear from article 54 of the Charter of Fundamental Rights, the abuse occurs not because the right is used contrary to its purpose but because its use affects excessively the other legally recognized interests, taking into account the circumstances. This means that the test could certainly not be applied with regard to the abuse of law in the strict sense. This, however, appears to be, in the opinion of the writer, the inevitable result of the plurality of meanings that can assume the prohibition of abuse in the most diverse contexts.

229 This aspect is underlined by AG Lenz in his Opinion of 16 June 1994 in case: C-23/93, TV10 v. Commissariaat voor de Media of 5 October 1994, ECLI:EU:C:1994:251, I-04795, par. 60, which states: "(...) in the face of the legally significant activity of a legal person acting by means of one's own organs, the realization of subjective elements takes on fundamentally different connotations. The legal person is not in itself capable of developing a subjective behavior. Only natural persons act with responsibility from an ethical point of view, which is of fundamental importance, for example as regards the punishment of a subject. In a system that recognizes the existence of legal entity and capacity, there are generally rules of imputation on the basis of which the activities of the bodies, carried out through natural persons, are considered as activities of the legal person. This imputability may extend to the attribution to the legal person of a capacity under the criminal profile. These rules of imputation present significant differences in the various member states legal systems (...)".

230 D. WAELBROECK, La notion d'abus de droit dans l'ordre juridique communautaire, op. cit., pp.

On the other hand, the emerging data should not be underestimated that the intention to obtain advantages from a rule cannot be considered reprehensible in itself, since it is perfectly legitimate to try to plan one's own business in the light of the applicable law. The case is different in which a particular activity is put in place for the sole reason of obtaining an advantage and, to this end, pure construction is used, as occurred in C-110/99, Emsland-Stärke case of 14 December 2000. However, since actions are usually carried out by more than one purpose, it is not always easy to determine the boundary between use and abuse, interpreting each time the adjectives "unique", "principal" and "essential" that accompany the purpose[231].

These criticisms inevitably catch the eye. Yet, it cannot be overlooked how, by eliminating the ascertainment of the subjective element and looking only at the rationale of the norm, it would be possible, as already pointed out, to substantially assimilate the prohibition of abuse to the restrictive interpretation of the Union law. From this, it follows that the subjective element must necessarily be safeguarded, but at the same time reinterpreted in an objective key, as CJEU will have a better way to explain in C-255/02, Halifax and others case of 21 February 2006, so that a central role in verifying its existence, it will be assumed by the presence of a series of circumstances, precisely objective, such as, for example, in the case of artificial operations in the CAP sector, links or affiliations, of a personal or economic nature. In fact, if the subjective intention is certainly difficult to determine, the right is (sufficiently) prepared to identify this will on the basis of objective elements, including primarily the artificial nature of the operation.

In other words, it can hardly be denied that the application of the subjective criterion proves to be an extremely complex operation. On the other hand, to admit that, because the abuse of law exists, suffice the mere presence of the objective element, would in fact lead to putting aside the European provision that is supposed to be abused, even going against its literal tenor, as long as the supposed objective of the same is not achieved. This would lead to an extension

---

603ss. No further concern is given to a further criticism of the configuration in the test of a subjective element, namely that the element of intention to obtain advantages from the legislation would not always be appropriate. This would happen, for example, in the case of abuse of property rights or legal proceedings, against which a more appropriate criterion could be the intention to harm, as indicated by art. 54 of the Charter of Fundamental Rights of the European Union. In fact, the same considerations are already expressed above: it is not really possible to imagine a test applicable both to the abuse in the strict sense that to the abuse intended as fraud to the law.

231 D. WAELBROECK, La notion d'abus de droit dans l'ordre juridique communautaire, op. cit.

of the concept of abuse that is hardly compatible with the principle of legal certainty[232].

It should be noted, in conclusion, that CJEU, after referring to the objective and subjective elements of the abuse, stated that it is for the national court to establish their existence, in accordance with the national legislation on the subject of proof, but on condition to respect a series of guidelines, paying attention to the effectiveness of Union law is not compromised. In this regard, it should be noted that, given the extremely general wording of the Emsland-Stärke test, because it assumes a real, preceptive meaning, it must be related to the specific circumstances of the event. As pointed out by the AG Sharpston in C-279/05, Vonk Dairy Products case of 11 January 2007, it claims that CJEU has developed a broad and pragmatic concept of abusive practice. In this last regard, it is noted that, in any case, CJEU, although formulating a test of deliberately broad and general scope, does not seem to have been forced to expressly consecrate the existence of a general principle prohibiting the abuse of law, showing itself more cautious both of the EC. The written observations had considered the art. 4 n. 3 of Regulation 2988/95 "expression of a general principle of law already in force in the community legal order"[233], given the existence of such a principle in the legal system of almost all member states, as well as its application in the constant case law of CJEU, both from AG Alber and, referring to a "simulated legal shop"[234], had confirmed the existence of a general principle prohibiting the abuse of their rights, common to member states and consecrated in the Union's legal order.

According to the writer, from the described jurisprudential evolution two notions of the concept of abuse of right/tax avoidance, a valid one in the field of the harmonized taxation and another operating in the field of non-harmonized taxes can be derived. One, therefore, pertains to the hypotheses of abuse in the strict sense, while the other concerns cases of abuse in the broadest sense. As mentioned in the previous paragraph, the two concepts diverge only as to the degree of intensity that must characterize the subjective element and, consequently, the valid economic reasons. With reference to the abuse in a broad

232 J. SNELL, The notion of and a general test for abuse of rights: Some normative reflections, in R. DE LA FERIA, S. VOGENAUER, Prohibition of abuse of law: a new general principle of EU law?, op. cit., pp. 225ss.

233 CJEU, C-110/99, Emsland-Stärke of 14 December 2000, op. cit.

234 CJEU, C-110/99, Emsland-Stärke of 14 December 2000, op. cit., par. 38.

sense and to the non-harmonized taxation sector, it is necessary that the purpose of avoiding the tax is exclusive and that therefore any economic reasons are completely marginal and irrelevant[235]. With regard to the abuse in the strict sense and to the sector of harmonized taxation, however, the pathological situation is integrated when the purpose of evading the tax is essential, not necessarily exclusive. As a consequence, any extrafiscal economic reasons may also reach a certain degree of importance, provided that they do not open the way to an alternative justification path for the operation carried out, in the sense that the latter would have been carried out even without the prospect of obtaining of a tax advantage.

Moreover, although CJEU has always stated that two are the constituent elements of the abuse, the traditional "objective" and subjective elements should be flanked by the "anomalous" construction, i.e. the distorted use of legal instruments. On the basis of Italian and European jurisprudence, a distorted use of legal instruments occurs when the taxpayer uses acts, facts or contracts which make it possible to produce the same economic effect as that which could have been achieved through the completion of any operation or a more direct and linear operation, not directly contrasting in any case with the rules of the legal system. Thus, in C-110/99, Emsland-Stärke case of 14 December 2000, the anomalous operation was the exportation of products from Germany to Switzerland and the re-importation thereof, shortly thereafter, to another member state of the Union, where they were actually released for consumption. In order to achieve the same economic effect, i.e. to put products into consumption in a given EU member state, the tax payer could have carried out a more linear operation, consisting of the direct exportation of the products to the latter state. In the C-255/02, Halifax and others case of 21 February 2006, the anomalous operation consisted in entrusting the construction of the call-centers to companies controlled by the same bank (the Halifax). The latter could have obtained the same economic effect (the construction of call centers) by paying directly to the contractors. In the C-223/03, University of Huddersfield Higher Education Corporation v. Commissioners of Customs & Excise case of 21 February 2006, the anomalous situation established by the university consisted in having leased the property through the establishment of a trust, linked to it and controlled by it, and in using the property good on the basis of a subsequent sublease

235 CJEU, C-108/17, Enteco Baltic of 20 June 2018, ECLI:EU:C:2018:473. C-533/16, Wolkswagen of 21 March 2018, ECLI:EU:C:2018:204, above published in the electronic Report of the cases.

concluded between the trust and the university. The same economic effect (use of the real estate consisting of a mill, for restructuring purposes) would have been produced even if the university had not concluded any contract aimed at guaranteeing the direct use of the asset, given that it already owned it. In the C-419/02, BUPA Hospitals Ltd and University of Huddersfield Higher Education Corporation v. Commissioners of Customs and Excise case of 21st February 2006, the anomalous operation consisted in agreeing with suppliers to receive invoices of payment, with recourse VAT charge, in relation to operations (of sale of medicines and prostheses) that would have been performed later. The same economic effect (the provision of a supply of medicines and prosthetics) also in this case would have been achieved if the hospital had not agreed to do so with the suppliers, waiting for the actual execution of the operation to receive the invoices. In C-196/04, Cadbury Schweppes and Cadbury Schweppes Overseas case of 12 September 2006, the anomalous operation consisted of setting up the two subsidiaries in Ireland, given that the same economic effect (raising funds and making them available to of the parent company and other group companies) could have been produced by setting up subsidiaries directly in the United Kingdom. In C-321/05, Kofoed v. Skatteministeriet case of 5 July 2007, CJEU denied that the operation carried out by the taxpayer constituted a circumvention of art. 2, letter d) of Directive 90/434/EEC and therefore, in essence, has denied the configurability of an artificial operation. Finally, in the C-425/06, Part Service case of 21 February 2008, the anomalous operation consisted of the splitting into several contracts of a single leasing transaction. It is clear, therefore, that these contracts allowed to produce the same economic effect as a unitary leasing contract and, lastly, compared to the use of several contracts, is a more direct and linear operation.

As can be seen from the examples just mentioned, in assessing whether or not there is a misuse of legal instruments, it is essential to examine the objective economic substance underlying the disputed operation. One must ask, in other words, what economic effect the latter was able to produce and whether this economic effect could have been achieved through a more direct and linear operation. If an alternative operation can be identified, more direct and linear than the one implemented and producing an identical economic effect, it is correct to conclude that there is a misused use of legal instruments, devoid of economic substance. The evaluation of the distorted use implies, therefore, an examination of the presence or absence of any economic objectives that justify the use of a more convoluted operation. The latter is justified, that is, and therefore does not fall into the category of distorted use, if it is likely to produce a different or additional economic effect compared to what would be obtained with the most direct operation. To conclude in the sense of the existence of a distorted use, the interpreter must be able both to identify the most direct operation and to exclude the presence of a different economic substance between "normal" and "abnormal" operation.

Obviously, the analysis that the interpreter is called to perform under this last profile regards the objective economic substance of the concrete case, that is, that emerges from an examination of the operation conducted, however, by those who remained foreign to it. In other words, the investigating subject, to affirm the existence of a distorted use, must be able to conclude that between "abnormal" operation, concretely put into being, and "normal", which should have been completed or even not completely completed, there is an objective identity of economic substance. This is clear from an initial analysis of the case, without prejudice therefore to any clarifications that the taxpayer will provide in a procedural dispute to prove the existence of subjective economic motivations (such as marketing) of which only he initially knew and that were "unpredictable" and not evaluable, in a first phase, by the interpreter. In fact, the viewpoint on which the anomalous nature of an operation is assessed is a "comparatistic", not "finalistic", or "teleological" viewpoint.

The economic substance must therefore be kept distinct from the element of valid economic reasons. The first concerns the objective plan of the operation, namely that of the coherence between legal forms employed and economic objectives to be achieved. From this point of view, there is no economic substance when the use of "anomalous" legal instruments is not suitable, from an objective point of view, to produce economic effects different from those that would be obtained through the use of a more direct and linear operation. In short, this is the expression behind which there is a judgment of adequacy between form and substance, insufficient to prove circumvention or abuse alone. The valid economic reasons, on the contrary, pertain to the subjective profile of the case and respond to the need to identify the reasons for which the operation, syndicated on the level of abuse, was put in place.

For example, in C-425/06, Part Service case of 21 February 2008, if the Luxembourg judges had adopted a finalistic or teleological approach, the operation carried out could not have been considered as anomalous. It should have been considered that the plurality of linked contracts allowed the tax payer, as he himself indicated, to obtain economic effects such as those related to marketing (launch of a new financial product with compressed premiums), to the organization (division of risk management functions: insurance, sureties and loans entrusted to the C-425/06, Part Service case of 21 February 2008, management of the car park entrusted to the operating companies) and the guarantee (the loan served as a security deposit for the fulfillment of the obligations of the user) that could not have been produced with the stipulation of a single leasing contract, but adopting an exclusive approach comparatively, such purposes cannot be taken into account when assessing the element of distorted use. The operation was anomalous in that, compared to that consisting in the conclusion of a single leasing contract, it allowed to achieve the same objective economic effect and, beyond the specific aims pursued in the specific case, was configured as less linear and direct. Therefore, if the specific economic purposes pursued by the tax payer were considered genuine, the circumvention should have been denied in this case. But in any case, in a first phase, the one in which it is only the financial administration to assess the occurrence of an abuse and the objective element of distorted use could have been considered integrated.

In conclusion, it is true that, in assessing the requirement of artificial construction, the financial administration must be able to conclude that the anomalous transactions are devoid of economic substance, but it is also true that the latter is (or does not appear) in objective manner from an analysis of the operation conducted from outside, by those who, like the revenue authorities, have remained foreign to it. If from this first investigation it emerges that the less linear and direct transaction cannot produce economic effects different from those deriving from the most direct transaction, the revenue can conclude in the sense of the existence of a distorted use of legal instruments. It will then be up to the taxpayer to provide full evidence of the existence of subjective and valid economic reasons that justify the "anomalous" path he has undertaken. According to the modest opinion of the writer, in the investigation on the element of the distorted use and, in particular, on the absence of the economic substance, it is opportune to use the canon of good faith and the parameter of judgment of the average businessman. In fact, from the aforementioned review of jurisprudence it emerges that CJEU has reconstructed the conduct (the abusive and the "normal") in economic terms, applying the criterion of the "economic reasonableness" of the behavior and therefore referring to generally accepted standards and to the behavior of the average economic operator. From this point of view, due to the manner in which it is implemented, the abuse of law translates into an "abnormal" exercise of the law itself, or as an exercise of the same in a manner contrary to its economic-social destination[236]. Having defined the element of distorted use, a last notation concerns its relevance with respect to the two objective and subjective elements.

Beginning with the C-110/99, Emsland-Stärke case of 14 December 2000, CJEU has affirmed that the constitutive elements of the tax avoidance are objective and subjective, never speaking of an independent third element. However, in all cases where the EU judicature has been called upon to rule on the issue of circumvention, the modalities of conduct have always materialized in a distorted use of legal instruments. Finally, with the ruling in C-425/06, Part Service case of 21 February 2008, the weight attributed to this element also seems to have grown. On the basis of this consideration and looking at the various national anti-avoidance laws, which impose on the financial administration the increasingly stringent motivation obligations to identify the abusive ways of the conduct, it seems correct to consider that the element of distorted use legal instruments complete a real requirement constituting the abuse of the right, which joins the objective and subjective elements. By adhering to this thesis, the notion of abuse is better circumscribed and at the same time the effectiveness of the obligation to state reasons on the financial administration is guaranteed, as a guarantee of the tax payer and his right of defense. If, in fact, the constituent elements of the circumvention were only that objective and subjective, the revenue authority would need, from time to time, to demonstrate the fiscal advantage achieved and the essential purpose of obtaining it. Even when the operation carried out by the tax payer, it resulted in a distorted use of legal instruments (because it has real economic reality) and, therefore, even when the operation itself is fully approved by the legislator. On the other hand, if the distorted use is raised to the rank of a constitutive element of abuse, the financial administration is pushed to concentrate, in terms of motivation of the imposition, also on the precise identification of the abusive ways of the conduct and, therefore, on the proof of the inexistence of economic substance.

Another relevant theme concerns the identification of the object of abuse. In this regard the terminology "abuse of legal forms" is often used. The writer does not consider this expression to be completely correct, since it indicates that the object of abuse is the use of legal forms and therefore the exercise of contractual freedom. On the contrary, the exercise of contractual freedom is the subject of

236 R. SALEILLES, Etude sur la théorie générale de l'obligation dans la second rédaction du projet de code civil allemand, Paris, 1895.

a distorted use but is not, properly, the object of abuse. It must not be forgotten, in fact, that we are talking about the abuse of EU law in the field of taxation, so it is necessarily a right attributed by the legal system of the Union to having be the object of abuse in the proper sense. The legal form, used in a distorted way, is only the "mediated" object of the abuse, it being understood that the "final" object of the elusive conduct is an individual prerogative attributed by the EU (when we speak of Union) or national law (when reference is made to the dynamics purely internal to a state).

That said, to identify the object of the abuse, it is necessary to distinguish between abuse in a broad and in the strict sense. In abuse in a broad sense, a contractual legal form is used in an abnormal but formally lawful manner invoking a fundamental freedom guaranteed by the Treaty. This distorted use of the legal form takes place for the essential purpose of obtaining a tax advantage provided for by a rule of domestic law, which advantage, looking at the substance of the operation and its implementing modalities, contrasts with the rationale of a fundamental freedom guaranteed by the Treaty, and therefore it is configured as undue. In these cases, it is therefore the aforementioned fundamental freedom to be abused. For example, in C-196/04, Cadbury Schweppes and Cadbury Schweppes Overseas case of 12 September 2006, the enjoyment of the most favorable Irish regime on the taxation of corporate profits, looking at how it was obtained (establishment of two subsidiaries in Ireland to the sole purpose of enjoying this regime), contrasted with the objective of freedom of establishment, identified by CJEU in "allowing a citizen of a member state to set up a secondary establishment in another member state to carry out its activities and thus favor economic and social interpenetration in the territory of the community in the field of independent activities (...)"[237].

In the case of abuses in the strict sense, on the other hand, contractual freedom is used in a distorted but formally licit way, for the essential purpose of obtaining a tax advantage provided for by a EU law, which is contrary to the ratio of the same norm that foresees it or to the ratio of a different secondary European rule. In any case, to be abused is the right to the tax advantage provided by a secondary law and therefore the law of the Union itself. The same EU law that provides for tax advantage, which means that the taxpayer has artificially created the conditions to enjoy it, frustrates the objective. Thus,

237 F. VANISTENDAEL, Halifax and Cadbury Schweppes: One single European theory of abuse in tax law?, op. cit.

for example, in the C-110/99, Emsland-Stärke case of 14 December 2000, the taxpayer has artificially created the conditions to enjoy the benefit of export refunds, provided for in Regulation n. 2730/79 of 29 November 1979, importing its products into Switzerland and re-importing them into another state of the Union, in such a way as to obtain an undue tax advantage[238]. In fact, the granting of refunds was foreseen for the cases in which the product had actually been released for consumption in a third country. To be abused, therefore, was the right to get the payment of refunds, because exercised in a manner contrary to its ratio. If, on the other hand, it is a secondary EU regulation, different from that which provides for the tax advantage, it is usually a rule that provides for certain obligations, prohibitions or a specific tax discipline, which are unduly circumvented by the taxpayer through the creation of artificial assumptions that allow avoiding its application. Thus, in C-425/06, Part Service case of 21 February 2008, to be abused was the right to exemption provided for by art. 13 of the sixth Directive, in so far as it was exercised (in order also to cover elements that should have contributed to forming the taxable base for VAT purposes), contrary to the ratio not of the same article 13 but of article 11, which provides for "the imposition of everything that constitutes the counterpart obtained or to be obtained by the user"[239]. The circumvention of the ratio of art. 11 was recognized by the same CJEU in the comment.

EUROPEAN RECOMMENDATION ON AGGRESSIVE TAX PLANNING OF 2012, DIRECTIVE NO. 121/2015/EC AND THE "ANTI-CIRCUMVENTION" DIRECTIVE 2016/0011

The notion of abuse of right, enucleated above, was confirmed by the EC Recommendation of 6 December 2012 on aggressive tax planning[240].

EC first observed that, although countries around the world have always considered tax planning as a legitimate practice, over time this phenomenon has resulted in progressively more sophisticated structures, developing across

238 See in argument: E. MCKENDRICK, Force majeure and frustation of contract, ed. Routledge, London & New York, 2013.

239 CJEU, C-425/06, Part Service of 21 February 2008, op. cit.

240 Council Directive (EU) 2015/121 of 27 January 2015 amending Directive 2011/96/EU on the common system of taxation applicable in the case of parent companies and subsidiaries of different member states, OJ L 21, 28.1.2015, p. 1-3.

jurisdictions and allowing the transfer of taxable profits in states with more favorable tax regimes. The fundamental characteristic of the practices in question is that they reduce the amount of tax due through legal transactions in the strict sense, which are however contrary to the purpose of a standard. Despite considerable efforts, member States find it difficult to protect their tax bases from erosion due to aggressive tax planning, as national provisions are often not fully effective, mainly due to the transnational dimension of many tax planning structures and the major mobility of capital and people. With a view to achieving better functioning of the internal market, the EC, hoping that all member states follow the same general approach to aggressive tax planning, thus helping to reduce existing distortions, has recommended the introduction of a uniform general anti-abuse standard. It should be noted, however, that the latter does not contain a definition limited to the abuse of EU law, but delineates a more general concept, aimed at finding application to all the practices of aggressive tax planning that do not fall within scope of the specific national rules aimed at combating tax avoidance. The reference is therefore directed not only to practices that involve an abuse of EU law but, more generally, to all elusive practices (including national ones) that cannot be countered by the specific anti-avoidance rules already existing at state. This finding is relevant in that it explains the scope of the notion of the objective element, which focuses on the circumvention not of a rule of EU law but, more generally, of a tax provision.

As indicated in par. 4.2 the Recommendation contains the following proposal for a general anti-abuse clause: "a construction of pure artifice or an artificial series of constructions that has been put in place essentially for the purpose of circumventing taxation and which implies a fiscal advantage must be ignored. National authorities must treat these buildings for tax purposes by referring to their economic substance"[241]. Par. 4.4 states that "for the purposes of par. 4.2 a construction or a series of constructions is artificial if it lacks commercial substance"[242]. Then, it follows an exemplary indication of a series of objective criteria on the basis of which to assess the absence of commercial substance, among which are included, to name a few, the fact that "the legal qualification of the individual measures of which the construction is composed it is not

241 CJEU, C-425/06, Part Service of 21 February 2008, op. cit.

242 Council Directive (EU) 2015/121 of 27 January 2015 amending Directive 2011/96/EU on the common system of taxation applicable in the case of parent companies and subsidiaries of different member states, op. cit.

consistent with the legal foundation of the building as a whole"[243] and the fact that "the construction or series of constructions is carried out in a way that would not normally be employed in what should be a reasonable behavior in the commercial sphere"[244]. It has, therefore, been reiterated that a constituent element of the elusive phenomenon is the presence of an artificial construction, that is of a distorted use of legal instruments. This requirement implies, as clarified in the previous paragraph, the absence of commercial substance, to be ascertained on the basis of objective criteria. From the Recommendation, the other two fundamental requisites constituting the abuse emerge, that is the objective element and the subjective one.

As for the first, it is the essential purpose of circumventing taxation. The clarification that the elusive purpose should be essential is important for two reasons. The EC aligning itself with the jurisprudence of CJEU, has set the minimum threshold of elusiveness of a conduct in the essentiality of the purpose of avoiding the tax, not requiring a necessarily exclusive purpose oriented in this sense. Secondly and above all, it should be noted that the aforementioned European Recommendation concerns aggressive tax planning in the field of direct taxation and in this field CJEU has defined the abuse of EU law as the practical one aimed exclusively (not, therefore, only essentially) to evade tax[245].

The European Recommendation could therefore provide an opportunity for a revocation of the same court of Luxembourg as regards the definition of the concept of abuse of EU law in the field of non-harmonized taxation. On the evaluation of the essential character of the elusive purpose, par. 4.6 states that "for the purposes of par. 4.2, a given purpose must be considered fundamental if any other purpose that is or could be attributed to the construction or series of buildings appears to be mostly irrelevant in the light of all the circumstances of the case"[246]. It must therefore be the purpose that led the taxpayer to act and without which the operation would not have been completed.

243 Council Directive (EU) 2015/121 of 27 January 2015 amending Directive 2011/96/EU on the common system of taxation applicable in the case of parent companies and subsidiaries of different member states, op. cit.

244 Council Directive (EU) 2015/121 of 27 January 2015 amending Directive 2011/96/EU on the common system of taxation applicable in the case of parent companies and subsidiaries of different member states, op. cit.

245 CJEU, C-251/16, Cussens and others of 22 November 2017, ECLI:EU:C:2017:881, published in the electronic Reports of the cases.

246 CJEU, C-251/16, Cussens and others of 22 November 2017, op. cit.

With regard to the objective element, it cannot be inferred having regard only to the definition contained in par. 4.2, which refers to obtaining a tax advantage, without qualifying it as undue. The latter element, however, is evident from par. 4.5, which states that the purpose of artificial construction "is to evade taxation when, irrespective of any personal intentions of the taxpayer, it conflicts with the objective, spirit and purpose of the tax provisions that would otherwise be applicable"[247]. Even in clarifying this point, the EC has shown that it has implemented the indications deriving from the jurisprudence of CJEU, identifying the undue tax advantage with that advantage obtained in contrast with the rationale of a rule of the legal system. However, while the hypothesis of abuse of EU law to be frustrated is the ratio of a European rule (primary or secondary), in cases of abuse of domestic law the contrast concerns the purpose pursued by a state tax provision, consisting of a tax or facilitative law.

In more recent times, the EU legislator has transposed the main guidelines on the abuse of rights expressed by CJEU.

In fact, in 2015, with the Directive n. 121/2015/EU, an anti-abuse clause was included in the "mother-daughter" directive, modifying art. 1, paragraphs 2 to 4. The new anti-illusion standard, on the one hand, incorporates the expressions contained in the "mergers" and "interests and royalties" directives (referring to the "main purpose" or "one of the main purposes" of obtaining an advantage tax), on the other hand it incorporates the principles established by CJEU jurisprudence. Following the change in comment, art. 1, parr. 2 ss. of the "mother-daughter" directive is as follows: "2. Member states shall not apply the benefits of this Directive to a construction or a series of constructions which, having been put into place for the main purpose or one of the main purposes of obtaining a tax advantage which is contrary to the object or purpose of the Directive, is not genuine having regard to all the relevant facts and circumstances. A building can include more than one phase or part; 3. For the purposes of paragraph 2, a construction or series of constructions shall be considered to be non-genuine to the extent that it has not been put in place for valid commercial reasons which reflect economic reality; 4. This Directive is without prejudice to the application of national or conventional provisions necessary to avoid tax evasion, tax fraud or abuse (...)"[248].

247 CJEU, C-251/16, Cussens and others of 22 November 2017, op. cit.

248 CJEU, C-251/16, Cussens and others of 22 November 2017, op. cit.

First of all, also in the anti-abuse clause in comment appears the reference to the concept of artificial constructions, elaborated for the first time in C-196/04, Cadbury Schweppes and Cadbury Schweppes Overseas case of 12 September 2006. From a strictly literal point of view, not one speaks of artificial but rather of non-genuine constructions, but the difference is not to be overestimated. From the combined provisions of the second and third paragraphs, it is clear that the element in question corresponds to the distorted use and lacking the economic substance of legal instruments. It must be ascertained on the basis of a strictly objective judgment, as is clear from the reference to all relevant facts and circumstances and to valid commercial reasons which reflect economic reality[249].

As for the subjective element, as we have mentioned, the present regulation takes up the expressions contained in the "mergers" and "interests and royalties" directives, referring to the "main purpose" or "one of the main purposes" of obtaining a fiscal advantage and not for an essential aim, required by the most recent CJEU jurisprudence.

Finally, the classic objective element is recalled, represented by the undue character of the fiscal advantage to which the taxpayer's action is aimed, namely the contrast between this advantage and the object and purpose of the same European Directive. Finally, the principles contained in Directive n. 121/2015/EC have been extended by the EC as they are considered suitable to establish a genuine general anti-abuse clause.

On 28 January 2016, the EC presented to the Council of the Union a draft directive (anti-circumvention Directive n. 2016/0011)[250] setting out rules against tax avoidance practices that directly affect the functioning of the internal market. The proposal was approved by Ecofin on 12 July 2016, with the obligation for member states to implement new measures to combat tax avoidance by 31 December 2018, unless equivalent measures are already in force in their internal laws. Among the remedies that member states will be required to adopt there is also a general anti-abuse rule which, in accordance with the acquis, is designed to take account of CJEU's artificiality tests.

This rule, applicable to all taxpayers who are subject to corporation tax in one or more member states, including the permanent establishments located in one

249 The same seventh recital of Directive 2015/121 states that "in assessing whether a construction or a series of constructions is abusive, it is appropriate that the tax administrations of member states undertake an objective analysis of all the relevant facts and circumstances".

250 Council Directive (EU) 2016/1164 of 12 July 2016 laying down rules against tax avoidance practices that directly affect the functioning of the internal market, OJ L 193, 19.7.2016, p. 1-14.

or more member states of entities resident for tax purposes in a third country, provides that: "1. Non-genuine or a series of non-genuine constructions carried out essentially for the purpose of obtaining a tax advantage that runs counter to the object or purpose of the tax provisions that would have otherwise been applicable are ignored for the purposes of calculating the tax on the companies due a building can include more than one phase or part; 2. For the purposes of paragraph 1, a construction or series of constructions shall be regarded as not genuine to the extent that it has not been put into place for valid commercial reasons which reflect economic reality; 3. When buildings or a number of buildings are ignored in accordance with paragraph 1, the tax due shall be calculated by reference to the economic substance in accordance with national law(...)"[251].

As anticipated, the general anti-abuse rule accurately acknowledges, by extending its scope, the principles that were introduced in the "mother-daughter" directive at the beginning of 2015. To modest opinion of the writer, however, a significant difference regards the description of the subjective element: confirming the tendency to enhance the essential (and not necessarily exclusive or main) character of the abusive conduct, the new standard refers to constructions not genuine "essentially for the purpose"[252] to achieve an undue tax advantage.

THE DISTORTED USE OF LEGAL INSTRUMENTS

According to the writer, there is no doubt that the element in question is a fundamental prerequisite constituting tax avoidance or abuse of law. We may consider that the use of anomalous, inadequate or unusual paths is merely an indicator of the willingness of the taxpayer to obtain an asystematic advantage, not rising to the rank of a true constitutive element. The taxpayer, therefore, could circumvent the tax rules also by performing perfectly linear and "normal" operations. According to the subdued opinion of the writer, however, this address cannot be shared. Indeed, it is beyond doubt that in some cases the abnormal use of legal instruments is a symptomatic factor in the taxpayer's desire to circumvent the tax rules. However, first of all this is not always true, in the sense that in many

251 For further details: A. VALDESALICI, F. PALERMO, Comparing fiscal federalism, ed. Brill, The Hague, 2018.

252 As we can see in the case of CJEU: C-456/12, O. Of 12 March 2014, ECLI:EU:C:2014:135, par. 58; C-364/10, Hungary v. Slovak Republic of 16 October 2012, ECLI:EU:C:2012:630, above the cases published in the electronic Reports o the cases, par. 58.

cases the taxpayer puts in place operations that are configured, yes, as anomalous or distorted, but which, on the other hand, are justified by valid economic reasons. Moreover, and apart from this, the distorted use cannot be considered as a simple indicator revealing the desire to obtain an undue tax advantage (of which it could also be missing in the concrete case), as it is an element that indestructibly characterizes any case in point of tax avoidance and therefore must be elevated to the rank of indispensable prerequisite constituting the abuse of the right.

As is known, in many jurisdictions, the latter institute was born from the civil elaborations on the subject of fraud to the law and, in this sense, was taken up and used by CJEU. The most recurring references to the fraudulent legal procedure are found in the Justinian compilation, which contained two well-known fragments of Paul and Ulpian that first identified the case under examination in the phenomenon for which the agent "salvis legisisis substantiam eius circumvenit". To evade means to get around. The circumvenire legem, in fiscal field, describes the phenomenon for which the taxpayer puts in being an artificial behavior (not in the sense of simulated but in the sense of anomalous, abnormal), exploiting the gaps of the legal system. In other words, through circumvention, "the main road is bypassed, which is legally blocked, with a tendentious combination of side streets"[253], in order to "strike" the law with "an occult and unnoticed attack on the hips, to the real content, which is the weaker side, because it is not defended by any word"[254]. It is therefore considered that the distorted use of legal instruments integrates one of the three elements constituting the abuse of the right, of which the financial administration must necessarily provide proof. In fact, the necessity of this assumption is denied, arguing that it can be circumvented even without some kind of distorted or otherwise abnormal operation, omitting to give any example to support one's thesis. On the other hand, it is believed that the distorted use is only an index indicating the lack of valid economic reasons for the operation carried out by the tax payer and not a constitutive element of the abuse. However, apart from the critical issues (which will be explained later) inherent in the choice to place the lack of valid economic reasons among the constituent assumptions of the circumvention, the discourse is similar to the one just done. The anomalous use of the legal instrumentation is an element fundamental and indefectible of any abusive case. Irrespective of the

253 CJEU: C-456/12, O. of 12 March 2014, op. cit.

254 CJEU: C-456/12, O. of 12 March 2014, op. cit.

symptomaticity that it may possibly express with respect to other elements, it is certainly to be raised to an autonomous assumption constituting tax avoidance.

Having said that, in the proposed law, this element would be defined (paragraph 2, letter a) as "the use of facts, deeds and contracts that produce the same economic effect that could have been achieved through a more direct and linear, non-contrasting operation with the rules of the legal system"[255]. As can be seen from this expression, in defining in discursive terms "the distorted use" it was decided not to repeat attributes such as "abnormal", "anomalous", and so on[256].

Any such definition would be too general and indeterminate and would leave to the most varied interpretations (and prevarications). As has been repeatedly stated, a general anti-elusive clause should try to minimize the margin of uncertainty and discretionary appreciation in head of the investigating body, even though this discretion is to some extent unavoidable.

In trying to define the element represented by distorted use, a question arises spontaneously: when we talk about a distorted, anomalous or abnormal negotiation path, what is the comparison between distortion, anomaly or abnormality? In essence, it is necessary to identify a term of comparison, which is a "normal" operation (which the taxpayer could have made) with respect to which the concretely put in place is configured as abnormal, distorted, etc. But how can one arrive at such a distinction between two operations, qualifying one to be as normal and the other as anomalous and distorted? In the slightest warning of the writer, it is necessary to have regard to the economic result produced in concrete by the operation carried out by the taxpayer and question whether the same result could have been produced by a different operation, still in line with the regulatory provisions but more linear and direct and that it would be accomplished by the average businessman. If the answer to this question is negative (that is, if the average businessman would not have performed the operation considered by the entrance authority as more linear and direct), this means that the tax payer's operation is not anomalous and distorted and therefore is precluded any possibility of qualifying his conduct in elusive terms. In this case, the taxpayer pursues a legitimate tax saving, as it uses negotiation instruments which, being in no way distorted or altered with respect to the normal market logic, fall into one of the "different optional schemes offered from the law" and

255 CJEU: C-456/12, O. of 12 March 2014, op. cit.

256 A. VALDESALICI, F. PALERMO, Comparing fiscal federalism, op. cit.

therefore, simply, between "operations involving a different tax burden"[257]. Conversely, if the answer to the question is positive (that is, if the average businessman would have performed the most direct and linear operation, identified by the tax authority, to achieve the same concrete economic result), the necessary consequence is that the case in point made by the tax payer is to be considered as anomalous, distorted or at least "abnormal"[258].

This does not mean, that the tax payer has therefore only put in place a situation of tax avoidance. Contrary to what has happened frequently in many jurisdictions in the past, the financial administration must exclude itself from issuing notices of assessment based on the simple consideration of the distorted nature of the acts performed by the taxable person; the abuse of law presupposes, in fact, a distorted use of juridical instruments, but the verification of this last element is not absolutely sufficient to found the claims of the revenue authority.

A final clarification must be made with reference to the element of the distorted use of legal instruments. It has been previously argued that, for the purposes of its assessment, it is necessary to have regard to the result produced concretely by the operation carried out by the tax payer. But what is the result? Is it legal or economic? The writer believes that one can refer to the economic result of the concrete negotiating scheme. If, in fact, it is assumed as a reference point the purely legal result of the operation, it is easy to note that no other case of negotiation, different from that actually implemented, would produce the same, identical, legal effects; each operation is different from each other, in this respect. Consider, for example, the comparison between a sale of controlling interests in a company, whose assets are represented by a company, and a direct sale of the company itself. Having regard to the strictly legal effects, the two transactions are not comparable, since the former involves not only the transfer of ownership of a good from one person to another, but also the loss of the quality of shareholder for the seller and, specularly, the purchase of this status for the buyer. It is clear that, on the contrary, these last two effects are not produced through direct sales of the company. On the contrary, if we only have regard to the final economic effect, the two cases are comparable, as both ensure the buyer the possibility of managing the production complex according to their needs and in line with their expectations.

257 A. VALDESALICI, F. PALERMO, Comparing fiscal federalism, op. cit.

258 A. VALDESALICI, F. PALERMO, Comparing fiscal federalism, op. cit.

In conclusion, for the purposes of ascertaining the distorted use of legal instruments, it is the economic effect that needs to be referred to. In other words, it is necessary that between the (anomalous) operation concretely carried out and the (normal) operation that the taxpayer could have carried out there is an economic substitution, which is to say that the transaction carried out by the taxable person of imposed, compared with the "normal" one, which would have been implemented by the average businessman, has no objective economic substance.

The criterion of economic substitutability was also used by the German tax system. In particular, par. 5 of the Reichsabgabenordnung of 1919, in specifying the conditions that integrated an "abuse of civil forms" (and, therefore, tax avoidance), referred to the case in which, taking into account the nature of the relationships. Also considering the manner in which it was carried out or it was necessary to proceed, the parties obtain substantially the same result from the economic point of view, which they would have obtained if the legal form corresponding to the events, facts and relationships had been adopted.

It is evident that, applying the two meters of judgment of the reference to the average businessman and of the substitutability in the economic sense, the judgment on the recurrence of a distorted use of legal instruments has an objective character, significantly reducing the scope of appreciation discretionary to the investigating office.

THE UNDUE TAX ADVANTAGES

In the general anti-illusion clause proposed, "undue tax advantages" would complement the second, objective element of the abuse of law. The element of undue recourse is to terminologies such as, for example, contrasting the operation carried out by the tax payer with the general principles of the system, or with the regulatory principles of the various tax laws, or with the principles that inspire the rule evaded in the concrete case. There has also been talk of advantages that the legal system disapproves, or of advantages realized in contrast with the purposes of tax regulations or with the principles of tax law.

The reason that inspires the will to raise the element of the indebted to a prerequisite constituting the abuse of right is appreciable. The necessary undue character of the tax reductions, reimbursements, or facilitations achieved implies that the simple prosecution does not constitute tax avoidance of a fiscal advantage, since the latter must have a pathological connotation. However, the definitions that have been given over time are, in the slightest warning of the writer, too general, ending with the attribution, to the financial administration and to the judge, an absolute discretion in the qualification as undue of a tax saving. Through the formulation of a general anti-elusive clause, any legislator should try to minimize the element of indeterminacy, which indefectibly characterizes any measure aimed at combating borderline operations such as abusive ones. Therefore, the definition of the element of the indebted must therefore be as objective as possible.

The solution here shared, which recognizes, first of all, that in general a tax advantage can be considered undue when it is in contrast with the aims pursued by the tax rules. However, unlike what happens in EU, where the fundamental aims of the provisions of EU law are objectified in the preambles of the Treaties, the corresponding aims in the internal sphere do not find such objectification in the normative formulation and therefore cannot be inferred from specific obligations or prohibitions provided for by the evaded laws, which have as their object conduct that allow to achieve results equivalent to those pursued by the taxpayer and challenged by the financial administration.

Concluding, therefore, the undue tax advantages are reimbursements, tax reductions or benefits obtained by circumventing the specific obligations or prohibitions provided for in the tax rules effectively circumvented. In the formulation of the proposed anti-illusion standard, we have chosen to use the word "bypass" in place of "contrast" meaning to emphasize that the tax advantage should not be obtained through a direct violation of specific tax rules (integrating the conduct, in these hypothesis, an evasive case), but through their circumvention. Assuming a comparative perspective, we note that the objective element, like the distorted use of legal instruments, is also present in most of the foreign anti-abuse clauses analyzed in the previous paragraphs.

THE ESSENTIAL PURPOSE OF CIRCUMVENTION

A subjective assumption has always been considered as a constitutive element of tax avoidance or abuse of rights, with some exceptions found, for example, in German and Spanish law, where the concept of abuse of rights is defined in strictly objective terms. In other words, for the purposes of qualifying a conduct in elusive terms, it has always been required that between the transaction carried out by the taxpayer and the undue advantage obtained there should be an element (subjective, in fact) of preordering the first to the achievement of the second. The tax payer must put in place a specific case to (for the time being we do not clarify the degree of intensity) obtain an undue tax advantage.

Turning, once again, a look at the foreign legal systems analyzed, even the subjective element is included in the anti-fraud clauses in most of these.

Moreover, with the famous C-255/02, Halifax and others of 21 February 2006 sentence, the subjective element was taken over by CJEU and elevated to the rank of requirement constituting the abuse of right. In more recent times, the Recommendation of the EC of 2012 on aggressive tax planning has called for the adoption (by member states) of an anti-abuse clause aimed at striking the operations carried out "essentially for the purpose" of circumventing the imposition, expression, the latter, also taken up by the recent "anti-circumvention" directive, approved by Ecofin on 12 July 2016.

Art. L 64 of the Livre dé procedures fiscales in France refers to transactions with the tax avoidance as "sole reason". At the same time, the anti-abuse clauses in force in Germany and Spain are formulated in strictly objective terms (although it must be remembered that the Spanish law, in the past, focused on "(tried) purpose" to circumvent the tax law). The new anti-exhaust clause introduced in the United Kingdom, in line with the evolution of EU law, refers to transactions with the "main objective" or "one of the main objectives" of obtaining a tax advantage.

Given this, unequivocal solutions have been adopted on the subject concerning the degree of intensity that the subjective requirement must assume, in order to qualify the behavior in terms of abuse. Within the Union, the recently introduced "anti-circumvention" directive refers to the essential purpose of obtaining an undue tax advantage and the concept of essentiality.

Moreover, given the principle of the prevalence of EU law on domestic law which is incompatible with it (given that the United Kingdom, at the time of writing, is still formally a member state of the Union), by virtue of legislative developments and European jurisprudential, it is correct to conclude that the abusive purpose at the base of the taxpayer's conduct must be characterized by the character of essentiality, on penalty of the attribution to the tax authorities and the tax court of an excessive margin of discretion on the choices made by the tax payer. Moreover, in the general anti-exhaustive clause proposed here, the emphasis would be placed on making the assessment of the subjective element dependent on the analysis of the psychological process as such, which bases the action of a given subject, but on the basis of analysis of the psychological process to the extent that the latter is reflected in external circumstances, of a univocal and objective nature (therefore verifiable by the financial administration and by the judge). Otherwise, in fact, it would be possible to attribute to the financial administration and to the judge a margin of discretional appreciation that is too broad, incompatible with the constitutional principles in force in the various legal systems. In other words, what is proposed here is the adoption of a subjective theory tempered by connotations of objectivity.

THE VALID EXTRA-TAX REASONS

In the anti-evasive norm proposed here, the taxpayer would be recognized as having the opportunity to demonstrate that the transaction, specifically carried out and contested by the financial administration, is justified by valid non-marginal reasons. In fact, it is an element generally shared by the various legal systems analyzed. However, it cannot be considered as a constitutive element of tax avoidance or abuse of rights, but rather as an exemplary invocable by the taxable person in his favor.

Initially, from the literal formulation of the "almost-general" anti-avoidance clauses, the absence of valid economic reasons appeared to be configured as a constitutive element of the concept of circumvention, with the consequence that the burden of furnishing proof of it, at first view (beyond that of the jurisprudential oscillations) seemed to burden the financial administration, when it proceeded to the contestation of an elusive conduct.

However, according to the writer, this is an improper formulation, not to be confused with the absence of valid economic reasons, but to be understood as the distorted, abnormal use of legal instruments. In other words, the necessary absence of an objective economic substance, not to be confused with the absence of valid extrafiscal reasons, recalls the criterion of economic fungibility between "anomalous" operation, concretely realized, and "normal", which would have had to be accomplished.

The relevance of the jeopardizing constituted by valid economic reasons is also recognized in the other legal systems analyzed in the previous chapters. Thus, in the French legal system, art. L 64 of the Livre des procédures fiscales refers to acts motivated solely for the purpose of circumventing the tax law, implicitly opening the way for the taxpayer to prove that the purpose of reducing the tax debt was not exclusive, in the specific case, but concurrent with valid economic reasons. In Germany, par. 42 provides that the qualification of a conduct in elusive terms is bound to fail if the taxpayer demonstrates the recurrence of "extrafiscal reasons worthy of protection. In Spain, from the reading of art. 15 of the Ley general tax office, it is clear that the taxpayer has the right to demonstrate that the transaction involves "significant legal or economic effects, other than tax savings". Finally, the anti-abuse clause recently introduced in the United Kingdom, like the French one, implicitly offers the taxpayer the opportunity to prove that obtaining a tax advantage was not one of the main objectives of the operation he carried out, by virtue, therefore, of the existence of valid economic reasons[259].

In conclusion, to the modest opinion of the writer, a general anti-consumer clause, shared at international level, should establish a definition of tax avoidance or abuse of right formed by three constitutive elements: the misuse of legal instruments, the obtaining of advantages undue taxes and the fact that the transaction is essentially aimed at producing such tax advantages. On the other hand, the tax payer should be allowed to prove the existence of valid economic reasons, understood as simple.

As anticipated, the general anti-abuse rule accurately acknowledges, by extending its scope, the principles that were introduced in the "mother-daughter" directive at the beginning of 2015. To the modest opinion of the writer, however, a significant difference regards the description of the subjective element: confirming the tendency to enhance the essential (and not necessarily exclusive or main) character of the abusive conduct, the new standard refers to constructions not genuine "essentially for the purpose" of obtaining an undue tax advantage.

Some examples of the most recent jurisprudence regarding the Common Agricultural Policy confirm the test.

It was noted that CJEU, in C-110/99, Emsland-Stärkesentence of 14 December 2000, faced with the fictitious preconstitution of the conditions for obtaining an advantage directly descending from an EU Regulation, applied the related prohibition. From what has been observed, it can well be asserted that the distinctive connotation of such a technique is the taking into account, alongside an objective element consisting in the non-respect of the purposes of the law, of a subjective element. Regarding the mechanism for the operation of the prohibition, in

259 A. VALDESALICI, F. PALERMO, Comparing fiscal federalism, op. cit.

this context, the same seems to be conceived as an exception to EU law, which allows not to assign the right to payment of the amount or which in any case determines ex post the repayment.

Well, the abuse test as outlined in C-110/99, Emsland-Stärke case of 14 December 2000 has found constant confirmation and application in subsequent rulings on CAP[260]. Although this is not surprising, since the situations faced by such jurisprudence can be subsumed in the same case, so that the application of the same prohibition is not particularly significant, it is useful to mention those passages of the decisions in question which clarify the application methods of the test used by CJEU. To this end, a series of cases referring to the element that most characterizes the prohibition, that is to say, the subjective one will be briefly taken into consideration to then focus on a pronunciation that has better clarified the burden of proof.

ABUSE AS AN EXCEPTION TO THE RULE: C-515/03, EICHSFELDER SCHLACHTBETRIEB GMBH V. HAUPTZOLLAMT HAMBURG-JONAS OF 23 JULY 2005, COMPARED TO THE C-114/99, ROQUETTE FRÈRES CASE OF 17 OCTOBER 2000

In this regard, the sentence in C-515/03, Eichsfelder Schlachtbetrieb GmbH v. Should be mentioned first. Hauptzollamt Hamburg-Jonas case of 23 July 2005, concerning the EC Regulation, n. 3665/87[261] of 27 November 1987, laying down

260 EC cites the next cases: Cremer, C-250/80, Schumacher of 27 October 1981, op. cit. C-8/92, General Milk Products v. Hauptzollamt Hamburg-Jonas of 3 March 1993, op. cit. The conclusions of AG Tesauro presented in cases: C-441/93, Panagis Pafitis and others v. Trapeza Kentrikis Ellados A.E. and others, op. cit., it should be noted that the Commission refers to art. 4, par. 3, reg. n. 2988/95 cit., even if it is not applicable ratione temporis to the main cause, precisely because it considers the norm the expression of a "general principle of law already in force in EU system (...)". See in particular: C-279/05, Vonk Dairy Products of 11 January 2007, op. cit., C-515/03, 0 C-515/03, Eichsfelder Schlachtbetrieb GmbH v. Hauptzollamt Hamburg-Jonas of 23 July 2005, Schlachtbetrieb GmbH v. Hauptzollamt Hamburg-Jonas of 23 July 2005, ECLI:EU:C:2005:491, I-07355. C-116/12, Ioannis Christodoulou and others v. Elliniko Dimosio of 12 December 2013, ECLI:EU:C:2013:825, published in the electronic Reports of the cases: C-434/12, Slancheva sila EOOD v. Izpalnitelen direktor na Darzhaven fond "Zemedelie" Razplashtatelna agentsia of 12 September 2013, ECLI:EU:C:2013:546, published in the electronic Reports of the cases. C-155/13, Società Italiana Commercio and Servizi srl (SICES) and others v. Agenzia Dogane Ufficio delle Dogane di Venezia, of 13 May 2014, ECLI:EU:C:2014:145, published in the electronic Reports of the cases. For further details see: K. LIMBACH, Uniformity of customs administration in the European Union, Hart Publishing, Oxford & Oregon, Portland, 2015.

261 For further details see: E. MC KENDRICK, Force majeure and frustration of contract, ed. Routledge,

common rules for the application of the system of export refunds for agricultural products[262]. Beyond the case in itself considered, the cause is of interest if correlated with the previous C-114/99, Roquette Frères of 17 October 20003 referred to by the national court.

In both cases, export refunds related to a product which had undergone a substantial transformation were highlighted before being re-exported to the then community.

As is known, in C-114/99, Roquette Frères case of 17 October 2000[263], CJEU had held that the payment of an export refund could not be subject to the burden of producing additional evidence to show that it had actually been injected on the market of the third country of import a product which was then used in that country for the manufacture of another product which, in turn, could be exported to a member state. The referral court in C-515/03, Eichsfelder Schlachtbetrieb GmbH v. Hauptzollamt Hamburg-Jonas case of 23 July 2005, however, while calling the precedent, questioned that the goods for which export refunds had been paid, in consideration of its re-export to Germany shortly after its importation and transformation into Poland and the reimbursement of Polish customs duties, could be considered imported into Poland "in order to be released there"[264].

What is of interest here is like CJEU, in answering, while doing what was already stated in C-114/99, Roquette Frères of 17 October 2000 case, takes care to distinguish the hypothesis in which the exporter takes part in a practice unlawful, citing art. 4, n. 3, of Regulation n. 2988/95, as well as the Emsland-Stärke

London & New York, 2013.

262 On the fourth recital, Regulation No 3665/87 (OJ, L 25, page 39) recalls that "some exports may give rise to abuse; in order to avoid them, it is appropriate to make payment of the refund for these exports, in addition to the condition that the product has left EU customs territory, also on the condition that the product has been imported into a third country and, if necessary, actually placed on the "last market".

263 CJEU, C-114/99, Roquette Frères of 17 October 2000, ECLI:EU:C:2000:568, I-08823.

264 National CJEU therefore asked whether the requirement for the granting of a differential export refund pursuant to the regulation-that is to say the completion of customs formalities for release for consumption of the product in the third country of destination-was satisfied when the product itself, after having been subjected to the payment of import duties in that country, had been subjected to substantial processing or in accordance with article 24 of the Customs Code and subsequently re-exported to the then Union with the repayment of duties collected in the same country and the payment of customs duties on imports into the then Union.

test[265], and delegating the verification of these elements to the national judge for this purpose[266].

The rule is therefore that already enunciated at the time in C-114/99, Roquette Freres sentence of 17 October 2000 , the right to the export refund exists, without a restrictive interpretation of secondary legislation, as proposed by the national court. However, this ruling is an exception to the case where the exporter has taken part in an unlawful practice.

Precisely from the parallel with this last sentence, it is therefore confirmed that the prohibition of abuse is of an exception nature.

In this regard, the sentence in C-515/03, Eichsfelder Schlachtbetrieb GmbH v. Hauptzollamt Hamburg-Jonas case of 23 July 2005, on the one hand, specifies on the contrary a supporting element of the Emsland-Stärke test, excluding the existence of an abuse when there is no artificiality, absence identified in the substantial and non-reversible transformation suffered by products previously exported[267]. On the other hand, it enhances the verification of the constituent elements of the test by the national court.

---

265 More specifically, citing the case C-114/99, Roquette Frères of 17 October 2000, the CJEU recalls that "such a process or transformation, involving the creation of a new product, excludes the risk, provided for by art. 5, n. 1, of Regulation n. 3665/87 and that art. 17, n. 3 of the regulation itself tends to prevent, an illegal re-importation of initial goods in EU, in violation of the purpose pursued by the refund system, whether they are differentiated or not (...)". (par. 30).

266 On the other hand, AG Ruiz-Jarabo Colomer had tried instead to make a differentiation between the case in question and C-114/99, Roquette Frères of 17 October 2000 in his conclusions submitted on 25 May 2005, an indication which was not accepted by CJEU. AG, in fact, states, in paragraph 57, that "the decisive feature of the present case lies in the fact that the import duties were repaid, which retroactively prevented the goods from satisfying the requirement of article 17, n. 3, of Regulation n. 3665/87; the question underlying Roquette Frères was limited to determining whether, where there is a substantial change, the payment of an export refund may be subject, pursuant to article 5, n. 1, of Regulation n. 3665/87, to the burden of producing additional evidence to show that the goods were actually placed as such on the market of the importing third country. CJEU found that re-importation into EU of goods which had undergone irreversible transformation was acceptable as it became a new product. It was then limited, as stated in paragraph 19 of the sentence, to deny the existence of the risk of abuse (...)".

267 This affirmation was included in case: C-116/12, Ioannis Christodoulou and others v. Elliniko Dimosio of 12 December 2013, op. cit., in which CJEU states, even more clearly, that the abuse consisting in particular of the risk of reintroducing the exported product into the Union cannot exist when the product concerned has undergone a substantial and irreversible transformation, involving its failure as such and the creation of a new product falling under another heading (C-114/99, Roquette Frères of 17 October 2000, op.cit., paragraph 19, and C-515/03, C-515/03, Eichsfelder Schlachtbetrieb GmbH v. Hauptzollamt Hamburg-Jonas of 23 July 2005, Schlachtbetrieb GmbH v. Hauptzollamt Hamburg-Jonas of 23 July 2005, op. cit., par. 31). In the same judgment, CJEU, in answering the subsequent questions of national CJEU, concerning the determination of customs value of a commodity which benefited from an export refund, obtained by implementing a practice consistent with the application of EU law provisions in order to obtain an abusive advantage, he states: "in the present case, it

On this point, it is interesting to note that the national court, once summarized the case, has shown extreme caution in applying the test. As the objective element, in fact, it is pointed out that the purpose of the relevant legislation had been achieved since the customs formalities they had been fulfilled and the product had been marketed through processing. Alternatively, with reference to the subjective element, he noted that no involvement of the exporter or his participation and influence on the behavior of the importer had been proven, just as it was not clear whether the importer was engaged in artificial operations and whether these operations aimed at benefiting from lower costs in the preparation of the product[268].

(FOLLOWS)THE OBJECTIVE AND SUBJECTIVE ELEMENT OF THE TEST: ANALYSIS OF C-434/12, SLANCHEVA SILA EOOD V. IZPALNITELEN DIREKTOR NA DARZHAVEN FOUNDER "ZEMEDELIE" RAZPLASHTATELNA AGENTSIA OF 12 SEPTEMBER 2013 AND C-155/13, SOCIETÀ ITALIANA COMMERCIO AND SERVIZI SRL (SICES) AND OTHERS V. CUSTOMS OFFICE OF THE CUSTOMS OFFICE OF VENICE, OF 13 MAY 2014 PRONUNCIATIONS

If the pronunciation in C-515/03, Eichsfelder Schlachtbetrieb GmbH v. Hauptzollamt Hamburg-Jonas case of 23 July 2005 confirms the classification of the prohibition of abuse as an exception to the application of EU legislation. In cases: C-434/12, Slancheva sila EOOD v. Izpalnitelen direktor na Darzhaven founded "Zemedelie" Razplashtatelna agentsia of 12 September 2013[269] and

is common ground that the applicants intended to conceal the fact that the goods are, in the form of definitive exportation and an alleged substantive transformation, in reality, the object of a passive perfection. Through this practice, they have circumvented the application of article 146 (1) of the Customs Code, by virtue of which goods which give rise to export refunds cannot be subjected to the outward processing procedure" (par. 62) and that, using the Emsland-Stärke test, "it is for the national CJEU to establish the existence of those two elements, the evidence of which can be provided in accordance with the rules of national law, provided that this does not affect the effectiveness of Union law" (Par. 65). As to the consequences to be drawn from the ascertainment of an irregularity deriving from such an abusive practice, CJEU considers the art. 4, par. 3, of Regulation n. 2988/95, defined as "general scope" (par. 66).

268 C-434/12, Slancheva sila EOOD v. Izpalnitelen direktor na Darzhaven fond "Zemedelie" Razplashtatelna agentsia of 12 September 2013, op. cit.

269 CJEU, C-155/13, Società Italiana Commercio and Servizi srl (SICES) and others v. Agenzia Dogane

C-155/13, Società Italiana Commercio and Servizi srl (SICES) and others v. Customs Office of the Customs of Venice, of 13 May 2014, the indispensable interdependence between objective and subjective element. Thus, the prohibition of abuse cannot operate in the presence of the sole desire to obtain an undue advantage and, vice versa, more importantly is not enough that the objective of the norm cannot be respected, since the proof of the subjective element is also necessary.

The C-434/12, Slancheva sila EOOD v. Izpalnitelen direktor na Darzhaven founded "Zemedelie" Razplashtatelna agentsia of 12 September 2013 pronunciation starts from a dispute arising from the refusal of the Bulgarian administration to accept the investment project proposed by the applicant company in support of the creation and development of micro-enterprises, as it intended to benefit from the granting of such aid abusively[270].

CJEU, citing the sentences: C-515/03, Eichsfelder Schlachtbetrieb GmbH v. Hauptzollamt Hamburg-Jonas of 23 July 2005, and C-279/05, Vonk Dairy Products of 11 January 2007 points out that in this context it is necessary first of all to interpret the notions of "artificial creation" conditions required to receive payment and "non-compliant advantage" contained in the anti-abuse clause pursuant to art. 4, par, 8, of Regulation n. 65/2011[271]. This establishes methods of application of Regulation (EC) n. 1698/2005, which excludes the granting of payments to beneficiaries who are found to have artificially created the conditions necessary to obtain such payments, in order to derive an advantage that does not comply with the objectives of the support scheme.

On this point, CJEU resumes the abuse test, showing to interpret the anti-abuse clause in the light of the more general prohibition and paying attention to distinguish the two constituent elements of the test. It, thus, notes that the company's intention to circumvent the restrictions on the reduction of eligible projects and the maximum amount of aid per beneficiary "does not in itself exclude that the investment project presented by C-434/12, Slancheva sila EOOD

Ufficio delle Dogane di Venezia, of 13 May 2014.

270 In particular, the national competent authority considered, in the light of circumstances of the main proceedings, that the company had intended to circumvent the limits laid down by the national legislation by agreeing with third parties, also requesting aid under the same support scheme, to proceed with the artificial division of a single project into three smaller projects.

271 Regulation (EU) n. 65/2011 of the Commission of January 27, 2011, which establishes methods of application of Regulation (EC) no. Council Regulation (EC) No 1698/2005 on the implementation of control procedures and conditionality for rural development support measures (OJ L 25, 8).

v. Izpalnitelen direktor na Darzhaven founded "Zemedelie" Razplashtatelna agentsia case of 12 September 2013 would have contributed to achieving the objectives set by Regulation n. 1698/2005"[272], that is to support the diversification measures of the rural economy, with the aim of promoting entrepreneurship and strengthening the economic fabric. In this regard, according to the European Union courts, it is up to the referring court to examine whether by that will it achieves that the objectives set out in art. 52, lett. a), ii), of Regulation n. 1698/2005 cannot be achieved. In this passage, it is therefore better explained a concept underlying the abuse test, i.e. that the elusive will is not enough to establish an abusive practice, being however required that the objectives of the legislation are not achieved[273].

CJEU then specifies, referring to C-110/99, Emsland-Stärke case of 14 December 2000 that, to ascertain artificial nature of the creation, the national court may take into consideration a number of factual elements, including legal, economic and/or personal constraints between the persons involved in the investment transaction concerned[274].

CJEU thus reaches the important conclusion that the application of the codified anti-abuse clause requires in any case the presence of an objective and a subjective element. With reference to the first of these elements, it is up to the referring court to consider the circumstances objective of the present case that allow the conclusion that the purpose of the support scheme cannot be achieved; as regards the second element. On the other hand, the referring court must consider the objective evidence to conclude that by artificially creating the

272 Council Regulation (EC) No 1698/2005 of 20 September 2005 on support for rural development by the European Agricultural Fund for Rural Development (EAFRD), OJ L 277, 21.10.2005, p. 1-40, no longer in force from 31 December 2013.

273 Paragraph 40. In the specific case, then, the existence of that subjective element can also be corroborated by evidence of collusion, which may take the form of intentional coordination, between different investors who request aid under the support scheme, particularly when the investment projects are identical and there is a geographical, economic, functional, legal and/or personal link between these projects (par. 41).

274 CJEU specifies at parr. 46 and 47 that the existence of a legal link between the applicants, or even the absence of functional autonomy between the various investment projects concerned, certainly constitute clues from which the artificial creation of the conditions can be inferred requests to benefit from a payment pursuant to art. 4, par. 8, but they are not enough alone. As CJEU takes care to clarify in response to the second preliminary question, indeed, the assessment by national CJEU must always be made with reference to all circumstances of the case. In other words, it must be apparent from all the objective elements of the main proceedings that the essential purpose of the choice of the modalities relating to the investment project in question is the payment of aid under the support scheme, so that any other justification which has a link with the objectives of the scheme.

conditions required to benefit from the payment, the applicant only intended to derive an advantage which did not comply with the objectives of that regulation regime[275].

In this way, the principle that the anti-abuse clauses must be interpreted in the light of the general prohibition is also confirmed in recent times. Even more relevant are the statutes of CJEU in C-155/13, Società Italiana Commercio and Servizi srl (SICES) and others v. Customs Office of the Customs Office of Venice case of 13 May 2014, concerning certain import operations of garlic of Chinese origin in the European Union carried out by the C-155/13, Società Italiana Commercio and Servizi srl (SICES) and others v. Customs Office of the Customs Office of Venice, of 13 May 2014 and other companies considered fraudulent. The preliminary question of the Italian appeals court was aimed at verifying whether Regulation n. 341/2007[276] and in particular its art. 6, par. 4, where, as a result of which they constitute an abuse of rights, they are prevented by operations by which a "new importer", who holds a reduced rate of import licenses, purchases a product, before its importation into the operator who is a traditional importer within the meaning of the same regulation but who has exhausted his reduced import licenses and then resells it after importing it into the Union[277].

Beyond the specific affair, for real complex, what is interesting to underline is the reasoning developed by CJEU with reference to the subjective element. In fact, after having reconfirmed the need for the national court to ascertain the abuse by making use of the abuse test, the Union judge comes to affirm, with regard to the objective element, that the objective of the provisions of the regulation herein concerned. That is to say, the protection of competition between the actual importers, in order to prevent a single importer from controlling the market, is not achieved by the operations described[278].

275 Regulation (CE) n. Commission Regulation (EC) No 341/2007 of 29 March 2007 opening and providing for the administration of tariff quotas and the establishment of a system of import licenses and certificates of origin for garlic and certain other agricultural products imported from third countries (OJ L 90, p.12).

276 Under which "By way of derogation from art. 9, par. 1, of the regulation (CE) n. 1291/2000, the rights deriving from the "A" securities are not transferable".

277 The companies involved, in their capacity as "new importers" pursuant to art. 4, par, 3, of Reg. n. 341/2007, were holders of "A" licenses issued in accordance with that regulation, which allowed the imports in question to benefit from the duty exemption. The Customs Agency, however, censured the execution of a series of mechanisms, considered fraudulent, aimed at circumventing the ban on the transfer of rights deriving from the "A" securities through consecutive sales of garlic.

278 Such operations, in fact, may allow the buyer, who is also a traditional importer who has exhausted his "A" licenses and is therefore no longer able to import garlic at a subsidized rate and extend its

CJEU, hereinafter referred to verify the subsistence of the subjective element, does not detect its existence and therefore comes to exclude the abuse, thus demonstrating the key function of this element. In particular, CJEU notes that, at the same time as, as in the present case, the provisions of secondary legislation, which are considered to be abused require importers to effect certain imports under penalty (here, using the "A" certificates issued to them), importers have a real interest in making such imports, even in the context of artificial operations. The operations in question therefore do not prove to be devoid of any economic or commercial justification for the importers. However, CJEU does not exclude that, in some cases, operations such as those at issue in the main proceedings have been artificially designed for the essential purpose of benefiting from the subsidized duty[279].

In the light of these observations, the distinction usually made by CJEU emerges with extreme clarity, as will be seen, also in the fiscal sphere, between the purchaser's desire to benefit, even in bad faith. From an advantage alongside the pursuit of other economic and commercial goals, this distinction is not relevant in terms of abuse, and essentiality of the purpose of benefiting the subsidy linked on the objective level to the absence of economic justification of operations, element that allows to affirm the existence of an abuse. In other words, if there is an economic and commercial justification, the subjective element cannot be considered integrated, and, consequently, the prohibition of abuse cannot be applied.

THE THIRD ELEMENT OF THE TEST. CASE: C-279/05, VONK DAIRY PRODUCTS OF 11 JANUARY 2007 AND DISTRIBUTION OF THE EVIDENTIAL BURDEN

The same attention already given in other pronunciations, including in particular in C-515/03, Eichsfelder Schlachtbetrieb GmbH v. Hauptzollamt Hamburg-Jonas

influence on the market beyond the quota of the tariff quota allocated to it (par. 36).

279 Paragraphs 38 and 39. In that sense, one of the factors which could make it possible to ascertain the artificial nature of the transactions is, as the European Commission has pointed out in its observations, the fact that the importer who holds 'A' securities has not commercial risk, since the latter was actually covered by its buyer, who is also a traditional importer. Such an artificial character may also result from the fact that the profit margin of importers is insignificant or that the prices of the sale of garlic by the importers to the purchaser in EU are lower than the market price.

case of 23 July 2005, the role of the national judge in assessing the circumstances of the present case can be found in the C-279/05, Vonk Dairy Products sentence of 11 january 2007[280]. This case sets out important clarifications concerning the distribution of burden of proof of abusive behavior. That question was raised in the main proceedings because the exporting company complained that the national authorities had refused the refunds due to them without proving the existence of an abusive practice against it pursuant to C-110/99, Emsland-Stärke sentence of 14 December 2000. In fact, the national customs authority had failed to prove the abuse[281] and, therefore, posed a problem in relation to the allocation of the burden of proof.

As suggested by AG Sharpston[282], CJEU affirms that the undue nature of the refunds must be demonstrated by the proof of an unlawful practice of the exporter. This proof, which must be provided according to the rules of national law, must be ascertained by the referring court, through an overall analysis of the circumstances of the case.

On this basis, the referring court, alleging that the evidence showing the abuse had not been mentioned in detail in the recovery decision taken by the national authority, then ordered the annulment of the contested decision once the case was summarized adopted by the national authorities[283].

280 CJEU, C-279/05, Vonk Dairy Products of 11 January 2007, op. cit. In summary, national judge asked CJEU to interpret the provisions governing the recovery of refunds granted to promote exports of milk products. When these products were subsequently re-exported to a different destination country (in this case from the United States to Canada), taking into account that exports made directly by EU in Canada would have benefited from a lower refund rate compared to the one payable for exports to the United States.

281 Paragraph 35 reads "the Netherlands Government maintains in this regard that proof of an unlawful practice of the exporter, according to the judgment in Emsland-Stärke, must be furnished only if all the conditions are satisfied for the granting of refunds, which would not be the case in the main proceedings, since, due to the fact that the consignments of cheese re-exported to Canada were released for consumption on the US market, the condition of release for consumption in the third country pursuant to art. 17, n. 3, of Regulation n. 3665/87 has not been satisfied (...)".

282 According to paragraph 61, "it is clear from this case-law that the finding of such an abusive practice entails an overall examination of the circumstances of case and evidence. Only on the basis of this overall analysis can the national CJEUs determine whether an abusive practice has been perpetrated". See also par. 64: "it is clear from the definition of abusive practice outlined by CJEU that the assessment of whether a particular conduct, properly understood, corresponds to an abusive practice involves an overall examination of species and evidence. If, and to what extent, this assessment should be carried out by the competent authority for the examination of refund payments (the Productschap) or by the national CJEU responsible for reviewing the legality of decision of the competent authority, or both sequentially, are matters concerning the legal system of the member state concerned (...)".

283 The companies claimed that, "once the internal customs formalities for entry into the destination

The case also assumes importance in the face of the claims of the companies regarding a violation of legal certainty[284]. As CJEU points out, however, the prohibition of abuse and the fact that the application of European regulations cannot extend to the protection of abusive practices by economic operators raises an exception to the principle of legal certainty. If the principle according to which the payment of a refund is final is generally valid in exceptional cases, and even if the formal conditions giving entitlement to refunds have occurred, the obligation to reimburse the refund received may arise, despite its definitive character. Moreover, as also clarified in C-110/99, Emsland-Stärke sentence of 14 December 2000, the obligation to repay the refunds received, if the existence of the two constituent elements of an abusive practice is confirmed, does not infringe the principle of legality. Indeed, the obligation to reimbursement does not constitute a sanction, for which a clear and unambiguous legal basis is necessary. But, the mere consequence of the finding that the conditions required for obtaining the benefit deriving from the European legislation were created artificially, rendering the refunds granted unduly and thus justifying the reimbursement obligation.

Summing up what has been observed so far, the post-case ruling of C-110/99, Emsland-Stärke of 14 December 2000, confirm first of all that abuse of rights is an element to be taken into consideration precisely where Union law would otherwise be applicable, thus representing a limit to its application. Indeed, the problem of abuse arises when formally all the requirements prescribed by the relevant legislation are met. The judgments cited, then, in applying the test drawn up in C-110/99, Emsland-Stärke case of 14 December 2000, confirm that, to admit the presence of an abuse, it is essential to preliminarily identify the purposes that justify the attribution of the right by EU legislation, or the interests protected by the provision invoked[285]. This is indeed the application of a more general principle, according to which legal rules constitute the product of certain causes and serve certain objectives, the ratio legis, which

---

country have been completed, often (even if not always), the control over the goods has passed from the operator to his client. In principle, therefore, the interest in legal certainty would lead to the finalization of the attribution of the refund (...)" (par. 40 of the Opinion of AG Sharpston, op. cit.).

284 CJEU, C-43/93, Van Schijndel v. Stifting Pensioenfonds voor Fysiotherapeuten of 14 December 1995, ECLI:EU:C:1995:441, I-04703, par. 21. CJEU, C-452/09, Tonina Enza Iaia of 19 March 2011, ECLI:EU:C:2011:323, I-04043, parr. 20, 21 and 23. B. THORSON, Individual rights in European Union law, op. cit., pp. 22ss.

285 A. ILIOPOULOU-PENOT, Libertés de circulation et abus de droit in E. DUBOUT, A. MAITROT DE LA MOTTE (a cura di), L'unité des libertés de circulation: in varietate concordia?, op. cit., p. 187.

the interpreters must identify[286]. It will not suffice, therefore, as made clear by C-434/12, Slancheva sila EOOD v. Izpalnitelen direktor na Darzhaven founded "Zemedelie" Razplashtatelna agentsia case of 12 September 2013, the abusive intent to apply the related prohibition, whether it is descended from a general principle or from an anti-abuse clause that encodes it. The verification of the abuse in this regard implies a legal classification of the set of objective circumstances showing that the objective pursued by the European legislation has not been achieved, which in turn requires an interpretation of EU law and its purposes, with the consequence, not irrelevant, that the national judge, if necessary, will have to address CJEU. The teleological method thus allows CJEU to maintain a central role in determining the existence of the abuse in such a way as to avoid that the primacy of the Union system risks to weaken.

Vice versa, failure to achieve the goal is not sufficient to qualify an operation as abusive, where it is supported by other motivations than the abusive will. This is a particularly relevant statement, in that it highlights one of the differentiating elements of the prohibition of abuse compared to restrictive interpretation, which will be analyzed funditus in the following paragraphs.

286 D. TRIANTAFYLLOU, L'interdiction des abus de droit en tant que principe général du droit communautaire, op. cit., pp. 611ss.

PART B

Abuse of EU law in the tax area

BRIEF INTRODUCTION. THE MULTIPLE ASPECTS OF INTEREST IN TAX SECTOR

A few years after its elaboration on CAP, the abuse test has also been applied in the field of indirect taxes, which is also largely harmonized and which involves financial resources specific to the European Union, traits common to CAP. On this point, it must be clarified that the interest of the Union for the tax system derives not so much from the fact that it is a tax in part to European revenue, but from the need to ensure as much as possible the tax identity and application of the tax, which directly affects internal competition. In fact, any differentiation of tax treatment in the sale of goods or services entails a price differentiation that does not depend on the quality of the product, being due to mere tax artifices. It is therefore a factor of potential alteration of competition[287].

The study of abuse in the fiscal field[288] more generally, takes on particular importance for several reasons. First of all, the "European" tax law has adopted multiple anti-abuse clauses with the common characteristic of attributing to national authorities the power to deny the benefits deriving from the distorted application of the existing provisions. This codification reveals to the extent that it makes more evident the dual role that the prohibition of abuse of law assumes in the jurisprudence of CJEU. In general, CJEU is asked to rule on the applicability of the prohibition of abuse of law, in the presence of a clause that already

287 J. FREEDMAN, The anatomy of tax avoidance counteraction: Abuse of law in a tax context at member state and European Union level, in R. DE LA FERIA, S. VOGENAUER (a cura di) Prohibition of abuse of law: A new general principle of EU law?, op. cit., pp. 368ss.

288 P. PIANTAVIGNA, Tax abuse in European Union law, op. cit., pp. 138ss.

deals with tax avoidance or tax fraud within the legislation subject to attention, instead, CJEU will limit itself to verifying the applicability of the latter, interpreting it in a reflex manner in light of the general prohibition. However, it is necessary to ask how the codification relates to the prohibition, understood as an autonomous principle. In particular, it is a question of understanding whether the general prohibition can operate even where the member state has chosen not to transpose the anti-abuse clause into its national legislation.

Secondly, in this area the fundamental distinction between those abusive manifestations that occur only in the legal Union system and those that are expressed in an evasion of national legislation, thus involving several jurisdictions, clearly emerges. The prohibition of abuse, in fact, has been the subject of attention from the European jurisprudence both with reference to the abuse of law and to the different hypothesis of abuse of right. In the first case, the abuse involves an agendi norm belonging to the national tax system, which the taxpayer circumvents through a distorted use of European provisions, to obtain advantages not foreseen by the fiscal legislator or a reduction of tax burdens (to bring us back to our distinction, a case of cross-border abuse of law). In the second case, the abusive operation is carried out through a facultas agendi guaranteed by a "European Union" legislation, which the taxpayer uses to obtain a result, the reduction of tax, which is prohibited (according to our distinction, a case of internal abuse of law)[289].

As already mentioned, the two hypotheses outlined above differ not only with regard to the behavior performed by the private sector, but also and above all to the number of systems involved and to the rules that are relevant to the operation. In the defined hypothesis of abuse of law, the taxpayer uses the freedoms of circulation attributed by the Treaties to move to a more favorable order, in the absence of harmonization. In the case of abuse of right, instead, to be used in a distorted manner is a harmonized discipline, contained in a text of secondary law, which provides for certain benefits in favor of taxpayers. This last hypothesis will be discussed in this paragraph. As for the first type of abuse, it is useful only here to anticipate that the target result is twofold. On the one hand, the taxpayer circumvents national legislation, and on the other hand, abuses a European Union freedom, which constitutes the instrument for move into another more favorable legal system. This situation cannot be accepted from

289 D. WAELBROECK, La notion d'abus de droit dans l'ordre juridique communautaire, in Mélanges en hommages à J.V. Louis, op. cit., pp. 603ss.

two points of view (national and Union), but they do not always correspond. CJEU can in fact consider non-abusive what is prohibited by the evaded national tax system.

The tributary sector, more generally, constitutes a privileged point of view of the parallel between positive integration, where a harmonization of taxes has been achieved, and negative integration, established through the jurisprudence on free movement.

The areas described above both count a landmark decision, respectively C-196/04, Cadbury Schweppes and Cadbury Schweppes Overseas of 12 September 2006[290] sentence and C-255/02, Halifax and others case of 21 February 2006[291]. The comparison of which may be useful to highlight the different perspective that adopts CJEU with reference to the two meanings of abuse. This section will be the subject of an in-depth analysis of the latter ruling, which marked one of the most significant stages in the application of the prohibition on the abuse of law, both because it fully affirmed the extension of this prohibition to a key (fiscal) area to EU law and because it reiterated, with a series of clarifications and with the criteria for using the prohibition already outlined in C-110/99, Emsland-Stärke sentence of 14 December 2000.

PROHIBITION OF ABUSE APPLIED TO VAT. THE JURISPRUDENCE INAUGURATED BY THE PRONUNCIATION OF C-255/02, HALIFAX AND OTHERS CASE OF 21 FEBRUARY 2006

The C-255/02, Halifax and others case of 21 February 2006 assumed central importance in the construction of the abuse doctrine in the European Union as it provided an opportunity to broaden the scope of the prohibition of abuse. It was outlined in the matter of the common agricultural policy, just one sector, that of indirect taxes, until then considered immune from the limitations related to fraud and circumvention, confirming the fact that advanced harmonization is not obstacle to invoking the ban.

Likewise, this pronunciation has marked a further evolution of the concept of abuse of rights attributed by the EU law, launching a debate that has allowed

290 CJEU, C-196/04, Cadbury Schweppes and Cadbury Schweppes Overseas of 12 September 2006, op. cit.

291 CJEU, C-255/02, Halifax and others of 21 February 2006, op. cit.

to clarify the subjective element of the abuse test, thanks to the work of CJEU, but also of the AG Poiares Maduro, whose conclusions undoubtedly mark an important stage in the process of evolution of a complete theory of abuse[292].

JURISPRUDENTIAL CONTEXT REFERENCE: THE AMBIVALENT ATTITUDE OF CJEU

If certainly C-255/02, Halifax and others case of 21 February 2006 constitutes the point of arrival of the jurisprudence in the matter of CAP, the evolution of reflections that had already been sketched out by CJEU cannot be ignored as signs, by member states. In some cases decided in the early 2000s, the EU decided that transactions. which according to the member state concerned, were characterized by being elusive for VAT purposes.

The sentences that will be mentioned below, in particular, highlight the alternative between the use of prohibition of abuse and a given interpretation of the discipline, both of which allow the abuse to be punished. In this context, there was an ambivalent attitude on the part of CJEU. In fact, in two pronunciations, supported by the formulation of the referring court's questions and using the restrictive interpretation, he skillfully avoided addressing the issue of abuse of rights. While in another decision, concomitant, he laid the groundwork for the reasoning he will develop in C-255/02, Halifax and others case of 21 February 2006.

As an example of CJEU's self-restraint attitude, the Chancery Division RAL[293] ruling, issued in 2005 on the back of a United Kingdom judge, asked CJEU to interpret some articles of the sixth Directive concerning the provision of services, and to establish whether, in this case, the prohibition on abuse of right could be applied[294]. The Union judge, as anticipated, does not answer this last question, rephrasing the numerous questions referred for a preliminary

292 O. ROUSSELLE, H.M. LIEBMAN, The doctrine of the abuse of European Union law: The sword of damocles hanging over the Head of EC corporate tax law?, in European Taxation, 46, 2006, pp. 559ss. F. MARIATTE, Taxe sur la valeur ajoutée et abus de droit, in Europe, 128, 2006, pp. 27-28.

293 CJEU, C-452/03, RAL (Channel islands) and others of 12 May 2005, ECLI:EU:C:2005:289, I-03947.

294 Exactly the referring CJEU, with the fourth question for a preliminary ruling, asked "whether there is a principle of abuse of rights (irrespective of the interpretation given to VAT directives), which precludes the benefits pursued in a case such as the present. In the case of an affirmative solution, how does it work in a case like the one in question".

ruling in order to consider that "by its questions the referring court seeks essentially to determine the place of reference for that provision of services"[295]. In this regard, CJEU states that the provision of services[296] consisting in allowing the public to use, against remuneration, gambling machines installed in gambling halls located on the territory of a member state, must be regarded as one of recreational or similar activities pursuant to art. 9, n. 2, lett. c) of the sixth VAT Directive[297], so that the place of reference for this provision of services corresponds to that where it is physically carried out. In this way, it comes to believe that the subsidiary of the RAL group was a taxable person in the United Kingdom, as services located outside the Union could not be considered.

The same year in C-63/04, Centralan Property Ltd v. Commissioners of Customs & Excise case of 15 December 2005[298], although the EC in its written observations drew the attention of CJEU on the possible presence of an abuse of right[299], the latter merely remembers on the point that "in the hearing, the EC has recognized, as regards the possible application of the concept of abuse of rights, that this problem had not been discussed before the national institutions"[300].

In this way, CJEU avoids answering the question about the applicability of the prohibition, considering the interpretation given in the Directive to be sufficient to rule out any abuse. It points out, in fact, that because "in circumstances

295 R. DE LA FERIA, "Game over" for aggressive VAT planning?: RAL v. Commissioners of customs & excise, in British Tax Review, 55, 2005, pp. 394ss.

296 CJEU, C-3/17, Sporting Odds of 28 February 2018, ECLI:EU:C:2018:130, published in the electronic Reports of the cases.

297 Sixth Council Directive 77/388/EEC of 17 May 1977 on the harmonization of the laws of member states relating to turnover taxes- Common system of value added tax: uniform basis of assessment (OJ, L 145, p 1). The directive was subsequently repealed by Council Directive 2006/112/EEC of 28 November 2006 on the common system of value added tax (OJ, EU L 145, p.1).

298 CJEU, C-63/04, Centralan Property Ltd v. Commissioners of Customs & Excise of 15 December 2005, ECLI:EU:C:2005:773, I-11087.

299 In particular, according to the Commission, as stated in paragraph 46 of the judgment, "if CJEU were to establish that the concept of abuse of rights may be applied in a case such as that in the main proceedings, it would be necessary to add to the solution given to the point that if a taxable person or a group of persons who have links with each other undertake one or more transactions which do not have economic justification but which produce a fictitious situation whose sole purpose is to create the conditions necessary to recover upstream VAT, these transactions should not be taken into consideration (...)".

300 Paragraph 47. Continues by recalling that the Commission erroneously assumed that, given the short period which has elapsed between the construction of the Harrington building and its resale for twenty years and the conclusion of the two transactions at issue in the main proceedings, it was necessary to consider that all these elements together constituted a system developed in advance.

such as those in the main proceedings, in the event that the referring court reaches the conclusion, mentioned in par. 64 of the present judgment, that each of the two transactions in question has transferred the power to dispose of the investment property in question as owner, the correction provided for in art. 20, n. 3, of the sixth Directive must be made taking into account the two assignments in consideration proportionally to their respective values, there is no need to examine the question of the possible application of the principle of abuse of rights in such circumstances"[301].

The close correlation between prohibition of abuse and restrictive interpretation is already highlighted in the Kokott AG's conclusions, which in this sense precede those of the AG Poiares Maduro in C-255/02, Halifax and others case of 21 February 2006. The AG Kokott, in fact, although recognizing the existence of fictitious transactions, deems it superfluous to analyze the applicability of prohibition of abuse to the present case, being sufficient, in his opinion, to adopt a teleological interpretation of the provisions of the Directive.

In fact, even through this tool, the result would be to exclude "that such fictitious transactions entail a tax exemption that contrasts with the objectives of the Directive and that should be corrected by the use of unwritten principles, such as the prohibition of the abuse of right"[302].

The AG, therefore, not only detects the opportunity to combat the phenomenon of aggressive tax planning, but also recognizes the prohibition of abuse of law as a potentially suitable instrument to combat such operations.

CJEU has proved more inclined to address the issue in the joined cases: C-487/01 and C-7/02, Gemeente Leusden and Holin Groep BV of 29 April 2004 in which it was necessary to establish whether a Danish law enacted to combat artifice aimed at tax evasion, on the basis of article 20 of the sixth Directive,

301 Paragraph 61. For the sake of completeness, this quotation has been taken from the English text, compared with the French text, which is reported here: "the interpretation of the Sixth Directive which I am here advocating, however, precludes these artificial transactions from the point of view of the scope of the directive and of the prohibition on the abuse of rights"; "(...) interpretation de la directive que nous avons proposée exclut cependant que ces opérations artificielles ouvrent le droit à une exonération contraire aux objectifs de la directive et qu'il conviendrait de corrige en se fondant sur des principes non écrits tels que l'interdiction de the abus de droit". Otherwise, in the Italian text, there was an inconsistency: "the interpretation of the Sixth Directive provided in this context does not exclude that such fictitious transactions result in a tax exemption which runs counter to the objectives of the Directive and which should be corrected by the use of unwritten principles such as the prohibition of abuse of rights (...)".

302 CJEU, joined cases C-487/01 and C-7/02, Gemeente Leusden and Holin Groep BV of 29 April 2004, ECLI:EU:C:2004:263, I-05337.

could be considered proportionate to the objective pursued, as well as respectful of the legitimate expectations of the taxable persons.

In this regard, CJEU invokes the anti-abuse clause contained in art. 13 B of the Directive, according to which, member states exempt the letting of immovable property from the conditions established by them to ensure the correct and simple application of the exemption and to prevent any possible fraud, evasion, and abuse. Such establishment is to derive the consequence that "the fight against any possible fraud, evasion, and abuse is an objective recognized and promoted by the sixth Directive "and that, therefore" would be against this objective to prohibit a member state from imposing the immediate application of a law that suppresses the right to opt for the imposition of specific leases of real estate, having as corollary the obligation to correct the deductions made, if that state realized that the right of option was exercised within the framework of the elusive mechanisms of the tax (...)"[303]. Once the conformity of the anti-abuse legislation to the objectives of the Directive is recognized, CJEU deepens the notion of abuse, citing for this purpose the Emsland-Stärke test and its constituent elements, to then observe, more specifically, with reference to evasion and the legitimate expectation invoked by the private sector. Then, "even if, under the law of a member state, a taxable person cannot be criticized for having benefited from a provision or a regulatory gap, which enabled him to pay less tax without. However, if there is an abusive practice, the deletion of the regulatory framework of which a VAT payer has benefited cannot, in itself, violate legitimate expectations based on community law (...)"[304].

In light of this brief overview, it can therefore be concluded that a few years before the C-255/02, Halifax and others case of 21 February 2006 had been identified the need to prevent the phenomenon of tax avoidance in the field of indirect taxes. The latter which invokes for this purpose the anti-abuse clauses contained in the European Union regulations on the standardization of the principles of tax discipline. Likewise, the impossibility of censoring the behavior of taxpayers had already been underlined, except that they had not used techniques suitable for frustrating the objectives pursued by the European Union legislation. CJEU had already drawn the boundary between the choice to take advantage of a law

303 CJEU, joined cases C-487/01 and C-7/02, Gemeente Leusden and Holin Groep BV of 29 April 2004, op. cit.

304 CJEU, joined cases C-487/01 and C-7/02, Gemeente Leusden and Holin Groep BV of 29 April 2004, op. cit.

or the gaps in legislation with the objective of tax savings and the use of elusive methods, through the creation of artificial operations aimed at obtaining a tax advantage, situation, the latter to be labeled as abusive[305].

NATIONAL JUDGE'S QUESTIONS AND CONCLUSIONS OF THE AG: THE ALTERNATIVE BETWEEN RESTRICTIVE INTERPRETATION AND PROHIBITION OF ABUSE OF LAW

Furthermore, it is only with the C-255/02, Halifax and others sentence of 21 February 2006 that the prohibition of abuse is not only invoked but also fully applied by the EU judicature with regard to the field of indirect taxes. Before dwelling on the sentence, it should be noted that Directive n. 77/388/EEC[306], so-called sixth Directive VAT, in force at the time of the facts, contained an anti-abuse clause in art. 27, par. 1, under which the Council could authorize each member state to introduce special measures derogating from the Directive, in order to avoid certain frauds or tax evasion.

The story, as well as complex, is known, which is why it will be reported only in summary. The British banking institution Halifax, having to build four call centers for its business, could have recovered less than 5% of the input VAT paid for the construction works, as an almost totally exempt operator. The company, therefore, decided to delegate the construction work to its subsidiaries, so that they were able to deduct the VAT due for these works in the same year in which they had performed other taxable transactions. As a result of these choices, he was able to fully deduct the VAT paid on invoices received from his suppliers for the construction works. Similar operations with the same objective were carried out by the University of Huddersfield[307] and by Bupa Hospital[308].

---

305 R. DE LA FERIA, Prohibition of abuse of (European Union law), op. cit., pp. 421ss.

306 Sixth Council Directive 77/388/EEC of 17 May 1977 on the harmonization of the laws of member states relating to turnover taxes-common system of value added tax: uniform basis of assessment, OJ L 145, 13.6.1977, p. 1-40, no longer in force from 31 December 2006. For further details see: B. PECI, F. MORINA, The legal framework for harmonization of Value Added Tax (VAT) in European Union, in Acta Universitatis Danubius. Juridica, 13 (1), 2017.

307 CJEU, C-223/03, University of Huddersfield Higher Education Corporation v. Commissioners of Customs & Excise of 21 February 2006, op. cit.

308 CJEU, C-419/02, BUPA Hospitals Ltd and University of Huddersfield Higher Education Corporation v. Commissioners of Customs and Excise of 21 February 2006, op. cit.

In essence, with such constructions, the companies aimed to take advantage of a more favorable taxation.

A dispute arose with the British tax authorities, who refused to grant reimbursement in all three cases, the referring court submitted two closely related questions to CJEU. Firstly, it asked whether transactions carried out solely with the intention of obtaining a tax advantage and without a commercial purpose could be regarded, for VAT purposes, as "services" put in place by the persons involved in the course of their economic activities[309]. Secondly, it questioned whether the principle of abuse of rights established by CJEU case-law was applicable to prevent the company from recovering input VAT.

In this regard a first important notation is required. The two proposed questions reflect, in reality, the alternative that is proposed more generally to CJEU in the presence of an EU legislation between the restrictive interpretation of the field of application of the Union legislation and use of the prohibition of abuse of right to counter fraudulent behavior or abusive individuals. In other words, the referring court asked to first verify the application, in such circumstances, of the EU legislation and, subsequently, in case of a positive reply, if the prohibition to abuse their rights could be triggered, which excludes their allocation. As you can see, the two floors are different.

The imperfect coincidence of the choice between restrictive interpretation and the application of the prohibition of abuse is well highlighted in the conclusions of the AG Poiares Maduro. The latter observes first that, by opting for the thesis advocated by the United Kingdom, CJEU would deviate from its current orientation. In any case, "for an effective treatment of VAT evasion plans, it should be considered that there are less drastic solutions, more in keeping with the spirit and nature of the common VAT system"[310].

Accepted an extensive interpretation of the sixth Directive and therefore discarded the thesis advocated by the United Kingdom, the AG recognizes that, in the case where the right invoked is not in line with the purposes of the rules. From which it formally springs, it is possible to apply also in the VAT area the notion of abuse of law, as recognized by the case law in other areas of EU law.

---

309 According to the United Kingdom, since the only real intention of the participants in such transactions was to implement a tax avoidance plan, the activities carried out were completely outside the scope of the Sixth Directive and could not be classified as economic.

310 Opinion of AG Poiares Maduro presented in case: C-255/02, Halifax and others of 21 February 2006, ECLI:EU:C:2006:200, I-01609, par. 53. This is an observation which will be repeated over time, as will be seen from now on.

Indeed, the AG from the analysis of previous European Union jurisprudence, deduces the existence of a general principle of EU law which prohibits the abuse of its rights, as such also applicable to the VAT system[311].

More precisely, the prohibition of abuse, as an "interpretative principle of community law"[312], would apply once the two criteria elaborated in the C-110/99, Emsland-Stärke of 14 December 2000 sentence, were revisited here in an objective sense. The AG specifies, in fact, that "the artificiality of certain events or operations must not be based on an assessment of the subjective intentions of those who invoke Union law, but must be proven with certain objective circumstances verified on a case-by-case basis. This is also in line with CJEU's reference, again in its C-110/99, Emsland-Stärke sentence of 14 December 2000, to the "sole purpose" of an activity or a behavior as a central element in support of the conclusion that an abuse of community law has been committed"[313]. In other words, such events "should not be subjective elusive intentions of the parties to supplement the subjective element referred to in C-110/99, Emsland-Stärke sentence of 14 December 2000. On the contrary, the intent of the parties to obtain an undue benefit from the order of the Union it can be simply inferred from the artificial character of the situation, to be judged in the light of a series of objective circumstances"[314]. In the light of these observations, the subjective element

311 Par. 62 et seq. are reported here. Of the conclusions, in which a review of the previous jurisprudence on abuse is carried out: "an analysis of CJEU case studies reveals a conspicuous series of converging elements regarding the notion of abuse in EU law. CJEU stated that the deception of egislation of a member state through the exercise of these freedoms is inadmissible. This principle has been reiterated by CJEU in other areas such as social security, where it has also said that benefits cannot be derived from abuse or fraud. In other disputes, as regards the common agricultural policy, CJEU has stated, following the same logic, that the application of the relevant legislation on export refunds "could not in any case be extended to include abusive practices of economic operators (...)". In a different order of cases, in the field of company law, CJEU also acknowledged that a shareholder should not be able to invoke European law in order to obtain unlawful advantages that are clearly extraneous to the objective of the provision in question. In case: C-212/97, Centros of 9 March 1999, which concerned an alleged abuse of the right of establishment, CJEU reiterated its position by stating that "a member state has the right to take measures to prevent that, thanks to the possibilities offered by the Treaty, some of its citizens try to escape the empire of national laws, and that those concerned cannot abusively or fraudulently use EU law (...) a general principle of European law can undoubtedly be inferred from the cases examined. CJEU summarized it by stating that "individuals cannot abusively or fraudulently use EU rules (...)".

312 CJEU, joined cases C-487/01 and C-7/02, Gemeente Leusden and Holin Groep BV of 29 April 2004, op. cit.

313 Paragraph 70, continue: "It is true that those objective elements reveal that those who put in place such activity most likely intended to abuse EU law. Yet it is not this intention that is the decisive factor for the evaluation of the abuse, but the activity itself objectively considered (...)".

314 See, paragraph 87 of the same case of analysis. Consequently, this element can be considered an

is therefore equivalent to the absence of any other economic justification for the activity, other than to provide a fiscal advantage[315].

The AG supports the thesis that, in such circumstances, the prohibition of abuse must also apply to the common VAT system, which certainly cannot be considered as a sort of "immunity" from abuse in the system of the Union, so that the rule of law must be interpreted, notwithstanding its letter, in the sense that it does not actually confer the right.

It should be noted that, in this sense, the fact that the AG indicates the prohibition of abuse as an interpretative principle does not seem to influence the mode of operation of the technique. In fact, even here, as in the CAP, the consequence is the non-attribution of the right.

If anything, considering the prohibition in question as an interpretative principle allows AG Poiares Maduro to state that the application of the prohibition of abuse in the context of the sixth Directive cannot necessarily depend on the adoption by the individual member states of adequate anti-fraud provisions, to the procedure described in art. 27 of the Directive. It is necessary to distinguish, in fact, the application of the interpretative principle of EU law that prohibits abuses in the common system of VAT, from the procedure described in art. 27 for the introduction by member states of special measures derogating from the sixth Directive, aimed at preventing certain forms of evasion or fraud.

In any case, the prohibition of abuse in the VAT system must necessarily coordinate with the freedom to choose the form of conduct of business subject to lower tax[316], in order to minimize costs, as well as with the principles of legal certainty and protection of legitimate expectations of taxpayers. By virtue of these principles, the scope of the interpretative principle of EU law that prohibits abusing VAT legislation must be defined in such a way that it does not prejudice legitimate transactions. In particular, its potential negative impact will be averted if the prohibition is interpreted as meaning that the right invoked by a taxable person is excluded only when the corresponding economic activity has

---

element of autonomy. In fact, when applying it, national authorities must determine whether the activity at issue has an independent basis which, leaving aside the considerations of a fiscal nature, provides it with an economic justification in the circumstances of the case.

315 S. DOUMA, F. ENGELEN, Halifax Plc and others v. Commissioners of customs & excise: The ECJ applies the abuse of rights doctrine in VAT cases, in British Tax Review, 51, 2006, pp. 429ss. P. PISTONE, Abuse of law in the context of indirect taxation, in R. DE LA FERIA, S. VOGENAUER, Prohibition of abuse of law: a new general principle of EU law?, op. cit., pp. 145ss.

316 As we can see in case: C-606/15, Aviva of 21 September 2017, ECLI:EU:C:2017:718, published in the electronic Reports of the cases.

no other explanation than to pre-establish that right against the tax authorities and the recognition of law would collide with the aims and results of the relevant provisions of the common VAT system. Such economic activities, even if not illegal, do not deserve to be protected by invoking the European principles of legal certainty and protection of legitimate expectations, because they respond to the sole purpose of subverting the purpose of the same legal system[317].

The prohibition in question will no longer be valid on the other hand if the economic activity carried out can be explained otherwise than with the mere achievement of tax benefits to the detriment of tax authorities. In such circumstances, in fact, interpreting a provision of law in the sense that it does not confer any rights on the basis of an unwritten general principle would mean giving too much discretionary powers to the national authorities to decide which purposes of a given transaction to consider predominant. This would entail, among other things, a high level of uncertainty for the legitimate choices of economic operators and an impairment of economic activities that are clearly worthy of protection, provided they are implemented, at least to a certain extent, for ordinary commercial purposes[318].

(FOLLOWS) THE PRONUNCIATION OF CJEU: THE "OBJECTIFIED" SUBJECTIVE ELEMENT

The indications of the AG concerning the answer to the question whether operations, such as those at issue in the main proceedings, could fall within the scope of application of the sixth Directive, are accepted by CJEU. First of all, the judges state that from the consolidated interpretation of the concepts of "supplies of goods", "services", and "economic activities", it follows that "operations such as those in the main proceedings constitute the sale of goods or services, and an economic activity pursuant to arts. 2, par. 1, 4, no. 1 and 2, 5, n. 1, and 6, n. 1, of the sixth Directive. They meet the objective criteria on which these concepts are

317 F. VANISTENDAEL, Halifax and Cadbury Schweppes: One single European theory of abuse in tax law?, op. cit., pp. 193ss.

318 Paragraph 58. CJEU adds, in paragraph 59, "Of course, these criteria are not met in the case of tax fraud, for example by making false declarations or issuing irregular invoices. Nevertheless, ascertaining whether the transaction in question is carried out for the sole purpose of obtaining a tax advantage is irrelevant to establishing whether it constitutes a supply of goods or of services and an economic activity (...)".

based, although they have been carried out for the sole purpose of obtaining a tax advantage, without any other economic objective"[319].

The Luxembourg judge then focused on the question of the possibility of invoking the prohibition of abuse of right, also accepting in this respect, in principle, the approach made by the AG Poiares Maduro, even if with a more nuanced reasoning. Thus, the existence of a "community-law theory"[320] of abuse of law is admitted even in the VAT sector, without however being unbalanced in describing the prohibition of abuse as a principle of interpretation, or even as a general principle.

On the other hand, CJEU, as before the AG, not only proves very careful to balance the prohibition in question with the principle of legal certainty, which is imposed with particular rigor when it comes to deciding the application of an appropriate legislation to entail financial burdens. But it also recognizes the right of the taxable person to choose the form of conduct of business that allows him to limit his tax contribution. Such a choice is clearly distinguished from the abuse, defined on the basis of the two usual criteria borrowed by C-110/99, Emsland-Stärke case of 14 December 2000 but partly revised. CJEU, in fact, confirms in such a case that "in the VAT sector, in order to talk about abusive conduct, the transactions in question must, notwithstanding the formal application of the conditions laid down by the relevant provisions of the sixth Directive and the transposing national legislation, to obtain a tax advantage whose concession would be contrary to the objective pursued by these same provisions"[321].

However, it accomplishes a change of perspective in relation to the subjective element, stating that "it must also result from a set of objective elements that the purpose of the transactions at issue is essentially to obtain a fiscal advantage"[322]. Thus, as also underlined by the AG Poiares Maduro, the prohibition of abusive behavior ceases to be valid where the operations in question can be explained

319 F. VANISTENDAEL, Halifax and Cadbury Schweppes: One single European theory of abuse in tax law?, op. cit.

320 R. GEIGER, D.E. KHAN, M. KOTZUR, EUV/AEUV, op. cit., M. DECHEVA, Recht der europäischen Union, op. cit., C. BARNARD, S. PEERS, European Union law, op. cit., pp. 586ss. N. FOSTER, European Union law directions, Oxford University Press, Oxford, 2016. A. THIES, International trade disputes and European Union liability, Cambridge University press, Cambridge, 2013.

321 CJEU, C-606/15, Aviva of 21 September 2017, op. cit.

322 Indeed, the question reflects the divisions that exist at national level. In fact, there has always been a strong division between the proponents of the subjectivist conception, which would require the presence of the animus fraudandi, and of the objectivist theory, for which the concrete would suffice suitability of the operation to achieve the result prohibited by the mandatory rule.

otherwise than with the mere achievement of tax advantages. Ultimately, what matters is the rationality (or otherwise) of the economic operation, deduced from objective elements.

Before resolving the issue in the sense of the applicability of prohibition of abuse of law in the sixth Directive system, CJEU, while delegating to the national court the verification of the actual content and significance of the transactions, establishes itself, in substance, the presence of the subjective element of the abuse in the concrete case, where it states that "in any case, the decision to refer shows that for the VAT and Duties Tribunal the operations subject of the main proceedings had the sole purpose of obtaining a fiscal advantage"[323].

With regard to the recovery of VAT, CJEU confines itself to pointing out that it is for the member states to determine the conditions under which the tax authority can levy the tax due ex post facto. However, it does not omit to point out that the finding of the existence of an abusive behavior should not lead to a sanction, for which a clear and unambiguous legal basis would be necessary, but simply a reimbursement obligation, in order to re-establish the situation that would be existed without the operations in which that behavior materialized.

A not inconsiderable fact emerges from the pronunciation in comment: since the notion of abuse is defined in extremely general terms, it requires, in the various areas in which the prohibition may be applied, an incessant and inevitable "adjustment" in relation to the concrete case. Indeed, the need for more developed criteria to make operational a general principle of EU law is not a question of easy solution, but it is necessary to proceed by trial.

In the C-255/02, Halifax and others case of 21 February 2006, CJEU questioned the need to maintain a subjective element based on intentions. On this point, certain doctrine has rightly highlighted the danger of a reduction in the subjective element, that is to say the excessively broad application of the notion, which also affects behavior in non-abusive realities. This is an observation which also emerges from the conclusions of the AG Poiares Maduro and which, added here, would lead to the elimination of any distinction between a restrictive interpretation of EU law and the prohibition of abuse of rights. In the C-255/02, Halifax and others case of 21 February 2006, however, CJEU, on closer inspection, does not give up entirely to a subjectivist view, but, aligning itself with the conclusions of the AG, only perfects such criteria, according to what

323 F. VANISTENDAEL, Halifax and Cadbury Schweppes: One single European theory of abuse in tax law?, op. cit.

already it was possible to derive from the C-110/99, Emsland-Stärke case of 14 December 2000, specifying the terms in which the evaluation of what is objective can be included. This replaces the element of the will to obtain an advantage with the objective proof of the actual content and meaning of the operations in question, which can be achieved by using a series of indices, such as, for example, the purely artificial nature of the operations or the links of legal, economic or personal nature among the operators involved in the reduction of tax burden. The objective of the operation must be to obtain a fiscal advantage, instead sufficient for the presence of an economic objective for the activity to be considered legitimate. Using a terminology that was not entirely precise, however, the ruling left some doubts to the interpreter about the uniqueness or essentiality of the abusive objective, then clarified by the jurisprudence of a little later.

THE CONFIRMATION OF THE APPLICABILITY OF PROHIBITION IN THE SUBSEQUENT JURISPRUDENCE AND THE FURTHER REFLECTIONS ON THE SCOPE OF THE SUBJECTIVE AND OBJECTIVE ELEMENTS

In the wake of the C-255/02, Halifax and others sentence of 21 February 2006 are inserted, after a few years, the C-162/07, Ampliscientifica srl and others v. Ministry of Economy and Finance of 22 May 20081 and C-425/06, Part Service of 21 February 2008[324] sentences, both rendered in 2008, as well as the pronouncements of cases: C-277/09, RBS Deutschland Holdings GmbH of 22 December 2010[325] and C-103/09 and, the Commissioners for Her Majesty's Revenue & Customs v. Weald Leasing Ltd of 22 December 2010[326], which deserve attention as they provide the interpreter with explanations concerning the subjective and the objective element respectively.

324 CJEU, C-298/05, Columbus Container Services of 6 December 2007, ECLI:EU:C:2007:754, I-10451.

325 CJEU, C-277/09, RBS Deutschland Holdings GmbH of 22 December 2010, ECLI:EU:C:2010:810, I-13805 and case C-103/09, The Commissioners for Her Majesty's Revenue & Customs v. Weald Leasing Ltd of 22 December 2010, ECLI:EU:C:2010:804, I-13589.

326 CJEU, C-103/09, The Commissioners for Her Majesty's Revenue & Customs v. Weald Leasing Ltd of 22 December 2010, op. cit.

THE C-162/07, AMPLISCIENTIFICA SRL AND OTHERS V. MINISTRY OF ECONOMY AND FINANCE OF 22 MAY 2008 SENTENCE, PART SERVICE OF 21 FEBRUARY 2008: UNIQUE OR ESSENTIAL ADVANTAGE?

In C-425/06, Part Service case of 21 February 2008, CJEU was able to clarify the scope of the test element which, although objectified, can continue to be defined as subjective. The case proves to be interesting because the request for a preliminary ruling was specifically aimed at obtaining a clarifying interpretation of the previous C-255/02, Halifax and others case of 21 February 2006, thus giving CJEU the opportunity to think more deeply about a constituent element of the abuse.

For our purposes, it is sufficient to remember that the case concerned the fragmentation of vehicle leasing contracts in two fictitious shops. According to the financial administration, the separate contracts concluded between the parties masked the conclusion of a single contract, so as to artificially reduce the tax base (given by the amount of the rent) on which VAT was to be applied. On the contrary, the company involved in the transaction alleged the existence of valid economic reasons capable of justifying the conclusion of a plurality of related contracts, as well as the absence of any elusive intent. CJEU, in an Appeal Chamber Court in charge of the dispute, wondered whether the notion of abusive operation, defined by the judgment of the C-255/02, Halifax and others case of 21 February 2006 as essentially accomplished in order to achieve a tax advantage, coinciding, broader or more restrictive than the notion of transaction that does not have economic reasons other than a tax advantage, an expression also used in the same ruling.

The Luxembourg judge, with the intention of explaining the inconsistency noted by the referring court, emphasizes that the sentence subject to interpretation refers on two occasions, respectively to par. 74 and 75 and in par. 81, to a set of objective elements from which "it appears that the purpose of the transactions at issue is essentially the obtaining of a tax advantage"[327]. First, in order to outline the abuse test in general terms and, subsequently, to provide the judge of the direct reference to direct him in his interpretation in the main proceedings.

327 CJEU, C-103/09, The Commissioners for Her Majesty's Revenue & Customs v. Weald Leasing Ltd of 22 December 2010, op. cit.

That said, underlines that CJEU, when it found "that, in any case, the operations in the main proceedings had the sole purpose of obtaining a tax advantage, in par. 82 did not transform this circumstance into a condition for the existence of an abusive practice, but simply pointed out that, in the case pending before the referring court, the minimum threshold for qualifying an abusive practice was even exceeded"[328].

The question raised is therefore answered by stating that the correct interpretation of the sixth Directive must be to recognize the existence of an abusive practice if the pursuit of a tax advantage constitutes the essential purpose of the transactions at issue, which is a minimum threshold because you find an abuse. He then took the opportunity to specify that, in assessing the essentiality, "the national court may take into consideration the purely fictitious nature of the transactions, as well as the legal, economic and/or personal links between the operators involved cases (C-255/02, Halifax and others of 21 February 2006, par 81), being such elements capable of proving that obtaining the tax advantage is the essential objective pursued, despite the possible existence, on the other hand, of economic objectives inspired by considerations, for example, of marketing, organization and guarantee"[329].

The ruling gives clarity in this way on a central aspect of the abuse of tax tests. To assess whether the operations carried out by a taxpayer can integrate an abusive practice after verifying that the result is a tax advantage whose grant, despite the compliance with the formal data, is contrary to the rationale of the legislative provisions, it will have to be evaluated above all if, on the basis of objective elements derived from the operation carried out, this advantage constituted the essential, not necessarily exclusive, purpose of the chosen economic solution.

---

328 CJEU, C-162/07, Ampliscientifica srl and others v. Ministero dell'Economia e delle Finanze of 22 May 2008, op. cit.

329 Do not require a particular deepening, at least in the Italian context, criticism of the English jurists to the Part Service judgment (C-425/06, Part Service of 21 February 2008) for having formulated a broader idea of abuse, using the expression "principal aim", with an adjective therefore susceptible to include more situations than the term "essential". It would indeed be a difference in translation, given that in the Italian version, the language of the case respectively, the expression "essential purpose" is used in the French version, the working language of CJEU, the expression "but essentiel". Actually, as R. LYAL, Cadbury Schweppes and Abuse observes: Comments, in prohibition of abuse of law, op. cit., pp. 429-430, dwelling on every expression used by CJEU would be over-interpreting precisely because a sentence cannot be considered as a text of law in which every word must be given its exact meaning.

In other words, in practice, an illegal tax and an economic-business reason can coexist, but the tax savings must be the ultimate motivation that determined the choice of the subject in completing a transaction according to particular modalities, that is the purpose overall activity performed.

It must be concluded that, by referring to C-255/02, Halifax and others case of 21 February 2006, to the fact that the transactions in question had the sole purpose of obtaining a tax advantage, CJEU did not alter the condition of essentiality, but indicated only that, in the concrete case, it had even been overcome.

Thus, the question is raised about the necessity of the uniqueness or the essentiality of the evasive purpose in the field of indirect taxation, which, in C-255/02, Halifax and others case of 21 February 2006 left open, inclining for the second definition, that, although certainly more complex and less certain (requiring a thorough balancing of the objectives pursued) leaves more room for national administrations to combat practices deemed to be abusive.

For the sake of completeness, it should be noted that, after a few months, CJEU once again ruled on the abuse in an Italian case, (C-162/07, Ampliscientifica srl and others v. Ministry of Economy and Finance of 22 May 2008) showing on that occasion not to take account of its previous C-425/06, Part Service case of 21 February 2008.

More in detail, CJEU was asked to assess the substantial compatibility inter alia with the prohibition of abuse of law. This Italian law of 1979 provided for the possibility for an institution or a parent company to proceed with the declaration and payment of the VAT according to the simplified procedures established by the Regulation only if it held more than 50% of the shares or units of legally dependent subjects, such as subsidiaries, from the beginning of the calendar year preceding that of the declaration. What we are interested in pointing out here is how CJEU in this regard observes that the prohibition of abuse of rights is aimed in the VAT sector, that European Union legislation is not extended to include the abusive behavior of economic operators, namely operations carried out not in the context of normal commercial transactions, but solely for the purpose of unlawfully benefiting from the advantages provided for by Union law[330].

This principle is aimed, according to CJEU, to prohibit the construction of pure artifice, devoid of economic effectiveness, carried out solely for the purpose of obtaining a tax advantage.

330 CJEU, C-255/02, Halifax and others of 21 February 2006, op. cit. parr. 69, 70.

CJEU, therefore, excludes that it infringes the principle of prohibition of the abuse of law a national legislation requiring economic operators to prove. Through a certain continuity of their activity and their operations, the use of a simplified declaration and payment regime VAT does not proceed exclusively from the desire to obtain a tax advantage, notably by accounting for a debt or a VAT credit to the institution or to the parent company, but is the result of a longer-term economic choice.

The examination of the two pronunciations shows a certain discordance: the one in fact welcomes a more detailed definition of the subjective element, which coincides with the essentiality of the purpose. The other, however, coincides with the uniqueness of the purpose. Nevertheless, taking into account a part of the short distance between each other, of the C-255/02 citation of Halifax and others case of 21 February 2006, without particular detail and reflection in C-162/07, Ampliscientifica srl and others v. Ministry of the Economy and Finance case of 22 May 2008 as opposed to an exhaustive and reasoned explanation, in C-425/06, Part Service case of 21 February 2008, it is considered appropriate to give prevalence to the interpretation proposed in the latter.

Among other things, it seems preferable to understand the essential term aim in a substantialistic perspective. Through the use of this phrase, it would simply emerge the intention of CJEU to avoid that taxpayers have a good game to argue that in addition to the true purpose of transaction (tax avoidance) there are other more or less plausible economic reasons.

JUDGMENTS OF CASES: C-277/09, RBS DEUTSCHLAND HOLDINGS GMBH OF 22 DECEMBER 2010 AND C-103/09, THE COMMISSIONERS FOR HER MAJESTY'S REVENUE & CUSTOMS V. WEALD LEASING LTD OF 22 DECEMBER 2010. THE WILL TO GAIN AN ADVANTAGE IS NOT ENOUGH

The judgments of cases: C-277/09, RBS Deutschland Holdings GmbH of 22 December 2010 and C-103/09, the Commissioners for Her Majesty's Revenue & Customs v. Weald Leasing Ltd of 22 December 2010 concerning both leasing transactions, which had the potential effect of reducing or even avoiding the taxability of the lease fees, deserve to be recalled. They corroborate with a concrete application what was already affirmed only in the abstract in C-255/02, Halifax and others case of 21 February 2006, i.e. that also in the tax area, as in the matter of the common agricultural policy, the arrangement of artifices aimed at obtaining the benefits deriving from the use of the Union in accordance with their objectives. This demonstrates that it is always necessary, in order to invoke the prohibition of abuse, for a joint application of both criteria.

In C-277/09, RBS Deutschland Holdings GmbH case of 22 December 2010, in particular, CJEU excludes the existence of an abusive case, since the financial and leasing services had actually been provided in the context of a real economic activity. Thus CJEU, referring to the judgment in C-255/02, Halifax and others case of 21 February 2006, states that "the principle of the prohibition of abusive practices does not preclude, in circumstances such as those at issue in the main proceedings, where an undertaking established in one member state it decides to make leasing transactions on assets to a third-party company established in the first member state through its subsidiary established in another member state, in order to avoid the application of VAT on the fees for such operations, where they qualify, in the first member state, as rental services in the second member state and instead, in that second member state, as supplies of goods carried out in the first member state, to the right to deduct VAT set by art. 17, n. 3, lett. a), of the Directive (...)"[331]. These are not transactions of an artificial nature, they are operations that are the result of real economic activity, which at the same time legitimately limit tax contribution. It was simply a matter of a corporate choice regarding organizational structures and operating procedures aimed at pursuing the most advantageous economic option to limit tax burdens, as such fully legitimate[332].

Similarly, in C-103/09, the Commissioners for Her Majesty's Revenue & Customs v. Weald Leasing Ltd case of 22 December 2010, CJEU considered that the choice of a banking group to assign leasing operations to a company belonging to the group, to benefit from the non-imposition of such transactions, was an expression of the right of the taxable person to choose the more suitable form for carrying out their business. The "European Union" judges, after having found

331 CJEU, C-255/02, Halifax and others of 21 February 2006, op. cit. parr. 69, 70.

332 M. POULSEN, Treaty/Directive shopping and abuse of EU law, in Intertax, 2013, pp. 244ss. The author notes that one of the main differences between the pronunciations of Halifax and RBS Deutschland Holdings GmbH lies in the existence of (or lack of) commercial risks in the transactions. In Halifax, since the transactions were carried out exclusively between related parties and were exclusively aimed at ensuring a tax advantage, there were very few risks associated with the "intermediate" companies used by the Halifax Group to obtain the VAT deduction. In contrast, the risks assumed by RBS Deutschland Holdings GmbH corresponded to the normal risks borne by companies involved in banking and leasing activities.

that, in the specific case, the essential purpose of the leasing transactions was actually the obtaining of a tax advantage and that therefore the second element of the test was satisfied, ruled that, as regards the first element, "tax advantage deriving from the fact that a company uses leasing transactions on assets such as those at issue in the main proceedings, rather than on the direct purchase of such assets, does not constitute a tax advantage which would be contrary to the objective pursued the relevant provisions of the sixth Directive and of the national legislation transposing the latter, provided that the contractual conditions relating to such transactions, in particular those relating to the fixing of the amount of rental payments, correspond to normal market conditions and the involvement in such transactions a third-party intermediary company is not likely to hinder the application of the aforementioned provisions, which is a matter for the referring court to verify (...). The fact that this company does not carry out leasing operations in the context of its normal commercial operations is irrelevant in this regard"[333].

In short, because each subject is free to choose the organizational structures and the most suitable operating procedures for the conduct of their business, do not integrate unauthorized cases all those operations that only allow limiting the tax contribution as the result of an adequate and reasoned business management. In fact, in these cases, obtaining the tax advantage is only a "side effect" of normal business management, contrary to what happened in C-255/02, Halifax and others case of 21 February 2006, where the operations apparently had no real commercial purpose other than obtaining a VAT deduction.

CASE STUDY ANALYSIS OF C-321/05, KOFOED V. SKATEMINISTERIET CASE OF 5 JULY 2007. PROHIBITION OF ABUSE OF LAW IN THE FIELD OF HARMONIZED DIRECT TAXATION

In order to complete the casuistry of the form of abuse of right that can synthetically be defined as internal abuse of law, in addition to the rulings on VAT, the C-321/05, Kofoed v. Skateministeriet sentence of 5 July 2007[334] on

333 M. POULSEN, Treaty/Directive shopping and abuse of EU law, op. cit.

334 CJEU, C-321/05, Kofoed v. Skateministeriet of 5 July 2007, op. cit., For a comment see: A. ZALASINSKI, Case-law-based anti-avoidance measures in conflict with proportionality test-Comment on the

the interpretation of Directive 90/434/EEC, aimed at eliminating national tax restrictions which hinder mergers, divisions, transfers of assets and exchanges of shares concerning companies of different member states, and in particular the anti-abuse clause contained therein[335]. The case in question, although related to one sector, that of direct taxation, for the most part not covered by Union legislation, is an excellent demonstration of the leading role that harmonization can play in determining the application of the prohibition of abuse. In this case, the alleged abusive benefits stemmed from an improper use not of the fundamental freedoms of circulation, but of secondary legislation.

Unlike the lodging in C-196/04, Cadbury Schweppes and Cadbury Schweppes Overseas case of 12 September 2006, which also fits into the field of direct taxation, even this hypothesis can therefore be included in the category of abuse that occurs in a single judicial system, since the abusive operation, perpetrated through an improper use of the aforementioned Directive, aimed at pursuing an undue advantage descending from the same EU legislation.

THE FIRST APPLICATIONS OF THE ANTI-ABUSE CLAUSE. BRIEF REFERENCES TO THE PREVIOUS C-28/95, LEUR-BLOEM CASE OF 17 JULY 1997

It must briefly state that Directive 90/434/EEC pursues the objective of eliminating tax obstacles to cross-border restructuring within the European Union, excluding for this purpose an imposition at the time of a merger, a division, a transfer of assets or an exchange of shares between companies of different member states. The Directive started from the observation that in most tax systems transfers of shares and contributions of assets from one company to another give rise to profits for the shareholder or the transferring company that are subject to tax, but that when the transaction is linked to a grouping or restructuring operation is often granted a tax exemption.

Since, as is to be understood, this exemption varied from one member state to another and sometimes did not extend to all transactions carried out within the Union, the Directive aimed at achieving harmonization of the tax system in this regard. In other words, it was decided to set up neutral tax rules for

---

ECJ decision in Kofoed, in European Taxation, 12, 2007, pp. 572ss.

335 D. LIAKOPOULOS, A comparative analysis of EU and US transnational mergers regulation, op. cit.

competition in respect of competition, to enable companies to adapt to the needs of the common market, to improve their productivity and to strengthen their international competitive position by introducing a common tax regime that avoids taxation at the time of a merger, a spin-off, a transfer of assets or an exchange of shares, while protecting the financial interests of the receiving state of the transferring or acquiring company[336].

The objective in question was pursued in essence by requiring member states to defer taxation on profits from the sale of assets or shares in connection with such transactions, while allowing them the possibility of collecting the deferred tax at a later stage, upon the definitive disposal of assets by the receiving company or upon the sale by the shareholders of the new shares received on the basis of an exchange of shares[337].

In the text, however, we find, as already mentioned, a limitation on the application of the tax benefits contained in the Directive, through the introduction of an anti-abuse clause. In this regard, recital n. 9 states that "it is necessary to provide for the possibility for member states to refuse the benefit of the application of this Directive when the merger, division, transfer of assets or exchange of shares aims at fraud or evasion tax"[338]. Article 11, then, authorizes the member state not to apply the provisions of the Directive when the operation carried out by the company has as its main objective tax fraud or evasion, specifying that the fact that one of the operations in question "is not carried out for valid economic reasons, such as the restructuring or rationalization of the activities of the companies participating in the transaction, it may constitute the presumption that the latter has as its main objective or as one of the main objectives the

336 Thus, the Opinion of AG Jacobs presented in case: C-28/95, Leur-Bloem of 17 July 1997, ECLI:EU:C:1997:369, I-04161.

337 CJEU, C-28/95, Leur-Bloem of 17 July 1997, op. cit., Mrs Leur-Bloem, in the context of a merger by shares, ceded her shares, as a sole shareholder of two companies, to a third-party company. In doing so, it made it possible to compensate for losses between the two companies. The question, raised by a Dutch judge, concerned the interpretation of the condition of bringing together, from a financial and economic point of view, the business activity of the two companies in one and the same and of art. 11, n. 1, lett. a), member states must grant the tax benefits provided for by the Directive in the case of share exchange operations pursuant to art. 2, lett. d), unless these transactions have as their main objective or as one of the main objectives, fraud or tax evasion. In particular, CJEU clearly states that member states may provide that the absence of valid economic reasons for the operation legitimizes a presumption to that effect. For further details see: A. BARAV, Judicial of enforcement and implementation of European Union law, ed. Bruylant, Bruxelles, 2017.

338 D. LIAKOPOULOS, A comparative analysis of EU and US transnational mergers regulation, op. cit.

tax fraud or evasion"[339]. The same art. 11, however, does not regulate any form of verification of fraud or tax evasion.

CJEU has been able to comment on the scope of this clause already a few years after the entry into force of the Directive in the sentence of the C-28/95, Leur-Bloem case of 17 July 1997. Recalled first of all is how, from the combined disposed of art. 2, lett. d) and h), entity, condition added by the Netherlands legislator, upon the transposition, to the definition resulting from the Directive of the "mergers by exchange of shares" (article 2, letter d). This condition had been inserted precisely in order to exclude, as permitted by art. 11 of the Directive, from the granting of tax concessions provided for by the Directive, operations that primarily had for objective fraud or tax evasion.

However, to ascertain whether the operation to be carried out has such an objective, the competent national authorities cannot confine themselves to applying predetermined general criteria, but must in each case carry out an overall examination of the operation, which must to be subject to judicial review[340].

Having noted the absence of more precise European Union provisions on the matter, CJEU then provides a series of indications. From these, it is recalled that, if it is for states to prepare the internal procedures necessary for this purpose, while respecting the principle of proportionality, "a rule of general scope which automatically excludes certain categories of transactions from tax relief (...) regardless the existence of effective tax evasion or fraud, would exceed what is necessary to avoid such tax fraud or evasion and would undermine the objective pursued by the Directive"[341].

In any case, in responding to the second question by the referring court, CJEU concludes that "from the formulation and objectives of art. 11, as from those of the Directive, it appears that the notion of valid economic reasons transcends the mere search for a purely fiscal facilitation. Therefore, a merger by exchange of shares solely for the purpose of achieving that objective cannot constitute a valid economic reason within the meaning of that article (...)"[342].

---

339 CJEU, C-28/95, Leur-Bloem of 17 July 1997, op. cit.

340 P. DEROUIN, Fiscalité des fusions de sociétés et échanges d'actions, in Droit Fiscal, 46, 1997, pp. 1100ss. F. HOENJET, The Leur-Bloem judgement: the jurisdiction of the European CJEU and the interpretation of the anti-abuse clause in the Merger Directive, in EC Tax Review, 6, 1997, pp. 206ss.

341 F. HOENJET, The Leur-Bloem judgement: the jurisdiction of the European CJEU and the interpretation of the anti-abuse clause in the Merger Directive, op. cit.

342 F. HOENJET, The Leur-Bloem judgement: the jurisdiction of the European CJEU and the interpretation of the anti-abuse clause in the Merger Directive, op. cit.

THE DISTINCTION BETWEEN RESTRICTIVE INTERPRETATION OF THE SCOPE OF THE DIRECTIVE AND PROHIBITION OF ABUSE OF LAW IN THE CONCLUSIONS OF THE ADVOCATE GENERAL KOKOTT

The C-321/05, Kofoed v. Skateministeriet sentence of 5 July 2007 should not be understood as a mere confirmation of a more recent setting, although there are some contact aspects. On the contrary, it presents profiles of indisputable novelty, also in relation to the changed context in which it is related to the evolution of the doctrine of the abuse of law, which deserve to be underlined.

The case concerned the tax treatment to be applied, according to EU legislation, to a distribution of profits carried out in close connection with a cross-border exchange of company shares realized immediately before. Two Danish nationals had contributed their units in a Danish to an Irish company, in exchange for shares in the latter. A few days later, the Irish company, as already planned, had made a distribution of profits to the two Danish taxable persons. The problem that arose was whether the Directive 90/434/EEC could apply to the transaction, which, among other things, provided that, if the assignment was accompanied by a cash balance, the latter could not exceed 10% of the nominal value of the securities for the exchange to benefit from the exemption[343].

In fact, in the tax return, the subjects assigned to the shares assumed that the exchange of shares should be exempt from tax[344]. On the contrary, the national authorities argued that the aforementioned exchange could not benefit from the exemption, since the distribution of the dividends which took place soon after, the amount of which exceeded the 10% ceiling, had to be considered as part of the exchange transaction.

First of all, the question arose of understanding whether distribution could be considered a cash balance. Also, in this case, as in C-255/02, Halifax and others case of 21 February 2006, there was the alternative between a given

343 D. LIAKOPOULOS, A comparative analysis of EU and US transnational mergers regulation, op. cit.

344 Former art. 8, lett. 1 and 4, "the assignment, during a merger, demerger or exchange of shares, of securities representing the share capital of the company receiving or acquiring to a shareholder of the transferring or purchased company, in exchange for securities representing the share capital of the latter company must not in itself imply any taxation on the income, profits or capital gains of this shareholder. Paragraphs 1, 2 and 3 do not preclude the holding of the cash balance that may have been paid on the occasion of the merger, the demerger or the exchange of shares for the taxation of the shareholder".

interpretation of the Directive, aimed at excluding from its field of application the abusive case, and the use of prohibition of abuse of law.

With regard to this aspect the conclusions of the AG Kokott are very clear, where it is emphasized that, in its practical effects, the case goes far beyond the mere clarification of the concept of a cash balance. "Indeed, the interpretation of that concept ultimately gives rise to another question, namely how the applicable law of the Union allows national authorities to take into account a possible intention to evade tax on the occasion of restructuring of joint-stock companies"[345].

Therefore, it confirms the assumption that, in order to react adequately to a possible tax evasion, two solutions can be assumed in the context of Directive 90/434/EEC: "the first consists in a relatively broad interpretation of the concept of balance in cash pursuant to art. 2, lett. d), of Directive 90/434/EEC; the second in the use of the possibility, recognized by art. 11, n. 1, lett. a) of the aforementioned Directive, to refuse, in whole or in part, the application to a specific case of the tax benefits envisaged or to revoke the benefit"[346]. The AG dismisses the first option, believing that, on the one hand, the need to protect the financial interests of member states concerned against fraud or tax evasion has already been taken into account by the EU legislator, who, precisely at this purpose, has inserted a special rule in the Directive, art. 11. On the other hand, a general extension of the concept of a cash balance would go beyond what is necessary to counter tax fraud and evasion, while at the same time jeopardizing the necessary predictability of the common tax scheme for the undertakings concerned.

In making such a choice between the two proposed solutions, a choice subsequently endorsed by CJEU, the conclusions also highlight another interesting element of differentiation between the interpretation of rules and the doctrine of abuse, as a means of reacting the order before abusive or fraudulent transactions.

Taking into consideration the C-28/95, Leur-Bloem sentence of 17 July 1997, the AG notes, in fact, that "the possible reasons for the transaction from time to time in question must not already affect the interpretation of the concept of a

345 Opinion of AG Kokott presented on C-321/05, Kofoed v. Skateministeriet of 8 February 2007, ECLI:EU:C:2007:86, I-05795, par. 41.

346 Par. 42. Also, the final note of the AG is interesting: "The preference given by the Danish authorities to the first of these two alternatives is not least due to the fact that at the time of the facts, Danish law did not contain any specific provision of transposition of art. 11 Directive 90/434/EEC (...)".

cash balance as such, but can only come to the fore when checking for possible abuses in the individual case, pursuant to art. 11 of Directive 90/434/EEC (...)"[347].

The reasoning can be so developed: to state that the reasons why the private individual performs a specific action are not in themselves relevant when interpreting the rule, means to say that the same reasons should not be taken into account to define which actions fall within the scope of the standard. Hence, the short passage to state that the reasons do not even influence the definition of the purpose of the standard.

Only when the objective of the provision is not reached, then can an investigation be made about the intention, based on objective elements, as specified in C-255/02, Halifax and others case of 21 February 2006.

This is in fact a conclusion which appears to be in line with what CJEU has already affirmed with regard to the common agricultural policy and thus confirms the permeability of one sector to another of the "community" concept of abuse. Indeed, when the AG Kokott refers to the prohibition of abuse, understood as an instrument attributed by the legal system to react to abusive behavior, here explained in an anti-abuse clause, which nevertheless expresses the principle already recognized by CJEU's jurisprudence, faces immediately the theme of the reasons. In fact, he points out that the mere fact of taking advantage of the opportunities offered by EU law, in this case, by Directive 90/434/EEC, cannot in itself justify the suspicion of an abuse. However, this does not apply if one of the main objectives of the transaction is fraud or tax evasion, the typical example of which is the absence of valid economic reasons justifying the transaction in question.

This is exactly what happens, according to the AG, in the case submitted to its examination: from the factual findings made by the national court it appears, in fact, that there was no specific commercial reason for the exchange of quotas, aimed rather at a saving tax. Moreover, the extreme temporal proximity between the distribution of profits and the exchange made, moreover, may suggest an abuse of the opportunities offered by Directive 90/434/EEC. The same can be said with reference to the fact that the participants in the operation had acted knowing the imminent amendment of the Danish-Irish double taxation convention.

347 D. LIAKOPOULOS, A comparative analysis of EU and US transnational mergers regulation, op. cit.

DEFINITION OF PROHIBITION OF ABUSE OF LAW AS A GENERAL PRINCIPLE OF "UNION" LAW IN THE PRONUNCIATION OF CJEU: LIGHTS AND SHADOWS

If the conclusions by the AG assume a certain importance for having clearly highlighted the alternative between restrictive interpretation and abuse doctrine, both techniques to combat the abusive behavior of private individuals, but with well clarified differentiating elements, CJEU ruling, more concise on point[348], deserves further study in other aspects.

Already in C-255/02, Halifax and others case of 21 February 2006, CJEU referred to a "principle of prohibition of abusive behavior", but here, for the first time, the prohibition of abuse of rights is defined as a general principle of Union law[349]. More in detail, CJEU states that "article 11 (1) (a) of Directive 90/434/EEC reflects the general principle of Union law, according to which (...) individuals cannot use fraudulently or abusively the rules of EU law. The application of the latter cannot be extended to include abusive practices, i.e. transactions carried out not in the context of normal commercial transactions, but solely for the purpose of unlawfully benefiting from the advantages provided for by community law (...)"[350].

This statement, which at first sight seems to constitute a formal consecration of the existence of a general principle of EU law that prohibits the abuse of law, presents profiles of problems that must be taken into account before reaching

348 The CJEU clarifies, in paragraphs 33 and 34, that the dividend "cannot be included in the calculation of the cash balance", lacking any indication that such dividend is an integral part of the counter party to be paid for the acquisition of shares, and that "therefore, the exchange of the shares in question falls within the scope of article 8, n. 1, of Directive 90/434/EEC, which implies that its taxation is, in principle, prohibited".

349 R. DE LA FERIA, Prohibition of abuse of (European Union law), op. cit., pp. 433, it is noted that EU judge refers specifically to two precedents. In particular, Halifax, a case of abuse of EU law, and Cadbury Schweppes, a case of circumvention of national legislation, thus marking a line of continuity that could constitute the confirmation of the new unitary approach to the abuse of tax law. Consider, however, that, as will be shown below, chap. III, the citation by CJEU of previous jurisprudence in other areas is often nothing but an empty formula. The affirmation does not correspond, in fact, to its application.

350 Par. 38. At the same conclusion, even without specifying the general nature of the principle, AG Kokott had arrived at par. 57, where he stated "that provision (art. 11 (1) (a)) expresses in depth what is also recognized by the constant jurisprudence. It is not allowed to make fraudulent or abusive use of EU law. The application of EU legislation cannot, in fact, be extended to include the abusive behavior of economic operators, that is to say transactions carried out not in the context of normal commercial transactions, but solely for the purpose of illegally benefiting from the advantages provided for by EU law (...)".

an affirmative conclusion in on the generality of the ban. The present case, in fact, presented a not inconsiderable peculiarity, consisting in the fact that the Danish legislation applicable at the time of the facts of the case, did not contain a specific provision for the transposition of art. 11, n. 1,). Therefore, the problem arose of understanding whether the anti-abuse clause could still operate even in the absence of transposition.

CJEU recalled that the principle of legal certainty precludes directives from being able, independently of a national transposition law, to create obligations on the part of individuals and that therefore they cannot be relied on as such as by the member state against individuals. Thus, CJEU resolves the question by stating that "it is however recognized that the state can, in principle, impose a consistent interpretation of the national law against individuals"[351]. It is therefore up to the national court to examine whether there is a provision or a general principle in Danish law on the basis of which the abuse of right is prohibited or whether there are other provisions on fraud or tax evasion which can be interpreted in accordance with article 11, n. 1, lett. a) of Directive 90/434/EEC.

CJEU, even admitting that the anti-abuse clause contained in art. 11 reflects a general principle that prohibits the abuse of law, does not recognize the latter self-executing[352] character of the general principles of law, circumstantially. This was invoked by the doctrine in support of the fact that the consecration of CJEU

351 L. CERIONI, The "abuse of rights" in EU company law and EU tax law. A re-reading of ECJ case law and the quest for a unitary notion, op. cit., pp. 809ss, notes that CJEU's reference to the general principle of abuse of law in Kofoed would not contradict the fact that it considers a national anti-abuse provision to be necessary since, in the case of Mergers Directive, the financial interests to be safeguarded directly are the interests of member states, rather than of EU. The final choice of whether and how to safeguard its financial interests, which is then left to member state, which can decide whether the introduction of national anti-abuse provisions is the most appropriate means to protect these interests.

352 A. ARNULL, What is a general principle of EU law?, in R. DE LA FERIA, S. VOGENAUER, Prohibition of abuse of law: a new general principle of EU law?, op. cit., p. 20, in support of his thesis points out that CJEU thus diverged from the previous case: C-144/04, Mangold of 22 November 2005, ECLI:EU:C:2005:709, I-09981, in which, as is known, it had established that the prohibition of discrimination on the grounds of age was a general principle of unwritten law and therefore endowed with a full horizontal direct effect. The author then notes that the decision in question was taken from the first and not from the large section and that the language used in case: C-321/05, Kofoed v. Skateministeriet of 5 July 2007 is certainly more equivocal than the one used in Mangold, which left no doubt about the elaboration in that of a new general principle. It would seem, however, that the recognition by CJEU in large sections, although it may constitute a strengthening, is not a necessary condition for the emergence of a general principle.

was, in reality, more formal than revolutionary from a substantial point of view, as at first sight it could appear[353].

Starting from the observation that CJEU has certainly proved to be prudent in attributing a direct effect to the prohibition of abuse in the present case[354], a clearer indication of the reasons for such an approach can be found in the conclusions of the AG Kokott[355]. Indeed, it is stated that the national authorities "could not directly invoke a possible general principle of already existing Union law against the individual, which prohibits the abuse of law, as, in relation to cases falling within the scope of Directive 90/434/EEC, such a principle has already found specific expression and realization in art. 11, n. 1, lett. a) of the Directive"[356]. In fact, if, next to the possibility of appeal to art. 11, n. 1, lett. a) "it would also allow direct recourse to a general principle of law with decidedly less clear and precise content, there would be a risk of frustrating the harmonization objective of Directive 90/434/EEC and of undermining the legal certainty it pursues the restructuring of limited companies"[357].

The AG, and with it CJEU, although in a less explicit manner, privileges in this way the principle of legal certainty, also referring, in a note, to the "situation of confusion and uncertainty created by the former Mangold case strongly criticized by the commentators and by legal operators"[358].

---

353 Contra T. TRIDIMAS, Abuse of Right in EU law, op. cit., pp. 11-12, underlines how Kofoed and Mangold are distinguished in many ways. Firstly, while in Mangold it was a private dispute, in Kofoed, on the other hand, a state authority was involved in enforcing a directive against an individual. Secondly, Mangold (C-144/04, Mangold of 22 November 2005) was concerned with equal treatment, a fundamental constitutional principle receptive to a dynamic interpretation, while Kofoed concerned the abuse of law, a principle of an exceptional and defensive nature, which limits the rights of individuals. This last point would explain why CJEU was more prudent in attributing to the prohibition of abuse in the present case a direct effect which would not only have clashed with legal certainty but would also have been resolved in imposing an obligation for the individual. The same statement is found it in A. ZALASINSKI, Some basic aspects of the concept of abuse in the tax case law of the European Court of Justice, op. cit., pp. 573-574: "Bearing in mind that anti-avoidance clauses do not grant rights to individuals but, conversely, permit tax authorities to restrict the rights granted in other provisions of directives, it appears to be evident that these clauses do not have direct effect (...)".

354 D. CHALMERS, G. DAVIES, G. MONTI, European Union law, Cambridge University Press, Cambridge, 2014.

355 T. TRIDIMAS, Abuse of Right in EU law, op. cit.

356 D. CHALMERS, G. DAVIES, G. MONTI, European Union law, op. cit.

357 D. LIAKOPOULOS, A comparative analysis of EU and US transnational mergers regulation, op. cit. D. CHALMERS, G. DAVIES, G. MONTI, European Union law, op. cit.

358 D. CHALMERS, G. DAVIES, G. MONTI, European Union law, op. cit.

The point that we want to highlight here is another one. The AG seems to suggest, in fact, that the introduction of an anti-abuse clause excludes the possibility of invoking from scratch a general principle of abuse of jurisprudential law. As we will see, this is a reasoning also taken with regard to Directive 2004/38/EC[359] and art. 35 contained therein. In fact, by referring to the gap-filling function attributed to a general ban, it seems acceptable that, when a legal text has established an alternative system with the capacity to prevent abusive practices, also taking into account the principles of certainty law and effectiveness, the general prohibition cannot operate[360]. To conclude on this point, it should therefore be stated that the general principle in question is not applied when the problem of abuse is regulated in the same and exhaustive manner by specific rules.

It should be noted, however, that CJEU, dealing with a case in which a national anti-abuse transposition law was also lacking in more recent times, has accepted a wider interpretation option. In the judgment of the C-131/13, C-163/13 and C-164/13, Schoenimport "Italmoda" Mariano Previti of 18 September 2014 joined causes dealing with some fraudulent transactions in the field of VAT, the Union judge has stated in an innovative way that even if it were established that, in this case, national law does not include rules which can be interpreted in accordance with the criteria of EU law in the fight against tax evasion; "however, it could be inferred that national authorities and courts are prevented from (...) denying the advantage deriving from a right provided for by the sixth Directive in the event of fraud"[361]. In fact, the denial of the benefit of a right complies with the principle that no one can use fraudulently or abusively the rules of EU law,

359 See in argument: T. SZABADOS, National courts in the frontline. Abuse of rights under the citizens rights directive, in Utrecht Journal of International and European Law, 33, 2017, pp. 89ss.

360 CJEU, joined cases, C-131/13, C-163/13 and C-164/13, Schoenimport "Italmoda" Mariano Previti of 18 September 2014, ECLI:E:C:2014:2455, published in the electronic Reports of the cases. The Dutch tax authorities, considering that Italmoda had consciously participated in a fraud designed to evade VAT in Italy, denied the right to exemption for intra-European Union supplies made in that member state, the right to deduct the tax paid to upstream, as well as the right to reimbursement of the tax paid for goods coming from Germany.

361 Par. 56-57. In paragraph 58, CJEU concludes that "it is rather, in that case, that it is impossible for the taxable person to make use of a right provided for by the Sixth Directive, of which the objective criteria for granting are not met owing to either fraud concerning the transaction carried out by the same taxable person, or the fraudulent nature of a chain of transactions considered as a whole, to which he participated, as explained in paragraph 50 of this judgment (...)".

the application of which cannot be extended to include abusive or fraudulent practices[362].

Thus, by ruling, CJEU admits, in essence, the possibility for the member state to invoke the prohibition of abuse even in the absence of a national anti-abuse legislation transposing the corresponding clause contained in the text of secondary legislation. On the basis of the reasoning that, since the abusive or fraudulent facts cannot establish a right under the Union legal order, the refusal of an advantage envisaged in the present case by the sixth Directive is not equivalent to imposing an obligation to charge the individual concerned by virtue of this Directive. However, it is nothing more than the mere consequence of the finding that the objective conditions required for the purpose of obtaining the advantage to be achieved, provided for by that Directive in relation to said right, do not they are, in fact, satisfied[363].

It, therefore, seems that the member state can still apply the general prohibition, regardless of the internal transposition of an anti-abuse clause, even if cannot be excluded the opening of CJEU is dictated by the different configuration of the relevant legislation. Indeed, while in joined cases: C-321/05, Kofoed v. Skateministeriet case of 5 July 2007 discussed the failure to transpose a specific anti-abuse clause, in the judgment of the C-131/13, C-163/13 and C-164/13,

362 T. TRIDIMAS, Abuse of Right in EU law, op. cit.

363 The case: C-321/05, Kofoed v. Skateministeriet of 5 July 2007 was the first and most famous statement of the general character of prohibition abuse, but not the last. The same explanation, in fact, is found in the most recent sentence: C-126/10, Foggia-SGPS of 10 November 2011, ECLI:EU:C:2011:728, I-10923. CJEU recalls, in fact, citing the previous C-212/97, Centros of 9 March 1999 Halifax and Kofoed, that " art. 11, n. 1, lett. a) Directive 90/434/EEC reflects the general principle of Union law according to which the abuse of right is prohibited (...)"(par. 50), thus confirming its propensity for the assertion of prohibition of abuse as a new EU general principle, at least when it is understood as an abuse of EU law. The case is also relevant from another point of view, given that it gave CJEU the opportunity to once again rule on the notion of "valid economic reasons", the absence of which may suggest the existence of a principal objective of fraud or tax evasion, also highlighting the distinction with the legitimate tax advantage. CJEU underlines, in fact, how the restructuring or rationalization of a group, carried out in order to reduce administrative and management costs, which have become unsustainable for the continuation of economic activity, which consequently makes it possible to reduce the tax burden, it cannot be considered an abusive practice, but constitutes a valid economic reason that legitimizes the operation in question, thus excluding a possible legal redevelopment in terms of abusive practice. A merger can therefore constitute a valid economic reason based on several objectives, among which tax considerations may also be included, provided that the latter are not preponderant in the context of the planned transaction. On the other hand, "it may constitute a presumption that such transaction was not carried out for" valid economic reasons "within the meaning of this provision the fact that, at the time of the merger transaction, the company does not exercise any business, does not hold any interest and only transfers to the acquiring company only tax losses of a high amount and of undetermined origin, even if this operation has a positive effect in terms of the economy of structural costs for that group (...)" (par. 52).

Schoenimport "Italmoda" Mariano Previti of 18 September 2014, the objective, recognized by the sixth VAT Directive, of the fight against tax evasion, tax avoidance and possible abuses was more generally upheld. So much so that the Dutch government had insisted that there were no gaps in Dutch law concerning the transposition of the sixth Directive.

In any case, for our purposes, the sentence in C-321/05, Kofoed v. Skatteministeriet case of 5 July 2007 deserves to be remembered precisely because it constitutes the first occasion in which CJEU recognized the prohibition of abuse as a general principle. On the other hand, it shows that, even in the field of direct taxation, the notion of abuse used by the legislator and then interpreted by CJEU, through cross referrals to judgments rendered in other areas, is the same as the abuse test as specified in C -255/02, Halifax and others case of 21 February 2006. In particular, it emerges in this context the centrality of the absence of valid economic reasons that justify the operation, intended as an objective element of proof that one of the main objectives of the transaction is to from fraud or tax evasion.

SOME THOUGHTS AND SHORT OBSERVATIONS

The examination of the jurisprudence of CJEU on the abuse of law in harmonized sectors, such as that of CAP, VAT and corporate restructuring, corroborates the assumption from which we started in the introduction to the Chapter. In fact, the existence of a consolidated jurisprudence that recognizes and applies the prohibition of abuse of law is confirmed, where the abuse is realized by creating an artificial situation for the sole purpose of formally meeting the conditions laid down by EU legislation and, in in this way, to benefit from the related advantages, involving only the supranational order.

Going further, it can be said that in this context there has certainly been an evolution of the jurisprudence of CJEU, which has gradually refined and clarified the concept of abuse of rights, through the co-publication of a general test[364].

What must be emphasized in this regard is how CJEU not only mentioned in principle the prohibition in question, but at the same time admitted the possibility for the national court to apply it to the case under consideration, in the event of circumstances very precise and very often predetermined and verified in the

364 T. TRIDIMAS, Abuse of Right in EU law, op. cit.

concrete case by CJEU itself. In this regard, on the basis of the overall picture just outlined above, the conditions under which the prohibition in question may operate may first be recalled.

Already in the cases of the early 1980s, concerning the accession compensatory amounts and export refunds, the Luxembourg court, in dealing with artificial operations of export and importation, carried out for the sole purpose of formally meeting the conditions imposed by the Union legislation and in this way to benefit from the related financial advantages, while not yet using the technique of the prohibition of abuse, had denied the exporters the right to obtain payment of the amounts requested. This, by enhancing the contrast of non-actual operations with the aims of the legislation allocating aid, as well as the intention to make an unfair profit from the technical defects of the aid system.

These indications were then incorporated into a broader test, which requires the national court to double check: that the objective of the law was not achieved and that the private individual wanted to obtain an advantage deriving from European Union legislation, by creating artificiality of the conditions necessary for obtaining it. The verification of a question of law is therefore required, that is to say if the purpose of the legislation would be frustrated if the right was granted; and of a quaestio facti, that is, if the right derives from the carrying out of a non-artificial economic activity[365].

As we have seen, the subjective one proved to be the most problematic element, even only in terms of proof, so as to require some clarifications over time. In particular, it seems that CJEU has valued, rather than the aspect of the subjective will to obtain an advantage, that of "artificial creation", as an index of this will, thus arriving at what is defined as an objectification of the element in question. Already in C-110/99, Emsland-Stärke of 14 December 2000 and later. For example, in C-434/12, Slancheva sila EOOD v. Izpalnitelen direktor na Darzhaven founded "Zemedelie" Razplashtatelna agentsia of 12 September 2013, CJEU had specified that evidence of the presence of such an element could be given, in particular, demonstrating a collusion between the exporter of the Union, beneficiary of the refunds, and the importer of the goods in the third country.

In C-255/02, Halifax and others case of 21 February 2006, it was finally clarified how the intent of the parties to obtain an undue benefit from the Union's order can be inferred from the absence of a justification economic and

365 P. PIANTAVIGNA, Tax abuse in European Union law, op. cit., pp. 143ss.

commercial, to be judged in the light of a series of objective circumstances[366]. The proof of the artificiality thus entails an investigation into the economic rationality of the operation. To define artificiality as an absence of economic rationality is also necessary to avoid a common misunderstanding, which assimilates the artificiality to the absence of economic reality[367].

However, bearing in mind that the element of artificiality has been expressed differently in the numerous rulings of CJEU, it can be said that, in practice, an operation lacks economic rationality, when it involves costs that could otherwise be avoided. This is clear from the comparison of the transactions carried out respectively in cases: C-110/99, Emsland-Stärke of 14 December 2000 and C-515/03, Eichsfelder Schlachtbetrieb GmbH v. Hauptzollamt Hamburg-Jonas of 23 July 2005, in which CJEU ratified the cross-border operation, highlighting the fact that a substantial modification of the asset had taken place[368].

If in the first cases relating to CAP[369], CJEU, preferably, referred to the uniqueness of the purpose of obtaining benefits from the Union legislation by using pure construction, the rulings given in the field of VAT, allowed CJEU to take a position on the point. It stated in C-425/06, Part Service case of 21 February 2008 that, in practice, an illegal tax reason and an economic-business reason can coexist, but tax savings must prove to be the ultimate motivation which

366 F. VANISTENDAEL, Halifax and Cadbury Schweppes: One single European theory of abuse in tax law?, op. cit., pp. 195ss.

367 Linked but distinct problematic aspect appears to be the configuration of the subjective element on which CJEU has also focused. That is to say the alternative between the essentiality or the uniqueness of the abusive purpose which must animate the private. From the beginning it became clear that the intention to obtain advantages from a rule could not be considered reprehensible in itself, since it is perfectly legitimate to try to plan one's own business in the light of the applicable law. Nevertheless, since actions are usually carried out by more than one purpose, the problem has been posed to determine the boundary between use and abuse by interpreting each time the adjectives "unique", "principal", "essential" that they accompany the purpose.

368 A. SAYDÉ, Defining the concept of abuse of Union law, in Yearbook of European Law, 33, 2014, pp. 149ss.

369 The exact delimitation of test's subjective element assumes considerable importance, bearing in mind that it constitutes the cornerstone of the differentiation between the prohibition of abuse of law and the different technique of protection of the Union system. As highlighted by AG Poiares Maduro in case: C-255/02, Halifax and others of 21 February 2006, in the presence of a text of secondary law (id est in a harmonized sector), CJEU, in order to counter the fraudulent or abusive behavior of private individuals, has the possibility to opt for the restrictive interpretation of the field of application of Union law, as for the use of prohibition on the abuse of the right, where it considers upstream the applicable EU legislation that attaches the right. Similar reasoning has been brought forward by AG Kokott in the case: C-321/05, Kofoed v. Skateministeriet of 5 July 2007.

determined the choice of the subject in completing a transaction in particular ways, the overall purpose of the activity carried out.

Also, in C-155/13, Società Italiana Commercio and Servizi srl (SICES) and others v. The Customs Office of the Customs Office of Venice case of 13 May 2014, moreover, has been highlighted as the essentiality of the purpose of benefiting from the subsidy, which is linked on the objective level to the absence of economic justification of the operations, allows to affirm the existence of an abuse. In this regard, it should be noted that the two plans that of the prohibition and that of interpretation do not prove to be perfectly coinciding. In order for the prohibition in question to apply, in fact not only does the fact not fall within the purpose of law, but there must also be a creation without economic justification, indicating the desire to obtain an abusive advantage. Thus, in C-515/03, Eichsfelder Schlachtbetrieb GmbH v. Hauptzollamt Hamburg-Jonas case of 23 July 2005, the existence of an abuse was excluded, since the artificiality was absent, the absence identified in the substantial and non-reversible transformation suffered by the products previously exported. Equally, in C-155/13, Società Italiana Commercio and Servizi srl (SICES) and others v. Customs Office of the Customs of Venice case of 13 May 2014 the real interest of importers not to be sanctioned, which showed the presence of an economic and commercial justification, was valued. The driving role of the subjective element in the construction of the prohibition must not be brought to the extreme consequences: it is worth remembering in this regard how the same is not sufficient in itself to prove the existence of an abuse of right. The pronunciation of the cases: C-277/09, RBS Deutschland Holdings GmbH of 22 December 2010 and C-103/09, The Commissioners for Her Majesty's Revenue & Customs, may be cited in this regard. Weald Leasing Ltd of 22 December 2010, where CJEU recalls that the preparation of devices aimed at obtaining the benefits deriving from the application of EU rules in accordance with the objectives of the same does not constitute abuse, thus demonstrating that it is always necessary, because the prohibition of abuse is applicable, a joint application of both criteria[370]. It can

370 Although some indications are already found in the cases under analysis, it is considered appropriate to postpone the examination of the effects deriving from the application of the prohibition on the abuse of right to previous paragraphs. It is only clear that CJEU, neither here nor elsewhere, seems to have firmly opted for the classification of prohibition as a rule that would allow delimiting the scope of application of Union law or as a rule limiting the exercise of a right conferred by Union law. For example, Cremer states that "the application of regulation in question, together with the commission Regulation no. 171/64, could not in any case be extended until you get back abusive practices of economic operators"; on the contrary, in Halifax (C-255/02, Halifax and others of 21 February 2006) it is specified that where there is evidence of abuse, the rule of law must be

therefore be concluded that the prohibition of the abuse of law as a technique of protection of the European Union's legal order is fully operational in areas where there is total or almost no harmonization and member states no longer retain the possibility to take anti-abuse measures, other than those authorized by the secondary legislation itself[371]. What needs to be highlighted is how the two-phase approach outlined above lends itself well to tracing the abusive operations described. It is, in fact, well able to distinguish the cases of real economic activity, from those of pipelines artificial resources aimed at obtaining undue advantages[372]. This proves to be a central aspect, since, as will be explained in previous paragraphs, CJEU shows instead of the difficulties in transposing the same two-phase approach, which verifies the subsistence before an objective element and then a subjective one, when it comes to verify the existence of the abuse involving more than one legal system.

---

interpreted, in spite of its letter, in the sense that it does not actually confer the right.

371 R. IONESCU, L'abus de droit en droit de l'Union européenne, in C. KESSEDJIAN, Autonomie en droit européen Stratégie des citoyens, des entreprises et des Etats, op. cit., pp. 221ss.

372 V. J. FREEDMAN, The anatomy of tax avoidance counteraction: Abuse of law in a tax context at member state and European Union level, in R. DE LA FERIA, S. VOGENAUER, Prohibition of abuse of law: a new general principle of EU law?, op. cit.

CHAPTER 3

Abuse of law involving multiple legal systems. Free circulation as a vehicle of abuse

Short introduction

As we have said, the abuse of law consists in a formally correct behavior, but implemented artificially, in order to derive an unfair advantage from the application of Union rules or another national system. If involving more than one system, this operation presupposes a "complex" choice in the private sector. It is now necessary to clarify that a triangulation between legal systems takes place when the private sector, avoiding the national provisions that would otherwise find application, invokes the freedom of movement to move to another legal system, either national or of the European Union.

In this case, the cross-border element assumes a determining scope, since the circumvention is achieved precisely through the invocation of the freedoms of movement. What can change is the order of belonging of the norm from which derives the advantage that the private individual aims to obtain through the artificial construction. From this point of view, it is useful to distinguish the cases in which the illegal construction is put into place in order to apply a more advantageous national law or a provision of EU law, in the presence of secondary legislation that attributes certain benefits. It should be noted that, in both cases, and beyond the legislation invoked in this case, the abusive construction consists in the use of freedom of movement to move from the country of origin to another, in order to obtain certain benefits. As we can see, two national regulations are involved (the starting and the arrival), as well as the EU system, which acts as a "vehicle". In this sense, the metaphor of the "flight" used by the doctrine well describes the phenomenon under examination[373].

373 The expression "flight into" was used from: S. VOGENAUER, The prohibition of abuse of law: An emerging general principle of EU law, in R. DE LA FERIA, S. VOGENAUER, Prohibition of abuse of law: a new general principle of EU law?, op. cit., pp. 526ss.

As a partially different construction, as we will see, it does not determine a differentiation in the contents of the solutions provided by the jurisprudence, is that in which there are only two systems involved. This happens when the private person invokes the rights that are attributed to him by the freedom of movement in a member state other than that of citizenship, in order to be able to apply the discipline of that state, without a specific intent elusive of the legislation of the state of origin.

It is therefore necessary to dwell on the jurisprudence of CJEU, which has dealt with the constructions described above. The hypothesis in which the subject seeks to obtain an advantage from another national system, and the one in the second section, in which the application of EU legislation to affect the private sector, are analyzed.

In this regard, it must be borne in mind that, as will be shown through the analysis of CJEU jurisprudence, in all these cases there is a close correlation between the invocation of the prohibition of abuse and the invocation of a "purely internal situation" on the part of member states. This is not surprising since the subject agent, in fact, aims first of all to artificially create an element of strangeness in order not to apply the national discipline. It is then necessary to ask whether the effects differ. As we shall see, if it is certain that the provisions of the Union ratione loci derive from the purely internal situation, in the presence of an abuse, it is not always clear whether the related prohibition hypothetically involves the denial of the right or the non-applicability of EU law.

Another affirmation of principle that must be kept in mind in the analysis of this jurisprudence is the following. CJEU, in deciding the causes in which the issue of abuse of freedom of movement was raised, freedoms that, at this juncture, constitute "channels of connection" between distinct national laws. While recognizing the abuse in principle, it tends not to apply the prohibition on the abuse of law, as elaborated in the context of abuse of EU law, for the reasons that will be outlined below. In particular, the examination of the most relevant rulings of CJEU shows that the reference to abuse by CJEU itself must often be considered improper: in other words, the affirmation of the principle is not equivalent to recognizing the use of prohibition. This does not mean that in all the cases that will be analyzed, an abusive behavior intended lato sensu must be excluded. On the contrary, the casuistry of pseudo-foreign corporations shows well how, from the point of view of the member state, there was an abuse[374]. In the following analysis, it will be necessary to pay particular attention to two elements: first, one cannot disregard a close comparison with the constituent elements of abuse of EU law; and second, it must be borne in mind that the reconstruction of the operation and its traceability takes place in a new and original context, that of several closely related arrangements. Moreover, the existence of a principle, which to a certain extent collides with the prohibition at issue, cannot be ignored in such a context. The case-law has in fact repeatedly stated without hesitation the legitimacy of the exercise of the rights to free movement, order to benefit from a more favorable legal regime in another member state. Since these decisions are functional to the internal market, obviously, the tension between legitimate choice and abuse of law lends itself to systematic considerations, which will be continued hereinafter

374 See in argument: A. CAHN, D.C. DONALD, Comparative company law: Text and cases on the laws governing corporations in Germany, the UK and the USA, Cambridge University Press, Cambridge, 2010, pp. 93ss.

PART A

Circumvention of the most stringent national legislation in order to apply the provisions of another national system

The case of primary plant in countries with more favorable legislation: the jurisprudential branch of the pseudo-foreign corporations

Freedom of movement constitutes the "vehicle" used by private individuals to move from one order to another. In particular, private individuals have the possibility of carrying out an abusive "U" operation, which enables them to apply the most favorable legislation of another member state, invoking both freedom of establishment[375] and to provide services. In the following paragraphs, the newly defined buildings will therefore be analyzed, focusing first on the abuse of secondary freedom of establishment, and then on the abuse of freedom to provide services.

In particular, the phenomenon of pseudo-foreign corporations can be summarized as follows. These are juridical persons who are constituted in an order considered, for various reasons[376], more favorable, and then operate exclusively in the member state of citizenship of the member or administrator of the society-organization endowed with a more severe discipline-by means of a main activity center, "disguised" as a branch. The head office, in this way, ends up being, in fact, a "phantom society", not carrying out any activity in the country

375 CJEU, C-504/16, Deister Holding of 20 December 2017, ECLI:EU:C:2017:1009, published in the electronic Reports of the cases.

376 The expression "flight into" used from S. VOGENAUER, The prohibition of abuse of law: An emerging general principle of EU law, in R. DE LA FERIA, S. VOGENAUER, Prohibition of abuse of law: A new general principle of EU law?, op. cit., pp. 526.

in which it is established. In this sense the artificiality profile of the whole operation is well understood[377].

C-212/97, Centros case of 9 March 1999[378] is certainly the one that best illustrates the position taken by the EU judge in this regard. Indeed, it can be said that this ruling marked a turning point in the recognition of commercial companies between member states, as well as indirectly on the relevant conflict rules. Precisely for this figure among the most cited and studied cases in doctrine[379].

However, the same problem had already been addressed by CJEU about ten years earlier in the less well-known C-79/85, Segers pronunciation of 10 July 1986[380], in which some analogous conclusions were reached. It is therefore necessary to move from this first ruling, keeping in mind how the dates show a not inconsiderable coincidence with respect to the first pronouncements made on CAP, and then dwell more in detail on the C-212/98, Centros case of 9 March 1999 and arrive at the most recent jurisprudence.

The analysis that follows does not want to describe the attitude of CJEU with regard to abuse of rights, but aims to highlight the gap between statute of principle and application of the principles themselves, showing how the same operation, considered abusive with the "lens" of the member state of origin, cannot in fact be qualified as such by the EU. And this for mainly structural reasons, as will be observed.

377 CJEU, C-89/17, Banger of 12 July 2018, ECLI:EU:C:2018:570, published in the electronic Reports of the cases.

378 In Segers case (C-79/85, Segers of 10 July 1986) the private individual considered that the Anglo-Saxon appellation favored the image; in the Centros and C-167/01, Inspire Art of 30 September 2003 cases (on which see below), on the other hand, the rules on minimum capital were considered to be more favorable.

379 P. CABRAL, P. CUNHA, "Presumed innocent": Companies and the exercise of the right of establishment under European Union law, in European Law Review, 25, 2000, pp. 158ss. L. CERIONI, The "abuse of rights" in EU company law and EU tax law. A re-reading of the ECJ case law and the quest for a unitary notion, op. cit., pp. 790ss. M. LAUTERFELD, Centros and the EC regulation on insolvency proceedings: The end of the real seat approach towards pseudo-foreign companies in german international company and insolvency law?, in European Business Law Review, 12, 2001, pp. 79ss. A. LOOIJENSTIJN-CLEARIE, Centros ltd, a complete U-turn in the right of establishment for companies?, in International and Comparative Law Quarterly, 49, 2000, pp. 636ss. J. P. OMAR, Centros, Überseering and beyond: A European recipe for corporate migration: Part 1, in International Company and Commercial Law Review, 15 (4), 2004, pp. 404ss.

380 CJEU, C-79/85, Segers of 10 July 1986, ECLI:EU:C:1986:308, I-02375. For further details see: Y. LOUSSOUARN, Le droit d'établissement des sociétés, in Revue Trimestrielle de Droit Européen, 27, 1990, pp. 229ss. N. TRAVERS, The right of establishment of companies which are economically inactive in their member State of registration, in Commercial Law Practitioner, June 1999, pp. 162ss.

THE ORIGINS: A FIRST AFFIRMATION OF THE RIGHT TO ESTABLISH THE MAIN OFFICE IN THE MEMBER STATE WITH THE MOST FAVORABLE LEGISLATION

With the ruling of C-79/85, Segers case of 10 July 1986, CJEU had the opportunity to rule on a typical case of pseudo-foreign corporation[381]. A citizen of Dutch nationality decided to set up a private company limited by shares in the United Kingdom, at the same time transforming the existing Dutch company into a subsidiary of the new British company, according to a mechanism by which, in practice, the Dutch company continued to carry out all the activities, while the UK registered office did not take place. According to the national legislation at the time, according to which only the national administrations could benefit from the national sickness insurance scheme, the Netherlands national authority consequently denied that social security benefits to Mr. Segers. It was therefore necessary to clarify whether such a refusal was compatible with the freedom of establishment. However, it was not a simple case of unequal treatment on grounds of nationality. In fact, the Dutch enforcement authority argued inter alia that the differentiation in question found its justification in preventing abuses and in the interest of the proper implementation of the Netherlands social security legislation[382].

Referring to what the EC sustained in this regard[383], the Luxembourg judge, as usual when it comes to verifying the existence of an unjustified restriction on fundamental freedoms, focuses on the exact delimitation of the right that is considered to be overused. This reasoning is also suited to the verification of the abuse, which, as is known, requires first of all a check on the exact consistency and the limits of the law that is taken into consideration. It thus recalls that "freedom of establishment includes, in accordance with art. 58 of the Treaty

381 A. CAHN, D.C. DONALD, Comparative company law: Text and cases on the laws governing corporations in Germany, the UK and the USA, op. cit.

382 First of all, on the basis of a defense frequently relied on member states, it argued that the provisions of the Treaty on the freedom of establishment and the provision of services did not apply to the case in point, by not prescribing the classification of companies constituted under the law of other member states to those established under Netherlands law. There was no difference in treatment since anyone would have been free, regardless of their nationality or place of establishment, to set up a company under Netherlands or foreign law.

383 See par. 10. Thus, the Dutch authority: "It should, in fact, be avoided that the directors choose the form of the company under foreign law only to avoid the restrictions imposed by the Dutch laws on the establishment of limited liability companies (...)".

(now article 54 TFEU), for companies established under the laws of a member state and having their registered office, central administration or principal place of business within the community, the right to their activity in another member state through an agency, branch"[384]. Therefore, "admitting that the member state of establishment can freely reserve a different treatment for the sole reason that the registered office of the company is located in another member state would deprive art. 58 (now article 54 TFEU)"[385].

CJEU then takes another step, noting that the content of the right as described cannot be affected by the fact that the company under English law manifestly does not carry out any commercial activity in the United Kingdom. Indeed, "article 58 (now article 54 TFEU), for the application of provisions relating to the right of establishment, requires only that companies be established under the laws of a member state and have their registered office, the administration central or central place of business within the community: if these conditions are fulfilled, the fact that the company carries on its business, through an agency, branch or subsidiary, only in another member state is irrelevant (...)"[386].

CJEU, therefore, welcomes a formalistic interpretation of art. 54 TFEU, without drilling the corporate veil, while at the same time creating a first recognition of the possibility for EU economic operators to choose the law regulating their commercial activity. This is indeed better explained in the conclusions of the Darmon AG, where it is stated that "a member state benefits from the elasticity of the British company law and makes use of an Anglo-Saxon company name, which in his view is more attractive to customers"[387]. Moreover, this situation is congruent with the purpose for which the freedom of establishment in the EEC Treaty was established: to promote the free movement of persons and, thereby, the establishment of a common market[388].

---

384 In argument see: CJEU, C-504/16, Deister Holding of 20 December 2017, ECLI:EU:C:2017:1009, published in the electronic Reports of the cases.

385 D.A.O. EDWARD, R. LANE, Edward and Lane on European Union law, Edward Elgar Publishers, Cheltenham, 2013. C. NOWAK, Europarecht nach Lissabon, ed. Nomos, Baden-Baden, 2011. D. CHALMERS, G. DAVIES, G. MONTI, European Union law, op. cit., J. TILLOTSON, N. FOSTER, Text, cases and materials on European Union law, Cavedish Publishing, New York, 2013.

386 T. OPPERMANN, C.D. CLASSEN, M. NETTESHEIM, Europarecht, C.H. Beck, München, 2016. R. SCHÜTZE, T. TRIDIMAS, Oxford principles of European Union Law, Oxford University Press, Oxford, 2018. C. BARNARD, S. PEERS, European Union law, op. cit., pp. 788ss.

387 R. SCHÜTZE, T. TRIDIMAS, Oxford principles of European Union Law, op. cit.

388 CJEU, C-265/16, VCAST of 29 November 2017, ECLI:EU:C:2017:913, published in the electronic Reports of the cases.

In replying then to the justification put forward by the Dutch state with regard to the need to prevent possible abuses, CJEU first refers to the derogations formally provided for in the Treaty, noting that "article 56 of the Treaty effectively allows, within certain limits, the application of a special regime for companies constituted under the law of another member state. Provided that this regime is justified on grounds of public policy, public security, or public health"[389], it is concluded that "although the fight against fraudulent practices may, under certain circumstances, justify unequal treatment, the refusal to pay sickness benefits to the director of a company established under the law of another member state cannot, however, constitute an adequate provision in this respect"[390].

In this way, CJEU seems to admit, purely hypothetically, that member states can counter the abuse of law with appropriate measures. Not only that, it does not specify what should be understood by the terms "certain circumstances" and "appropriate measures", but (note) reconnects this possibility of reaction to the derogations expressly provided for in the Treaty. From this point of view, the conclusions of AG Darmon come to the rescue again, which stresses that the mere possibility of fraud cannot justify a general restriction on the right of establishment of natural or legal persons. Although, it cannot be denied to the authorities the right to check, from time to time, whether the companies have been established, as expressly prescribed by the current art. 54 TFEU, pursuant to the provisions of the law. Similarly, the member state will be able to monitor their activities with regard to the requirements of public policy[391].

The AG and, more concisely, also CJEU seem, in other words, to admit two types of controls: one in which the national laws on the constitution have been complied with; and second in which the commercial activity is exercised in compliance with the limit of public order.

The grievance of national authority in relation to an alleged abuse, however, is not accepted by CJEU, which does not apply the prohibition. Although the reasoning on this point is not explicit, it can be considered, in light of the

389 A. CAHN, D.C. DONALD, Comparative company law: Text and cases on the laws governing corporations in Germany, the UK and the USA, op. cit.

390 CJEU, C-504/16, Deister Holding of 20 December 2017, op. cit.

391 T. CORTHAUT, EU ordre public, Kluwer Law International, The Hague, 2012. D. LIAKOPOULOS, European integration and its relation with the jurisprudence of European Court of Human Rights and private international law of European Union, in Homa Publica. Revista Internacional de Direitos Humanos e Impresa, 2 (2), 2018.

passages concerning the scope of the right of establishment, that, in this case, the objective element of the abuse, that is a behavior contrasting with the ratio of the norm, was absent. In this regard, it has been argued that CJEU in C-79/85, Segers case of 10 July 1986, has come to a paradoxical result because, on one hand, the exercise of the right of establishment implies by its very nature a genuine integration into the economy of the receiving state. On the other hand, according to this ruling, this same right does not seem to presuppose an effective economic link with the state of origin. This would lead to a logical inconsistency incompatible with the provisions of the Treaty, which provide for the possibility of a secondary establishment depending on the primary establishment in another state[392]. In response, we can for the moment anticipate how the problem actually derives from the need to ensure a coherence of EU's legal system, which incidentally touches the "traceability" of abuses by a third-party system compared to national ones. The invocation of prohibition of abuse of law and its contextual non-application: some notation on the C-212/97, Centros Ltd v. Erbevervs-og Selskabsstyrelsen sentence of 9 March 1999.

Already in C-79/85, Segers case of 10 July 1986, the characteristic traits of what will be established as the jurisprudence of C-212/97, Centros case of 9 March 1999. However, in the first case, it was highlighted restrictive national legislation of general scope and only incidentum tantum judges had pointed out how states could take appropriate measures to counter abuse and fraud, in C-212/97, Centros case of 9 March 1999, CJEU was called to rule on the legitimacy or otherwise of an individual restriction, thus addressing a hypothesis that in C-79/85, Segers case of 10 July 1986 was confined abstractly to the plane. The case is known. A limited liability company established in England by two Danish spouses, although never engaged in business in the member state of origin, requested the registration of a branch in Denmark in order to carry out all of its activities there. The registration, however, was refused by the competent administration, alleging that in that way the company aimed to circumvent the Danish legislation on the establishment of a rigorous society especially in terms of the minimum capital required for the purpose of the constitution by an abusive exercise of the right to secondary establishment[393]. The facts thus referred to a trivial case of pseudo-foreign corporation, so as to be, already at

392 L. CERIONI, The barriers to international mobility, op. cit., pp. 64ss.

393 CJEU, C.106/16, Polbub-Wykonawstwo of 25 October 2017, ECLI:EU:C:2017:804, published in the electronic Reports or the cases.

first sight, "singular contrast between the scope of the principles affirmed by CJEU and the mediocrity of the case before the national court"[394].

Despite not particularly noteworthy facts, the case has provided fundamental indications regarding the application of prohibition of abuse, as already noted in the conclusions of the AG La Pergola[395]. These, as well as the previous ones that have been recalled, have been accepted by CJEU without hesitation, demonstrating how the C-212/97, Centros case of 9 March 1999 represents in reality a further element of a jurisprudence partly already consolidated and shared[396].

First, it must be noted that the case in question takes on particular interest for our purposes where it clearly shows the close correlation between the abuse of rights and purely internal situations, which was already highlighted in the introduction. The national authority claimed, in fact, that the situation at issue was purely internal, which is why the provisions of the Treaty should not have been applied. Given the illegal purpose of the operation implemented by Danish nationals, to avoid the application of the Danish legislation on the setting up of limited liability companies, the establishment of a company in another member state could not have constituted an element of extraneousness relevant from the point of view of EU law[397].

CJEU replies to this first statement by noting that such a situation, on the contrary, falls within the scope of EU law, since it is not relevant in this regard that the company was established in the first member state solely for the purpose to settle in the second. In latter, it would carry out the essential, if not all, of its economic activities, as already stated in C-79/85, Segers sentence of 10 July 1986. The question of the applicability of the Treaty is, in fact, separate from the question of whether a member state can take measures to prevent abuse[398].

394 C. TIETJE, The status of international in the European legal order: the case of international Treaties and non-binding international instrument, in J. WOUTERS, A. NOLLKAEMPER, E. DE WET (eds.), The Europeanization of international law: The status of international law in the EU and its member state s, Cambridge University Press, Cambridge, 2008.

395 Opinion of AG La Pergola, presented on 16 July 1998, op. cit.

396 It should immediately be pointed out that in this judgment, as in many others that will be analyzed, the invocation by the member state of the prohibition of abuse of right is accompanied by the invocation of overriding reasons of public interest, as in the case of species, the need to protect creditors and to fight fraudulent bankruptcy. These are issues that will not be analyzed here, but hereinafter, where we will be able to reason on the other techniques used by EU's legal system to limit the abuse.

397 A. HATJE, J.P. TERHECHTE, P.C. MÜLLER-GRAFF, Europarechtswissenschaft, ed. Nomos, Baden-Baden, 2018.

398 CJEU, C-123/11, A Oy of 21 February 2013, ECLI:EU:C:2013:84, published in the electronic Reports

Only after having clarified this aspect does the EU judge address the issue of abuse which, according to the Danish authorities, would make it impossible for the spouses to avail themselves of the right of establishment. The choice of such an order to deal with the matters implies the considered diversity of the effects of the abuse: not the non-application of EU law, but the possibility for the member state to invoke its derogability. Indeed, CJEU recognizes in principle that "a member state has the right to take measures to prevent, thanks to the possibilities offered by the Treaty, some of its citizens trying to escape the empire of national laws, and that those concerned cannot abusing or fraudulently engaging in Union law (...) national courts may take account, on the basis of objective factors, of the abusive or fraudulent behavior of the person concerned in order to deny him the possibility of benefiting from the provisions of community law invoked"[399]. However, when assessing such behavior, it must take account of the objectives pursued by the European provisions which are the subject of abuse[400].

To the affirmation of the principle, however, it does not follow, as already in C-79/85, Segers of 10 July 1986 the application of the same to the case in speciem. CJEU, in fact, takes care to underline that "the national provisions of which the parties try to avoid the application are rules relating to the establishment of companies and not rules concerning the exercise of certain professional activities"[401]. It is noted that the purpose of the first is precisely that of allowing companies established in accordance with the legislation of a member state, having their registered office, central administration or their main establishment within the European Union, to carry out activities in the other member states through an agency, branch or affiliate. This means that "the fact that a citizen of a member state wishing to set up a company chooses to set it up in the member state whose company law rules seem less stringent and creates branches in other

---

of the cases, par. 27.

399 A. KACZOROWSKA-IRELAND, European Union Law, ed. Routledge, London & New York, 2016.

400 CJEU, C-33/74, Van Binsbergen v. Bestuur van de Bedrijfsvereniging voor de Metaalnijverheid of 3 December 1974, op. cit., C-148/91, Veronica Omroep Organisatie v. Commissariaat voor de Media of 3 February 1993, op. cit.On the matter of freedom of establishment, judgments C-115/78, Knoors v. Staatssecretaris van Economische Zaken of 7 February 1979, op. cit .; C-61/89, Bouchoucha of 3 October 1990, op. cit., On the subject of free movement of goods, houses C-229/83, Leclerc/Au blè vert and others of 10 January 1985, ECLI:EU:C:1985:1, ECR 00001; in the field of social security, C-206/94, Brennet AG v. V. Paletta of 2 May 1996, op. cit. on the free movement of workers, C-39/86, Lair v. Universität Hannover of 21 June 1988, op. cit. on the common agricultural policy, C-8/92, General Milk Products v. Hauptzollamt Hamburg-Jonas of 3 March 1993, op. cit. in the field of company law, C-367/96, Kefalas and others of 12 May 1998, op. cit., par. 24-25.

401 CJEU, C-367/96, Kefalas and others of 12 May 1998, op. cit.

member states cannot in itself constitute an abuse of the right of establishment. The right to set up a company in accordance with the law of a member state and to establish branches in other member states is inherent in the exercise, within the framework of a single market, of the freedom of establishment guaranteed by the Treaty"[402]. This is also true when, as already stated in C-79/85, Segers case of 10 July 1986, the company does not carry out any activity in the member state in which it has its headquarters and instead performs all its activities only in the member state of its branch.

Nor can it point out, in the opinion of CJEU, the fact that company law is not completely harmonized in the Union, "also taking into account the fact that the Council can always, by virtue of the powers conferred on it by art. 54, n. 3, lett. g) of the EC Treaty, complete this harmonization"[403].

Discarded the possibility of invoking the prohibition of abuse to deny the right of secondary establishment, CJEU analyzes the possible existence of an overriding requirement of general interest that could justify the measure at issue, and then excludes it in the specific case. This is an issue that will be explored in the following paragraphs.

SOME IDEAS ON THE ROLE OF HARMONIZATION IN THE FIGHT AGAINST ABUSE. THE C-167/01, INSPIRE ART CASE OF 30 SEPTEMBER 2003

The conclusions reached by CJEU in the C-212/97, Centros sentence of 9 March 1999 have been confirmed over the years by numerous rulings: CJEU continued to deny the presence of an abuse where the company was created in one member state only in order to benefit from more advantageous legislation, even

402 Paragraph 27. At the same time AG La Pergola, in paragraph 20, in replying to the Danish authorities' argument that in the present case there was an abusive and fraudulent exercise of the right of establishment, as such without protection, while identifying the prohibition of abuse of law as a general principle in EU law, considers that it is inherent to the freedom of establishment that "the newly established company (has) the right to settle-primarily and possibly also secondary-wherever it prefers within EU, neither "the motives, calculations, and individual interests of the interested party underlying this choice" can be syndicated.

403 CJEU, C-167/01, C-167/01, Inspire Art of 30 September 2003, ECLI:EU:C:2003:512, I-10155, par. 96. In the same spirit see also the case: C-411/03, SEVIC Systems of 13 December 2005, ECLI:EU:C:2005:762, I-10805. For further details see also: P. MÄNTYSAARI, The law of corporate finance: General principles and European Union law, op. cit., pp. 254ss. J. BORG-BARTHET, The governing law of companies in European Union law, Hart Publishing, Oxford & Oregon, Portland, 2012, pp. 136, 143ss.

if the company in question carries out the essential, if not the whole, of its economic activities in the secondary state of establishment[404]. This shows, inter alia, the fallacy of attempts to pursue a "significant" evolution in the jurisprudence of the EU judge.

In particular, it is worth mentioning C-167/01, Inspire Art pronunciation of 30 September 2003, under two profiles. This was also the case with a Danish citizen who had set up a company in the United Kingdom, which exercised the entire business through a branch in the Netherlands. In asking the C-167/01 Inspire Art of 30 September 2003 to comply with a set of national rules, the Dutch authorities relied on the need to protect creditors and to combat the abuse of freedom of establishment, fairness in commercial relations and the effectiveness of tax controls, leading the national judge to doubt their compatibility with the freedom of establishment. A peculiarity of the present case, which distinguishes it from the C-212/97, Centros case of 9 March 1999, was above all the fact that the Dutch authority in this case did not refuse to register the branch. Instead, since it was a "Formally foreign" company, it required establishment abroad but actually operated exclusively in the Netherlands, which complies with a number of Dutch company law rules, including that concerning minimum capital, providing otherwise for the fine a regime of liability of directors in solidarity with that of the company.

CJEU declares that such a system is incompatible with Union law by imposing a series of additional obligations on formally foreign companies, which, while not compromising their recognition, are intended to make the exercise of the right of a less convenient establishment. In this respect, while reaffirming the conclusions already reached in the past, it realizes a widening of the Centros doctrine. It is enough, in fact, the application, by the host country, to the companies constituted according to the law of another member state, of any national legislation that replicates the conditions of constitution envisaged for national companies, even when these are purely administrative rules, for a restriction of the freedom of establishment to be realized. CJEU thus seems to recognize a "pure mutual recognition", while at the same time radicalizing the principle of "freedom of regulatory option", never previously theorized so explicitly.

However, a second consideration is more important for our purposes. It should be noted, in fact, that in this case was indirectly affected by secondary

404 CJEU, C-225/15, Politanò of 08 September 2016, ECLI:EU:C:2016:645, published in the electronic Reports of the cases.

legislation, the eleventh Directive on corporate matters, of which many provisions of the Dutch law were transposed. These data allow to observe the position of CJEU regarding the recognition of a possible abuse perpetrated in a sector (at least in part) harmonized. The judges of the Union, in fact, after having highlighted that the program of harmonization of company law at Union level has given rise to some fundamental rules to correct the divisions between the legal systems within the Union. They consider that the eleventh Directive on company law can be considered exhaustive and that member states consequently do not have the right to add further disclosure requirements according to C-167/01, Inspire Art of 30 September 2003, which has the effect of even more severe limitation on the freedom of member states to build their own legislative regimes as protection measures[405].

THE CASE OF SECONDARY ESTABLISHMENT IN MEMBER STATES WITH MORE FAVORABLE TAX LEGISLATION

Through the "lens" of the jurisprudence of CJEU, the hypothesis of the primary is established in a country with the legislation regarding a more favorable society. Therefore, it is now necessary to dwell on the hypothesis in some ways specular of corporate groups having their headquarters (society mother) in a particular member state, which transfer taxable profits to companies controlled by them, established in those states where there is a lower level of taxation, so as to gain a tax advantage. Here, we refer to tax advantages in the area of direct taxation, non-harmonized matter, except by reference to specific sectors[406], since it is a sector closely related to the sovereignty of member states.

Under this last point, it is useful to start from the observation that, inevitably, the lack of harmonization affects the functioning of the internal market.

405 J. LOWRY, Eliminating obstacles to freedom of establishment: the competitive edge of UK company law, in The Cambridge Law Journal, 63 (2), 2004, pp. 342ss.

406 Council Directive 90/434/EEC of 23 July 1990 on the common system of taxation applicable to mergers, divisions, transfers of assets and exchanges of shares concerning companies of different member states, op. cit.; Council Directive 90/435/EEC of 23 July 1990 on the common system of taxation applicable to parent companies and subsidiaries of different member states (OJ, L 225, pag. 6); Council Directive 2003/48/EC of 3 June 2003 on taxation of savings income in the form of interest payments (OJ, L 157, pag. 38); Council Directive 2003/49/EC of 3 June 2003 on the common system of taxation applicable to interest and royalty payments made between associated companies of different member states (OJ, L 157).

Even in this area, as in the hypotheses examined above, private individuals are led to invoke freedom of movement for move into the field of application of the national laws that offer greater advantages[407].

More in detail, freedom of establishment is used in this context in order to apply another national legislation that is fiscally more favorable, exploiting the absence of harmonization. Differently than in the cases just analyzed, however, the artificiality element enforced by the national legislation concerns not the primary office but the secondary one, to which the taxable profits generated by the parent company are transferred. This leads to a reversal of roles: it will no longer be the country of secondary establishment to complain about the circumvention, but the primary state of establishment[408].

With this distinction in mind, it will then be necessary to examine whether the invocation of the abuse of law by the member states is admissible in this case, a question which CJEU gave a clear and coherent answer in C-196/04, Cadbury Schweppes and Cadbury Schweppes Overseas case of 12 September 2006.

C-196/04, CADBURY SCHWEPPES AND CADBURY SCHWEPPES OVERSEAS CASE OF 12 SEPTEMBER 2006. CHOICE OF MOST FAVORABLE TAX SYSTEM V. ABUSE

The jurisprudence, which has dealt with the prohibition of abuse of law as an "overriding reason of general interest" invoked by member states to oppose artificial constructions carried out by taxpayers, aimed at exploiting the provisions of the Treaty relating to free movement for the purpose of circumvention tax; it is somewhat dating. However, only in 2006, in C-196/04, Cadbury Schweppes and Cadbury Schweppes Overseas of 12 September 2006, CJEU examined the possibility for national authorities to apply the prohibition of abuse[409]. It is in

407 In recent years, the issue of law shopping seems to have reached the agenda of tax authorities and legislators in many member states. G. AIRS and others, abuse of tax law across Europe (part I and part II), in EC Tax Review, 19, 2010, pp. 85ss. See also the Commission Recommendation of 6 December 2012 on aggressive tax planning, C (2012) 8806 final.

408 CJEU, C-594/14, Kornhaas of 10 December 2015, ECLI:EU:C:2015:806, published in the electronic Reports of the cases.

409 CJEU had indeed already deal with that issue in case: C-436/00, X and Y of 12 December 2002, ECLI:EU:C:2002:704, I-10829.The national authority, in fact, claimed that there was a risk of tax evasion and, referring to Centros judgment, it found that in such a situation it was could doubt the applicability of the freedom of establishment, because, in this case, there would have been indica-

fact a unicum, since in a tendential line also in the following jurisprudence, as in the most recent one, CJEU will tend to bring back the abuse in the bed of imperative reasons of general interest.

This is true of one of the issues that are part of the more general issue of compatibility with the fundamental freedoms of national measures relating to controlled foreign companies' legislations[410].

With reference to the possible presence of an abuse of the freedom of establishment, CJEU does not even address the merits of the question, merely stating that "the national provision at issue in the main proceedings, excluding in a categorical and generalized way any A or B type from the benefit of deferment of tax, does not allow national courts to carry out such an examination on a case-by-case basis, taking into account the particularities of each case. It must also be noted that the criterion adopted by the national provision at issue in the main proceedings in order to exclude the sales of A and B type shares from the aforementioned tax advantage, namely the fact that the transfer is made to a company constituted under the legislation of another member state or in favor of a subsidiary established in Sweden by that company, is related to the exercise of the freedom of establishment guaranteed by the Treaty and cannot therefore constitute in itself an abuse of the right of establishment. Consequently, the fact that a member state excludes from a tax advantage any transfer of shares to a company established under the law of another member state or to a company controlled by that company established in its territory, as provided for in the national provision the case in the main proceedings cannot be justified on the grounds of an abuse of the right of establishment"(paragraphs 43 to 45)[411].

---

tions of a possible abuse of this freedom.

410 CJEU, C-524/04, Test Claimants in the Thin Cap Group Litigation of 13 March 2007, op. cit. C-298/05, Columbus Container Services of 6 December 2007, op. cit. C-105/07, Lammers & Van Cleeff of 17 January 2008, ECLI:EU:C:2008:24, I-00173; C-330/07, Jobra of 4 December 2008, ECLI:EU:C:2008:6856, I-09099; C-182/08, Glaxo Wellcome GmbH & Co. KG v. Finanzamt München II of 17 September 2009, ECLI:EU:C:2009:559, I-08591. C-311/08, SGI of 21 January 2010, ECLI:EU:C:2010:26, I-00487.

411 These legislative measures, whose adoption was recommended by the Organization for Economic Cooperation and Development (see Harmful Tax Competition-An Emerging Global Issue, OECD, Paris, 1998, pp. 44ss), have as their object the fight against tax evasion, and more specifically, are aimed at repressing the practice of transferring taxable profits generated by companies established in a member state to companies controlled by them established in other states where there is a lower level of taxation. These measures are therefore intended to be applied when the profits earned by SEC (acronym for a controlled foreign company) of a company which is tax resident in the member state in question are subject to a much lower tax than that applied in that member state. By way of derogation from the common law and provided that the conditions of one of the normally accepted exceptions are not met, these regulations provide that such profits are included in the taxable base

Cadbury Schweppes, the parent company of the international group of the same name, resident in the United Kingdom, controlled indirectly 100%, through a corporate chain headed by the subsidiary, also British, Cadbury Schweppes Overseas, two financial companies incorporated in Ireland, in an offshore tax facilitated (IFSC). Following the imputation by the UK tax company, Cadbury Schweppes Overseas of the profits earned by one of the Irish subsidiaries and the subsequent taxation in the United Kingdom in application of the rules on the controlled foreign companies, the company acted in court, claiming the incompatibility of the rules on controlled foreign companies with the freedom of establishment[412].

The referring court wondered, first, whether by establishing and financing companies in another member state for the sole purpose of benefiting from a more favorable tax system than the one in force in the United Kingdom, the company had abused the fundamental freedoms established by the Treaty. In the alternative, if it were concluded that the company had actually exercised those freedoms, the legislation on the controlled foreign companies could be justified on grounds of combating tax evasion.

The EU judge, having to answer the question concerning the existence, in this specific case, of an abuse by the company, first of all, qualifies such a request by the referring court as a "preliminary question" to be examined before the legislation on the European Cooperative Society (SECs) of articles 49 and 54 TFEU[413]. In this way, it seems to admit that in this context the issue of abuse is resolved to exclude the application of EU law, departing from C-212/97, Centros case of 9 March 1999.

---

of the parent company from the moment they are realized. For further information, see also M. HELMINEM, Is there a future for Cfc regimes in EU ?, in Intertax, 2005, pp. 117ss. T. RONFELDT, E. WERLAUFF, Cfc rules go up in smoke-With retroactive effect, in Intertax, 2007, pp. 45ss. T. O'SHEA, CFC reforms in the UK-Some EU law comments, in The EC Tax Journal, 13, 2012-2013, pp. 65ss. W. SCHON, CFC legislations and European European Union law, in the British Tax Review, 51, 2001, pp. 250ss. N. VINTHER, E. WERLAUFF, Tax motives are legal motives, in the European Taxation, 46, 2006, pp. 385, which highlighted a possible erosion of the post-Cadbury OECD legislative models. A.P. MORRISS, L. MOBERG, Cartelizing taxes: Understanding the OECD's campaign against harmful tax competition, in Columbia Journal of Tax Law, 4 (1), 2012, pp. 12ss.

412 R. SCHÜTZE, T. TRIDIMAS, Oxford principles of European Union Law, op. cit.

413 G.T.K. MEUSSEN, Cadbury Schweppes: The ECG significantly limits the application of CFC rules in the member states, in European Taxation, 47, 2007, pp. 13ss. T. O'SHEA, The UK's CFC rules and the freedom of establishment: Cadbury Schweppes plc and its IFSC subsidiaries-tax avoidance or tax mitigation?, in EC Tax Review, 7, 2007, pp. 13ss. P. SIMPSONS, Cadbury Schweppes Plc v. Commissioners of Ireland Revenue: the ECJ sets strict test for CFC legislation, in British Tax Review, 56, 2006, pp. 678ss.

This statement confirms the well-known assertion that, in theory, citizens of a member state cannot try, by means of the possibilities offered by the Treaty, to abusively evade the empire of their national laws, nor can they abuse or do it fraudulently. In an immediate contrast, there is another principle already affirmed by the jurisprudence in the past, namely that "a community natural or legal citizen cannot be deprived of the possibility of using the provisions of the Treaty only because he intended to take tax advantages offered by the rules in force in a member state other than the one in which it resides"[414]. This leads to the conclusion that the fact that the company was set up in a member state to benefit from a more advantageous legislation does not in itself constitute an abuse of that freedom.

In a few clear jokes, CJEU denies that the prohibition of abuse can be invoked, as assumed by the national court, giving substance to the impression that it was a discounted solution. Moreover, the same conviction can be drawn from the conclusions of the AG Léger, which has not shown any uncertainty in excluding the creation of a subsidiary in another member state for the declared purpose of benefiting from the more favorable tax regime enacted in itself an abuse of the freedom of establishment by the parent company, relying on the fact that the subsidiary carried out an effective economic activity. Therefore, the objective of freedom of establishment had to be considered achieved.

As in C-212/97, Centros case of 9 March 1999, the AG embraces such conviction on the basis of a formalistic interpretation of the aforementioned articles. These give a company the right to open agencies and/or branches or to create subsidiaries in the territory of another member state under the conditions defined by the legislation of that country towards its own nationals, consistent with the objectives of freedom of establishment. This implies the possibility for a citizen of the European Union to participate in a stable and continuous economic life of a member state other than the state of origin and to take advantage of it. In this regard, the AG recalls a cardinal principle of the abuse test in the C-110/99, Emsland-Stärke pronunciation of 14 December 2000, which has already been highlighted several times with regard to the abuse of EU law. Namely, "if the aim pursued by the freedom of establishment is achieved, the reasons why the community citizen or the company concerned wanted to exercise their freedom cannot influence the protection accorded to them by the Treaty"[415]. In essence,

414 CJEU, C-212/97, Centros case of 9 March 1999, op. cit.

415 A. DE GRAAF, M. EVERS, Limiting benefit shopping, op. cit., pp. 286, affirms that: "The ECJ applies

where the subsidiary actually and effectively operates in the member state in which it was created, the reasons why the parent company decided to set it up on that territory cannot affect the rights it derives from the Treaty.

On this point, the conclusions of the AG Léger are closed with an interesting relief. This sums up the underlying question of the invocation by member states of the concept of abuse, intended as circumvention of national legislation in order to benefit from another more favorable national legislation and to the strictly circumscribed use of CJEU. In fact, it stresses that "in the absence of community harmonization, it must be stated that the tax systems of the various member states can thus compete. Competition, which notably through the great disparity between member states of rates applied to corporate profits, can have a significant impact on the choice of companies in the territory of the European Union to set up their businesses. Legitimately, it is regrettable that in this sector interstate competition knows no limits. However, this is a question of a political nature (...)"[416].

In other words, CJEU is always attentive to the removal of any obstacles that impede greater integration, risking in some cases to favor unjustified use of European Union legislation, which is detrimental to the integration process itself. Excessive responsibility cannot be imposed on CJEU, which does not have the competence to promote the whole process of integration in a coherent way. Instead, legislative institutions are better equipped for this purpose. In this respect, the ultimate responsibility for the fallout of legislation, desirable or not, lies with the member states[417].

What for now is worth highlighting once again is the affirmation of the principle that the parent company has set up a subsidiary in Ireland in order to benefit from a more convenient tax system cannot in itself constitute abuse, since, in this case, paraphrasing, "tax motives are legal motives"[418]. Although the intention to benefit from lower taxation in Ireland was probably the only reason Cadbury Schweppes wanted to set up a branch in that country, CJEU was clear in stating that this does not trigger the prohibition of abuse of right, which

---

a rather formal approach to assessing whether a party is a beneficiary of the right of establishment (...)".

416 A. KACZOROWSKA-IRELAND, European Union Law, op. cit.

417 R. KARIMERI, A critical review of the definition of tax avoidance in the case law of the European Court of Justice, in Intertax, 2009, pp. 315-316.

418 N. VINTHER, E. WERLAUFF, Tax motives are legal motives, op. cit., pp. 384-385.

could potentially lead to the establishment of a subsidiary outside the scope of the freedoms guaranteed by the Treaty. Once again, the "European Union" jurisprudence confirms that the prohibition of abuse of rights cannot operate as a criterion capable of delimiting the application of EU law[419].

SOME CONSIDERATIONS ON THE ABUSE OF FREEDOM OF ESTABLISHMENT: THE CENTRAL ROLE OF THE OBJECTIVE ELEMENT IN THE CONSTRUCTION OF THE ABUSE AND THE DIFFICULTIES OF CJEU IN DETECTING THE "U-SHAPED" OPERATION

The description of the most relevant jurisprudence regarding pseudo-foreign corporations and SEC allows us to draw some conclusions about the application of the prohibition of abuse in this context. If we wanted to draw from what we have observed, it can be said that in the EU legal system the fact that a company exercises its right of establishment to benefit from a preferential corporate law regime or a more advantageous tax system does not in itself constitute formula often used, without its clear meaning being always clear-an abuse. Consequently, CJEU does not believe that a national authority can invoke the related prohibition, denying the right descending from EU law, that in the national perspective it would be the object of abuse[420]. On the contrary, the need to prevent internal legislation from being circumvented may express a public interest assessed in

419 The same conclusions are found in a more recent sentence case: C-123/11, A Oy of 21 February 2013, op. cit., with which CJEU reapplied the scheme of case: C-196/04, Cadbury Schweppes and Cadbury Schweppes Overseas of 12 September 2006, among other things without being asked a specific question on the possible applicability of the prohibition of abuse, as instead it had happened with reference to the latter one. The Luxembourg judge, in fact, considers that it must provide an accurate reply to the findings of German, Finnish, Italian and United Kingdom governments, according to which the freedom of establishment would not have been applicable to the case at issue in the main proceedings, as the company incorporated its economic activity prior to the merger and the corporate restructuring carried out was in fact motivated solely by the pursuit of a tax advantage, consisting in deducting the losses of the merged subsidiary from the taxable income of the parent company that had incorporated it. In this regard, CJEU notes that "the fact that a merger operation is exclusively motivated by tax reasons and that, in this way, the companies concerned actually seek to avoid abusively the application of their national legislation, cannot alone, lead to the exclusion of application of these provisions (...)". This is because "the question of the applicability of such articles is distinct from the question of whether a state can assume, according to CJEU, a different role in justifying a possible restriction, by way of an overriding reason of public interest.

420 W.H. ROTH, From Centros to Überseering: Free movement of companies, private international law, and European Union law, in International and Comparative Law Quarterly, 52, 2003, pp. 177-178.

the light of other imperative requirements which may limit the freedoms recognized by the Treaty.

In the cases that have been analyzed first, concerning the pseudo-foreign corporations, the perspective of national laws is very clear: the private, artificially creating the conditions to change a purely internal situation in a cross-border situation, abuses the freedom of establishment, realizing thus the goal of circumventing national legislation. For these reasons, the state where the branch is located, that is, the "national" state in which all the elements of the case are located with the exception of the main office, considers it legitimate to prohibit the private individual from relying on the freedom of establishment or, depending on, of the principle of national treatment by this descendant.

The same applies to the SEC case. The legislation of ES as the state of establishment of the parent company aims to combat a particular form of tax avoidance, based on the fictitious transfer of corporate profits from the member state in which they were made to a low-tax, creating a controlled subsidiary and concluding transactions primarily intended to allow such a transfer for the benefit of the subsidiary.

CJEU, alternatively, shows that it has a completely different perspective than the one adopted by member states, and with it also the AG who assist them in the cases in question.

The conclusions reached by the jurisprudence in this area could reasonably be justified by the acceptance of a concept of "restrictive" abuse in the context of free movement. This is in line with the objectives of economic integration of the internal market, which inevitably entails an effect deregulation and arbitrage, in itself economically advantageous. The jurisprudence, in this perspective, would be oriented only to incorporate in the system "safety valves", where this is necessary to limit the excesses in the arbitrage, which are identified precisely in the doctrine of abuse and in a wise use of the principle of proportionality[421].

As already mentioned, it could be argued that CJEU, in interpreting the Treaty provisions concerning the freedoms of movement, has difficulty in identifying those elements that we have already mentioned in the previous paragraphs as constitutive of the abuse test. Particularly in this context, it is the objective element that is always absent (the objective of the norm is always satisfied), which is why CJEU does not even go so far as to make the next step to ascertain the

421 T. TRIDIMAS, Abuse of right in EU Law: Some reflections with particular reference to financial law, op. cit., pp. 12.

existence of the subjective element, i.e. the desire to derive an undue advantage[422]. In the vein of the pseudo-foreign corporations[423], as well as the one on the SEC, the question arises of how it is possible that the objective of the norm can be said to be respected, in the presence of an artificial situation from the point of view of the member state. Analyzing the factual data from another perspective, it may be useful then to ask "under what circumstances CJEU would have accepted the limitations imposed by the host state"[424], or better, under what circumstances the prohibition of abuse could apply. It should be noted from this point of view that there were no rumors that cited sentences: C-212/97, Centros of 9 March 1999 and C-196/04, Cadbury Schweppes and Cadbury Schweppes Overseas pf 12 September 2006 as an example of the recognition of the ban on abuse of law in the Union legal system[425], that in the concrete case, only CJEU has not found an abuse in other hypotheses instead abstractly configurable. The same CJEU, moreover, called to deal with the doctrine of the abuse of law quotes several times what was stated in principle in C-212/97, Centros case of 9 March 1999.

In order to respond satisfactorily to the question, in the opinion of the writer, it is necessary to start from an inescapable fact, already highlighted on several occasions. For the European Union, it is extremely difficult, if not impossible, to identify abusive behavior and apply the related prohibition in relation to the hypotheses described above. In fact, since this is an abuse of rules concerning the constitution of the company and the possibility of carrying out an activity through a secondary center. It must be ruled out that CJEU, in interpreting them, cannot take a formal approach, such that the purpose of norm is inevitably respected when the latter applies. In other words, by borrowing the words of the AG Darmon, it must be borne in mind that "the [elusive] operation made possible by the concomitance of the right, granted to natural persons, to set up a company in another member state and that, for the legal entities including the companies thus constituted, to carry out their activity through a subsidiary in the country of origin of the natural person. Even though it may seem

422 L. CERIONI, The "abuse of rights" in EU Company law and EU tax law. A re-reading of the ECJ case law and the quest for a unitary notion, op. cit.

423 A. CAHN, D.C. DONALD, Comparative company law: Text and cases on the laws governing corporations in Germany, the UK and the USA, op. cit.

424 A. CAHN, D.C. DONALD, Comparative company law: Text and cases on the laws governing corporations in Germany, the UK and the USA, op. cit.

425 A. LENAERTS, The general principle of the prohibition of abuse of rights, op. cit., pp. 1132ss.

paradoxical, such a situation is the logical consequence of the rights guaranteed by the Treaty[426], as such conforms to the objectives of the rules that come into relief.

Even more important, however, is another consideration. When a company with its headquarters in one member state crosses the border for the first and only time, setting up a branch in another member state, as was the cases: C-79/85, Segers of 10 July 1986, C-212/97, Centros of 9 March 1999 and C-167/01, Inspire Art of 30 September 2003, or as subsidiary in C-196/04, Cadbury Schweppes and Cadbury Schweppes Overseas case of 12 September 2006, the elements to determine a "U-shaped" operation[427] from the perspective of EU law, an operation that can be considered abusive. In this sense, CJEU accepts the thesis that juridical persons benefit from fundamental freedoms as such, independently of the natural persons behind them.

With greater explicative effort, the right of the Union to look closely does not come to light until the company already established in the state of origin decides to open a secondary office in another country, invoking for this purpose its freedom of movement. The movement of the legal person is only one, which determines the opening of the secondary office; while evidently, the nationality of the director or of the shareholder of the company cannot in any way detect an unjustified discrimination on the basis of nationality.

With regard to the Centros strand (C-212/97, Centros of 9 March 1999), there are two elements that prevent the application of the ban. One refers to the purpose of the rule that cannot be said to be respected, since it is a matter of constitution rules and not on activity[428]. Second, when EU law comes into play, i.e. when the company crosses the border, exercising for the first time the freedom

426 Conclusions of AG Darmon in case: C-79/85, Segers of 10 July 1986, ECLI:EU:C:1986: 233, I-02375, par. 6.

427 M. REHBERG, C-167/01, Inspire Art of 30 September 2003-Freedom of establishment for companies in Europe between "abuse" and national regulatory concerns, in European Legal Forum, 6, 2004, pp. 4ss. The author notes that these are cases in which a company is incorporated in England and then, for the first and only time, crosses the border, either by transferring its registered office, or by setting up a branch in another member state. In the same spirit see also the next cases: C-371/10, Grid Indus of 28 November 2011, ECLI:EU:C:2011:785, I-12273; C-378/10, Épitèsi Kft of 12 July 2012, ECLI:EU:C:2012:440, published in the electronic Reports of the cases.

428 M. BROBERG, N. HOLST-CHRISTENSEN, Free movement in the European Union, ed. Djøf Forlag, Copenaghen, 2007, pp. 776ss. Goods shall benefit by EU provisions on free movement, once they have been legally produced or marketed in a member state but the states of destination, according to the principle of mutual recognition, must accept these goods in their internal markets, unless they are successful to justify the imposition of its own rules.

of establishment, that which for the member state is a "purely internal" situation artificially made intra-state, it becomes the case of a foreign company requesting registration of its branch in the host member state.

In this regard, it must be borne in mind that the element of national citizenship of the private, often invoked by member states to explain the purpose of circumvention which must necessarily exist for abuse, can in no way be taken into account in the EU legal order. Thus, invoking the distinction between norms of behavior and of constitution, CJEU, in essence, seems to start from the assumption that, in principle, it should be the state of origin to regulate the societies and their activities. The state of destination should be allowed to impose its rules only if there are adequate justifications in terms of overriding requirements in the general interest, an approach which presents, inter alia, similarities not inconsiderable with the model adopted by CJEU on the free movement of goods[429]. The key question then becomes the following: if the rules of the state of origin offer adequate protection to the interests of the state of destination and taking into account that the laws of member states often pursue objectives fundamentally different in the fiels of company law, do the rules of the state of origin may also prove insufficient to protect the interests of, for example, the creditors, employees or tax authorities of the host state. A possible solution to the problem could be, once again, harmonization.

With regard to the strand C-196/04, Cadbury Schweppes and Cadbury Schweppes Overseas of 12 September 2006, then, the situation is even simpler, as in these cases the lack of activity of the main office is not deduced, but simply of elusive reasons[430]. Well, as already pointed out, when the right of establishment has been correctly exercised at least on a formal level, the reasons are not relevant.

429 See also in argument the case from the CJEU: C-210/06, Cartesio of 16 December 2008, ECLI:EU:C:2008:723, I-09641. A. JOHNSTON, P. SYRPIS, Regulatory competition in European company law after Cartesio, in European Law Review, 6, 2009, pp. 386ss.

430 See also in argument: C-388/14, Timac Agro Deutschland of 17 December 2015, ECLI:EU:C:2015:829, published in the electronic Reports of the cases.

"U-SHAPED" OPERATIONS CARRIED OUT BY MEANS OF FREE PROVISION OF SERVICES

CJEU has adopted a stricter approach to constructions based on the abuse of the freedom to provide services, called "U-shaped" operations. These include transactions involving the movement, by a natural or legal person, of residence or any other connecting factor, such as the seat, in a member state other than the one of origin, with the aim of avoiding the application of certain stricter national rules, and then carrying out its activity in the state of origin in its capacity service provider.

The study of the cases that will be examined is relevant not only to highlight the different approach of the "European Union" jurisprudence with regard to the circumvention of national legislation, but also, as usual, from a chronological point of view, fundamental in the perspective of a comparison with that abuse of the right analyzed in its essential characteristics in the previous paragraphs. The freedom to provide services, in fact, is the subject in which CJEU has ruled for the first time on such an evasion[431], with the well-known C-33/74, Van Binsbergen v. Bestuur van de Bedrijfsvereniging voor de Metaalnijverheid sentence of 3 December 1974 although without explicitly referring to the abuse of rights doctrine.

THE ORIGINS: C-33/74, VAN BINSBERGEN V. BESTUUR VAN DE BEDRIJFSVERENIGING VOOR DE METAALNIJVERHEID CASE OF 3 DECEMBER 1974 AND THE ROLE PLAYED BY THE LOCATION OF THE ACTIVITY

In C-33/74, Van Binsbergen v. Bestuur van de Bedrijfsvereniging voor de Metaalnijverheid case of 3 December 1974, the question of the abuse of right by the service provider was not directly examined by CJEU, bearing in mind that the national authority did not invoke it either. Nonetheless, such a pronouncement assumes importance for our purposes because it allows us to underline the role assumed in the theory of abuse by the location of the activity in a given member country. The case concerned a Dutch lawyer, to whom the local court

431 C-33/74, Van Binsbergen v. Bestuur van de Bedrijfsvereniging voor de Metaalnijverheid of 3 December 1974, op. cit.

had challenged the legitimacy to fulfill his mandate, as he, during the course of the case, had transferred his residence to Belgium. Indeed, the Netherlands legislation provided that only persons residing in the Netherlands could take up the defense before that court. Since the applicant in the main proceedings relied on the provisions of the Treaty concerning the freedom to provide services, it was necessary to establish whether the contested national provision was compatible with the prohibition of any restriction on the freedom to provide services laid down in articles 59 and 60 TEC (now articles 56 and 57 TFEU)[432].

CJEU, in agreement with what was observed by the AG Mayras in its conclusions[433] regarding the scope of the provisions of the Treaty, starts from the finding that "the requirement of residence in the state where the service is provided may, at times, remove all practical relevance of art. 59, which, instead, proposes precisely to eliminate obstacles to the free provision of services by non-residents in the state in whose territory the service is provided (...)"[434].

However, in the light of special characteristics of the provision of services, the specific requirements which the provider must possess pursuant to the rules on the exercise of his profession, which are justified by the public interest and are binding on anyone residing in the service do not appear to be incompatible with the Treaty state where the service performed. In particular, "this applies if the provider fails to comply with these rules through his residence in another member state"[435]. Likewise, CJEU recognizes that the member state has the right to ensure that a service provider whose activities are carried out entirely or principally in the territory of that state cannot use the freedom guaranteed by the then art. 59 of the EC Treaty[436] in order to escape the rules governing the exercise of his profession. The observance of which would be imposed if he established himself in the state in question: "such a situation must in fact be

432 A. KACZOROWSKA-IRELAND, European Union Law, op. cit.

433 Opinion of AG Mayras, presented on 13 November 1974, op. cit. The AG does not mention the question of abuse of rights but, insisting on the need to make a distinction between freedom of establishment and freedom to provide services, states that the national law of the state in which he provides his services cannot be imposed on the service provider. It therefore concludes that the national measure in question, by restricting this freedom, runs counter to the provisions of the Treaty, since, although the possibility exists for national authorities to put in place control measures in order to protect private individuals, less stringent rules could be adopted in this case.

434 A. KACZOROWSKA-IRELAND, European Union law, op. cit.

435 A. KACZOROWSKA-IRELAND, European Union law, op. cit.

436 A. HATJE, J.P. TERHECHTE, P.C. MÜLLER-GRAFF, Europarechtswissenschaft, op. cit.

regulated by the rules on the right of establishment and not by the rules on the provision of services (...)"[437].

CJEU, on the basis of these findings, concludes that it is impossible to exclude the incompatibility with the provisions of the Treaty of national legislation. The Treaty requires those who exercise a profession connected with the administration of justice to establish their residence in the constituency of certain judiciary bodies, when the same appears to be objectively necessary to ensure compliance with professional provisions linked, in particular, with the functioning of justice and compliance with deontology. Interests that fall under those "imperative reasons of general interest" will be better specified by the subsequent jurisprudence and which will be examined more carefully in the following paragraphs.

Focusing for the moment on the prohibition of abuse of law, as was already anticipated, CJEU in the ruling in question does not mention it, let alone its application. Nevertheless, this is perhaps why it is agreed in the doctrine in pointing out the C-33/74, Van Binsbergen v. Bestuur van de Bedrijfsvereniging voor de Metaalnijverheid sentence of 3 December 1974 as the first recognition of the prohibition of abuse within the Union. It is right to anticipate how the Union judge proves to be aware of the fact that the freedoms of circulation are susceptible of abuse by that of private individuals, showing a different orientation from the one that emerged in the cases of establishment of the secondary office first examined, in which instead CJEU categorically excludes the abuse.

The sentence clearly identifies some points that will persist in the subsequent jurisprudential elaboration, including, in particular, the basic elements of the supplementary situation of the circumvention of the national legislation.

First of all, the fact that a service provider established in one member state addresses his activity "in whole or mainly in the territory" of another state of destination. Secondly, the fact that the operation was carried out by the subject "in order to avoid the rules on the exercise of his profession"[438], the observance of which would have been imposed on him if he were established in the state of destination.

In this sense, CJEU's perspective seems to coincide or in any case partially overlap with that of the national state. CJEU takes care to clarify that "however is different the situation in the case where the member state does not submit the provision of certain services to any kind of qualification or professional

437 A. KACZOROWSKA-IRELAND, European Union law, op. cit.

438 A. KACZOROWSKA-IRELAND, European Union law, op. cit.

discipline and establishes the residence requirement with reference to its territory in general. If indeed, within a member state, the exercise of a given activity is absolutely free, claiming residence in the state means imposing a restriction incompatible with articles 59 and 60 of the Treaty, since the proper functioning of justice can be guaranteed with less heavy obligations, for example by prescribing the election of a domicile where judicial communications can be sent" (paragraphs 15-16)[439].

In other words, EU law, dealing with situations in which a Union citizen makes use of the freedom to provide services, in order to exercise a professional activity on the basis of the rules of the new state of origin in which he/she is established, thus avoiding compliance with the more stringent requirements of the host statehood (id est eludendo national legislation), is prepared to point out that the citizen should, in fact, make use of another freedom, that of establishment[440]. In fact, structural requirements are lacking to make use of the freedom to provide services, bearing in mind that all activity is carried out in the state of performance. On this point, it should be noted that, as is known, the right of establishment and freedom to provide services are two sides of the same coin, differentiating only because in the first case there is a requirement of stability[441], vice versa absent in the second hypothesis. He who declares himself lender, but actually carries out all his activity in another member state, therefore lacks one of the requirements required to be considered lender. It is clear that EU law is prepared to take such a distinction and that therefore in these cases the member state is more easily authorized to intervene with restrictive measures.

BROADCASTING CASES: ABUSE OF LAW AS A JUSTIFICATION FOR RESTRICTIVE NATIONAL REGULATIONS COMPARED TO MINIMAL HARMONIZATION IN TELEVISION WITHOUT FRONTIERS/TVWF DIRECTIVE

The reasoning already present in nuce in the C-33/74, Van Binsbergen v. Bestuur van de Bedrijfsvereniging voor de Metaalnijverheid sentence of 3 December 1974

439 A. KACZOROWSKA-IRELAND, European Union law, op. cit.

440 As we can see in the case: C-208/00, Überseering of 5 November 2002, ECLI:EU:C:2002:632, I-09919.

441 CJEU, C-575/17, Sofina and others of 22 November 2018, ECLI:EU:C:2018, published in the electronic Reports of the cases.

has been replicated with greater clarity in several cases, called by the doctrine with an evocative expression, broadcasting cases. Such cases involved a series of television broadcasters, who had placed their registered office in another member state than the one of origin, while continuing to provide all its services in the latter; this in order to avoid the application of the most stringent regulations in force in the state of destination of the emissions.

In such cases, therefore, the companies involved aimed to circumvent the national legislation, invoking the freedom to provide the services provided by the Treaty in order to subject the exercise of the activity to the less stringent law of a different member state. In this regard, note that television broadcasters have an advantage in seeking the state from the most favorable provisions, thanks to the possibility of settling where they prefer, independent of the customer of the product being supplied, as long as they retain the possibility of accessing a satellite.

The broadcasting cases, which addressed for the first time the issue of restrictive measures for the free provision of services and the transmission of television programs adopted by member states to combat the shopping-law practices of television broadcasters, deserve attention in two respects.

As already pointed out, we see a different attitude of CJEU compared to the cases concerning the right of establishment, which can be better highlighted by analyzing the salient passages of the rulings. Alternatively, the causes in question provide useful indications regarding the role that harmonization can play in combating abusive behavior. While the first judgments on the matter were made before the "television without frontiers" Directive[442], CJEU had the opportunity to comment on transactions indicated as abusive by member states also following the regulation of the sector. It is therefore necessary to verify how the harmonization of the connection criteria of the issuers with a given system has influenced the considerations of the Union judge, indeed in many ways "obscure".

442 Council Directive 89/552 of 3 October 1989 on the coordination of certain laws, regulations and administrative provisions of member states concerning the pursuit of television broadcasting activities (OJ, L 298, p.23). See, in this regard, the opinion of AG Lenz, presented on 16 June 1994, in case: C-23/93, TV10 v. Commissariaat voor de Media of 5 October 1994. "Before passing on to the legal examination of the present case, I should allow a preliminary observation. The facts of the case date back to a period when there was still no obligation to transpose Directive 89/552/EEC, nor did the Dutch legislation on media change to allow commercial broadcasting. The legal criteria in the light of which the present case must be assessed would be essentially different if the facts in question had occurred at a later date. The legal assessment of the case in question thus assumes a limited value with regard to analogous cases which have subsequently occurred (...)" (par. 9).

THE PRONUNCIATIONS MADE BEFORE THE DIRECTIVE. CASES: C-148/91, VERONICA OMROEP ORGANISATIE V. COMMISSIONER FOR MEDIA OF 3 FEBRUARY 1993 AND C-23/93, TV10 V. COMMISSARIAAT VOOR DE MEDIA OF 5 OCTOBER 1994

CJEU is confronted for the first time[443] in depth with the problem of abuse of television broadcasters in C-148/91, Veronica Omroep Organisatie v. Commissariaat voor de Media case of 3 February 1993[444], an association under Dutch law, which carried out radio-broadcasting activities on the national territory. From which, a commercial broadcaster was set up in Luxembourg, RTL-Véronique, in contrast with article 57 of the Dutch law on the media, which prohibited the bodies of antenna time to carry out other commercial activities outside those provided by law. The referring court wondered whether the provisions of the treaty relating to the free movement of capital and the freedom to provide services precluded such a prohibition contained in the national legislation.

After reaffirming, citing the previous C-33/74, Van Binsbergen v. Bestuur van de Bedrijfsvereniging voor de Metaalnijverheid case of 3 December 1974 the

443 Indeed, already a year earlier, in case: C-211/91, Commission v. Belgium, op. cit., the Belgian Government, to justify national legislation restricting access to domestic cable TV to broadcasters established in other member states, had invoked the abuse doctrine, but CJEU, while reaffirming what was in case C-33/74, Van Binsbergen v. Bestuur van de Bedrijfsvereniging voor de Metaalnijverheid of 3 December 1974, he noted that "even if, according to paragraph 13 of the grounds for that judgment, the recipient state may provide that a service provider whose business is carried out entirely or principally in the territory of that state may not the freedom guaranteed by art. 59 for the purpose of avoiding the rules on the exercise of his profession whose observance would be imposed on him where he established himself in the state in question, it does not follow that a member state may generally rule out that certain services may be provided by operators established in other member states, which would be tantamount to abolishing the freedom to provide services (...)" (par. 13).

444 Already AG Tesauro, in his conclusions presented on 24 November 1992, had thus commented on Belgian Government's invocation of the case: C-33/74, Van Binsbergen v. Bestuur van de Bedrijfsvereniging voor de Metaalnijverheid of 3 December 1974. "(...) The Belgian Government nevertheless maintains, quite rightly, that the measure in question would not unlawful inasmuch as, as CJEU itself acknowledges in the Van Binsbergen judgment, a member state has the right to provide that a service provider whose activity is wholly or mainly directed towards its territory cannot use the freedom guaranteed by art. 59 for the purpose of avoiding the rules on the exercise of his profession, the observance of which would be imposed on him if he were to settle in the state in question. In this regard, it is hardly necessary to point out that such a case-law authorizes a member state to take particular measures in an individual case of abuse and certainly not to exclude, in a generalized way, a category of operators from its own market. The prohibition in question is not constructed in such a way as to prevent circumvention of the internal rules on the right of establishment: it applies to the dissemination of all programs not issued in the language of the state in which the issuer is established independently by the "quantitative" relevance of emissions released in Dutch by a particular broadcaster established in another member state (...)" (par. 4).

right of a member state to take measures to prevent the freedoms guaranteed by the treaty from being used by a service provider whose activity is wholly or essentially directed towards its territory. In order to avoid the rules which would be imposed on him if he were to settle in the state in question, CJEU specifies here that "by prohibiting national broadcasting organizations from giving aid for the creation of commercial radio and television companies abroad, in order to provide services to the Netherlands. The Netherlands legislation at issue in the main proceedings essentially prevents the exploitation of the freedoms guaranteed by the treaty from abusing the obligations deriving from the national legislation on the pluralistic and non-commercial content of the programs"[445].

Thus, the legitimacy of the adoption of preventive measures against national broadcasters is recognized, if such measures are inscribed in a system coherently aimed at achieving a general objective, such as the maintenance of a pluralistic and non-commercial system[446].

CJEU has returned to comment on the same subject, one year later, in C-23/93, TV10 v. Commissariaat voor de Media case of 5 October 1994[447]. The facts of the case are of particular interest because here, unlike in the case just examined, the single provision of the Dutch supervisory authority on the broadcasting sector had denied a commercial broadcasting agency established in Luxembourg. The authorization for access to the Dutch cable network, based on the fact that this entity, could not be considered as a "foreign broadcasting body" with the possibility of benefiting from the preferential treatment accorded by the Dutch foreign institutions, as it was established in Luxembourg exclusively for the purpose of avoiding the Dutch legislation applicable to national

445 CJEU, C-148/91, Veronica Omroep Organisatie v. Commissariaat voor de Media of 3 February 1993, op. cit. For a comment see: W. HINS, Case C-148/91, Vereniging Veronica Omroep Organisatie v. Commissariaat voor de Media, Judgement of 3 February 1993, in Common Market Law Review, 31, 1994, pp. 901ss. I. KATSIREA, The transmission State principle: The end of the broadcasting sovereignty of the member states?, in Cambridge Yearbook of European Legal Studies, 2003-2004, pp. 105ss.

446 CJEU, C-23/93, TV10 v. Commissariaat voor de Media of 5 October 1994. For a comments see: G. STRAEMANS, C. GOEMANS, TV10, in Columbia Journal of European Law, 2, 1995, pp. 319ss. P. WATTEL, Case C-23/93, TV10 SA v. Commissariaat voor de Media, Judgement of 5 October 1994; Circumvention of national law; Abuse of European Union law?, in Common Market Law Review, 32, 1995, pp. 1257ss.

447 The application was worded as follows: "If there are services of a cross-border nature relevant to EU law in the event that a broadcasting agency not authorized in the member state A for broadcasting radio and television programs, transmits programs from member state B on a manifest basis, inferred from objective circumstances, to circumvent the legislation of the member state to whose territory the transmissions themselves are principally, though not exclusively, direct".

broadcasting organizations. The referring court therefore asked CJEU whether the circumstances, taking account of the elements of circumvention of national law, were nevertheless considered to fall within the concept of provision of services[448] and, if so, whether those provisions were compatible with the measure adopted by the Dutch authority.

Indeed, interesting insights can already be found in the conclusions of the AG Lenz[449]. When questioning the legal consequences deriving from the circumvention by a service provider of regulations aimed at regulating the related business sector, the AG interprets the decisions of CJEU in C-33/74, Van Binsbergen v. Bestuur van de Bedrijfsvereniging voor de Metaalnijverheid of 3 December 1974 in the sense that the potential applicability in the event of an attempt to circumvent the legislation of a member state, also of the rules in force in the state of destination in the relevant professional or commercial sector, does not in itself preclude the applicability in the individual cases of the rules on the freedom to provide services[450]. The cross-border transmission of television programs in the present case, as objectively presented, must therefore be understood as the provision of services under Union law[451]. Hence the need, in the opinion of the AG, to analyze the issue from the point of view of justification by way of derogation from the prohibition of restrictions.

The conclusions of the AG are also noteworthy from a different point of view: the circumstances in which it is inferred that the service provider made use of the freedom to provide services in order to avoid the rules in force in the country in which he intended operate. He, in particular, proves skeptical about the verification of the intentional element of a juridical person "who is not able to develop a subjective behavior per se"[452]. On the contrary, and even

448 It is interesting to note that the AG Lenz puts the emphasis here on a fact that will be taken up again by the following jurisprudence: the existence of the abuse must be assessed by national CJEUs but CJEU will remain competent to establish the elements to be taken into account in this evaluation (par. 22).

449 See parr. 60 and 61. The circumvention should therefore only be ascertained on the basis of objective criteria, "such as, for example, the initial starting point of company's activity, its content and aims", as well as "any connections between companies".

450 CJEU, C-213/89, The Queen/Secretary of State for Transport, ex parte Factortame of 19 June 1990, ECLI:EU:C:1990:257, I-02433.

451 For further details see: J. SCHWARZE, U. BECKER, A. HATJE, J. SCHOO, EU-Kommentar, ed. Nomos, Baden Baden, 2019.

452 See par. 62 and 64: "On the other hand, it cannot be denied that, in the event of potential circumvention of law, the constitution of a legal person may already be part of the circumvention maneuver.

more important, some objective characteristics brought to light by the referring court must be excluded, such as the citizenship of the members of the applicant company, the citizenship of the directors, as well as that of the personnel. The AG claims, in fact, citing in this regard the sentence in C-213/89, the Queen/Secretary of state for Transport, ex parte Factortame case of 19 June 1990, the opposition to the Union law of the connection to the citizenship of the owners, as well as the directors of a company, as it would carry out illicit discrimination based on citizenship. This means that the connection to the citizenship of natural persons acting behind a company cannot be considered allowed, at least with regard to EU citizens.

The analysis of the conclusions leads us to underline two aspects. Firstly, the idea that an activity, even if abusive, must in any case be considered to fall within the scope of the provisions on free movement, and consequently, that the principle of abuse constitutes an exception to those rules. The view that the circumvention of national rules is not necessarily abusive, in fact, necessarily presupposes that, even in the event of circumvention, the provisions on free movement can hypothetically be applied.

Equally relevant is the reference to the need to define the criteria for determining the existence of the abuse, and in particular the possibility of using objective and /or subjective criteria, at the origin of the abuse test, established by CJEU in C-110/99, Emsland-Stärke of 14 December 2000, excluding those elements that would allow the member state to qualify the situation as purely internal.

On the contrary, some objective characteristics brought to light by the referring court must be excluded, such as the citizenship of the members of the applicant company, the citizenship of the directors, as well as that of the personnel. The AG claims, in fact, citing in this regard the sentence in C-213/89, the Queen/Secretary of State for Transport, ex parte Factortame case of 19 June 1990, the opposition to the law of the Union of the connection to the citizenship of the owners, as well as the directors of a company, as it would carry out illicit discrimination based on citizenship. This means that the connection to the citizenship of natural persons acting behind a company cannot be considered allowed, at least with regard to EU citizens.

Nevertheless, I believe that the link to citizenship of natural persons should be avoided, since there is a danger of discriminating against EU citizens on the basis of citizenship, discrimination whose prohibition has the status of fundamental right in European law (...)".

The analysis of the conclusions leads us to underline two aspects. First, the idea that an activity, even if abusive, must in any case be considered to fall within the scope of the provisions on free movement, and consequently, that the principle of abuse constitutes an exception to those rules. The view that the circumvention of national rules is not necessarily abusive, in fact, necessarily presupposes that, even in the event of circumvention, the provisions on free movement can hypothetically be applied.

Equally relevant is the reference to the need to define the criteria for determining the existence of abuse, and in particular the possibility of using objective and/or subjective criteria, at the origin of the abuse test, established by CJEU in C-110/99, Emsland-Stärke of 14 December 2000, excluding those elements that would allow the member state to qualify the situation as purely internal.

CJEU, in a more concise manner, excludes the fact that the elusive nature of the case is such that it immediately puts it outside the scope of the provisions of the Treaty, as this only happens when "all relevant elements are locally restricted to of a member state". Taking up the previous C-148/91, Veronica Omroep Organisatie v. Commissariaat voor de Media case of 3 February 1993 states that "a member state may legitimately equate to a national broadcasting agency or television and radio agency established in another member state for the purpose of providing direct services to its territory, as such a measure aims to prevent the institutions established in another country from using the freedoms guaranteed by the Treaty. Otherwise, both the Dutch and the German governments argued that, in view of CJEU's case-law on circumvention, it could not be considered to be in the presence of services under the Union law, with the consequence that, in purely internal relations, only the legislation of the state in which the programs are to be received should have been applied[453]. On the other hand, both the French government and the EC stated that there was a provision of services within the meaning of Union law, emphasizing the difference in the question of the measures which a state may legitimately adopt in order to prevent the provider from services evades national rules. The member state may unlawfully evade the obligations imposed by national legislation, in particular those relating to the pluralistic and non-commercial content of programs (...)"[454].

In more detail, CJEU follows a two-stage reasoning. The judges of the Union, in fact, first recall the objective of the national law to safeguard the freedom

453 See par. 12 of the conclusions of the AG.

454 A. KACZOROWSKA-IRELAND, European Union law, op. cit.

of expression of the different social, cultural, religious or philosophical components existing in the Netherlands and recognize that, since it is an objective of general interest, could legitimately be pursued by a member state. They then apply the reasoning of the C-33/74, Van Binsbergen v. Bestuur van de Bedrijfsvereniging voor de Metaalnijverheid sentence of 3 December 1974, concluding that a member state may treat the national broadcasting organization as equivalent to another member state to circumvent the most restrictive legislation of the state of origin, a legal fiction which allows to the state of destination to apply its provisions to the established organization illegally abroad.

Notice how, in the application of this legal fiction in C-23/93, TV10 v. Commissariaat voor de Media case of 5 October 1994, the first sanction of CJEU for circumvention can be identified[455]. As in C-148/91, Veronica Omroep Organisatie v. Commissioner of Media case of 3 February 1993, CJEU also adopts an intermediate position, partly focusing on the fact that national legislation had been circumvented and partly on the characteristics of the national legislation circumvented. It is not easy, therefore, to establish what the "European Union" judges would have decided if the objective of the national measures had not been of general interest.

455 L. IDOT, Libre prestation de services, in Europe, 464, 1994, pp. 13ss. In this regard, however, it remains to be clarified whether the issuing company, in addition to following the rules of the member state in which it provides its services, is also obliged to comply with the rules of member state in which it is legally established. An answer in the negative sense would inevitably interfere with CJEU's consistent case-law according to which the seat of a company serves as a link with the legal system of a particular state (see case: C-79/85, Segers of 10 July 1986, op. cit. C-330/91, Queen v. Inland Revenue Commissioners, formerly part Commertzbank AG of 13 July 1993, ECLI:EU:C:1993:303, I-04017. In addition to being in contrast with the first paragraph of art. 54 of the Treaty. It is therefore strongly preferable to give an affirmative answer, so that the interference with the question of corporate veil is less evident (L.H. HANSEN, The development of the circumvention principle in the area of broadcasting, in Legal Issues of Economic Integration, 25, 1998, pp. 126ss), although it should not be forgotten that this interpretation carries with it the considerable risk that the rules of the two states involved prove to be irreconcilable, thus giving rise to problems of difficult solution, which the same Lenz conclusions, without, however, giving an answer. As we have seen, the reasoning carried out by the jurisprudence focuses largely on the merit of national legislation, where it is accepted the compatibility with the EU right of measures which, in fact, equates societies only fictitiously established abroad to those national laws, allow the application of legislation that pursues general interests.

THE ADVENT OF "TELEVISION WITHOUT FRONTIERS/TVWF DIRECTIVE" AND THE CHANGES REGISTERED. COMMISSION V. BELGIUM, C-56/96, VT4 V. VLAAMSE GEMEENSCHAP CASE OF 5 JUNE 1997 AND JOINED CASES: C-34/95, C-35/95 AND C-36/95, KONSUMENTOMBUDSMANNEN (KO) V. DE AGOSTINI AND TV-SHOP OF 17 JULY 1997

Such a construction is destined to change where partial harmonization of the sector comes into play, in that, in this case will be the derived secondary rule that sets out exhaustively the criteria for establishing the application of a specific national legislation. Confirmation comes from the different attitude taken by CJEU in dealing with the establishment of television broadcasters in countries other than the one of origin, to which service provision is principally directed[456].

The main objective of the present examination is then to highlight such change, through a focused analysis of the contents of the sentences, which is best understood in relation to the conclusions of the advocates-general, who have paid more attention to this aspect.

First of all, it should be noted that the television sector was governed by the "television without Frontiers" Directive (TVWF Directive) of 11 December 2007"[457], with the primary objective of guaranteeing the free circulation of television programs, through the provision of minimum requirements for transmissions transmitted by the European Union collected in the same area, as can be seen from the 13th and 14th recitals of the Directive. In summary, the technique used to achieve the stated objective is to establish minimum criteria to be observed by broadcasters under the jurisdiction of a member state and general bans for member states to submit transmissions from another member state to further checks before receipt or retransmission.

With reference to the causes that will be analyzed in this paragraph, art. 2 of the aforementioned Directive, according to which each member state shall ensure that all television broadcasts of the issuers under its jurisdiction comply

456 CJEU, C-621/18, Wightman and others of 4 December 2018, ECLI:EU:C:2018:999, published in the electronic Reports of the cases.

457 Directive 2007/65/EC of the European Parliament and of the Council of 11 December 2007 amending Council Directive 89/552/EEC on the coordination of certain provisions laid down by law, regulation or administrative action in member states concerning the pursuit of television broadcasting activities, OJ L 332, 18.12.2007, p. 27ss. For further details see: I. KATSIREA, The television without frontiers directive, in K. DONDERS, C. PAUWELS, J. LOISEN (eds.), The Palgrave handbook of European media policy, ed. Palgrave Macmillan, London, 2014.

with the law applicable to broadcasts intended for the national public. At the same time, member states ensure freedom of reception and not hinder the retransmission on their territory of television broadcasts from other member states for reasons relating to the areas coordinated by this Directive.

In particular, it is worthy of attention to our purposes of the Commission v. Belgium case of 10 September 1996[458], on the compatibility of the system for issuing an authorization for broadcasting by other radio and television broadcasters of other member states of commercial advertising and teleshopping programs specially intended for the public of the French community, art. 2, n. 2, of television without frontiers Directive. The Belgian Government, in fact, defended itself by claiming that the legislation in question was justified, since it was designed to prevent the national rules from being circumvented. It was stated, in particular, that by broadcasting commercial advertising from another member state, in particular to viewers of the French community, television networks circumvented the law in force in the French community, that is to say in the receiving state, and therefore could not claim the application in their comparisons of art. 2, n. 2, of Directive 89/552/EEC[459]. The requirement of a prior authorization would therefore have enabled the competent authorities to check whether an issuer was actually managed by a television company to which the Directive would be applicable.

CJEU does not agree with the Belgian Government's approach, stating that it does not even wish to examine whether, under Directive 89/552/EEC, a member state, pursuant to article 59 of the Treaty (now article 56 TFEU)[460], may still take measures to prevent the freedoms guaranteed by the Treaty from being exploited by a service provider whose activity is wholly or mainly directed towards its territory[461]. This is because, C-33/74, Van Binsbergen v. Bestuur van

458 CJEU, C-11/95, Commission v. Belgium of 10 September 1996, ECLI:EU:C.1996:316, I-04115. For further details see: B. HANNIGAN, Company law, Oxford University Press, Oxford, 2012.

459 Directive 89/552/CEE du Conseil, du 3 octobre 1989, visant à la coordination de certaines dispositions législatives, réglementaires et administratives des États membres relatives à l'exercice d'activités de radiodiffusion télévisuelle, OJ L 298, 17.10.1989, p. 23-30, no longer in force from 4 May 2010. For further details see: D. WARD, The European Union and the culture industries. Regulation and the public interest, ed. Routledge, London & New York, 2016. R. DENUIT, Politique culturelle européenne, ed. Bruylant, Bruxelles, 2017.

460 F. JONGEN, A. STROWEL, Droit des mèdias et de la communication: Presse, audiovisuel et internet, ed. Larcier, Bruxelles, 2017.

461 AG Lenz in his opinion, presented on 30 April 1996, in paragraphs 71 and 73, considers that the Directive has not deprived states of the right to take measures, under certain conditions, in order to avoid circumvention of their rules; nevertheless agrees with the Commission that the restrictive

de Bedrijfsvereniging voor de Metaalnijverheid of 3 December 1974 and C-23/93, TV10 v. Commissioner of Media case law of 5 October 1994, although cited by Belgium, "does not authorize a member state to generally rule out that certain services may be provided by operators established in other member states, since this would be tantamount to suppressing the freedom to provide services (...)"[462]. The question concerning the consistency of the prohibition of abuse following the adoption of a secondary law text remains unresolved.

Otherwise, in the judgment of the C-56/96, VT4 v. Vlaamse Gemeenschap case of 5 June 1997[463], CJEU, in one passage, expressly ruled on the issue of abuse of rights, greatly restricting its scope as a justification for restrictive national measures. According to the national authority, in fact, VT4 was in fact a Flemish body established in another member state in order to circumvent the application of the Flemish legislation.

The question also referred to the interpretation of article 2 of Directive 89/552/EEC: the referring court asked, in essence, what were the criteria for identifying television broadcasters under the jurisdiction of a member state pursuant to the aforementioned art. 2, n. 1. CJEU, to decide the matter. This operates in parallel with the previous European Commission v. United Kingdom[464] case, in which he had already examined the interpretation to be given to the

---

rules in force in Belgium cannot be justified by the need to avoid circumvention of the law of the receiving state, as this would assume that all companies transmitting their commercial advertising programs or teleshopping from other member states, directing them particularly to the French-speaking public, may be accused of trying to circumvent the rules of the receiving member state", while the circumvention charge, in the opinion of AG, is justified only if the issuer television commits an abuse. It should be noted immediately that in this last passage the AG seems to fall into a tautology, without being able to explain when the avoidance can be defined as abusive; what is certain is that, in any case, it cannot be "assumed that any television company in another member state that issues advertising or sales programs particularly addressed to the French-speaking public commits an abuse for this reason alone" (paragraph 74), as already stated by CJEU in the Commission judgment v. Belgium of 1992, op. cit. Once again, therefore, indications are given on what the abuse is not, more than on its ontological essence, with the exception of the reference to the concrete, trend confirmed by the jurisprudence success.

462 As we can see in the case: C-580/15 Van der Weegen and others of 8 June 2017, ECLI:EU:C:2017:429, published in the electronic Reports of the cases.

463 CJEU, C-56/96, VT4 v. Vlaamse Gemeenschap of 5 June 1997, ECLI:EU:C:1993:584, I-031143. For a comment see: B. EDELMAN, Note sur l'arrêt VT4, Recueil Dalloz, 1999, pp. 192ss.

464 VT4, based in London, was a company incorporated under English law, the main activity of which consisted on the transmission of radio or television programs. VT4 programs were intended for the Flemish public and therefore registered or subtitled in Dutch. However, the television signal was sent to the satellite from the United Kingdom territory; VT4 then had a branch office in a Flemish locality in Belgium, which maintained relationships with advertisers and production companies.

notion of "jurisdiction" in the expression "television broadcasters subject to the (...) jurisdiction (of a member state)"[465] pursuant to art. 2, n. 1 of the Directive. This reiterates that the latter provision should be interpreted as meaning that a television broadcaster is subject to the jurisdiction of the member state in which it is established and in the event that there are several offices, of the state in which the issuer center of activity, with particular reference to the place where the planning policy is decided and the final composition of the programs to be broadcasted[466].

Such reasoning is not affected by the assertion of the national authority that, in order for the rules concerning the freedom to provide services to apply, it is not sufficient for the provider to be established in another member state, but it is also necessary that this provider is not established also in the host country.

CJEU objects, inter alia, that "the mere fact that all transmissions and advertisements are exclusively intended for the Flemish public does not allow, contrary to what is claimed by the national authority, to demonstrate that VT4 cannot be considered established in the United Kingdom. The Treaty does not prohibit an undertaking from exercising the freedom to provide services if it does not offer services in the member state in which it is established (...)"[467].

In this way, the Union judge seems to operate a significant change of perspective with respect to his way of reasoning before the Directive. As in other precedents, it seems to interpret the text of the Directive, and in particular the criterion for determining the seat pursuant to art. 2, taking into account the prohibition of abuse. The prohibition of abuse therefore becomes a principle that governs the interpretation of the jurisdiction clause provided for by the Directive. Then again, it excludes the fact that a company offers all its services in the member state of destination and some in that of the establishment proves an abuse, thereby diverging from what was stated in C-23/93, TV10 v. Commissariaat voor de Media case of 5 October 1994.

In the conclusions presented on 6 February 1997, the AG Lenz also has access to a restrictive view, but on the basis of partly different considerations. Even

465 CJEU, C-56/96, VT4 v. Vlaamse Gemeenschap of 5 June 1997, op. cit.

466 CJEU, C-222/94, Commission of the European Communities v. United Kingdom of Great Britain and Northern Ireland of 10 September 1996, ECLI:EU:C:1996:314, I-04025. For further analysis see: J. OSTER, European and international media law, Cambridge University Press, Cambridge, 2016, pp. 125ss.

467 D. DOUKAS, Free movement of broadcasting services and abuse of law, in R. DE LA FERIA, S. VOGENAUER Prohibition of abuse of law: A new general principle of EU law?, op. cit., p. 77.

admitting that the jurisprudence on abuse is applied even after the adoption of Directive 89/552/EEC, comes to exclude the abuse in this case. In particular, the AG specifies that the fact that the VT4 program is aimed at Flanders is in itself irrelevant: in fact, "a company established in a member state can exercise the freedom to provide services even if in the state in which it is established it does not provide itself no service" (paragraph 28)[468]. He then goes on to say that VT4's business has relations with both the United Kingdom and Belgium, on the basis that VT4 is a company established under English law, established in the United Kingdom, from where it broadcasts its programs. Thus, even if all other activities were carried out in Belgium, it would have, according to the case-law cited above, a registered office in the United Kingdom, even if it were only a subsidiary, which, according to the Treaty, is a registered office (par. 29). The change in perspective is clear: the AG no longer looks at the performance of the activity under the freedom to provide services in the territory of the state of destination, but at the formal data of the establishment of the company in the state of origin.

Lastly, the conclusions of the AG Jacobs in the C-34/95, C-35/95 and C-36/95, Konsumentombudsmannen (KO) v. De Agostini and TV-Shop case of 17 July 1997, which deal with the abuse in reply to one of the defenses of the Swedish government, which referred, in fact, to the abuse doctrine to justify the restrictive measures of free movement of services[469]. The case, in short, concerned the compatibility with EU law of television advertising rules established by the Swedish legal system, which came into play with reference to certain television stations established in the United Kingdom, which broadcast television programs via satellite from this state to Denmark, Sweden and Norway.

The AG recalls that the principles established in cases: C-33/74, Van Binsbergen v. Bestuur van de Bedrijfsvereniging voor de Metaalnijverheid of 3 December 1974, C-148/91, Veronica Omroep Organisatie v. Commissioner for Media of 3 February 1993 and C-23/93, TV10 v. Commissioner of Media of 5 October 1994 are the expression of the more general principle of abuse of rights. Because of such qualification, the principles must still be considered to be in force in the television broadcasting sector, despite the implementation of the television without frontiers Directive. However, it must be remembered that

468 See in argument also: CJEU, C-18/15 Brisal e KBC Finance Ireland of 13 July 2016, ECLI:EU:C:2016:549, published in the electronic Reports of the cases.

469 CJEU, joined cases: C-34/95, C-35/95 and C-36/95, Konsumentombudsmannen (KO) v. De Agostini and TV-Shop of 17 July 1997, ECLI:EU:C:1996:344, I-03843.

the same must in any case be construed restrictively, constituting an exception to one of the freedoms that make up the internal market. He then makes an interesting consideration when he observes that allowing such a principle to be invoked in a case "where the interests protected by the rules that are claimed to be circumvented fall within the scope of the Directive, would undermine in a fundamental way the principle of the state of transmission constituting itself the primary expression of the Directive's aim to abolish obstacles to the free movement of services with a view to establishing the internal market"[470]. This shows that, where EU law intervenes in the regulation of a given sector, the approach necessarily changes, in the sense that, correlatively, the remedies must be found in the secondary legislation itself[471]. The AG is firm in excluding the abuse by the issuer, noting that the circumvention of the legislation applicable in the member state cannot be inferred from "the mere fact that an issuer established in a member state transmits programs for the purpose of have them received in another member state" (paragraph 47)[472]. It should be noted in closing as in the dispute just described, two revisions of the television without frontiers were followed, first in 1997 and then in 2007, which explicitly sanctioned the legitimacy of anti-abuse measures adopted by member states, thus consolidating the norms of the jurisprudence just described.

In particular, Directive 97/36/EC[473] recognized in the preamble the function of the prohibition of abuse as an overriding reason, where it is stated in recital

470 It should be noted that the Consumer Ombudsman claimed that TV3 should be considered essentially a Swedish television broadcaster, which is why the Directive would not be applicable in this case; this because all of its programs broadcast in Sweden were produced there, dubbed or subtitled and presented in Swedish, advertisements were exclusively produced for the Swedish market, taking into account the language in which they were prepared and the products marketed. The AG shows that he does not share this view, recalling how CJEU, in the Commission v. United Kingdom, considered that member state under whose jurisdiction an issuer is located in the member state in which the issuer is established.

471 For further details see: B. J. DRIJBER, The revised television without frontiers directive: is it fit for the next century?, in Common Market Law Review, 36, 1999, pp. 87ss. A. MEYER-HEINE, Les apports de la nouvelle directive Television sans frontiéres du 30 juin 1997 entrée en viguer le 31 décember 1998, in Revue Trimestrielle du Droit Européen, 35, 1999, pp. 95ss.

472 B. J. DRIJBER, The revised television without frontiers directive: is it fit for the next century?, op. cit.

473 Directive 97/36/EC of the European Parliament and of the Council of 30 June 1997 amending Council Directive 89/552/EEC on the coordination of certain provisions laid down by law, regulation or administrative action in member states concerning the pursuit of television broadcasting activities, OJ L 202, 30.7.1997, p. 60–70, no longer from 4 May 2010. In fact, in the vigor of Directive 89/552, the place of television broadcaster establishment was determined on the basis of various criteria, which, considered fully equivalent to each other, left room for possible abusive phenomena. In modifying the aforementioned article, the legislator has defined the criteria more precisely precisely in order

14 that "according to the constant jurisprudence of CJEU, a member state retains the right to take action against a television agency which, although it has established its headquarters in another member state, directs its whole or part of its business to the territory of the first member state, where the choice to settle in the second member state has been made in order to avoiding the legislation that would have been applied if it had been established on the territory of the first member state"[474]. Similarly, recital 19 states that "the necessary provisions should be taken, within the community, to avoid any legal uncertainty and distortion of the market and to reconcile the free movement of television services with the need to prevent possible circumvention of measures national laws designed to protect a legitimate general interest"[475]. The aforementioned art. 2 on jurisdiction, including four new paragraphs (from 2 to 5), with the aim of clarifying the exact scope of the concept of establishment of the television station so as to limit abusive phenomena. The introduction of more punctual criteria for delimiting the jurisdiction on issuers has considerably reduced the risk of abuse of the freedoms of circulation, without however eliminating it; for this reason, Directive 2007/654/EC introduced to art. 3 new forecasts which codified the role of prohibition of abuse as an imperative reason capable of justifying the

to establish precisely when an issuer could be considered located in the territory of a state. Firstly, the criterion of issuer's principal place of residence is linked to the criterion for the place where editorial decisions on programming are taken. In the alternative, in the event that there is no coincidence between the place of editorial decisions and the head office, we look at the territory of the state in which a significant part of the operators working in broadcasting operates; in the alternative, where a significant part of the staff operates in each of those member states, the issuer is then deemed to be established in the member state in which it has its principal place of business. Finally, if the broadcaster does not operate a significant part of the broadcasters in either of the two member states, it is considered established in the first member state in which it has started to broadcast, provided that there is a stable and effective link with the economy of that state. It emerges that the set of the aforementioned criteria represented a great innovation compared to the previous regulation, since the latter, not including any order to be respected in applying the criteria for identifying the establishment of the television company, was easily circumvented: See in argument: I. KATSIREA, The circumvention principle: An effective defence of national Broadcasting system against abuse?, in Communications Law & Policy, 23, 2005, pp. 130ss. E. GUILD, C. GORTAZAR ROTAECHE, D. KOSTAKOPOULOU, The reconceptualization of European Union citizenship, ed. Brill, Martinus Nijhoff Publishers, Leiden, Boston, 2014, pp. 268ss.

474 Directive 97/36/EC of the European Parliament and of the Council of 30 June 1997 amending Council Directive 89/552/EEC on the coordination of certain provisions laid down by law, regulation or administrative action in member states concerning the pursuit of television broadcasting activities, op. cit.

475 I. KATSIREA, The circumvention principle: An effective defense of national Broadcasting system against abuse?, op. cit.

restrictive measures of member states[476]. It was indeed provided in par. 3 which, the member state of destination of services, if it considers that the issuer has established itself in the member state exercising jurisdiction to circumvent, in the areas coordinated by the Directive, the stricter rules that would be applicable if it were established in the first member, may take appropriate measures against the concerned issuer, which are objectively necessary, applied in a non-discriminatory and proportionate manner to the objectives pursued, after having notified them to the EC that it must verify their compatibility with EU law.

A COMPARISON WITH THE LODGING OF C-212/97, CENTROS CASE OF 9 MARCH 1999 REGARDING THE OBJECTIVE ELEMENT

It has just been observed that the television without frontiers Directive has led to a change in CJEU's approach to interpreting the prohibition of abuse of law, which takes on particular significance for our purposes, as it is clearly determined, as just demonstrated, by the adoption of the Directive. In particular, it was noted that the jurisprudence, after the implementation of the Directive, is characterized by two trends. On the one hand, CJEU uses the prohibition of abuse to interpret the Directive and in particular the provision pursuant to art. 2, as in cases: C-11/95, Commission v. Belgium of 10 September 1996 and C-56/96, VT4 v. Vlaamse Gemeenschap of 5 June 1997. On the other hand, CJEU, while not expressly denying the application of the prohibition in the field covered by the Directive as a ground for justifying exceptions by member states, adopted a restrictive interpretation, which limited the discretion of member states and has retained the effectiveness of the principle of jurisdiction of the state of transmission, as can be inferred from the analysis of the Commission v. Belgium, C-56/96, VT4 v. Vlaamse Gemeenschap case of 5 June 1997 and the joined cases: C-34/95, C-35/95 and C-36/95, Konsumentombudsmannen (KO) v. De Agostini and TV-Shop of 17 July 1997[477].

Apart from such observations, which more properly pertain to the relationship between prohibition and harmonization, it is now useful to dwell on the

476 See in argument: C. BARNARD, O. ODUDU, The outer limits of European Union law, Hart Publishing, Oxford & Oregon, Portland, 2009.

477 J. HORNLE, Country of origin regulation in cross-border media: One step beyond the freedom to provide services?, in International and Comparative law Quarterly, 55, 2005, pp. 115-118.

scope of the prohibition in this area, a problem that revolves, once again, around the verifiability or not of the objective element. The analysis of the most significant jurisprudence concerning the freedom to provide services shows that CJEU initially legitimated the restrictive measures of the state justified by the abuse. Considering that it is an "embryonic" jurisprudence, which first was related to the abuse doctrine, certainly inaccuracies are found. It is not clear how the prohibition of abuse correlates with the imperative reasons of general interest: in C-148/91 case, CJEU, departing from the conclusions of the AG Tesauro, does not take into account the proportionality aspect which is also inherent to the overriding reasons of general interest, thus demonstrating the application of the prohibition. In the reasoning carried out in C-23/93, TV10 v. Commissioner of Media case of 5 October 1994, on the other hand, the merit of the interests pursued by the national eluded legislation assumes a preponderant role, since the European Union courts considered it necessary to analyze the existence of legitimate objectives capable of justifying the measures. It becomes uncertain, in the interpreter's eyes, if the restrictive attitude of the member state, in order to overcome the assessment of compatibility with the provisions of the Treaty, must pursue a legitimate objective of public interest, or whether it is sufficient for a national provision to be circumvented on purpose[478].

What we are interested in here is how CJEU, in this context, did not limit itself to the formulation of principles in principle, but, in practice, found abuse in the behavior of the private who acts as a service provider when instead it was in fact established in the country of destination of the services, with this admitting the application of national law evaded. The change in perspective with respect to the C-212/97, Centros case law of 9 March 1999 is thus evident. If, in fact, in both cases, CJEU recognizes in principle the prohibition of abuse, only with reference to the free provision of services reconnects the possibility for the member state to penalize it, thereby demonstrating that it has clear the artificial operation.

The first case law on the provision of services suggests that the notion of abuse is wider in the freedom to provide services than in the freedom of establishment. It is therefore necessary to understand if there is a coherent explanation of such differentiation. In this regard, it was noted that this different approach is a reflection of the difference between the two freedoms: while a

478 L. H. HANSEN, The development of the circumvention principle in the area of broadcasting, op. cit., pp. 120-122.

citizen of the Union exercising the freedom of establishment becomes subject to the law of the host state, a person providing services remains in principle beyond the competence of the authorities of the state where the services are provided. This means that the risk of "arbitrage" and the use of interstate mobility to circumvent national requirements is much higher in relation to the freedom to provide services, which would also justify greater vigilance of CJEU[479].

If this affirmation certainly captures an aspect of truth, it reveals itself at the same time partial, since, as we have seen, in the establishment, the state that complains about the abuse is not so much what governs society, that is, the one in which it takes place the primary establishment, but the state of the real primary headquarters, "disguised" as a branch.

In reality, it can be observed that in this hypothesis there would seem to exist those elements suitable for identifying a "U-shaped" operation also in the perspective of EU law. In cases: C-23/93, TV10 v. Commissioner for Media of 5 October 1994, C-148/91, Veronica Omroep Organisatie v. Commissioner for Media of 3 February 1993 and C-33/74, Van Binsbergen v. Commissioner. In fact, we are assisting two movements, that of the natural or legal person who settles first in another member state invoking the freedom of establishment, and then exercising all the services in the state of origin.

However, this does not seem to be the perspective adopted by CJEU, which gives weight to another key element, namely the fact that a freedom has been used improperly in place of another. In this way, it is clear how EU's legal system has here the means to find that, instead of the free provision of services, freedom of establishment should have applied, starting from the structural comparison between the constituent elements of two cases.

Here the described case law can be easily harmonized with the jurisprudence on the freedom of establishment, which outlined the principle according to which, when the objective conditions exist for invoking the right of primary establishment and therefore the objective of the norm is satisfied, intentions do not detect. While, in fact, as regards the freedom of establishment, as already

479 "(...) Segers and TV 10 cases form a sort of mirror image of each other. Mr Segers used a foreign legal entity in order to manoeuvre himself within the scope of national legislation he wished to benefit from, whereas TV 10 used a foreign entity in order to manoeuvre itself outside the scope of national legislation it did not wish to comply with. Consequently, Mr Segers was denied the national treatment he desired, whereas TV10 was subjected to the national treatment it did not desire (...). TV 10 absolutely needed to be established outside the Netherlands, because it needed a cross-border situation in order to be able to invoke the Treaty freedom to supply services. For the purposes pursued by Mr Segers, on the other hand, the foreign establishment of his company was immaterial (..)". T. TRIDIMAS, Abuse of right in EU law, op. cit, pp. 19ss.

noted, the abuse had as its object the rules on the establishment of the company, in the freedom to provide services to take a leading role is the activity carried out. Therefore, if it proves that an institution is established in a state other than the one to which it belongs. From this address, totally or mainly, its activity towards the same country in which it should have settled, it is at that precise moment that the objective plan of abuse occurs, but then verifies the existence of the subjective element, which, in truth, in this case law seems to be deduced from the sole misuse of the freedom of establishment. CJEU, in fact, does not verify in any of the cases examined whether it is actually an artificial establishment set up in order to circumvent the legislation.

Ultimately, as has just been noted, it is unclear whether in these cases the prohibition of abuse really found application in its essence, remaining the doubt that in reality CJEU wanted to reconnect the abuse to an imperative reason of general interest. What cannot be revoked in doubt is the fact that the objective element of the test was integrated.

A logic not unlike would seem to have oriented the reasoning of CJEU in C-113/89, Rush Portuguesa case of 27 March 1990 then resumed in C-445/03, Commission v. Luxembourg case of 21 October 2004, where it is stated that "CJEU has already had occasion to declare, however, that a member state can ascertain that an undertaking established in another member state which is seconded to the territory of the first worker of a third state does not make use of the freedom to provide services for a purpose other than the performance of the service in question, for example that of bringing in its staff for the purposes of the placement or the making available of workers(...) (par.39)"[480].

480 In the same spirit see: C-527/16, Apenrid and others of 32 January 2018, ECLI:EU:C:2018:669, published in the electronic Reports of the cases.

PART B

Circumvention of national legislation. Contextual application of Union law

Part B of this paragraph is aimed at examining the behavior of individuals who aim to circumvent the national legislation by simultaneously invoking the application, not of another national legislation, but of the EU law, which brings certain advantages.

As in the hypothesis analyzed in part A, there is also a triangulation here, in the sense that three systems are involved, that of the member state of origin, that of the EU and of the member state of destination; equally, the tool used to keep abusive construction in place is freedom of movement, which allows them to invoke the benefits deriving from EU law. Also in this case, the question of abuse inevitably intertwines with the different question of understanding whether, in reality, we are dealing with a purely internal situation, since the private has created "artificially" the presuppositions of transnationality.

What changes is precisely the discipline that requires application, which, in these cases, is that "European Union" and not that of another member state. Thus, while, for example, in the case already analyzed of the pseudo-foreign corporations, the private individual seeks to obtain the application of the most favorable national law, in the cases that will be examined, such as that of the "professional tourist", the private sector aims to achieve certain benefits arising from Union law[481].

The statement, as formulated, is however incomplete, and a further bipartition is appropriate. On this point, it is certainly easier to rely on concrete exemplification, which is why we refer all the details to the following paragraphs.

481 J. SCHWARZE, U. BECKER, A. HATJE, J. SCHOO, EU-Kommentar, op. cit.

For the time being, it is sufficient to distinguish between two typical situations. In one, the private sector engages in an abusive construction in order to obtain certain benefits from a certain member state, different from that of origin, benefits which can only be acquired through application of Union law, which therefore plays a central role. In the second, the private person, traveling to another member state, pre-establishes the requirements for the direct benefit of the application of a given Union framework[482].

The first hypothesis described can be defined as "hybrid". Here the choice of the most favorable national law is taken first, but once this choice is made, the private individual then wants to apply the law of the Union, whose discipline it allows him certain advantages, which otherwise he would not have.

In the second hypothesis described, the national system is different from that of origin, is involved only to create the element of extraneousness that allows the application of EU law, thus assuming the role of mere instrument, so that, to put it simply, one member state holds the other.

As will be seen shortly, not even with reference to these situations, CJEU is used to apply the prohibition of abuse of right, preferring possibly to accept a restrictive interpretation of the "European Union" discipline, a technique for the protection of EU law that will be analyzed in the next paragraphs.

ABUSE WITH REFERENCE TO THE RECOGNITION OF PROFESSIONAL QUALIFICATIONS

Parallel to the story of elusive behaviors perpetrated in the service sector, CJEU in conjunction with the adoption of the first sectorial directives on the mutual recognition of professional qualifications was called to deal with those constructions aimed at circumventing the most of the state to which they belong in the field of access to regulated professions. This invokes the right to the recognition of a professional title acquired in another member state by the most favorable

482 We remember that, in the mind of art. 57 TCEE (now article 53 TFEU), "in order to facilitate access to the autonomous activities and exercise of these activities, the European Parliament and the Council, acting in accordance with the ordinary legislative procedure, shall establish directives aimed at the mutual recognition of diplomas, certificates and other evidence and coordination of laws, regulations and administrative provisions of member states relating to the access of autonomous activities and the exercise of these activities. The aim of the former is to oblige member states to recognize the diplomas obtained by nationals of other member states, while the latter prescribe the training requirements necessary for the acquisition of securities to which the exercise of specific activity is subject, and the essential content of the training.

legislation, a right descending from the secondary EU legislation. As is known, in fact, in this context, the harmonization of the conditions for obtaining titles[483] has left room for codification in directives, first sectorial and then general, of the principle of mutual recognition based on the equivalence of titles. This postulates precisely the persistence of divergences between the laws of member states and from which it follows that the host state can impose only in exceptional cases, rigidly predetermined, measures aimed at a substantial verification of the knowledge of the citizen who intends to settle on its territory.

In fact, private individuals have not hesitated to exploit the differences between the various national laws to access regulated professions to which they would not have had access to the law of the country of origin, using the rules of a member state other than the one of origin. The risk of such behavior is even higher if one considers that national citizens can enforce the secondary EU legislation with respect to their member state of origin, choosing to train abroad, to subsequently pursue their professional activity at home[484].

The construction, characterized by a certain complexity, is so congenital. The individual is directed primarily towards an order different from that of origin, in which rules are less strict regarding the acquisition of the diploma or professional title; then moves from the state in which he acquired the qualification to the state of origin, enforcing the EU legislation to obtain recognition of the title and thus access the regulated profession.

---

483 See, for doctors, directives 75/362/EEC and 75/363/EEC of 16 June 1975, (OJ, L 167), then replaced by Directive 93/16/EEC of 5 April 1993 (OJ, L 165) and subsequent modifications; for nurses, the directives 77/452/EEC and 77/453/EEC of 27 June 1977 (OJ, L 176); for midwives, the directives 80/154/EEC and 80/155/EEC of 21 January 1980 (OJ, L 33); for pharmacists, Directives 85/432/EEC and 85/433/EEC (OJ, L 253); for veterinarians, directives 78/1026/EEC and 78/1027/EEC of December 1978 (OJ, L 362); for architects the directive 83/384 / EEC of 10 June 1985 (OJ, L 223). The general directives are then followed, namely Council Directive 84/48/EEC of 21 December 1988 on a general system for the recognition of higher education diplomas which sanction professional training with a minimum duration of three years (OJ, L 19) and then Council Directive 92/51/EEC of 18 June 1992 on a second general system for the recognition of vocational training, which complements Directive 89/48 / EEC (OJ, L 209). This directive has extended the mutual recognition to diplomas that sanction professional training for less than three years. Both directives were amended by Directive 2001/19 of the European Parliament and of the Council of 14 May 2001 amending Council Directives 89/48/ EEC and 92/51/EEC concerning the general system for the recognition of professional qualifications and directives 77/452/EEC, 77/453/EEC, 78/686/EEC, 78/687/EEC, 78/1026/EEC, 78/1027/EEC, 80/154/EEC, 80/155/EEC, 85/384/EEC, 85/432/EEC, 85/433/EEC and 93/16/EEC of the Council concerning the professions of nurses responsible for general care, dentist, veterinary surgeon, midwife, architect, pharmacist and doctor.

484 J. CAVALLINI, Reconnaissance sur reconnaissance ne vaut, in La Semaine Juridique Social, n. 13, 24 March 2009, pp. 1134ss.

From the described steps, we can grasp the different vision that animates the applicant's member state of nationality and EU system, respectively. In fact, the national system clearly identifies the "U-shaped" operation of its citizen, from which the refusal by the member state to recognize the titles thus obtained and to allow the exercise of the service, to prevent their citizens may otherwise escape the application of national provisions on vocational training. Contrarily, for the EU system, the state which, from a national point of view, is the destination, becomes the state of origin, and that which is the state of origin the state of destination, without taking into consideration the nationality of the applicant identification.

THE C-115/78, KNOORS V. STAATSSECRETARIS VAN ECONOMISCHE ZAKEN CASE OF 7 FEBRUARY 1979: THE DIRECTIVE'S PRESENCE EXCLUDES THE ABUSE

CJEU addressed for the first time the problem described above in a 1979 ruling. The case concerned a Dutch national residing in Belgium, who had been denied by the competent Dutch authorities to carry out the same profession as an installer of heating systems in the Netherlands that he had carried out for seven years in Belgium, since he was considered not in possession of the professional training required by national laws. Faced with such a refusal, Mr. Knoors claimed the application of Directive 64/427/EEC in the field of industry and craftsmanship[485], pursuant to which a member state, if he makes access to certain activities subject to the possession of specific qualifications professionals, the effective exercise in another member state of the activities in question for a given period of time must be recognized as sufficient proof of such qualifications.

According to the usual pattern already found throughout the course of the present discussion, the Netherlands government argued first of all that Mr. Knoors, being of Dutch nationality, could not benefit from European Union legislation, but was subject to the relevant national provisions governing access to specialized trade. He also referred to CJEU's attention to the risk that nationals

485 Council Directive 64/427/EEC of 7 July 1964 on the modalities of transitional measures in the sector of non-salaried transformation activities of the classes 23-40 C.I.T.I. (Industry and crafts) (OJ, L 117, p.1863). The Directive was repealed by Directive 99/42/EC of the European Parliament and of the Council of 7 June 1999 establishing a mechanism for the recognition of qualifications for professional activities governed by the liberalization directives and transitional measures which completes system's general recognition of qualifications, (OJ, L 201, pag. 77).

of a member state, using the provisions of the Directive, would avoid the application of national provisions on professional preparation in case they were authorized to invoke, in respect of their national authorities, the possibilities offered by the Directive.

CJEU discards, as usual, the argument of "purely internal situation", stating that the provisions of the Treaty on the right of establishment cannot be interpreted "so as to exclude from the advantages of EU law the citizens of a given member state, where, by virtue of having regularly resided in the territory of another member state and acquired a professional qualification recognized by EU law, they are in a situation similar to that of their member state of all the others who benefit from the rights and freedoms guaranteed by the treaty"[486]. In other words, the Directive can be invoked by the citizens of all member states, who find themselves in the concrete situations contemplated by the Directive itself, and this also with regard to the state of which they are citizens.

The EU judicature also ruled on the question of circumvention, but without a request to that effect addressed to him by the national court, stating, in principle, that the member state had a legitimate interest in preventing to the possibilities offered by the treaty, some of its citizens, try to avoid abusively the empire of national laws on professional preparation, but then rule out the existence of a risk of abuse in the specific case.

Since the denial of ex application if in no way deviates from what was observed in the first section, CJEU statute becomes relevant from the point of view of the motivation. CJEU observes that the possibility of abuse is actually avoided by the mandatory conditions laid down by the Directive concerning the duration of the periods of professional occupation for the sectors covered, thus accepting the conclusions of the AG Reisch[487] on this point. The latter stated that he did not share the fears of the Netherlands government, precisely because "the conditions for recognition of the exercise of the corresponding profession in another member state, as regards their duration and the position required, are already not easy to so that it is not to be assumed that a large number of

486 C-115/78, Knoors v. Staatssecretaris van Economische Zaken of 7 February 1979, op. cit.

487 See from the CJEU in particular the next cases: C-274/05, Commission v. Greece of 23 October 2008, ECLI:EU:C:2008:585, I-07969. C-286/06, Commission v. Spain of 23 October 2008, ECLI:EU:C:2008:585, I-07969. C-84/07, Commission v. Greece of 4 December 2008, ECLI:EU:C:2008:679, I-00171, C-151/07, Chatzithanasis of of 4 December 2008, ECLI:EU:C:2008:680, I-09013. For further details see: E. ELLIS, P. WATSON, European Union anti-discrimination law, Oxford University Press, Oxford, 2012, pp. 321ss.

nationals of the host state can use this system to escape national provisions on education and exams"[488]. Lastly, CJEU adds that in any case it is always possible for the Council to eliminate, on the basis of the powers conferred upon it by the then art. 57 TFEU[489]. Lastly, CJEU adds that in any case it is always possible for the Council to eliminate, on the basis of the powers conferred upon it by the then art. 57 TFEU[490], the cause of possible fraud against the law, providing for the harmonization of the methods of professional preparation in the various member states[491]; affirmation that it would seem to delegate to the legislator the task of countering abuses.

As in the broadcasting case, here the need to treat the present sentence in full without making the usual distinction between protection techniques, despite the risk of repetition in the following paragraph, derives from the fact that the first rulings on abuse of CJEU appear somewhat stringent and less conscious in the logical succession of the passages, so that often they do not explicitly dwell on the prohibition in itself and on the possibility of its application as an autonomous principle. It would therefore be simplistic to limit ourselves to reporting that the ruling excluded the application of the ban. The sentence, indeed, is relevant exactly where it correlates abuse and harmonization in this context. The presence of a Directive, in fact, leads both the CJEU and the AG to exclude the abuse of the freedom of establishment. In the presence of a legislative text of secondary legislation which fully regulates the recognition of certain professional qualifications, in fact, the room for maneuver left to the member state in deciding the same recognition policies, in implementation of the principle of the primacy of the right of Union, and, consequently, also its power to take anti-abuse measures, since it is assumed that the rules put in place by the Union text are the most appropriate to prevent the possibility of an abuse of the national citizen. Here then, in a system governed by EU law, already just because it is possible to find an abuse, we need, as we will see, "something more". A different question is then that concerning the technique considered most appropriate to combat it.

Focusing now on the first aspect, it may be useful to analyze two different situations: that of 286/06, Commission v. Spain case of 23 October 2008 and

488 E. ELLIS, P. WATSON, European Union anti-discrimination law, op. cit.

489 A. KACZOROWSKA-IRELAND, European Union law, op. cit.

490 J. SCHWARZE, V. BECKER, A. HATJE, J. SCHOO, EU-Kommentar, op. cit.

491 A. KACZOROWSKA-IRELAND, European Union law, op. cit.

that of C-311/06, National Council of engineers of 29 January 2009 on the most evident situation of abuse, the case of recognition.

THE C-286/06, COMMISSION V. SPAIN CASE OF 23 OCTOBER 2008: THE RIGHT TO CHOOSE THE MEMBER STATE IN WHICH ONE WISHES TO ACQUIRE THEIR PROFESSIONAL QUALIFICATIONS DOES NOT KNOW THE ABUSE

In the last months of 2008 CJEU made a series of rulings concerning causes that were all characterized by the fact that the courses aimed at obtaining the diploma were followed by the interested party partly in the same host states, but outside their formal education system, so as to raise doubts about an abusive invocation of recognition procedures. In particular, an appeal by the 286/06, Commission v. Spain of 23 October 2008 that had failed in the obligation to recognize diplomas[492]. The Kingdom of Spain, in fact, in defense of national legislation, invoked, among other things, the prohibition of abuse.

The question arose because Spain complained about the circumvention of the Spanish legislation, which provided for a distinction between "official" and "own" diplomas. This circumvention resulted from the automatic recognition by a university of another member state of its own diplomas issued by a Spanish university, a recognition which took place in application of a mere private convention concluded between two universities. In the present case, in particular, the complainants claimed a diploma as a civil engineer, which was not an official diploma, but only a diploma from the University of Alicante. As such, in accordance with national law, it was devoid of the effects attributed by law to official diplomas and therefore was not valid in Spain for academic or professional purposes. Such a diploma would not have enabled the complainants to practice the profession of bridge and road engineer in Spain. However, the applicants, after completing their studies in Spain, had gone to Italy and, after passing the state

492 CJEU specifies that "as regards the condition referred to in art. 1, lett. (a) third indent of Directive 89/48, it should be noted that the documents annexed to the application show that the complainants were awarded a diploma of civil engineer ('degree in civil engineering') from "Università Politecnica delle Marche", on the basis of equivalence between the studies that they have followed at the University of Alicante and those leading to the undergraduate degree. The fact that said complainants obtained this diploma and passed the Italian state examination, following which they obtained the qualification to practice as an engineer, shows that they possess the professional qualifications required to gain access to a profession regulated in Italy (...)".

exam to become an engineer, invoked the provisions of Directive 89/48/EEC to access the aforementioned profession in Spain, an operation that was considered abusive by the Spanish authorities.

CJEU firstly advocates for the applicability of Directive 89/48/EEC[493] to the case submitted to its examination, considering the requirement for the possession of "diplomas" to be integrated, pursuant to art. 1, lett. a) first indent of the Directive itself, and therefore recognized the right of the complainants, without prejudice to any compensation measures, to exercise in Spain the profession which, by virtue of the said diplomas, they are qualified to practice in Italy. Moreover, underlining CJEU, from Directive 89/48/ECC, no condition can be deduced on the basis of which the parties concerned should have followed their training, in whole or in part, in a member state other than the Kingdom of Spain.

As for the prohibition of abuse, CJEU, as usual, while remembering the principle, in light of the purpose assigned to the general system of recognition referred to in Directive 89/48/EEC, considers that "the fact that a citizen of a member state who wishes to exercise a regulated profession chooses to access it in the member state of his preference cannot in itself constitute an abuse of the general system of recognition established by Directive 89/48/EEC"[494], since "the right of a member state to choose the member state in which they wish to acquire their professional qualifications is inherent in the exercise, in a single market, of the fundamental freedoms guaranteed by the EC Treaty"[495]. This means that the member state, under the Directive, is obliged to recognize diplomas obtained in another member state not only when the training received to achieve them has been carried out entirely or partially in the same state, but also where the diplomas have been issued by the competent authorities of that member state at the end of a training given entirely in the state of origin. CJEU first highlights the elements that allow to frame the situations under examination in the scope of the Directive, since the certificates issued by the authorities of the other member states well attest to the pursuit of the training necessary to access the professions. As regulated in question, once the notion of diploma

493 Council Directive 89/48/EEC of 21 December 1988 on a general system for the recognition of higher-education diplomas awarded on completion of professional education and training of at least three years duration, Official Journal L 019, 24/01/1989 P. 0016-0023. For further details see: L. KORTESE, Exploring professional recognition in the EU: A legal perspective, in Journal of International Mobility, 1 (4), 2016, pp. 45ss.

494 L. KORTESE, Exploring professional recognition in the EU: A legal perspective.

495 L. KORTESE, Exploring professional recognition in the EU: A legal perspective.

is satisfied, it affirms in principle the existence of a prohibition, but leaves no margin to the member state for its application, even in the presence of a construction, from the perspective of the latter, clearly abusive.

(FOLLOWS) CASES: C-311/06, NATIONAL COUNCIL OF ENGINEERS OF 29 JANUARY 2009 AND C-118/09, KOLLER OF 22 DECEMBER 2010. THE "GAME OF MIRRORS" AS AN EXCEPTION TO THE APPLICATION OF EU LAW

The controversy C-311/06, National Council of engineers of 29 January 2009[496] on the recognition that the latter had granted to Mr. Cavallera, an Italian citizen, of a Spanish degree of engineer, obtained through the approval of an Italian diploma, for the purpose of his registration in the register of Engineers in Italy.

The story of Mr. Cavallera can be summarized as follows. He first asked the Ministry of Education and Science in Spain for the approval of his Italian degree, so that the latter was recognized as equivalent to the corresponding Spanish university degree, in application of the provisions of the Royal Decree n. 86/1987. Taking advantage of the certificate attesting the homologation of his Italian diploma, Mr. Cavallera then entered in the register of one of the "colegios de ingenieros técnicos industriales" of Catalonia.

As can be seen, in this first phase, as also in the case at the origin of 286/06, Commission v. Spain case of 23 October 2008, EU law is not yet involved, since it is acknowledged on the basis of national regulations or agreements between states or institutions that operate independently of EU law.

Only in a second phase did Mr. Cavallera apply for recognition of the Spanish qualification in Italy, for the purpose of registering in the member state, in the register of Engineers, this time invoking an EU regulation, Directive 89/48/ EEC.

As stated in the same sentence, there was no doubt that Mr. Cavallera had never carried out a professional activity outside Italy, nor had he undergone training, nor, still, passed examinations required by the Spanish education system. Equally, it was not disputed that he had not taken the state examination provided for by the Italian legislation in order to obtain the qualification to practice as an engineer.

496 CJEU, C-311/06, Consiglio Nazionale degli ingeneri of 29 January 2009/National Council of engineers case of 29 January 2009: national state v. state of acquisition of the title, ECLI:EU:C:2009:37, I-00415.

The referring court therefore asked whether the provisions of Directive 89/48/EEC could be invoked to enter a regulated profession in a host member state by the holder of a license issued by an authority of another member state who did not penalties for any training foreseen by the education system of that member state and is not based on an examination or on professional experience acquired in that member state.

It is anticipated here that CJEU, in answering the question of the national judge, verifies, as in 286/06, Commission v. Spain of 23 October 2008, if the set of qualifications held by the applicant can be considered a "diploma" according to Directive 89/48/EEC. Referring to the following paragraph for a funditus analysis of the motivation of CJEU, as the same will propose for the application of a different technique to combat the abuse, it is useful here to pay particular attention to the conclusions of the AG Poiares Maduro. These take on particular importance for our purposes because, in deepening the interpretation to be given to the notion of "diploma" under the Directive, they suggest to the CJEU two options, which underlie the alternativeness of the techniques available to combat abuses. According to the AG, accepting a restrictive interpretation, the approval decision would not be comparable to a diploma and could not therefore give rise to an operation of mutual recognition. On the contrary, by proposing for an extensive interpretation the notion diploma would also include homologation, "the question of the possibility of Mr. Cavallera, to invoke the rights conferred by the Directive"[497]. While underlining how both orientations of equal value represent two instruments that CJEU can indifferently use to reach an identical result, preference of the AG goes to the thesis of extensive interpretation, offering the latter the advantage of preserve the discretionary power of member states and avoid the exclusion from the scope of the Directive of situations that would fully fall within the objective of free movement[498], as well as preserving the principle of mutual trust. The AG is however firm in believing that the applicability of the Directive does not coincide with the possibility of invoking it, finding in this case strong evidence. This includes the coincidence between the state of origin and the host state, of an abuse of the right, abuse which, according to the AG, can be "traced" using the Emsland-Stärke abuse test. With

497 Conclusions of the AG Poiares Maduro presented in case C-311/06, Consiglio Nazionale degli ingeneri of 29 January 2009, ECLI:EU:C:2009:130, I-00415, par. 24.

498 M. HORSPOOL, M. HUMPHREYS, European Union law, Oxford University Press, Oxford, 2012, pp. 552ss. T. OPPERMANN, C.D. CLASSEN, M. NETTESHEIM, Europarecht, op. cit. R. SCHÜTZE, T. TRIDIMAS, Oxford principles of European Union Law, op. cit.

regard to the existence of the objective element, given that the Directive in question explicitly intends to facilitate the effective exercise of the free movement of persons to promote economic and social interpenetration in the territory of the Union, the AG notes that "if a citizen intends to use in member state A where he has completed his entire academic training, which does not allow him access to the profession he wishes to practice in that state, or wishes to apply in another member state C, a diploma obtained in member state B he grants him access in that state, but without the latter having acquired professional or academic experience connected to the member state which issued him the diploma, in other words, without his having studied it there in the formations he received or worked in that state B, one can reasonably doubt the existence of an exercise effective free movement, as no activity took place in the host member state"[499]. As regards the subjective element, the approval and recognition operation carried out, in the opinion of the AG, does not seem to possess a different justification with respect to the sole interest in circumventing the applicable national regulations, but is purely artificial, since "far from favoring economic and social interpenetration, the result achieved is to enable a European Union citizen to enter a profession in his member state of origin without having obtained the qualifications required in accordance with the requirements of that member state and without that it was necessary to acquire professional and/or academic skills in the context of a training system offered by another member state"[500]. This makes use of advantages deriving from EU law in a purely internal situation, which was only artificially made intra-Union. As already mentioned, CJEU opts for the most restrictive solution proposed, considering the requirements not to be integrated so that the notion of diploma could be configured. In this way, a "technical" explanation is given to the refusal to qualify the certificate of homologation of the diploma, while the justification given by the need to fight against fraud is invoked only implicitly.

499 "The general system for the recognition of diplomas must in fact be capable of applying to an approval decision when it has been adopted by a member state in which professional competence has been acquired which results in particular from the exercise of that profession in the territory of that member state. In fact, under these conditions, the type approval attesting to the academic qualifications of the citizen and the professional experience gained in the territory of that state must allow that person to practice his profession in another member state by virtue of a mutual recognition of his qualifications under the directive" (par. 32).

500 See in argument: C-2/17, Crespo Rey of 28 June 2018, ECLI:EU:C:2018:511, published in the electronic Reports of the cases.

Although in practice the national court has allowed the elusive maneuver to be stopped, the decision in question does not therefore bring any new legal element to the theory of abuse of rights[501]. If not in negative terms, that is to say, not to apply the prohibition, the decision was made even more evident by the fact that on the point CJEU has diverged from the conclusions of the AG. The divergence confirms what has already been noted in C-286/06, Commission v. Spain case of 23 October 2008, or that, when it comes to evidence of secondary legislation that is presumed to be abused, the reasoning carried out by the "European Union" jurisdictional bodies first requires the verification of the applicability of the legislation itself and only at a later time that of abuse. From this point of view, the hypotheses that are being analyzed in this section seem to be closer to the abuse of EU law, deviating from the cases in which the abuse of freedom of movement is presumed. Here again, the element of artificiality echoes in disguising a purely internal situation in intra-Union, an element that assumes a not indifferent centrality, even if often neglected, in the reasoning of member states and of the CJEU itself.

The logical succession just described between the applicability of law and the prohibition of abuse could at first sight lead us to believe that the CJEU in C-311/06, National Council of Engineers case of 29 January 2009 did not decide on the abuse, having chosen the more radical solution, which excluded such possibility at its root.

Well, this statement finds a first denial already in C-118/09, Koller case of 22 December 2010, of a few years later, having as its object a similar scheme, albeit with a fundamental difference: the acquisition of an additional professional qualification in Spain, given that some complementary examinations have been carried out on the spot[502].

In his conclusions, the AG Trstenjak, citing the 286/06, Commission v. Spain sentence of 23 October 2008 reaffirms that it is necessary not to confuse the applicability of a Directive with the possibility of invoking it, which must be excluded if there is an abuse. Starting from the premise that "the fact that a

501 L. DRIGUEZ, Reconnaissance des diplômes: réaction a minima contre une pratique abusive, in Europe, 126, mars 2009, pp. 15-16.

502 CJEU, C-118/09, Koller of 22 December 2010, ECLI:EU:C:2010:805, I-13627. For further details see: V. J. CAVALLINI, Homologation sur homologation peut valoir, in La Semaine Juridique, 12, 2011, pp. 13-14. V. MICHEL, Détermination du diplôme pertinent pour l'accès à la profession d'avocat, in Europe, février 2011, pp. 25ss. T. HEREMANS, Professional services in the European Union internal market: Quality regulation and self regulation, Hart Publishing, Oxford & Oregon, Portland, 2012, pp. 229ss.

citizen of the Union wanted to take advantage of the most advantageous access to a profession in a member state other than that in which he pursued his studies cannot be interpreted as an abuse of right" and that "in this case an abuse of law would be rather recognizable only in the absence of any effective exercise of free movement by the citizen of the Union"[503], comes to deny the presence of an abuse in the present case, having already been ascertained that Mr. Koller had obtained a professional qualification corresponding to a post-secondary course of studies.

What is relevant here, apart from a non-innovative reaffirmation of the right to choose the member state in which one wishes to acquire their professional qualifications as a protected right without any limitation in EU law, is that CJEU, once admitted the applicability of the Directive on recognition. It is not even possible to check whether the right is invokable or whether there is a margin to find an abuse of the law, as the member state sustains against a clearly elusive construction, thus demonstrating that even if the applicability of the Directive is allowed, only the control over abuse is excluded.

THE ADMISSIBILITY OF THE SPANISH STREET. JOINED CASES: C-58/13 AND C-59/13, TORRESI OF 17 JULY 2014

The last and most convincing confirmation of the non-configurability of the abuse of right in the field of professional qualifications, whose minimum requirements are harmonized, occurred with the Torresi1 ruling, with which CJEU defined the well-known affair of Italian abogados, already subject in recent years to several internal rulings, which had left a rather confusing picture on the applicability to the "Spanish way"[504] of the prohibition of abuse of rights. The national court, referring explicitly to the prohibition of abuse, which is reconstructed in terms

503 An Austrian citizen, after obtaining a diploma in law in Austria and after passing a series of complementary examinations at a Spanish university, obtained the homologation of his diploma in Spain, becoming automatically abogado and then subtracting from the compulsory five-year internship expected in Austria to enter the legal profession. He then asked the competent Austrian authority for authorization to take the aptitude test in order to obtain recognition of the diploma, at the same time presenting the application for exemption for all tests, which was however rejected, on the basis, inter alia, of the prohibition of abuse of law. Thus, a dispute arose, in which the national CJEU first asked CJEU whether Directive 89/48 was applicable to the main proceedings.

504 CJEU, joined cases: C-58/13 and C-59/13, Torresi of 17 July 2014, ECLI:EU:C:2014:2088, published in the electronic Reports of the cases.

of the general principle of pre-trial origin, asked the Luxembourg judge whether the Italian authorities could refuse, due to an abuse of right, the registration of the Italian graduate who obtains the title of abogado in Spain, and then engages in the profession in Italy, in the register of lawyers established by Directive 98/5/EC[505]. The second possibility is linked to the one already regulated in general terms by Directive 2005/36 on the basis of the comparison of the securities. Directive 98/5/EC supports, to the general system of Directive 2013/553 (former Directive 2005/36)[506] based on the comparison of qualifications, a simplified discipline for the legal profession, thanks to which it is exempted from the compensation measures pursuant to art. 14 of the Directive 2005/36[507] based on the comparison of qualifications, a simplified discipline for the legal profession. From which, it is exempted from the compensation measures pursuant to art. 14 of the Directive 2005/364 the AG which proves to have exercised with the title of origin, thus using the derecho, the Torresi, as indeed all the aspiring abogados, had to overcome a dozen additional examinations, as required by Spanish legislation, so that some integration into the Spanish system was present.

Also, in this case, at least according to the perspective of the member state of belonging, the "U-shaped" operation carried out to avoid the Italian state examination is clear enough. The citizen of the member state in question, after obtaining a degree within the latter, he goes to another member state in order to acquire the professional qualification of a lawyer, and then returns, immediately after, to the state of origin and practice the profession of lawyer with the professional title obtained in the member state in which the professional qualification was acquired, using Directive 98/5/EC.

505 Directive 98/5/EC of the European Parliament and of the Council of 16 February 1998 to facilitate practice of the profession of lawyer on a permanent basis in a member state other than that in which the qualification was obtained, OJ L 77, 14.3.1998, p. 36-43.

506 Directive 2013/55/EU of the European Parliament and of the Council of 20 November 2013 amending Directive 2005/36/EC on the recognition of professional qualifications and Regulation (EU) no 1024/2012 on administrative cooperation through the Internal Market Information System ("the IMI Regulation"), OJ L 354, 28.12.2013, p. 132-170. For further details see also: L. WOODS, P. WATSON, M. COSTA, Steiner & Woods European Union law, op. cit., pp. 494ss. S. DE VRIES, E. IORATTI, O. GUARDA, European Union citizens economic rights in action: Re-thinking legal and actual barriers in the internal market, Edward Elgar Publishers, Cheltenahm, 2018, pp. 253ss. S. MORANO-FOADI, J. NELLER, Fairhurst's law of the European Union, op. cit.

507 Directive 2005/36/EC of the European Parliament and of the Council of 7 September 2005 on the recognition of professional qualifications, OJ L 255, 30.9.2005, p. 22-142.S. MORANO-FOADI, J. NELLER, Fairhurst's law of th European Union, op. cit.

In answering the question, CJEU, like the AG, in a few places limits itself to applying, indeed in a linear manner, its own precedents. Firstly, the EU judge established that Directive 98/5/EC created a mechanism for the mutual recognition of professional qualifications of migrant lawyers wishing to exercise with the qualification obtained in the member state of origin[508], fully harmonizing the prerequisites required for the exercise of the right of establishment conferred by the Directive. It is necessary and sufficient, that is, presentation to the competent authority of the host member state of a certificate of registration with the competent authority of the home member state, the only condition to which the registration of the data subject in the host member state must be made subject to his being able to pursue his activity in that member state by his professional title of origin.

On the basis of the previous C-506/04, Wilson case of 19 September 2006[509], he concludes that nationals of a member state such as Torresi, who submit to the competent authority of that member state the attenuated establishment machinery-activity "effective and regular" for at least three years in the host state (article 10). As CJEU has stated in the Ebert judgment, these different methods of access to the profession of lawyer in a host state with the professional title of the latter are complementary to each other, so that the lawyer can choose one or more other option depending on the circumstances and their integration needs.

In this way, as we can see, the applicability to the present case of the legislation of the Union is not questioned, and only at a later stage one wonders whether such an application can be undermined by the abuse of law.

Entering the issue, CJEU does not fail to remember, as usual, that, according to settled case law, individuals cannot use fraudulently or abusively the rules of the Union, but, in this case, excludes the configurability of an abuse. In more detail, as regards the objective element, it is first noted that "the fact that a national of a member state who has completed a degree in that state goes to another member state in order to acquire the professional qualification of a lawyer and following return to the member state of which he is a national to practice the profession of lawyer, with the professional title obtained in the member state in which that qualification was acquired, constitutes one of the

508 As we can see in the case from the CJEU: C-168/98, Luxembourg v. European Parliament and Council of 7 November 2000, ECLI:EU:C:2000:598, I-09131, par. 56.

509 CJEU, C-506/04, Wilson of 19 September 2006, ECLI:EU:C:2006:587, I-08613. For a comment see: E. MEISSE, Modalités d'inscription des avocats citoyens communautaires à un barreau d'un État membre, in Europe, 315, novembre 2006, pp. 20-21.

cases in which the objective of Directive 98/5/EC "facilitating the permanent exercise of the profession of lawyer in a member state other than that in which the professional qualification was acquired" is achieved and cannot in itself constitute an abuse of right of establishment resulting from article 3 of Directive 98/5/EC(...)"[510].

This would be enough, as already noted, to exclude the right of national authorities to deny the descending right from the Directive which is assumed as abused. CJEU, however, takes care to reiterate, with reference to the subjective element, what already stated in the pronunciation of 286/06, Commission v. Spain case of 23 October 2008 cited above: "the fact that a citizen of a member state has chosen to acquire a professional title in another member state, other than that in which he resides, in order to benefit from more favorable legislation does not allow per se, to conclude in the sense of the existence of an abuse of right"[511]. Nor, such finding "can be undermined by the fact that the submission of an application for registration in the register of lawyers established with the competent authority of the host member state it took place a short time after obtaining the professional title in the member state of origin"[512], since the registration is not subject to the condition that a period of practice as a lawyer in the state of origin be carried out.

Thus affirmed, CJEU does not even examine the possible hypotheses of abuse, nor the measures concretely adoptable to combat the phenomenon, so that in the perspective of the remitting judge the demand remains substantially unanswered. The Luxembourg judge thus seems to take the opportunity to firmly deny the equation between such operations and the abuse, categorically closing the doors to a control space, also cut in the concrete case, by the competent national authorities.

An extra glimmer would seem at first sight to be hypothesized from the AG Wahl, which, in its conclusions, has admitted a residual possibility of a more in-depth investigation by the authorities of the host state (possibly in collaboration with the authorities of the state of origin) on the possible existence of abusive behavior, in some specific cases, which gave rise to a legitimate suspicion of

510 A. KACZOROWSKA-IRELAND, European Union Law, op. cit.

511 A. KACZOROWSKA-IRELAND, European Union Law, op. cit.

512 By way of example, one could think of the case of those who have acquired the title of abogado without passing the qualification examination now expected in Spain after the entry into force of the ley 34/2006, using the assistance of Spanish lawyers' orders. "Condescending", referred to the order from circular 7.3.2013 n. 35 of the Consejo General de la Abogacia Espanola.

abusive or fraudulent conduct. As can be seen from the exemplification made, which includes counterfeiting, corruption or even false declaration, it is actually only an impression of greater openness. The AG, in fact, refers to the abuse of the right in a sense if he wants to be improper. In reality, this refers to the different hypothesis of fraud, which, as already pointed out, consists in the direct violation of the norm, thus distinguishing himself from the abuse, and presupposes the apparently formal respect of the same, but its violation in substance, that is its purposes.

In reality, even the phrase "in itself" used by the Union judge in several points (also) of this pronunciation always leaves open the question whether it is possible to imagine an abuse in hypotheses that present some specific anomaly indices, a certain quid pluris which would legitimize a power to control national authority. As usual, however, we must ask ourselves, from a pragmatic point of view, if and when, in practice, this can occur. An example not too much of the school, taking into account the business that took place around this phenomenon in Italy, could be that of the non-existent stay in Spain of the Italian citizen who, relying on some Italian commercial organizations, carries out the additional university exams required in only a day in Rome. However, this is actually a purely internal situation, so that it is not even said that at this juncture the prohibition of abuse can play an autonomous role in limiting the allocation of rights arising from Directive 98/5/EC.

In any case, beyond this example, the answer to the question, once again, seems to be negative. Even in the latter case, in fact, the perspective of EU law can hardly coincide with that of national law. In this regard, it is necessary to start from the fact that the first of the formalities necessary for the Italian graduate to undertake the "Spanish way" is represented by the homologation of its degree, according to the procedure provided for by the Spanish legislation[513], which provides for the passing of additional examinations. Once the homologation has been obtained, according to the legislation prior to the Ley 34/2006, the graduate in derecho could practice the legal profession as abogado[514], while now

513 See Real Decree of 20 February 2004, n. 285, in BOE n. 55 of March 4, 2004, pursuant to which the homologation is carried out by submitting a special request to the Ministerio de Educación, Subdirección General de Títulos y Reconocimiento de Cualificaciones; the request is evaluated by a board formed by the representatives of all Spanish universities, which, through a comparative evaluation between the applicant's and national's title, establishes whether there are substantial differences in the training courses and determines the possible conditions further to be satisfied in order to obtain academic recognition (article 17, par. 3).

514 As of today, when a new discipline of access to the profession has arisen, a graduate who intends to

the prior attendance of a master is required and the passing of an exam. This first phase, however, is governed exclusively by national and not by EU law, which comes into play only when the abogado invokes Directive 98/5/EC to register in the register of established lawyers of another state member.

From the point of view of the member state, if it is clear that the intent of Italian citizens, who graduate in law in Italy, is to circumvent the limit represented by the state examination for obtaining the status of lawyer, acquiring such title in member states which issue the qualification in question with greater generosity, the same evidence is not required in the EU legal order.

The moment in which EU law comes into play is intimately linked to the regulation operated by Directive 98/5/EC. Once the requisites necessary for the establishment of a professional in possession of a qualification acquired in a member state have been set, therefore, or it is excluded that the qualification falls within the scope of the Directive in question, or it is not clear how establishment can deny itself. On the other hand, if no experience is required, no aptitude test or period of forensic practice to exercise as abogado in Spain, it is not permissible for such requirements to be required to migrate with the same professional title in another member state[515].

---

become abogado is required to attend an eight-month Oficial de Abogacia Master Course to be held in a presidential or semi-presidential manner, to carry out a period of practice at least quarterly, also contextual to Master's degree, at law firms or public institutions affiliated with the University that organizes the Master and, finally, pass a test consisting of a multiple choice test, composed of 75 questions, and in the drafting of an opinion on of a practical case concerning a subject previously chosen by the candidate (see Royal Decree of 3 June 2011, No. 775, por el que se aprueba el Reglamento de la Ley 34/2006, de 30 de octubre, sobre el lit profesiones de Abogado y Procurador de los Tribunales, in BOE of 16.6.2011, No. 163, 1st century).

515 CJEU, C-61/89, Bouchoucha of 3 October 1990, op. cit., The case concerned a French citizen who, in possession of a French diploma of masseur-cinesiterapista and a diploma of osteopath released in Great Britain, returned to the country of origin to carry out this same profession, had been convicted of abusive medicine, being in France osteopathy a profession reserved for medical graduates. However, the question arose whether this prohibition was at odds with the freedom of establishment. In this context there was no EU legislation governing the exercise of paramedical activities, such as osteopathy, so that the professional qualification in question could not be considered as recognized by EU law, and, on the other hand, directives concerning medical activities they did not even contain a EU definition of the activities to be considered as a medical activity.

THE LEGITIMACY OF "PROFESSIONAL TOURISM" UNDER THE AEGIS OF HARMONIZATION, A DEMONSTRATION TO THE CONTRARY FROM C-61/89, BOUCHOUCHA CASE OF 3 OCTOBER 1990

The analysis of the jurisprudence in this field has shown how, in the presence of a text of secondary law that establishes the conditions for recognition of the title, CJEU, beyond a mere statement of principle, denies in its root the usability of the technique of the prohibition of abuse, without dwelling, even when expressly requested, on the possible hypotheses of abuse, or on any measures that can be adopted to combat the phenomenon.

As for the factual plan of the manifestation of abuse, in most of the hypotheses analyzed, CJEU excludes, explicitly or implicitly, the presence of an abusive situation. Only in C-311/06, National Council of Engineers case of 29 January 2009 seems to detect an avoidance, but, as will be discussed later, to counteract it uses the different technique of restrictive interpretation of the law. With reference to protection techniques, the game is played in any case on the application or not of secondary legislation. CJEU always examines this profile first and, if the required conditions are met, does not go further. From some pronunciations, like C-115/78, Knoors v. Staatssecretaris van Economische Zaken of 7 February 1979 and C-118/09, Koller of 22 December 2010, shows the basic idea that member states cannot demand the application of a more stringent internal regulation, since the risk of abuse is avoided. Hence, in the presence of harmonization of the minimum requirements for obtaining recognition, there is no room for the prohibition of abuse. If the abusive manifestation is macroscopic, CJEU prefers to opt for a restrictive interpretation of the Directive that has come to light.

Moreover, the relevance of the role played by the harmonization, is inferred from a previous judgment, made with reference to a professional qualification not yet covered by a secondary law, the C-61/89, Bouchoucha sentence of 3 October 1990[516], without wishing to go over the details of CJEU in detail. Just remember that, in the absence of a European Union regulation of the osteopath profession, the diploma in question could not be considered as a professional qualification recognized by the provisions of EU law, and therefore in the

516 J. LONBAY, Picking over the bones: Rights of establishment reviewed, in European Law Review, 2, 1991, pp. 510ss.

opinion of CJEU, each member state remained free to regulate the exercise of this activity on its territory, provided it was non-discriminatory.

In particular, CJEU has recognized the interest of a member state in preventing its citizens, through the possibilities offered by the Treaty, from evading national laws on professional preparation, a situation that would occur, in particular, "if the fact, for a national of a member state, having obtained a diploma in another member state, the extent of which and the value of which is not recognized by any European Union provision, could oblige the member state of origin to allow him to carry out on his territory activities related to this diploma, where the performance of such activities is reserved for holders of higher qualifications mutually recognized at Union level and that this reserve does not appear to be arbitrary"[517], admitting the legality of the refusal.

In this case, the greater space left for national anti-avoidance maneuvers emerges, which seems to have as a premise the absence of coordination directives on the matter. This last aspect would make the pronunciation "delphic and obscure" according to some doctrine[518], since the reason why CJEU has introduced nuances regarding the type of recognition, according to whether it is based on the provisions of the treaty or is automatic, is unclear since it is based on secondary law, a distinction which should not influence the possibility of reacting to any abusive behavior. In order to clarify the point, the finding that in the absence of harmonization, as has already been shown, CJEU does not actually use the technique of the prohibition of abuse of law, while allowing member states to adopt national measures, helps to clarify the point justified by overriding reasons in the public interest. It is clear that an area of intervention of member states thus conceived cannot be applied in the presence of a "European Union" discipline, where not expressly permitted, having to find within the

517 Directive 2004/38/EC of the European Parliament and of the Council of 29 April 2004 on the right of citizens of the Union and their family members to move and reside freely within the territory of member states, amending Regulation (EEC) No 1612/68 and repealing Directives 64/221/EEC, 68/360/EEC, 72/194/EEC, 73/148/EEC, 75/34/EEC, 75/35/EEC, 90/364/EEC, 90 /365/EEC and 93/96/EEC (Official Journal L 158, page 77). As is well known, the sector has been regulated by several texts of secondary legislation, until the entry into force of Directive 2004/38/EC: see Council Directive 64/221/EEC of 25 February 1964 for the coordination of special measures concerning the transfer and residence of foreigners, justified on grounds of public policy, security and health (OJ, 56, p. and Regulation (CEE) n. 1612/68 of the Council of 15 October 1968 on the free movement of workers within the European Union(OJ, L 257, p.2).

518 The case of the communication of false data to enter the Union, which more properly falls within EU law fraud, is different: C-285/95, Suat Kol v. Land Berlin of 6 March 1997, op. cit. C-235/99, Kondova of 27 September 2001, op. cit. C-303/08, Bozkurt of 22 December 2010, ECLI:EU:C:2010:800, I-13445. C-186/10, Oguz of 21 July 2011, ECLI:EU:C:2011:509, I-06957.

system and not outside it the means to react to abuse, such as, with reference to the recognition of professional qualifications, the possibility of providing for the so-called compensatory tests.

ABUSE WITH REFERENCE TO THE CASE OF STAY OF A THIRD NATIONAL COUNTRY MARRIED TO AN EU CITIZEN

The prohibition of abuse of law was frequently invoked by member states to deny the right of residence granted by Directive 2004/38/EC to a non-EU citizen married to an EU citizen. In particular, in this way, the national legal systems have tried to stem not so much and not only the practice of "comfortable" marriages, then sanctioned by art. 35 of Directive 2004/38/EC, but also the construction carried out by the "authentic couple", who moves to another member state to create an intra-Union situation, so as to benefit from the provisions of EU law that attribute the right of residence to non-EU spouses, while circumventing national provisions concerning the entry and residence of applicants from third countries.

This hypothesis has some peculiar characteristics. In fact, with regard to the recognition of professional qualifications, the triangulation between legal systems depends on the fact that the citizen of a member state moves to the state with the most favorable legislation to acquire the professional qualification. In this context, the triangulation is given by the temporary transfer of the couple to a member state other than that of residence, for the sole purpose of benefiting from the European provisions on family reunification once they have returned to their state of residence. In other words, as already pointed out, in these cases the member state of destination is involved not so much to derive benefits directly from its more favorable national legislation, but only to artificially create that intra-state situation required to benefit from the provisions of the Directive 2004/38/EC. This implies, inter alia, the indifference of the destination state. The problem of abuse in this area has affected both the Council, which adopted a resolution already in 1997, and the EC, which in 2014 published a kind of vademecum available to national authorities[519].

519 Article 35, in regulating the hypothesis of "abuse of rights", states that "member states may take the necessary measures to refuse, extinguish or revoke a right conferred by this Directive, in the event of abuse of rights or fraud, such as example a fictitious marriage".

For its part, as will be shown, the Luxembourg judge has adopted the same approach that we found with regard to the recognition of diplomas: it refers to abuse of right only in the context of fictitious marriages, citing art. 35 of the Directive. Otherwise, when the marriage is authentic, even if the circulation is manifestly elusive, it prefers, in the case, to adopt a restrictive interpretation, rather than to make use of the prohibition of abuse of rights, thus tracing a clear border line between the fraudulent marriage, to which art. 35, and the authentic marriage, even if invoked for essentially elusive purposes.

THE REACTION OF CJEU TO THE PARADIGMATIC EXAMPLE OF ABUSIVE CIRCULATION OF SPOUSES: THE C-109/01, AKRICH CASE OF 22 SEPTEMBER 2003 AND THE IRRELEVANCE OF ABUSIVE INTENTIONS

The C-109/01, Akrich case of 22 September 2003[520] is probably the most fitting example of the approach followed by the CJEU in the area of free movement of persons, then governed by Regulation (EEC) no. 1612/68[521] and by some complementary directives. On the one hand, the referring court explicitly asked the CJEU whether the behavior of the spouses could be regarded as abusive and for that reason it was possible for the national authorities to deny the right of residence in the country of origin, which the spouses claimed to EU law. On the other hand, the facts of the case did not indicate that it was a fictitious marriage, but only that the right of circulation had been used artificially, with the sole purpose of invoking Union law, more favorable than the Anglo-Saxon Immigration Act.

As stated by the national authority, the spouses, a Moroccan national and an English citizen, had moved to Ireland with the clear intention of returning to the

520 CJEU, C-109/01, Akrich of 22 September 2003, ECLI:EU:C:2003:491, I-09607. For further details see: R. PLENDER, Quo vadis? Nouvelle orientation des règles sur la libre circulation des personnes suivant l'affaire Akrich, in Cahiers de Droit Européen, (1-2), 2004, pp. 261 ss. C. SCHILTZ, Akrich: A clear delimitation without limits, in Maastricht Journal of European and Comparative Law, 12, 2005 (3), pp. 241ss. E. SPAVENTA, Case C-109/01, Secretary of State for the Home Department v. H. Akrich, judgment of the Full CJEU of 23 September 2003, ECR 1- 9607, in Common Market Law Review, 42, 2005, pp. 225ss.

521 Regulation (EEC) no 1612/68 of the Council of 15 October 1968 on freedom of movement for workers within the Community, OJ L 257, 19.10.1968, p. 2–12, no longer in force from 15 June 2001. For further details see: A. SAYDÉ, Abuse of European Union: Law and regulation of the internal market, op. cit.

United Kingdom using EU law, so that Mr. Akrich could enter into that country as a spouse of a citizen of the Union, who had used its freedom of movement. In other words, a purely internal intra-Union situation was transformed. The judge in charge of the dispute therefore wondered whether Mr. Akrich was actually entitled to reside in the United Kingdom under the provisions on the free movement of workers in accordance with the C-370/90, The Queen/Immigration Appeal Tribunal and Surinder Singh, Former Secretary of State for the Home Department case law of 7 July 1992[522], having regard to the fact that the two spouses had moved to Ireland with the express purpose of subsequently exercising European Union rights, in order to be able to legally return to the United Kingdom.

Already, the AG Geelhoed recognizes that Mr. Akrich has used the free movement of persons as an instrument to enter EU, when he would not have been entitled to it on the basis of immigration rules that should have been applied[523]. However, the United Kingdom's argument that EU law could not apply in the present case is disputed, since a person who seeks to avail himself of the Union's

522 Indeed, the evidence to detect an abusive construction by the spouses involved, at least from the point of view of the member state of origin- the United Kingdom-was evident from the couple's movements. A Moroccan citizen, married to an English citizen, after having lived in Ireland for six months with his wife, he applied for residence in the United Kingdom. More in detail, Mr Akrich had married a British citizen in August 1996 while illegitimately residing in the United Kingdom, and, at the end of the same month, had applied for a residence permit as a spouse of a United Kingdom citizen. After being detained in early 1997 under the Immigration Act, Mr. Akrich was expelled at his request to Ireland, where his wife had been established since June 1997. Mr Akrich requested the removal of the deportation order in January 1998 and, the following month, a permit to enter as a spouse of a person established there.

523 In this regard, the referring CJEU recalls that the United Kingdom immigration law did not initially contain a specific provision relating to the situation considered by CJEU in case: C-370/90, The Queen/Immigration Appeal Tribunal and Surinder Singh, ex parte Secretary of State for the Home Department of 7 July 1992, ECLI:EU:C:1992:296, I-04265. The admission to the United Kingdom of a person who should normally have an entry permit and who wishes to enter as a spouse of a United Kingdom national who is a member of the United Kingdom or who wishes to return to the United Kingdom after having exercised his rights under EU law as a worker in another member state. However, in the light of the case: C-370/90, The Queen/Immigration Appeal Tribunal and Surinder Singh, ex parte Secretary of State for the Home Department of 7 July 1992, that person enjoyed a "EU law which he can enforce directly" under Section 7 (1) of the Immigration Act 1988 and Section 2 of the European Communities Act 1972, and was not in this capacity to obtain an authorization to enter the United Kingdom. Conclusions presented on 27 February 2003, par. 129. It also notes that it is necessary to prevent EU legislation from being used to circumvent the national immigration rules and in particular the individual preventive assessment. "This applies even more to the case at issue in the main proceedings, in which EU legal order is invoked to circumvent a previous expulsion order adopted by a member state" considering it plausible that "the persons concerned will increasingly seek to circumvent national legislation on immigration, choosing EU law as a means of securing residence in your member state (...)" (see parr. 140-142).

legal system to circumvent national law cannot make claims deriving from European Union law[524].

The fact that Akrich falls within the material scope of Regulation 1612/68 is not sufficient to accept the reasons. In fact, in the opinion of the AG, in this case there is a prevailing imperative national interest for the United Kingdom that can be invoked in order to deny entry to the worker's spouse, following a prior individual assessment. Based on the legislation national immigration program, the AG does not explain how and why a right formulated in unconditional terms can be limited by invoking the doctrine of imperative reasons of general interest. Indeed, by conceding that the Akrich spouses fall within the scope of the Treaty and Regulation n. 1612/68, difficult to understand how their rights pursuant to art. 10 of the aforementioned Regulation may be limited for imperative reasons of general interest.

Beyond these critical points, what is most interesting to note is how even the AG can see the difficulty of applying the theory of abuse of law to the concrete case. This is because the subjective criteria are unreasonable and easily manipulated and the objective criteria, if knowable, can be circumvented[525] and also because the border between abuse and use for a purpose not pursued by the legislator is difficult to establish[526].

524 On the one hand, he observes that a national of a member state who has worked as a EU worker in another member state, such as Mrs Akrich, also continues to be entitled under the legislation, even after returning to the country of origin (paragraph 159).

525 The AG in parr. 180-181 states that "the establishment of the Akrich spouses in Ireland can be regarded as a use of EU law for a purpose which, if not pursued by the EU legislator, is nevertheless inherent in EU law. In fact, the legislator did not intend to create a right that could be used to circumvent the national legislation on immigration, but gave the citizen of a member state the right to settle in another member state together with his spouse. This very establishment in another member state is the essence of the freedom conferred by EU law on the union citizens (...)".

526 Paragraph 173. More in detail, the AG notes with reference to the subjective criteria that "the jurisprudence is very reluctant to attribute value to such criteria. In principle, as the Levin judgment states, (C-53/81, Levin v. Staatssecretaris van Justitii of 23 March 1982) the intentions of the worker are irrelevant. From my preliminary observation it follows that the caution of CJEU is inevitable, since the subjective criteria, and especially the intention of the interested ones, are easily manipulated. Nor is it necessary to make use of the declared will, as the Greek government wishes, or of an objectified will (...)" (par. 174). As regards the objective criteria, he then states that "in the present case, the duration of the stay in Ireland could constitute an objective condition. Both in Lair and Knoors the importance of the length of stay is emphasized (...). It could be argued otherwise that, in the absence of a minimum duration established by EU law, such an interest could instead exist (...)" (par. 175). Remember, however, that "the objective criteria are liable to be circumvented. Legal certainty requires, in my view, that the factors taken into consideration by national authorities in ascertaining the existence of an abuse are known. However, such factual knowledge presents the risk that those concerned may adapt the circumstances in which they are found in such a way as to satisfy the required conditions (...) "(paragraph 176). In the light of C-370/90, The Queen/Immigra-

Discontinuing the opinion of the AG, CJEU excludes the applicability of EU law by adopting an interpretation of the restrictive Directive. On the issue of abuse, which, as usual, where there is a text of secondary law, is taken into consideration, it is examined only after verifying the applicability of the Regulation, the CJEU confines itself to affirming, citing the previous C-370/90, the Queen/ Immigration Appeal Tribunal and Surinder Singh, Former Secretary of State for the Home Department case of 7 July 1992, that "the reasons that may have prompted a worker from a member state to look for work in another member states have no relevance as regards the right of entry and residence in the territory of that state, provided that the worker exercises or intends to carry out an effective and genuine activity (...) nor are these reasons relevant for assessing the legal situation of the couple upon their return to the member state of which the worker is citizen. Such behavior cannot constitute an abuse (...) even if the spouse did not have, when the couple has settled in another member state, the right to remain in the member state of which the worker is a citizen (...)"[527].

It should be noted here that, in reality, the attention given by the sentence to the abuse doctrine, partly justified by the formulation of the application by the national court, shows the clear desire of CJEU to suppress any doubt about the applicability of the ban in such hypotheses. Indeed, CJEU had already excluded the applicability of the Directive in the present case, due to the fact that Mr. Akrich could not claim a prior "legal stay" in a member state.

Wanting to draw the strings of what has been observed, the case described above is paradigmatic of the hypothetical behavior as abusive, held by a third-country national, who, to avoid the application of national immigration law, once married to a citizen of the Union, moves with the latter in a different member state, in order to ensure, on return, the invocation of the less stringent European discipline on residence. It should be borne in mind that, from the perspective of the member state concerned, the situation is aggravated by the fact that, when the third-country national comes under the right of residence descending from the provisions of EU law, in most cases, the national authority

---

tion Appeal Tribunal and Surinder Singh, ex parte Secretary of State for the Home Department of 7 July 1992, it is also irrelevant, according to the AG, "that Ms Akrich, having left Ireland, settles with her husband in a third member state. In this case there can of course be no abuse or return to the United Kingdom, as is the case here (...)" (par. 182).

527 CJEU, C-138/02, Collins of 23 March 2004, ECLI:EU:C:2004:172, I-027093. C-459/99, MRAX of 25 July 2002, ECLI:EU:C:2002:461, I-06591. For further details see: E. GUILD, S. PEERS, J. TOMKIN, The European Union citizenship directive: A commentary, Oxford University Press, Oxford, 2014.

he had already denied that the right of residence on the basis of national legislation and possibly already expelled.

Even in the face of such constructions, CJEU denies the existence of abuse "at a high price". In fact, it finds itself in an extremely restrictive solution, which substantially sacrifices fundamental freedoms and respect for family life, by excluding at the root the possibility of availing itself of fundamental freedoms and their corollaries in the absence of prior legal residence in a member state. This is a solution that is not acceptable on the level of principles, which is not only difficult to reconcile with other precedents of CJEU[528], but will be shortly afterwards exceeded by C-127/08, Metock and others sentence of 25 July 2008, as deemed to be no longer acceptable.

It is then necessary to question the reasons for this choice, bearing in mind also what observed from the AG about the difficulties of applying the ban in question. The reasons why the worker moves, when the subordinate activity turns out to be effective, cannot be completely irrelevant, given the difficulty in ascertaining with certainty the motivations, often multiple and not univocal, that pushed an individual to move from one place to another. In other words, the refusal by CJEU to take into account the allegations of abuse of law, shows how, in his eyes, there cannot be a case in which you go to "create abusively" a situation for which you become a worker for fall within the scope of Union law. Also, in this hypothesis, the CJEU is called to use another technique to protect against abuses, that of restrictive interpretation.

528 Consider, for example, partner proximity, best climate and pay abroad, a better welfare system, and so on. CJEU only three years earlier in case: C-110/99, Emsland-Stärke of 14 December 2000 had mentioned the presence of an objective and subjective element as key criteria for determining the existence of abuse. In the judgment in question it was instead clearly refused to take into account party's motivations to determine the legal position of EU citizens and their spouses. However, he considers that in a closer look, CJEU has in fact kept the two elements of the abuse test, underlining that the reasons why a worker seeks employment in another state are not relevant, provided that he intends to conduct an effective activity.

(FOLLOWS) C-456/12, O. V. MINISTER VOOR IMMIGRATIE, INTEGRATIE EN ASIEL AND MINISTER VOOR IMMIGRATIE, INTEGRATIE EN ASIEL V. B CASE OF 12 MARCH 2014 AND TIME'S FACTOR RELEVANCE

The construction described above involves more and more systems: law of the state of origin, whose legislation is tried to circumvent; that of EU, from which the right of residence is drawn; that of another member state, which is involved not so much because they want to draw direct benefits, but only for the purpose of creating that intra-Union situation that allows for EU rights. As noted, the reasons appear not to be relevant in this sector. However, one wonders if time element, with reference to the length of stay in a state other than the residence of the Union citizen, can instead take on some significance. On this point, it has already been observed that in Torresi CJEU has discarded the relevance of time element with reference to the period of work practice carried out in Spain by two brothers. Yet, the solution can change in this context, due to the particular role played by the law of the second member state involved, no longer a destination for the purchase of a favorable situation, but a simple vehicle of transnationality. While, in fact, in C-58/13 and C-59/13, Torresi case of 17 July 2014, EU regulations considered Torresi brothers to be equal to any other Spanish abogado, here the EU classification qualify the Union citizen married to a third-country national, as a migrant worker, when he moves for the first time from the state of origin to the second member state involved, since the worker already uses the right of movement during the first movement[529].

CJEU dealt with time factor in C-456/12, O. v. Minister voor Immigratie, Integratie en Asiel and Minister voor Immigratie, Integratie en Asiel v. B case of 12 March 2014[530], in relation to the case of a third-country national married to a Union citizen, who had exercised freedom of movement, moving from one state to another, before returning to the country of origin accompanied by the spouse, for which an intra-state case was created. Mr. O., a Nigerian citizen, who married a Dutch national in 2006, claimed to have lived in Spain between 2007 and April 2010 as a family member of a Union citizen. During the same period,

529 J. SCHWARZE, U. BECKER, A. HATJE, J. SCHOO, EU-Kommentar, op. cit.

530 CJEU, C-456/12, O. v. Minister voor Immigratie, Integratie en Asiel e Minister voor Immigratie, Integratie en Asiel v. B of 12 March 2014, ECLI:EU:C:2014:135, published in the electronic Reports of the cases.

his wife had stayed for two months with Mr., O., in Spain, but, having failed to find a job there, she had returned to the Netherlands, although she continued to spend holidays in Spain on a regular basis. Mr. O., who had returned to the Netherlands, was refused the request to obtain the residence permit as a family member of a Union citizen in 2010. The referring court therefore asked whether this refusal was contrary to Directive 2004/38/EC and article 21 TFEU. CJEU first excludes the applicability of Directive 2004/38/EC, noting that it provides "a derived right of residence in favor of third country nationals, family members of a Union citizen, in accordance with article 2 of that Directive, only when the latter has exercised his right to free movement, settling in a member state other than the member state of which he is citizen"[531]. On the other hand, he admits that a derived right of residence can be based on art. 21, par. 1, TFEU and, with regard to the conditions for concession, points out that the same, in principle, should not be stricter than those provided for by Directive 2004/38/EC. This is because "although such a return case does not fall under Directive 2004/38/EC, it must be applied by analogy with regard to the conditions of residence of the Union citizen in a member state other than that possesses citizenship, given that, in both cases, it is the Union citizen who is the contact person so that a third-country citizen who is a family member of the Union citizen in question can be granted a secondary right of residence"[532]. However, CJEU is careful to point out that the obstacle to leaving the member state of which the spouse is a citizen is realized only when the residence of the Union citizen in the host state is sufficiently effective to allow him or her to develop or consolidate a family life in that member state. In other words, not every stay of a citizen of the Union in the host state, in spouse's company, necessarily involves the granting of a right of residence derived from that family member. CJEU distinguishes, in this regard, the case of citizen who makes use of the rights granted to him by art. 6, par. 1, of Directive 2004/38/EC, which does not aim to establish itself in the host member state in a manner favorable to the development or consolidation of a family life in the latter member state, and the one proposing to make use of the rights deriving there from art. 7, par. 1, of Directive 2004/38/EC. Indeed, a stay in the host member state in accordance with and in compliance with the conditions

531 CJEU, C-456/12, O. v. Minister voor Immigratie, Integratie en Asiel e Minister voor Immigratie, Integratie en Asiel v. B of 12 March 2014, op. cit.

532 CJEU, C-456/12, O. v. Minister voor Immigratie, Integratie en Asiel e Minister voor Immigratie, Integratie en Asiel v. B of 12 March 2014, op. cit.

set out in article 7, par. 1, proves, in principle, the settlement and, therefore, the actual character of the stay. Only in this last hypothesis, whose existence must be ascertained by the national judge, art. 21 requires that the family life that the said citizen has led to the host member state may continue on his return to the member state of which he is a national, by granting a derived right of residence to the family member concerned, a third-country citizen[533].

CJEU adds that the application of rules of EU law cannot extend to the protection of abusive practices, recalling the elements of the abuse test. At the point immediately following, with an extremely abrupt transition, which necessarily imposes to correlate the previous statement with the subsequent one, it is then specifies that "what is the assessment whether the cumulative effect of various short-term stays in the host member state? is such as to give rise to a derived right of residence for a family member of the Union citizen (...). It must be remembered that only a residence that meets the conditions set out in par. 1 and 2 of art. 7 or of art. 16 of Directive 2004/38/EC is suitable for creating such a right of residence. In this regard, short-term stays, such as weekends or holidays spent in a member state other than that of which that citizen is a national, even if considered jointly, fall within the scope of article 6 of Directive 2004/38/EC and do not meet the conditions in question"[534].

The two points are now taken into consideration, and examining correlations between them show that: a) CJEU does not exclude the abuse of right, reconnecting it to the time element; b) does not, however, apply the prohibition but is based on a restrictive interpretation of the Directive, to exclude that short stays, though accumulated, may fall within art. 7 of the Directive and thus assign a derived right of residence.

533 AG Sharpston, in his Opinion of 12 December 2013 in case: C-456/12, O. v. Minister voor Immigratie, Integratie en Asiel e Minister voor Immigratie, Integratie en Asiel v. B of 12 March 2014, ECLI:EU:C:2013:837, published in electronic Reports of cases. See in particular paragraph 42 which is affirmed that: "(...) on the basis of the facts, nothing suggests that were marriages of convenience, nor that there was fraud or abuse of rights. In other circumstances, the finding of such an abuse could, in fact, make it unnecessary to further examine whether a derived right of residence can be legitimately refused. However, the mere fact that, at a certain point, both O and referent O, and B and referent B, have moved to another member state, where more favorable treatment is guaranteed, does not constitute an abuse of rights (...)".

534 K. ZIEGLER, "Abuse of law" in the context of the free movement of workers, in R. DE LA FERIA, S. VOGENAUER (a cura di), Prohibition of abuse of law: a new general principle of EU law?, op. cit., pp. 299-300.

A COMPARISON WITH THE HYPOTHESIS SUB A): B). THE "SOCIAL TOURISM" PHENOMENON

The constructions aimed at circumventing the restrictive national legislation do not exhaust the category of illegal constructions. In fact, it is possible to involve only two systems, where the private person does not set as main objective to avoid the national legislation considered unfavorable, but simply obtaining certain social benefits in another member state by placing itself "artificially" in the condition of invoking a certain status of Union law, such as that of a worker or a citizen, and of benefiting from the prohibition of discrimination on grounds of nationality.

The element of differentiation just highlighted does not change the conclusions reached by CJEU with regard to the hypotheses examined above involving three systems. In fact, even in the context of free movement of the Union worker and, subsequently, of the EU citizen, the case law does not recognize the prohibition of abuse of law as an autonomous technique of protection against the abuses reported by member states, possibly reaching legitimize the measures taken by the general or specific member states, as appropriate, through a certain interpretation of the Union law which is relevant.

More specifically, in this sector too, two trends pertain to the abuse related to time element, which would occur when a person who has worked in another member state for a very limited period of time requests the grant of a series of co-essential rights to the status of worker, and to the abuse related to the subjective element of motivation, which, from the perspective of the member state, could occur when a person requests social assistance, after becoming a worker at all the effects. It is reasonable to assume that he has entered the member state already for the purpose of deriving a further benefit resulting from the status of worker. What then characterizes the constructions put in place in these cases is that to be invoked abusively is a status descending from EU law, while the right to be obtained is attributed directly by the member state.

Otherwise, in the hypotheses previously analyzed, which also concerns the construction of individuals, relating to the right of residence of the non-EU spouse, if EU law and in particular the freedom of movement was abused, the advantage of illegal construction derives from EU law itself. As we have seen, in fact, the host state served only as an "instrument" to trigger the application of freedoms of movement.

In this case, CJEU denies the application of prohibition, but does not completely reject the presence of an abuse, making use of the time element to assess whether an effective activity has been put in place and completely discarding the relevance of the reasons[535]. What unites this hypothesis to that described in the previous paragraph is therefore the irrelevance of the intentions of individuals who move from one country to another for work. On the other hand, it is clear that the member state retains a wider margin of maneuver, justified by the fact that the benefits which "social tourist"[536] are to benefit from are guaranteed by their own legislation. Exactly for this reason, CJEU seems to be more inclined to recognize an abuse, although the technique used is not that of the prohibition of abuse, understood as an autonomous principle based on the two elements, objective and subjective.

In order to substantiate such statements, using the usual scheme that distinguishes between the motives and time factor, a group of well-known, more time-related judgments will be considered, which dealt with "social tourism" of European Union workers[537], and then analyze the most recent case of "social tourism" of the EU citizen, which consists in the practice of EU citizens moving from one member state to another in order to benefit from non-contributory benefits, i.e. system of performance of a social security system to which they have not contributed.

535 This term refers to EU citizens who move from one member state to another for the sole purpose of benefiting from non-contributory benefits, i.e. a system of benefits for a social security system to which they do not have contributed. The term used by AG Ruiz-Jarabo Colomer in his opinion in case C-138/02, Collins of 23 March 2004, Collins cited above, ECLI:EU:C:2004:446, I-06591, par. 75.

536 CJEU, C-39/86, Lair v. Universität Hannover of 21 June 1988, op. cit.

537 CJEU, C-306/16, Maio Marques da Rosa of 9 November 2017, ECLI:EU:C:2017:844, published in electronic Reports of cases.

THE ORIGINS: "SOCIAL TOURISM" OF COMMUNITY WORKERS. NOTES TO SENTENCES: C-39/86, LAIR V. UNIVERSITÄT HANNOVER OF 21 JUNE 1988, C-53/81, LEVIN V. STAATSSECRETARIS VAN JUSTITII OF 23 MARCH 1982 AND C-413/01, FRANCA NINNI-ORASCHE OF 6 NOVEMBER 2003. THE ROLE OF TIME FACTOR

In order to understand the scope of time element and the role it can play in this area, it may be useful to deepen C-39/86, Lair v. Universität Hannover case of 21 June 1988. In short, the case concerned a French citizen who, after having worked for a short period in Germany, had been refused the grant of a study grant from the University of Hannover, on the ground that the Federal law on education subordinated the assignment of the allowance to foreigners upon the provision of at least a five-year work activity. The question that arose essentially was whether member states could unilaterally make the granting of social advantages for the workers, in this case, the advantages of a system of national assistance for students to achieving a previous period of employment.

Having noted that the subsidy in question constitutes a "social advantage" pursuant to art. 7, n. 2, of Regulation n. 1612/68, which must therefore be enjoyed, without any discrimination, by workers who are nationals of other member states, CJEU in providing a reply concerning the possibility for the member state to request a minimum period of prior work as a condition for granting social advantages, we focus first on the notion of worker. On this point, he points out that, in principle, the rights guaranteed to migrant workers do not necessarily depend on the existence or continuation of an employment relationship. Moreover, since the concept of worker has a European scope and its definition cannot depend on criteria established by national legislation, member states cannot unilaterally make the grant of social advantages provided for by article 7, n. 2, of said Regulation, to a certain period of working activity.

He adds, however, that "to the extent that the arguments of the three member states in question are motivated by the concern to prevent certain abuses, which might arise, for example, when objective elements allow the establishment of a worker entering a member state in order to benefit from the student benefits system, after a very short period of work, it should be noted that such abuses are not covered by the community rules in question (...)"[538].

538 Conclusions of the AG Slynn, presented in case C-39/86, Lair v. Universität Hannover of 21 June

It is not easy to interpret the meaning of this statement, which closes cryptically the ruling of CJEU, just before it is reiterated that the right to social advantages under article 7, n. 2, of Regulation n. 1612/68 cannot be subjected to the condition imposed by the host member state of a minimum period of previous work carried out in the territory of that state.

Of course, no precise indications can be drawn regarding the possibility of applying the prohibition on the abuse of rights in a situation such as the one described above. From this point of view, it is useful to state that this is a theoretical decision, since, in the concrete case, there was not a question of abuse, as pointed out by the AG in its conclusions, where it is stated that " it seems clear to me of the present proceedings (and, according to the order for reference, the national court was also persuaded) that the applicant went and stayed in the Republic of Germany as a worker economically inserted in the host state"[539]. It must also be borne in mind that this is one of the first rulings in which CJEU referred to the abuse of law, which therefore appears to us, "rudimentary", in some ways.

What interests us here is to highlight how CJEU has linked the assessment of abuse to the "very short period of work", understood as an objective element. It is unclear, however, whether this element rises due to a restrictive interpretation of the concept of worker, as the AG seems to suggest, or whether, on the other hand, the member state is authorized to adopt certain measures on a case-by-case basis, the possibility of adopting which requires a minimum period of work, as per device.

1988, ECLI:EU:C:1988:377, I-03161.

539 CJEU, C-53/81, Levin v. Staatssecretaris van Justitii of 23 March 1982, ECLI:EU:C:1982:105, I-01035. Mrs Levin, a British national married to a third country, applied for a residence permit in the Netherlands, but the request was rejected on the grounds that, inter alia, Mrs Levin exercised a professional activity in low countries that do not allow the minimum subsistence, so it could not be considered "privileged CEE citizen" in accordance with this discipline. The national court asked CJEU essentially whether the rules of EU law on the free movement of workers could also apply to the national of a member state who pursues an employment activity on the territory of another member state, but obtains a lower income from what the law of the host state considers the minimum vital.

REASONS' IRRELEVANCE: FROM C-53/81, LEVIN V. STAATSSECRETARIS VAN JUSTITII OF 23 MARCH 1982 TO C-413/01, FRANCA NINNI-ORASCHE OF 6 NOVEMBER 2003

If already in the C-53/81, Levin v. Staatssecretaris van Justitii pronunciation of 23 March 1982[540] CJEU had the opportunity to affirm the irrelevance of the reasons that push the individual to move from one country to another, in the face of a question to that effect of the national court constructed in hypothetical terms only, the same principle is reaffirmed and applied in the concrete case with the C-413/01, Franca Ninni-Orasche sentence of 6 November 2003, after twenty years. In the first case, the EU judge must answer inter alia to the question whether the right of access and residence in the territory of a member state could be denied to a worker who was pursuing, by entry and stay in a member state, mainly for purposes other than the exercise of a subordinate activity, had already highlighted two key aspects. In general, the principle that the European rules at issue express the need, inherent in the principle of free movement of workers, that the advantages conferred by EU law can only be demanded by those who actually they intend to carry out a subordinate activity. On the other hand, Union rules do not imply that the enjoyment of that freedom may be subordinated to the aims pursued by a citizen of a member state with his application for entry or residence in the territory of another member state, condition that he exercises or intends to exercise an activity that meets the criteria specified above, that is, a real and effective subordinate activity. If there is a real and effective activity then, the reasons that may have led the worker to look for work in the member state in question "are irrelevant and should not be taken into consideration"[541]. Nothing new, in short, on this front.

540 On this point, CJEU held that EU provisions relating to freedom of movement for workers also apply to the national of a member state who, on the territory of another member state, exercises a subordinate activity from which he derives income inferior to it is regarded as a minimum vital in the second member state, irrespective of whether the person concerned complements the proceeds of his subordinate activity with other revenues which enable him to dispose of the aforementioned minimum or are satisfied with means of subsistence lower than the minimum, provided that the subordinate activity is actually and effectively exercised (par. 18).

541 Par. 22. CJEU thus departs in part from the reasoning of AG Slynn who, by analyzing the relevant EU legislation, had concluded that the right of citizen to enter and reside in the member state is subject to proof of genuine intention to work in that member state, even if for the person concerned that intention does not constitute the main reason for the transfer.

C-413/01, Franca Ninni-Orasche case of 6 November 2003[542] concerned instead an Italian student who, after having worked for a short period in Austria before starting her university studies, had asked for the grant foreseen for those studying in Austria, denied by the national authority. In particular, the referring court relied on three specific elements of the present case, namely the fact that the person concerned had only worked as a waitress several years after entering the host member state, that she had acquired, shortly after the conclusion of her short employment relationship, a diploma which gave her the right to access university studies in that state, and had sought, at the conclusion of this employment relationship, to find a new job.

The Austrian government pointed out that all the circumstances of the main proceedings should be assessed on the basis of objective criteria to determine whether the person concerned, instead of trying to exercise his right of free movement for the effective purpose of working, actually had to study in a member state other than the member state of origin and therefore attempted to create a situation which would make it appear as a worker for the sole purpose of gaining advantages, such as a scholarship.

CJEU, for its part, recalls the irrelevance of the elements relating to the behavior held by the interested party before and after the working period to ascertain the quality of the worker in the sense of what today is art. 49 TFEU[543], since they are not related either to the eventual accessory nature of the activity exercised, nor to the nature of this activity or of the employment relationship.

Starting from this premise, CJEU goes on to address specifically the argument that the referring court would have to verify, on the basis of the circumstances of the present case, whether the appellant in the main proceedings misused an attempt to create a situation, which allows the claim of the status of worker in the Union in order to obtain the benefits associated with that status. First of all, it points out that "any abusive use of rights granted by the Union legal system by virtue of the provisions concerning the free movement of workers presupposes that the person concerned falls within the scope ratione personae of that Treaty, satisfying the conditions to qualify as a "worker" within the meaning

542 CJEU, C-413/01, Franca Ninni-Orasche of 6 November 2003, ECLI:EU:C:2003:600, I-13817.

543 A. KACZOROWSKA-IRELAND, European Union law, op. cit. M. POIARES MADURO, M. WIND, The transformation of Europe: Twenty-five years on, Cambridge University Press, Cambridge, 2017, pp. 321ss. A. MANGAS MARTÍN, Tratado de la Uniòn Europea, Tratado de Funcionamiento ed. Marcial Pons, Madrid, 2018.

of that provision"[544], thus excluding the fact that the problem of abuse of rights affects the answer to the question of the national court. The factual elements mentioned by the referring court could indeed be relevant to the examination of the question whether, in the present case, "the appellant in the main proceedings exercised a short-term work for the sole purpose of benefiting from the system of grants to students in the host member state (...), but such an hypothesis is immediately rejected by CJEU, where it detects, (...) on the one hand, the fact that the applicant in the main proceedings appears to have entered the host member state for the sole purpose of benefiting from it the system of student subsidies, but to live there with your husband, a citizen of that state, and, secondly, the fact that you are legally residing therein"[545].

This last observation clearly demonstrates the impasse in which the reasoning of CJEU is found, since, even here, the gap between principle and application emerges clearly: CJEU admits that a short-term work activity (objective element) exercised solely for the purpose of abusive (subjective element) can make an abuse, except in the application, being necessarily to exclude the "only purpose", since it is clear that the purposes that move the individual may be the most disparate, from cohabitation, to a better climate and so on. However, according to CJEU, the legal stay, objective element, excludes necessarily subjective motivation, which is equivalent to a refusal, in substance, to verify the abuse. Once again, it is shown that, in CJEU's vision, there cannot be a case in

544 CJEU observes: "it is for the referring CJEU to make the necessary findings in order to determine, in accordance with the case-law referred to in paragraphs 34 to 36 of this judgment, whether there is a continuity link between the work previously carried out by the applicant in the case in the main proceedings and the studies undertaken thereafter, if the latter were in an involuntary state of unemployment and if the labor market situation forced it to carry out a professional reconversion, or if it exercised that activity solely to benefit from the student benefits scheme in the host member state. It is, however, important to point out in this regard that the mere fact that a contract of employment is originally concluded as a fixed-term contract cannot necessarily lead to the conclusion that, when that contract expires, the worker concerned automatically finds himself in a state of voluntary unemployment. In fact, if it is true that a contract of employment is normally the result of negotiations, it is not true that it is not rare cases in which the worker has no influence on the duration and type of employment contract that he can stipulate with an employer of work. On the other hand, the elements referred to by the referring CJEU, namely the fact that the person concerned has obtained, after the termination of her employment relationship, a diploma conferring her the right to enroll at university in the host member state, and the immediate search for a new employment after the end of the employment relationship, or the nature and level of the new work sought, are not necessarily relevant in this regard. Indeed, these circumstances may characterize both the case of involuntary unemployment of the applicant in the main proceedings and that of his voluntary unemployment (...)" (parr. 41 to 45).

545 A. KACZOROWSKA-IRELAND, European Union Law, op. cit.

which a situation such as that for which someone becomes a worker for the purposes of EU law is created abusively.

THE NEW FRONTIER OF "SOCIAL TOURISM" OF EU CITIZENS: THE PARADIGMATIC EXAMPLE OF C-333/13, DANO CASE OF 11 NOVEMBER 2014 (POSTPONEMENT)

In the famous C-333/13, Dano sentence of 11 November 2014, with which "a decade of jurisprudential developments" was weakened[546], CJEU once again ruled on the delicate balance between the fundamental right of Union citizens to move freely within the Union and to claim equal treatment with the nationals of the host state, and the willingness of member states to protect their public finances from "social tourism"[547]. In short, the EU judge was called upon to assess whether national legislation excluding, in whole or in part, citizens of other member states not economically active from the benefit of certain "special non-contributory cash benefits"[548]. Instead, the legislation is recognized to

546 CJEU, C-333/13, Dano of 11 November 2014, ECLI:EU:C:2014:2358, published in the electronic Reports of cases. Mrs Dano, a Romanian citizen holding a residence permit of unlimited validity for Union citizens issued by the city of Leipzig, was living with her son Florin, born on 2 July 2009 in Germany, in the apartment of a sister, the which provided for the livelihood of both. Mrs Dano received, for her son Florin, dependent child benefits from the family allowance fund in Leipzig on behalf of the Federal Employment Agency for an amount of € 148 monthly, in addition to an advance on food part of the social assistance service for youth and children in Leipzig for an amount of € 133 per month for this child, being the father unknown. The competent authority rejected the applications made by Ms Dano and her son for the purpose of obtaining basic insurance benefits under the national legislation. Ms Dano and her son appealed lastly against that decision on the basis of articles 18 and 45 TFEU and Vatsouras and Koupatantze decisions (joinjed cases: C-22/08 and C-23/08 of 4 June 2009) before the national CJEU (Sozialgericht Leipzig), which suspended the proceedings, asking CJEU whether art. 4 of Regulation n. 883/2004 on the coordination of social security systems, the general principle of non-discrimination resulting from art. 18 TFEU and the right of residence resulting from art. 20 TFEU, preclude the provisions of German law which do not confer entitlement to basic insurance benefits in the present case, as an economically non-active citizen. For details see: V. D. DUMONT, Arrêt Dano: fin du tourisme social ou de la citoyenneté européenne?, in Journal de Droit Européen, 9, 2015, pp. 196ss. W. KOWALCZYK, Dano: A right to freedom of movement or protection against an unreasonable burden imposed upon member state's social security systems?, in European Law Reporter, 2014, pp. 248ss. D. THYM, When Union citizens turn into illegal migrants: The Dano case, in European Law Review, 2015, pp. 535ss. H. VERSCHUEREN, Preventing "benefit tourism" in the EU: A narrow or broad interpretation of the possibilities offered by the ECJ in Dano?, in Common Market Law Review, 52, 2015 (2), pp. 363ss.

547 See also in argument: H. VERSCHUEREN, Free Movement or Benefit Tourism: the Unreasonable Burden of Brey, in European Journal of Migration and Law, 2014, pp. 147ss.

548 CJEU, C-133/15, Chavez-Vilcez and others of 10 May 2017, ECLI:EU:C:2017:354, published in the

nationals of the host member state who are in the same situation, whether or not it is compatible with Union law and in particular with Regulation n. 883/2004 on the coordination of social security systems[549] and with Directive 2004/38/EC, as well as the prohibition of discrimination and the right of residence resulting from articles 18 and 20 TFEU[550].

The sentence applies another legal technique. Reasoning, for the moment, on what CJEU excludes more than what it affirms in positive, even in this case, there was the refusal of CJEU to invoke the prohibition of abuse of rights. To meet the demands of member states, CJEU is increasingly fearful of seeing their welfare state affected by opportunistic behavior and has, thus, preferred to reinterpret Union legislation, giving centrality to the conditions of "economic self-sufficiency" provided for in article 7 of Directive 2004/38/EC, to which the right of residence of the inactive European citizen is subject, instead of using the general principle of prohibition of abuse.

In the present case, the prohibition of abuse of rights had not been expressly invoked by the German government, nor did the referring court refer to it. The central point, however, was to avoid opportunistic behavior of EU citizens, aimed at taking advantage of the social security system of certain member states, is first apparent from the conclusions of the AG, where it is stated that "by denying basic insurance benefits to people who come to Germany for the sole purpose of benefiting from the social assistance scheme of that member state and that they do not intend to integrate into the labor market in any way, national legislation (...) avoids abuses and a certain form of tourism"[551]. CJEU itself, moreover, in interpreting article 7 (1) (b) restrictively, finds its rationale in preventing the

---

electronic Reports of the cases.

549 H. VERSCHUEREN, Preventing "benefit tourism" in the EU: A narrow or broad interpretation of the possibilities offered by the ECJ in Dano?, op. cit., pp. 388ss.

550 A. KACZOROWSKA-IRELAND, European Union law, op. cit.

551 CJEU, C-200/02, Zhu and Chen of 19 October 2004, ECLI:EU:C:2004:639, I-09925. For comments see: J. Y. CARLIER, Case C-200/02, Kunqian Catherine Zhu, Man Lavette Chen v. Secretary of State for the Home Department, Judgement of the CJEU of 19 October 2004, in Common Market Law Review, 42 (4), 2005, pp. 1121ss. M. GAUTIER, Cour de justice, 19 octobre 2004, Kunqian Catherine Zhu et Man Lavette Chen v. Secretary of State for the Home Department, in Revue des Affaires Européennes, 1, 2003-2004, pp. 673ss. B. HOFSTÖTTER, A cascade of rights, or who shall care for little Catherine ? Some reflections on the Chen case, in European Law Review, 30 (4), 2005, pp. 548ss. B. KUNOY, A Union of National Citizens: The origins of the CJEU's lack of avant-gardisme in the Chen case, in Common Market Law Review, 43 (1), 2006, pp. 179ss. A. TRYFONIDOU, Case C-200/02, Kunqian Catherine Zhu, Man Lavette Chen v. Secretary of State for the Home Department: futher cracks in the 'great wall' of the European Union?, in European Public Law, 11 (4), 2005, pp. 528ss.

economically inactive citizens of the Union from using social security's protection system of the host member state to finance their livelihoods.

In the pronunciation are then specified some factual elements relating to the specific situation of Mrs. Dano, which demanded precisely those non-contributory social benefits referred to by the national court, which may have influenced the innovative interpretation given by CJEU. In fact, the town had attended school for three years in Romania, without obtaining any degree of study, which included spoken German and was able to express itself in a simple manner in that language, but could not write in that language and could understand texts written in German only to a limited extent; who did not have any vocational training and did not work in Germany or in Romania; that even if his suitability for work had never been challenged, there was no evidence that he had sought employment.

From this framework, CJEU comes to the conclusion that "a member state must have the possibility, pursuant to that art. 7, to deny the granting of social benefits to Union citizens, economically inactive, who exercise freedom of movement for the sole purpose of obtaining the benefit of social assistance from another member state even if they do not have sufficient resources to be able to claim the benefit of the right of residence"[552], proposing, in substance, a reasoning very similar to that of the abuse test.

(FOLLOWS) ABUSE OF NATIONAL LEGISLATION TO APPLY EU LAW: THE CASE OF ACQUISITION OF EU CITIZENSHIP

Reverse hypothesis compared to what we have just described and which deserves to be reported for the various conclusions reached by CJEU, is that which is realized when the private individual, in order to obtain a benefit from the EU legal system deriving from a particular status, uses abusively the national legislation of a member state. This is what happened in C-200/02, Zhu and Chen case of 19 October 2004, in which a Chinese citizen had planned the birth of her second daughter in Belfast, Northern Ireland to obtain Irish citizenship. Then, she would use the status of citizen of the Union acquired by the daughter, known as the

552 N. SHUIBHNE, Free movement of persons and the wholly internal rule; time to move on?, in Common Market Law Review, 39 (4), 2002, pp. 731ss. R. E. PAPADOPOULOU, Situations purement internes en droit communautaire: un instrument jurisprudentiel à double fonction ou une arme à double tranchant?, in Cahiers de Droit Europeén, 38 (1), 2002, pp. 95ss.

"little Catherine", and stay in the United Kingdom as a non-self-sufficient minor child's parent. It must be premised that, under the law then in force in Ireland, the Irish Nationality and Citizenship Act of 1956, a person born on Irish territory is Irish citizen by birth, if he does not aspire to obtain the citizenship of a different country. Therefore, the attribution of citizenship on the basis of jus soli was foreseen. However, the United Kingdom refused to apply for a residence permit on its territory, invoking an alleged abuse of EU law by Ms. Chen. It was clear, in fact, that the latter had requested and obtained a temporary residence permit in Ireland in order to allow the child who was waiting to acquire Irish nationality and, consequently, to allow herself and her daughter to acquire the right to reside in the United Kingdom.

The referring court therefore asked whether Directive 73/148/EC[553], Directive 90/364/EC[554] or article 18 EC (now article 21 TFEU)[555] conferred, in circumstances such as those of the present case, on the minor citizen of a member state, at the expense of a parent, and in favor of the parent, who is a citizen of a third member state, the right to reside in another member state, where the child is the recipient of childcare services.

CJEU dismisses United Kingdom's argument that the situation of a national born in a member state and that he did not avail himself of the right to free movement, for that reason, should only be assimilated to a purely internal situation. Then, the aforementioned citizen would be deprived of the benefit, in the host member state, of the provisions of EU law on the free movement and residence of persons. Does not he also doubt that the right of residence on the territory of member states is invoked by little Catherine under article 18, n. 1, EC (now article 21 TFEU)[556], providing the latter with both sickness insurance and sufficient resources provided by its mother.

CJEU then addresses the allegation raised by the United Kingdom that Mrs. Chen's abusive displacement to Northern Ireland would mean that she would

---

553 Council Directive 73/148/EEC of 21 May 1973 on the abolition of restrictions on movement and residence within the Community for nationals of member states s with regard to establishment and the provision of services, OJ L 172, 28.6.1973, p. 14-16, no longer in force from 29 April 2006. For further details see: G. CONWAY, European Union law, op. cit., pp. 464ss.

554 Council Directive 90/364/EEC of 28 June 1990 on the right of residence, OJ L 180, 13.7.1990, p. 26–27, no longer in force from 29 April 2006. For further analysis see: A. KACZOROWSKA-IRELAND, European Union Law, op. cit.

555 A. KACZOROWSKA-IRELAND, European Union Law, op. cit.

556 A. KACZOROWSKA-IRELAND, European Union Law, op. cit. A. MANGAS MARTÍN, Tratado de la Uniòn Europea, Tratado de Funcionamiento, op. cit.

not be able to rely on EU law, as the objectives pursued by those European provisions would not be achieved. On this point, EU judicature is clear in stating that if the stay in Northern Ireland was intended to create the necessary conditions to allow her birth to acquire the nationality of a member state, a circumstance which Mrs. Chen accepted subsequently in the end obtaining a long-term residence permit for themselves and their daughter in the United Kingdom. However, the determination of the methods of acquisition and loss of citizenship falls within the competence of each member state, in accordance with international law. He adds that "none of the parties who submitted observations to CJEU questioned either the legitimacy or the actuality of Catherine's acquisition of Irish citizenship (...) and that in any case"[557] it is not for a member state to limit the effects of the attribution of citizenship of another member state, "demanding a further requirement for recognition of that citizenship for the purpose of exercising the fundamental freedoms provided for by the Treaty (...)"[558].

CJEU therefore recognizes the right of residence to both Catherine and, on the basis of the principle of useful effect, to the mother, since it is clear that the enjoyment of the right of residence by a child at an early age necessarily entails that the child has the right to be accompanied by the person who actually guarantees custody[559]. In responding to the exception raised by the United Kingdom according to which Catherine's Irish citizenship would have an "artificial" character, being the result of a precise design put in place by parents to acquire a right of residence in the Union, the AG, after having highlighted, whereas the reference parameter for finding an abuse consists in establishing whether or not there has been a misrepresentation of the aims and objectives of European

557 R. DE LA FERIA, S. VOGENAUER (a cura di), Prohibition of abuse of law: A new general principle of EU law?, op. cit.

558 Paragraph 39. "Now, this would be exactly the case if the United Kingdom had the right to deny to citizens of other member states such as Catherine the enjoyment of a fundamental freedom guaranteed by EU law simply because the acquisition of the citizenship. In reality, a member state seeks to provide a third-country national with a right of residence in accordance with EU law (...)" (paragraph 40). Approve this reading C. COSTELLO, Citizenship of the Union: Above Abuse?, in R. DE LA FERIA, S. VOGENAUER (a cura di), Prohibition of abuse of law: A new general principle of EU law?, op. cit., pp. 321ss.

559 Paragraph 115: "It seems to me that the system of relations between EU legal order and the legal systems of member states, as has been delineated for several decades by CJEU's case law, necessarily implies that the abuse of a right conferred by the Treaty can occur only in exceptional circumstances, because the fact that the application of a national rule is excluded as a result of the invocation of a right conferred by EU law is the normal consequence of the principle of supremacy of EU law (...)" (paragraph 112).

Union law which gives the right in question[560], and excludes its existence in the present case, because, when a future parent decides that the good of his minor daughter requires that it acquires European Union citizenship in order to then enjoy the relative rights, and in particular the right of establishment as per art. 18 EC, there is nothing "abusive" in the fact that he activates, in compliance with the law, to ensure that the child meets, at the time of birth, "the conditions for the acquisition of citizenship of a member state (...)"[561].

He then grasps the observation that, in reality, the problem, if we want to talk about the problem, would be "in the criterion of attribution of citizenship adopted by Irish legislation, jus soli which lends itself to provoke situations such as in this case"[562], which could have been avoided by adding a condition of permanent residence of the parent in the territory of the island of Ireland. However, this condition does not exist in Irish legislation[563]. In other words, it was a national not a Union problem.

In fact, this seems to be the focal point of the story. Ireland was the only member state that used jus soli as the sole criterion for the acquisition of nationality, without any connection with Ireland being required, which gave rise to a phenomenon that can be summarized with the formula of "tourism of citizenship"[564], i.e. a migratory flow of citizens from third countries, willing to give birth to their children in Ireland, so that children, as EU citizens (and themselves, through their children), get the full range of rights derived from European citizenship. In this context, Chen, far from being an isolated case[565],

560 Par. 120. "In fact, we are not in the presence of persons" who invoke for EU purposes illegitimate or fraudulent, distorting the scope and purposes of norms of that system, but of people who, knowing the content of the freedoms provided for by EU law, they use it with legitimate means, precisely to achieve the objective that EU law wants to guarantee: the right of residence of the child (par. 122).

561 A. KACZOROWSKA-IRELAND, European Union law, op. cit.

562 A. KACZOROWSKA-IRELAND, European Union law, op. cit.

563 A. TRYFONIDOU, op. cit., p. 531. J.Y. CARLIER, op. cit., pp. 1122-23.

564 CJEU, C-342/17, Memoria e Dall'Antonia od 14 November 2018, ECLI:EU:C:2018:906, published in the electronic Reports of the cases.

565 CJEU, C-34/09, Ruiz Zambrano of 8 March 2011, ECLI:EU:C:2011:124, I-01177. For further details see: S. CORNELOUP, Citoyenneté européenne: la Cour de justice apporte une nouvelle pierre à son édifice, in Recueil Le Dalloz, 2011, pp. 1325ss. D. DITTERT, Les droits des citoyens de l'Union: vers un statut détaché de tout élément transfrontalier?, in Revue des Affaires Européennes, 2, 2011, pp. 223ss. K. HAILBRONNER, D. THYM, Case C-34/09, Gerardo Ruiz Zambrano v. Office national de l'emploi (ONE), Judgment of the CJEU (Grand Chamber) of 8 March 2011, in Common Market Law Review, 48, 2011, pp. 1253ss. R. MORRIS, European citizenship and the right to move freely: Internal situations, reverse discrimination and fundamental rights, in Maastricht Journal of European

seems to constitute only "the tip of an iceberg" in relation to the problematic nature of the way in which Irish citizenship was conferred[566].

The decision assumes a certain importance not only from the quantitative but also from the qualitative point of view. With reference to this second aspect, the novelty of the Chen case consists precisely in the "Europeanization" of the problem, since Ms. Chen also had in mind invoke the right to free movement The United Kingdom wanted to condemn this "artifice". However, CJEU noted that it is sufficient that there be a difference between the nationality of the citizen and the place of residence and that the legitimacy and reality of acquisition of the nationality in question were not questioned. In these terms, we are witnessing an evolution of the concept of "movement", as it is not the person who has to physically move, but is enough that it is nationality that moves.

With the C-34/09, Ruiz Zambrano ruling of 8 March 2011, for the truth, such reasoning will be further developed. Considering CJEU, even in the case of a situation at least at first sight "purely internal", the status of a Union citizen of young children object to decisions taken by the member state against the non-EU parent, such as denial of residence permit, may deprive children of the "real and effective enjoyment of the rights attached to the status of Union citizen", as they force them to abandon the territory of the Union to accompany their parents. CJEU, inter alia, in this last sentence does not even address the issue of a hypothetical abuse committed by Mr. Zambrano, a Colombian citizen, in making his sons acquire Belgian citizenship. This question has been peacefully overcome by the AG Sharpston, that resolves it in a few lines reminding that "deciding not to expressly express the Colombian citizenship for his children and choosing instead to let them acquire the citizenship of the member state in which they were born, Mr. Ruiz Zambrano made use of a possibility that he was entitled by law. From this point of view, his behavior can very well be

and Comparative Law, 18, 2011, pp. 179ss. P. VAN ELSUWEGE, Shifting the Boundaries? European Union Citizenship and the Scope of Application of EU Law-Case No. C-34/09, Gerardo Ruiz Zambrano v. Office national de l'emploi, in Legal Issues of Economic Integration, 38, 2011, pp. 263ss.

566 See, on this point, the opinion of AG Sharpston, presented on 30 September 2010, in case C-34/09, where it is stated, in paragraph 96, that "like Catherine Zhu, Diego and Jessica cannot exercise their rights as citizens of the Union (specifically, their right to move and reside in any member state) fully and effectively without the presence and support of their parents. By applying the same link that CJEU accepted in Zhu and Chen ruling (allowing a minor to effectively exercise his citizenship rights), it follows that the situation of Mr Likewise, Ruiz Zambrano is not a "purely internal" situation in the member state. It too falls within the sphere of Union law (...)". It must be noted that in reality, however, in the Chen case at least one nationality was found different from that of the country of stay.

compared with that of Messrs. Zhu. CJEU has made it clear that there is nothing reprehensible in using a possibility granted by the law and that this is clearly something different from an abuse of rights"[567]. CJEU thus arrives, even in the absence of an element of extraneousness, to recognize the residence of the third-country, who takes charge of their children at an early age. As citizens of the Union in the member state of residence of the latter of which they are citizens, such a decision could deprive those children of the actual and effective enjoyment of the rights attached to the status of citizen of the Union.

(FOLLOWS) INTENTIONS THAT DO NOT CONSIDER A COMPARISON WITH THE HYPOTHESES SUB B) AND C).

The study of the various abusive manifestations of individuals moving within the Union leads us to carry out a series of considerations aimed at highlighting points of contact and differentiation between the different situations examined. The hypotheses described are distinguished both with regard to the number of systems involved, only two in the case of sub b), with regard to the system to which the abused standard belongs, the national one in the hypothesis sub c). What unites them, once again, however, is the refusal of CJEU, beyond a mere statement of principle, to admit the prohibition of abuse. From this point of view, it must be underlined how, in the hypothesis sub c), the motivations appeared rather clear, but to be abused was the national legislation and not the Union, which is why the EU system could not but disregard it. In other words, CJEU could not have decided otherwise in the Chen case, since Mrs. Chen had committed an abuse not of EU law but of transnational law, which the EU system cannot absolutely punish.

In the hypotheses sub a) and b), on the other hand, the difficulty of CJEU emerged to investigate the motivations that could have led the individual to exercise his rights, motivations of which the irrelevance was repeatedly and constantly stated. This implies a necessary removal from the prohibition of abuse: it is a fact acquired in the jurisprudence of CJEU that the abuse implies, in addition to an improper use of European liberties to circumvent the legislation, also a psychological element, so the reason that pushes the bearer of a right

567 A. KACZOROWSKA-IRELAND, European Union law, op. cit.

to exercise it, acquires a central weight to determine whether there is abuse or not[568].

In this context, CJEU, where it has to deal with abusive situations, prefers therefore to opt for another technique, that of restrictive interpretation, which has undoubted advantages, including that of disregarding the reasons that move individuals. Thus, what is relevant here is not so much the motivations as the effectiveness, which can be deduced from the element of time. Compared to member states, this solution is also consistent with the obligation imposed on them to ensure the effective application of Union rules if the conditions required for this purpose, such as citizenship or residence, are met without the need for unions (except in cases of fraud) the circumstances under which these conditions were acquired.

At this point, it would seem to be concluded that the hypotheses sub a) and b) are superimposable. This is not entirely true, however. As we have seen that not only would it seem that the member state concerned has a wider margin to adopt restrictive regulations in case b), but in the latter case the role of effectiveness circulation becomes key, while in a) it does not seem to be sufficient, as Akrich clearly demonstrates.

THOUGHTS AND OBSERVATIONS

If we want to bring the above considerations into line with the system, it is worth remembering how the established jurisprudence was established, which recognizes and applies the prohibition on the abuse of law in the harmonized sectors, where only the EU system is relevant.

In particular, an evolution has been reported in the jurisprudence of CJEU, which has gradually refined and fine-tuned the concept of abuse of law, coining a general test, which can be replicated in many contexts, albeit with the necessary clarifications. The test, as has been shown on several occasions, requires a double check to the national court: that the objective of the law has not been achieved and that the private person wanted to obtain an advantage deriving from the European legislation by artificially creating the necessary conditions for obtaining it.

568 E. SPAVENTA, Comments on abuse of law and the free movement of workers, in R. DE LA FERIA, S. VOGENAUER (a cura di), Prohibition of abuse of law: a new general principle of EU law?, op. cit., pp. 315ss.

On the other hand, analyzing the cases in which a "triangular" situation, which involves several systems, is artificially created, it has been observed that CJEU has difficulty in transposing the same biphasic approach in the verification of the existence of the abuse. Thus, if the doctrine advocated by CJEU can be easily summarized in the formula "Union law cannot be invoked for abusive or fraudulent ends", the practical implications of this ruling remain obscure[569]. Moreover, the implications of the lemma "in itself" are not clear at all, which makes it possible to exclude abuse in the concrete case, while at the same time implying the possibility of recognizing it when other facts of life occur.

Such an attitude cannot be surprising, given that, unlike the cases referred to in the preceding paragraphs, in which it has ended up adapting to the scope of the Union a concept already known and used in national legislation, here we are dealing with situations in a certain original measure, precisely because of the transnationality that distinguishes them. In particular, it has been emphasized on several occasions that CJEU's perspective does not always coincide with that of the member state concerned.

Dwelling on the reasons for the orientation that tends to exclude the applicability of the ban, it can be observed that certainly the systematic favor for intra-Union mobility through the strengthening of freedom of circulation may have played a role. This is because the prohibition of abuse implies a sanction, precisely, the denial of the abused right or, according to another perspective, the non-application of EU law.

However, this explanation remains insufficient. Indeed, other factors, more fundamental, explain such an orientation, and, in particular, allow us to understand the oscillations that sometimes show CJEU in its judgments. The main obstacle to the entry of prohibition of abuse seems in fact the necessary differentiation of the parameters used by the member state, on one hand, and the EU, on the other, to verify the abuse, which determine the "traceability" of the operation by the EU legal order. Thus, those constructions that, under the "lens" of the member state, appearing to be abusive, often are not abusive to that of the EU legal order.

From this point of view, it has been observed that the nationality of the interested party can hardly operate as a marker of the complexity of the operation,

569 A. KJELLGREN, On the border of abuse: The jurisprudence of the European CJEU on circumvention, fraud and other misuses of European Union law, op. cit., pp. 190. A p. 192. AG questions on the usefulness of preparing such a prohibition in EU law, note that: "Fair outcomes might in most cases be reached through interpretation of the relevant EU provisions, in much the same way CJEU usually resolves the cases today (...)".

which, for the "U-shaped" operations leads almost automatically to exclude the satisfaction of the test, since the abusive constructions described so far have in common an effective circulation, nor can the motivations, once the objective element is satisfied, be detected. Moreover, we cannot fail to remember how the first assumption of the abuse, able to differentiate it from fraud, is precisely the formal respect of the norm, which often suffices however EU order to give freedom of movement. In other words, the fact of falling within the scope of EU law is sufficient to rule out the abuse.

According to our opinion from a pragmatic point of view, it does not seem important whether the principle of abuse is considered an exception to EU law or whether it regulates the interpretation of the scope of European Union law. In the decision of the cases, the approach would be slightly different, but the result identical (see, however, infra in the text for some additional consideration on the relationship with the teleological interpretation). In fact, the emphasis attributed makes sense only considering the abuse as a general principle of EU law, but, as will be seen, such a qualification, at least in a cross border situation, must be excluded.

It has already come to light as CJEU on several occasions, for example in the judgments: C-311/06, National Council of Ingivers of 29 January 2009, and C-109/01, Akrich of 22 September 2003, excluding the possibility of applying the prohibition of abuse did not choose the solution that most encouraged mobility, resulting in an unjustifiably restrictive interpretation. If anything, the encouragement of mobility can be read in reverse, to explain the cases, indeed sporadic, in which CJEU has tried to apply the ban[570].

It has also been observed how to admit in such contexts the relevance of the abuse, as congenital, would lead in practice to recognize the existence of a "purely internal situation". The private, in fact, through the abusive construction, changes the location of the case, modifying the connection criterion, so as to arrive at the application of a different right from the otherwise applicable one, in order to avoid the imperative rules of the latter[571]. In this perspective, recognizing the abuse, would also mean excluding the relevance of the element

570 CJEU, C-456/04, Agip Petroli of 6 April 2006, op. cit.

571 A. LOOIJESTIJN-CLEARIE, Centros ltd, a complete U-turn in the right of establishment for companies?, op. cit., pp. 639ss, affirms that: "In its judgments, CJEU has been extremely lenient with regard to the existence of a relevant cross-border or EU element. In many of the "U-turn" cases, CJEU has found the relevant provisions of EU law to apply and has rejected arguments concerning purely internal situations (...)".

of extraneousness, since the artificiality is perceived exactly in relation to the improper use of freedom of movement[572].

Thus, for example, without taking into consideration the element of nationality, which makes it possible to "trace" the "U" operation of companies established in a country with the most favorable legislation, and then carry out all their activities in the state of origin, it is clear that the objective of the Union rules on the establishment of companies is respected. The same reasoning can be replicated with reference to the securities acquired in the country with the most favorable legislation, without prejudice to the clarifications that will be made shortly, as well as with regard to the circulation of the Union citizen who moves with the non-EU spouse.

The objective element of the test, in these terms, is unlikely to be satisfied, since with this type of operation it will be difficult to go against the objectives of EU legislation. Thus, the right to set up a company in accordance with the legislation of a member state and setting up branches in other member states is inherent in the exercise, within the framework of a single market, of the freedom of establishment guaranteed by the Treaty. Likewise, the effective movement in another member state as an EU worker or citizen respects the objective pursued by the provisions relating to the right of residence, to eliminate any restriction on the movement and residence of European Union citizens. Furthermore, acquiring a diploma in another member state does not conflict with the objective of facilitating the permanent exercise of the profession in a member state other than that in which the professional qualification was acquired. If, in reality, many of the "U-shaped" operations are united by an "irrational" transfer, the Union's legal system makes it harder to catch it.

The only case in which the barrier given by the objective element seems to have been overcome is that of the abuse of the freedom to provide services, first in C-33/74, Van Binsbergen v. Bestuur van de Bedrijfsvereniging voor de Metaalnijverheid case of 3 December 1974 and then in broadcasting cases, "television without frontiers", but only if and because in which it was clear that the private individual had actually invoked the freedom to provide services in place of the freedom of establishment. The parameter of the activity carried out entirely or mainly on the territory of the state of origin, in this sense, is very

572 A. SAYDÉ, Abuse of EU law and regulation of the internal market, op. cit., p. 86: "in short, artificial transactions typically entail avoidable real-life costs, or at the very least do not create any real-life value (...)".

effective. In any case, it is not clear how the prohibition is placed in relation to the overriding reasons of general interest.

Looking more closely at these hypotheses, then consider that CJEU, once the objective element has been ascertained, that is to say the use of a freedom for an end that is not its own, has not made a real verification of the subjective element, even only in its "objectivized" form, coined in C-255/02, Halifax and others case of 21 February 2006. It has not been questioned about "the artificiality" of the abusive construction, nor has it identified of the indexes apt to prove it, referring only in formal way to the fact that the operation had been realized by the subject in order to avoid the relevant norms.

It should be noted that, even with reference to the free movement of goods, CJEU seems to have had no difficulty in identifying the objective element of the test, although in only one isolated case which concerned a possible "U-shaped" construction. However, it was a peculiar situation, more like any other than a purely internal situation, since there was no connection with another member state. In more detail, in C-229/83, Leclerc/Au blè vert and others sentence of 10 January 1985, EU judicature was concerned with assessing the compatibility with EU law, and in particular with free movement of goods, a French law that obliged all retailers to observe the price set by the publisher or importer for the sale of books. In this regard, CJEU examines two different situations: firstly, that of books published in another member state and imported into France, and secondly, that of books published in France itself and reimported after exportation to another member state. With reference to this second hypothesis, CJEU points out: "the rule requiring, for the sale of these books, to observe the selling price set by the publisher does not constitute a discipline that distinguishes between national and imported books. However, that provision prevents the sale of reimported books because it deprives the importer of those books of the possibility of passing on the price per minute the advantage derived from a more favorable price which has been seen in the exporting member state. It therefore constitutes a measure having an effect equivalent to a quantitative restriction on imports prohibited by article 30" (paragraph 26)[573]. He adds, however, that "what has been said does not extend to cases in which objective evidence proves that the books were exported for the sole purpose of re-importing them, with the intention of circumventing a law such as the one in question" (paragraph 27)[574].

573 C-229/83, Leclerc/Au blè vert and others of 10 January 1985, op. cit.

574 C-229/83, Leclerc/Au blè vert and others of 10 January 1985, op. cit.

The subjective element, in fact, does not prove to be a good parameter even with reference to the hypotheses involving the circulation of individuals. Since the reasons do not reveal, the possibility of applying the prohibition in the case in which natural persons are involved must be excluded, moving to the EU to get certain benefits. On one hand, it is unlikely that the exercise of one's rights by an individual, in order to enjoy the related rights conferred by EU, may have importance in defining the scope of these rights, otherwise would reach the paradoxical conclusion that the intention to enjoy the rights would exclude the possibility for the interested party to take advantage of these rights. On the other hand, it would be illogical, in this sector, to take motivation into account, since there are infinite variables that can influence individual choices, from economic to individual ones, such as, to name but a few, personal preferences, family, or even friends, it is consequently impossible to find a common logic capable of determining how and when these personal preferences are relevant to define the legitimate or abusive exercise of the right in question. If anything, "artificiality" could be inferred from the time element, which represents an ineffective parameter, taking into account the impossibility of predetermining a priori a useful term and the possibility for private individuals, to adapt easily the prescriptions gradually given by CJEU on the point, circumventing them.

On the other hand, it is not clear how the prohibition of abuse in hypothesis can operate if the same involves the non-application of EU law in an interpretative way to circumvent the national legislation, but without wanting to take advantage from another national legislation. It is not clear if this means that, for there to be effective trade, books must have been the subject of retail sale, a rather restrictive interpretation, or if a serious transaction with a distributor in another member state is sufficient[575]. Here, the crossing of a border is realized as a means of trying to evade the rules of what was the state of origin and that the migration has transformed into the host state but without subjugation to the rules of the new state of origin. This is a fiction, not a cross-border situation at all. However, this situation is rare and cannot occur if the company intending

575 P. J. KUYPER, Case 229/83, Association des Centres Distributeurs Edouard Leclerc, Paris and Thouars Distribution & Autres S.A., Sainte Verge, v. Au Blé Vert S.a.r.l., in Common Market Law Review, 22, 1985, pp. 808ss. Y. GALMOT, J. BIANCARELLI, Les réglementations nationales en matière de prix au regard du droit communautaire, in Revue Trimestrielle de Droit Europèen, 21, 1985, pp. 269ss. On closer inspection, however, we are dealing with a purely internal, easily verifiable situation, starting from the absence of effective trade. In particular see: S. WEATHERILL, Fitting "abuse of rights" into EU Law governing the free movement of goods and services, in R. DE LA FERIA, S. VOGENAUER, Prohibition of abuse of law: a new general principle of EU law?, op. cit., pp. 56ss.

to make use of free movement needs to set up some distribution or production center, albeit limited, in another member state.

Thus, for example, while in C-212/97, Centros case of 9 March 1999, CJEU clearly distinguished the question of applicability of the Treaty with respect to the question of the measures that a member state can take to prevent the abuse, in C-196/04, Cadbury Schweppes and Cadbury Schweppes Overseas case of 12 September 2006, on the other hand, deals with the question as a preliminary point, as member states would like, which invoke the abuse precisely to exclude the concrete situation from the field of application of EU law. Instead, there is a text of secondary law, the question does not pose particular problems, since as we have seen, the verification of abuse is always made subsidiary, once the Directive has been interpreted.

In this section, we wanted to show how CJEU, even in the cases cited as the foundation of abuse doctrine law, first of all by CJEU itself, but also by numerous AG conclusions, has never actually applied the correlative prohibition[576]. We tried to explain the reasons for this choice, which, as mentioned, was in many cases obligatory[577].

In fact, from the analysis carried out, several problematic issues emerged of the prohibition of abuse, intended as a technique to protect the legal system from abusive conditions, which inevitably affect the effectiveness of the remedy. This confirms the impression that, at present, jurisprudence, in reality, aims at a varied use of different legal techniques compared to that of the prohibition of abuse. Indeed, the EU system seems to have adequate protection techniques to combat extreme situations. It is therefore necessary to elaborate on these alternative protection techniques: where the next paragraphs will be dealt with, namely the use by member states of the overriding reasons relating to the general interest and the restrictive interpretation of the Union rules.

576 P. SIMPSONS, Cadbury Schweppes Plc v. Commissioners of Ireland Revenue: ECJ sets strict test for CFC legislation, in British Tax Review, 56, 2006, pp. 680, has stated that: "it is important to note the limit of this point. It has nothing to do with whether the national provisions in question are compatible with European law, but concerns simply whether the person seeking to rely on provisions of the EC Treaty may do so (...)".

577 So it is considered appropriate to deviate from the position that the prohibition of abuse was used to limit the exercise of economic activities, while in terms of free movement of persons and citizenship rights judges have proved more sensitive to the values of integration and expansion of welfare policies, avoiding the configuration of abusive conduct (see, R. DE LA FERIA, Prohibition of abuse of (European Union law), op. cit., pp. 417ss. J. SNELL, And then there were two, op. cit., pp. 62).

CHAPTER 4

Alternative techniques for combating the abuse of law employed by EU law

SHORT INTRODUCTION

The analysis of the jurisprudence concerning cases in which the abusive construction involves more than one system, resulting in the "artificial" creation of a connecting element, has led us to give a negative answer to the question whether the prohibition of abuse in such a context can be considered an operative legal technique in EU. This is because, beyond the statements of principle, CJEU shows not leaving space for the application of the prohibition, as outlined in the context in which a single system was involved, with the characters crystallized in the abuse test elaborated by the jurisprudence starting from C-110/99, Emsland-Stärke judgment of 14 December 2000.

The EU system, however, seems to have other techniques to combat abuse, the analysis of which is the subject of this paragraph. As already mentioned, in cases where individuals, through the exercise of freedom of movement, pre-establish the conditions to circumvent the legislation of the member state of belonging and apply other national legislation to the most favorable ones, CJEU has, for the most part, admitted as a palliative the appeal by the state concerned to the overriding reasons of general interest.

With reference to the invocation of the freedoms of movement by private individuals in order to circumvent the otherwise applicable national legislation and at the same time seek the application of the secondary legislation of EU, or in cases where the private individual invokes an advantage deriving by a status conferred by EU law on the exercise of the freedoms of movement, the Luxembourg court has shown a certain propensity for the restrictive interpretation of Union rules, in place of the application of the abuse doctrine.

It is necessary, however, to verify whether these techniques, in contrast to the prohibition of abuse, prove to be effective, in the sense of allowing an effective contrast to the abuse. To this end, a targeted analysis will be carried out of the application mechanisms of imperative reasons of general interest, verifying their functioning in concrete terms, and then analyzing the use of the restrictive interpretation of "European" freedoms or secondary legislation, focusing on free movement of persons.

PART A.

Abuse of law as an overriding reason of general interest

The theory of imperative reasons of general interest has found fertile ground for development concurrent with the emergence of the prohibition of indistinctly applicable restrictive measures, also defined as the principle of access to the market. The pretense claim that the measures which, although without any discriminatory effects, in substance, are nevertheless a non-justifiable obstacle to circulation are also prohibited, is tempered by the possibility offered to the member state to justify such measures, where certain conditions are satisfied. The overriding reasons relating to the public interest must therefore be conceived as the counterpart of the extension of the concept of an obstacle to measures which are applicable without distinction.

This balance is well explained in terms of negative integration[578], a method of removing obstacles to the freedoms of movement, which consists in entrusting the courts of the Union with the task of deciding whether the requirements of free movement or the regulations of member states prevail. In particular, the negative integration is achieved when the rules adopted at national level are not applied, as they are considered incompatible with the freedoms of movement and with free competition in the internal market[579]. This technique has allowed CJEU to bring an ever-increasing number of national regulations under its control, at the same time extending, through its own jurisprudence, the number of potential justifications that member states can invoke in defense of the rules subject to control.

578 B. BERTRAND, Que reste-t-il des exigences impératives d'intérêt général?, in Europe, janvier 2012.

579 P. J. OLIVER, Oliver on Free Movement of Goods in the European Union, Hart Publishing, Oxford & Oregon, Portland, 2010, pp. 135ss.

As is known, over time the jurisprudence established a parallelism between the rules on the freedom of establishment and the free movement of goods[580], and the rules on the freedom to provide services[581], so that today we can refer to a global approach to all the freedoms of movement. In other words, there is a tendency towards a unitary discipline of the different freedom of circulation of productive factors in the European area, fundamentally based on the principle of mutual recognition of the regulatory choices of member states, as a next step, and more evolved at least in the prospect of building up an effective internal market, compared to the mere national treatment[582].

In particular, the method used by CJEU to determine whether a non-applicable legislation constitutes a restriction on the freedom of establishment or the freedom to provide services, strongly recalls the formula developed in the judgment of C-120/78, Cassis de Dijon case of 20 February 1979[583] in relation to goods. According to which, a restriction is contrary to the free movement of goods even if applied in a non-discriminatory way, unless it is justified by imperative requirements and satisfies the proportionality test[584].

Bearing in mind the whole of the approach adopted by CJEU, it will then be necessary to focus first on the structure and on the salient characteristics of the exception of the imperative requirements invoked by the member state. CJEU has thus come to consider that even the application to the nationals of other member states of professional rules without distinction applicable to all those engaged in a given activity and thus without albeit indirectly, discriminatory

580 V. HATZOPOULOS, Le principe communautaire d'équivalence et de reconnaissance mutuelle dans la libre prestation de services, Sakkoulas/Bruylant, Atene-Bruxelles, 1999, pp. 107ss. N. BERNARD, La libre circulation des marchandises, des personnes et des services dans le Traité CE sous l'angle de la competence, in Cahiers de Droit Européen, 34, 1998, pp. 11ss. S. DEAKIN, Regulatory competition in European company law, in D. C. ESTY, D. GERADIN (a cura di), Regulatory competition and economic integration, Oxford University Press, Oxford, 2001, pp. 198ss.

581 J.G. HUGLO, Liberté d'établissement et libre prestation des services, in Revue Trimestrielle de Droit Européen, 32 (4), 1996, pp. 742ss.

582 P. OLIVER, W. H. ROTH, The internal market and the four freedoms, in Common Market Law Review, 41 (4), 2004, pp. 407ss, contra: V. HATZOPOULOS, Exigences essentielles, impératives ou impérieuses; une théorie, des théories ou pas de théorie du tout?, in Revue Trimestrielle de Droit Européen, 34, 1998, pp. 201-202.

583 ECLI:EU:C:1979:42, ECR I-00649. For further details see: A. TRYFONIDOU, Further steps on the road to convergence among the market freedoms, in European Law Review, 16, 2010, pp. 36ss.

584 A.H. TÜRK, Judicial review in European Union law, op. cit., L. WOODS, P. WATSON, M. COSTA, Steiner & Woods European Union law, op. cit., pp. 37ss C. BARNARD, S. PEERS, European Union law, op. cit., pp. 788ss.

effects, may constitute a restriction on the right to establishment, unless the state proves that these are rules justified by reasons of general interest. It follows that the free movement of persons and services does not end with the mere prohibition of discrimination, but also entails the prohibition of applying to beneficiaries of that freedom all those regulations, which although without distinction, have the effect of hindering exercise of the rights included in the free circulation. CJEU jurisprudence, since the 1980s and even more in 1990 with regard to the right of establishment[585], has brought a decisive step towards a broader concept of restrictions that must be eliminated by virtue of the freedoms in question.

Attention will then be paid, more specifically, to the paradigmatic case of tax avoidance, in relation to which a consolidated jurisprudence has been built. Once the application of the technique in question has been analyzed and, in particular, the elements of differentiation with respect to the prohibition of abuse, it will be necessary to evaluate its effectiveness in combating abuse.

Measures are legitimate if and to the extent that two other conditions are met, which at the same time incorporate a qualitative element, namely the control of the need for the measure at issue, and a quantitative element, namely the control of the adequacy of the measure to the objectives prosecuted, even if often jointly treated[586]. The national restrictive measure must, in other words, be objectively suitable to guarantee the realization of the objective of protection it sets itself. This means, according to what is stated in the Pretoria, that, in order to satisfy the requirement of eligibility, restrictive measures must pursue the general interest objective in a consistent and systematic way. It is therefore a matter of verifying that the application of the law is not so strict as to nullify, in specific cases, the achievement of the general interest objective that is intended to be guaranteed.

The last condition of eligibility, which is also the most relevant, because it is better able to make a strict selection of national measures, is compliance with the principle of proportionality[587]. In the majority of the cases brought to the

585 CJEU, C-55/94, Gebhard v. Consiglio dell'Ordine degli avvocati e Procuratori di Milano of 30 November 1995, ECLI:EU:C:1995:411, I-04165 and in the same spirit see: C-120/78, Rewe-Zentral of 20 February 1979, ECLI:EU:C:1979:42, ECR 00649.

586 V. HATZOPOULOS, Exigences essentielles, impératives ou impérieuses; une théorie, des théories ou pas de théorie du tout?, op. cit., pp. 204ss.

587 A. HARTKAMP, C. SIEBURGH, W. DEVROE, Cases, materials and text on European law and private law, op. cit.

attention of CJEU, the disputed measures were censored as they went beyond what was necessary to achieve the desired result. It is therefore the latter criterion that deserves greater attention[588]. Moreover, the submission of measures to strict control of proportionality explains why CJEU quite easily accepts the wide variety of grounds of general interest invoked by member states.

The national measure, in a nutshell, should not impose any restrictions beyond what is strictly necessary to achieve the general interest of objective pursued. Therefore, if a state has a choice between several measures suitable to achieve the goal, it must choose the means which would reduce the freedom to trade. This is, as can be seen from the vague wording, a requirement that can take on the most varied facets in individual cases of species.

Lastly, it should be noted that it is up to the member state which maintains a restrictive measure in its law to justify it on the grounds of overriding reasons of general interest, and to the internal judge, with the aid of the interpretation of CJEU, to verify the reliability of justification. This introduces a relative presumption of incompatibility with the Treaty of national regulations, which can be overcome by the member state by demonstrating the presence of conditions just examined, interpreted in a restrictive way by the jurisprudence of CJEU.

THE IMPERATIVE MOTIFS' TECHNIQUE IN THE JURISPRUDENCE THAT DEALT WITH ABUSIVE CONSTRUCTIONS: SOME FIRST CONFLICTING INDICATIONS

As CJEU has already observed, in addition to verifying the abuse of private sector's behavior, when questioned on this point by the national court, it has also sought to establish the compatibility with Union law of restrictive measures adopted by the member state, in light of the doctrine of imperative reasons of general interest.

It is now necessary to deepen this aspect, noting first of all how the jurisprudence, on this point, proved to be rather fluctuating and not always precise in the analysis of the constitutional elements of the test coined from the judgment of C-120/78, Cassis de Dijon case of 20 February 1979.

588 CJEU, C-33/74, Van Binsbergen v. Bestuur van de Bedrijfsvereniging voor de Metaalnijverheid of 3 December 1974, op. cit., par. 12. C-76/90, Sager v. Dennemeyer of 25 July 1991, ECLI:EU:C:1991:331, I-04221 par. 12-15.

It must be emphasized here that inevitably the attitude of CJEU in this regard is influenced by the questions that are asked from time to time by the national court and the defense invoked by the member state concerned. However, one can try to reach a systematization. Indeed, it may be noted that, rarely, the only reason of general interest in the fight against abuse was the object of attention; more frequently, the same state flanked by other justifications, other times it was not invoked at all. Starting from the latter hypothesis, the previously C-212/97, Centros analyzed case of 9 March 1999, in which Denmark, in addition to invoking the prohibition of self-abuse, had put forward as a justification obligation, for limited liability companies, to set up and release a minimum share capital, the need to protect potential creditors of the company itself, preventing the risk of fraudulent bankruptcy due to the insolvency of companies whose initial capital was insufficient[589]. Consequently, CJEU submitted the restrictive measures to the Gebhard test, to conclude that the required conditions were not met in the present case.

First of all, the restrictive measures did not appear to be able to meet the stated objective of protecting creditors, as it would have been sufficient to carry out some activity by the company in the United Kingdom in order to obtain registration, without thereby protecting creditors[590]. Secondly, since C-212/97, Centros case of 9 March 1999 presented itself as a company under English law, creditors should have been adequately informed that it was governed by foreign law; in any case, they could have referred to European rules to protect them, such as the fourth and the eleventh companies' directives.

The legislation in question did not pass the proportionality test, since, according to CJEU, it would have been possible to adopt less restrictive measures of the right of establishment, such as giving the public creditors the legal possibility of constituting the necessary guarantees.

---

589 L. CERIONI, The "abuse of rights" in EU company and tax law. A re-reading of ECJ case law and the quest for a unitary notion, op. cit., pp. 791ss, considers that CJEU would suggest in this way that, without negative effects for the protection of creditors, there can be no abusive behavior, despite the choice of a less restrictive company regime for the establishment of the company which would then carry out all the activities through a branch in another member state.

590 Thus, paragraph 37. CJEU accordingly establishes that the refusal to register the branch of the company incorporated in another member state is incompatible with EU provisions, while underlining, again, in closing, that such an interpretation "does not rule out that the authorities of the member state concerned may take all appropriate measures to prevent or penalize fraud both with regard to the company itself, possibly in cooperation with the member state in which it is constituted, and to other members (...)", (par. 38).

More interesting for our purposes are those cases already analyzed under the different profile of the prohibition of abuse, intended as an autonomous protection technique, in which CJEU has taken into account the fight against abuse also as justification for restrictive national measures.

It should be noted here that, in many of the cases analyzed in the previous chapters, the analysis of the abuse is placed in a "limbo", in the sense that the "imperative reasons of general interest" justify, in turn, the restrictive measures adopted from time to time by the member state to combat abuse. In other words, measures to combat abuse are admissible, where the abuse is being circumvented by particularly deserving standards of protection.

To better understand this statement, it may be appropriate to proceed with an exemplification, citing first of all C-33/74, Van Binsbergen v. Bestuur van de Bedrijfsvereniging voor de Metaalnijverheid case of 3 December 1974. CJEU with this ruling, has ruled out incompatibility with the provisions of the Treaty of national legislation, which requires those who exercise a profession connected with the administration of justice to establish their residence in the circumscription of certain judicial bodies. When the same appears to be objectively necessary to ensure compliance with professional provisions linked, in particular, with the functioning of justice and with respect for deontology, interests fall precisely within the category of imperative reasons of general interest, stating that, in particular, "this applies if the provider fails to comply with these rules through his residence in another member state"[591]. In this passage, we can understand the role played, in CJEU's thought, by the particular merit of the interests protected by the legislation that we intend to circumvent.

Moreover, this conception is even clearer from the continuation of the judgment, where a distinction is made with the case in which "the member state does not subject the provision of certain services to any kind of professional qualification or discipline and establishes the residence requirement with reference to its territory in general. If indeed, within a member state, the exercise of a given activity is absolutely free, claiming residence in the state means imposing a restriction incompatible with articles 59 and 60 of the treaty[592], since the proper functioning of justice can be guaranteed with less burdensome obligations, for

591 C-33/74, Van Binsbergen v. Bestuur van de Bedrijfsvereniging voor de Metaalnijverheid of 3 December 1974, op. cit.

592 M. POIARES MADURO, M. WIND, The transformation of Europe: Twenty-five years on, op. cit. pp. 321ss. A. MANGAS MARTÍN, Tratado de la Uniòn Europea, Tratado de Funcionamiento, op. cit.

example by prescribing the election of a domicile where the judicial communications can be directed (...)"[593].

CJEU thus adopts an intermediate position, partly focusing on the fact that national legislation could be circumvented, and partly on the characteristics of the national legislation circumvented.

Likewise, in the already analyzed broadcasting cases and in C-148/91, Veronica Omroep Organisatie v. Commissioner of Media case of 3 February 1993, CJEU first focuses on the objective of national law to safeguard freedom of expression of the different social, cultural, religious, or philosophical components existing in Netherlands, recognizing that, as a general interest, the same could legitimately be pursued by the state concerned. It is only at a later stage that it admits that a member state can treat the national broadcasting organization as being established in another member state to circumvent the more restrictive legislation of the state of origin.

In other words, CJEU recognizes the legitimacy of the adoption of restrictive measures that have the effect of preventing abuse, if they are placed in a system coherently aimed at achieving a general objective, such as maintaining a system pluralistic and non-commercial or the proper administration of justice. We are dealing with a peculiar application of the principle of abuse. In these cases, the measures granted to the host state in application of the prohibition of abuse, which in fact result in the equivalence, for the purpose of the applicable legislation, of the lender to subjects performing the same activity as established, must be justified in the need to guarantee objectives of general interest[594].

It is not easy, therefore, to establish what the "European" judges would have decided if the objective of the national measures had not been of general interest. However, it has already been stressed that this is an "embryonic" jurisprudence, in which it is at least hypothetical an application, however inaccurate, of the prohibition of abuse.

With the Kraus[595] sentence, the fight against abuse in the particular field of diplomas was instead invoked by the member state as the only reason justify-

593 A. MANGAS MARTÍN, Tratado de la Uniòn Europea, Tratado de Funcionamiento, op. cit.

594 For further details see: C. DENYS, Affaire no C-19/92, Dieter Kraus et Land Baden- Württemberg, in Cahiers de Droit Européen, 32, 1994, pp. 638ss. L. J. SMITH, Postgraduate degrees, vocational training and reverse discrimination: the narrow divide, in European Law Review, 19, 1994, pp. 67ss. W.H. ROTH, Case C-19/92, Dieter Kraus v. Land Baden-Württemberg, Judgement of 31 March 1993, in Common Market Law Review, 30, 1993, pp. 1251ss.

595 CJEU, C-19/92, Kraus of 31 March 1993, op. cit. Mr. Kraus, a German national, and Land Baden-

ing the state measures which made the use of a university degree obtained in another member state subject to the issue of authorization by the competent administration, without the autonomous prohibition being emphasized[596].

CJEU recalls that, although in the absence of harmonization concerning the conditions of use of the postgraduate diploma, the power to determine the modalities for the use of the aforementioned title to be subject to the individual member states, the provisions on freedom of establishment "preclude any provision concerning the conditions for the use of a supplementary university degree obtained in another member state, which, even if it applies without discrimination on grounds of nationality, may hinder or discourage the exercise by European Union citizens, including those of the member state which issued the measure itself, of the fundamental freedoms guaranteed by the Treaty"[597].

Wuerttemberg, opposed the dispute as to latter's refusal to recognize that the use of the postgraduate university degree obtained by Mr Kraus in the United Kingdom in the absence of prior authorization, prescribed by the German legislation. Mr Kraus, in fact, had refused to formally request authorization, claiming that the fact of requiring prior authorization for the use of a university degree obtained in another member state constituted an obstacle to the free movement of persons and a discrimination, prohibited by the EEC Treaty, since such authorization was not required for the use of a diploma issued by a German institute.

596 CJEU had already ruled in a similar case, C-61/89, Bouchoucha of 3 October 1990, op. cit., legitimizing the French legislation which, in the absence of harmonization, reserved osteopathy only for holders of the medical degree. At that juncture, CJEU noted that, lacking a EU regulation of the osteopath profession, each member state is free to regulate the exercise of this activity on its territory, without giving rise to discrimination between its own citizens and those of other member states (par. 12). In particular, a member state has a legitimate interest in preventing some of its citizens from escaping the empire of national laws in the field of vocational training, thanks to the possibilities offered by the Treaty. "This would occur in particular if the fact, for a national of a member state, of having obtained in another member state a diploma, the extent and value of which is not recognized by any EU provision, could oblige the origin member state to allow him to carry out activities related to that diploma on his territory, where the performance of such activities is reserved for holders of a higher qualification mutually recognized at EU level and that this reserve does not appear to be arbitrary (...)" (par. 15). It therefore resolves the question raised by the Cour d'appel of Aix-en-Provence in the sense that, in the absence of harmonization at EU level of activities pertaining exclusively to the exercise of the medical profession, article 52 of the Treaty (now article 49 TFEU) does not preclude a member state from reserving a paramedical activity, such as osteopathy in particular, solely for holders of the medical degree.

597 Paragraph 35. It should be noted that CJEU, thus ruling, does not accept the thesis proposed by AG Van Gerven in his opinion of 13 January 1993, according to which "the prohibition, punishable by penalties, of using false diplomas is sufficient in itself to broadly protect public's good faith", which would be enough to make such national legislation contrary to the principle of necessity and/or proportionality (paragraph 13). It is interesting to note that, from the point of view of the abuse, the AG distinguished the present from the Bouchoucha case: "This reservation of the Bouchoucha judgment to the general principle set out in the Knoors ruling does not seem relevant to me in this case. It should be read in relation to the subject-matter of the dispute, which, as I have already noted (par. 15), concerned the use of a diploma (British) which, according to the holder's claims, gave access to a regulated profession (in France). Well, so it is not in the present species, since Mr. Kraus does not

However, according to the usual scheme, the member state may call for justification of non-discriminatory restrictive measures, overriding reasons of general interest, provided that, of course, the measures in question guarantee the achievement of the aim pursued and do not go beyond what is necessary to achieve this purpose.

In the present case, CJEU acknowledges that the national measure "aims to protect the public against the misuse of university degrees obtained outside the territory of the member state concerned"[598]. Having recalled that "even" EU law does not prevent a member state from adopting, in the absence of harmonization, measures to prevent the possibilities offered by the Treaty from being abused and contrary to the legitimate interests of that state, further confirming the rationale of the state ban. CJEU concludes that "the need to protect a public not necessarily competent against the abusive employment of university degrees that have not been issued in accordance with the rules issued for this purpose in the state in which territory the holder of the diploma intends to use it is a legitimate interest to justify a restriction, by the member state concerned, of the fundamental freedoms guaranteed by the Treaty"[599].

However, it states that a national regulation establishing such a procedure must satisfy certain conditions in order to be compatible with the principle of proportionality. In this regard, CJEU specifies how the authorization procedure should have the sole purpose of verifying whether the postgraduate university degree has been regularly issued, as well as being easily accessible and not entailing the payment of excessively high administrative rights. Furthermore, decisions that deny authorization must be susceptible to judicial review and, to

try to use his LL.M. for the purpose of exercising a regulated profession in the Federal Republic of Germany, but only intends to take advantage of the degree connected to the diploma. Furthermore, the reservation made in the Bouchoucha judgment is motivated by the concern to avoid that, thanks to the possibilities offered by the Treaty, national citizens attempt to circumvent, in a sector as sensitive as the medical and para-medical one, the application of internal laws in access to a regulated profession. The judgment in question should rather be read in the light of the CJEU's case-law referred to in paragraph 13: case-law, from which it is inferred that the national rules designed to prevent the fundamental freedoms guaranteed by the Treaty from being abused are compatible with the purpose, for example, to circumvent the mandatory internal rules on vocational training. As I have pointed out in this connection, however, the protection and authorization, claiming that the fact of requiring prior authorization for the use of a university degree obtained in another member state constituted an obstacle to the free movement of persons and discrimination, forbidden by the EEC Treaty, since such authorization was not required for the use of a diploma issued by a German institute.

598 CJEU, C-61/89, Bouchoucha of 3 October 1990, op. cit.

599 CJUE, C-61/89, Bouchoucha of 3 October 1990, op. cit.

this end, the interested party must be able to know the reasons on which they are based. Finally, the penalties imposed for failure to comply with the authorization procedure must not be disproportionate to the gravity of the infringement. Ultimately, a set of rules must be observed to ensure the satisfaction of the principle of proportionality[600].

The examination of these cases shows how jurisprudence has made a variable use of the reason for the fight against abuse, so that this brief consideration cannot lead to conclusive conclusions.

In particular, if it is clear that the abuse can be invoked by member states at different levels, the attitude of CJEU with regard to the fight against the abuse as a reason of general interest is not as sure. To be honest, even from Kraus pronunciation there is a greater propensity to invoke the abuse as a justification for the restrictive measures adopted. It is not understandable, however, whether, over and above the statements of principle, to consider justification abuse can be said to be effective. Moreover, it would be inappropriate to draw a general rule from an isolated case.

Starting from these considerations, we explain the need to analyze a particular strand, that of tax avoidance, in which the jurisprudence of CJEU is not only consolidated, but has made an effort to analyze the constituting elements of the significant test.

APPLICATION OF THE TECHNIQUE OF IMPERATIVE REASONS IN RELATION TO CIRCUMVENTION IN DIRECT TAXATION

As was already observed in the area of direct taxation, which, it should be recalled, is a largely non-harmonized matter, EU has had the opportunity to deal with abusive situations perpetrated by companies established in a particular member state that, in order to circumvent the tax legislation of the same and move towards more favorable regulations, the so-called tax havens have invoked the freedom of secondary establishment, creating in these last states secondary centers of "convenience", to which transfers taxable profits.

As you will see, in the first cases in which the case law was compared with this phenomenon, before C-196/04, Cadbury Schweppes and Cadbury

600 A. HARTKAMP, C. SIEBURGH, W. DEVROE, Cases, materials and text on European law and private law, op. cit.

Schweppes Overseas of 12 September 2006, abuse was always[601] and only talked about in terms of fight against tax evasion, which justifies restrictive measures by national authorities.

C-196/04, Cadbury Schweppes and Cadbury Schweppes Overseas case of 12 September 2006 was intended, from a certain doctrine, as a watershed towards an autonomous notion of abuse of right[602], also on the basis of the overall view that transpires from the operated references from CJEU itself, first of all to C-255/02, Halifax and others case of 21 February 2006. However, it has already been observed that consistent claims are not always applied to the principle statements of the case law. In this sense, it can be assumed, on the contrary, that this pronunciation represents the proof of the incapacity, at present, of CJEU to attribute such autonomy to the concept. In fact, we have already seen how CJEU has promptly excluded it. The same abuse was instead brought back to the imperative reasons of general interest. It therefore appears useful, for our purposes, to examine first the case law before the C-196/04, Cadbury Schweppes and Cadbury Schweppes Overseas case of 12 September 2006, in which the constitutional elements of the technique were already present in the nuce, which will then be subsequently replicated, at the same time verifying the operating conditions of the ban on a case-by-case basis.

In this regard, a methodological clarification must first be carried out. The study of the jurisprudence in this paragraph will focus less on the facts of the case as the basis of the judgment. This choice is justified by the fact that the previous paragraphs responded to the need to first outline the presence and characteristics of the abusive manifestations, and then analyze CJEU's response to the same, as well as the underlying reasons. On this occasion, however, having established that there is a detachment between abusive behavior and the application of the related prohibition, we want to investigate the alternative techniques employed by the law, with a view to providing an overview of the consequences of choosing to bring the doctrine back of the abuse of law in terms of justifications against tax avoidance.

In this regard, it can already be anticipated that the prohibition of restrictive fiscal measures has traditionally been framed by CJEU as a prohibition of

601 CJEU, joined cases C-397/98 and C-410/98, Metallgesellschaft and others, of 8 March 2001, ECLI:EU:C:2001:134, I-01727, par. 37. For further details see: N. BAMMENS, The principle of non-discrimination in international and European tax law, IBFD, Leidend, 2012.

602 CJEU, C-307/97, Saint-Gobain ZN of 21 September 1999, ECLI:EU:C:1999:438, I-0616, par. 35. A. DE GRAAF, M. EVERS, Limiting benefit shopping cit., p. 281 ss.

discriminatory measures that treat cross-border situations in a manner that is less comparable to internal situations. Indeed, according to settled case-law, while it is true that the matter of direct taxation falls within the competence of member states, it is also true that the latter must exercise that power in compliance with Union law. As far as we are concerned, the freedom of establishment of companies established in accordance with the legislation of a member state, having their registered office, central administration or principal place of business in EU territory, consists of the right to carry out their activity in another member state through a branch, or an agency. As stated, the rules on freedom of establishment aim to ensure the benefit of national legislation of the host member state; as noted in case law, however, they also preclude the state of origin from impeding the establishment in another member state of its own national or of a company constituted according to its own legislation. In view of this, CJEU's orientation is constant in considering that the national regulations restricting the freedom of establishment can be justified in an abstract way in the fight against tax avoidance, which is an overriding reason of general interest, but only if they possess precise characteristics, including first of all proportionality and selectivity. The national measures, in fact, must be suitable to "hit" the only abusive constructions. In other words, they must take what has been called a shotgun approach[603]. In this, as we can see, CJEU does nothing more than apply to the present case more general considerations which fit the grounds of general interest according to CJEU jurisprudence.

C-196/04, CADBURY SCHWEPPES AND CADBURY SCHWEPPES OVERSEAS CASE LAW OF 12 SEPTEMBER 2006: NARROW LIMITS WITHIN WHICH IMPERATIVE GROUNDS OF GENERAL INTEREST OPERATE

CJEU jurisprudence is consolidated by accepting in principle that member states can take remedies to counter tax evasion of taxpayers who take advantage of the Treaty provisions relating to freedom of movement and, in particular, those on freedom of establishment, to take advantage of the more favorable tax regime of another member state.

603 See, N. VINTHER, E. WERLAUFF, Tax motives are legal motives-The borderline between the use and abuse of the freedom of establishment with reference to the Cadbury Schweppes Case, in European Taxation, 6, 2006, pp. 385ss.

However, it recognizes this possibility within very narrow limits.

Thus, in ICI[604], EU judicature was called upon to rule on the possibility of justifying the difference in treatment created, with reference to the freedom of establishment, by a national legislation which used the criterion of the seat of subsidiaries to provide differentiated taxation treatment of these companies, direct, inter alia, to reduce the risk of tax evasion. Such risk, as claimed by the United Kingdom government, was determined by intra-group transactions aimed at organizing a transfer of charges from non-resident subsidiaries to a subsidiary resident in the United Kingdom and, on the other hand, to make profits appear to subsidiaries residents. According to this approach, the legislation at issue aimed therefore at preventing the creation of subsidiaries abroad for the purpose of subtracting taxable assets from the British tax authorities.

CJEU, in reply, excludes that the fight against tax evasion may be invoked in the present case, by concisely observing that "the legislation at issue in the main proceedings does not have the specific objective of excluding purely artificial constructions from a tax advantage whose purpose is to evade the UK tax law, but generally considers any situation in which companies controlled by a group are in majority established, for any reason, outside the United Kingdom"[605]. It notes that "the establishment of a company outside the United Kingdom does not in itself entail tax evasion, given that the company in question is nevertheless subject to the tax law of the state of establishment"[606].

604 CJEU, C-264/96, Imperial Chemical Industries plc (ICI) v. Kolmer, of 16 July 1998, ECLI:EU:C:1998:370, I-04695. The referring CJEU essentially asked whether the freedom of establishment precluded a legislation of a member state which, as regards the companies established in that member state and forming part of a consortium through which they hold a company, subordinated the right to remission tax on the condition that the holding company was to hold exclusively or principally the shares of subsidiaries established in the member state concerned. For analysis see: S.E. BÄRSCH, Taxation of hybrid financial instruments and the remuneration derived therefrom in and international cross-border context: Issues and options for reform, ed. Springer, Berlin, 2012.

605 S.E. BÄRSCH, Taxation of hybrid financial instruments and the remuneration derived therefrom in and international cross-border context: Issues and options for reform, op. cit.

606 CJEU, C-324/00, Lankhorst-Hohorst GmbH of 12 December 2002, ECLI:EU:C:2002:749, I-11799. The referring CJEU doubted the compatibility with the freedom of establishment of national legislation adopted to combat under-capitalization, which substantially offset a subsidiary from the fiscal point of view on account of the fact that the parent company was established in another member state to the subsidiary. For further analysis see: O. F. GRAF KERSSENBROCK, In the wake of Lankhorst-Hohorst, in Intertax, 2004, pp. 306ss. D. GUTMANN, L. HINNEKENS, The Lankhorst-Hohorst case. ECJ finds German thin capitalization rules incompatible with freedom of establishment, in EC Tax Review, 3, 2003, pp. 90ss. L. IDOT, Un régime différencié pour l'octroi du credit d'impôt en matière d'impôt sur les sociétés est contraire à l'article 43 CE, in Europe, 55, février 2003, pp. 17ss. N. VINTHER, E. WERLAUFF, The need for fresh thinking about tax rules on thin capitalization: the consequences of the judgment of the ECJ in Lankhorst- Hohorst, in EC Tax Review, 3, 2003, pp. 97ss.

In these first affirmations of European Union jurisprudence, it seems to be seen to be contrary to the recognition in principle that the fight against tax evasion may rise to the rank of a plea capable of justifying measures which are restrained as restrictive. However, CJEU clearly points out that the lack of any selectivity in UK legislation is essentially equivalent to considering the establishment itself in another member state as elusive, which is why it can only be defined as an unjustified restriction on the establishment of subsidiary companies in another member state.

This last statement will be taken up in the subsequent jurisprudence. Suffice it to cite the C-324/00, Lankhorst-Hohorst GmbH sentence of 12 December 2002 with which CJEU, resuming the previous ICI, sanctioned the incompatibility with the freedom of establishment of the German discipline on funding by non-resident members. While the same objective was not to avoid that, through artificial constructions, tax advantages otherwise unreachable could be obtained, it was suitable to include any legitimate situation in which the parent companies had their headquarters outside the German Republic a situation which does not in itself entail a risk of tax evasion, given that the company in question is nevertheless subject to the tax legislation of the state in which it is established[607].

These decisions marked the start of a long series of rulings in which the Luxembourg judge, in a manner that was truly less cryptic, repeatedly considered the need to combat tax evasion as a valid justification for restrictive national measures, initially intended as part a wider range of justifications, normally the cohesion of tax system and the effectiveness of fiscal controls, and subsequently also appreciating it as the only justification[608].

A particular mention in this regard is given by ruling C-436/00, X and Y sentence of 12 December 2002[609], in which CJEU affirmed positively that the need to safeguard the coherence of tax system, the fight against tax evasion and the effectiveness of tax controls are overriding reasons of general interest capable

607 Paragraph 37. Moreover, CJEU adds in paragraph 38, according to the findings of the referring CJEU itself, that in this case there is no abuse, since the loan actually intervened to reduce, in favor of the appellant in the main proceedings, the burden of financial interests resulting from your bank credit. Furthermore, it is apparent from the documents that Lankhorst-Hohorst was, for the years 1996 to 1998, at a loss, for amounts largely higher than the interest paid to LT BV.

608 Judgment of CJEU in case C-436/00, X and Y of 21 November 2002, op. cit., concerning Swedish legislation concerning the sale of shares in companies constituted in accordance with the legislation of a member state in which the transfer holds an investment of a subsidiary established in the Kingdom of Sweden by that company.

609 CJEU, C-436/00, X and Y of 12 December 2002, op. cit.

of justifying regulations that restrict the fundamental freedoms guaranteed by the Treaty[610].

The referring court wondered about the compatibility with the freedom of establishment and the free movement of capital of the discipline that applies to the transfer of shares of companies to a different tax treatment depending on the nature of the transferee. The national authority argued that in the present case the only objective of the transfer to a Swedish company established for that purpose, rather than to a Belgian company, was to enjoy tax advantages. In this regard, he recalled that, according to CJEU jurisprudence, a member state has the right to take measures to prevent, thanks to the possibilities offered by the Treaty, that some citizens attempt to evade the empire of national laws abusively and that, furthermore, data subjects cannot abusively or fraudulently use Union law. The national authority claimed that the risk of tax evasion would first of all have raised doubts as to the applicability of the freedom of establishment because, in this case, there would have been indications of a possible abuse of that freedom. Only in the alternative, he argued that that risk could have been relied upon to justify a possible restriction on the freedom of establishment, by way of overriding reason of public interest. CJEU follows the suggested biphasic approach, first excluding the abuse and then verifying if the reasons could be justified by imperative reasons of public interest.

He, however, judged the norm submitted to his unsuitable[611] and necessary attention in relation to the objective pursued. In this latter regard, in particular,

---

610 CJEU considers that: "the measure adopted by the Kingdom of Sweden is not suitable for achieving the objective that should be pursued, i.e. that the transfer is effectively taxed in Sweden for the capital gains realized on the shares sold, in particular if the sale is produced before a definitive transfer of the latter abroad. In fact, it must be stated that, in the event of the sale of Type C shares, the transfer benefits in any case of a postponement of the tax payment on the capital gains realized on the shares sold. Now, in response to a question put by the CJEU, the Swedish government has not been able to show that, for this type of assignment, there are different objective situations from which it can be deduced that the potential risk resulting in a permanent transfer abroad of the transfer, with regard to its tax liability, is essentially in different terms for the sale of type A and type B shares (...)" (par. 63).

611 Judgment of CJEU: C-9/02, Hughes de Lasteyrie du Saillant of 11 March 2004, ECLI:EU:C:2004:138, I-02409. The national court asked whether art. 52 TEC (now 49 TFEU) opposed the establishment, by a member state, for the purpose of preventing the risk of tax evasion, of an imposition system, on the date of transfer of the domicile of a tax payer outside France, of capital gains on social rights, where the latter were determined by the difference between the value of these rights on the date of said transfer and their purchase price. This tax only applied to taxpayers who held rights in the social profits of a company that exceeded 25% of such profits at any time during the last five years preceding the aforementioned date. The peculiarity of the wording lay in the fact that it concerned the imposition of latent capital gains. CJEU immediately notes that the taxpayer wishing to transfer the domicile outside French territory, in the exercise of the right guaranteed to him by art. 52 of the

CJEU reiterated that a general presumption of tax evasion or fraud cannot be based on the fact that the transferee company or its parent company is established in another member state, or justify a measure tax that undermines the exercise of a fundamental freedom guaranteed by the Treaty, whereas this was precisely the case of the legislation under examination. The latter, in fact, did not have the specific purpose of excluding purely artificial transactions whose purpose was to circumvent the Swedish tax legislation from a tax advantage, but concerned, in a general manner, any situation in which the sale underpaid was made in favor of a company established in accordance with the legislation of another member state in which the originator held an investment or a subsidiary established in the Kingdom of Sweden by that company[612].

The ruling in C-9/02, Hughes de Lasteyrie du Saillant case of 11 March 2004 also specified that the national regulations cannot, without exceeding what is necessary to achieve the intended purpose, presume the intention to circumvent the tax legislation by part of any taxpayer who transfers his domicile outside the member state of belonging.

Although this statement does not present particular traits of innovation in itself considered, it is interesting to note the factual context in which it was made. In fact, to justify the obstacle posed to the freedom of establishment by national legislation, the French government referred the objective of avoiding

---

Treaty (now art. 49 TFEU), is subject to unfavorable treatment compared to a person who retains his residence in France. However, it checks whether this provision can be justified. For further details see: S. KODANIS, French exit tax incompatible with the freedom of establishment, in European Taxation, 4, 2004, pp. 375ss. J.P. MAUBLANC, Liberté d'établissement- Incompatibilité aves les traités communautaires de la taxation à la sortie par l'article 167 bis du CGI CJCE 11 mars 2004 no 9/02 de Lasteyrie du Saillant, in Revue du Marché Commun et de l'Union Européenne, 444, 2004, pp. 684ss.

612 Paragraph 24. The French Government stated that the adoption of the provision at issue was inspired by the behavior of certain taxpayers consisting in temporarily transferring their tax domicile before securities for the sole purpose of avoiding the payment of capital gains tax due in France. Even more clearly, as reported in the opinion of AG in paragraphs 53 and 54, "The French Government, which has presented the most detailed arguments on this point, explains that the contested provision seeks to prevent what should be defined as an abuse of law, i.e. the fraudulent use by a taxpayer of the freedoms conferred on him by EU law. In this regard, government points out that a member state is free to define the way in which capital gains are taxed, particularly as regards tax rates. It would therefore be entirely legitimate for each member state to take appropriate measures to prevent the taxation of capital gains from being deprived of substance because of abusive behavior. In the present case, that behavior consists in the fact that a taxpayer temporarily transfers his tax residence outside France before transferring securities for the sole purpose of avoiding the payment of capital gains tax payable in France. In this case it would not be a normal exercise of the freedom of establishment, but of an abusive use of this freedom, in order to circumvent the tax legislation (...)".

an abusive use of this freedom in order to circumvent tax legislation, expressly linking it to the prohibition of abuse. It noted that "it would be an application in the tax area of what CJEU considered as "abusive exercise" of a right conferred by Union law[613]. CJEU, in response, does not limit itself to excluding proportionality in negative, but provides very precise indications on the question of how to avoid the risk of evasion with less restrictive measures of freedom of establishment, in particular suggesting to provide "taxation of the taxpayer who, after a relatively brief stay in another member state, returns to France after having realized his capital gains, which would avoid jeopardizing the situation of taxpayers whose sole objective is to exercise in good faith the freedom of establishment in another member state"[614].

This option had already been proposed by the conclusions of the AG Mischo, where it was pointed out that a taxpayer's decision to settle abroad does not in itself imply a tax fraud and, as a consequence, it is up to the tax administration of the member state concerned to try, on a case by case basis, the existence of a risk of tax evasion. In particular, regarding the French government's claim that the transfer of securities shortly after departure from France constituted a sure indication of the desire to evade the tax, the AG very pragmatically finds that the departure for another member state. In order to undertake a new professional activity, it can involve considerable expenses, which may be linked to this new activity or derive from the need to buy, for example, accommodation. Therefore, it cannot be assumed that the mere transfer of shares shortly after the transfer of the domicile is sufficient to reveal the fraudulent intention. On the other hand, he admits that a criterion based on the speed of return to France would be, a priori, a closer relationship with the aim of preventing the taxpayer from circumventing the tax through the simple expedient of a short stay in another member state, during which the securities would be sold[615].

---

613 CJEU, C-370/90, C-370/90, The Queen/Immigration Appeal Tribunal and Surinder Singh, ex parte Secretary of State for the Home Department of 7 July 1992, op. cit., and the conclusions presented on 13 March 2003, par. 64. The AG, while acknowledging that the case-law recognized the fight against tax evasion as an overriding reason of general interest, points out that the national provision in question determines, an "irrefutable presumption of tax fraud".

614 M. LANG, The Marks & Spencer case-The open issues following the ECJ's final word, in European Taxation, 6, 2006, pp. 54ss. T. O'SHEA, Marks and Spencer v. Halsey (HM Inspector of Taxes): Restriction, justification and proportionality, in EC Tax Review, 6, 2006, pp. 66ss.

615 Parr. 49-51. A. ZALASINSKI, Some basic aspects of the concept of abuse in the tax case law of the European Court of Justice, op. cit., pp. 163ss, notes how this ruling shows that the court is increasingly inclined to recognize that cross-border activities can increase the risk of tax avoidance for member states. Therefore, in principle, the prevention of tax abuses appears to be a valid justifica-

Finally, in the pronunciation of C-446/03, Marks & Spencer, Plc v. David Halsey case of 13 December 2005[616] which precedes less than a year Cadbury Schweppes, CJEU has the opportunity to apply in a more organic way the compatibility test, in relation to the legislation that introduces a different tax treatment between the losses suffered by a subsidiary resident and those by a non-resident subsidiary. Thus, in regards to the justification for tax evasion, CJEU recognizes that the possibility of transferring the losses of a non-resident subsidiary to a resident company carries the risk where, within a group of companies, losses are organized in management of companies registered in member states where the rates of taxation are higher and in which, consequently, the tax value of losses is higher. Thus, restrictive legislation, such as the one in question, pursues legitimate objectives compatible with the Treaty and guarantees the realization of these objectives[617].

It states, however, that the legislation cannot be applied, exceeding what is necessary for the attainment of the objectives pursued, in the case in which "the non-resident subsidiary has exhausted the possibilities of taking into account the losses existing in its state of residence for fiscal year considered in the application for remission, as well as previous fiscal years, possibly by transferring such losses to a third party, or attributing such losses to profits made by the subsidiary during the previous financial years, and losses of the foreign subsidiary they may be taken into account in its state of residence for future tax purposes either by itself or by a third party, particularly if the subsidiary is sold to the latter"[618].

tion for restrictions on free movement, provided that the measures are proportionate.

616 ECLI:EU:C:2005:763, I-010837. K. DZIURDZ, C. MARHGRABER, Non discrimination in European and tax treaty law. Open issues and recent challenges, op. cit.

617 Paragraph 55. "At a time when, in a member state, the parent company demonstrates to the tax authorities that these conditions are met, it is contrary to articles 43 EC and 48 EC to exclude the possibility for the latter to deduct from its taxable income in that member state the losses incurred by its non-resident subsidiary. In this context, it is still necessary to clarify that member states remain free to adopt or maintain in force rules having the specific objective of excluding purely artificial constructions from a fiscal advantage, the purpose of which is to circumvent national tax legislation (see in this sense, cited judgments par. 26, and de Lasteyrie du Saillant, par. 50)" (parr. 56 and 57).

618 A. ZALASINSKI, Some basic aspects of the concept of abuse in the tax case law of the European Court of Justice, op. cit.

The indications that can be drawn from these first pronunciations are manifold. First of all, it is beyond doubt that, in the view of CJEU, the fight against tax avoidance could be an overriding reason of general interest capable of justifying, in the abstract, a restrictive national measure. In this sense, the abuse of law rises to the role of justification for the inequalities of treatment caused by national legislation, as an imperative reason of general interest[619].

However, the fact that none of the national laws subject to examination by EU judicature has emerged unscathed from the proportionality test is a fact. It has been pointed out that CJEU, sometimes not even on the merits of question, other times providing more precise indications to member state, has come to deny compliance with national law of such congenital national measures, finding mostly the too broad scope of their formulation, which also led to hitting non-elusive operations. Indeed, control by Union's legal system regarding the constituent elements of justification proves to be severe, affecting all the laws that establish a general presumption of circumvention or fraud, on the basis that the assignee company or its parent company is based in another member country. This seems reasonable, because otherwise it would end up nullifying the freedom of establishment itself. In short, it serves an element of selectivity, because otherwise the establishment in another member state would be considered in essence to be in itself elusive. On the other hand, it is necessary to highlight immediately the difficulties faced by a norm, necessarily abstract and general, in precisely defining the operations that are certainly abusive. On this point, this case law, with the exception of what was said in Lasteyrie du Saillant with reference to the element of "rapidity of return", offers, among other things, little hint as to what constructions should be considered abusive, the national measure is justified.

This can be explained by taking into account what has just been stated. CJEU may not have felt the need to establish the criteria for identifying an abusive situation, given that the national measures in question had such a wide margin

619 V. EDWARDS, P. FARMER, The concept of abuse in the freedom of establishment of companies: A case of double standards?, op. cit., pp. 213ss, they point out how, in reality, this first jurisprudence did not provide a certain answer to the question about the possibility of a "doubling" of the concept of abuse, which can be understood as a tool to limit the concrete application of fundamental freedoms, in based on the consideration that certain constructions are not worthy of protection, either as justification.

of application, to be clear that they had not been specifically designed to counteract abusive behavior[620].

In any case, what is already evident is how member states and CJEU demonstrate that they have different perceptions about what may or may not be considered abusive. While the former tend to qualify any taxpayer conduct that is abusive as a reduction of tax revenue for the state, CJEU accepts that a certain transaction is considered abusive only when the loss of tax revenue is the result of a purely artificial construction, the purpose of which is to circumvent tax law.

Problems that have just been brought to light regarding the definition and verification of abuse, as well as the related satisfaction of the proportionality element, will indeed be more fully developed in C-196/04, Cadbury Schweppes and Cadbury Schweppes Overseas sentence of 12 September 2006, which represents, compared to previous jurisprudence, a coherent evolution of CJEU's thought, a "form of linear development". C-196/04, Cadbury Schweppes and Cadbury Schweppes Overseas case of 12 September 2006 offered CJEU a good opportunity to explain what the expression "construction of pure artifice" actually meant.

C-196/04, CADBURY SCHWEPPES AND CADBURY SCHWEPPES OVERSEAS CASE OF 12 SEPTEMBER 2006 AS A STARTING POINT FOR A CLEARER DEFINITION OF "PURELY ARTIFICIAL CONSTRUCTION"

In C-196/04, Cadbury Schweppes and Cadbury Schweppes Overseas case of 12 September 2006, CJEU has been able to deal with the controlled foreigner companies legislations, legislative measures aimed at repressing the practice of transferring the taxable profits generated by companies established in a member state to companies controlled by them and established in countries with a lower level of taxation. In short, these are measures intended to be applied when the profits earned by the controlled foreign company of a company that is tax-resident in the member state in question are subject to a much lower tax than that applied in that member state. By way of derogation from the common law and provided that the conditions of one of the normally accepted exceptions are not

620 K K. LENAERTS, The concept of "abuse of law" in the case law of the European Court of Justice on direct taxation, in Maastricht Journal of European and Comparative Law, 22, 2015, pp. 336ss.

met, these regulations provide that such profits are included in the taxable base of the parent company from the moment they are realized.

Under that provision, Cadbury Schweppes company, tax resident in the United Kingdom, was also taxed on profits made by its subsidiaries, which had been established in Ireland solely because their financing activities of the Cadbury Schweppes group could benefit from a more favorable tax regime.

CJEU, once rejected the possibility of invoking the prohibition of abuse in this case, has been called, in the alternative, to establish whether such legislation is congenital, restrictive only of the freedom of establishment, where it leads to an unequal treatment among resident companies based on the level of taxation applied to the company in which they hold a controlling interest, could be justified on grounds of combating tax evasion.

Such a restriction, abstractly justifiable if there are overriding reasons of general interest, must overcome the usual test established by CJEU jurisprudence. The protective measure must therefore be suitable to ensure the achievement of the aim pursued and not exceed what is necessary to achieve it. In particular, since the British legislation in the "for theft" procedure of exempt cases used inter alia the motive test, making an assessment about the absence of elusive purposes by resident members[621], CJEU has posed the problem of understanding if the same test, as conceived, was or not suitable to limit the application of anti-avoidance rules only to purely fictitious constructions.

CJEU, after recalling that a restriction on freedom of establishment must have the specific purpose of hindering conduct consisting in creating purely artificial constructions, designed to circumvent the normal tax on profits, considers it useful to make a parallel with the abusive practices of Marks & Spencer. This parallel consists of organizing transfers of losses, within a group of companies towards companies established in member states that apply the highest tax rates. Consequently, the tax value of the losses is higher, noting that both behaviors described are such as to violate the right of member states to exercise their tax jurisdiction in relation to activities carried out on their territory.

Such importance is not of little importance: in Marks & Spencer, in fact, the legislation was so suitable to repress tax avoidance, but not proportionate to this

621 In essence, it requires that the resident company demonstrates, on the one hand, that the significant decrease in UK tax which would result from the transactions between that company and SEC was not the objective, or one of the main objectives, of the transactions and, secondly, that the obtaining of a reduction of the tax by distraction of profits in the sense of that legislation was not the main or one of the main reasons, of the establishment of SEC.

end. What is interesting to note, therefore, is how CJEU, in principle, labeled the constructions described as abusive. The abusiveness of the former construction, however, is not sufficient to establish the legitimacy of the law, from which it is clear that the control of the legislation is placed at a different level from that of factual reality, a significant element of differentiation between technique of imperative reasons of general interest and the prohibition of abuse.

What makes the pronunciation commentary innovative compared to the jurisprudence just analyzed is however the following. CJEU, after having also ascertained the suitability of legislation to combat the circumvention[622] in verifying its proportionality, recalls the abuse to be understood as an imperative reason that justifies the adoption of a national restrictive measure, as already established in all other context[623].

Consider the test coined in C-110/99, Emsland-Stärke case of 14 December 2000 and then reiterated in C-255/02, Halifax and others case of 21 February 2006, CJEU judges UK legislation on SEC compatible with EU law only insofar as the inclusion. The latter includes the taxable base of a company resident in a member state and profits made by a controlled foreign company established in another state, when such profits are there subject to an imposition level lower than the one applicable in the first state, concerning pure construction designed to circumvent national tax. On the contrary, application of such tax measures must be excluded if, from objective and verifiable elements by third parties, it appears that, even if there are reasons of a fiscal nature, the subsidiary is actually implanted in the state of establishment and exercises effective economic

622 In this regard, CJEU notes that "by providing for the inclusion of profits of a SEC subject to a very favorable tax regime in the taxable base of the resident company, the said legislation allows counteracting practices aimed at nothing other than circumventing the tax normally due on profits generated by activities carried out on the national territory. As noted by the French, Finnish and Swedish governments, such legislation is therefore appropriate for achieving the objective for which it was adopted (...)"(par. 59).

623 G.T.K. MEUSSEN, Cadbury Schweppes: The ECG significantly limits the application of CFC rules in the member states s, op. cit., pp. 19, criticizes CJEU view regarding the burden of proof. According to the author, in fact, CJEU should have clearly stated that it is the member state in question that has to provide proof of the existence of a construction of pure artifice (and not, vice versa, that the company resident to provide proof which is not a purely artificial construction). In the same spirit see also: par. 67. It should be noted that CJEU recalls in detail only the first of the three criteria detailed in AG's opinion, namely the level of physical presence of the subsidiary in the state of establishment, linking it to the effectiveness of the activity it provides. In particular, according to the lawyer in general, "even if the subsidiary proves to be just a simple executive instrument, because the decisions necessary to perform the services for which it is paid are taken at other levels, it is legitimate to consider the reconditioning of such benefits are a mere artifice of the state of establishment (...)" (par. 113).

activities. On this point, it is stated that such a finding must rest on objective and verifiable elements on the part of third parties, "relating, in particular, to the level of physical presence of SEC in terms of premises, personnel and equipment"[624].

In other words, the national legislation in question can be applied only if SEC turns out to be a "phantom" or "screen" company, that is to say, a fictitious installation, which does not exercise any effective economic activity on the territory of the member state of establishment[625].

The conclusion reached by CJEU, from the point of view of artificiality, is nothing more than the logical result of definition of establishment and its ratio, which is clearly evident from the Treaties, as interpreted by the Union jurisprudence[626]. The absence of the aforementioned human and technical equipment, in

---

624 The value added by subsidiary's activity should also be verified. This is undoubtedly the most delicate criterion to be implemented if the services provided by the latter actually correspond to the exercise of real activities in the state of establishment, but nevertheless useful for taking account of the objective situation in which the services provided by the subsidiary are missing of any economic interest in relation to the activity of the parent company, to derive a totally artificial creation, given that the price paid by the parent company for the services in question seems, in some way, without compensation (...)" (par. 114).

625 CJEU adds that "on the other hand, as AG observed in par. 103 of his opinion, the fact that the assets corresponding to the profits of SEC could well have been carried out also by a company established in the territory of the member state in which it is located. The resident company cannot permit the conclusion that there is a construction of pure artifice"(paragraph 69). Must agree with R. KARIMERI, A critical review of the definition of tax avoidance in the case law of the European Court of Justice, op. cit., pp. 308-310, when he states that, at first sight, the fact that the element of artificiality has been used to define in negative the purpose of freedom of establishment and correlatively the activities not covered on the basis of the objective element could be anomalous, both as an objective index of the desire to obtain an improper advantage, it is easy to repeat that the purpose of a rule, objective evidence and motives, in practice, are closely related. It is clear, in fact, that CJEU will have to decide whether there has been an advantage contrary to the purposes of the rule, following which it may be relevant to assess whether abusive motivations exist, but, in practice, the verification of the reasons and the achievement of the purpose the norm takes place simultaneously, since it is largely based on the same objective evidence of artificiality. The great virtue of the test of purely artificial construction consists precisely in providing clear and unequivocal evidence of the abusive will, while demonstrating that the purpose of the tax rule in question has not been met.

626 Note that case: C-196/04, Cadbury Schweppes and Cadbury Schweppes Overseas of 12 September 2006, was not an isolated ruling but was also applied in UK in Vodafone 2 case (C-203/05, Vodafone 2 of 20 August 2008, ECLI:EU:C:2008:460, not published), in which CJEU of Appeal ruled that CFC legislation could be interpreted in such a way as to comply with EU law, adding a new one exception, according to which the restrictive measure does not apply if CFC is actually established in another member state and carries out effective economic activities there. After being "received" by the national jurisdiction, this same ruling has then contributed to take a larger step, starting the legislative reform of CFC legislation in UK in EU since 2011. Perhaps a weight may have had the request of May 2011 Commission to the United Kingdom to make further changes to CFC rules, considering the inadequate response to Cadbury Schweppes (see Case No. 2009/4105, IP/11/606 of 19/05/2011). See in argument: T. O'SHEA, CFC Reforms in the UK-Some EU Law Comments, in EC Tax Journal, 13, 2012-2013, pp. 65ss. M. BROBERG, N. FENGER, Preliminary references to the

fact, would prevent the setting up of objective elements that would help third parties to recognize the establishment and would therefore not allow the exercise of an economic activity having an indefinite duration. Consequently, the enjoyment of freedom of establishment would have no justification and would require the need to find natural arrangement of the secondary establishment in the state where the primary is exercised.

Apart from considerations related to the impact on provisions of SEC on such a ruling, which is reasonably clear in excluding the legislation in question from being applied in its original form[627], the innovativeness of the judgment can be found, in conclusion, under two different and linked profiles. One being the formula "constructions of pure artifice", already used but not yet defined precisely by the previous jurisprudence, and the second be the transposition to imperative reasons of general interest of the criterion elaborated in C-110/99, Emsland-Stärke case of 14 December 2000 with regard to the prohibition of abuse of law.

However, it is necessary to ask whether such a transposition proves to be appropriate. Before tackling this issue, however, it is necessary to check whether the test used by CJEU to establish the proportionality of the measure has been confirmed in subsequent rulings.

To date, the jurisprudence, on this point is consolidated[628]. The judgments which dealt with proportionality after C-196/04, Cadbury Schweppes and

---

European Court of Justice, Oxford University Press, Oxford, 2014. M. HELMINEN, European Union tax law: Direct taxation, IBFD, Leidend, pp. 102ss.

627 J. PETEVA, Abuse under EC tax law and the standard of review of the European Court of Justice, in M. LANG, P. MELZ, Value added tax and direct taxation: Similarities and Differences, IMFD, Amsterdam, 2009, pp. 498ss. It is recalled that "the mere fact that a resident company obtains a loan from a related company established in another member state cannot establish a general presumption of abusive practices, or justify a measure that jeopardizes the exercise of a fundamental freedom guaranteed by the Treaty", but "to be justified by reasons for combating abusive practices, a restriction on the freedom of establishment must have the specific purpose of hindering conduct consisting in creating purely artificial constructions, devoid of economic effectiveness and aimed at circumventing the normal tax on profits generated by activities carried out in the national territory (...)".

628 Paragraph 82. The question was raised about the compatibility with the freedom of establishment of UK legislation which limited the possibility for a resident company to deduct the interest paid on loans granted by a parent company, whether directly or indirectly, for tax purposes, resident in another member state, if the resident company would not have suffered such a restriction if the interest had been paid on loans granted by a parent company established in the United Kingdom. In particular, the national CJEU wondered whether the solution to such a question would change if it could be shown that the loans supplemented an abuse of rights or formed part of an artificial construction intended to circumvent the tax legislation of the member state of residence of the borrowing company.

Cadbury Schweppes Overseas of 12 September 2006, have in common the fact that they adopted the same approach with regard to the notion of "purely artificial" construction, which becomes an indispensable starting point for tax measures to be justified.

However, this notion constitutes the starting point for arriving at more meditated results. First of all, CJEU specifies that where tax legislation does not allow the scope of its application to be determined a priori and with sufficient precision and, consequently, does not meet the requirements of legal certainty. According to which, the rules of law must be clear, precise and predictable in their effects, particularly when they may have negative consequences on individuals and companies, it cannot be considered proportionate to the objectives pursued.

Jurisprudence, then, in the judgment of proportionality, clarifying what has already been established in C-196/04, Cadbury Schweppes and Cadbury Schweppes Overseas case of 12 September 2006, gives a decisive weight to the distribution of the burden of proof, evaluating the legitimacy of national anti-fraudulent measures adopted in this regard. In particular, it has been reiterated that the existence of artificial constructions creates per se the conviction of the presence of a willingness to avoid the payment of tax normally due following the exercise of an economic activity; however, the taxpayer must be given the opportunity to prove the absence of any abusive practice.

In order to be compatible with treaty provisions, national regulations, in short, must regulate the examination of objective and verifiable elements, which make it possible to identify the existence of a construction of pure artifice implemented solely for tax purposes, providing for the possibility of taxpayer to produce, without excessive administrative burdens, elements relating to commercial reasons underlying the transaction in question.

This is a discriminating factor in the eyes of CJEU, and demonstration is given by the test Claimants ruling, the first case in which the Luxembourg judge was called upon to apply the concept of abuse explained in C-196/04, Cadbury Schweppes and Cadbury Schweppes Overseas case of 12 September 2006.

The Anglo-Saxon tax measure object of attention aimed at countering the practice of "undercapitalization", under which a corporate group tries to reduce the taxation of profits generated by one of its subsidiaries, choosing to finance this subsidiary through loans rather than own funds. This allows it to transfer profits to a parent company in the form of deductible interest when calculating its taxable profits, and not in the form of non-deductible dividends. In this way, when the parent company is based in a country where the rate of taxation is lower than that applicable in the subsidiary's country of residence, the tax debt is transferable to a country where the tax burden is lower.

CJEU seems to admit the compatibility of EU law with the Anglo-Saxon legislation, which passes the proportionality test. Having recalled, on the basis of the C-196/04, Cadbury Schweppes and Cadbury Schweppes Overseas case of 12 September 2006, that the requirement of proportionality is not satisfied by a national legislation that does not have the specific objective of excluding from a fiscal advantage purely of artificial constructions designed to steal the company from such legislation, CJEU observes that, on the contrary, "legislation of a member state can be justified on grounds of the fight against abusive practices when it provides that the interests paid by a subsidiary resident to a non-resident holding company are qualified as distributed profits only if and to the extent that they exceed what they would have agreed in a competitive environment, that is, commercial conditions that could have been applied by such companies if these had not belonged to the same corporate group (...). The circumstance and the loan was obtained on terms other than those that would have been applied in a fully competitive regime, constitutes for the member state of residence of the borrowing company "an objective and verifiable element by third parties to establish whether the transaction in question represents, in whole or in part, a construction of pure artifice, fundamentally aimed at removing the company from the tax legislation of that member state (...)"[629].

Such legislation must be considered as not exceeding what is necessary to prevent abusive practices on the double condition. Under one, when the verification of these elements shows that the transaction in question corresponds to a construction of pure artifice devoid of real commercial logics, and without excessive administrative burdens, the tax payer must be able to produce elements relating to any commercial reasons for which such transaction has been concluded. Under the second, the retraining of interest paid as distributed profits is limited to the part of such interest that exceeds what would have been agreed in the absence of special relations between the parties or between the latter and a third one[630].

629 Paragraph 81. In this regard, the question is whether, in the absence of special relations between the companies concerned, the loan would not have been granted or if it would have been granted for a different amount or interest rate.

630 In contrast, in case: C-105/07, Lammers & van Cleeff of 17 January 2008, op. cit., CJEU excludes the compatibility of the Belgian legislation aimed at combating under capitalization, as it went beyond

It corroborates this approach in C-311/08, SGI case of 21 January 2010, in which CJEU, even more clearly, considers proportionate to the objectives pursued by the Belgian tax measure, always based on three elements: the suspicion that a transaction exceeds what the companies concerned would have agreed in a system of full competition; the possibility for the tax payer, without excessive administrative burdens, to produce elements relating to any commercial reasons for which this transaction has been concluded; and a correction limited to the fraction that exceeds what would have been agreed in the absence of a situation of interdependence between companies[631].

SOME CONSIDERATIONS REGARDING THE MEANING OF "PURELY ARTIFICIAL" CONSTRUCTION

From the study of jurisprudence in this field, it emerges that CJEU has dealt with national tax laws that were going to hit the most disparate infragroup operations judged by the elusive state, fragmentary inevitably involving differentiated responses. However, the indications provided allow us to carry out some system considerations.

It is certain that the national legislation can be a bulwark of imperative reasons, provided that it refers to a concept of "Europeanized" abuse, not necessarily in line with what is found and sanctioned nationally[632]. From this point

---

what was necessary to achieve that objective: "even if interests granted to non-resident companies are retrained as dividends as soon as they go beyond such limit, it cannot be ruled out that this redevelopment also applies to interests recognized as remuneration for loans granted under conditions of full competition"(paragraph 33).

631 Similarly, in the judgment of case: C-182/08, Glaxo Wellcome GmbH & Co. KG v. Finanzamt München II of 17 September 2009, op. cit., CJEU observes, in conclusion, that "since legislation such as that in the main proceedings does not permit the limitation of its application to pure construction on the basis of objective factors, but extends to all cases in which the resident taxpayer has acquired shares in a company resident by a non-resident shareholder at a price which, for whatever reason, exceeds the nominal value of such shares, the effects of such legislation must be beyond what is necessary to achieve the objective of preventing frames of pure artifice, devoid of economic effectiveness and made for the sole purpose of unduly benefiting from a tax benefit "(paragraph 100). Normative by virtue of which an" extraordinary "benefit or "without consideration" was subject to taxation by the resident company, if the company had granted it to a company in another member state, against which that first company is linked, directly or indirectly, by interdependence. The legislation in question made it possible to adjust for tax purposes situations in which the companies concerned had been affected in their relationships by conditions which did not correspond to what they would have applied in a fully competitive regime (...)".

632 F. VANISTENDAEL, Halifax and Cadbury Schweppes: One single European theory of abuse in tax

of view, everything is played on the selectivity of the norm: the same must be suitable to contain the artificially constructed cases and not those characterized by an effective exercise of fundamental freedoms and, therefore, responding to the objectives underlying them.

The concretization of what is meant by "purely artificial construction" depends on legislation that from time to time is subject to examination[633]. On the negative side, it is not enough to hit those practices suggested by the finding of significant differences between tax bases or tax rates applied in different member states, which are designed to circumvent the tax normally payable in the member state in which it is established the company that granted this advantage. In fact, as already stated, in essence, taxes are legal motives.

Union order, to admit the legitimacy of national legislation, therefore requires a quid pluris, fully delineated only starting from the pronunciation of C-196/04, Cadbury Schweppes and Cadbury Schweppes Overseas case of 12 September 2006. Thus, tax measures cannot provide for any absolute presumption, but to strike only those operations that prove to be artificial. The assessment of artificiality changes, however, depending on the legislation that is relevant. We now look at the lack of activity of subsidiaries, when the conditions of full competition and when the absence of the state of necessity[634], all considered objective elements and verifiable by third party to establish whether the transaction represents, in fact, a construction of pure artifice. In fact, these are indices that can be traced back to the rationality and normality of the operation, which is not surprising given the role it assumes in the assessment of the absence of economic effectiveness.

---

law?, op. cit., pp. 194ss. The author points out that a construction that a member state considers tax evasion only because it does not receive income, can be classified by CJEU simply as an exercise of fundamental freedoms, which thus acquire the role of "saving clauses" for abusive practices think in a national perspective; in terms of taxation, this same theory can eventually lead to inequalities, always according to the same perspective, interfering with the distribution of the tax burden.

633 For example, in case: C-123/11, A Oy of 21 February 2013, op. cit., the CJEU, following the case: C-446/03, Marks & Spencer, Plc v. David Halsey of 13 December 2005, op. cit., established that the legislation of a member state which excludes, in the event of a merger between a parent company resident in that state and a subsidiary resident in the possibility for the parent company established in that member state to deduct from its taxable income the losses of the incorporated subsidiary established in another member state, goes beyond what is necessary to achieve the essential part of the objectives pursued, in a situation where the non-resident subsidiary has exhausted the possibility of accounting for losses in its state of residence, which is the responsibility of the parent company to demonstrate.

634 A. SAYDÉ, Defining the concept of abuse of Union law, op. cit., pp. 151-152.

In this regard, it should be noted that there is not always a one-to-one correspondence between the construction of pure artifice and the elements just described. Indeed, the language of CJEU, which is not exempt from this point of ambiguity, feeds the misunderstanding that assimilates artificiality to the absence of economic reality[635]. Defining artificiality as an absence of economic reality would, however, excessively reduce the scope of anti-consumer legislation. Taking the C-524/04, test Claimants in the Thin Cap Group Litigation cause of 13 March 2007, it is indisputable that "real" amounts of money have been transferred from the subsidiary to the parent company. The test of artificiality thus questions only the economic rationality of the operation, that is to say, a payment of interest, rather than a distribution of dividends, given its tax profitable consequences. Ultimately, therefore, the question raised by the test of artificiality is not whether there is a real economic transaction (economic reality) in place, but if the legal construction chosen to carry out this operation has a rational economic explanation, beyond to the regulatory benefit pursued (economic rationality).

What is striking, starting from the examples that have been made, is then how the statements CJEU imply a requirement that for a regulation is very difficult to satisfy. It requires, in fact, that it is "stitched" exactly on the unlawful case. This is even more so given that, in the view of CJEU, it must be the legislation itself and not the administration proceeding to provide for such a selection, as a tribute to a principle of legal certainty. Where the standard also affects operations whose economic effectiveness is indisputable, proportionality is to be excluded. Going even further, it could also be said that CJEU actually requires a kind of codification of anti-abuse clauses to the national legal system.

635 The dichotomy between case: C-196/04, Cadbury Schweppes and Cadbury Schweppes Overseas of 12 September 2006, on the one hand, and the Centros vein (C-212/97, Centros of 9 March 1999), on the other, would in truth be only apparent. In fact, the creation of a company in a certain state solely for the benefit of more advantageous legislation does not constitute an abuse, even when the institution carries out all its activities in the state of establishment, it is a fact that it is questioned in case: C-196/04, Cadbury Schweppes and Cadbury Schweppes Overseas of 12 September 2006. If then there is no abuse even if the institution does not carry out any activity in the legal system whose law the private individuals have decided to exploit, when, as in Cadbury, the subsidiary actually and effectively operates in the member state in which it is been created (Ireland), the choice to locate the company in a system different from the one of origin can not even more be considered an abusive conduct. The exercise of real economic activity in the member country of establishment then automatically excludes the abuse of EU law, but its absence does not only imply an abuse, representing only a presumption of abuse. The reason for which the right of establishment implies the actual exercise of an economic activity must then be understood as the recognition of the possibility of overcoming possible presumptions of abuse by proving the exercise of an effective activity in the member country whose law there you want to benefit.

In conclusion, one last point to be explored remains. Given that the use purely artificial construction formula, even with the criticalities just highlighted, seems incontestable, has raised the problem of understanding how the same is compatible with the jurisprudence on pseudo-foreign corporations[636]. Several solutions have been proposed in doctrine, which can however be traced back to two great lines of thought: there are those who have argued that the two jurisprudences could be reconciled[637] and who, on the contrary, considered it preferable to exclude it[638].

In particular, the position of those who, like the AG Poiares Maduro, supported a trend reversal in CJEU jurisprudence: while in cases of pseudo-foreign corporations, in fact, the artificiality of operations had been considered irrelevant to establish the existence of an abuse, in C-196/04, Cadbury Schweppes and Cadbury Schweppes Overseas case of 12 September 2006, on the contrary, abuse and artificiality are considered two closely related concepts[639]. Similar facts to those examined in C-212/97, Centros case of 9 March 1999 therefore could not

636 There are those who argued that, in CJEU's opinion, what matters is that real economic activities are carried out in relation to secondary establishment activity, such as T. O'SHEA, The UK's CFC rules, op. cit., pp. 30. Precisely from this observation it would therefore be possible to reach a conciliation. Cases: Segers (C-79/85, Segers of 10 July 1986), Centros (C-212/98, Centros of 9 March 1999) and C-167/01, Inspire Art of 30 September 2003, in fact, concerned all companies that were taxed in the United Kingdom under the tax rules of the country and that, although they had moved of the branches of activity in other member states, in any case they remained Anglo-Saxon companies that carried out an effective economic activity.

637 According to other scholars, the various conclusions reached by CJEU should be motivated by looking at the consequences of operations on a case-by-case basis for the interests of third parties, a prospect that could demonstrate the similarity of the concept of abuse in the field of company and tax law. The use of a different terminology, such as L. CERIONI, The "abuse of rights" in EU company law and EU tax law. A re-reading of the ECJ case law and the quest for a unitary notion, op. cit., pp. 795-796. How the choice of a more favorable company law is not alone enough to prove the existence of an abuse if not accompanied by proven prejudice for the protection of specific interests of third parties, for example of creditors, in equal measure the choice to exercise the freedom of establishment in a member state with tax legislation which is more favorable than that of the member state of origin alone is not sufficient to prove the abuse, that is to say a "construction of pure artifice", but can become so if the absence of genuine economic activity in the host member state demonstrates that the sole objective and result is to cause injury to the economic interests of the home member state.

638 In particular see: N. VINTHER, E. WERLAUFF, Tax motives are legal motives, op. cit., pp. 384-385, make a distinction upstream, between subjects, to conclude that tax law should draw the boundary line between use and abuse differently from company law to prevent the exercise of European Union freedoms degenerate into a pure "cherry-picking" tax, so the dividing line should be set according to whether the structure is genuine or not in the sense already specified above.

639 J. VELLA, Sparking regulatory competition in European company law: A Response, in R. DE LA FERIA, S. VOGENAUER (a cura di), Prohibition of abuse of law: a new general principle of EU law?, op. cit., pp. 129ss.

fall into the new test, as CJEU in C-196/04, Cadbury Schweppes and Cadbury Schweppes Overseas case of 12 September 2006 explicitly refers to "screen" companies as examples of purely artificial constructions.

In this way, CJEU would have wanted to overcome the Centros doctrine, so that the new test would apply to company law, even if, in any case, the use by CJEU of the adverb "purely" would indicate that the required requisites to companies not to be considered fictitious, they should not be viewed in an excessively restrictive manner[640].

This thesis does not fully convince, presenting, among other things, some incongruities under the temporal profile. It has already been observed, as it is not in the pronunciation in C-196/04, Cadbury Schweppes and Cadbury Schweppes Overseas case of 12 September 2006, that CJEU uses for the first time the expression "purely artificial constructions", already in mind, a formula already presented, among other things, in ICI sentence of 1998. Well, CJEU, in C-167/01, Inspire Art case of 30 September 2003, does not seem to have paid the slightest attention to ICI sentence and the pure artifice construction that appears there. This could mean, on a speculative basis, that "European" judges understood the two parallel jurisprudences.

However, it seems that a high consideration is relevant to the reasoning followed by CJEU, which first identifies the applicable provisions, as well as their object and purpose, and deals only with the question of artificiality of the buildings, in the moment it goes to analyze the justification for restrictive measures and the fee for proportionality. Following this reasoning, CJEU may not have felt the need to distinguish C-196/04, Cadbury Schweppes and Cadbury Schweppes Overseas case of 12 September 2006, by sentences: C-212/97, Centros of 9 March 1999 and C- 167/01, Inspire Art of 30 September 2003. In fact, the element that best resolves the apparent contradiction between these decisions always seems to be the same: we are faced with a further demonstration of the fact that the prohibition of abuse of law and the overriding reasons of general interest are two techniques, which lead to distinct results. The question, indeed, is closely linked to the more general problem pertaining to the elements of distinction between these two techniques, which will now be examined.

640 L. CERIONI, The "abuse of rights" in EU company law and EU tax law. A re-reading of the ECJ case law and the quest for a unitary notion, op. cit., pp. 795ss.

LIGHTS AND SHADOWS OF IMPERATIVE REASONS OF GENERAL INTEREST: A COMPARISON WITH THE PROHIBITION OF ABUSE OF LAW

In the preceding pages, it was observed that CJEU used the technique of imperative reasons of general interest to admit the restrictive measures of member states aimed at protecting their legal system from the elusions made possible thanks to the triangulation of legal systems.

This has emerged with particular clarity with reference to the regulations used at national level to combat tax avoidance. The doctrine has questioned the reasons why the cases mentioned were not decided by the use of prohibition on the abuse of right[641], bearing in mind that the state concerned asserted the fight against tax avoidance to justify its own legislation, so that CJEU clearly the invocation by the member state of the abuse is considered legitimate. In fact, it is even more difficult to understand why the approaches in these cases differ when looking at how CJEU defined, starting from the C-196/04, Cadbury Schweppes and Cadbury Schweppes Overseas case of 12 September 2006, the criteria for verifying the proportionality of measure, using the same Emsland-Stärke test. Such an attitude, at first sight indecipherable, is nothing but the confirmation that CJEU does not use the prohibition of abuse of law not so much (and not only) to promote competition between jurisdictions and to exclude arbitrary limitations of freedoms of movement by member states, but above all for "structural" reasons, already exposed in the previous paragraphs. EU system, in other words, does not have the right tools to select in these cases the abusive situations, differentiating them from those that are not, since the test of abuse, for how thought out, does not respond to the purpose.

This statement leads us to illustrate the differences that have emerged, in the study of their respective applications, between the two techniques, starting from C-196/04, Cadbury Schweppes and Cadbury Schweppes Overseas sentence of 12 September 2006, particularly interesting because it examines them both.

641 F. VANISTENDAEL, Halifax and Cadbury Schweppes: One single European theory of abuse in tax law?, op. cit., pp. 423. According to which the underlying economic idea is that if a member state develops competitive and attractive economic infrastructures for investors, including through the reduction of taxes, so that the appeal of its tax system is growing, another member state cannot to think about introducing compensatory tax levies that burden on their residents established in the state with the most captivating legislation. This would result in a fragmentation of the single market in a variety of markets, thus hindering fundamental freedoms. Nevertheless, the "market splitting" criterion must balance itself with the legal notion of abuse of law to avoid excessive compression of the national interest.

The C-196/04, Cadbury Schweppes and Cadbury Schweppes Overseas case of 12 September 2006 describes the same test applied in cases: C-110/99, Emsland-Stärke of 14 December 2000 and C-255/02, Halifax and others of 21 February 2006. Paradigmatic hypotheses of application of the prohibition of abuse of right to constructions involving a single legal system. This cross-reference was read, from a certain doctrine, as a concrete embodiment of the intention of CJEU to create a notion of abuse of unit law at EU level, so that the same concept of abuse, with the same characteristics, could be used with reference to all cross-border transactions occurring within the internal market. This would have led to a "denationalization" of this notion.

These statements are only partially correct. Certainly, it can be considered that a test with the same characteristics has been invoked, just as it can be said that CJEU, without a shadow of a doubt, has taken a different approach from that of member states, which often fall into the temptation to "label" as abusive all those constructions united by the obtaining of a tax saving. However, this does not mean that the notion of abuse is unitary. In fact, C-196/04, Cadbury Schweppes and Cadbury Schweppes Overseas case of 12 September 2006 does not show that CJEU is inclined to carry out the same test to identify abusive practices that occur in different areas of EU law.

On this point, it should be noted first that the issue of abuse is treated as a restriction on freedom of movement, justified only on certain conditions.

Already here, we find a distinctive trait, particularly clear, inter alia, in C-196/04, Cadbury Schweppes and Cadbury Schweppes Overseas of 12 September 2006, with the prohibition of abuse: applying the latter, in fact, to the person or to the company that seeks to avail itself of a Union law for an improper or fraudulent end, the right itself is denied, so that one could not properly speak of a restriction on free movement.

More important is the fact that, in the hypotheses described above, one no longer looks at the operation itself, but at how the normative, necessarily general and abstract, has been constructed. All the reasoning of CJEU aimed at verifying the legitimacy of the restriction is centered on the suitability and proportionality of the national legislation, which must specifically concern the construction of pure artifice, devoid of economic effectiveness, whose sole purpose is to obtain a tax benefit. The advantage of the approach that makes the sanction to abuse a reason for justification, moreover, is precisely that of allowing the exercise of a control of proportionality of the legislation[642].

In this respect, the fact that in some of the cases studied, the member state, and consequently CJEU, did not even investigate the abuse of the behavior or even excluded it[643] cannot be overlooked. From here, we can understand how the two arguments, on the norm and on the abusive manifestation, are carried out in parallel, in a disjointed way: the Union judge, in other words, does not deal with the construction in itself, nor asks the national judge to do so, but only with the legislation, regardless of whether or not is in presence of an abusive manifestation.

What has just been affirmed allows us to highlight even the greatest limits to the effectiveness of the theory of imperative motives. This legal technique, in fact, presents as its main drawback the very fact of focusing on the control of national anti-abuse measures, and therefore on the behavior of member states, rather than on the control of abusive behavior in question. From this point of view, the problem arises to limit ex ante the general legislation to pure construction, which is not an easy solution for the member state. As proportionality control is congenial, member states, in fact, encounter strong limitations in introducing specific legislation or in invoking general principles in order to combat the phenomenon of law shopping[644]. If CJEU jurisprudence shows how the restrictive national rules applicable "to every situation" (in other words, measures that do not take into account the specific circumstances that indicate an abuse), "for any reason" (therefore without taking into account the subjective will of abusing) are, according to CJEU, a too general means of combating abuses, it is difficult to determine how extensive or how narrow the anti-abuse rules should be from time to time to pass the compatibility test with EU law[645]. As it was said, CJEU

642 A. ILIOPOULOU-PENOT, Liberté de circulation et abus de droit, op. cit., pp. 196ss.

643 Suffice it to mention Kraus, in which it is clear from the facts of the case that the question was not so much the abuse of Mr Kraus, but rather his refusal to seek authorization, or the pronunciation Lankhorst-Hohorst GmbH, in which CJEU, in paragraph 38, explicitly excludes the presence of an abuse.

644 According to M. POULSEN, Treaty/Directive shopping and abuse of EU law cit., pp. 236, underlining how two opposing interests clash in this area: on the one hand, the legitimate need of member states to effectively counter such behavior; on the other, the implementation of integration and the related need not to introduce unjustified restrictions on free movement and the right of the tax payer to legitimately benefit from favorable tax legislation in other member states.

645 D. WEBER, Abuse of law in European tax law: An overview and some recent trends in the direct and indirect tax case law of the ECJ-Part 2, in European Taxation, 13, 2013, pp. 313ss.

seems "surgical" in its statutes, requiring among other things, for the purpose of compliance with legal certainty, that the legislation itself should provide for that selectivity that allows it to be proportionate, without leaving discretionary spaces to the national administration. In other words, what emerges is how CJEU refuses to unify if in the concrete case under its attention there can be an abuse, while requiring, at the same time, that the national legislation looks to the concrete case. Hence, the second limit of the technique in question is that we cannot neglect how the private who abuses EU law in a state, in which there is no anti-abuse legislation, benefits from a wider application of EU law compared to a private individual operating in a state where such provisions have not been adopted[646]. In other words, in almost identical circumstances, that is to say abusive, the private individual will be sanctioned or not by admitting the restriction on his freedom of movement, depending on whether the member state has adopted legislation prohibiting abuse, a finding that helps understand the fallacy of the thesis that the concept of abuse would be Europeanized.

646 See, W. SCHÖN, Abuse of rights and European tax law, in J. A. JONES, P. HARRIS, D. OLIVER (a cura di) Comparative perspectives on revenue law-Essays in honour of John Tiley, Cambridge University Press, Cambridge, 2008, pp. 78ss.

PART B.

The technique of restrictive interpretation of provisions of EU law

In order to try to limit the abusive behavior of individuals, in addition to allowing the member state to invoke imperative grounds of public interest, the EU judge makes use of another technique, that of teleologically oriented interpretation. As such, it is possible to delimit the scope of a provision of the Treaty or of secondary legislation, in such a way as to exclude it from having regard to abusive conditions. This is true of a technique that is certainly familiar to him, since CJEU, in fact, is institutionally responsible for interpreting the rules of the Treaties[647]. In so doing, CJEU can avoid coming to the point of declaring the existence of an abuse of EU law. It is sufficient, in fact, to give a specific definition of the scope of application of the Union rules, to exclude the case of private individual who tries to re-enter illegally under EU law.

However, this inclination should not lead to the view that the prohibition of abuse governs the interpretation of EU law. If it is true, in fact, that CJEU, in the face of possible cases of abuse, has responded to the questions posed by delimiting the scope of application of law, at the same time in many of these cases has made clear, sometimes explicitly, sometimes implicitly, through the arguments carried out, the existence of a different and independent prohibition of abuse.

647 M. POIARES MADURO, Interpreting European law: Judicial adjudication in a context of constitutional pluralism, in European Journal of Legal Studies, 1, 2007, pp. 8ss. It must be borne in mind that the interpretation of a EU provision provided by CJEU is limited to clarifying and specifying the meaning and scope of provision, as it should have been understood and applied from the moment of its entry into force. It follows that the rule thus interpreted can and must be applied by the judge also to legal relationships which arose and developed before the interpretative sentence, provided, on the other, the conditions exist for submitting to the competent CJEU a dispute concerning the application of that rule.

On this point, it should be pointed out that, from a pragmatic point of view, it does not seem so important to establish whether the prohibition of abuse should be considered an exception to EU law or a principle that regulates the interpretation of the scope of EU law, since the result we reach is ultimately the same[648], the opposite is not true.

It is, in fact, important to verify whether the scope of application of the law is outlined through the technique of teleological interpretation or on the basis of an independent prohibition of abuse. This is because, only in this second case a verification of the existence of the subjective element, that is to say elusive or fraudulent motivation, which allows, inter alia, to circumscribe the restrictive scope of interpretation.

It is therefore clear that these are two separate instruments, but the close link must not be underestimated. Indeed, it is apparent that, by intending the prohibition of abuse as an exception to EU law, the scope of this principle depends directly on the scope attributed to the freedoms of movement. Reducing the scope of law means to say, in substance, that some potentially abusive practices do not fall under the law and, as such, are not permitted[649]. At the same time, from a quantitative point of view, the probability that there are behaviors that fall within the prohibition of greatly reduced abuse.

In this section, without pretension of exhaustiveness, a paradigmatic series of pronunciations will be considered, adopting an approach that focuses more on the method used by CJEU, than on the single case, for the same reasons that have already been exposed in the first section. It is appropriate to clarify in this regard how, in the context of freedom of movement, sometimes the reasoning

648 Likewise, judgment of case: C-202/97, FTS of 10 February 2000, ECLI:EU:C:2000:75, I-00883, with reference to the problem of temporarily posted workers, deserves to be mentioned. In par. 43, in fact, CJEU has clarified the meaning of the phrase "to exercise normally the activity in the territory of the state in which they are established", emphasizing the necessity that the enterprise carries out in an effective way, or preponderant, its activity in the place of settlement.

649 According to: A. ILIOPOULOU-PENOT, Liberté de circulation et abus de droit, op. cit., pp. 188ss, "(...) it will therefore look at both cases that mention the abuse, and in cases where CJEU could have referred to the abuse, but did not do so, even in spite of the fact that the issue had been raised by the governments of member states. As a paradigmatic example, CJEU's judgment in joined cases: C-267/91 and C-268/91, Kech and Mithouard of 24 November 1993, ECLI:EU:C:1993:905, I-06097, in the matter of free movement of goods, in which CJEU, in arriving at the conclusion that article 30 of EEC Treaty must be interpreted as not applying to the legislation of a member state which generally prohibits the resale below cost, points out in paragraph 14 that economic operators increasingly invoke art. 30 of the Treaty in order to challenge any legislation which, while not involving products from other member states, has the effect of limiting their commercial freedom, CJEU considers it necessary to review and clarify its case law on the matter (...)".

underlying the restrictive interpretation, that is, the desire to exclude abusive situations from the protection of EU law, is made explicitly, as in many of the judgments already analyzed in terms of the prohibition of abuse. Other times, the issue of abuse is so present, but without the concept being explicitly invoked. The goal, however, also in this context, is to understand the functioning of the technique of restrictive interpretation, the differences with the prohibition of abuse and its effectiveness.

"U-SHAPED" CONSTRUCTIONS COMPARED TO THE RESTRICTIVE INTERPRETATION OF SECONDARY LEGISLATION

The technique of teleological interpretation has sometimes been used by CJEU to deal with the "U" operations denounced by the state of origin, which sees the national citizen re-enter the territory with the new "dress", depending on the working citizen, of a qualified professional, or a provider of services or companies in another member state. The citizen, thus, invoking EU law, acquires a subjective legal position or advantages which otherwise would not have been entitled in the state of origin. It is then well understood that, in these cases, the invocation by the private individual of the EU-primary law[650] or derivative towards the state of origin may alter the division of the regulatory powers at the base of the internal market, being the state in question, on the basis of the principle of mutual recognition, called to recognize the rules on products, qualifications, services and all that is in conformity with the rules of the state of origin[651].

Such a construction, as already noted above, always involves three systems; however, it can change the role played by the state system involved, different from the one of origin: a destination for the purchase of an advantageous

650 Reference is made to cases in which the recognition of professional qualifications (previous paragraphs) and of the right of residence pertaining to the family member of a third country was discussed.

651 K. AMSTRONG, Mutual recognition, in C. BARNARD, J. SCOTT, The law of the single European market: Unpacking the premises, Hart Publishing, Oxford & Oregon, Portland, 2002, pp. 225. For an analysis of C-56/96, VT4 v. Vlaamse Gemeenschap of 5 June 1997, in which CJEU provided a restrictive interpretation of the criteria for identifying television broadcasters subject to the jurisdiction of a member state pursuant to art. 2, n. 1, of the Directive, in the sense that a television broadcaster is subject to the jurisdiction of the member state in which it is established and where there are several offices, of the state in which the broadcaster has the center of activity, with reference, in particular, to the place where the planning policy is decided and the final composition of the programs to be broadcast.

situation, a case that is part of the phenomenon of system shopping, or simply a vehicle of transnationality.

It is considered relevant to examine, taking up some of the profiles illustrated in the previous paragraph, two cases that best demonstrate the conscious choice of CJEU to interpret EU law strictly and which highlight the different role of the state other than the original as we can see in cases: C-311/06, National Council of the engineers of 29 January 2009 and C-109/01, Akrich of 22 September 2003, studying now the mechanism of operation[652].

C-311/06, NATIONAL COUNCIL OF ENGINEERS CASE OF 29 JANUARY 2009: NATIONAL STATE V. STATE OF ACQUISITION OF THE TITLE

C-311/06, National Council of engineers of 29 January 2009, takes on particular importance as it allows to highlight the distinction between the technique of restrictive interpretation and the prohibition of abuse, as well as the favor of CJEU in the context of species, well highlighted by the contrast with the arguments of the AG Poiares Maduro, in favor of the application of the prohibition of abuse.

In order to avoid unnecessary repetition, it is necessary here only to recall how the construction put in place by Mr. Cavallera was beyond doubt in the perspective of the member state, since the move to Spain could not be motivated except by the desire to circumvent the more restrictive Italian legislation about the requirements for access to the profession of engineer. It was therefore pertinent to establish whether it could invoke Directive 89/48/EC on the mutual recognition of diplomas for its own benefit[653].

652 The question of the national court is also recalled: in particular, it was necessary to determine whether or not a EU citizen could make use of the provisions of the Directive on the recognition of professional qualifications in his member state of origin in order to have a diploma which was the result of mere homologation of a three-year university degree course followed in his home member state, without however requiring the citizen in question to have completed additional academic or professional training in the member state of graduation.

653 Directive 2005/36/EC of the European Parliament and of the Council of 7 September 2005 on the recognition of professional qualifications in OJEU L 255, 30.9.2005, p. 22ss. (hereinafter amended by Directive 2013/55 of the European Parliament and of the Council of 20 November 2013), has adopted the following definition of "training qualification" They must include "diplomas, certificates and other qualifications issued by an authority of a member state designated in accordance with the laws, regulations and administrative provisions of that member state and which enshrine

To this end, CJEU was asked to verify the existence of the three cumulative conditions required by art. 1, lett. a), so that the qualification or professional experience for which recognition is sought can be considered a diploma, which is the keystone of the general system of recognition of higher education diplomas provided for by the Directive.

More specifically, the Directive requires that the diploma be issued by the competent authority of a member state; establish a cycle of post-secondary studies with a minimum duration of three years; and finally give access to a profession in the country of origin.

In the present case, the problematic condition was evidently the second: it was, in fact, undisputed that the defendant had not followed any professional or academic training in Spain, so that the diploma of mechanical engineer obtained in Spain was the result of a mere homologation of the Italian university degree with the title of Spanish engineer. Therefore, the problem was posed of deciding whether to accept a notion of "diploma" that would include the aforementioned hypothesis. CJEU, as already mentioned, excludes it, adopting an interpretation of the Directive, defined restrictive primarily from the AG Poiares Maduro. In this case, the first and third requirements had certainly been fulfilled. The diploma, in fact, had been issued by the Spanish Ministry of Education and Science, authorized, in the light of Spanish legislation, to award diplomas as an industrial technical engineer. Similarly, the Spanish diploma relied on by the defendant, in fact, authorizes him to practice as a mechanical engineer in the state issuing the diploma, namely Spain.

More precisely, starting from the aim of Directive 89/48/EC, which is to eliminate obstacles to the exercise of a profession in a member state other than the one issued the diploma which confers the professional qualifications in question, the Luxembourg states that a qualification which establishes professional training, such as that of an engineer, cannot be assimilated to a "diploma", pursuant to the Directive, in the absence of the acquisition, total or partial, of qualifications in the context of the education system of the member state which issued the title de quo. That is because, by reasoning to the contrary, it would

professional training acquired predominantly in EU". However, recital 12 specifies that the Directive does not concern "the recognition by member states decisions taken by other member states in accordance with this Directive. Therefore, holders of professional qualifications which have been recognized under this Directive may not use that recognition in order to obtain, in their member state of origin, rights other than those conferred by the professional qualification obtained in that member state, unless demonstrate that they have obtained additional professional qualifications in the host member state (...)".

be possible for a person who has exclusively received a license issued by that member state which, in itself, does not give access to that regulated profession to access it equally, without however having the type-approval certificate obtained in Spain certifies an additional qualification or professional experience. A result, it would be achieved "contrary to the principle enshrined in Directive 89/48/EC, and set out in its fifth "recital", according to which the member states retain the right to establish the minimum qualification level necessary to guarantee the quality of services provided on their territory"[654].

CJEU therefore resolves, in a few lines, the question submitted to it, without admitting the slightest temperament, in a perspective focused exclusively on the organization of the state of origin and on the consequences that the recognition of the invokable nature of the Directive would entail for it, which clearly shows how CJEU had a clear idea of the abuse committed by the Italian citizen. It is interesting to note that this reasoning, seen from the perspective of the "host" state, on closer inspection, after the homologation becomes and according to the EU legal system, shows some incongruity, rightly highlighted by the conclusions of the AG Poiares Maduro, which was inclined towards a wider interpretation of the Directive, accompanied by the use of the prohibition of abuse.

The AG in particular pointed out the risk that such an interpretation of the Directive, such as to exclude the approval decision from the notion of diploma, would have determined exclusion from the scope of the Directive of situations which, on the other hand, would fully covered by the objective of free movement, for example the cases in which such a decision was taken by a member state in which the profession was later exercised.

654 It should be noted that EC, to support the thesis of the restrictive interpretation of the concept of diploma, referred to the twelfth recital of Directive 2005/36/EC, which excludes from its scope "(...) recognition by member states decisions taken by other member states under this Directive (...) in order to obtain, in their member state of origin, rights other than those conferred by the professional qualification obtained in that member state, unless (the persons concerned) prove that they have obtained additional professional qualifications in the host member state (...)". However, the AG points out that this approach is not convincing because the decision relied on by Mr Cavallera is not a "recognition decision" based on the directive, but a type approval decision taken on the basis of national law. The Italian diploma, in fact, is not a "diploma" pursuant to art. 1, lett. a) of the Directive. This is precisely the problem in this case, given that the title obtained by Mr Cavallera in Italy, although sanctioning a three-year cycle of studies, does not however allow access to the profession of engineer in that state (...) the type approval and then the registration of engineers in Spain took place solely on the basis of national law and did not take place on the basis of Directive 89/48 (...)" (par. 27).

It was then established that an overly restrictive interpretation of the Directive could have undermined the principle of mutual recognition of diplomas based on the principle of mutual trust[655].

In fact, based only on a literal interpretation of the second requirement, it does not seem to reveal the modalities or procedures on the basis of which the diploma was issued, nor in which territory the training activities were followed, provided that they took place in overwhelming majority in Union territory. It corroborates such an interpretation art. 3, first paragraph, lett. a) of the Directive, which prohibits member states from refusing to grant access to a profession to a citizen even in cases where he "holds the diploma prescribed in another member state for access (a) to that profession on its territory(...)"[656]. Applying such a reasoning to the specific case, since Spain believed that Mr. Cavallera had the professional skills necessary to exercise in his territory, it is not clear how it was possible to deny the qualification of the diploma that the state had issued to him.

Looking back on some considerations regarding the effectiveness of this technique, the analysis of this case clearly demonstrates how CJEU used the restrictive interpretation to sanction abusive behavior, thereby demonstrating the adoption of a vision that favors the national state; otherwise, he would be deprived of his skills in accessing professions. However, it was also shown that another interpretation would have been plausible and how certainly it would have been more in line with the principle of mutual trust that must animate relations between member states, repeatedly invoked by CJEU itself[657].

---

655 See parr. 31-33 of the conclusions. With this in mind, Spain must be considered free to determine access to the profession of engineer in Spain either on the basis of a decision to approve a training carried out on the territory of another member state or on the basis of a diploma certifying its formation since the only requirement in the Directive is to impose that the certificate states that the holder has successfully completed a cycle of post-secondary studies of a minimum duration of three years (...) showing that (...) possesses the professional qualifications required for access to a regulated profession in that member state (...)" (par. 34).

656 Conclusions of the AG Poiares Maduro, op. cit., par. 36.

657 In particular, the judgment of case: C-130/88, Van de Bijl of 26 September 1989, op. cit., is recalled here, in which CJEU, faced with national authority objection concerning certification's validity issued by the United Kingdom, stated that, in principle, the host State is "normally bound by the declarations contained in the certificate issued by the member state of origin" and "cannot call into question the accuracy of the indication of the activities exercised by the person concerned or their duration (...)" (parr. 22 to 23), except in cases where the attestation produced contains a manifest inaccuracy. On this point, AG Darmon in his conclusions presented on 19 April 1989 referred to the maxim fraus omnia corrumpit as a general principle common to member states, stating that, since fraud spoils everything, "a host state which does not have them wanted, of a certain number of elements proving that the competent authority of the state of origin was misled when the certificate is issued can oppose such fraud (...)" (par. 17).

C-311/06, National Council of engineers case of 29 January 2009 analyzed the hypothesis in which the choice of private to go to another member state to acquire a new role is determined by the most favorable discipline of the same, so that there is a case of system shopping. C-109/01, Akrich case of 22 September 2003. On the other hand, represents the paradigmatic case in which the private person moves to any other order whose legislation is indifferent to the sole purpose of creating that intra-Union situation that allows to benefit from EU rights.

The EU judge excluded the applicability of Regulation n. 1612/68 to the case under examination, as Mr. Akrich, citizen of Morocco, married to a citizen of the Union, could not claim a prior "legal stay" in a member state at the time it was its transfer to another member state. In particular, even in this case, CJEU considered that such an interpretation was "in line with the economy of European Union provisions aimed at guaranteeing the freedom of movement of workers within the Union, the exercise of which cannot penalize the migrant worker and his family"[658]. This is based on the assumption that "when a Union citizen established in a member state and married to a third-country citizen who does not have the right to reside in that member state, moves to another member state to subordinate employment, the fact that his spouse does not have the right, deriving from art. 10 of Regulation n. 1612/68, to settle with him in that other member state, cannot constitute a less favorable treatment than that enjoyed before that citizen of the Union enjoyed the possibilities offered by the Treaty on the movement of persons"[659]. In other words, the absence of such a right, in this case, would not be such as to dissuade the citizen of the Union from exercising the traffic rights recognized by art. 45 TFEU.

658 CJEU, C-109/01, Akrich of 22 September 2003, op. cit.

659 CJEU, C-1/05, Jia of 9 January 2007, ECLI:EU:C:2007:01, I-00001. For details see: F. KAUFF-GAZIN, Droit de séjour de l'ascendant à charge, membre de la famille du ressortissant communautaire, in Europe, 86, 2007, Comm. n. 86, pp. 14-15. J. H. REESTMAN, No legal residence requirements for the admission of family members with a third-country nationality of migrated Union citizens, in European Constitutional Law Review, 3, 2007, pp. 463ss. A. TRYFONIDOU, Jia or "Carpenter II": the edge of reason, in European Law Review, 32, 2007 pp. 909ss.

Such conclusions undoubtedly have some similarities with those just analyzed in C-311/06, National Council of engineers case of 29 January 2009: the teleological interpretation carried out by CJEU conflicts with the literal interpretation, since the prior legal stay was not required from the Regulation between the mandatory requirements of the stay. From this perspective, CJEU makes its own is that of the state of origin, whose competence in attributing or not the residence permit to non-EU citizens would otherwise be scratched; finally, it is evident how this technique has been used to counteract what was perceived as an abusive behavior.

This last aspect is confirmed, if ever there was need, in some passages of C-1/05, Jia sentence of 9 January 2007[660]. CJEU, in fact, in answering the question of the referring court on the possibility of transposing in the case brought before him for reviewing the judgment in Akrich, he first points out that the factual background of the dispute which gave rise to the Akrich judgment was different, since, in C-1/05, Jia case of 9 January 2007, "is not charged the member of the family in question to stay illegally in a member state or to try to avoid abusively the application of national immigration legislation"[661]. Exactly from such considerations, it is excluded that the condition of prior legal residence in another

660 Paragraph 31. CJEU recalls in paragraph 30 that in Akrich case with reference to a situation of a couple, he intended to return to the United Kingdom using EU law, so that Mr Akrich could enter that country as a spouse of a union citizen who had used his freedom of movement, "the referring CJEU before which the dispute was pending had asked CJEU what measures member states could take to combat the behavior of EU family citizens who did not fulfill the conditions established by national law for entering and staying in a member state.

661 CJEU, C-459/99, MRAX of 25 July 2002 and the case: C-60/00, Carpenter of 11 July 2002, ECLI:EU:C:2002:434, I-06279. In the MRAX ruling the CJEU had stated, inter alia, that "article 4 of Directive 68/360 and 6 of Directive 73/148 must be interpreted as meaning that they do not authorize a member state to refuse to issue a residence permit and to take a measure of expulsion against a third-country national who can provide proof of his identity and of his marriage to a national of a member state, for the sole reason that he entered the territory of the member state concerned illegally (emphasis added)" (par. 80). See in argument for further analysis and details: S. ACIERNO, The Carpenter judgement: fundamental rights and the limits of the European Union legal order, in European Law Review, 28, 2003, pp. 398ss, it is noted, with regard to Carpenter, that if the specific circumstances relating to the two cases could well explain the different reasoning followed by CJEU, it is difficult to draw a general rule in relation to the rights and status of family members of Union citizens who are illegally present on the territory of the Union. As rightly stated by the question remains to understand whether irregular migrants fall within the scope of EU law. Article 49 EC, read in light of the fundamental right to respect for family life, must be interpreted as meaning that it precludes the member state of origin of a service provider established in that state, who provides services to recipients established in other member states, deny the right of residence in its territory to the spouse of that lender, a national of a third country, even if he does not have a residence permit in any member state (see par. 46). For further details see: N. ROGERS, R. SCANNEL, W. ROBINSON, Free movement of persons in the enlarged European Union, Sweet & Maxwell, London, 2012, pp. 190ss.

member state, as formulated in C-109/01, Akrich sentence of 22 September 2003 can be transposed sic et simpliciter in C-1/05, Jia case of 9 January 2007, resulting in the absence of the element of abuse.

C-1/05, Jia case of 9 January 2007, as well as proving the fear of abusive behavior that led CJEU to adopt an extremely restrictive interpretation that is not in line both with the literal content of the rules, and with the previous C-60/00, Carpenter of 11 July 2002 and in C-459/99, MRAX case of 25 July 2002[662]. This case also demonstrates the will of CJEU to delimit as much as possible the application of the Akrich pronunciation "sewing it on" those cases in which it is possible to verify, in practice, an abuse. Well, this also seems to be the greatest limit to which the adoption of a restrictive interpretation can lead: the latter, to be honest, does not fit the concrete case, being instead generalized; as such, it can be taken literally by the national authorities, without them incurring an infringement of EU law.

This could also be the most plausible reason why, in less than five years, CJEU has been forced to overturn the previous expansive jurisprudence of the free movement of workers with the C-127/08, Metock and others case of 25 July 2008[663], which found it incompatible with Directive 2004/38/EC for national legislation requiring the family member to have previously resided legally in another member state prior to his arrival in the host member state[664]. CJEU, justifying the assumption, points out that no provision of Directive 2004/38/EC subordinates the application of the latter on the assumption that the family members have previously resided in a member state. He then admits that he declared "in par. 50 and 51 of the aforementioned C-109/01, Akrich sentence of 22 September 2003 which, in order to enjoy the rights referred to in art. 10 of Regulation n. 1612/68, a third-country citizen, spouse of a Union citizen, must legally reside in a member state when he moves to another member state, in

662 It is also noted that AG Geelhoed in his conclusions in Akrich proposed a solution based on MRAX and Carpenter, suggesting that third-country nationals who entered the territory of an unlawful member state should fall within the scope of Regulation n. 1612/68, even if their state was illegal and therefore the refusal of the member state should have been valid as an exception invoking reasons of public interest.

663 CJEU, C-127/08, Metock and others of 25 July 2008, ECLI:EU:C:2008:449, I-06241. The referring CJEU emphasizes that none of the marriages at issue in the main proceedings was a fictitious marriage.

664 C. COSTELLO, Metock: Free movement and "normal family life" in the Union, in Common Market Law Review, 46, 2009, pp. 587ss. J. FAULL, Prohibition of abuse of law: A new general principle of EU Law, in R. DE LA FERIA, S. VOGENAUER (a cura di), Prohibition of abuse of law: a new general principle of EU law?, op. cit., pp. 291-293.

which the Union citizen emigrates or has emigrated", to then say clearly that "this conclusion must be rethought". This is because "the enjoyment of such rights cannot depend on a prior legal residence of such a spouse in another member state"[665]. This can be interpreted that, a fortiori, it is required in relation to the new Directive 2004/38/EC, which aims to strengthen the free movement and residence rights of all Union citizens.

This leads to an antithetical conclusion with respect to Akrich, whereby the refusal by the host member state to recognize the rights of entry and residence of family members of a Union citizen is such as to dissuade the latter to move or reside in that member state, even if his family members do not already reside legally in the territory of another member state.

A COMPARISON: THE TEST OF EFFECTIVENESS OF THE CONNECTION WITH THE HOST COUNTRY IN THE CASE OF "SOCIAL TOURISM"

In the previous paragraph, the main limitations that the jurisprudence encounters in the use of the restrictive interpretation of the secondary legislation to combat U-shaped operations analyzed, where sometimes it comes to solutions not entirely consistent with the principles that inform the Union legal framework. It is now necessary to verify whether these same limits are also found with regard to the use of the restrictive interpretation contrary to social tourism.

CJEU has ruled on several occasions on disputes that are in fact linked to the claims of individuals, nationals of a member state, to have access to certain social benefits in the host state, claims based on the assumption of being part of a social category, as that of worker, student, or even, with the development of Union law on this front, of Union citizen, with the possibility of asserting the principle of equal treatment descending from EU law.

It is recalled from these cases, in which the hypothesized abuse affects only two systems, that of EU and that of the host state, while in no way the state of

665 Thus, CJEU concludes that "since the third-country national, family member of a Union citizen, derives from Directive 2004/38/EC entry and residence rights in the host member state, the latter may limit such rights only in compliance with articles 27 and 35 of the said directive (...)", thereby relying on the jurisprudence according to which, where there is a secondary legislation, the tools against the abuse must be sought within the same discipline, and not be entrusted to restrictive initiatives by member states. In this way, the notion of abuse in this area seems to have been mainly attributed to the abuse of family law, with the help of a fictitious marriage.

origin is involved: the private, that is, the tip to obtain a benefit granted by the member state, by unduly invoking a subjective position attributed by EU law, which entitles equal treatment with national citizens.

Initially, when the individual was still considered "productive factor", from a purely economic point of view, it was a matter of understanding whether the individual could claim the status of worker, the only category that could benefit from free circulation and to which, by virtue of principle of non-discrimination, certain benefits were due to the host state, such as grants or scholarships.

As is well known, the requirement to carry out an economically significant activity has since disappeared with the introduction of Union citizenship, which has led to the prohibition of discrimination on grounds of nationality to play a central role in the framework of the rules on free movement of persons. However, differences remain of considerable importance as regards the right of residence and equal treatment, depending on whether it is a simple citizen or an economically active person. Even today, therefore, the question is raised whether a particular subject can invoke the provisions concerning the free movement of economically active subjects, or only those concerning citizens[666].

Indeed, precisely the presence of significant differences in EU law, with reference to the attribution of the right of residence and equal treatment, between active and non-active citizens, has created in the past, and still creates, an incentive for certain individuals to try to be recognized as active citizens, in particular subordinate workers, in order to gain access to a wider range of social benefits in the host state[667].

---

666 The same happened with reference to the freedoms attributed to self-employed workers. As is known, in fact, the established worker is required to comply with national provisions, unlike the service provider, who, however, is in principle subject to the law of the state of origin and not to that of the state destination of the service. Having to distinguish the two freedoms, CJEU used the interpretative technique. See, in particular, the judgment of case: C-55/94, Gebhard of 30 November 1995, in which CJEU has established the temporary nature of provision of services, must be assessed taking into account the duration, frequency, and continuity of the service itself.

667 Thus, for example, in the judgment of case: C-344/87, Betray of 31 May 1989, ECLI:EU:C:1989:226, I-01621, CJEU ruled out that they can be regarded as real and effective, those activities which represent only an instrument for the re-education or reintegration of those concerned (paragraph 17); furthermore, in the judgment of case: C-197/86, Brown v. Secretary of State for Scotland of 21 June 1988, ECLI:EU:C:1988:323, I-03205, he excluded that a national of a member state obtains the right to a grant in another member state as a worker, when it is undisputed that he has become solely as a consequence of his admission to the university in order to undertake the studies in question (parr. 27 to 28). For further details see: S. WEATHERILL, Law and values in the European Union, Oxford University Press, Oxford, 2016. G. ROBINSON, Optimize European Union law, ed. Routledge, London & New York, 2014, pp. 137ss.

This type of behavior has required EU to define and, consequently, the national authorities to put into practice a clear and coherent border between the different categories of citizens. CJEU, in this regard, applied the test of effectiveness of the activity carried out to assign the status of worker, resolving the issue of possible abuse of a given social condition in order to obtain social benefits, otherwise not due.

Likewise, the case law has been asked to establish when the citizen of the Union, irrespective of the active role he plays, can access the welfare services of the host state[668]. In response to member states fear regarding an expansion of "social tourism"[669], CJEU has adopted the criterion of effective integration, which requires verification of the existence of real links between the migrant citizen and the company that welcomes it[670]. It has been observed that such a concept of real connection serves, on the one hand, to base the claims of Union citizens who are not workers at equal treatment and, on the other, as a guarantee against social tourism[671], since it is legitimate that member states require a real

668 We remember the landmark decisions of CJEU: C-184/99, Crzelczyk of 20 September 2001, ECLI:EU:C:2001:458, I-06193. C-456/02, Trojani of 7 September 2004, ECLI:EU:C:2004:488, I-07573. For further details see: F. PENNINGS, M. SEELEIB-KAISER, European Union citizenship and social rights: Entitlements and impediments to accessing welfare, Edward Elgar Publishers, Cheltenham, 2018. E. CLOOTS, National identity in European Union law, Oxford University Press, Oxford, 2015.

669 In the Grzelczyk judgment (C-184/99, Grzelczyk of 20 September 2001, ECLI:EU:C:2001:458, I-06193) CJEU, passing the previous case C-197/86, Brown v. Secretary of State for Scotland of 21 June 1988, op. cit., admitted that "the fact that a union citizen conducts university studies in a member state other than that of which he is a national cannot, in itself, deprive him of the possibility of using the ban of any discrimination based on citizenship "(paragraph 36), after having noted that" the status of a union citizen is intended to be the fundamental status of nationals of member states which allows those of them in the same situation to obtain, regardless of citizenship and subject to the exceptions expressly provided for in this regard, the same legal treatment (...)" (par. 31). For further details see: S. CURRIE, Migration, work and citizenship in the enlarged European Union, ed. Routledge, London & New York, 2016. F. PENNINGS. M. SEELEIB-KAISER, European Union citizenship and social rights. Entitlments and impediments to accessing welfare, op. cit.

670 In the Trojani ruling, (C-456/02, Trojani of 7 September 2004) CJEU also concluded that "a EU citizen who does not have a right of residence in the host member state under articles 39 EC, 43 EC or 49 EC (now arts. 45, 49 and 56 TFEU) can, by virtue of his status as a citizen of the Union, enjoy a right of residence for the direct application of art. 18, n. 1, EC"(paragraph 46), after reiterating that "the host member state may find that a national of another member state who has made use of social assistance no longer meets the requirements to which his right of residence is subject. In that case, the host member state may adopt a removal measure, subject to the limits imposed by EU law. However, recourse to the social assistance system by a union citizen cannot automatically lead to such a measure (see, to that effect, Grzelczyk, (C-184/99, Grzelczyk of 20 September 2001, op. cit., parr. 42 and 43) (...)" (par. 45).

671 See, for example, the judgment of the case C-209/03, Bidar of 15 March 2005, ECLI:EU:C.2005:169, I-02119, where it is stated, in paragraphs 57 and 59: "As regards aid to cover student maintenance costs, it is also legitimate whereas a member state grants such aid only to students who have dem-

and effective connection with the territory or with the company of the state in which access to social benefits is requested[672].

In this way, the need for genuine integration is used to resolve the tension between the right of migrant citizens to transnational solidarity and the power of member states to shape their social security system and to avoid abuses of law of the host state, in the form of social tourism[673].

The line that dealt with the complex problems generated by the interaction between the freedom of movement and the restrictions made by the member states with reference to their social system, resolving them by defining what is meant by real and actual activities or even by sufficient degree of integration, it is extremely substantial[674]. Suffice it to recall some cases that are of particular interest to our purposes, considering the problem of abuse.

First of all, remember the C-53/81, Levin v. Staatssecretaris van Justitie case of 23 March 1982[675]. In this judgment, CJEU was able to state that, while part-time

---

onstrated a certain degree of integration in the society of that state (...). The existence of a certain degree of integration can be considered to have been proven following ascertaining that the student in question stayed for a certain period in the host member state (...)". See in argument: O. GOLYNKER, Jobseekers' rights in the European Union: challenges of changing the paradigm of social solidarity, in European Law Review, 30, 2005, pp. 117ss. C. O'BRIEN, Real links, abstract rights and false alarms: the relationship between the ECJ's real link case law and national solidarity, in European Law Review, 33, 2008, pp. 643ss.

672 R. WHITE, Free movement, equal treatment, and citizenship of the Union, in International and Comparative Law Quarterly, 55, 2005, pp. 905ss, it is noted that the test of the real and effective connection is a fair and effective way of recognizing the legitimate concerns of member states. He noted that this test is in fact a way to enable member states to rely on a potentially indirectly discriminatory precondition, by limiting the access of EU citizens to social assistance. See, P. J. NEUVONEN, In search of (even) more substance for the "real link" test: comment on Prinz and Seeberger, in European Law Review, 39, 2014, pp. 134ss, considers that this diversity of approach is partly due to the fact that the test of the actual link can justify different outcomes, depending on how the substance of the link is defined.

673 A. SAYDÉ, One law, two competitions: An enquiry into the contradictions of free movement law, in Cambridge Yearbook of European Legal Studies, 2010-2011, pp. 395ss.

674 It is recalled here that CJEU had been called, inter alia, to determine whether the right of access and residence in the territory of a member state could be denied to a worker who was pursuing, by entry and stay in a member state, mainly for purposes other than the exercise of a subordinate activity. In part. 16 affirms that: "from the wording of the principle of the free movement of workers and the placing of the relevant provisions in the Treaty, it is clear that these rules guarantee only the free movement of persons who exercise or intend to "economic activity" (...)".

675 See par. 21. Levin's ruling (C-53/81, Levin v. Staatssecretaris van Justitii of 23 March 1982) was then resumed in the judgment of case C-66/85, Lawrie-Blum v. Land Baden-Württemberg of 3 July 1986, ECLI:EU:C:1986:284, I-02121, where, in providing the concept of worker, the CJEU states that "even the fact that the trainee only performs a reduced number of hours per week and receive only a wage below the minimum salary of a tenured teacher at the beginning of the career precludes his qualification as a worker. In the aforementioned Levin ruling (C-53/81, Levin v. Staatssecretaris van

working is not excluded from the scope of rules relating to the free movement of workers, these rules apply only to exercise of real and effective activities. However, the activities being so small as to be considered purely marginal and accessory are excluded from this sphere[676]. These are formulas that express nothing other than the need, inherent in the same principle of free movement of workers, that the advantages conferred by EU law on the basis of this principle can be demanded only by those who actually do or intend to actually carry out a subordinated activity[677].

In C-39/86, Lair v. Universität Hannover case of 21 June 1988, then, CJEU took care of the thin border line between the figure of the worker who, as such, has the right to receive the benefits expected in the host state, and that of the student who created a situation to make it appear as a worker, for the sole purpose of accessing those advantages, such as a scholarship. Here too, CJEU adopts the same modus operandi, delimiting ex ante the perimeter of the provisions of the treaties and referring to the "very short period of work" to exclude the

---

Justitii of 23 March 1982), CJEU has in fact declared that the concepts of "worker" and "subordinate activity" must be understood so as to include those who, not carrying out a full-time activity, receive only a lower remuneration than contemplated for full-time activity, provided that this involves the exercise of real and effective activities.

676 CJEU, C-138/02, Collins of 23 March 2004, op. cit. Mr. Collins, a US and Irish citizen, after working part-time and occasionally in the United Kingdom between 1980 and 1981, returned there in 1998 to find work in the social services sector, asking for compensation for job seekers, who was refused because he did not usually reside in that member state. See, E. MUIR, Statut et droits du demandeur d'emploi-travailleur-citoyen: confusion ou rationalisation?, in Revue du Droit de l'Union Européenne, 2004, p. 249ss.

677 C. COSTELLO, Citizenship of the Union: above abuse?, in R. DE LA FERIA, S. VOGENAUER (ed. by), Prohibition of abuse of law: a new general principle of EU law?, op. cit., pp. 348ss. G. DAVIES, The high water point of free movement of persons: Ending benefit tourism and rescuing welfare, in Journal of Social Welfare and Family Law, 26, 2004, pp. 211-222. Contra M. DOUGAN, Some comments on the idea of a general principle of Union law prohibiting abuses of law in the field of free movement for Union citizens, in R. DE LA FERIA, S. VOGENAUER (a cura di), Prohibition of abuse of law: a new general principle of EU law?, op. cit., pp. 359 notes that Collins was cited as an example of the conduct of an individual who would constitute an abuse of the right of movement on the grounds that an economically inactive citizen had made unjustified demands for a financial subsidy from the host state's welfare resources. However, Collins is only one of the judgments that enter into a substantial jurisprudence (see judgments C-184/99, Grzelczyk of 20 September 2001, op. cit., C-456/02, Trojani of 7 September 2004, C-209/03, Bidar of 15 March 2005, C-158/07, Förster of 18 November 2008, C-224/98, D'Hoop v. Office National d'emploi of 11 July 2002, ECLI:EU:C:2002:432, I-06191) which deals with such problems. For further details see: N. ROGERS, R. SCANNELL, J. WALSH, Free movement of persons in the enlarged European Union, Sweet & Maxwell, London, 2012. E. GUILD, S. PEERS, J. TOMKIN, The European Union citizenship directive. A commentary, op. cit., P. LOUTRAKOS, M. NIC SHUIBHNE, P. SYRPIS, Exceptions from European Union free movement law. Derogation justification and proportionality, Hart Publishing, Oxford & Oregon, Portland, 2016.

application of Union law[678]. The same concept of the exercise of the work activity only for a short period, as such not suitable for framing the individual in the category of worker of the Union, has been resumed, after many years, in C-413/01, Franca Ninni-Orasche sentence of 6 November 2003[679].

C-138/02, Collins case of 23 March 2004, with which, according to a part of the commentators, CJEU invoking the necessity to verify the effectiveness and the reality of the connection, would have clearly wanted to social tourism. In this sense, they would point to the need to avoid abuse by both the EC and the AG Colomer. In particular, CJEU considered it acceptable that the unemployment allowance provided for nationals is granted to the national of another member state in search of first employment only after it has been possible to

---

678 EC observed that the condition of habitual residence could constitute indirect discrimination, justifiable as it was aimed at avoiding "social tourism" and thus preventing possible abuses by people who are falsely seeking work, to be excluded, however, in the present case, because the authenticity of the search for an occupation of Mr. Collins was not disputed. Even AG Colomer, according to par. 75 of his opinion submitted on 10 July 2003, noted that the imposition of a condition relating to residence could be justified on the basis of the need to avoid the phenomenon of social tourism, practiced by those persons moving from one state to another for the purpose of benefiting from non-contributory benefits and, therefore, in order to prevent abuse, concluding that "in so far as the application of this condition is accompanied by an examination of the situation particular of the applicant in each specific case, it does not seem to me that such a measure goes beyond what is necessary in order to achieve the objective pursued".

679 See paragraph 69. CJEU reiterates D'Hoop judgment (D'Hoop v. Office National d'emploi of 11 July 2002, op. cit., par. 38), in which it had already ruled that it is legitimate for the national legislature to be sure of the existence of a real link between those requiring compensation which has the character of an advantage social security pursuant to art. 7, n. 2, of Regulation n. 1612/68 and the geographic market of the concerned work. Specifies here that the existence of such a link could be verified, in particular, by ascertaining that the person in question actually sought employment in the member state in question for a reasonable period of time. See in argument: M. DOUGAN, The bubble that burst, in M. ADAMS (a cura di), Judging Europe's Judges, Oxford University Press, Oxford, 2013, pp. 127ss. J. HUNT, C. J. WALLACE, The high water point of free movement of persons: Ending benefit tourism and rescuing welfare, op. cit., According to the author with Collins it can be said that the free movement of people has entered a mature phase (as was the case with the free movement of goods, with the Keck and Mithouard ruling (joined cases C-267/91 and C-268/91, Kech and Mithouard of 24 November 1993). Such statements are also found in the judgment of 4 June 2009 in joined cases C-22/08 and C-23/08, Vatsouras and Koupatantze of 4 June 2009, ECLI:EU:C.2009:344, I-04585. The CJEU stated that, although taking into account the establishment of European citizenship, it can no longer be excluded from the scope of article 39, n. 2 EC, a benefit of a financial nature intended to facilitate access to employment on the labor market of a member State is in any case "legitimate for a member State to award such a benefit only after having established that there is a real link between is looking for a job and the labor market of the same state (...)", specifying how" the existence of such a link could be verified, in particular, by ascertaining that the person in question actually and concretely looked for a job in the state member concerned for a period of a reasonable duration [emphasis added] (...)" (parr. 38-39). See also in argument: U. LIEBERT, A. GATTIG, Democratizing the European Union law below? Citizenship, civil society and the public sphere, ed. Routledge, London & New York, 2016.

ascertain the existence of a real link between those seeking labor and the labor market of that state[680]. In these terms, it was highlighted how the ruling opted for a reductive reading of the right to social benefits, "saving" the national legislation that introduced indirect discrimination[681].

Some of the indirect discriminations admitted as a pre-trial were then resumed in Directive 2004/38/EC and transformed into real regulatory exceptions to the principle of equal treatment. Here, reference is made, in particular, to the hypotheses contemplated in art. 24, par. 2, by way of derogation from par. 1, concerning jobseekers and students, which was the subject of attention already in the Förster case[682], although the Directive was not applicable to the present case. Indeed, CJEU reminds that, pursuant to art. 24, n. 2 of Directive 2004/38/EC, a host member state is not required to grant aid for the maintenance of studies, including for professional training, in the form of scholarships or loans to students who have not acquired a right to permanent living room. Also, this relief could have determined the more restrictive attitude followed in C-158/07, Förster case of 18 November 2008 compared to the previous C-209/03, Bidar case of 15 March 2005, where instead the condition of the residence had

680 Decision of case: C-158/07, Förster of 18 November 2008, ECLI:EU:C:2008:630, I-08507. CJEU, having to judge the national legislation that provided a condition of residence to students in order to benefit from a series of subsidies, found that it was legitimate for a member state to grant aid to cover student maintenance costs only to those who have proved to be a certain degree of integration into the society of that state, admitting the compatibility of the five-year residency condition. See, S. DE LA ROSA, La citoyenneté européenne à la mesure des intérêts nationaux. A propos de l'arrêt Förster (aff. C-158/07 du 18 novembre 2008), in Cahiers de Droit Européen, 45, 2009, D. MARTIN, Comments on Förster (case C-158/07 of 18 November 2008), Metock and others (case C-127/08 of 25 July 2008) and Huber (case C-524/06 of 16 December 2008), in European Journal of Migration and Law, 11, 2009, pp. 95ss.

681 In his conclusions presented on 10 July 2008, AG Mazák noted that "the decisive element is whether the person has actually carried out a specific work activity, that is, an effective and real work activity and not merely marginal or accessory in the sense of the concept of "worker". If it is shown that a person fulfills these conditions objectively, the fact that he must simultaneously be considered as a student does not deprive him of the status of worker and the rights deriving from it"(paragraph 81). He then adds that "there is no evidence of abuse in this case. In particular, given that Ms Förster had been employed for more than three years before terminating her, it cannot be said that she entered another member state solely for the purpose of using the student benefit scheme. Furthermore, at the hearing it emerged that Ms Förster went and started working and studying in the Netherlands because of her personal relationship with a Dutch national. This circumstance could serve as an indication that it did not enter that state solely for the purpose of using the system of student subsidies (...)" (parr. 86 to 87).

682 Although CJEU does not follow the lawyer either with regard to the continued effect of the status of worker or with regard to the disproportion of five years, he follows it in excluding the relevance of the grounds and therefore the abuse (paragraph 44: For this purpose, the fact that Ms Förster came to the Netherlands mainly for reasons of study is irrelevant.

been considered an indirect discrimination. CJEU, in other words, seems to have reformulated its own jurisprudence to adapt to the Directive.

The restrictive tendency of CJEU, which refers to secondary legislation to limit the rights of non-active citizens, has reached its peak in C-333/13, Dano case of 11 November 2014. CJEU, in this case, has reinterpreted the European Union legislation, giving central importance to the conditions of "economic self-sufficiency" provided for in art. 7 of Directive 2004/38/EC, which is subject to the right of residence of the inactive European citizen.

More in detail, CJEU first reads the principle of non-discrimination pursuant to art. 18 TFEU[683] in the light of article 24 of Directive 2004/38/EC and art. 4 of Regulation n. 883/2004, both relevant in this case. In this way, he comes to affirm that, as can be seen from art. 24, par. 1, a citizen of the Union, regarding access to social benefits such as those at issue in the main proceedings, "may request equal treatment with respect to nationals of the host member state only if his stay on the territory of the host member state respects the requirements of Directive 2004/38/EC (...)"[684].

However, the stay of more than three months but less than five years is subject to the conditions set forth in art. 7, par. 1. These include the obligation for the economically inactive Union citizen to have sufficient financial resources for himself and his family members. Hence, it is inferred that "recognizing that people who do not benefit from a right of residence under Directive 2004/38/EC can claim the right to social benefits under the same conditions as those applicable to nationals would run counter to an objective of that Directive, set out in its recital 10, which is to prevent citizens of other member states from becoming an excessive burden on the social assistance system of the host member state"[685]. Precisely art. 7, according to CJEU, the possibility is established for the member state to refuse to grant social benefits to economically inactive Union citizens who exercise freedom of movement with the sole aim of obtaining the benefit of social assistance from another member state, even if they do not have sufficient resources to be able to claim the right of residence. Otherwise, it would lead to the paradoxical consequence, detected by CJEU, as well as from the AG

683 A. HATJE, J.P. TERHECHTE, P.C. MÜLLER-GRAFF, Europarechtswissenschaft, op. cit.

684 Paragraph 74. "It must therefore be noted that Article 7, par. 1, lett. b) of Directive 2004/38/EC aims at preventing economically inactive Union citizens from using the social protection system of the host member state to finance their livelihoods (...)".

685 C-333/13, Dano of 11 November 2014, op. cit.

that people who do not have sufficient resources to meet their needs when they enter the territory of another member state would automatically to dispose of it, thanks to the granting of a special non-contributory cash benefit, whose objective is to provide for the beneficiary's existence.

From these passages the role that the restrictive interpretation can play in excluding any kind of abuse can be very well understood: an interpretation of the Directive, as described above, necessarily leads to the exclusion of the possibility of any subsidy for non-nationals citizens that could have an abstract right. On the other hand, the answer given to the national court leaves no doubt that the motivation of the person involved is irrelevant for the attribution of the right of residence and equal treatment. Basically, the benefits deriving from the Directive, according to CJEU, were not invoked by Mrs. Dano when she did not have sufficient resources, not because of her abusive intentions: Mrs. Dano could not apply for social benefits, regardless of the fact that his behavior could (or not) be qualified as abusive[686].

It is therefore clear that with this ruling two different citizenship statuses are reintroduced, profoundly different from each other: on the one hand, that of economically active subjects, which are fully recognized as having access to the social protection systems of member states, on the basis of their contribution to the economic development of the host country. On the other hand, that of citizens who, not exercising an economic freedom, are in contrast excluded, in principle, from the possibility of cross-border access to the national social solidarity circuits.

Wanting to draw the thread of what has been said, it can be seen how the jurisprudence that looks at real and effective activity, as well as sufficient integration in the host country, to determine the right to social benefits assured there, at first sight, may prefer to use of the notion of abuse, the test of which offers few indications in this context. By linking integration and solidarity, on the other hand, CJEU grasps the nature of the underlying social status relationship, so as to effectively prevent social tourism[687]. Indeed, unlike in the hypothesis referred to in the paragraph concerning U-shaped operations, it is not a

686 As pointed out in the opinion of AG Poiares Maduro on 7 April 2005 in the case C-255/02, Halifax and others of 21 February 2006, op. cit., with regard to the solution of restrictive interpretation, the prohibition of abuse of rights represents a less drastic solution, more suited to the spirit and nature of the common VAT system (par. 53).

687 CJEU, C-340/14, Trijber of 16 July 2014, ECLI:EU:C:2015:505, published in the electronic Reports of the cases.

question of favoring one state (that of nationality) over another, since the whole construction is focused on establishing a link with the host state, whose legislation want to take advantage of. The level of integration in the state seems a good parameter. The case is different in CJEU, as in Dano, regardless of integration in the host country, of which true trace is not found in the reasoning followed, interpret the primary law and in particular the principle of equal treatment in light of the provisions of the Directive, specifically excluding those who do not benefit from a right of residence under the same, can claim the right to social benefits under the same conditions applicable to nationals. Indeed, it cannot fail to notice how the reasoning carried forward, however justified on the basis of an allegedly teleological interpretation of the Directive, although certainly effective in safeguarding the social assistance system of the host member state, proves to be excessively restrictive in some respects. This concerns the member state that requires social benefits such as those discussed in Dano, in fact, by force of things does not have sufficient economic resources for their livelihood and, consequently, cannot be considered legally resident, at least before the five years required to trigger the right of permanent residence. In this way, unnecessarily rigid interpretation of real integration is accepted, making it in fact coincide with the aforementioned term.

SOME BACKGROUND OBSERVATIONS. IS RESTRICTIVE INTERPRETATION AN EFFECTIVE TECHNIQUE? A COMPARISON WITH C-456/04, AGIP PETROLI SENTENCE OF 6 APRIL 2006

In the cases just analyzed, CJEU has avoided the danger of abuse by opting for the interpretative tool, which allows to find within the norm the limits beyond which the abuse is configured. More specifically, CJEU refers to the objective pursued by the European Union provision to exclude from its scope artificially constructed operations, which, even if they comply with the letter of the standard, have as their sole purpose to benefit from the advantages attributed by the standard itself.

It is worth highlighting once again that there has been no question of conscious choice: indeed, CJEU has explicitly taken into consideration, as in Akrich, or implicitly, as in C-311/06, National Council of Engineers case of 29 January 2009, the possibility of invoking the prohibition of abuse, discarding it and instead favoring a restrictive interpretation.

In this regard, it cannot be discounted that the option adopted by the EU judicature is exactly the same as the one chosen in the hypothesis of fraud on EU law. On the other hand, where CJEU followed certain rulings based on restrictive interpretation, he finally proposed for the use of the ban. Suffice it to say here that, in C-255/02 Halifax and others case of 21 February 2006 (leading case concerning the abuse of rights), the national court itself proposed, with the questions referred, the alternative between restrictive interpretation of the application field of the sixth Directive and use of the prohibition of abuse of rights. The same thing happened in the famous pronunciation in C-321/05, Kofoed v. Skateministeriet case of 5 July 2007.

This is evidently two distinct plans[688]. Indeed, the consequences arising from the use of one or the other technique are not insignificant: to sanction the abuse through the interpretative tool ignores the consolidated presence of the subjective element in the abuse test. According to which, in addition to establishing that the application of a particular rule to the present case would be contrary to its purpose, we must also prove the animus fraudandi. Although to be demonstrated on the basis of "objective elements", the necessity of the subjective element is constant in CJEU jurisprudence and involves the consequence, not indifferent, that the decision not to apply a rule based on the prohibition of abuse of law requires more rigorous assessments compared to those inherent in the process of interpretation of the rule itself.

If certainly this technique allows CJEU, as already mentioned, to maintain the monopoly in the definition of abusive situations, without risking to leave to the national authorities an excessively wide maneuvering space[689], it does not

688 See the conclusions presented by AG Mazak in the case: C-277/09, RBS Deutschland Holdings GmbH of 30 September 2010, ECLI;EU:C:2010:566, I-13805, where it is stated that the interpretation of the Sixth Directive and the relevance, in this case, of the prohibition of abuse of rights are issues "conceptually distinct and should, therefore, to be dealt with one after the other rather than jointly "and that" only if the conditions laid down by the relevant provisions of the Sixth Directive for obtaining the deduction in question are met, at least formally, it will be necessary to consider, as a second if the taxable person concerned intends, in the circumstances of the case, to make use of the aforementioned provisions for fraudulent or abusive purposes, that is to say if the activities in question are, in the light of the subjective and objective criteria which CJEU has made in this regard in its case-law, to be considered equivalent to abusive behavior (...)" (parr. 29 and 31).

689 From this point of view, as we have seen, the Akrich saga is instructive. See also the restrictive interpretation adopted in O and B, already analyzed in the previous chapter. It is recalled here that CJEU adopts an interpretation of the directive which would preclude that short stays, although accumulated, may be included in its art. 7 and thus assign a derived right of residence. In other words, it requires sufficient effectiveness to enable EU citizen to develop or consolidate family life in the host state. E. SPAVENTA, Family rights for circular migrants and frontier workers: O and B, and S and G, in the Common Market Law Review, 52, 2015, pp. 763, 776ss, notes how the union judge,

seem the motivations that bring the AG Tesauro in C- 367/96, Kefalas and others case of 12 May 1998 to advance reservations about the possible existence of the prohibition of abuse as an autonomous principle in EU law. The AG in fact, after discarding the possibility of a general definition of the category of abuse, due, among other things, to a difficult conceptualization even at national level, does not hesitate to affirm that the issue of abuse is always resolved. The use of a mere instrument of interpretation proves to be entirely acceptable, since, from the practical point of view, the technique of interpretation can involve various problems, already emerging in the specific treatment of the causes. In fact, in addition to limiting the areas of private autonomy[690], precisely the absence of verification as to the subjective element, determines a gap between interpretation and the fight against abuse. This is because, on one hand, the interpretation looks to the rule abstractly considered; and on the other hand, the abuse must necessarily be reconstructed in concrete terms. In other words, faced with these situations, the Achilles' heel of restrictive interpretation is found precisely in its "rigidity" and immutability in the face of individual situations.

This gives the national authorities a weapon that allows them to deny the protection given by EU law without having to worry about looking at the individual case, with all the problems that also derive from it in terms of division of powers between the member states[691].

---

thus ruling, has tried to limit the benefits of circular migration (U-shaped construction) and that, although this may constitute a reasonable intention, there are problems regarding the way in which CJEU realizes it. He, however, notes the critical issues in this approach: in particular, to pp. 769-770, observes as CJEU, insisting that, in order to benefit from the rights in question, it is not sufficient to have resided legally in the host state, perhaps even for a considerable period of time, but rather, the citizen of the Union must have satisfied the conditions laid down by Directive 2004/38/EC throughout its stay, even when the host state had granted more generous conditions to the migrant citizen, also calling into question the rights of workers in search of employment, such as the applicants, who they have a hybrid status in EU law, in the sense that, although they may remain beyond the first three months if they show a good chance of finding a job, they are not however resident in accordance with art. 7, par. 1, but rather "present" pursuant to art. 14 (4) (b).

690 CJEU, C-456/04, Agip Petroli of 6 April 2006, op. cit.

691 Council Regulation (EEC) of 7 December 1992, n. 3577, concerning the application of the principle of freedom to provide services to maritime transport between member states (maritime cabotage), in OJ, L 364, p. 7. Art. 3 of the regulation provides: 1. For vessels carrying out continental cabotage and cruise ships, all matters relating to the crew are the responsibility of the state in which the vessel is registered (flag State); 2. In the case of vessels which carry out island cabotage, all matters relating to the crew are the responsibility of the state in which the vessel is engaged in a maritime transport service (Host State). 3. However, as from 1 January 1999, for cargo ships of more than 650 gross tonnage carrying out island cabotage, when the trip in question follows or precedes a journey from or to another state, all matters relating to the crew are the responsibility of the state in which the vessel is registered (flag State).

If this is one of the side effects deriving from an imprudent use of restrictive interpretation, one could even hypothesize cases in which it is not in the sole definition, by CJEU, of the intrinsic limits of the subjective juridical positions attributed by EU law the possibility of denying its invoking is therefore allowed only when it is shown that those limits have been exceeded. Since CJEU essentially "gives the national court the possibility of penalizing a distorted or excessive use of Union law only where the objectives pursued are not jeopardized (...), the question of the abuse is based on the provisions of national law and ends up resolving, when a legal situation assigned by EU law is at stake, in a question of interpretation of the community law in question" (paragraph 25)[692].

In order better to make such a statement, C-456/04, Agip Petroli sentence of 6 April 2006[693] may be cited. The case, which concerned the interpretation of art. 3 of the Regulation on maritime cabotage, saw the Agip Petroli company as opposed to the Port Authority of Syracuse regarding a decision by which the harbor master's office had refused to permit a vessel, flying the Greek flag, to carry out an insular cabotage, without load, between Magnisi and Gela. Agip Petroli appealed against this decision, invoking art. 3, n. 3 of Regulation, which provides for the application of the law of the flag state. National authority, on the other hand, narrowly interpreting art. 3, n. 3, claimed that the provision could not be invoked in the present case, since the vessel had made a ballast prior to the insular cabotage voyage, which could not therefore have been included in the "journey which follows or precedes a journey coming from or going to another state", referred to in 3[694]. This led the referring court, who claimed the necessity to avoid that, by means of fake consecutive cabotage, the provisions of art. 3, n. 2, to request clarification on the notion of "journey that follows or precedes"[695] the cabotage voyage referred to in article 3, no. 3, that is, if it included only the journey with cargo on board or if it could be extended to the hypothesis of a journey in ballast.

CJEU replies that, since the Regulation does not contain any definition of the concept of "journey", nor does any element suggest that EU legislature intended

692 CJEU, C-456/04, Agip Petroli of 6 April 2006, op. cit.

693 The authorization had been refused because they were part of the crew of seafarers of Filipino nationality and this was prohibited by Italian law, which according to the national authority should have been applied under article 3 n. 2.

694 CJEU, C-456/04, Agip Petroli of 6 April 2006, op. cit.

695 CJEU, C-456/04, Agip Petroli of 6 April 2006, op. cit.

to allow for additional criteria to be taken into account, such as the need for a cargo on board or the existence of a functional and commercial autonomy of the international voyage, this notion must be understood as comprising. In principle, any journey regardless of the presence of a cargo on board is supported in maritime transport where sometimes ballast trips[696] are carried out.

CJEU adds that "despite this finding, ballast journeys undertaken abusively for the purpose of circumventing the provisions of art. 3 of the Regulation and the objective of the Regulation itself"[697]. Hence, CJEU admits that national courts can take account of the abusive behavior of the person concerned in order to deny him the possibility of benefiting from the provisions of Union law invoked.

The sentence is certainly singular in its specificity. The application of the prohibition of abuse should therefore not be surprising, as shown in par. 20 of the sentence, where c) judgments: C-125/76 are cited as above, Peter Cremer v. Bundesanstalt für landwirtschaftliche Marktordnung of 11 October 1977, C-8/92, General Milk Products v. Hauptzollamt Hamburg-Jonas of 3 March 1993 and C-255/02, Halifax and others of 21 February 2006, state that the circumvention of rules laid down by Union law is not permitted. At the basis of the reasoning of CJEU, well highlighted when it comes to applying the abuse test, which considers the objective of art. 3 of the Regulation, as well as the desire to apply a provision of the Regulation in place of another, CJEU seems to not refer to the circumvention of national legislation, but to fraud EU law, which takes the form of an artificial construction, in order to be applied a given rule of conflict in place of another, allowing the application of the most favorable national law. In other words, CJEU, in the presence of a Regulation indicating the conditions for application of a specific national law, respectively that of the host or flag state, considers that the prohibition of abuse can be applied, setting it entirely on the European conflict law, whose circumvention necessarily involves the circumvention of national law.

696 CJEU recalls at point 23 that the assessment of an abusive practice of this kind requires, on the one hand, that the international voyage in ballast, despite the formal application of the conditions set out in article 3, n. 3 of Regulation, has the result that the shipowner, for all matters relating to the crew, is responsible for the application of the flag state rules in disregard of the objective of art. 3, n. 2 of Regulation, which consists in allowing the application of the rules of the host state to all matters relating to the crew in the case of insular cabotage (objective element). On the other hand, it must also result from a set of objective elements that the essential purpose of this international ballast voyage is to avoid the application of art. 3, n. 2 of the regulation, for the benefit of that of no. 3 of the same article (see, to that effect in case C-255/02, Halifax and others of 21 February 2006, op. cit., par. 86) (subjective element).

697 CJEU, C-456/04, Agip Petroli of 6 April 2006, op. cit.

What interests us here to highlight, beyond the specificity of the sentence, is how CJEU, in this case, could not make use of the technique of restrictive interpretation, simply because such a choice would have led to a de facto repeal of the Regulation provision subject to attention. As pointed out by the AG Kokott, in fact, to require that a cargo be transported on international travel would have considerably limited the possibilities of cabotage, almost to the exclusion of it with reference to some sectors, such as that of oil[698].

Therefore, the technique of restrictive interpretation is not always feasible. On the contrary, where there is a text of secondary law that provides for well-defined rules of conflict so as to indicate the national legislation that applies to one case rather than to another, the prohibition of abuse seems a viable path in how elusive design is clearly visible even at the level of EU system.

The referring court also made it clear that this would have made most of the insular cabotage in the oil sector in Italian islands impossible.

CONCLUDING REMARKS

Referring to the conclusions of the individual sections for a more in-depth analysis of the characteristics and the limits of the protection techniques of the legal system taken into consideration in this paragraph, it can be stated here, in summary, how the cases object of attention have confirmed that "European" jurisprudence, in the presence of a triangulation between legal systems, has largely solved the problem of abusive demonstrations of individuals using techniques other than the prohibition of abuse.

In the face of "U" operations carried out using the freedoms of circulation to circumvent national legislation and move into a more favorable national system, CJEU, in the absence of any form of harmonization, has consented, under conditions defined, to the invocation by the member state of the fight against abuse as an overriding reason of public interest.

Alternatively, in the presence of "U-shaped" constructions aimed at applying Union law in place of national law, the jurisprudence has shown itself inclined to interpret the scope of the rights conferred by EU law in such a way as to exclude the root situations that were outside the objectives of the legislation.

698 R. IONESCU, Abus de droit en droit de l'Union européenne: nouvelles applications, notamment en matière de transport, in Journal de Droit Européen, 221 (1), 2015, pp. 100ss.

It has indeed been pointed out that in all sectors, the concept, albeit different, has a constant characteristic: the teleological criterion, which consists in the failure to respect the objectives pursued by the relevant EU law provision. If this element unites the three techniques, this cannot lead to affirm that they can be included under the umbrella of prohibition of abuse intended as an autonomous concept. As already highlighted, in fact, the first technique differs from the abuse of law as it focuses on the suitability and proportionality of the national anti-abuse legislation and not on the abusive behavior considered in itself, which translates into requiring the legislation considered to be just consider constructions of pure artifice already in the abstract. As for the technique of restrictive interpretation, it must be reiterated that the plans for the prohibition of abuse and interpretation are not perfectly coinciding. In order for the prohibition in question to apply, in fact, not only does the fact not fall within the purpose of law, but must also be a creation without economic justification, indicating the desire to obtain an abusive advantage.

More generally, it was observed that CJEU, in essence, to combat the most obvious manifestations of abuse, claims to use techniques that focus on legislation, general and abstract, when the same badly fit the concrete case. This applies to the imperative reasons, as well as to the restrictive interpretation. In the first case, in fact, through a very strict proportionality test, we end up allowing the national authority to apply the legislation only if it is aimed at opposing specific constructions outlined ex ante with extreme precision. Among other things, the most nourished jurisprudence with reference to the fight against abuse is found in the field of tax avoidance, which has undeniable particularities compared to other hypotheses of circumvention that have been analyzed. In these cases, it is not so much a connecting element with another national order to be created fictitiously, but the operation itself. One might ask, therefore, if the same principles can be valid in other cases of circumvention, including the pseudo-foreign corporations, in which the element of artificiality is very difficult to trace according to the parameters set by jurisprudence, without taking into consideration the nationality of the private individual. Even the teleological interpretation, on the other hand, is inevitably not very flexible, insofar as it pertains to the letter of the law.

This last section, which unites restrictive interpretation and imperative reasons, together with other problematic aspects already highlighted during the course of the discussion in this paragraph, first of all the risk of excessively affecting the division of powers between the state of origin and that of destination, leads to believe that CJEU is "ill-equipped" in the difficult task of answering the questions that are submitted, where it is to verify an abuse or otherwise to provide the national court with the coordinates to do so, considering the relative lack of experience on the subject, outside the realm of the law.

The described attitude of CJEU is at the origin of a series of problems, which also affect the relationships between negative and positive harmonization. In this regard, it cannot be overlooked that the abuse involving several jurisdictions finds its raison d'être in regulatory competition. If, in fact, the introduction of the principle of mutual recognition has allowed resources, companies and individuals to travel to states which offer them more advantageous conditions, specularly, member states have had the opportunity to offer economic actors an advantageous regulation in order to attract investment[699]. Where member states are free to define the content of their national provisions that do not influence circulation, an arbitrage opportunity for individuals is created.

Apart from considerations related to the risk of a leveling down national protection standards, what we would like to highlight is how the difference between territorial unity and regulatory diversity favors the emergence of abusive practices aimed at choosing the most favorable order; which are distinguished from simple arbitrage due to the high artificiality component that characterizes the latter.

On the contrary, harmonization eliminates the possibility of comparison between national laws and ipso facto of abuse involving multiple jurisdictions, as evidently no choice of applicable law can be made in the presence of a single legal regime.Thus, legislative institutions could be better equipped to combat large-scale abuses, also taking into account that member states, which are the first to request the application of the abuse ban, would ultimately be responsible for the consequences, desirable or less, descendants of legislative choices. In this regard, the link that can exist between the difficulties faced by CJEU in sanctioning the abuse and the harmonization reflected by the legislators of member states must not be underestimated. They also have a certain interest in the anti-abuse provisions introduced by EU legislator in several texts of secondary legislation, called anti-abuse clauses, and their mechanisms of functioning, as well as the role that can be played by EC in presence of a text of secondary law that imposes certain rules in order to limit law shopping. These are issues that deserve further study, the subject of the subsequent and final paragraph.

699 N. BERNARD, Flexibility in the European Single Market, in C. BARNARD, J. SCOTT, The law of the single European market, op. cit., pp. 101ss.

CHAPTER 5

ABUSE OF LAW, PROCEDURAL PREROGATIVES AND DOMINANT POSITION

INTRODUCTION

Antitrust law should be fully applied to that type of behavior that, although formally compliant with the regulatory framework of a given prerogative, is aimed at pursuing an objective different from, or contrary to, that for which the prerogative in question has been recognized by the law. The investigation of the functional limits of law (and the alignment, or otherwise, of the behavior challenged to the function for which the prerogative was recognized) clearly refers to the figure of abuse of rights.

The experience of US law in exercise of participatory prerogatives and application of antitrust law shows that even in US law the distinction about the application of antitrust law is represented by the genuineness or otherwise of the use of an antitrust law determined participative prerogative with respect to the function recognized by the legal system. Regarding the main lines of the figure of abuse of rights, both at national level and within the European legal system. With reference to the legal system (and, in particular, to the jurisprudence) of EU, it will be the object of our continuous investigation of the interaction between the abuse of procedural prerogatives, and application of article 102 TFEU. This is the case: T-111/96, ITT Promedia v. Commission of 17 July 1998[700], on the subject of access to justice by the dominant undertaking and cases: T-321/05, AstraZeneka UK v. Commission of 1st July 2010[701] and C-373/17P, Agria Polska and others v. Commission of 20 September 2018[702], relating to

700 T-111/96, ITT Promedia v. Commission of 17 July 1998, ECLI:EU:C:1998:183, II-02937.

701 T-321/05, AstraZeneka UK v. Commission of 1st July 2010, ECLI:EU:T:2010:266, II-0285. For further details see: D. GERARD, M. MEROLA, B. MEYRING, The notion of restriction of competition: revisiting the foundations of antitrust enforcement in Europe, ed. Bruylant, Bruxelles, 2017.

702 CJEU, C-373/17P, Agria Polska and others v. Commission of 20 September 2018, ECLI:EU:C:2018, published in the electronic Reports of the cases.

the abuse of procedural rights by the company in a dominant position. In this regard, the analogy between the test used in these cases by EU institutions on the application of prohibition of abuse of a dominant position and the general test emerging from EU jurisprudence on the prohibition of abuse of rights. The peculiarity of cases: T-111/96, ITT Promedia v. Commission of 17 July 1998 and T-321/05, AstraZeneka UK v. Commission of 1st July 2010 is represented by the fact that the figure of the abuse of right does not assume an autonomous role, but is inserted within the case of abuse of a dominant position.

Taking advantage of the lessons from the previous EU jurisprudence, our survey represents an emblematic case in which the abuse of a dominant position was read in light of the figure of abuse of rights[703]. In this regard, it will be highlighted that the position is: (i) erroneous and, (ii) clearly diverges from EU jurisprudence (in particular, from the previous case: T-321/05, AstraZeneka UK v. Commission of 1st July 2010) and (iii) ends up implying a substantial disregard of article 102 TFEU, since the Council of State has judged the facts of the case directly in the light of the figure of the abuse of rights, without proving its subsumption within the prohibition of abuse of a dominant position (contrary to what is required by Union jurisprudence).

The double "dimension" shows the relationship between the figure of abuse of law and the prohibition of abuse of a dominant position. On a first (mainly theoretical) level, the figure of abuse of rights can be useful as a tool for reading the logic underlying the prohibition of abuse of a dominant position. The latter could very well be considered in fact a specification of the prohibition of abuse of law. The figure of abuse of rights does not detect autonomously, but becomes part of the case of prohibition of abuse of a dominant position, acting as a distinctive criterion between the genuine exercise of procedural prerogatives and their abuse by the company in dominant position[704].

---

703 CJEU, C-373/17P, Agria Polska and others v. Commission of 20 September 2018, op. cit.

704 See, Federal Trade Commission, Staff Report: Enforcement Perspectives on the Noerr-Pennington Doctrine, 2006: "(...) although the court has not provided a consistent source for the doctrine, it appears to be rooted in a construction of the Sherman Act to avoid conflict with the constitutional right to petition the government for redress of grievances and the principle of effective government decision-making (...) (p. 6).

PARTICIPATION AND ANTITRUST LAW IN US EXPERIENCE: THE NOERR-PENNINGTON JURISPRUDENCE

The theme of interaction between antitrust law and participation of companies in public decision-making processes has been carefully treated by both jurisprudence and US antitrust doctrine.

Through the Noerr-Pennington doctrine, which takes its name from two rulings of the first half of the 1960s, the Federal Supreme Court has traced the scope of immunity of the public decision-making arena from the interference of antitrust law. In speciem, the ratio of Noerr-Pennington doctrine is to prevent the application of antitrust law from conflicting: (a) with the right of petition, understood as the right of every citizen to ask the Government to protect their interests, and (b) with the principle of effectiveness of public decision-making process[705].

The crucial point to avert the conflict between these values is identified in the correct definition of the field of application of antitrust law. The jurisprudence and the best American doctrine agree in considering, at least in principle, that [the scope] of antitrust laws is not to correct failures in political markets, but only in traditional private markets[706]. Antitrust law therefore has as its object exclusively the behavior of companies regarding the economic process, that is, the entrepreneurial conduct of the market. Instead, the conduct retained, even by dominant companies, within the political process (i.e. public decision-making) lies outside the scope of the Sherman Act. These principles are better understood if contextualized in cases where they are they have been expressed and analyzed below.

705 P.E. AREEDA, H. HOVENKAMP, Antitrust law: An analysis of antitrust principles and their application, Wolters Kluwer, New York, 2018, pp. 146ss. See also the sentence from the American Supreme Court: Eastern Railroad Presidents' Conference v. Noerr Motor Freight, Inc 365 U.S. 127 (1961). For further details see: D.F. BRODE, U.S. Antitrust law and enforcement. A practice introduction, Oxford University Press, Oxford, 2010. E. ØSTERUD, Identifying exclusionary abuses by dominant undertakings under EU, Kluwer Law International, The Hague, 2010.

706 E. ØSTERUD, Identifying exclusionary abuses by dominant undertakings under EU, op. cit.

PUBLIC DECISION-MAKING PROCESSES ARE IMMUNE FROM THE APPLICATION OF ANTITRUST LAW: THE NOERR CASE

The leading case in the matter is the Supreme Court ruling in the Eastern Railroad Presidents' Conference v. Noerr Motor Freight, Inc. ("Noerr")[707]. The Noerr case is the result of the hard comparison between the railway industry and that of land transport by road. In this case, the railway undertakings were associated with each other for the purpose of undertaking strong lobbying activities against the expansion of the road transport sector (in particular, transport of goods by truck and by people on buses). The companies of the railway industry, with the help of a company specialized in public relations, launched a tough lobbying campaign aimed at manipulating public opinion on the alleged dangerousness of road transport, in order to invoke the adoption of legislative measures that penalized this mode of transport.

A consequence of the lobbying campaign was the decision of the Governor of the State of Pennsylvania to veto the adoption of a legislative measure (the "Fair Truck Bill") which, raising the weight limits of the load transportable from the trucks, would increase competition between road and rail freight transport. In response to this decision, 41 lorry transport companies operating in the State of Pennsylvania have sued 24 railway companies, their trade association and the lobbying public relations company, requesting that they be ordered to pay compensation, punitive damages (treble damages) for attempting to monopolize the long-distance freight sector. The plaintiffs complained, in particular, of the existence of an agreement (conspiration) between the resisting parties, aimed at obtaining the adoption of legislative measures unfavorable to land transport by road, as well as disseminating disparaging information on the sector to the public and customers of land transport by road.

In more detail, among the means used by the association of railway and by the public relations company, we can list: (a) the organization of protest demonstrations that may appear to be the result of spontaneous initiatives by groups of citizens, but in reality, were organized by the consulting firm, (b) the dissemination of documents, studies or pamphlets, not always truthful and apparently

707 S.A. GARRETSON,The hazards of doing business with the government: Expanding exceptions to Noerr {Eastern R.R. Presidents Conference v. Noerr Motor Freight, Inc., 81 S. Ct. 523}-Pennington {United Mine Workers of Am. v. Pennington, 85 S. Ct. 1585}, in Washington University Journal Urban & Contemporary Law, 26, 1984, pp. 198ss. G. MINDA, Interest groups, political freedom, and antitrust: A modern reassessment of the Noerr-Pennington doctrine, in Hastings Law Journal, 41, 1990, pp. 908ss.

coming from independent organizations and/or civic groups. In fact, they were produced from sources related to railway undertakings (or public relations company assumed by the latter); (c) intense lobbying with the authorities and legislative bodies in various states of the Federation.

The US Supreme Court, by reforming the decisions of the lower courts, decided that antitrust law could not be applied in this case. According to the court, no violation of antitrust law could be envisaged in the case of "mere attempts to influence the passage or enforcement of laws"[708]. The antitrust law, in the same way, cannot be considered violated whenever "a restraint upon trade or monopolization" is the result of a "valid governmental action, as opposed to private action"[709].

The representation of interests by companies within the legislative process is therefore, in principle, immune from the intervention of antitrust law and the possible restriction of competition produced by legislative acts, adopted as a result of lobbying initiatives of companies, is attributable exclusively to public power and not to private conduct[710].

(FOLLOWS) THE PRINCIPLE EXPRESSED BY THE SUPREME COURT IS BASED ON TWO SETS OF ARGUMENTS

Firstly, the immunity from the application of the antitrust law necessary to guarantee the effective functioning of the public decision-making process (in this case, the legislative one). From this perspective, the US judges have observed that "the very heart of a system of representative democracy" is at the heart of

708 P.C. WARD, Federal Trade Commission. Law, practice and procedure, Law Journal Press, New York, 2018.

709 P.C. WARD, Federal Trade Commission. Law, practice and procedure, op. cit.

710 In the same spirit see the next cases: Matossian v. Fahmie, 161 Cal. Rptr. 532 (Cal. Ct. App. 1980); Long Beach v. Bozek, 645 P.2d 137 (Cal. 1982)). Eaton v. Newport Bd. of Educ., 975 F.2d 292, 293 (6th Cir. 1992) (lobbying); Christian Gospel Church, Inc. v. City & Cty. of San Francisco, 896 F.2d 1221, 1226 (9th Cir. 1990) (zoning); United States v. Hylton, 710 F.2d 1106, 1111 (5th Cir. 1983) (filing a complaint with law enforcement); Arim v. Gen. Motors Corp., 520 N.W.2d 695, 700 (Mich. Ct. App. 1994) (cooperating with law enforcement). E.R.R. Presidents Conference v. Noerr Motor Freight, Inc., 365 U.S. 127, 136 (1961). Venetian Casino Resort, LLC, 357 N.L.R.B. 1725 (2011), rev'd sub nom. Venetian Casino Resort, L.L.C. v. NLRB, 793 F.3d 85 (D.C. Cir. 2015).

the concept of "the ability of the people to make their wishes known to their representatives"[711].

Of this, the judges continued, "to hold that the government retains the power to act in this representative capacity and yet hold, at the same time, that the people cannot freely inform the government of their wishes would impute to the Sherman Act a purpose to regulate, not business activity, but political activity, a purpose which would have no basis whatever in the legislative history of the Sherman Act (...)"[712].

Secondly, the conduct of railway undertakings was "mere solicitation of governmental action with respect to the passage and enforcement of laws"[713], i.e. they were placed within the scope of application of the right of petition, protected by the First Amendment of the US Constitution. Antitrust law must therefore be interpreted in such a way as not to interfere with the constitutionally guaranteed right of petition to public authority and participation in public decision-making processes[714].

The recognition of immunity from the application of antitrust law in the legislative process also contains two important implications. Firstly, antitrust law does not apply even when there is evidence that the adoption of legislative measures has been invoked by a given company in order to penalize its competitors, or to gain a certain advantage over it. It is therefore irrelevant that, for the purposes of liability by unlawful antitrust, the intent with which the legislator is required to adopt certain measures. Secondly, the immunity from the application of antitrust law also covers ancillary anti-competitive effects (i.e., collateral) to activities aimed at obtaining the adoption of legislative measures penalizing for competition. It must be treated, however, of collateral anti-competitive effects ("incidental effects", according to the terminology of the

711 P.C. WARD, Federal Trade Commission. Law, practice and procedure, op. cit.

712 P.C. WARD, Federal Trade Commission. Law, practice and procedure, op. cit.

713 P.E. AREEDA, H. HOVENKAMP, Antitrust law: An analysis of antitrust principles and their application, op. cit., in case. Noerr "the Court did not actually applied the First Amendment. It merely held that, given the lack of any congressional mandate in the Sherman Act's legislative history to apply the statute to political activity issue, it would not warrant such an application" (p. 150).

714 According to the Supreme Court: "the right of the people to inform their representatives in government of their desires with respect to the passage or enforcement of laws cannot properly be made to depend upon their intent in doing so" (case Noerr, pp. 139). This also because: "(...) the construction of the Sherman Act that would disqualify people from taking a public position on matters in which they are financially interested would thus deprive the government of a valuable source of information and, at the same time, deprive the people of their right to petition in the very instances in which that right may be of the most importance to them" (par. 139).

court) to activities whose main purpose is "to obtain legislation and nothing more"[715] and not instead of "interfere directly with the business" relationships of a "competitor"[716].

PUBLIC DECISION-MAKING PROCESSES ARE IMMUNE FROM THE APPLICATION OF ANTITRUST LAW. THE JURISPRUDENCE FOLLOWING THE NOERR CASE

With the jurisprudence following the Noerr ruling, the Federal Supreme Court has extended the principles set out therein to other public decision-making areas. There are two judgments that have contributed most to this effect.

The first is the United Mine Workers of America v. Pennington ("Pennington")[717], adopted by the Supreme Court 4 years after the Noerr decision. In the Pennington case, the Supreme Court expressed itself on the compatibility with the antitrust law of the decision to increase the minimum wage in the mining sector, adopted by the US Government, accepting the requests in this direction received from a miners' union and the main active companies in the mining sector, in implementation of a collective bargaining between them previously intervened[718].

715 P.E. AREEDA, H. HOVENKAMP, Antitrust law: An analysis of antitrust principles and their application, op. cit., pp. 52ss.

716 See case: Noerr, p. 144. the supreme Court affirmed that: "it is inevitable, whenever an attempt is made to influence legislation by a campaign of publicity, that an incidental effect of that campaign may be the infliction of some direct injury upon the interests of the party against whom the campaign is directed. And it seems equally inevitable that those conducting the campaign would be aware of, and possibly even pleased by, the prospect of such injury. To hold that the knowing infliction of such injury renders the campaign itself illegal would thus be tantamount to outlawing all such campaigns (pp. 143-144).

717 Sentence of the American Supreme Court: United Mine Workers of America v. Pennington, 381 U.S. 657 (1965). For further analysis see: T. KÄSEBERG, Intellectual property, antitrust and cumulative innovation in the EU and the US, Hart Publishing, Oxford & Oregon, Portland, 2012.

718 The American Supreme Court has also affirmed that: "(...) such conduct is not illegal, either standing alone or as part of a broader scheme itself violative of the Sherman Act" (ibid.); mining industry (and the resulting redundancies), in exchange for an increase in the minimum wage of miners. Both parties, in implementation of the agreement, have requested the (and obtained from) government (in particular from the Secretary of State for Labor) the adoption of a decision that would increase the minimum wage at the level agreed between the social partners. The overall agreement was clearly more favorable for large mining companies, because they were the only ones with the financial capacity to invest in the mechanization of mining activities and thus to offset the higher cost resulting from the increase of the minimum wage with the savings cost obtained from the mechanization

The case, in particular, originated from a collective bargaining between a union of miners and the companies active in the mining sector, according to which the former would not oppose the further mechanization of the Supreme Court. Deciding on the part of the collective agreement to the lobbying activities at the Executive for the achievement of the minimum wage increase, he considered the principles expressed in the Noerr case fully applicable in this case. The judges have, in this view, affirmed that "joint efforts to influence public officials do not violate the antitrust laws even if intended to eliminate competition"[719]. The immunity from the application of antitrust law was therefore explicitly extended also to activities aimed at invoking the intervention of the executive power[720].

The other important ruling for the purposes here is that adopted by the Supreme Court in the California Motor Transport Trucking Unlimited case ("California Motor")[721]. The applicant (a company active in intra-state road transport) complained that the respondent, together with other companies (all active in the field of inter-state road transport), would put in place activities aimed at preventing the entry of new competitors in the inter-state road transport market. According to the appellant, the defendant (and other companies operating in the inter-state road transport sector) was systematically opposed to administrative proceedings aimed at examining the appellant's claims for obtaining the necessary authorizations for access to the inter-state transport segment.

In the present case, the court took the opportunity to state the principle that immunity from antitrust law is applicable, both with regard to proceedings before the "administrative agencies" and the arms of the executive, both with reference to those before the judicial bodies (called" the third branch of Government")[722]. According to the Court, it would be "destructive of rights of association and of petition to hold that group with common interests may not,

---

of the activities in question. For this reason the collective bargaining was not respected by several small mining operators, including the company Phillips Brothers Coal Company whose president, Mr. Pennington, was sued by the miners' union, precisely because of the failure of the aforementioned collective agreement.

719 Sentence of the Supreme Court: California Motor Transport v. Trucking Unlimited, 404 U.S. 508 (1972).

720 A.S. GOLUB, The exception of Noerr-Pennington materials from discovery under the petition clause of the first amendment, in St. John's Law Review: 66 (4), 1993, pp. 1099ss.

721 K.N. HYLTON, Antitrust law: economic theory and common law evolution, Cambridge University Press, Cambridge, 2010, pp. 370ss.

722 P.C. WARD, Federal Trade Commission. Law, practice and procedure, op. cit.

without violating the antitrust laws, use the channels and procedures of state and federal agencies and courts to advocate their causes and points of view respecting resolution of their business and economic interests towards their competitors"[723].

The immunity from the application of antitrust law in public decision-making processes is not absolute. If it is true that in the California Motors judgment the Supreme Court extended the application of the Noerr-Pennington immunity also to administrative/judicial proceedings. It is true that in the same decision the federal judges have identified the boundaries of the Noerr-Pennington doctrine, defining the exceptions to its application. In California Motors, the Supreme Court has in fact denied that the Noerr-Pennington doctrine could apply to the facts of the case.

Therefore, the Noerr-Pennington immunity is not absolute. A first indication in this sense is indeed already found in the Noerr judgment, in which the United States Supreme Court affirmed, albeit in an obiter, that "(...) there may be situations in which a publicity campaign, ostensibly directed toward influencing governmental action, is a mere sham to cover what is actually nothing more than an attempt to interfere directly with the business relationships of a competitor and the application of the Sherman Act would be justified"[724].

It should therefore be distinguished, according to the court, between activities that represent "genuine" attempts to influence public institutions and those which constitute a mere pretext to hinder (and/or interfere) the activity of the competitor[725]. The former is immune from the application of antitrust law, while the latter is not.

723 The Supreme Court affirmed also that: "the right of access to the courts is indeed but one aspect of the right of petition".

724 In Noerr case was declared: "(...) no one denies that the railroads were making a genuine effort to influence legislation and law enforcement practices. Indeed, if the version of the facts set forth in truckers' complaint is fully credited, as it was by the courts below, that effort was not only genuine, but also highly successful. Under these circumstances, we conclude that no attempt to interfere with business relationships in a manner proscribed by the Sherman Act is involved in this case (...)".

725 This distinction clearly emerges in the California Motors ruling, in which the Supreme Court highlighted that "[m]is representations, condoned in the political arena, are not immunized when used in the adjudicatory process (...)" (par. 513).

THE EXCEPTIONS TO THE NOERR-PENNINGTON IMMUNITY: OBTAINING ANTI-COMPETITIVE MEASURES THROUGH THE USE OF "IMPROPER PARTICIPATORY MEANS"

In the first category of exceptions we can list all the cases in which the adoption of a restrictive competition decision is requested from the public authorities, using improper, incorrect, or somehow (even ethically) reprehensible means. An emblematic example is that in which the public decision-maker is provided with false information, or the circumstances that are relevant to the adoption of the provision favorable to the applicant are kept aside.

In these cases, it is believed that the immunity provided for by the Noerr-Pennington doctrine should not apply because, although any anti-competitive effect will only be produced by the final decision of the public decision maker, the latter's will may have been manipulated through improper means used by the dominant undertaking.

On the theoretical level, to conclude on the inapplicability of the immunity provided by the Noerr-Pennington doctrine, one must demonstrate both the improper nature of company's behavior (or the means used by the latter in the decision-making process), or recourse to the aforementioned improper means constitutes a "non genuine" attempt to influence the public authority (that is, it is not a simple mistake).

On a practical level, it is certainly not easy to prove the existence of the two elements. The jurisprudence is able to distinguish, in this regard, the behaviors held in the political/ legislative field from those carried out in the context of adjudicatory or quasi-adjuratory proceedings[726]. As a general rule, it is extremely difficult to demonstrate that a given behavior in the context of the political-legislative confrontation process is to be considered improper for the purposes of the application of antitrust law[727]. The Noerr-Pennington immunity will therefore find its maximum extension in the political-legislative arena.

726 P.E. AREEDA, H. HOVENKAMP, Antitrust law: An analysis of antitrust principles and their application, op. cit., "(...) the minimum teaching of Noerr is that unethical political conduct in the legislative context is irrelevant for antitrust purposes, and that result is reinforced by the recognition that the government learns about reality and appropriate policy responses through a complex battle of contending political forces that speak truths and partial truths and exert diverse pressures upon various persons and institutions. Society recognizes that politics is often a rough and tumble affair (...)" (pp. 167ss).

727 See, Federal Trade Commission, Staff Report , Enforcement Perspectives on the Noerr-Pennington Doctrine, 2006, pp.18ss.

Within the administrative procedures, it distinguishes between restricted procedures (ministerial proceedings) and discretionary proceedings. As for the former, it is believed that misleading, improper or improper behavior will hardly be covered by the Noerr-Pennington[728] immunity. Similar evaluations also seem to apply to judicial proceedings.

Firstly, incorrect, misleading and/or improper behavior should not be the result of a mere mistake, but must be a deliberate and conscious procedural conduct on the part of the company[729]. Secondly, the conduct of the company must have a direct impact on the outcome and content of the decision taken by the public administration[730]. In any case, a clear limit is placed on the intervention of antitrust law, i.e. that its application cannot and must not be transformed into a re-exercise of the power assigned to the administration which has adopted the anti-competitive decision[731].

---

728 P.E. AREEDA, H. HOVENKAMP, Antitrust law: An analysis of antitrust principles and their application, op. cit.

729 According to Federal Trade Commission, "(...) the courts have made this last factor an essential element in the inquiry, with some requiring that the misrepresentation "'deprive the litigation of its legitimacy,'" others asking whether he misrepresentation "infect[s] "the very core" of the case", and still others asking "whether the government action would have resulted 'but for' the misrepresentation or omission." (pp. 27-28).

730 Federal Trade Commission confirmed that: "(...) application of the exception also must protect governmental decision-making. It should be clear that antitrust enforcement in these circumstances is not challenging government action itself, but rather attacking a private misrepresentation that "effectively supplanted government action (...)". Similarly, application of the misrepresentation exception must not interfere unnecessarily with the governmental decision-making process. For example, there should not be any reassessment of the governmental entity's determination of public welfare or after-the-fact regulation of the outcome of that entity's political processes" (p. 28). Note that it should be distinguished from the Noerr-Pennington doctrine, cases concerning the adoption of intellectual property rights through the use of misleading information. The latter hypotheses are in fact governed by a specific line of case law, according to which the antitrust law infringes the dominant company which operates intellectual property rights which it knows to have obtained in a deceptive manner. (see: Walker Process Equipment v. Food Machinery & Chemical 382 US 172 (1965). For further details see: V. GUIMARAES DE LIMA E SILVA, Sham litigation in the pharmaceutical sector, in European Competition Journal, 7 (3), 2011, pp. 471-472. S. GALLASCH, Astrazeneca v the Walker process-A Real EU-US Divergence or just an attempt to compare apples to oranges, in European Competition Journal, 2011, pp. 505-526. C.R. LESLIE, Antitrust law and intellectual property rights. Cases and materials, Oxford University Press, Oxford, 2011. C.A. NARD, M.J. MADISON, M.P. MCKENNA, The law of intellectual property, Wolters Kluwer, New York, 2017. N. DUNNE, Competition law and economic regulation: making and managing markets, Cambridge University Press, Cambridge, 2015.

731 P.E. AREEDA, H. HOVENKAMP, Antitrust law: An analysis of antitrust principles and their application, op. cit., "(...) [s]trictly speaking, the term "sham" refers to a petition to the government that is improper in that it is intended not to obtain the requested relief from the government entity but only to exclude a rival, raise rival's costs and constrain its output, or cause similar competitive harm (...)" (pp. 215ss).

THE NOERR-PENNINGTON IMMUNITY EXCEPTIONS (SHAM EXCEPTION)

The second category of exceptions to the application of the Noerr-Pennington immunity includes cases in which participation in public decision-making procedures is a purely emulative or obstructive act. It is a case in which the dominant undertaking participates in a given decision-making process essentially to cause damage to its competitors, typically through the increase of their costs (to resist the action/obstruction of the dominant undertaking). We are in the presence of that exception that commonly jurisprudence and the doctrine call the "sham exception"[732]. The notion of "sham exception" (or the exception of emulation) includes cases in which the company resorts to public authority or participates in public decision-making procedures without having any interest in the final outcome of the decision-making process, having instead as essential objective that of causing damage to the competitor by increasing the costs of the latter[733].

From a conceptual point of view, the "sham exception" is different from the use of improper means, referred to in the first category of exceptions[734]. In the case of the sham exception, the company is disinterested in the final provision and participates in the decision-making process essentially to hinder competitor's action. The previously examined exception of the use of improper means refers instead to all those situations in which the company participates in a particular decision-making process just to obtain a certain type of provision

---

732 Prof'l Real Estate Inv'rs, Inc. v. Columbia Pictures Indus., Inc. (PREI), 508 U.S. 49, 60–61 (1993). For further details see: S.N. SENATOR, G.M. SERGI, Noerr-Pennington: Safeguarding the first amendment right to petition the government, in Competition Journal of Antitrust & Unfair Competition Law, 23, 2014, pp. 86ss. M. PEMSTEIN, The basis for Noerr-Pennington immunity: An argument that federal antitrust law, not the first amendment, defines the boundaries of Noerr-Pennington, in Thuergood Marshall Law Review, 40, 2014, pp. 80ss.

733 P.E. AREEDA, H. HOVENKAMP, Antitrust law: An analysis of antitrust principles and their application, op. cit., it's represented as: "(...) a regulated firm's request to a regulatory agency for a tariff excluding or injuring rivals when the firm has no expectation that the requested tariff will actually be approved, but the rivals will face significant costs in opposing it (...)".

734 For cases in which the Supreme Court specifically addressed Noerr-Pennington arguments, see Octane Fitness, LLC v. ICON Health & Fitness, Inc., 134 S. Ct. 1749 (2014); BE & K Constr. Co. v. NLRB, 563 U.S. 516 (2002); PREI, 508 U.S. 49; City of Colom. v. Omni Outdoor Advert., Inc., 499 U.S. 365 (1991); Allied Tube & Conduit Corp. v. Indian Head, Inc., 486 U.S. 492 (1988); Cal. Motor Transp. Co. v. Trucking Unlimited, 404 U.S. 508 (1972); United Mine Workers of Am. v. Pennington, 381 U.S. 657 (1965); E.R.R. Presidents Conference v. Noerr Motor Freight, Inc., 365 U.S. 127 (1961). Noerr-Pennington was argued, but not addressed in the following cases, because the Court decided them on other grounds: F.T.C. v. Ticor Title Ins. Co., 504 U.S. 621 (1992).

(anti-competitive), but does so by using improper means or in some way, reproachable (from a legal and/or ethical point of view). In the first case, the anti-competitive restriction thus derives exclusively from the dominant undertaking's participation in the decision-making process. In the second case, the restriction of competition derives from the provision of public authority[735].

With regard to the application of the sham exception, in analogy to what was observed for the exceptions relating to the use of improper means, it is believed that the very nature of political-legislative process makes it extremely difficult to demonstrate the exception in question. In the administrative proceedings, however, particular attention will be paid to the ways in which participation is made, or to the (obviously unfounded) nature of the provision that is required[736]. In the first case, an indication in favor of the application of sham exception could be represented by the demonstration of the awareness of the dominant company to intervene in the proceeding exclusively to hinder the competitor. In the second case, the nature of the requested measure should be examined, concluding for the applicability of the exception in cases where the request of the dominant company aims at the adoption of objectively and manifestly unfounded provisions, null and void of competence of another authority. The Supreme Court has argued in that regard in California Motors that the sham exception would apply in all those cases where it was possible to prove that the participatory instances of the dominant undertaking are objectively "baseless" and that therefore "the administrative and judicial processes have been abused"[737].

---

735 The American Supreme Court in case: California Motors, op. cit., affirmed that: "(...) opponents before agencies or courts often think poorly of others tactics, motions, or defenses and may readily call them baseless. One claim, which a court or agency may think baseless, may go unnoticed; but a pattern of baseless, repetitive claims may emerge which leads the fact finder to conclude that the administrative and judicial processes have been abused. That may be a difficult line to discern and draw. But once it is drawn, the case is established that abuse of those processes produced an illegal result, effectively barring respondents from access to the agencies and courts. Insofar as the administrative or judicial processes are involved, actions of that kind cannot acquire immunity by seeking refuge under the umbrella of "political expression" (...) (par. 514).

736 BE & K, 536 U.S. at 525; Bill Johnson's, 461 U.S. at 743. BE & K and Bill Johnson's provided the Court the opportunity to formally extend Noerr-Pennington into the labor law realm, but the Court never explicitly did so.

737 P.E. AREEDA, H. HOVENKAMP, Antitrust law: An analysis of antitrust principles and their application, op. cit.

CONCLUDING REMARKS ON THE NOERR-PENNINGTON DOCTRINE: THE DISTORTED USE OF PARTICIPATORY PREROGATIVES RAISES THE APPLICATION OF ANTITRUST LAW

According to my opinion, antitrust law cannot sanction the mere exercise by the dominant company of its rights. The application of antitrust law in the same way cannot be transformed into a re-exercise of a power assigned to the competence of another public administration.

Precisely for these reasons that in US experience it emerges more clearly that the scope of antitrust law is alien to the exercise of rights (prerogatives) that are part of public decision-making processes[738]. On the other hand, antitrust law applies whenever there is a misused use of participatory law. Thus emerges, in US experience, the substantial reference to the idea of abuse of law (in the form of abuse of process), as a criterion for the application of antitrust law with reference to apparently (and formally) behaviors conforming to the implementation schemes of the prerogatives recognized by sorting.

It should be noted that in US antitrust experience there is not a dogmatic-expressed reference to the notion of abuse of law, which is instead known to the legal traditions of civil law. The jurisprudence, called upon to rule on the application of antitrust law to the specific case, uses those that could be considered symptomatic indices, or single cases, of abuse of law. Notions, such as "genuineness" in the exercise of rights, emulation and/or recourse to improper participatory means, thus delineate the boundary between the exercise of a prerogative recognized by the law and its abuse[739].

---

738 Octane Fitness, LLC v. ICON Health & Fitness, Inc., 134 S. Ct. 1749, 1756–58 (2014).

739 It is affirmed that: "the various legal systems adopt different approaches to abuse of procedural rights: while common law countries use "rich and complex typologies of specific instances of APR (abuse of process) and of sanctions, civil law systems use different approaches, among them vague rules stating abuse, or else specific rules without calling them abuse. Sham litigation can easily be considered part of the mentioned specific typology under US common law system; among the procedural rights listed as abusive in a report, frivolous claims and also repetitive claims, which characterize sham litigation, were mentioned". Recognition of a link between sham and abuse of process, although not always clearly assessed, has also been provided by US Courts. In PRE, the Supreme Court clarified the origins of the concept of sham litigation by establishing "sham" as the opposite of "genuine", as defined by the Federal Rule of Civil Procedure, in order to justify the objective prong of the test. In its turn, in the US case CR Bard Inc, the Federal circuit stressed that to "invoke sham exception the claimant must show "some abuse of process", as well as "clear and convincing evidence of bad faith". For further details see: V. GUIMARAES DE LIMA E SILVA, Sham Litigation in the pharmaceutical sector, op. cit, pp. 494-495.

The substance of the problem, however, does not change even in US law: what must be proved, for the purposes of applying antitrust law to a behavior that apparently constitutes the exercise of a prerogative, is essentially its deviation from the purpose, or from the function assigned by the order to the aforementioned prerogative.

As we will see in the following paragraph, this is also the basic rationale of the figure of abuse of rights, elaborated in national and European law.

THE ABUSE OF LAW AS AN INSTRUMENT OF CONTROL AND CONTAINMENT OF PRIVATE POWER

Before attempting to provide some possible criteria for resolving the conflict between the application of antitrust law and the exercise of prerogatives (including those that are constitutionally guaranteed), it is considered appropriate to conduct a brief investigation into the figure of abuse of rights.

Conceptually, there is no difficulty in accepting the formula "abuse of law" in its current meaning, that is, as a deviation from the substantial purposes assigned to the prerogative by virtue of normative recognition. In this light, the abuse of law does not affect behavior that would be contrary to other precise bans of law (even not of positive law): on the contrary, in these cases it is undisputed that the figure would have no reason to exist. Likewise, it is argued that the abuse of law is different from the excess of law: the latter is an illicit figure that should not give rise to particular problems, since it can easily be placed in the traditional category of civil liability. Non-exercise or exercise according to criteria other than those imposed by the nature of function can be considered abuse in relation to that power. But, a function must also be found in private autonomy in its normal aspects of free autonomy, which is nevertheless linked to the care of interests. Only that this function must primarily be perceived in the connection of act with the limits of the same power that with that act of exercise. The concept of abuse of law is susceptible of assuming a meaning in all those cases in which an alteration occurs in the objective function of the act with respect to the power of autonomy that configures it in relation to the conditions attached to the exercise of power itself. Such an alteration of the objective function of the act would occur: "a) in the form of an alteration of the causal factor which is reflected in an alteration in the structure of the act itself;

b) in the form of a conduct of legal relations contrary to good faith or otherwise detrimental to the good faith of others.

The abuse of right, or rather the prohibition against abusing a prerogative, is instead emphasized in all those situations in which the exercise of the prerogative, even if formally compliant with the ordering scheme, is activated by its owner for a different purpose/function from what the law assigns to such a prerogative. In other words, the abuse of law far from assuming a violation in the formal sense of law, outlines the altered use of the formal scheme of law, aimed at achieving further and different objectives than those indicated by the Legislator. Deviation which, according to the different doctrinal conceptions, is considered to be sanctionable with the non-granting of protection or according to the rules of civil tort.

The problem of the theory of abuse of rights is not a conceptual problem, but rather, as has been pointed out, a positive and consists in the identification of an autonomous juridical principle that is, first of all, inferable in a generalization from normative norms of positive law; and, secondly, such to add a quid pluris of a preceptive value, with respect to the normative content of each of it. On this point the doctrine was strongly divided between those who doubted the presence of the figure or its usefulness and those who admit the existence of a general principle of prohibition of the abuse of rights.

Whoever admits the existence of this principle in the legal system strives to identify the cases of positive law from which it can be inferred. From this point of view, the prohibition of emulation acts is called into question; the treatment of the illicit reason that induces to contract; the principle of correctness; the repression of oppressive clauses; the rule on the threat to assert one's own right; the rule of objective good faith. It is precisely in the inseparable connection with the objective good faith that administrative jurisprudence currently reconstructs the presence in legal system of the principle of prohibition of abuse of rights. In this sense, the prohibition of abuse of law, through the connection with the obligations of good faith, objective and correct, is considered to be founded in the duty of social solidarity.

It is good to point out that the attempt, which can in principle be agreed, to find a positive right to the prohibition of abuse of rights does not in the least detract from its peculiar function of acting as a "valve" of acceptance (or if you prefer contamination of) of instances emerging from the society in which it operates. These instances, in fact, in a given historical period could highlight the contrast with the duty of solidarity (and with the obligations of good faith and correctness) of behavior that cannot be blamed in previous historical periods. According to the writer, the controversial principle of the prohibition of abuse of rights emerges precisely from the auscultation, to which the jurist is called, of ethical and political needs manifested in a particular society in contrast with beliefs that are declining. It is with reference to this aspect that also emerges the ancient recurrent concern regarding the figure of abuse, namely the distrust of powers of control and appreciation of the invasive judge with respect to prerogatives recognized to private individuals and above all dangerous for legal certainty.

Recognizing such a power to judges does not constitute, however, a reason for excessive alarm, especially in a system dotted with the provision of general clauses.

It must be immediately clear, however, that by definition this control function cannot be carried out in the abstract, but must always be anchored to circumstances of a particular conduct or a concrete relationship. The abuse presupposes the right (or the subjective position of advantage) and its (apparent) exercise. Thus, the task of the judge is to unify the presence of those concrete circumstances which render abusive what apparently would be the exercise of the right, namely those circumstances which indicate the deviation of exercise of the right by the purpose assigned by the law.

In this direction, the jurisprudence we have seen so far seems to go, which alongside the (a) ownership of the right and (b) the discretion in its concrete exercise, lists among the constituent elements of the abuse, (c) the circumstance that (the exercise), even if formally respectful of the frame attributable to that right, is carried out according to censurable methods with respect to an evaluation criterion, legal or extra-juridical; the fact that, due to such a mode of operation, there is an unjustified disproportion between the benefit of the right holder and the sacrifice to which the counterpart is subjected[740].

FROM THE ABUSE OF RIGHT TO ABUSE OF (OR IN) PROCESS

As far as procedural prerogatives are concerned, the jurisprudence of legitimacy is now constant in considering the principle of abuse of law prohibition also applicable in the process. It is sufficient to point out how they came back to the

740 CJEU, C-373/17P, Agria Polska and others v. Commission of 20 September 2018, op. cit.

issue through Union jurisprudence, pointing out that the general nature of the principle derives from the fact that every system that aspires to completeness and functionality must "protect itself" to avoid that the rights guaranteed by it are exercised or realized, by a judicial intervention, in an "abusive" way, that is excessive and/or distorted.

For this reason, the need to identify a limit to abuse extends from the substantive law to the process, transcends the peculiar connotations of the various systems, finding wide response not only in the internal legal systems, but also in the supranational ones and being unequivocally resolved. Both are at a regulatory level that interpretative, in the sense that the distorted use of right to act or react in court, aimed at achieving a different advantage and/or contrary to the purpose for which the right or the procedural right is recognized, does not allow protection. It is therefore considered that the abuse of discretion, that is the improper and distorted use of discretionary power that the law confers on the trial, is in contrast with the principles of correctness and good faith and with the constitutional principle of due process. It has been correctly pointed out then that the abusive phenomenology can be realized both in the form of abuse of and in process.

The use of the notion of abuse of process has also assumed importance in administrative litigation, with a variety of cases now varied and complex, which, without any pretense of completeness, it is considered appropriate to briefly review. In one of the first cases, the notion of abuse was used to declare the appeal against a measure that granted exactly what was requested by the request of the addressee inadmissible. The abuse of the trial then had "greater visibility" on the consequences relating to the non-appeal of the administrative provision.

The abuse of trial was also identified in administration's behavior, which, having failed to execute the first-level protective order, decided to appeal the ruling on the merits that, in the erroneous conviction of compliance by the administration of the precautionary order, had declared the matter of contention ceased. Again, it was considered a procedural abuse and, therefore, inadmissible that reproduced those already as abuses of judicial protection as a whole, but also abuses that occur in the process and concern the completion of specific acts of the proceeding.

There are also cases in which the absence of abuse is considered among the conditions to establish the existence of interest to resort, namely the merit of the action. The massive and, moreover, a serious recourse to the abuse of the trial took place in the matter of lack of jurisdiction in the context of appeals, excluding the fact that the lack of jurisdiction of the court of jurisdiction in the judgments, prescribes that such a defect is detected if deducted for a specific reason against the head of the contested decision which, implicitly or explicitly, has established jurisdiction.

The peculiar trait of this last sentence is the analysis firmly anchored to the peculiarities of the specific case. The jurisprudence far from announcing a general and abstract rule about the inadmissibility of the appeal motive proposed by those who in the first instance established administrative jurisdiction, was asked to verify concretely the existence of circumstances that could indicate-prove the abusiveness of the procedural behavior of the appellant. However, this aspect has been completely neglected by the subsequent jurisprudence.

THE RIGHT OF ACCESS TO JUSTICE AND THE PROHIBITION OF ABUSE OF A DOMINANT POSITION

The right to access justice and to defend one's own interests are fundamental constitutional rights for any democratic society. This implies that the company in a dominant position must, like any other natural or legal person, be able to defend its interests, even against its competitors and/or its customers. It was also stated by EU institutions that a "dominant producer is not required to subsidize its competitors"[741].

However, the dominant company could use its own resources, deriving from its position of supremacy in the market, to carry out legal actions against its competitors, with the sole purpose of hindering and/or preventing their access to the market, increasing their costs. In these cases, in addition to the negative

741 See the decision of the European Commission of 29 July 1987, case IV/32.279, BBI/Boosey & Hawks, in OJ, L-286/1987, pp. 36ss. The procedure in question was then concluded by the European Commission with a final decision to close the case, because the investigation did not find a violation of article 102 TFEU (at the time, Article 86 EEC). For further details see: L. LOVDAHL GORMSEN, A principled approach to abuse of dominance in European competition law, op. cit., R. NAZZINI, The foundations of European Union competition law: The objective and principles of article 102, op. cit., R. O'DONOGHUE, J. PADILLA, The law and economics of article 102 TFEU, op. cit., P. NIHOUL, The ruling of the General Court in intel: Towards the end of an effect-based approach in European competition law?, op. cit., pp. 56ss. J. BOURGEOIS, D. WAELBROECK (eds), Ten years of effects-based approach in EU competition law: State of play and perspectives, op. cit., J. DREXL, W. KERBER, R. PODSZUN (eds), Competition policy and the economic approach: Foundations and limitations, op. cit., L. LOVDAHL GORMSEN, Are anti-competitive effects necessary for an analysis under article 102 TFEU?, op. cit., pp. 224ss.

effects on competition, the use of procedural strategies also produces a distortion of the judicial system, since it is used for purposes and functions different from those assigned by the law (in particular, the genuine protection of legal situations that the plaintiff considers to be injured by actions or omissions by the defendant).

In this way, all the complexity of choices that the interpreter has to carry out emerges whenever he is called upon to evaluate the application of article 102 TFEU[742] to judicial proceedings brought about by the undertaking in a dominant position.

If the right of the dominant firm to access justice in order to defend its interests is excessively limited, it ends up essentially to subsidize the competitors of the dominant undertaking and, therefore, carries out an operation of economic leadership there is a risk of leaving unpunished actions that substantially distort the judicial system and which, at the same time, undermine competition.

With this in mind, EU institutions seem to resort to the abuse of law as a distinctive criterion between the (genuine) exercise of procedural prerogatives, and therefore immune to antitrust law, and the abuse of such prerogatives, which, if instead put in place from a dominant undertaking, would fall within the scope of the competition rules.

THE RIGHT OF ACCESS TO JUSTICE AND THE PROHIBITION OF ABUSE OF A DOMINANT POSITION: T-111/96, ITT PROMEDIA V. COMMISSION CASE OF 17 JULY 1998

The issue of interaction between the right to access to justice and the abuse of a dominant position has been addressed by the EU Court in ITT Promedia v. Commission case[743], which is still the leading case in the matter in question[744].

742 L. LOVDAHL GORMSEN, Are anti-competitive effects necessary for an analysis under article 102 TFEU?, op. cit.

743 See decision of the European Commission (rejection of the complaint) of 21 May 1996, case IV. 35268, ITT Promedia/Belgacom. From the General Court sse: T-111/96, ITT Promedia v. Commission of 17 July 1998, op. cit. For further analysis see: R. WHISH, D. BAILEY, Competition law, Oxford University Press, Oxford, 2015.

744 It should be noted, however, that a first indication of the possibility that the abuse of the exercise of procedural rights could constitute an abuse of a dominant position is found in the decision of the European Commission's BBI/Boosey & Hawks (see, A. JONES, B. SUFRIN, EU Competition law: Text, cases and materials, Oxford University Press, Oxford, 2015, pp. 564ss). The case arose

ITT Promedia v. Commission of 17 July 1998 originated in a dispute between the former Belgian telephony monopolist, the Belgacom (the first RTT entity), and the ITT Promedia company, which was the first to publish telephone directories in Belgium. At the end of the contract between Belgacom and ITT Promedia, concerning the granting of the latter for the publication of telephone directories in Belgium, the parties did not find an agreement for the renewal collaboration. Following a period of unsuccessful negotiations, ITT Promedia announced that it would continue publishing its telephone directories, without being in possession the authorizations required by national legislation, which essentially recognized a monopoly position for Belgacom. For this reason, the Belgacom company, reacting to ITT Promedia campaign, warned its customers that the former concessionaire's initiative lacked any authorization from Belgacom itself and outside any contractual relationship.

ITT Promedia consequently sued Belgacom for unfair competition and infringement of article 102 TFEU (at the time 86 EEC)[745]. The Belgacom company reacted to ITT Promedia actions, proposing both counterclaims and independent judicial actions against its former concessionaire. Thus, a complex judicial dispute has been established between the two parties. In parallel with national

from the complaint lodged before the European Commission by the BBI company, the newcomer in the market for instruments for British brass orchestras, with which they complained that the dominant company Boosey & Hawks had put in place several practices excluding, between judicial proceedings with regard to copyright in relation to BBI and the interruption of supplies to its distributors that also promoted BBI products and also had debts with Boosey & Hawks. The European Commission, while focusing on the issue of supply disruption, carried out assessments applicable to all actions undertaken by Boosey & Hawks against the threat of the competitor BBI, believing that "a dominant undertaking can always take reasonable steps to protect its commercial interests, provided they are fair and proportionate to the threat (...)". This is because, as already mentioned in the text, "a dominant producer is not required to subsidize its competitors". It therefore follows that "if a client transfers its main activities to the promotion of a competing brand, even a dominant manufacturer may have the power to review its commercial relations with that customer and, after sufficient notice, stop any special relationship". In the present case, however, the Commission considered that "the refusal of any supply to GHH and RCH and the other actions taken against them in reaction to the possible threat of BBI would outweigh the legitimate defense of B & H's commercial interests" (decision by the Commission BBI/Boosey & Hawks, par. 19). For further details see: A. LOOIJETIJN-CLEARIE, C.S. RUSU, M. VEENBRINK, Boosting the enforcement of E competition law at the domestic level, Cambridge Scholar Publishers, London, 2017. O. AKMAM, The concept of abuse in EU competition law: law and economic approaches, Hart Publishing, Oxford & Oregon, Portland, 2012. E. ŞAHIN, Collective redress and European Union competition law, ed. Routledge, London & New York, 2018. A. JONES, B. SUFRIN, EU competition law. Text, cases and materials, Oxford University Press, Oxford, 2016. M.M. DABBAH, International and comparative competition law, Cambridge University Press, Cambridge, 2010.

745 L. LOVDAHL GORMSEN, Are anti-competitive effects necessary for an analysis under article 102 TFEU?, op. cit.

actions, ITT Promedia filed a complaint before the European Commission, complaining that Belgacom's procedural behavior constituted an abuse of a dominant position.

The European Commission, rejecting the complaint, considered that, in principle, "the act of bringing legal action, an expression of the fundamental right to judicial protection"[746], cannot be qualified as "abuse" unless "a case dominant undertaking intents judicial actions i) that cannot reasonably be considered aimed at asserting their rights, therefore only defatigatory, and ii) are conceived in the context of a plan aimed at eliminating competition"[747]. The Commission essentially considered that ITT Promedia complainant had not sufficiently proved the abusive and defatigatory nature of judicial actions proposed by the Belgacom company. The fact that the national courts had ruled out the vexatious nature of the aforesaid counterclaims with which it also complained about the violation by ITT Promedia of the legislation on unfair competition and anti-trust, since it would have carried out commercial activities in the absence of the required authorizations by the national reference legislation. The trial ended with the acceptance, both at first instance and on appeal, of the main application and with the rejection of the counterclaim introduced by Belgacom. Subsequently, ITT Promedia after having requested, without success, access to the data on its subscribers to Belgacom, has again sued it for violation of antitrust rules. The Belgacom company, also on this occasion, filed a counterclaim, similar to the first, for violation of antitrust regulations by ITT Promedia. The Belgian courts upheld the main claim, while they rejected Belgacom's counterclaim, notwithstanding its vexatious nature. Against the two legal actions initiated by ITT Promedia, the Belgacom company sued the latter asking for the fulfillment of a clause in the concession contract that obliged it to transfer, free of charge, to the grantor all information, patent licenses and, in general, all specifications and know-how acquired during the concession period and necessary for the publication of telephone directories. In the context of this third process, ITT Promedia was instead to propose a counterclaim, claiming the vexatious nature of Belgacom's actions. However, the judges rejected both applications.

746 L. LOVDAHL GORMSEN, Are anti-competitive effects necessary for an analysis under article 102 TFEU?, op. cit.

747 L. LOVDAHL GORMSEN, Are anti-competitive effects necessary for an analysis under article 102 TFEU?, op. cit.

The decision of the Commission was confirmed by EU Court, which, ruling on the appeal proposed by ITT Promedia, considered legitimate the two conditions used by the European Commission to establish the application of prohibition under article 102 TFEU to the proposed judicial actions from the company in a dominant position. The General Court also provided further indications regarding the actual application of the aforementioned test established by the Commission, with particular reference to the first requirement relating to the nature of the defatigation or non-action[748].

Firstly, the court held that, as regards the time period in which to place itself in order to analyze the vexatious nature of prosecution, only the situation existing at the time when the action in question is taken into consideration must be taken into consideration.

Secondly, what should be assessed at the time is not to establish whether the rights which the undertaking concerned were actually existed, or whether the latter was founded, but to establish if such action had the purpose to assert those that, at that moment, the enterprise could reasonably consider were its rights.

It follows, from the General Court in our days' judgment, that to satisfy the first test criterion established by the Commission, the unreasonableness of the action, that is its defatigatory nature, should be manifested by the action itself, by analogy it happens, for example, for issues of admissibility of the action. This is evidenced by the fact that on several occasions the court has held that the groundlessness of merits of the judicial action was not sufficient to establish the defatigatory/vexatious nature of the same[749]. The first test criterion therefore

748 L. LOVDAHL GORMSEN, Are anti-competitive effects necessary for an analysis under article 102 TFEU?, op. cit.

749 In this regard, the reasoning of the General Court must be interpreted in so far as it considered that "the examination of the question whether the Belgian legislation governing the publication of telephone directories was compatible with Community law could not have shown that the first two Belgacom's judicial actions were not intended to assert what the latter, at the time when it brought them, could reasonably be considered as their own rights, derived from that legislation, and that the two actions were merely defatigatory" (par. 94). This is because, "this matter belonged to the examination of the merits, which was the responsibility of the national court seised by Belgacom with the first two legal actions" and, therefore, the Commission was not considered competent (or even obliged) to conduct the aforementioned analysis, for the purpose of ascertaining the alleged abuse of company's conduct in a dominant position (ibid., § 95). According to the Court of First Instance, to support the opposite interpretation of the first of the criteria in the above mentioned test for the application of TFEU to the judicial proceedings brought by the dominant undertaking, "would make the judicial protection of dominant undertakings practically impossible, not to risk being guilty of infringement of art. 86 of the Treaty for the mere fact of having carried out a judicial action, should ensure, before proposing such action, that the legislation on which they base their rights is compatible with European law (...)". For analysis see: R. O'DONOGHUE, J. PADILLA, The Law

requires proof that the judicial action is, from an objective point of view, devoid of any foundation. The existence of abusive behavior should, a fortiori, be ruled out in all cases where the judicial applications proposed by the dominant undertaking have been accepted by the courts.

Lastly, the court observed that the two cumulative criteria, constituting an exception to the general principle of judicial protection, which guarantees respect for the law, must be interpreted and applied strictly, so as not to make the application of general principle impossible[750].

The teachings of ITT Promedia case v. Commission of 17 July 1998 were fully confirmed by the court in its judgment T-119/09, Protégé International v. Commission of 13 September 2012[751]. On that occasion, it was reiterated in an even more explicit way that the fact that the national courts declared the judicial action of the undertaking in a dominant position to be unfounded is not in itself sufficient to consider it defatigatory under of the first ITT Promedia test criterion.

THE RIGHT OF ACCESS TO JUSTICE AND PROHIBITION OF ABUSE OF A DOMINANT POSITION: CONCLUDING REMARKS

ITT Promedia v. Commission case of 17 July 1998 highlights, first of all, the affinity (if not the similness) between the test established there for the application of article 102 TFEU and that established by EU case law on the abuse of rights[752].

The first criterion of ITT Promedia test is the same criterion of objective reasonableness of the action, developed within EU jurisprudence on the subject of abuse of law. In both cases, it is required to demonstrate that a behavior

and Economics of article 102 TFEU, op. cit., which is affirmed that: "the fact that the dominant firm prevailed in litigation should be an absolute defence, unless, perhaps, there was some subsequent authority for saying that no reasonable court could have reached the conclusion that it reached" (p. 652).

750 T-119/09, Protégé International v. Commission of 13 September 2012, ECLI:EU:C:2012:422, published in the electronic Reports of the cases.

751 T-119/09, Protégé International v. Commission of 13 September 2012, op. cit., pp. 56-57. In the same way, to satisfy the first test criterion ITT Promedia, it must be demonstrated not only, and not so much, the groundlessness (in point of fact and / or law) of the legal action brought by the company in a dominant position, but the defatigatory/vexatious nature of the same (at the time when it was proposed) (paragraph 59).

752 L. LOVDAHL GORMSEN, Are anti-competitive effects necessary for an analysis under article 102 TFEU?, op. cit.

that is formally compatible with a prerogative recognized by EU law is actually aimed at achieving a contrary, or different, purpose from that for which it was recognized.

Regarding the second test criterion elaborated in ITT Promedia, it does not seem to be that ratione application the subjective criterion elaborated by the aforementioned EU jurisprudence in cases of abuse of law. The second criterion of ITT Promedia test refers essentially to the exclusionary intent of the dominant company, to be demonstrated through the evidence of the insertion of judicial action within a complex exclusionary strategy. Also, in this context, as required for the second test criterion elaborated by EU jurisprudence on the subject of abuse of law, a sort of objectification of the subjective element proceeds.

The reference to the figure of abuse in ITT Promedia case diverges, however, from EU jurisprudence on the abuse of right to a specific profile, which is that of qualifying the figure of abuse and, consequently, its sanction. This is the second reflection that comes from the ITT Promedia case.

In ITT Promedia v. Commission of 17 July 1998, the abuse of right of access to justice by the firm in position does not assume an independent function, but constitutes the subsumption in the specific case of the situation of abuse of a dominant position pursuant to article 102 TFEU. The application of ITT Promedia test does not therefore reveal the abuse of law as an autonomous figure of offense, instead constituting the applicative/specific criterion of the abusive case referred to in article 102 TFEU[753].

From this point of view, in this case the connection of the figure of abuse of right with the situation of dominant position (rectius, the subsumption of the first within the second) entails the application of sanctions provided for in article 102 TFEU, primarily, of those pecuniary ones.

In the jurisprudence, the prohibition of abuse of EU law emerges as an autonomous figure, and for this reason, the sanction against those who have abused the prerogative recognized by the law is one of those "typical" of the theory of abuse, that is the inefficacy towards the author of abuse of the benefits foreseen by the aforesaid prerogative[754].

753 P. NIHOUL, The ruling of the General Court in intel: Towards the end of an effect-based approach in European competition law?, op. cit.

754 See from the American Supreme Court the sentence: Professional Real Estate Investors (PRE) v. Columbia Pictures Industries, 508 U.S. pp. 60-61 (1993). According to the court: "(...) the lawsuit must be objectively baseless in the sense that no reasonable litigant could realistically expect success on the merits (...) if an objective litigant could conclude that the suit is reasonably calculated (...)".

The third reflection on ITT Promedia test is that it appears to be substantially identical to that developed by the Noerr-Pennington jurisprudence of the US Supreme Court[755]. According to the latter in fact the defendant in court to support the sham exception with respect to the judicial action of the company in a dominant position should demonstrate: (i) the objective and manifestly groundlessness of the action (which must therefore be "objective baseless"); and (ii) the anti-competitive intent of the actor[756].

Regarding the first part of the test, the respondent should show that no reasonable appellant would expect the acceptance of the action. Only if this first part of the test is proved, the judge will then have to assess the defendant's arguments about the existence of an anti-competitive intent on the part of the plaintiff. From this point of view, the respondent must prove that the actor has only acted to hinder the defendant's activities, using the process itself (and not its outcome) as an anti-competitive tool. In this case, it is also a mixed test, that is, that requires an appreciation both on the objective scope of the application and on the subjective one (linked to actor's intention)[757].

The difference between US jurisprudence and ITT Promedia doctrine seems instead to consist in the fact that, according to the American jurisprudence, the acceptance of the sham exception does not imply, obviously, the ascertainment of the responsibility from unlawful antitrust, but simply that a determined behavior it is not protected by the Noerr-Pennington doctrine. This means that the antitrust responsibility must also be demonstrated following the normal rules of procedure and evidence[758].

---

755 S. BIEZCZAT, First amendment protection for unfair labor practices. Reexaming the Noerr-Pennington doctine, in University of Illinois Law Review, 2017, n. 4, pp. 1586ss.

756 The Supreme Court emphasized that: "(...) only if challenged litigation is objectively meritless may a court examine the litigant's subjective motivation. Under this second part of our definition of sham, the court should focus on whether the baseless lawsuit conceals "an attempt to interfere directly with the business relationships of a competitor," Noerr, op. cit., par. 144 (emphasis added), through the "use (of) the governmental process-as opposed to the outcome of that process-as an anti-competitive weapon," Omni, 499 U. S., at (par. 14). This two tiered process requires the plaintiff to disprove the challenged lawsuit's legal viability before the court will entertain evidence of suit's economic viability (...)" (par. 61).

757 P. NIHOUL, The ruling of the General Court in intel: Towards the end of an effect-based approach in European competition law?, op. cit.

758 Note, in any case, that the doctrine that dealt with the AstraZeneca case suggested a reading of the abuse not only of the second abusive case, but also of the first claiming that "As the granting of SPC's is one of those IPS that have undergone a process of harmonization, AstraZeneca is a law enforcement agency, can be unlawfully extended to the SPC terms, could be construed as a financial gain (M. MAGGIOLINO, L. MONTAGNANI, Astrazeneca's abuse of IPR-related procedures: A

Also, for this reason, it is an extremely difficult test to satisfy. Also, in PRE judgment, the court held that "(...) of course, even a plaintiff who defeats the defendant's claim to Noerr immunity by demonstrating both the objective and the subjective components of a sham must still prove a substantive antitrust violation. Proof of a sham merely deprives the defendant of immunity; it does not relieve the plaintiff of the obligation to establish all other elements of his claim" (par. 61). This explains the low rate of acceptance, in US jurisprudence, of counterclaims based on the alleged infringement of the antitrust law by the plaintiff.

ABUSE OF PROCEDURAL RIGHTS OF LAW AND OF DOMINANT POSITION

Recourse to the figure of abuse of law can constitute a useful application criterion of article 102 TFEU to behaviors that, at least formally, appear to be the exercise of procedural prerogatives[759].

In T-321/05, AstraZeneka UK v. Commission case of 1st July 2010 the use of the figure of abuse of right is implicit in the reasoning of EU institutions, although influencing the analysis in a clear and decisive way. In the second case, the prohibition of abuse of right is raised to a general principle of national law and is expressly referred to by the Council of state as the decisive element of the dispute.

Anticipating the conclusions of the analysis that will be carried out below, it is noted that in T-321/05, AstraZeneka UK v. Commission case of 1st July 2010 the reasoning of EU institutions correctly uses the figure of abuse of law, since it focuses the analysis on the evidence related to behavior deviation censored by

hypothesis of ant-trust offense, Abuse of Rights, and IPR Misuse, in World Competition, 34, 2011, pp. 257ss). The thesis supported by the Authors, however, is difficult to reconcile with the notion of abuse of law. In the first case, in fact, the dominant company had provided untruthful information, or in any case misleading, to the national authorities, which leads to the conclusion for the non-compliance of the behavior challenged with the scheme of the prerogative recognized by the law. In other words, the behavior challenged in the context of the first type of abuse, precisely because in itself reproachful, also in light of the obligations of collaboration incumbent on the dominant undertaking, can not even be formally considered compatible with the scheme of the prerogative that it pretends to exercise, therefore placing itself outside the typical scheme of such a prerogative. This divergence between concrete behavior and the hypothetical scheme of prerogative is sufficient to place behavior outside the case of abuse of rights.

759 P. NIHOUL, The ruling of the General Court in intel: Towards the end of an effect-based approach in European competition law?, op. cit.

the function for which the prerogative, of which the contested behavior would constitute the exercise, has been recognized by the law. In the second case, instead, the figure (rectius, the principle) of the abuse of right is used, according to the writer, in a distorted way, since it seems to act as a slogan, or as an argument, to support an analysis that seems to resolve in the application article 102 TFEU or, at the very least, the requalification of the offense in question to the dominant undertaking[760].

ABUSE OF THE LAW, OF PROCEDURE AND OF A DOMINANT POSITION: T-321/05, ASTRAZENEKA UK V. COMMISSION CASE OF 1ST JULY 2010 READ IN TERMS OF ABUSE OF LAW

To analyze the use of abuse of rights in T-321/05, AstraZeneka UK v. Commission case of 1st July 2010 it is considered more interesting to dwell on the second abusive case. The reason for this choice is that - unlike the first unauthorized case, in which the behaviors per se were reprehensible, such as having provided untruthful or reticent information to the regulatory authorities - the second abusive case concerns behaviors (at least formally) compatible with (and complying with) the exercise of a prerogative granted by EU law.

As part of the second abusive case, the AstraZeneca group, as will be recalled, was held responsible for the violation of article 102 TFEU in order to have withdrawn in Sweden, Norway and Denmark the marketing authorizations for the capsule version of the Losec order to delay the entry of genericists and parallel importers into the aforementioned markets.

Even without explicitly mentioning the figure of abuse of rights, nor the test drawn up by the Court in ITT Promedia v. Commission of 17 July 1998, EU institutions considered that the withdrawal of the authorizations by the AstraZeneca group was not intended to protect their legitimate interests, nor was it supported by objective justifications.

First of all, EU judges highlighted the fact that at the time of the revocation of authorizations, AstraZeneca no longer had an exclusive right on their studies, having therefore used all the time necessary, according to the legislator, to recover the investments made. Secondly, the withdrawal of the marketing

760 P. NIHOUL, The ruling of the General Court in intel: Towards the end of an effect-based approach in European competition law?, op. cit.

authorization was not necessary for the introduction of a new line of the Losec drug.

On the profile of objective justifications, AstraZeneca's thesis about the necessity to avoid the penetrating requirements of pharmaco-vigilance was considered contradictory, (since the authorizations had not been revoked in other member states with heavy pharma-covigilance obligations), even before which is inadmissible, because it was raised for the first time before the court.

As a result, the entry of generic products is hindered or delayed onto the market. On closer inspection, the reasoning used in this case is none other than to demonstrate satisfaction with the first condition of ITT Promedia test. In regards to the second condition of ITT Promedia test, that is the subjective element, EU institutions have proved, through accurate documentary evidence, that with the behavior challenged AZ as the court stated in paragraph 814 of the ruling (first instance), intended to impede the introduction of generic products and parallel imports.

Finally, it should be noted that an important role in the conclusions of EU institutions was the fact that the disputed behavior, i.e. the revocation of authorizations, took place after the expiry of the exclusivity period on the use of their data, recognized by EU law to the AstraZeneca company. The system had therefore introduced a (temporal) limitation to the exclusive right of the dominant company over the use of its data and laboratory studies, thus recognizing a genuine right of genericists to access them in the event of marketing of products essentially similar to that to which the studies and data in question referred.

Precisely on this aspect, it should be noted that the key feature of the second abusive case in AstraZeneca is represented by the attempt by the dominant company to obtain a result contrary to EU legislation, i.e. a result that circumvented the application of the restriction on exclusivity of the dominant undertaking over its own data and thus, in fact, extended the exclusive period of the AZ group to the data and studies in question. The court highlights this fact clearly when it states that AstraZeneca's conduct had the consequence of "rendering the limitation that the European legislation on abbreviated procedures provides for the exclusive exploitation of information from pharmacological, toxicological, and clinical tests"[761].

761 T-321/05, AstraZeneka UK v. Commission of 1st July 2010, op. cit., par. 682. In an even clearer way, the Commission took the view that through its behavior "(...) it would have attempted to artificially preserve its exclusivity on the market, seeking to annul the right conferred by the regulatory framework to the second applicant and applicants subsequent to end of the data exclusivity period, not to

In other words, in T-321/05, AstraZeneka UK v. Commission case of 1st July 2010 was censored the attempt by the dominant company to go beyond the exclusive period that the system had recognized as a time of exclusive exploitation of its studies, necessary and sufficient for the recovery of investments made by the group in the field of research.

ABUSE OF LAW, OF PROCEDURE AND OF A DOMINANT POSITION: THE "SPECIAL RESPONSIBILITY" OF THE COMPANY IN A DOMINANT POSITION

The reading of T-321/05, AstraZeneka UK v. Commission case of 1st July 2010 in the light of the theory of abuse of rights raises the question of the ways in which one can legitimize, from a theoretical point of view, the use of the notion of abuse of law as a case in point in the application of competition law. In other words, it is a matter of understanding on what basis one could justify that the same action is potentially punishable by the imposition of heavy fines if implemented by an undertaking in a dominant position, while it may escape this sanction if carried out from an undertaking which does not hold such a position.

The answer to the question can be found in the aforementioned notion of special responsibility of the dominant undertaking. Since the Michelin I[762] ruling, Community and national judges have repeatedly stressed the existence of a duty of "special responsibility" incumbent on the dominant undertaking, stating that the dominant position "involves the subjection (of the company) to a particular statute of responsibility, by virtue of which (it) is bound to behaviors different from those normally allowed to market operators and to the observance of a greater degree of diligence and precaution in expanding its activity in the market, in order not to further compromise with its conduct the residual competitive confrontation, already affected by the significant market power of which it is held"[763].

---

provide the data contained in the files of the first applicant "(see judgment of the court, § 645, where the conclusions of the decision adopted by the Commission are reported).

762 CJEU, C-322/81, Michelin of 3 November 1983, ECLI:EU:C:1983:313, I-03461, par. 57. For further details see: W. VERLOREN VAN THEMAAT, B. REUDER, European competition law: A case commentary, Edward Elgar Publishers, Cheltenham, 2018. P. WILLIS, Introduction to EU competition law, CRC Press, New York, 2013.

763 The concept recalls the paradigm of the "as if" of ordoliberal matrix (even if not shared by all

It is all evidence of a notion, of liberal derivation[764], which clearly expresses that conception of the application of article 102 TFEU as a means of containing private economic power, according to the paradigm for which "whoever holds power has the right to be free and who wants to be free should not hold power"[765]. The rigidity of the duty in question is proportional to the degree of power held by the company in a dominant position[766].

As has been consistently held in doctrine and jurisprudence, the notion of special responsibility does not in itself pertain to the purpose of configuring the abuse of a dominant position, but simply implies that, "when they are able to restrict competition, even common and totally legitimate commercial behavior, if adopted by non-dominant companies can be abusive if adopted by a dominant

school affiliates), according to which to avoid the risks deriving from the concentration of private economic power in the hands of a given subject, the latter should behave "as if" operated in markets characterized by perfect competition. The standard "as if" moreover of an economic nature, then found legal basis in the distinction between "performance" and "impedement competition". The first is a form of permitted competition, the second is not. So, it has been observed that, according to this conception, "since the dominant firm will abuse its position if it engages in hindrance competition, it is under a duty to refrain from such, hence the special responsibility of the dominant firm (...)". For further details see: P. LAROOUCHE, M.P. SCHINKEL, The Oxford Handbook of international antitrust economics, Oxford University Press, Oxford, 2015, pp. 164ss. E. ROUSSEVA, Rethinking exclusionary abuses in EU competition law, Hart Publishing, Oxford & Oregon, Portland, 2010. K. MCMAHON, Interoperability: "indispensability" and "special responsibility", in high technology markets, in Tulane Journal of Technology & Intellectual Property, 9, 2007. R. NAZZINI, The foundations of EU competition law: the objective and principles of article 102, op. cit.

764 E. ROUSSEVA, Rethinking exclusionary abuses in EU competition law, op. cit., pp. 72ss. R.A. CORCHO, Can we finally say farewell to the "special responsibility" of dominant companies?, in C.D. EHLERMANN, M. MARQUIS, European Competition Law Annual: 2007-A reformed approach to article 82 EC, Hart Publishing, Oxford & Oregon, Portland, 2008, pp. 320-324, it had a "position of honor" in the Commission's Guidelines on Excluding Abuses. In fact, in § 1 of the aforementioned Guidelines we read that: "Article 82 of the EC Treaty (hereinafter" Article 82 ") prohibits the abusive exploitation of the dominant position. In accordance with the case law, it is not in itself illegal that an undertaking is in a dominant position and that undertaking has the right to compete on the basis of its own merits. However, the company in question has a special responsibility not to allow its conduct to prevent competition which is truly free of distortions in the common market (...)". This demonstrates that this is a concept strongly rooted in European competition law.

765 In CMB case, CJEU claimed that "the material scope of the particular responsibility incumbent on a dominant undertaking must be assessed in the light of case's specific circumstances, which reflect a situation of weakened competition" (joined cases: C-395/96 396/96, of 16 March 2000, I-01365, par. 114). Thus, in the cases of undertakings in a "super-dominance" position, the Community judicature considered the attempt by the aforementioned undertaking to avail itself of "a contractual exclusivity provided for in a given agreement with the public authority in order to expel the only competitor from the market.

766 T-191/98 and 212-214/98, Atlantic Container Line and others v. Commission of 30 September 2003, ECLI:EU:T.2003:245, II-03275, parr. 1461ss.

undertaking"[767]. This was recently reiterated by CJEU that "the level of market power affects, in principle, more on the extent of company's behavior effects in question than on the existence of the abuse as such"[768]. To argue the contrary would mean condemning the mere holding of a company's dominant position.

The role that the special responsibility of the company in a dominant position plays is that of a sort of open general clause, through which the behavior of the company in a dominant position contributes to different obligations and/or behavioral rules dictated by the function performed by article 102 TFEU and thus from the objectives assigned to competition order[769]. These are both general obligations, such as cooperation with the authorities, good faith and loyalty in behavior, as well as negative obligations of abstention from affecting the competitive structure of the market.

It is precisely in the light of its "particular responsibility" that the dominant company cannot abuse its procedural prerogatives, i.e. it cannot "use regulatory procedures to prevent or make it more difficult for competitors to enter the market, in absence of reasons relating to the defense of the legitimate interests of an undertaking engaged in competition based on merit or in the absence of objective justifications"[770].

To these obligations, the most recent jurisprudence has also added positive obligations, that is real duties of activation by the dominant company for the

767 T-191/98 and 212-214/98, Atlantic Container Line and others v. Commission of 30 September 2003, op. cit.

768 Contra, R. NAZZINI, The foundations of European Union competition law. The objective and principles of article 102, op. cit., which is affirmed that: "(...) special responsibility is not a legal doctrine because it does not define legal rules. It is a short-hand to describe and explain their operation. Importantly, the doctrine of special responsibility must not be used as a formula according to which duties and liabilities can be imposed on the dominant undertakings. Duties and liabilities can be imposed on the dominant undertaking only under tests that concretize the general precepts of article 102 in the light of its objective (...). Only to this extent can "special responsibility become a legal doctrine. But the nit would add nothing to the definition other abuse because it would only say that a dominant undertaking has a special responsibility not to abuse its dominant position within the meaning of article 102 (pp. 175) (...) the principle of "special responsibility", frequently invoked in the case law of the court (...) becomes so an independent source of obligations and prohibitions for the companies in dominant position; according to a logic of integration, of the typified obligations, and of balancing, of the conflicting interests, which belongs also to other general clauses, first of all, the rule of good faith which, as is well known, occupies a preminent role in European law of contracts (...)" (pp. 155ss).

769 J. BOURGEOIS, D. WAELBROECK (eds), Ten years of effects-based approach in EU competition law: State of play and perspectives, op. cit.

770 J. BOURGEOIS, D. WAELBROECK (eds), Ten years of effects-based approach in EU competition law: State of play and perspectives, op. cit.

purpose of collaboration with public authorities. Consider, for example, the obligation to correct the errors of the sector regulator enunciated by EU judges in C-280/08P, Deutsche Telekom case of 14 October 2010[771], i.e. those set out in T-321/05, AstraZeneka UK v. Commission case of 1st July 2010 and aimed both at informing the competent authority of the errors committed by the dominant undertaking in submitting an authorization application, and at adopting, between different interpretations of the sectoral legislation, the "more orthodox" one, or the one with lower incidence negative impact on the competitive situation of the market[772].

It is therefore necessary to impose on the dominant undertaking not only the incentive for a decentralized and responsible application of competition law, but also a requirement for active cooperation with the sectoral authorities. In this way, there is a sort of inversion of the traditional duty of aid to the public authorities, since the dominant undertaking has a special responsibility to take action so that the (sectoral) public authority adopts decisions compatible with competition law, or correct its previous decisions contrary to competition law.

In the aforementioned cases, the deviation of the disputed conduct with respect to the objective for which the prerogative has been recognized by the European legal system has been demonstrated. The exclusion from the market of competitors, for a determined time considered by the legislator as necessary for the recovery of the investments made by the inventor, actually represents the objective of the patent regulation in question.

The difference of the present case with the second case in T-321/05, AstraZeneka UK v. Commission case of 1st July 2010 is, in this light, evident.

---

771 C-280/08P, Deutsche Telekom of 14 October 2010, ECLI:EU:C:2010:603, I-09555.

772 F. MURPHY, F. LIBERATORE, Abuse of regulatory procedures-the AstraZeneca case, in European Competition Law Review, 2009, pp. 322-323, which is affirmed that: "in its most basic form, it appears that the Commission's case is that the special responsibility under art. 82 of EC Treaty extends to a dominant company being under a positive obligation to ensure that its marketing authorisations are maintained so that it is easier for generics and parallel imports to come on to the market and thereby compete with the dominant company. The special responsibility prevails regardless of whether or not the dominant company still has a commercial interest in selling the product to which the marketing authorisation relates. Special responsibility also prevails regardless of the fact that the maintenance of the marketing authorisations would impose upon the dominant company continuing updating pharmaco-vigilance obligations that it would have to fund (...) Commission's extension of the special responsibility on dominant companies goes way beyond existing case law. What the Commission is doing in AstraZeneca is introducing a form of compulsory licensing through the back door. If upheld, the Commission's AstraZeneca Decision will have the effect of placing dominant companies under a positive obligation to actively maintain rights (whether exclusive or non-exclusive) they have obtained to commercialise their products, if the maintenance of those rights would make it easier for others to compete with them (...)".

In T-321/05, AstraZeneka UK v. Commission case of 1st July 2010 the reason why the law (rectius, jurisprudence) EU admitted a limitation to the use of the shortened procedure for the marketing of generic products was to protect public health and not to exclude genericists from the market. In T-321/05, AstraZeneka UK v. Commission case of 1st July 2010 therefore had a real deviation from the objective pursued by the contested behavior, compared to that established by sectoral legislation, as interpreted by CJEU jurisprudence.

In T-321/05, AstraZeneka UK v. Commission case of 1st July 2010, the conduct complained of occurred after the expiry of the maximum period of exclusivity recognized by the legislature and had as their purpose to extend the protection beyond the aforementioned period. The behaviors challenged were aimed at benefiting from the maximum period of protection guaranteed by the legislator: nothing more nothing less!

CONCLUDING REMARKS

The "double dimension" represents the relationship between abuse of law and abuse of dominant position The investigation carried out until now leads us to identify, at least, two plans on which the relationship between abuse of a dominant position and law develops.

The first relationship plan can be defined, a little emphatically, of a dogmatic type. The abuse of a dominant position and of law are, in this perspective, in a relationship of specialty between them. This is, to be clear, the position that the prohibition of abuse of a dominant position is merely a specification of the general principle of abuse of rights. The prohibition of abuse of a dominant position is therefore read in light of the logic of the abuse of rights, understood as a deviation from the function assigned to a given position of power and/or supremacy.

From this perspective, the prohibition of abuse of a dominant position becomes one of the privileged fields in which to study the mutation of the concept of power and its source of legitimacy, that is, of subjective law. The market, as a container of various pluralistic interests best expresses the passage from the absolutist and monologic conception of subjective law, as a source of legitimization of power, to a "social" or "functional" and solidarity concept of individual position. of supremacy.

The abuse of a dominant position can therefore be constructed as the deviation of the dominant undertaking's action from the objectives pursued by a given competitive order, such as, for example, that of guaranteeing "equality before competition". In this direction, the principle, already established with reference to the competition law in the United States, remains firm, according to which it is not illegal to interfere in the economic objectives of the competitor if it is required for the achievement of its success. The purpose of those who pursue their own affirmation in the economic field constitutes justification, and discriminates from the responsibility for what, prima facie would be a tort, but the illicit injury begins there where invoking the privilege of competition appears as an abuse.

The analysis of the abuse, understood as a misuse of the function, is carried out on the basis of parameters, general clauses, or otherwise named, "evaluation standards". Suffice it to think, in this sense, of the recurring statements in the case-law concerning: a) normal competition, b) on merits, c) on (or based on) benefits, d) effective, and e) fair. Under this logic, to give a concrete example, offering lower prices than competitors represents the heart of competition based on merits. While applying predatory prices, i.e. below a certain cost threshold, this would be abnormal behavior, abuse of a competitive instrument, since such a policy would hardly find a justification other than the exclusion of competitors from the market. The figure of the abuse of right, that is the position/prerogative of advantage, could, in other words, act as a key to understanding the logic of abuse of a dominant position.

Observe, however, as we have just done, the prohibition of abuse of a dominant position can also be constructed in the light of the theory of prohibition of abuse of rights. The latter is useful for the purpose of the theoretical-dogmatic construction of abuse of dominant position, but nothing adds to the criteria for the concrete application of article 102 TFEU. The analysis on the abusiveness of the conduct by an undertaking in a dominant position will have to be carried out exclusively according to the modalities provided for in article 102 TFEU, as interpreted by EU jurisprudence. Therefore, this analysis cannot be substituted with that used by the jurisprudence on the prohibition of the abuse of right[773].

To be relevant, for the purposes of the concrete application of article 102 TFEU, the figure of abuse of right must be assumed in case of abuse of a dominant position. This is the second plane of relationship between the abuse of a

773 J. BOURGEOIS, D. WAELBROECK (eds), Ten years of effects-based approach in EU competition law: State of play and perspectives, op. cit.

dominant position and law. The abuse of law, in this perspective, detects as a criterion within the case of abuse of a dominant position[774].

With particular reference to behaviors held outside (or by means other than those of the) market, its role is to discriminate between what constitutes a genuine exercise of regulatory prerogatives and their abuse. In other words, as part of the case of abuse of a dominant position, recourse to the figure of abuse of rights assumes importance for the purpose of assigning a regulatory maladjustment to a conduct that is formally compatible with the regulatory framework of a given prerogative.

This is indeed the underlying logic of ITT Promedia v. Commission of 17 July 1998 and T-321/05, AstraZeneka UK v. Commission of 1st July 2010, decided by EU jurisprudence. From the same cases, we can also draw the two cumulative criteria that make possible the subsumption of the figure of abuse of law within the case of prohibition of abuse of a dominant position. The first criterion, more specifically regards the abuse of the prerogative, intended as a deviation from the function assigned to it by the order. This can be identified, either by obtaining an undue advantage, or by obtaining a result different from/contrary to that pursued by the legislation that recognizes the relevant prerogative, and by the defatigatory use of it. The second criterion concerns anti-competitive intent, that is the absence of an alternative justification to the detriment of competition (also intended as a strategy aimed at excluding a single competitor). It has already been noted that, according to EU case law, although it is a subjective requirement, its proof must be based on objective data, information and assessments. It is therefore proposed for the objectification of the subjective criterion, at least for what concerns its assessment.

774 J. BOURGEOIS, D. WAELBROECK (eds), Ten years of effects-based approach in EU competition law: State of play and perspectives, op. cit.

CHAPTER 6

Some critics and observations

REFLECTIONS OF THE DIFFICULTIES OF CJEU AND FUTURE PROSPECTS

We started from the consideration that, although the "European Union" jurisprudence has elaborated a complete definition of the circumstances necessary to ascertain the abuse of law, the concrete applications of the prohibition in question, of a pretoria nature, are very limited and extremely differentiated. From the beginning, it was highlighted how, in the face of the (apparent) inconsistency of the jurisprudence in this regard, the variety of situations in which the abuse is invoked and the multiple meanings that the same takes on from time to time. The question that it is more problematic, at present, is to understand not so much whether a general principle of abuse of law is to be found in EU legal system, but upstream, under what circumstances there is an abuse in the perspective of EU law and if in such cases, the related prohibition may operate. In fact, although in principle CJEU has repeatedly invoked the prohibition of abuse, also elaborating, starting from the pronunciation in C-110/99, Emsland-Stärke case of 14 December 2000, a test of general scope that can facilitate the national judge in verifying the existence of an abuse of the right, are far from the cases in which the prohibition in question was then concretely applied, or whose application has been delegated to the national court, even in the presence of situations manifestly abusive, at least from the perspective of member states. In other words, the abuse of right has been defined by European Union jurisprudence mainly in negative terms: CJEU, in fact, usually comes to believe that the situations of fact submitted to its judgment cannot be considered unfair from the point of view of the right of the Union[775].

775 N.N. SHUIBHNE, The coherence of EU free movement law, constitutional responsibility and the Court of Justice, op. cit., pp. 85ss. A. KJELLGREN, On the border of abuse: CJEU jurisprudence on circumvention, fraud and other misuses of European Union law, op. cit., has highlighted a: "stunningly low practical application value". In the same spirit see: B. HOFSTOFFER, A cascade of rights,

Thus, if "the principle according to which the interested parties cannot abusively or fraudulently avail themselves of community law is constant in the jurisprudence (...) specifying the exact contours is, however, far from easy"[776].

With the aim of systematizing the matter, we then started from an in-depth analysis of CJEU jurisprudence in which the issue of abuse was addressed, opting for a bipartite classification, only partly coinciding with that used by the traditional doctrine.

Starting from the consideration that the notion of abuse is configured as "polymorphic" in relation to the different (national and supranational) areas in which it is emphasized, so that it is almost impossible to give a single definition, it was found that the abuse in Union law took an original connotation, since, understood as synonymous with circumvention and elusion, invests the complex relations between EU and national laws. Particular reference is connected to the linking techniques that allow to go back to the normative discipline applicable to subjective legal situations of private subjects.

It was therefore considered that an interpretative framework aimed at clarifying the attitude of CJEU regarding the abusive manifestations, should take into account the element of marked originality of the context in which the prohibition of abuse of EU law is inserted. Thus, the chosen classification distinguishes the case in which the abusive manifestation involves only EU regulation ("internal abuse of law"), if the latter contains two or more alternative rules that regulate the same case, and the case involving more EU and national laws (cross-border abuse of law). In that regard, it must be borne in mind that, on the one hand, the advantageous situation which the objective of obtaining through abusive conduct may derive from the application both of a provision of the Union, whether it is contained in the Treaty or in provisions secondary legislation, as much as a law of a member state other than the one of origin, invoked as a result of Union law. On the other hand, even the means used to obtain such an advantage, that is to say the abused rule, can be identified in a national or Union standard.

In the case of internal abuse, the abusive behavior, like what happens for the abuse at national level, consists in creating an artificial situation with the sole purpose of formally meeting the conditions foreseen by EU legislation and,

---

or who shall care for little Caterine?, op. cit., pp. 548ss, has defined abuse as: "a frequently tested but ineffective argument (...)".

776 Conclusions of the AG La Pergola in case C-212/97, Centros, op. cit., par. 20.

in this way, benefit from the related benefits. In this case, a single regulation is highlighted: it abused the latter to obtain the advantage envisaged by the same. In the case of cross border abuse, on the other hand, abusive construction involves, or rather finds its foundation in more distinct legal systems, national and EU, where there are "channels of connection" between them, so that the right holder finds himself in the condition to use the norms of a different order in place of those of the order of belonging.

Case studies relating to the hypothesis in which the abusive operation only involves the supranational order has been analyzed first.

The examination of CJEU jurisprudence on the abuse of law in harmonized areas, such as the common agricultural policy, VAT and corporate restructuring, has shown that where the abuse takes place creating an artificial situation for the sole purpose of formally meeting the conditions laid down by EU legislation and, in this way, benefit from the related advantages. Involving only the supranational system, the prohibition of abuse not only finds a generalized application, but has also been elaborated in its current characteristics. It is with reference to the fact, that the jurisprudence has specified the conditions in the presence of which the presence of abusive behavior can be found, coining the abuse test in C-110/99, Emsland-Stärke sentence of 14 December 2000 applied (or sometimes only recalled) in other sectors.

Specifically, it has been observed that CJEU has defined over time, albeit with the hesitations and physiological oscillations in the praetorian law, uniform conditions in the presence of which abusive behavior can be found in the field of common agricultural policy. What must be emphasized in this regard is that in these cases CJEU not only mentioned in principle the prohibition in question, but at the same time gave the referring court the power to apply it directly to the case under consideration, in presence of very specific circumstances and very often predetermined by CJEU itself.

The same orientation was also found in the tax area, with case law: C-255/02, Halifax and others of 21 February 2006, and C-321/05, Kofoed v. Skateministeriet of 5 July 2007 pronounces the latter, in which the general scope of the principle was also recognized. Fiscal matter therefore represents a definitive turning point in the affirmation of the prohibition of abuse of rights, proving still today full of ideas. In particular, it should be remembered here that in this sector, faced with illegal constructions by private individuals, the alternative was between the use of prohibition of abuse and the adoption of a restrictive interpretation of the discipline subject to abuse, techniques, which allow (both) to sanction the abuse; this alternative was resolved by CJEU in the sense of preferring the application of prohibition of abuse, which operates at a time after the admissibility of legislation[777].

The prohibition of abuse, to be applied, requires a double verification to the national court: it is necessary to ascertain that the objective of law has not been achieved and that the private person wanted to obtain an advantage deriving from European Union legislation by creating artificial conditions necessary to achieve this advantage.

On this point, it was pointed out that the subjective element becomes the cornerstone of the prohibition in question, although, in the jurisprudential evolution, it has been progressively "objectified", valuing, more than the subjective will to obtain an advantage understood as the absence of an economic and commercial justification. Thus, in C-515/03, Eichsfelder Schlachtbetrieb GmbH v. Hauptzollamt Hamburg-Jonas case of 23 July 2005, the existence of an abuse was excluded, since the artificiality was absent, given the substantial and non-reversible transformation of the products previously exported. Equally, in C-155/13, Società Italiana Commercio and Servizi srl (SICES) and others v. Customs Office of the Customs of Venice case of 13 May 2014, the real interest of importers not to be sanctioned, which showed the presence of an economic and commercial justification, was valued[778].

As regards the consequences arising from the application of prohibition, it was noted, instead, that in this context CJEU did not firmly opt for the classification of prohibition as a rule allowing to delimit the scope of application of Union law or restrict the exercise of a right conferred by Union's legal order[779].

777 As can be seen, the plans are different. The non-perfect coincidence of the choice between restrictive interpretation and the application of the prohibition of abuse is well highlighted in the opinion of AG Poiares Maduro, presented in case: C-255/02, Halifax and others of 21 February 2006, op. cit., par. 53.

778 The driving role of the subjective element in the construction of the prohibition must not however be brought to the extreme consequences. It is worth remembering in this regard how the same is not sufficient in itself to prove the existence of an abuse of the right. In this sense, RBS Deutschland Holdings GmbH and Weald Leasing Ltd quotations referred to, in which CJEU recalls that the establishment of devices aimed at obtaining the advantages deriving from the application of Union rules in accordance with their objectives is not abusive, thus demonstrating how it is always necessary, because the prohibition of abuse is applicable, a joint application of both criteria.

779 For example, in Cremer ruling we read that "the application of the regulation in question, together with commission's Regulation n. 171/64, could not in any case be extended until you get back abusive practices of economic operators (...)"; on the contrary, in case: C-255/02, Halifax and others of 21 February 2006, it is specified that, where there is evidence of abuse, the rule of law must be interpreted, notwithstanding its letter, in the sense that it does not actually confer the right.

In this regard, from a theoretical point of view, it seems more correct to classify the prohibition in question as a limit to the exercise of the right, also in consideration of the function that it assumes, it does not seem, however, that the question, in practice, affects the sanction, consisting in the return or non-allocation of the advantage.

The picture changes significantly if the abusive construction involves more legal systems, realizing what in the course of the work has been defined as a "triangulation" between legal systems: these are the most problematic hypotheses, as they are extraneous to the abuse of law at the national level. For this reason, it is considered opportune, at the conclusion of the work, to dwell more deeply on the results of the analysis of the jurisprudence related to this second hypothesis, which, on the one hand, characterizes EU's legal system more, as a supranational system intrinsically connected to the national laws of member states and, on the other hand, it deals with nodal aspects of the functioning of the internal market and of policies aimed at favoring its development.

Taking into account the origin, respectively, of the abused norm and of the norm from which the advantage derives, in chapter 3 the cases in which the individual, through the exercise of the right of circulation, which represents the "vehicle" to move from one system to another, pre-establishes the conditions to circumvent the legislation of the member state of belonging and to apply another national legislation more favorable in itself.

The study of jurisprudence has highlighted the gap between statute of principle and application of themselves, demonstrating that the same manifestation, considered abusive under the "lens" of the member state of origin, cannot be qualified as such by EU law, for mainly structural reasons.

In more detail, the analysis of the cases relating to the pseudo-foreign corporations and the controlled foreign companies has shown that the reason why CJEU excludes the possibility of using the prohibition of abuse even in the face of clearly elusive constructions is that, in interpreting the provisions of the Treaty concerning the freedoms of movement, he has difficulty in identifying those elements that were mentioned in the paragraphs of Chapter II as constituting the so-called abuse test.

In fact, the Luxembourg judge has interpreted, with a formal approach, the rules concerning the establishment of a company and the possibility for it to carry out an activity through a secondary center. From this, it follows that the purpose of the rule is inevitably respected when the latter applies. On the other hand, when a company with headquarters in one member state crosses the border for the first and only time, setting up a branch in another member state, as was the case in C-79/85, Segers of 10 July 1986, houses C-212/97, Centros of 9 March 1999 and C-167/01, Inspire Art of 30 September 2003, or a subsidiary, as in the lodging of C-196/04, Cadbury Schweppes and Cadbury Schweppes Overseas case of 12 September 2006, there is no evidence to establish the existence of a "U-shaped" operation[780] from the perspective of EU law, that is to say the type of transaction that can be considered most abusive. The movement of legal person, for EU law, is only one. When the company incorporated in a member state B, even with the primary objective of operating in member state A, crosses the border, exercising for the first time freedom of establishment, that which for member state A is a "purely internal" artificially situation rendered intra-state, becomes instead the case of a foreign company requesting registration of its branch in the host member state.

On the other hand, the analysis of the most significant jurisprudence concerning the freedom to provide services shows that CJEU has found an abusive demonstration in the behavior of private individuals who, in fact, established in the country of destination of services, acts as a service provider. The change of perspective with respect to C-212/97, Centros case law of 9 March 1999 is evident. If in both cases the CJEU recognizes in principle the prohibition of abuse, only with reference to the free provision of services makes it possible for the member state to sanction it, thereby demonstrating that it recognizes the artificial operation.

In this regard, the examination of casuistry has shown that in this juncture EU's system, looking at the activity carried out, has the tools to verify that a freedom has been misused in place of another, starting from structural comparison between the constituent elements of the two cases.

Secondly, the case law concerning cases where the right of movement by a private individual was invoked in order to circumvent the otherwise applicable national legislation and at the same time investigate the application of the secondary EU legislation was analyzed. As such, the judgments that dealt with qualification shopping and circumvention in the context of free movement of persons were analyzed, in particular with regard to the right of residence of the non-EU spouse.

780 With regard to case: C-196/04, Cadbury Schweppes and Cadbury Schweppes Overseas of 12 September 2006 lodging, then, the situation is even simpler, as in these cases the lack of activity of the main office is not deduced, but simply elusive reasons. Well, as already pointed out, when the right of establishment has been correctly exercised at least on a formal level, the reasons are not relevant.

The examination of the case studies has shown how, even in these hypotheses, the perspective, respectively, of the member state of nationality of the applicant and of the EU legal system is different. In the presence of a text of secondary law that regulates the conditions for granting the right to recognition or stay, CJEU beyond a mere statement of principle, denies in its root the use of the technique of prohibition of abuse, without dwelling, even when expressly requested, on possible hypotheses of abuse, or on measures that may be adopted to combat the phenomenon. The pseudo-foreign corporations and for the factual plan of manifestation of abuse CJEU excludes, often based on the objective and subjective parameters of the prohibition, the presence of an abusive situation. Only in C-311/06, National Council of engineers case of 29 January 2009 seems to find an evasion of the national system uses the different technique of restrictive interpretation of the discipline. With reference to the protection techniques, in fact, the game is played in any case on the application or not of secondary law: CJEU always examines this profile first and, if the required conditions are met, does not go further.

The same orientation was found when the right of movement of the worker or of the citizen, invoked to benefit from the provisions of Directive 2004/38/EC or, again, when national provisions attributing particular benefits to the migrant, on the basis of the principle of non-discrimination. Even in these cases, CJEU beyond a mere statement of principle, did not apply the prohibition of abuse. In the cases examined, it emerged, in particular, the difficulty of CJEU to investigate the reasons that could have led the individual to exercise his rights, motivations of which he was repeatedly and constantly declared irrelevant.

Ultimately, the examination of "European" jurisprudence reveals the considerable difficulties faced by CJEU in detecting the abusive manifestation on the basis of the abuses test criteria. As already noted, the systematic favor for intra-union mobility may have played a role in determining an extremely restrictive application of the prohibition of abuse.

However, the main obstacle to the application of prohibition of abuse seems to be another: the non-coincidence of the criteria used by the member state, on the one hand, and the EU, on the other, to verify the abuse. Thus, those constructions that appear to be abusive in the member state are often not for the EU order. From this point of view, it has been observed that the nationality of the interested party can hardly operate as a marker of the artificiality of the operation. The "U-shaped" operations leads almost automatically to exclude the satisfaction of the test, since the abusive constructions described so far have in common an effective circulation, nor can the motivations, once the objective element is satisfied, be detected. Moreover, we cannot fail to remember that the first assumption of abuse, capable of differentiating it from fraud, is precisely the formal respect of the norm, which often (though) is sufficient for the EU order to give freedom of movement. In other words, the fact of falling within the scope of EU law is sufficient to rule out the abuse. Hence is the exclusion of the need to verify the presence of the subjective element.

On the other hand, even if the objective element is integrated, the subjective element does not always prove to be a good parameter. This happens in particular with reference to the hypotheses involving the circulation of individuals. In fact, it would be illogical to consider motivations here, as there are infinite variables that can influence individual choices, from economic to individual ones[781].

It has also been observed that, in such contexts, admitting the relevance of abuse, as congenital, would lead in practice to recognize the existence of a "purely internal situation": the private, in fact, through the unauthorized construction, changes the location of the case, so as to achieve the application of a different right from the otherwise applicable law, in order to avoid the mandatory rules of the member state of belonging. In this perspective, recognizing the abuse, would also mean excluding the relevance of the element of estrangement created by the private, since the artificiality is perceived exactly in relation to the improper use of freedom of movement.

In conclusion, from the analysis carried out various problematic issues of the prohibition of abuse emerged, understood as a technique of protection of the order from abusive conditions, which inevitably affect the effectiveness of the remedy. Not only does it not seem useful, at present, to question the scope of the general principle of prohibition. However, this does not mean that EU law does

781 It was also noted that the ways in which the prohibition of abuse would operate would not be clear: whether it involves the non-application of EU law in an interpretative way, as seems to emerge from some rulings, or the denial of the right, once that the relevance of Union law is established. It is recalled on this point that, for example, CJEU in case: C-212/97, Centros of 9 March 1999 clearly distinguished the question of Treaty's applicability with respect to the question of the measures that a member state can take to prevent the abuse, whereas case: C-196/04, Cadbury Schweppes and Cadbury Schweppes Overseas of 12 September 2006 dealt with the question in preliminary, as member states would like, which invoke the abuse precisely to exclude the concrete situation from the scope of EU law. On the other hand, where there is a directive, the question does not pose particular problems, since, as we have seen, the verification of the abuse is always made subsidiary, once the directive has been interpreted. As for the sanction that derives from the application of the abuse, the same, as we have seen, is found in denying the choice of the attempted right, which is undesirable. The prohibition of abuse, therefore, does not call into question the validity of the economic transaction carried out, but only the choice of the applicable law performed by the private.

not have other protection techniques to combat situations limit circumvention of national legislation from part of the private sector. In fact, the cases analyzed confirmed the impression that, jurisprudence, in reality, in the presence of a triangulation between legal systems, aims to use various legal techniques, different from that of the prohibition of abuse.

In many cases, it has been observed that, in the face of "U" operations carried out using the freedoms of circulation to circumvent national legislation and move to a more favorable national system, in the absence of any form of harmonization, CJEU, accepting the thesis of the member state, considered the fight against the abuse as an overriding reason of general interest, provided that certain well-defined conditions were met.

The case study showed that, often, CJEU, to verify the proportionality of the state measure has applied a test that has the same characteristics as the one coined to verify the presence of an abuse: the national legislation, in fact, must specifically concern buildings of pure artifice, devoid of economic effectiveness, whose sole purpose is to obtain a benefit. The two arguments on the norm and on the abusive demonstration, however, are brought forward in a disjointed way. The Union judge, in fact, does not deal with the construction itself, nor does it demand the national judge to do so, but only to how the normative, necessarily general and abstract, has been constructed, regardless of whether we are (or not) in the presence of an abusive manifestation.

On the contrary, in the presence of "U-shaped" constructions which aim at obtaining the application of EU law in place of national law, as well as in cases where the advantage of a private person derives from a status conferred by EU law by virtue of the exercise of freedom of movement, the Luxembourg court has shown a certain propensity for the restrictive interpretation of Union's rules. By doing so, CJEU can avoid coming to the point of declaring the existence of an abuse of EU law. It is sufficient, in fact, to provide a specific definition of the scope of application of "European Union" rules in order to exclude the case of the private individual who tries to re-enter illegally in the field of EU law. More specifically, CJEU referred to the objective pursued by the European Union provision to exclude from its scope artificially constructed operations which, even if they respect the letter of the standard, have as their sole purpose to benefit from of the advantages attributed by the standard itself. In this regard, it cannot be discounted that the option adopted by the EU judge is exactly the same as that chosen in the hypothesis of abuse of EU law, while after some rulings based on the restrictive interpretation of the applicable legislation, CJEU ultimately proposed for the use of the ban.

In comparing the three protection techniques, it was noted that they are united by the use of the objective-teleological criterion, which consists in the verification of the non-compliance with the objectives pursued by the provision of Union law concerned. This element, which alone cannot lead us to include such instruments under the umbrella of a broader and more independent notion of abuse. In fact, it has been pointed out that the imperative reasons differ from the prohibition of abuse as the verification focuses on the suitability and proportionality of the national anti-abuse legislation and not on the abusive behavior considered in itself, which translates into requiring the regulation considered to be limited to constructions of pure abstract artifice. As for the technique of restrictive interpretation, it was noted that the plans of prohibition of abuse and interpretation are not perfectly coinciding. In order for the prohibition in question to apply, in fact, not only the case is not included in the purpose of regulation, but there must also be a creation without economic justification, indicating the desire to obtain an abusive advantage.

More generally, it has been noted that the employment, to combat the most evident manifestations of abuse, of techniques that focus on general and abstract normative and therefore badly suited to the concrete case, has not always proved to be a convenient choice. In case of imperative reasons of general interest, in fact, through a very strict proportionality test, we end up allowing the national authority to apply the legislation only if it is aimed at countering specific constructions outlined ex ante with extreme precision[782]. On the other hand, private individuals who abuse EU law in a state where there is no anti-abuse legislation benefit from a wider application of EU law than a private individual operating in a state where such provisions have been adopted.

Teleological interpretation, on the other hand, in addition to limiting the spaces of private autonomy with respect to the prohibition as less selective, is inevitably not very flexible, insofar as it pertains to the letter of the law. As

---

782 Among other things, as already noted, the most nourished jurisprudence with reference to the fight against abuse is found in the field of tax avoidance, which has undeniable particularities compared to other hypotheses of circumvention that have been analyzed: in these cases, in fact, it is not so much the connecting element with another national order to be created fictitiously, but the operation itself. One might ask, therefore, if the same principles can be valid in other cases of circumvention, including first of all the pseudo-foreign corporations, in which the element of artificiality is very difficult to trace according to the parameters set by jurisprudence, without taking into consideration the nationality of the private individual.

a side effect, it may happen that the national authorities are given a weapon that allows them to deny the protection granted by EU law, without having to worry about looking at the individual case, with all the problems that also derive in terms of division of powers between member states. We could then even hypothesize cases in which the use of restrictive interpretation cannot be imagined, since, as the legislation of secondary legislation is structured, one would arrive at an interpretative abrogans of the same. In essence, the main limit that unites the imperative reasons of general interest and the restrictive interpretation, is precisely that of not having the ability to move from the plane for which they are congenital, that of the abstract to the concrete level in where the abuse is located, and can lead to a series of repercussions inconsistent with the system as a whole.

Precisely from these last considerations, we can finally say that CJEU has so far proved ill-equipped in the fight against abuse, even for structural reasons. In interpreting the rules of the Treaty concerning the freedoms of movement, in fact, the Union judge has difficulty in identifying the constituent elements of the abuse test for the reasons already illustrated. Thus, those constructions which, for the member state, appear to be abusive, are often not so for the EU order, due to the necessary differentiation of the criteria used by the member state on one hand and the EU on the other in performing the verification.

Alternatively, the use of "palliatives" also does not always lead to satisfactory results, as well as being consistent with the system as a whole. CJEU has often been based, in fact, on techniques that do not fit the concrete case, focusing on the general and abstract legislation.

OTHER AVENUES AVAILABLE TO LEGAL SYSTEMS IN ORDER TO LIMIT THE ABUSE OF LAW: THE LEGISLATOR'S INTERVENTION

The described difficulty of CJEU is at the origin of a series of problems, which also affect the relationships between negative and positive harmonization. In this regard, it should be noted that the abuse involving multiple jurisdictions finds its raison d'être in regulatory competition. If, in fact, the introduction of the principle of mutual recognition has allowed resources, companies and individuals to move to states that grant more advantageous conditions, member states have had the opportunity to offer regulatory benefits to economic actors in order to attract investments[783].

Where member states are free to define the content of their national provisions that do not influence circulation, an arbitrage opportunity for individuals is created.

Apart from the considerations related to the risk of a leveling down of national protection standards[784], what we would like to emphasize is how the difference between territorial unity within the Union and regulatory diversity, structurally favors the emergence of abusive practices aimed at choosing a more favorable order, which are distinguished from simple arbitrage because of the high component of artificiality that characterizes them.

On the contrary, harmonization eliminates the possibility of comparing legislation and ipso facto abuse, as evidently no choice of applicable law can be made in the presence of a single legal regime.

Then, legislative institutions both national and EU could be better equipped in the fight against large-scale abuses, which are the first to request the application of the ban on abuse, they would be responsible for the desirable or not consequences descending from their own legislative choices.

In this regard, it should not be underestimated the link between the difficulties that CJEU finds in sanctioning the abuse and what can be defined, in non-technical sense, a reflex harmonization, or rather forced, by member states legislators, which, with reforms adopted at national level, adjust their legislation to that of the most competitive states, with the aim of restricting arbitrage.

783 N. BERNARD, Flexibility in the European single market, in C. BARNARD, The law of the single European market, op. cit., pp. 101ss.

784 Not relevant to our review. Indeed, there is not necessarily a correlation between abusive and downward grading. Regulatory arbitrage is at the center of a heated debate about the benefits and costs of regulatory competition, starting with the experience of the United States, which was affected by the "Delaware" effect, the term used to refer to the risk of a downward trend compared to national standards, in order to attract investments. For further details see: D. CHARNY, Competition among jurisdictions in formulating corporate law rules: an American perspective on the "race to the bottom" in the European Communities, in Harvard International Law Journal, 32, 1991, pp. 422ss. S. DEAKIN, Legal diversity and regulatory competition, which model for Europe?, in European Law Journal, 12, 2006, pp. 440ss. M. SIEMS, Convergence, competition, Centros and conflicts of law: European company law in the 21st century, in European Law Review, 27, 2002, pp. 47ss. J. CARRUTHERS, C. VILLIERS, Company Law in Europe, condoning the continental drift?, in European Business Law Review, 11, 2000, pp. 91ss. J.M. SUN, J. PELKMANS, Regulatory competition in the single market, in Journal of Common Market Studies, 33, 1995, pp. 67ss. C. HOLST, European company law after Centros: is the EU on the road to Delaware?, in The Columbia Journal of European Law, 8, 2002, pp. 323ss.

Likewise, the key role that the EU legislator can take must be taken into account. They note not only positive harmonization in this regard, but also the provisions introduced by the EU legislator in numerous texts of secondary legislation to counteract abusive phenomena in various ways (called anti-abuse clauses), as well as the role that can be called to carry out the EC in the presence of a text of secondary law that imposes certain rules in order to limit law shopping.

It is therefore necessary to dwell (at the end of this work) that harmonization can play in the fight against the abuse of law, providing some ideas to the reader on a theme, such as harmonization, which inevitably crosses that of the abuse of law merits some brief considerations while falling outside the object of our examination.

NATIONAL LEGISLATOR'S ROLE: "REFLEX OR FORCED HARMONIZATION" TRIGGERED BY REGULATORY COMPETITION

The invocation of prohibition of abuse by member states whose legislation, considered by the most restrictive private circumvented, can be considered partial corrective to competition between legal systems, at least with reference to artificial behaviors. On this point, it is worth recalling what has already been reported on several occasions: namely that the issue of abuse is bound to a question of jurisdiction of a certain legal system rather than another in regulating a particular case. In "U" operations, in fact, the state of origin, whose legislation would be applicable in the absence of abusive construction, becomes a host state, without being able to demand the application of its provisions. It is well understood, therefore, how, from the private point of view, if both legal systems introduce an identical regulation, there will be no advantage to move from one system to another.

When CJEU does not want or cannot recognize the abuse, by denying the possibility for national jurisprudence to use the related ban, which would allow the individual abuses to be punished, member states, with a view to system, can be called to intervene, through the modification of its legislation (harmonization by way of reflection). It thus seems interesting to make some considerations regarding the link that can exist between the exclusion of abuse by CJEU and spontaneous or reflected harmonization of member states laws.

In this regard, it is worth pointing out that, theoretically, two hypotheses may occur: one in which the member state with the most restrictive legislation aligns with the member state to which the choice of the private individual is directed, and one in which, specularly, the arbitrary state of arbitration will change its legislation. Where there is a liberal attitude of CJEU, which aims to make mobility prevail in the Union and the objective of eliminating the obstacles to free movement with respect to the concern of each member state to protect its interests.

THE AFOREMENTIONED STRUCTURAL REASONS

As an example of the first case described, the reforms that have occurred in company law in the countries of civil law can be cited as a result of C-212/97, Centros case of 9 March 1999. In fact, we have seen, following the jurisprudence on pseudo-foreign corporations, an exponential growth of companies established in England and, at the same time, a multiplication of branches in continental Europe. In this regard, the close correlation between the liberal approach of CJEU to abuse was highlighted, as well as the fact that, consequently, almost all national anti-abuse regulations were declared to be contrary to EU law, on one side, and peak of corporate migrations, especially towards the United Kingdom, not only because of the differences concerning the minimum capital but also, for example, of limited establishment costs, rapid procedures, more flexible restructuring and bankruptcy laws, on the other. What we need to underline here is how continental member states, in response to the described migratory phenomenon, have been forced to revise their corporate law, in such a way as to maintain a certain attraction in competition with other systems[785].

785 V.W. G. RINGE, Corporate mobility in the European Union-a flash in the pan? An empirical study of the success of lawmaking and regulatory competition, in European Company and Financial Law Review, 10, 2013, pp. 230ss. Z. ADAMS, S. DEAKIN, Freedom of establishment and regulatory competition, in A. ARNULL, D. CHALMERS (a cura di), The Oxford Handbook of European Union Law, Oxford University Press, Oxford, 2015, pp. 545ss. W. BRATTON, J. MCCAHERY, E. VERMEULEN, How does corporate mobility affect lawmaking? A comparative analysis, in American Journal of Comparative Law, 57, 2009, pp. 347ss. It is no coincidence that the companies in CJEU in the Sergers, Centros and C-167/01, Inspire Art of 30 September 2003, op. cit., cases were all established in the United Kingdom: the Anglo-Saxon discipline of the Private Limited Company does not provide for a minimum capital or a requirement of initial contributions. To give an idea, the German government, in responding to a parliamentary question, estimated that the number of English companies established through agencies in Germany between January and August 2005 was equal to 3,200. Thus, for example, new and more deregulated forms of limited liability companies have been introduced in

As a result of the increase in regulatory competition in corporate law, CJEU's decisions have led, over time, to a "forced" harmonization[786] in relation to some of the aspects that had led the company to move to the United Kingdom. Indeed, it has been observed that, starting from the two-year period 2007-2008, the tendency to use fictitious companies seems to have reversed[787]. As the main reason for such a reversal, it should be sought not so much in the harmonization undertaken at EU level as in the reforms of national company law in the countries of civil law, which led to a reduction in the costs of establishment and in particular in the minimum capital requirement[788].

This first form of harmonization, that is to say, the one carried out by the state whose legislation is circumvented, which adapts itself to the most advantageous legal system, raises some problems. In fact, it has been observed that the result of an ex post harmonization at national level, carried out solely to avoid abuses, probably contributes more damage than benefits: if, in fact, market players develop a tendency to seek the country with the most permissive legislation, the fear that member states are obliged to eliminate those provisions that ensure higher levels of protection. Thus, the unilateral actions of member states in the regulation are likely to lead to a "leveling" downwards. However, the second hypothesis mentioned above may occur: in fact, it may happen that the member state with the most advantageous legislation modifies it so as to make it uniform to that of the other member states. Just think of the case of Ireland, which after the Chen case, changed its citizenship legislation with the Irish Nationality and Citizenship Act of 2004, harmonizing it with that of the United Kingdom, or that of the Spanish reform on access to the profession of lawyer.

In the first case, the new law replaced the original criterion for the attribution of Irish citizenship is focused solely on jus soli. The same can be said

France and Spain, with minimum capital and extremely limited formality. Reforms were also initiated in the Netherlands with the aim of ensuring greater freedom for entrepreneurs, as in Germany, which created a new GmbH without minimum capital. V. W. G. RINGE, Corporate mobility in the European Union-a flash in the pan? An empirical study of the success of lawmaking and regulatory competition, op. cit., pp. 239ss.

786 This expression is used to better highlight how often member states are forced to revise their rights, so as to maintain a certain attractiveness in competition with other jurisdictions.

787 V. K. SØRENSEN, The fight against letterbox companies in the internal market, in Common Market Law Review, 52, 2015, pp. 94ss. M. BECHT, C. MAYERAND, H. WAGNER, Where do firms incorporate? Deregulation and the cost of entry, in Journal of Corporate Finance, 14, 2008, pp. 241ss.

788 R. BRAUN, H. EIDENMÜLLER, A. ENGERT, L. HORNUF, Does Charter competition foster entrepreneurship? A difference-in-difference approach to European company law reforms, in Journal of Common Market Studies, 50, 2013, pp. 400ss.

with reference to the Belgian legislation: from the moment in which the facts of C-34/09, Ruiz Zambrano case of 8 March 2011, have been verified, Belgian citizenship has been subject to changes, so it would not be as much as possible, for a person in the position of Mr. Ruiz Zambrano, choose not to register their children under the diplomatic or consular protection of their country of jus soli and jus sanguinis. In this way, the children born in Ireland from non-citizen parents can obtain Irish citizenship and it must be demonstrated that at least one of the parents has a substantial connection with Ireland, residing regularly in the territory for a certain number of years[789]. To date, an effective connection is required of the third-country citizen with the member state whose citizenship is requested for their children.

In the second case, however, the Spanish legislator has modified the discipline to obtain the title of abogado, making the prior attendance of a master mandatory, after which the law graduate will take an aptitude test. The motivations that have pushed the Spanish legislator to a greater selectivity of the enrollment process, as illustrated in the preamble of ley 34/2006[790], which came into force in 2011, can be summarized in an awareness of the opportunity that graduates in jurisprudence they develop practical training before being able to practice their profession, as well as in the need to standardize the Spanish system of access to the profession of lawyer to that of other European countries[791]. As we can see, this last legislative change, in fact, precedes CJEU's rulings on the issue, so that it does not necessarily show the correlation between the lack of possibility to invoke the ban and national reforms. However, it is useful to underline the fungibility of jurisprudential and legislative instruments: the more the laws of member states converge, the lower the danger of abuses according to the "U-shaped" scheme.

789 A. TRYFONIDOU, Further cracks in the "great wall" of the European Union?, op. cit., pp. 531-32. Only here is the fact that the bill for the amendment of the Constitution was approved with a referendum in Ireland held in 2004.

790 Law of 30 October 2006 n. 34, "sobre el lit a las profesiones de Abogado y Procurador de los Tribunales", BOE 260, 31 October 2006, pp. 377ss., As amended by the law of July 6, 2012 n. 5, "de mediación en asuntos civiles y mercantiles", BOE 162, 7 July 2012, p. 49224 et seq., which introduced, in particular, an extension of the transitional regime until October 30, 2013.

791 Of the qualification shopping in Spain, moreover, the same Consejo General de la Abogacía Española seemed to know that, with circular dated March 7, 2013 n. 35, invited the Colegios de Abogados to adopt a restrictive criterion on the subject of registration as a lawyer for EU citizens who had applied for approval after October 30, 2011.

In light of the above, it is difficult to comment on the opportunity (or otherwise) of reflex harmonization, which includes too many hypotheses to make a unitary judgment possible. It is, however, a phenomenon that is certainly not very organic, more or less conditioned by contingent situations, which push the individual state to actions decided on from time to time. If anything, so delineated the possible indirect correlations between abuse of law and reflected harmonization and found that eventually even the reflected harmonization could constitute a palliative to be used by the member states to react to "massive" phenomena of abuse. From which, we can draw a further demonstration of how CJEU's orientation not to punish the abuse does not show the latter's will to promote competition between legal systems. The use of prohibition of abuse of law, in fact, acting as a flexible tool, would allow to "select" the behavior of private individuals not worthy of protection, while preserving the differences between national laws, leveled, on the contrary, by a structural reform implemented by the member state.

THE ROLE OF EU LEGISLATOR: OVERVIEW OF POSITIVE HARMONIZATION

The relationship between abuse of law and "European Union" positive harmonization is much more problematic, being dominated by contradictory tendencies, by centrifugal and centripetal forces: on the one hand, in a purely theoretical way, ex ante negotiated harmonization is one of the most effective instruments available to member states to counter the abuse of law intended as circumvention of national legislation. On the other hand, where some minimum conditions have been harmonized by the Union legislator, a clear-cut attitude is seen by the EU judge in admitting the possibility for member states to combat the abuse by using the relative prohibition. The extent of anti-abuse clauses codified by the EU legislator in various texts of secondary legislation is not entirely clear.

With regard to the first profile, it must be noted that the positive harmonization by the EU legislator is, in fact, the most intuitive way of resolving the problem of abuse at a regulatory level, as it consists in replacing all national legislation with a single legislation, adopted at European level[792]: the possibility

792 In this regard, the passage already cited by the AG La Pergola in case: C-212/97, Centros of 9 March 1999, op. cit., which states that: "in the absence of harmonization, in short, it is the competition between regulatory systems ("competition among rules") that should have free play, also in corporate

of comparison between national laws and ipso facto of abuse is eliminated, as evidently no choice as to the applicable law can be made in the presence of a single legal regime. Moreover, CJEU and the advocates-general who assisted it in resolving cases in which the abuse was invoked, have repeatedly recognized the role that positive harmonization can play in countering "unwanted" behavior by private individuals.

Thus, in C-115/78, Knoors v. Staatssecretaris van Economische Zaken judgment of 7 February 1979, CJEU stressed that "in the absence of harmonization of the conditions under which the holder of a postgraduate university degree can avail himself of it in member states other than the one in which the certificate was issued, the members remain, in principle, competent to define the modalities to which they make use of the same in their territory"[793]. In the pronunciation of C-212/97, Centros case of 9 March 1999, CJEU after having highlighted the fact that company law is not completely harmonized in Union, recalled that "the Council can always, by virtue of the powers conferred by art. 54, n. 3, lett. g) of the EC Treaty, to complete this harmonization"[794], thus urging member states" to come out of the process of harmonization"[795] to eliminate the serious disadvantages resulting from the disparity between national laws on corporate matters.

The AG Léger in its opinion in C-196/04, Cadbury Schweppes and Cadbury Schweppes Overseas case of 12 September 2006, after noting that "in the absence of European harmonization, it should be noted that tax systems of various member states can result in competition", he adds: "legitimately regrets that in

matters (...)" (par. 20).

793 Paragraph 28. Doctrine has also argued that in order to circumvent the possible harmful consequences of such a large liberalization in the corporate sector, a more complete harmonization of company law within the Union should be achieved. See in argument: J.P. OMAR, Centros, Überseering and beyond: A European recipe for corporate migration: Part 2, in International Company and Commercial Law Review, 13, 2005, pp. 23ss. C. D. EHLERMANN, Harmonization versus Competition Between Rules, in European Law Review, 19, 1995, pp. 333ss. M. POIARES MADURO, We the CJEU-The European Court of Justice and the European Economic Constitution, Hart Publishing, Oxford & Portland, Oregon, 1997, pp. 104ss. N. REICH, Competition between legal orders, in Common Market Law Review, 29, 1992, pp. 861ss.

794 M. POIARES MADURO, We the CJEU-The European Court of Justice and the European Economic Constitution, op. cit.

795 Paragraph 55. See also paragraph 60, which reads: "The damaging effects of an absolute lack of harmonization of tax rates on corporate profits are attributed, however, as I said before, to a political solution and I do not think justify calling into question the scope of the rights conferred by articles 43 and 48 EC (now art. 49 and 54 TFEU) as defined by the jurisprudence".

this sector interstate competition knows no limits. However, this is a question of a political nature (...)"[796].

Having said that, as is well known, an integration strategy based exclusively on the harmonization of member states law can be difficult to implement. Indeed, member states are not always inclined to make too radical changes to sectors considered to be crucial in terms of state sovereignty. In addition to the difficulties in finding a point of mediation, the costs of positive harmonization include the imposition of significant trading costs, as well as the impossibility for the member state to change the harmonized sector unilaterally.

What we are interested in emphasizing here is, in any case, how the technique of harmonization, unlike that of mutual recognition, allows to exclude at root the possibility of shopping system. With the due warning this does not mean the elimination of any form of abuse. In fact, where the harmonized legislation adopted at EU level establishes different legal regimes, an abuse of EU law could occur, as is the case with tax law or the common agricultural policy. The private, that is, could be led to put in place constructive constructions in order to unduly obtain the advantages descending directly from EU legislation. In these cases, however, as already mentioned, an intervention by CJEU would be easier to envisage: where the harmonization is more advanced, in fact, it is possible to apply the general principle of prohibition of abuse.

(FOLLOWS) ANTI-ABUSE CLAUSES

Even where the path of harmonization is not viable, the appearance of behavior apparently consistent with EU rules, but in reality, aimed at illegitimately benefiting from the advantages granted by such provisions, has led the EU legislator to provide preventive or repressive of possible abusive acts (so-called anti-abuse clauses) instruments in various legislative acts.

In this regard, it must be noted that these clauses do not always have the same function and operate with the same mechanisms. Indeed, some attribute the power to member states to adopt the most appropriate measures from time to time to combat abuse; others require the state to adopt a specific anti-abuse legislation, subject to control by EC. Certain clauses then delimit the concept

796 M. POIARES MADURO, We the CJEU-The European Court of Justice and the European Economic Constitution, op. cit.

of significant abuse ex ante in the specific sector and others, more laconic, do not provide a specific definition of the concept of abuse. In order to clear any doubt on the point, it should be noted at the outset that, if in any case there is obviously reference to rights attributed by secondary law, the anti-abuse clauses were introduced to counteract the behaviors that are substantiated so much in an internal abuse of law as in a cross border abuse of law. Here, we will analyze only the latter[797], consistent with the objective of the paragraph, to provide some ideas about the role in the fight against the abuse of alternative instruments to those of the magistrates.

In this sense, first of all, the anti-abuse clause already contained in the recital n. 8 of the second Directive, 89/646/CEE[798], remained unchanged in changes subsequently made to the text, which provides, in the context of the mutual recognition of authorizations and systems of prudential supervision and control exercised by the home member state, that these last principles require the competent authorities not to grant or withdraw credit authorization where a number of elements, including the activities actually performed, clearly indicate that the credit institution has opted for the legal system of that member state in order to avoid stricter rules in force in the member state in whose territory it intends to perform most of its activities. Member states are also required to require that the central administration effectively operate in the member state of origin. In truth, it is one of the many examples of the delegation of EU legislator to member states in the fight against the abuse of freedom of establishment

797 Here are some clauses aimed at limiting the abuse of EU law - which is therefore realized in a single system, hypothesis, as has been shown, less problematic-without pretension of exhaustiveness: paradoxically, in fact, where CJEU shows not to have difficulty applying the ban, the legislator has often been concerned with inserting anti-abuse clauses, especially with regard to the European agricultural policy. It seems therefore to be CJEU to play a leading role in this sense, delegating to the legislator more than anything else the "codification" of the pretestual statutes.

798 In this regard, art. 11 of the directive on the common tax regime to be applied to mergers and other corporate reorganisations (90/43/EC), Already analyzed, clause then transposed in art. 15 of Directive 2009/133/EC (in OJ, L 310 of 25.11.2009, p.38); article. 1, par. 2, of the so- called mother-daughter directive (90/435, in OJ, L 225 of 20.8.1990, p.6), which legitimizes member states to apply national or conventional provisions necessary to prevent fraud and abuse. The aforementioned art. 27, par. 1 of Directive 77/388/EEC (so-called Sixth VAT Directive), subsequently repealed by Council Directive 2006/112/EC of 28 November 2006 (Official Journal L 347, 11.12.2006, p.1), which contains a section 4 entitled "measures to prevent distortions of competition and tax evasion" (Article 342 et seq.). The clauses contained in EU legislation on tax matters are also capable of covering phenomena attributable to the conceptual category of abuse of rights. See, P. WATTEL, Circumvention of national law, op. cit., pp. 1279ss. Second Council Directive 89/646/EEC of 15 December 1989 on the coordination of laws, regulations and administrative provisions relating to access to and use of the business of credit institutions and amending Directive 77/780/EEC, in OJ, L 386 of 30.12.1989, p. 1 ss.

and freedom to provide services. Clauses of identical tenor are found, in fact, in various texts of derivative law which dealt with aspects that incidentally touch the right of establishment and freedom to provide services[799].

As you can see, EU legislator, in describing in broad terms the "U-shaped" construction, the legal person established in a given state, without carrying out any activity there, circumvent the most stringent regulations of the country in whose territory it intends to carry out most of the activities, legitimize, or better impose, on member states to refuse the attribution of the right.

Therefore, if the prerequisites for the identification of an abusive demonstration are the same that CJEU had already traced in the rulings, also dating, regarding the free provision of services[800], the penalty differs significantly, excluding the granting of credit authorization.

As you remember in the broadcasting case, it was emerged for the state of destination the activity to apply its own imperative rules to the company that is the protagonist of the abuse, through a fictio iuris such that it could be considered established in that state. It is not by chance that the same line was then followed by the clauses contained in the "television without frontiers" Directive, which, in codifying the previous jurisprudence of CJEU, allow the member state to which it is directed, in whole or in part, to take "appropriate" and objectively necessary measures, applied in a non-discriminatory and proportionate manner to the objectives pursued. This is one of the cases in which, presumably to compensate for the wide margin of action attributed to states, that includes not only negative measures, such as the revocation of a benefit, but positive and

799 See recital 9 of Directive 2000/12/EC of the European Parliament and of the Council of 20 March 2000; cons. 10 of Directive 2006/48/EC of the European Parliament and of the Council of 14 June 2006, in OJ, L 177, 30.06.2006, p. 1 ss ; cons. 16 of Directive 2013/36/EU of the European Parliament and of the Council of 26 June 2013, in OJ, L 176 of 27.6.2013, pp. 338ss. Although such a warning to states is not included in the directive, the anti-abuse perspective expressed in the preamble to the Directive makes it possible to better understand the importance of the provisions covering the supervisory mechanisms which member states should necessarily adopt to prevent and repress possible phenomena of circumvention of the national law through EU law (see in this regard the definition of a system of prior consultation between national authorities in order to identify, inter alia, concrete elements in the light of which it is decided that the credit institution has established itself in the other state in order to benefit from the most advantageous provisions guaranteed by the newly established national legal system).

800 Paragraph 14 of Directive 97/36 it is clear in this regard: "according to the settled case-law of the court, a member state retains the right to take action against a television agency which, although having established its seat in another member state, directs all or part of its business to the territory of the first member state, where the choice to settle in the second member state was made in order to avoid the legislation that would have been applied if it was established on the territory of the first member state (...)".

apparently undetermined, in these cases upon notification to EC, which must verify the compatibility of the measures with EU law[801].

Again regarding the provision of services between the freedoms of movement, which, in combination with the right of establishment, makes it possible to better exploit the differences between legal systems, the legislator has recently intervened with the objective to combat the practice of companies that establish themselves, through companies of convenience, in laws with the most advantageous labor law legislation, and then carry out their activity of sending staff in services, thereby bypassing the social security laws of the member state of effective employment. Directive 2014/67/UE[802], which has made significant changes to the application of Directive 96/71/EC[803], in fact, art. 4, entitled "identification of the authenticity of the posting and prevention of abuse and circumvention", provides for the possibility for national authorities to sanction the company by not applying Directive 96/71/EC, where an abuse is found on basis of the evaluation of a series of factual elements, aimed at determining whether an enterprise actually carries out substantial activities other than purely internal management and/or administration activities[804].

801 Thus art. 3 of Directive 2007/65. See then the art. 4, par. 3 of Directive 2010/13/EU of the European Parliament and of the Council of 10 March 2010 on the coordination of certain laws, regulations and administrative provisions of member states concerning the provision of audiovisual media services (Audiovisual Media Services Directive), in OJ, L 95 of 15.4.2010, p. 1ss. Paragraph 3 states that: "the first member state may take appropriate measures against the concerned issuer if it considers that: (a) the results achieved through the application of paragraph 2 are not satisfactory; and (b) the broadcaster in question has established itself in the member state exercising jurisdiction to circumvent, in the fields coordinated by this Directive, the stricter rules which would apply to it if it were established in the first member state. Such measures are objectively necessary, applied in a non-discriminatory and proportionate manner to the objectives pursued (...)". Pursuant to par. 4 "A member state may take measures pursuant to paragraph 3 only if the following conditions are met: (a) it has notified the Commission and the member state in which the television broadcaster is established its intention to take such measures, reasons on which it bases its assessment; and (b) the Commission has decided that these measures are compatible with Union law and, in particular, that the assessments of the member state adopting those measures pursuant to paragraphs 2 and 3 are properly justified (...)".

802 Directive 2014/67/EU of the European Parliament and of the Council of 15 May 2014 on the enforcement of Directive 96/71/EC concerning the posting of workers in the framework of the provision of services and amending Regulation (EU) No 1024/2012 on administrative cooperation through the Internal Market Information System ("the IMI Regulation") Text with EEA relevance, OJ L 159, 28.5.2014, p. 11-31. For further details see: F. WILMAN, Private enforcement of European Union law before national courts. The European Union legislative framework, Edward Elgar Publishers, Cheltenham, 2015.

803 Directive 96/71/EC of the European Parliament and of the Council of 16 December 1996 concerning the posting of workers in the framework of the provision of services, OJ L 18, 21.1.1997, p. 1-6.

804 Paragraph 2 mentions, for example, the place where the company carries out its main economic

Although no real definition of the concept of abuse is found, EU legislator assists the competent authorities in the checks and controls, predetermining some criteria useful for the perimeter of abusive behavior by the company, which must be taken into account in the assessment accomplished.

This is not an isolated technique: a predetermination of criteria useful for the national authorities to establish the abuse is also found in art. 35 of Directive 2004/38/EC, entitled "abuse of rights", under which "member states may take the necessary measures to refuse, extinguish or revoke a right conferred by this Directive, in the event of abuse of rights or fraud, such as a fictitious marriage"[805].

With reference to this clause, it must be noted that the same, on the assumption of its derogatory scope, is interpreted restrictively by CJEU, in the sense of being able to be invoked only in specific cases, such as those of fraud and fictitious marriages. With regards to the latter, in particular, a definition is found in the Council Resolution of 1997 on fictitious marriages, which shows that marriage can be considered as such, on the basis of a series of indications, where there is no effective morality and material communion between the spouses (artificiality), from which the sole purpose of allowing the person concerned to enter or stay in a member state transpires, so that in reality it would be a marriage of convenience.

A terminology that is not dissimilar is found in art. 16, par. 2, of Directive 2003/86/CE[806], inserted in the head dedicated to the sanctions and the remedies, which provides the power for member states to reject the application for entry and stay for the purposes of family reunification, or withdraw or refuse

activity and in which its administrative staff are employed; as well as the number of contracts executed and/or the amount of turnover achieved in the member state of establishment, taking into account the specific situation characterizing, inter alia, the newly established companies and SMEs. C. COSTELLO, Citizenship of the Union: Above abuse? op. cit., pp. 330. This can be inferred from the fact that the prohibition is subject to the limitation of proportionality.

805 C. COSTELLO, Citizenship of the Union: Above abuse? op. cit.

806 Thus in the judgment of case: C-202/13, Sean Ambrose McCarthy of 18 December 2014, CJEU has specified, referring to the Metock point that the member state may limit the right of entry and residence in the host state of the family member of EU citizen only in compliance with articles 27 and 35 of Directive 2004/38/EC (par. 45). He added that "in the absence of specific provisions in Directive 2004/38/EC, the fact that a member state is confronted, as the United Kingdom claims, with a high number of instances of abuse of rights or fraud committed by citizens of third countries, which use fake marriages or use false residence cards, cannot justify the adoption of a measure, such as that at issue in the main proceedings, based on considerations of general prevention, and which leaves aside any specific assessment of the behavior of the data subject (...)" (par. 55).

the renewal of the residence permit of the family in case of fraud or fictitious marriages[807].

In these hypotheses, the EU system goes further than merely indicating the parameters that the national authorities are invited to follow. In fact, it comes to delimit the concept of abuse, linking it to the notion of fictitious marriage, and provides for the possibility for the state not to apply EU law only in predefined cases. If the anti-abuse clauses unequivocally legitimize the member state to take anti-abuse measures, they restrict the scope of the concept, leaving aside the cases in which, even in the presence of a "real" marriage, the spouses, invoked the right of circulation for the sole purpose of circumventing national legislation. In this we see, as we said, the ambiguous role of anti-abuse clauses, which act as an instrument, on the one hand, to combat abuses and, on the other hand, to limit the notion of abuse.

This brief illustrative review of anti-abuse clauses aimed at limiting constructions aimed at circumventing national legislation confirms the existence of profound differences regarding the description of the concepts and the way of operating of these instruments, which was mentioned at the beginning of the discussion. Indeed, the particularity of situations in which an abuse of law may arise renders a normative solution of a general nature unprecedented, which would require a massive intervention of CJEU jurisprudence, as well as the technique of prohibition of abuse, but this does not preclude to those areas in which the risk of circumvention of the national laws can be more frequent, to the sectoral regulations an effective intervention space. This is possible not only with regard to the case where a given sector is governed by specific rules of EU law, so that allowing states to prohibit abuse first of all prohibits the abuse

---

807 Council resolution of 4 December 1997 on measures to be taken to combat fake marriages (97/C-382/01), in OJ, C 382 of 16.12.1997, p. 1 ss. Including the failure to maintain the relationship of cohabitation, the fact that the spouses have never met before the marriage or who make mistakes on their personal data, the circumstances in which they met or other important personal information that they concern, or the fact that spouses do not speak a language understandable to both, or the fact that a sum of money is paid for the marriage to be celebrated. In turn, the Commission, in its communication concerning the guidelines for better transposition and better application of this directive, identified, among the indicative criteria from which to infer the misuse of the abuse, the stability of the relationship between long-standing existence of the common domicile. Also, Council Directive 2003/109/EC of 25 November 2003 concerning the status of third-country nationals who are long-term residents, in OJ, L 16 of 23.1.2004, p. 44, cons. 11 states that the residence permit should also respond to high-level technical standards, especially with regard to safeguards against counterfeiting, to prevent any abuse in the member state that granted the status and in member states where it is exercised the right of residence. In Article 9 provides that "Long-term residents are no longer entitled to long-term resident status in the following cases: a) finding of fraudulent acquisition of long-term resident status (...)".

of the same EU legislation, but also with regard to the hypothesis in which a given sector is regulated solely by national regulations and only the freedoms of circulation act as a link. In this regard, at the end of the analysis, it is interesting to mention Directive 2016/1164/EC, which establishes a series of measures against aggressive tax planning, including a general anti-abuse rule, particularly relevant for our purposes, as specifically designed to prevent new attempts to circumvent tax rules from succeeding only because there is not yet a specific rule prohibiting that specific behavior[808].

Furthermore, art. 6, par. 1, gives member states the power to ignore "a series of constructions which, having been put into place for the main purpose or one of the main purposes of obtaining a tax advantage that is contrary to the object or purpose of the applicable tax law, is not genuine having regard to all relevant facts and circumstances"[809], specifying, in the paragraph immediately following, that the absence of genuineness is found in the case where the transaction has not been put in place for valid commercial reasons that reflect economic reality. The penalty, as explained in par. 3, is to calculate the tax due in accordance with national law.

As we can see, the law does nothing more than describe the objective and subjective elements of the abuse test, repeatedly described by the CJEU both in the application of the prohibition of abuse, and in assessing the proportionality of the measures to combat the tax avoidance adopted by individual member states. With the transposition of the Directive into national law, however, the criticalities encountered in the use of the imperative motif techniques will be eliminated.

First of all, through harmonization, there will no longer be any differentiation between systems that have anti-circumvention provisions and regulations that do not have them: the private sector will always be sanctioned. Secondly, the EU legislature thus instructs the national authorities to assess in practice, in relation to the individual case, the existence of an abuse, thus eliminating

808 This is evident from recital 11, where it is stated that "general anti-abuse rules are present in the tax systems to counteract abusive tax practices that have not yet been the subject of specific provisions. These rules are therefore designed to fill gaps and should not jeopardize the applicability of specific anti-abuse rules. Within the Union the general anti-abuse rules should be applied to constructions that are not genuine; It is also important to ensure that the general anti-abuse rules apply uniformly in national situations, within the Union and towards third countries, so that the scope and results of the application in national and cross-border contexts are identical member states that should not be prevented from imposing sanctions in cases where the general anti-abuse rule applies (...)".

809 Directive 2016/1164/EC, op. cit.

the problems linked to the rigidity of a pre-established ex ante regulation, at the time found. The legislation described above thus allows us to reflect on the importance of the role that the EU legislator can play in the fight against abuse.

(FOLLOWS) AN INNOVATIVE ROLE OF EUROPEAN COMMISSION IN THE FIGHT AGAINST THE ABUSE OF RIGHTS?

The relationship between positive harmonization and abuse of rights is ambivalent. On this point, it has already been observed that, where the anti-abuse clause has a definitive content, it also ultimately has the function of circumscribing the concept of abuse operating in a given sector. When a partial harmonization is then registered, regarding certain aspects considered more "sensitive" by the EU legislator, there is a more restrictive attitude of the Luxembourg judge to admit the possibility for member states to invoke the prohibition of abuse, even only in principle. That is, there is no record, that discrepancy highlighted on several occasions between a theoretical affirmation and an applicative denial. The changed attitude of CJEU in dealing with the prohibition or with the imperative measures of general interest in the presence of a text of secondary law, during the course of the discussion was repeatedly highlighted. In this sense, judgments, C-115/78, Knoors v. Staatssecretaris van Economische Zaken of 7 February 1979[810] and C-167/01, inspire Art of 30 September 2003[811], in which CJEU relied on the exhaustive character of directives which came to light in order to deny member states the right to add additional obligations to individuals. The same reasoning has been pursued by the jurisprudence concerning the provision of services of television broadcasters after the advent of Directive 89/552/EEC[812], as

810 It is recalled here how, in case: C-115/78, Knoors v. Staatssecretaris van Economische Zaken of 7 February 1979, CJEU affirmed that "the mandatory conditions formulated by art. 3 of the directive n. 64/427, as regards the duration of periods of professional occupation, have the effect of excluding, in the sectors covered, the risk of abuse reported by the Netherlands Government (...)" (par. 26, already cited)

811 In the C-167/01, Inspire Art of 30 September 2003 ruling, on the other hand, referring to the Eleventh Company Law Directive, he noted that additional reporting obligations could not be imposed by member states.

812 See, in addition to the already examined cases: C-11/95, Commission v. Belgium of 10 September 1996 and joined cases: C-34/95, C-35/95 and C-36/95, Konsumentombudsmannen (KO) v. De Agostini and TV-Shop of 17 July 1997, the judgment delivered by EFTA CJEU of 16 June 1995, joined cases: E-8 and 9/94, Matell Scandinavia, paragraph 49, which reads "it follows from the transmitting state principle, the corollary to which is the limitation on the possibility of restriction, that is,

well as with regard to the first corporate Directive[813]. In all these cases, it was highlighted that, in essence, the Directive already contained a certain level of protection of minors, so that member states could not take measures against advertisements that already met the criteria of the state of transmission.

An attitude of this kind is explained by referring to the gap-filling function attributed to a prohibition which, as an open clause, lends itself to being "flexible". It seems logical, in fact, where a legal text establishes an alternative system that can prevent abusive practices through the harmonization of the most delicate profiles of the discipline, or with the introduction of pre-established derogations, or again, through prior identification, on the basis of certain parameters, such as the residence or effective place of the member state whose rules are applicable in relation to a given situation[814],

try to limit the invocation by member states of a further derogation from the system. To conclude on this point, the operation of the prohibition should therefore be ruled out in its entirety when the problem of abuse is regulated in the same and exhaustive way by specific rules, also implicitly, as CJEU teaches.

However, even in these hypotheses, the equation between the intervention of the Union legislator mentioned above and the absence of abuse by the private sector is not obvious, as can be seen from the references for preliminary rulings by the national judges who exam. Inhibit the way of the initiatives of member states, so here in a new perspective, a more decisive role could be taken by EC, which has the power to penalize not so much the behavior of individuals as that of member states. In this sense, EC could use the instrument of the infringement procedure to prosecute those member states that have not properly transported

the cross-border transmissions fulfilling the criteria of the Directive must not be impeded. Action, based on the different rules enacted by the state of the United States, which fulfills the criteria of the transmitting, and is therefore contrary to the regime established by the Directive (...)".

813 Directive 68/151/EEC designed to coordinate, to make them equivalent, the guarantees that are required in member states for companies in accordance with the second paragraph of article 58 of the Treaty to protect the interests of members and third parties, in OJ, L 65, of 14.3.1968, p. 8 ss.

814 CJEU, C-106/89, Marleasing SA v. Comercial Intrrnacional de Alimentaciòn of 13 November 1990, ECLI:EU:C:1990:395, I-04135, of by which CJEU ruled the incompatibility with the objective of the directive in question of a national interpretation declaring null and void a company set up to carry out abusive transactions aimed at defrauding creditors, precisely in how abusive transactions were not among the justifications listed in art. 11 of the directive. In other words, the prohibition of abuse cannot be used to declare the invalidity of a company to which the first company directive applies, since it would otherwise contradict the purpose of the directive, i.e. limiting cases of invalidity to ensure legal certainty (see parr. 11-12).

EU regulations, where the latter set up, as was said, specific rules which, while not recalling the abuse, have the function to delimit it.

A good example is the appeal by CJEU in joined cases: C-329/06 and C-343/06, Widemann of 26 June 2008 for not correctly transposing the European legislation on driving licenses[815], with which the institution challenged the aforementioned member state has failed to fulfill its obligation to ensure that driving licenses are issued exclusively to residents in the national territory, "an essential requirement" for combating the so-called "driving license tourism"[816].

EC, therefore, ultimately, where fundamental values for the implementation of the market are raised, could play a role in the fight against abuses, not only in the upward phase, through recommendations and proposals for legislative acts containing anti-fraud measures useful, but also in the implementation phase, both through soft law acts that address the competent authorities[817], which as a controller of the policies of member states. In this case, EC would have more effective instruments than national courts called to apply the prohibition of abuse, having as its interlocutor the member state itself, whose legislation does not comply with the standards of protection of EU law. It emerges, concluding,

815 Directive 2006/126/EC of the European Parliament and of the Council of 20 December 2006 on driving licences (Recast), OJ L 403, 30.12.2006, p. 18–60. Legislation on the mutual recognition of driving licenses had already been set, among others, in the case decided by the judgment in joined cases: C-329/06 and C-343/06, Widemann of 26 June 2008, ECLI:EU:C:2008:366, I-04635, in which CJEU found that "the residence requirement contributes, in particular, to combating the "tourism of driving licenses", in the absence of complete harmonization of the laws of member states relating to the issuing of driving licenses (...)" (par. 69), has admitted that the host state may refuse to recognize the right to drive resulting from the driving license subsequently issued by another member state "where it is possible to demonstrate, not on the basis of information from the host member state, but on the basis of the entries on the driving license itself or other indisputable information from the issuing member state, that the residency requirement imposed by art. 7, n. 1, lett. b) of Directive 91/439 was not met at the time of issuing this license (...)" (par. 72). In the same sense also the case: C-1/07, Weber of 20 November 2008, ECLI:EU:C:2008:640, I-08571. See also in argument: C. JANSSENS, The principle of mutual recognition in European Union law, op. cit.

816 In this sense, see, for example, the Commission Recommendation of 6 December 2012 on aggressive tax planning of 6.12.2012, C (2012) 8806 final; and the Communication from the Commission to the European Parliament and the Council "helping national authorities to combat abuses of the right of free movement: Manual on how to deal with the alleged fictitious marriages between EU citizens and third-country nationals in the framework of Union legislation on free movement of EU citizens" of 26.9.2014, COM (2014) 604 final.

817 See also the Communication to the Council, the European Parliament and the Economic and Social Committee."The application of anti-abuse measures in the field of direct taxation within EU and towards third countries" of 10.12.2007, COM (2007) 0785, with which the Commission has invited member states to carry out a general review of their anti-abuse rules in the field of direct taxation, taking into account the principles that derive from the jurisprudence. See in argument: P. PIANTAVIGNA, Tax abuse in European Union law, op. cit., pp. 135ss.

that when the abuse of law involves more than one legal system, it is primarily the jurisprudential instrument that proves to be inadequate and, therefore, EU's system, in countering the abuse, must test alternative instruments, in which an essential role is played by the legislator.

CHAPTER 7

The abuse of law/process...in criminal approach

Introduction. The approach to law in the Anglo-Saxon world, as we know, is a case study

To this general approach, not even the doctrine of abuse of process does not escape. It seems appropriate to underline then that in the English system the institution cannot be crystallized in a rigid rule. At the most, it is possible to try to delimit its contents, to identify its foundation, to analyze its "clinical cases", useful for a diagnosis that, inevitably, will be carried out on a case-by-case basis. From here, as is well understood, a further difficulty arises for the jurist (but, probably, to such difficulty would not escape more generally the jurist of civil law systems): to detach from the usual syllogism, which is based on the subsumption of the concrete story within the abstract case. At the end of the reckoning if the final goal of the work would be to evaluate the possibility of reconstructing a general "prohibition of abuse" clause in the internal penal trial, in the absence of an explicit regulatory provision, we risk arriving at an instrument with contours far too wide, whose excessive latitude would risk to come back just against the purposes that would be at the base of his conception (process deflation on the one hand, corresponding to the one that founded the ruling of the Supreme Court, guarantee of the defendant, in our perspective, on the other).

Of course, these are considerations that, at the moment, are hasty, as it is impossible to foresee both the final results of the research, as well as the eventual transposition, if it ever happens, of the same in practice. But, it is a danger that must be taken into account. If, as practice has shown us, procedural legality has sometimes highlighted the limits of a system based on the rigor of abstract forms, then the excessive detachment from the same deprives the internal scholar of a "compass" fundamental, making it enter land where there is a wide range of application oscillations and a high mix of legal and metagiurid concepts.

Will also postulate, albeit briefly, an entry into supranational regulatory scenarios. Without dwelling on well-known aspects: the "if" European and international law (ECHR, first) is not a question here and is a model that we must always compare with today, but the assessment of "how much" it affects the indoor system.

The hermeneutical approaches of a "substantialistic" sign are a product of the recalled systems. Harmonization and uniformity (without delving into the semantic specificities of the terms) impose them in no uncertain terms and the national jurist can only take note of it. The real point lies in the penetrative capacity of these interpretative modules.

The internal system does not remain insensitive to such elaborations and, with a view to adapting to supranational obligations, the operator is led to "manipulate them". It seems obvious, but it is the truth: the obligation to adapt to international agreements (in a broad sense) makes possible what, in principle, for internal law would not be. Hence the need to evaluate, also in relation to the subject matter discussed here, the potential impact of European and international law (in particular, it is repeated, with reference to that deriving from the European Convention on Human Rights and the rulings of the Court of Strasbourg).

Looking at the Anglo-Saxon system, the overall theoretical abuse of process is based on the principle of fairness: if a fair trial cannot take place, or it would be unfair to continue a criminal trial against anyone, the basic concept is that we are facing a "false" process. The accused is no longer in a position to exercise his faculties and rights fully. To continue would be an outrage against the moral integrity of the system and, at the same time, unequal. On the side of European and conventional legislation, on the other hand, we are witnessing the progressive creation of minimum and uniform protection standards. If, at least at the current historical moment, the creation of a "European criminal trial" is inconceivable, it should at least provide a "hard" and essential core of guarantees, to protect the overall fairness of the procedure, which, therefore, would represent the final horizon towards which every (procedural) means is projected.

If, at the end of the reckoning, this is essentially what national justice systems ask, the question is consequential: is it necessary to develop a general clause ensuring compliance with the principle of fair trial, when the instruments provided by positive law are not enough? Could the abuse of process be useful in this sense? Judgments of merit or opportunity survey and passes and ends with a question: what is the "state of the art" in terms of procedural legality?

The question is of such magnitude and scope that it induces the risk of going beyond the aims and object of the discussion; however, it is so intimately connected to the central theme that it cannot be left out, even if (be granted) incidenter tantum. After all, the claims inherent in the analysis that will take place would be entirely imaginative, where completely removed from a look at the procedural legality as a whole, always being understood that it is the conformation and the degree of rigidity of the same that determines the possibility of solutions that they would like to propose, both their concrete articulation. This, inevitably, will also entail an overview of the "physiological" limits of the same; more concretely, we will try to identify "practical" cases that, going beyond the legal forecasts, would constitute a procedural abuse capable of leading to an overall mismatch of the balance of powers of the parties in the process and which is even more relevant, they are not expressly affected by any penalty. In essence, if any use of a clause prohibiting abuse of process could be, it would be to react to practical distortions not provided for by the system, but not tolerable for this.

PART A

The concept of abuse of process: origins and framing

Why "the abuse of process"?

Crisis of legality, decadence of forms, interpretative "substantialistic" approaches and rationality needs the system. We could go on for a long time. Not that they are expressions of equal meaning; it is the common thread that unites them to capture attention. Because, to carefully look, the object of the present discussion is the direct result of events such as those mentioned.

In short, we are cyclically witnessing the return of temptation to invoke the forms, since we do not have the principles. Even if we will go back to the point in greater detail, this is a statement with a deceptive charm: the authoritarian drifts often originate from the bending of forms to the demands of (self)-protection of the legal system.

One could say that the concept of "abuse" (better: the repression of abuse) is a requirement of the legal system. It is intuitive, whereby the rule of law, which is based on the freedom of the individual, always contains within itself the risk of a surreptitious use of recognized freedoms. Of course, the possibilities of misuse of a guarantee or of a freedom also depend on the technique of describing the case in point. In other words, the abuse is reconnected (also, but not only) to a legislative "programming" error. There is no doubt that at the level of conceptual genesis, at least according to domestic law, the notion (in the broad sense) of abuse of law is linked to the need for logic, efficiency, rationality of the legal system. The goodness of its foundation, always in general terms, could not be discussed; rather, the interpretative elaboration should be criticized, as well as the modalities of implementation or the areas within which it is inserted, including the penal process. It is precisely in this logical-argumentative context that particular important issues are inscribed: for everyone, the possibility of admitting an abuse of rights or procedural powers recognized by each Constitution, or the "abusability" of an obligation enacted therein (that of exercise of criminal proceedings).

Abuse of law is in some way connatural to the system. This is evident from the area within which it originates: the substantive right, from which moves the elaboration of a dogmatic category inherited from the process science (both the civil, as-subsequently-the criminal one). Without going into considerations that are too obvious and eccentric with respect to the topic, we know that the goal of the process is to compose a dispute that is not otherwise resolvable. It could then be said that the conception of the notion of abuse is connected to the need to guarantee both, on the substantial side, the social order and, on the procedural, the correct use of the process. The pre-juridical nature in law is expression of the neminem laedere.

It is therefore a notion (always in general terms) with rather indefinite outlines. With greater clarity, we mean that the conceptual framework of abuse, between law and sociology, is affected by this dual nature. Any attempt by the interpreter to define its connotations meets evident difficulty. Without exaggerating the hyperbole, every time we deal with abuse (including the abuse of the process), we have the constant feeling that "something does not come back".

It is not by chance that the accent has been placed on the "emotional" dimension of abuse, in particular in the field of procedural law: here, more than in substantive law, the problematic relationship between individual and authority is visible. In the penal process, then, the "abuse" lemma is charged with a particular meaning, awaiting the complex game of equilibrium that is established between the public (which inevitably leads to a position of physiological supremacy) and private part.

In criminal trial, the topic has an immediate political value. Indeed, while on the one hand it has a useful diagnostic function of the fundamental problems of procedural system and of an overall assessment of its "state of health", on the other it lends itself to dubious and inopportune political exploitation (accentuated by the media debate), which see the (often harsh) juxtaposition between those who would like to end the exercise of criminal prosecution to "political" intentions or, in any case, non-conferring with its institutional aims and those who would instead escape the course of justice through dilatory or obstructive tactics.

Hence, the immediate warning for the purposes of the discussion that will follow: as far as possible and, apart from everything, well aware of the difficulties that this will imply, the attempt to reconstruct will be operated in an exclusively juridical key, thus trying to avoid entry into complicated land, which, to exemplify, the terrain of legislative reforms and the contrast (very current in these times) between institutional forces (parliament and government) and magistrates.

This warning seemed necessary, since the whole theory of procedural abuse is based on a general obligation of correctness on the part of the parties, which, as is well understood, is often the cause of overshooting in extra-juridical dimensions, even projecting the discourse on the side of political dialectics. However, this aspect does not necessarily have to be looked on negatively; on the other hand, the (so to speak) transversality of abuse, capable of innervating different disciplinary areas of legal system, testifies both its relevance in legal science as its vitality.

COMPARING CATEGORIES: FROM THE ABUSE OF RIGHT TO THE ABUSE OF PROCESS. NEED TO "REWRITE" THE NOTION?

As already highlighted, the criminal procedure is a terrain in which the culture of the theme has been rather fragmentary. The lack of composite reconstructions in the aforementioned field also clearly emerges when one looks at civil procedural law, characterized instead by a copious literature on the subject, but not only, to want to look at the phenomenon also from a comparative point of view, on the subject, contrary to what we have observed in the internal legal system, the attention of many scholars of criminal procedural law has been concentrated (in this sense, we will see in particular the Anglo-Saxon system).

The need for a systematic reflection on the subject, then, is also linked to that of avoiding its "politicization", thus diverting attention from the real problems underlying the matter, channeling them to emotional drives completely divorced from the legal field. The need to build up a general theory of abuse was primarily felt in substantive law. It is the daily reality, in fact, that allows the observation of behaviors carried out in compliance with the "forms", but incongruent with the logic and purposes that are at the base. The emulation acts were, presumably, the starting point for each reconstruction on the category of abuse. However, the substantive matrix of the topic did not prevent the establishment of autonomous reflections in the field of trial, which led, as regards the civil procedural law (moving from the prohibition of reckless quarrel), to the reconstruction of a theoretical stand-alone. The conceptual autonomy of abuse of process compared to the abuse of law is appreciated first of all from the point of view of the function that the elaborated clause would carry out.

In terms of substantive law, in fact, the limitation of private autonomy is justified in light of the urgent circulation of rights in the economic-social fabric and certainty of traffic. We exemplify the imposition of a limit to the right of ownership (archetype of absolute real law) constituted by the prohibition of emulation acts logically serves both to delimit the owner's lordship on the thing (thus providing a certain content and extension), and to guarantee the "appeal" of rights recognized in the market, thus facilitating circulation. Otherwise, in the context of the trial, there is a need to contain the incorrect behavior of the party who, formally availing of the faculties recognized by the law, would tend to circumvent the ultimate goal of the process, that is to say the assessment of the matter. On the other hand, always with specific regard to the field of civilization, the opportunity has arisen right away, always moving from regulatory provisions that act as a "model" for a broader elaboration, to reconstruct a broad prohibition clause of abuse.

However, it is necessary to pay attention to the temporal context in which this reconstructive operation is carried out.

It was said that in substantive law, having as a reference center the economic and juridical traffic, there is the necessity to adapt the normative context to an extremely changeable reality and, above all, in very rapid evolution (especially at the current historical moment). At the procedural level, otherwise, the conception of a general prohibition of abuse would be a garrison of the efficiency of the judicial machine allowing it, following the activation by the parties, to reach its natural end. Now, if all that has been said above retains its current relevance (at least on a conceptual and principle level), what changes at the root is the regulatory framework of reference that, today, makes the attempt to reconstruct commentary to a great extent.

In short, the intersection of domestic law with that of supranational origin, the permeability (more generally) of national legal system compared to European (and not), places the interpreter in crisis in front of an operation like the one referred to: a speech, obviously, is reasoning in a "closed" system, where (in addition to the Constitution) the reference point is given by the code, self-sufficient body of discipline, capable of self-integration. Another is that which sees a "judge in the labyrinth", where the usefulness of a general clause of abuse must come to terms with heterogeneous legal systems, as well as with the incessant adjustment obligation to which the internal system is subjected to supranational/international system adherence.

The reasoning carried out would seem to be able to say, to call into question the terms and paradigms on the basis of which the previous theory of abuse (of law and of the process) was built. And (it seems equally evident that) if this discourse is correct on the civilistic side, it will certainly be also on the criminal one on which, even the overthrow of supranational law in recent times has assumed greater proportions and significance.

Focusing on the criminal process, then, we can say with good approximation that the "old" reconstructions of the theory of abuse are affected by a lack. An elaboration made without the "lens" of external law that, on balance, would be an indispensable technical armament and which, therefore, would in itself already lead to conceive the opportunity to "rewrite" the notion of abuse of process. Change the scenery, it can only change what is inside.

INAPPLICABILITY OF CIVIL LAW PERSPECTIVE TO THE EUROPEAN/INTERNATIONAL CRIMINAL PROCESS

Attempting to summarize, the parameters that inform the abuse of right are given by the impropriety of the private in the exercise of the right (subjective profile) and by the disproportion that is recreated between the injured interest and that belonging to the "abused" right.

As we can see, we are faced with rather broad criteria of identification, as well as being widely "acknowledged" in the tradition and in the technical arsenal of civilistic notions. Correctness, in fact, is a direct derivative of the obligation of good faith of the contracting parties, just as the principle of proportion innervates the whole matter of private autonomy, always requiring the judge to place in relation the protection of an interest of the contractual parties with his "merit" of protection of the legal system.

As soon as one tries to imagine the "translation" of these criteria on the procedural side, and especially the penal one, one realizes their evident inconsistency.

In civil law, the (so to say) principle of atypicality is essentially connected to the protection of legal traffic, tending therefore to adapt the law to practice its evolution. In this context, it does not seem a big problem to admit the elaboration of a general prohibition of abuse clause, which makes up for a lack of a system that, instead, is not found in other systems.

This cannot be valid for the criminal trial, strictly based on the principle of legality. Here, the scenarios are totally different, and not just compared to substantive law. The right to take legal action to protect one's own interests is very different from the obligation to prosecute. Yet, this is not enough because the rigor of legality must, in any case, relentlessly confront the dynamics of the accusatory process, which attributes in principle to the parties the lordship over the dispute and whose strategies are substantially replaced by the development of the process.

For this reason, any hypothesis of eliminating at root the danger of procedural abuse through a strict predetermination of the legal schemes for predicting the behavior of the parties and, at the same time, minimizing (if not canceling) the discretion of the same in relation to their concrete act, it would risk to involve the return to a ritual (basically corresponding to the previous inquisitorial model) characterized by the predominance of the figure of the judge who, as known, "directed" the actions of the parties themselves (in full coherence with the paternalistic conformation of the same within the previous code).

Therefore, it is worthwhile for the penal process, the metaphor, where the greater rigor in the repression of abuse would correspond to a restriction of the freedom of the parties and vice versa.

On the other hand, the distinction between the abuse of law and of process, in one with the opportunity to recreate an autonomous processing space for the latter with respect to the first, is also apparent from international law and, firstly, by ECHR, where the "distorted" exercise of one of the guarantees contemplated therein (article 17 ECHR)[818] is expressly distinguished from the proposition of an abusive appeal (article 35, which provides for the sanction of the inadmissibility of the same).

THE GENESIS IN PROCEDURAL LAW. AN ANSWER TO DIFFICULT PROBLEMS

What could be the added value of abuse in penal procedure or to what problems would one want to respond through the creation of a general notion in this sense?

818 C. TEITGEN-COLLY, La Convention europèenne des droits de l'homme: 60 ans et après?, ed. LGDJ, Paris, 2013. W.A. SCHABAS, The European Convention on Human Rights: A commentary, Oxford University Press, Oxford, 2015, pp. 1755ss.

It is not a new question; in general, a procedural system predisposes devices not only capable of guaranteeing the rights of the parties, but also of ensuring their proper functioning or, if one wants, that the latter is not put at risk by incorrect behavior of the parties. In short, it would be a question of assessing whether procedural invalidity constitutes sufficient protection for the protection of interests in dispute or, otherwise, the same are not able to summarize the needs represented above, opening the door to the opportunity to seek an extra-codic solution.

In general terms, the instrumental function of procedural law over substantive law would intuitively imply the necessity of elaborating an abuse clause on the first ground that is (to be clear) aimed at providing a correct convergence of the goals of the former. More simply, in terms of logic, the function of a general prohibition of abuse at the procedural level would guarantee an application of the substantive law within the ends that belong to it. On the criminal procedure side, this is not contradicted or in any case does not encounter a barrier in internal constitutional law. Indeed, a discourse would affirm the obligatory nature of prosecution, channeling it towards the protection of equality of citizens before the law, another that the prosecution cannot be abused and, therefore, that implement the intrinsic goals of substantive law.

It does not seem an eccentric consideration. The possible objection according to which, by reasoning, one assigns to a procedural notion a function (if we want to say) only a servant with respect to the substantive law, clashes with another fundamental fact: the criminal trial is not, like the civil composition of a controversy otherwise resolvable in practice through private autonomy (the civil trial is only a path that can be followed by the contenders who, therefore, may agree extra-judicial solutions). Criminal law only applies through jurisdiction. Hence, it would seem logical consequence, the function of procedural abuse in terms of "guarantee the fairness of purpose" of substantive law. In any case, the fact that this prohibition is assigned to the prohibition of abuse does not imply that it cannot cover it further at a properly procedural level.

In this last sense, one could derive from the profile relevant to the penalizing consequences that derive from the detection of abuse. In other words, the just reported profile would contribute to the identification of distortions that are to be avoided. Now, in terms of reaction, on the substantive ground, abuse of law generally involves a dual alternative.

The abusive act does not produce effects. Its fulfillment is ascertained for non-legal purposes, so it cannot benefit from any protection tamquam not esset.

Second option: incorrect conduct has such a seriousness as to integrate an offense. The author exposes himself to damages, or to a criminal proceeding, or to the payment of a pecuniary sanction.

One could imagine to "transplant" these solutions into a procedural (criminal) procedure. Thus, the abusive procedural act would not receive protection and, therefore, would fall into nothingness (effects never produced); again, it would constitute an illicit, exposing the author to liability (civil, criminal, or administrative).

However, it is easy to see that the second solution constitutes a remedy that has little use for the party affected by the abusive act: while not denying its deterrent capacity with respect to its authors, this approach would not have any effect on the injured party. "Thaumaturgical" on the procedural level (an effect to which, logically, it aspires). On the other hand, the framing of abuse within the penal process is not entirely correct as an aggression of the rational functioning of justice. Indeed, it would be short-sighted vision: empirical observation would immediately contradict it, showing how, in addition to the system, the guarantees and rights of the parties are a concrete target of the same.

Therefore, the first would remain. The idea that the most appropriate sanction for the abuse in the criminal trial may be the denial of efficacy to the vitiated act, essentially leads to the elaboration of a scheme of detection and consequences reaction such as the following. The P part performs an act formally legitimate, which pursues a non-institutional purpose; when the abuse is detected, the deed carried out does not produce the effects that the law would reconnect to it (those that may have already been produced would fall into nothingness, overwhelmed by the judicial declaration of ascertainment).

After all, we can say that we are dealing with an already known operative model: it follows that of codic invalidity (the first nullity). However, with the conception of a theory of abuse we would react to a physiological limit of the latter: taxability. Because there is not even a general prohibition, not even between the general nullity, for the judge and the other subjects of the trial, to perform "substantially" contrary acts to fairness or eccentric with respect to the legal purpose. If one wishes to continue the reasoning with regard to another form of disability, one can take the example of the uselessness; there is no explicit general prohibition on the acquisition of evidence for purposes that go beyond the intentio legis.

On closer inspection, the reasoning carried out allows us to arrive at a possible conclusion: that in the criminal trial, regardless of the interest that in the individual case you go to protect, the essential function of abuse would be to react to the gaps that inevitably recreate the legality. Basically, the idea (not entirely unlikely) arises that the abuse constitutes a sort of counter-limit to the principle in word that, beyond the function of guarantee, would represent the "problem" to which theoretical abuse should be answered.

On the other hand, the idea (of enlightenment matrix) for which the law in its entirety is compelled in the written law is completely illusory. The need for self-protection of the system, together with that of not end up imploding due to the voids that the legality inevitably leaves, radically reject this idea, setting the premises for a system that has to activate the valves of its values. However, in criminal matters, the question is extremely complicated.

In the civil trial, in fact, legality generally "softens" in the face of acts that, although not corresponding to the legal model, still achieve their purpose or that, lacking the necessary elements to achieve the purpose, are to be declared null even in the absence of specific forecast; in the penal one, otherwise, the overall balance of the partisan powers is based on legality. The freedom of action and strategy of the procedural actors is the rule, the limits to the same are the exceptions which, therefore, are in principle positively circumscribed.

In short, the conceptual difficulty faced by the abuse of process is that of interfering with a system pillar which, when questioned, leads directly to the possibility of significantly altering its structure.

THE LEGAL DIMENSION OF PROCEDURAL ABUSE IN CRIMINAL PROCEEDINGS: ASSUMPTIONS AND QUALIFYING ELEMENTS. HOW DO WE IDENTIFY AN ABUSE?

The casuistry on the subject is rather varied. Nonetheless, it is possible to trace an identifying connotation: the eccentricity of the purpose of the act with respect to that identified by the law, and we need some clarification on this. The qualifying attitude of the purpose of the act with respect to the notion of abuse would be supported by the fact that the element of purpose finds normative consecration in "adjoining" institutions. In establishing a nullity (relative or intermediate) when the party is interested in objecting to it, availed itself of the faculty to which the null act was preordained, the law would sanction an abusive, distorted use of the invalidity in question.

On the concept of purpose, three approaches converge: one can speak of it with reference to the act individually accomplished or, which is the same, as the institutional purpose of the same; a second meaning revolves around the legal effect that the law reconnects to the latter. Alternatively, it would identify itself with the objective concretely pursued by the party who performed the act. Now, on the second meaning of the noun in comment no particular perplexities would arise in relation to the content: here we have about the legal effect produced, which is predetermined by the law. The criterion in question, understood in this sense, would seem at first glance to the least exposed to interpretative uncertainties, since it is an element identified directly by the procedural law. However, on closer inspection, in the face of abuse it has only apparent heuristic efficacy: if the prosecutor exercises the criminal action, the effect of the definitive rooting of the jurisdiction is produced, so that the validity of the punitive pretension is examined. If, by hypothesis, the criminal action were dictated by "political" intent, the simple criterion of legal effect of the act would be of no use in this sense. On the contrary, the opposite would tell us that the magistrate has carried out an act (exercise of the penal action) from which the legislatively predetermined effect is derived, that is the rooting of the judicial screening on the punitive pretension.

On the first and third, therefore, attention should be focused on. The practical aim taken by the author would be a concept of empirical nature, for this very oscillatory and therefore too labile to found a useful qualifying and at the same time diagnostic element. Beyond that, there would be another difficulty for the interpreter: in some situations, there would be some difficulty in tracing the distinction between the two meanings.

Exemplify to be clear: the appeal, reduced the question to the minimum terms, has the institutional function of allowing the proposer to obtain a benefit not obtained in the previous degree. The presentation produces three effects: suspensive, devolutive and extensive. It is legitimate, however, to propose an appeal in order to obtain the prescription if the limit case is imagined. The accused will mature the term necessary to prescribe the immediate circumstances of the sentence of first instance and for which, therefore, the challenge would be the road obliged to get the acquittal? In this case, it cannot be doubted that the declaration of extinction of the offense due to a statute of limitations falls within the category of those benefits to which the party can legitimately aspire through the appeal. On closer inspection, a concretely and institutional purpose of the appeal (obtaining a benefit not achieved in the previous degree, where the prescription is, evidently, a benefit) coincide.

On closer inspection, within the theory of abuse of process, the meanings of institutional and of practical purpose are integrated and interact, becoming the one the comparison term for the other. With greater clarity and in order to verify that an act is carried out within the framework of the legislative purposes, a comparison would be needed which, for the purpose specifically aimed at, is that of the institutional purpose and vice versa. Of course, the identification of the purpose concretely pursued by the party exposes to significant probative difficulties, since it is an investigation into the psyche of the same. However, it seems like an inaccurate "tool" that is essential for the identification of abusive conduct. In fact, to be honest, one could not even conceive the notion of abuse without the implicit idea of the practical aim taken by the author.

POSSIBLE SANCTIONS FOR ABUSE

The attempt to reconstruct an abuse of process clause that is not simultaneously accompanied by the identification of remedies when it occurs, would deprive the prohibition in which it takes the form of any effectiveness. Operation completely useless, it would be better to say: imagine the irregularity, even with something less. This, although devoid of sanction, however, constitutes a discrepancy from a legal model "written", while the first, on the contrary, moves from the assumption that the procedural behavior is, albeit formally, adhering to the aforementioned model.

Comparatively, one could reasonably state that, in this regard, the profile inherent in the sanctions regime prevails over the identification of the conduct capable of integrating the pathology in question. We have said this before: the abuse of process is an institute that originates from strictly practical necessities, to react to the gaps in the "closed" system of procedural invalidity. It is therefore clear that it would be an operation as vain as (in practice and also on a scientific level) the attempt to compose a catalog of those acts that can be defined as abuse.

Hence, the choice to put the abuse treatment before that of the exemplary casuistry. The concept of abuse is intimately linked to the discretion of the judge (in the English system) to continue with the trial or, on the contrary, to arrest him. Ultimately, the power to block the continuation of the punitive pretension is a connatural aspect of jurisdiction. It is not the only form of reaction to procedural abuse, but certainly it is the most representative and, at the same time, of maximum rigor, reaching the limit beyond which the public interest in the repression of crimes cannot go or, in any case, in front of which he must yield.

There is no such remedy within the national system. The reasons why this solution is not in principle sustainable, and for which, in fact, has never been proposed or even hypothesized in practice, are multiple. This is not the place to dwell in depth. Here, however, the essential relief pertaining to the sensitive heterogeneity of the legal systems is sufficient.

The difference is the criminal action. In the Anglo-Saxon process, as is known, it is discretionary. The Crown Prosecution Service is assigned the selective capacity of what it deserves in practice to be prosecuted. In such a system, the abuse of process is the natural barrier to the possible "overflowing" of the prosecution in the exercise of the action. In short, the jurisdiction guarantees that the punitive pretension remains in the wake of the institutional ends. On the contrary, internally, criminal proceedings are mandatory: at stake the equality of citizens in the face of criminal law, being able to essentially say that the merit of the prosecution of offenses is carried out upstream by law. Clearly, therefore, a power corresponding to that developed in common law, not only is not justified in a systematic way, but would also risk to oppose with its own principles.

Given this, with the exception of what will be the object of reflection in the remainder, it is still possible to identify, within the internal practice, the remedies that, more or less frequently, have been used for the distorted uses of the process and the procedural instruments.

If we wanted to compare the sanctioning range in civil trial, we would deduce three fundamental types. The reactions will go from the application of a (in a broad sense) pecuniary sanction, to the penalties on the part of the parties and operating at the procedural level and, finally, to the disincentives arising from the defender[819].

With a good approximation, the first order would result in the imposition of restitutionary obligations (think of the charge of court costs). The second in the rejection of the application or, even more generally, of the request made by the party (this reaction would therefore find maximum expression in the declaration of invalidity of the deed). The last one would represent a synthesis of the two precedents, with the peculiarity that the directly affected subject is the sponsor

819 M. TARUFFO, General report, in A.A.V.V., Abuse of procedural right: Comparative standards of procedural fairness, Kluwer Law International, Hague-Boston-London, 1999, pp. 23ss.

(see, by way of example, which provides for the possibility of condemning to a pecuniary penalty the defendant-or even the part-who has proposed a recusal declared inadmissible).

In the criminal process, even in the profound diversity of the terrain, one would see, in terms of positive law, a certain "continuity" of solutions with respect to the processual-civil model. With a clarification, however: without prejudice to the appropriate interpretative emendations, possibly imposed by the "transplantation" in different sedes materiae. It is clear that only the second group of remedies is a strictly procedural legal instrument. Indeed, the pecuniary sanction is a threat that could be a deterrent, but does not "cancel" the effects materially produced by the abuse. Otherwise, the rejection of the application would operate properly on the procedure, producing the fall into nothing of the act.

Given this, the direction that the treatment regime, based on the model of the rejection of the application, could follow is twofold. One could react by rejecting the request of the part, "demolishing" the act in place and overwhelming its effects as well as the consequential acts (here the conjecture would borrow a mechanism designed for the nullity).

Otherwise, one could think of the neutralization of the benefit targeted by the author of abuse. It is clear: the two solutions place the judge in a different position according to the part to which the abusive conduct would lead: the prosecution and, in the final instance, of every act that constitutes its extrinsecation, would refer the judge to a control position on the conduct of public part; in the face of defense, on the other hand, it would operate in a disincentive key (in practice: a formally legitimate but abusive act could not receive recognition).

Nevertheless, if both the publicity of interests involved in the criminal trial, and the difficult coercibility of the partisan trial maneuvers, consistent with the accusatory model, would make the remedy constituted by pecuniary sanctions the one with a lower risk of "collision" with the principles of this option is understandably inadequate to ensure effective protection of rights of the parties, thus opening the way to the opportunity to conceive of remedies of a caducatory nature.

THE PARADIGM OF NEUTRALIZATION OF THE BENEFIT OBTAINABLE FROM THE ABUSE

It has an archetype in the discipline of suspension the terms of prescription of the crime and the duration of the precautionary custody. This, from the defense side: is an invitation to correctness the trial, when this is determined by the impediment of the defendant or his defender. Specularly, always to remain on the same ground, the possible abuse of "precautionary" application by the public prosecutor is a "corrective" system aimed at presiding over the interests of the party in process. In the argumentative context of work, otherwise, the term in question would emphasize the general-preventive effect that the proposed remedy would have on the trial actors, as well as on the orthopedics and ethics of their conduct.

One cannot doubt that these hypotheses are supported by a logic (so to speak) anti-abusive; however, the temptation to enumerate from the same rules generic prohibitions of abuse that are applicable in similar situations, must necessarily be measured with the reference terrain. Here, the soil is delicate: the good involved is personal freedom, whose rules of limitation if, in principle, can admit analogical applications in bonam partem, on the contrary they do not tolerate interpretative operations of opposite sign.

From this, more generally, it would follow that any attempt to reconstruct anti-abusive clauses should not be measured only with the limits imposed upstream by legality, but also with the context of reference and with the legal good "sacrificed" by the sanction of the conduct abuse. Yet, it is necessary to assess whether the legislator intended to limit the sanction of abuse to the specific situations described by the law and that, therefore, the remedy cannot be generalized.

(FOLLOWS) THE PARADIGM OF REJECTION OF THE ABUSIVE QUESTION

The theme must necessarily be tackled in separate perspectives, respectively related to the position of the public prosecutor and the accused. It is clear that some typical remedies, which constitute an expression of the paradigm in question, can establish a unitary reflection. Thus, the interest in the appeal acts as a filter useful for discerning the appeals pretestious or, in any case, markedly dictated by intent dilators, from those to the contrary founded. This, as we understand, would be as much for the prosecution as for the defense.

Let's go back to the starting methodology, proceeding with a separate analysis of the procedural parts.

Is there a way to syndicate, in a broad sense, the admissibility of the initiative in the exercise of prosecution or even more in general: does the judge have a generic power of rejection of the same when it is abusively proposed?

We return to what was said in the previous paragraph: a judicial attribution of this type is not present in the system. The criminal action is mandatory. If it is not founded, it is at most impracticable: in both cases, liberating formulas aside, we go to the acquittal that, apparently, would be the only remedy available for criminal actions conducted for extra-institutional purposes. However, despite the gaps left by the system, given that the accused, subject to the ordeal of a criminal action (by hypothesis) evidently dictated by "political" reasons, should still pass through the judicial screening of (in) the merits of the punitive pretension, not being able to invoke a general remedy for the arrest of the criminal trial because (the expression is allowed) of the eccentricity of the purpose of the action. In short, we cannot conceive a hypothetical judicial screening on the "congruity of the ends" of prosecution.

Changing point of observation, looking at the rejection of the presumptuous question of the accused, we would have the following examples.

The exception of nullity proposed by those who have no interest, or by whom caused it, goes to a denial. Likewise, an incident implementation proposed on the basis of grounds for the foundation of a previous request with the same content is inadmissible. As can be seen from an overall view, we react to maneuvers that lead to intolerable burdens of the judiciary, in relation to which the right of defense undergoes a contraction when the demand is not supported by founded reasons.

PART B

Abuse of trial and of procedural tools

When we talk about the abuse from the objective point of view (in this case we mean the behaviors that can integrate it), we can recall two macro categories. It is a bipartition which originates from the civil process but which, of course, retains its validity also in the criminal sphere: abuse of process in the strict sense, on the one hand; abuse of procedural tools, on the other.

This partition immediately informs us of a fact that the category of abuse essentially concerns the parts of the process, thus being worth excluding the judge, at least for two reasons. As one reason, the reference to the duty of correctness serves as a general limit for the conduct of trial parties, containing the perversions that could derive from the freedom of action and strategy they enjoy. Second, the general approach of the accusatory system, in one with the strict subjection of the judge, which would place him in principle in the position of arbitrator of the dispute, subtracts him from the notion in comment. At most, the exercise of a power that is not permitted by law, or anyway capable of leading to stasis of the procedure or to undue regressions, could produce another type of vice, that is to say the abnormality of the act.

Without obviously overemphasizing the comparison, it could be said that the abuse of process constitutes for the parties that "closure" of the system that for the judge is given by the abnormity. In both cases, therefore, we are outside the provisions of the code, within the jurisprudential creations.

Returning to the aforementioned bipartition, it should be said that in civil trial it is easy to hypothesize the abuse of process. The action is exercisable or not, directly subject to the availability of the parties (except in cases of exercise by the public prosecutor, when interests of obvious publicity are at stake). The same cannot be said in criminal cases, where, it would seem to be a first logical consideration, one would be able to conceive only the abuse of single acts (or rather, instruments) of the case.

Although this will be discussed later on, it should be pointed out that the difficulty of conceiving in criminal trial practical manifestations inherent to the first macro-category (process abuse) would arise only because of the principles of national (constitutional) system. In other words, nothing takes away that the one who has the power to start a trial does not promote the action for extra-institutional purposes, not animated by the intent to watch over the observance of laws. On the contrary, the instrumentalization of a "constitutional" obligation could be conduct (if desired) subtler than that of the right of defense, although more difficult to counteract, sensing how the adduction of the obligation due to the exercise of the action can be a convenient "coverage" of the sensuous side actions or of the real intentions to the same sub-asses. Yet, as we have said, stopping the continuation would be an intolerable invasion of the field, or aggression of the "reserve" of attribution made by every national system.

In addition to this, always with a view to delimiting the objective manifestations of abuse, the setting must always be considered valid, always invoked in civil law, which divides the related behavior on the basis of two criteria: that of functional deviation, on the one hand and of impropriety, on the other.

Basically, in adherence to this further partition, a discourse would be to exercise the action or perform an act for purposes other than those provided by law (i.e., to take action for the sole purpose of inducing the counterparty to a transaction, or compromising social "credibility", for example), another that of pursuing a legitimate aim, but in a manner contrary to fair trial (i.e., splitting up the credit into separate shares, subjecting the adversary to heavy burdens).

At first reading, one would be tempted to bring functional deviation and misconduct into unity by questioning: to the showdown, what would change? If the action or the act are subject in both cases to a distorted use, do you want with respect to the permitted purpose, or with respect to the duty of procedural correctness?.

At a closer look, however, we are aware of the difference between the two faces.

We exemplify in criminal process: if the public prosecutor exercises the action for the sole purpose of discrediting the image of someone, aware of the groundlessness of the punitive pretension, it would evidently owe the institutional purpose of attribution. Otherwise, if the same party voluntarily or negligently expands the timing of investigations, while working for the necessary collection of the elements that, in fact, determine the exercise of the action, there would be no rationale of purpose: the conduct complies with the legal purpose. It is a purely incorrect behavior. At most, the noteworthy question would be: what is meant by procedural correctness? The civil trial can count, unlike the criminal one, on case studies and a ten-year jurisprudential elaboration. There would be the problem of delimiting the contours of a concept which, in any case, would be more properly meta-juridical.

On the other hand, one can also image cases at the limit, where functional deviation and impropriety risk becoming confused. If the public prosecutor voluntarily or negligently does not carry out an investigation that would give rise to a piece of evidence to discharge the suspect, causing the loss of contribution during the assessment. Moreover, if the accused asks for the admission of a plurality of witnesses (imagine a large number), aware of the fact that many of them would make depositions of equal content (and therefore would be superfluous). In this way,would lengthening the time of education in such situations be distorted by legal or simply disloyal conduct?

Apart from this, the partition referred to above would also call into question the usefulness of the qualifying element i.e. the structure of abuse constituted by the purpose. As a criterion for identifying abusive conduct, it would certainly be decisive in the face of those characterized by a functional deviation. But in front of the others, does it have any practical utility in determining part's impropriety?

"CLINICAL" CASES OF ABUSE OF PROCESS. ABUSE OF TRIAL: EXERCISE OF CRIMINAL PROSECUTION. BETWEEN DEVIATIONS OF PURPOSE AND IMPROPRIETY

It is opportunely repeated: an exhaustive catalog is physically impossible. The cases taken as a reference, in the context of criminal trial, will be worth highlighting the characteristic traits and the physiognomy of the procedural abuse. The methodology of analysis will move from the partition operated in the previous paragraph. Therefore, we will proceed to a separate analysis of the two macro-categories of abuse of process and of procedural documents.

We are faced with conduct in relation to which we find the objective difficulty of measuring oneself with the "rigid" institutional obligations that refer to the figure of public prosecutor, while at the same time seeming completely detached from reality that we do not recognize the existence of deviant praxis, capable of configuring abuse in the strict sense. That's not all, because in this last sense, if we can abstractly conceive cases of abuse tout court of criminal prosecution, we also give situations in which the exercise of powers recognized to the public prosecutor, while not configuring an abuse in the first sense, affects the overall correctness or congruence of the purposes of his action. If during the investigations the requisite proceeds separately for two positions which, on the contrary, require a joint treatment, so surreptitiously causing an objective difficulty for the elaboration of defensive strategies, it could not be strictly speaking about abuse of criminal action. Nevertheless, the disloyalty of such behavior could undermine the overall correctness of the procedure that will follow, as a joint investigation ab initio would certainly have facilitated the determinations of defense.

Furthermore, the abuse can be commissive or omission. Within the first group, one can imagine those typical situations of use of the precautionary instrument (custody in prison, first) in order to obtain the collaboration of the accused; or, again, if the accused, reached by serious indications of guilt regarding several offenses, saw himself receiving more requests to apply the measure diluted over time, so as to protract the time of his detention. Here, as one guesses, it is a question of functional deviation: with the precautionary measure, a goal that is foreign to the system is pursued. In the second, the avoidance of legal obligations can be included in order to allow the participation of the accused in the proceedings and the implementation of the adversarial. We hypothesize the total or partial omission of the disclosure (at the end of the preliminary investigations or in those cases in investigations where it is required by law): the omission pursues ulterior purposes, to the detriment of the position of the accused. Differently, the inertia of prosecutor in carrying out the investigations or the delay in the exercise of the prosecution would be violations of the duty of loyalty.

On the other hand, a sort of "test bed" of this last group of hypotheses was found with the well-known problem of delay (voluntary or culpable) in the inscription of the notitia criminis in the register of crime reports. We know that the public prosecutor has the obligation to register when he finds the existence of evidence against someone. The omission is a source of responsibility for the same, not only on the disciplinary level, but also recurring the conditions on the criminal one. Is it also on a strictly procedural level? It is true that we are not properly faced with an improper exercise of criminal action, but it is equally true that the conduct in comment is a pathological manifestation capable of strongly affecting the subsequent act of impulse, substantially polluting its correctness (referred pathological manifestation that it is an example of a very useful point for our considerations, i.e. the objective practical difficulty of conceiving remedies or sanctions of abuse in the process).

Separate reflections deserve the hypotheses constituted by the choice of public prosecutor for certain simplified procedures (that is, in the opposite sense, by the lack of choice).

It is possible to hypothesize the appeal of public part to the procedure for a criminal decree (or, again, of an immediate judgment). The injury capable of recreating is immense, since the effect immediately produced is that of a "leap" of phase, while depriving the accused of the contradictory (better: postponing the implementation), being also plausible that the guarantee of judicial control imposed by law is not always sufficient protection.

Moreover, the issue relating to the choice of special forms of prosecution also invests that, opposed, not to use them: so, it can be assumed that the criminal magistrate, while aware of the concrete possibility of defining the procedure in the forms of the decree criminal conviction, opts for prosecution through the ordinary ways, for the sole purpose of prolonging the time of submission of the accused to the process.

From another view, the problem may be that the conduct of the public prosecutor aimed at "diverting" the defendant from the pre-constituted natural judge by national law could result in the genus of the improper exercise of criminal prosecution. With greater clarity, reference should be made here to the scenario in which the public prosecutor, in a proceeding concerning a crime that is connected with another operator, but in discussion at the judicial office, omits the reconditioning of proceedings at the "natural" headquarters. On closer inspection, there is no deviation of purpose, but unfair conduct. The remedies exist, but potentially insufficient (the defense could be aware of the defect of incompetence beyond the "temporal" limits set by the code, witnessing the crystallization of the foreclosure on the point).

As can be inferred, the exemplifying hypotheses represented would constitute the result of discretionary choices that are difficult to be examined according to positive instruments, when they are not even completely incontrovertible.

(FOLLOWS) ABUSE OF INDIVIDUAL PROCEDURAL ACTS

The macro category in comment is understandably more extensive. The accusatory approach established by national criminal system together with the exaltation of the maneuvering margins of the parties in the conduct of dispute, make this fertile ground, at least as much as the civil trial, for the cultivation of abuse of individual procedural instruments.

Because of its latitude, both the conduct of public prosecutor and those carried out by the defendant fall within it. If, in fact, it is not conceivable an abuse of the trial in the strict sense by the defendant, otherwise, the breadth of the range of action inherent in the right of defense makes it possible for the latter to use distorted procedural instruments. This is seen with regard to the public part, both in terms of functional deviation of the act, and in that of impropriety, so then, there will be "deviant" conduct both in commissive and in omission.

Here, however, we must take into account a peculiar aspect. The potential involvement of the accused, in one with the need to limit the "escapes" from the criminal trial to the detriment of the process economy, makes it appropriate to balance two opposed interests: the right of defense on one hand and the efficiency of criminal justice on the other.

The topic has been the subject of considerable attention not only in the doctrine, but also in constitutional jurisprudence, aimed at finding a reasonable balance between the reported needs and, at the same time, providing constitutional "coverage" to the value of procedural efficiency. Trying to identify the content of the latter, according to the perspective of the judge, it can be said that it coincides with the protection of achievement of the essential purpose of the criminal trial: id est, the verification of the merit claim. Therefore, the concept of abuse of procedural acts, where referred to the position of accused (as elaborated, as will be seen shortly, in view of the dilatory conduct put in place by the defense), is built in relation to those behaviors that have effect, due to procedural stasis recreated through the abuse of procedural guarantees, to prevent the assessment of the duty to punish. We are therefore faced with a concept of economic nature: it is linked to the need to contain judicial "expense", with a markedly utilitarian imprint. This concept, moreover, is firmly coupled with that of the rational use of process and of procedural instruments and which has therefore received a decisive "endorsement" of legislation due to the consecration of the principle of reasonable duration of process.

Now, if this was the conceptual and practical premise for the elaboration of abuse of procedural documents, it is necessary to emphasize the specific aspect of this macro category. If, in fact, on the basis of the above summarized approach, we can affirm the presence, within the system, of a principle (so to speak) of non-dispersion of procedural resources, but we must also go into the assessment of the abusive conduct of part, in the intimate ratio of the norm attributive of power or disciplinary accomplished act. In other words, it is necessary to carefully identify the value or the legal good protected by the law in question, thus placing it through a judgment of proportionality in relation to the need for cheapness the judicial machine. The question that arises at the end of this comparison operation, in short, is the following: does the efficiency of the process justify in that single case the compression of interest subtended to the conferring rule.

On closer inspection, we are faced with a reasoning which, in essence, refers to the balancing of conflicting interests which, as we see, should be solved case by case. The introduction of this operating module would logically function to avoid an interpretative reconstruction for which the identification of abuse would pass for the sole detection of the existence of its qualifying traits. In other words, faced with the abuse of procedural acts, it is not enough to say in premise that there is a functional distortion or impropriety in the exercise of power; we need more. It is necessary to establish whether the interest protected by the power of giving norm can succumb the economic nature of the court machine. Further, it is also evident that the problematic of the setting lies in determining the rank of the guarantee inherent in the provision governing power, which would be like saying: there are guarantees more or less "sacred" or, in any case, more or less susceptible to compression. While particular caution is needed in placing the interests at stake within the hierarchical scale of values, we have a judgment that, also because of the fact that it is conditioned by the ale of the concrete case, is inevitably affected by the relativism of values as well as by their extreme changeability over time.

That said, in an attempt to identify some symptomatic hypotheses of abuse of procedural tools, we can begin with that constituted by the overuse[820] of part instance. In other words, reference is made to the excess of reiteration of

820 L.S. MULLENIX, Discovery in disarray: The pervasive myth of pervasive discovery abuse and the consequences for unfounded rule making, in Stanford Law Review, 46, 1994, pp. 1393ss.

requests by parties to the judge, accompanied by a lack of substantial foundation or, in any case, by evident pretense.

One could almost say species of the broader genus of the manifestly unfounded request. However, if in this last case the abusive intent could be excluded from several reasons of manifest groundlessness (a request could be affected even if only due to the technical incompetence of the party in the use of the procedural means), the one mentioned above is relatively simpler. The pedestrian repetition of the same application, based on the same elements that would have supported the former already rejected or declared inadmissible (to cite the most frequent case), provides a fairly reliable index of the dilatory aims underlying the mechanism, beyond any forecasts of law that sanctions its rejection (see for example on the issue of inadmissibility of the proposed execution incident on the basis of grounds for the foundations of a previously rejected). It is, of course, harmful conduct in terms of system economics, subject to very serious forms of abuse that can sometimes even be concerted. One hypothesizes, in a multi-subjective process, the proposition "in turn" by the co-defendants of requests for deferment of the hearing due to a legitimate impediment, aimed at making the necessary for the prescription of the offense.

Still within the practice of the overuse, one can recall the phenomenon of abusive recourse or remission.

This is a distorted use of special alarm, so much to arouse the interest and the intervention of the Constitutional Court (national level)! Here, in hindsight, the degree of problematicity would be exacerbated by the apical importance of the interest protected by the procedural instruments in comment (impartiality) of the judge as opposed to that of procedural efficiency; which would translate, concretely, into the conflict between two basic principles of the system.

On the specific occasion (in particular on the referral), the judge had to remedy a lacuna in the system and a normative body that lent itself unreasonably to dilatory uses of requests for recusal and remission (the speech, moreover, would be more widely included in the Thematic of the relationship between the main and incidental process, where the need to avoid diachronic sequences would be opposed to that of not producing unnecessary slow-downs of the procedure).

The practice, faced with the evident vulnus, had developed extra-legal solutions, both technically dubious and exacerbated in rigor. In fact, the power of judge (rejected or remitted) to examine ex ante the admissibility of the requests of the party was established.

Intervening in order to compose the recreational conflict, he criticized the practice (it is a matter of attribution not allowed to most cases in the national system), he launched to "warning" the legislator, at the same time declaring the partial illegitimacy (thus removing the limit for the judge intervened the instance of remission or recusal, to pronounce sentence). In the work of normative planning, it is necessary to take into account the degree of "abusability" of an act or of a faculty. Therefore, in accordance with the principles of reasonableness and procedural efficiency, this degree should be as limited as possible, in order to prevent the process from being diverted from its natural end (response to the punitive pretension).

Putting content aside, to reflect well, the pronunciation gives us two essential indications for the purposes of this discussion. If on the one hand, we are faced with a reasoned attempt to reconstruct the category of abuse (at least with reference to that of the procedural documents), on the basis of guiding criteria of a constitutional matrix. On the other, it informs us of a cultural line and specific technical-legal address the basic distrust of the use of analogy and the tendency to leave "pretorias" in the hands of anti-abuse clauses elaboration not provided for by the law because it is necessary that the same clauses are established by a specific provision or, at least, they have a normative reference capable of acting as a conceptual basis.

In addition, careful consideration deserves the profile pertaining to the abuse of appeal. It is a phenomenon that is expressed in a heterogeneous range of hypotheses, within which the (sought) dilatation of the times aimed at the prescription is, probably, the most frequent.

One point must be clear. It is an area in which we must proceed with caution. Judgments of appeal, in principle refractory to the entry of nova (both as regards the tests, as for what concerns the thema decidendum, circumscribed in principle to the object devolved with the act of appeal) and, therefore, structurally closer to a "cartular" model than to one based on orality (as is the first degree), they are (so to speak) physiologically devoted to abuse. They constitute "appendices", procedural epilogues only possible and unnecessary (also keeping in mind that the only judgment for cassation has relevance-expressed-constitutional). Hence, one might say, the basic preconception that risks to meander through the system: the one for which, most of the time, the proposition of the same would be superfluous, useless.

From this reasoning, it would follow that the identification of "abusive" nature of the appeal must pass through a careful analysis of the reasons presented in support, where the parameter of interest assumes a determining value. The appeal is designed as a tool to check what has been done previously, which in itself, potentially, constitutes the basis for founding a judgment. The "physiological" risk of superfluity mentioned above, inherent in such an instrument, would make the abuse latent.

On the other hand, the system of appeals presents significant shortcomings in terms of abusive uses, in particular from the point of view of the proposition for the purposes of prescribing the offense. The lack of forecasts specifically aimed at neutralizing the dangers of distorted use of appeals led to reflections and perplexities on the normative approach, leading to the question of hypothetical reform if it were not necessary to intervene through the neutralization of the benefits that would automatically result to the proposition. To be clear: if the presentation of appeal automatically produces the lengthening of the time necessary for the prescription, we wondered if it was not appropriate to insert a mechanism to suspend the limitation period. In this same vein, the alternative idea of intervening had matured, precluding the judge of the appeal to declare the extinction of the crime where it matured as a result of the first instance ruling.

Beyond the range of possible remedies, the subject of abuse of appeals testifies to a fact. If, as we said, the complete availability of the relative power (which, at the end of the accounts, seems to establish a real potestative right in relation to the part) makes it a perfect venue for the proliferation of abuses, one could rationally arrive at a twofold conclusion. In one part, there seems to exist a relationship of direct proportionality between the extent of the discretion of the part inherent in the exercise of power, and the freedom of choice granted to the party as to whether to avail of a given prerogative, and the risk of abuse that can to derive. As the second part, given the fundamental approach of the accusatory system, which maximizes the strategic freedom minimizing the compression, the introduction of anti-abusive mechanisms (preferably by legislative means), for the need to bring back to logic the system, would present itself as a preferable solution.

CRITICAL OBSERVATIONS

There will be no observations on the actual need to develop the clause of abuse in the case submitted to the united sections: because, in any case, the wrong behavior of the accused is carried out in a closed hearing. Defensive terms, in short, were requested when the final discussion was terminated, also considering that the public prosecutor had renounced to make replies. Judge's response to the defense-related requests, therefore, would not have needed to "inconvenience" the diversion of guarantees and efficiency of the system: the trial was over, so the defense application had to be liquidated with a "non-place to provide".

However, the "nut (by now) is drawn": the solution is there, and the practical quantification of the immediate practical consequences is of little importance. The basic conceptual implications to which it could give rise and, even more, the hermeneutical drifts capable of being legitimized. We know the "classic" terms of the problem: the principle of legality, which is more rigid in terms of procedural invalidity, closes the possibility of creating others in an extra-legislative way.

The practice, however, highlighted trends of an antithetical sign: the gaps in the system were (as in the case under analysis) often exploited to the advantage of the parties. That of nullity is a perfect field of cultivation of such practices: for the sole purpose of making a profit from the procedure, the exception of nullity is an excellent expedient. In the face of such pretentious uses, judges' response is lapidary. Formally, the defect is integrated; substantially, there would be no harm or injury of any kind to be remedied through the declaration of invalidity. Thus, the exception must be rejected.

Equally known are the criticisms that these settings have attracted. With the maximum effort of synthesis, they constitute a subversion of the lines of the system: on the one hand, they manifest a recurrent anxiety to get rid of the formal apparatus; on the other hand, they would lead to the cancellation of the concept of perfection.

It will certainly not be wrong then, as already anticipated by observing that the abuse of process is inserted in the wake of anti-formalist interpretative tendencies which, running along the roads opened by an increasingly visible crisis of legality, are likely to lead to a (previously feared) justice "without commas". In fact, we can also add that the interpretative tendencies highlighted and the abuse of process (which is part of the first) share a basic aspect for both theories: the concept of the purpose of act.

Reduced the speech to the minimum terms, there is the underlying idea of a (so to speak) predetermination by law of purpose: each institution has a purpose, each act must achieve a "natural" end. The conduct that you mislead from it is incorrect. The essential feature of continuity lies in this: as in the context of the substantive tendencies in terms of nullity, the operation of sanction is denied if the act has in any case achieved its purpose, thus, faced with the abuse of process, the part deviates from the institutional purpose, bending an institution to unexpected logic from the rules, with the consequence that such behavior cannot receive any protection. In both cases, on closer inspection, there is an investigation that touches the volitional element of the author of the act, in particular that of the purpose concretely pursued, which, however, would be treated differently. In terms of nullity, misconduct is substantiated by the pretentious exception of the party, who wants to put in the void a procedural act that in any case has produced the legal effect required by law (a notification, by hypothesis invalid, can still produce effect of making the act known to the addressee). In the context of abuse tout court, however, the party realizes an act that deviates from its purpose or, in any case, contrary to the duties of correctness but that, in any case, complies with the provisions of law. Therefore, in abuse, there would be a lack of rigor, unlike nullity, of the opposition of a behavior to legal forms, which, at the end of the accounts, could be summarized in the following terms. In the context of exceptions of specious nullity, the interpretative address indicated would reach an expansion of the area of operation, in point of interest of the party to the observance of the disposition violated; in terms of abuse, otherwise, there is no reference paradigm (as there is on the first side) given by the provision of the law (formally) violated, indeed, the conduct would be formally unexceptionable on the contrary. Everything would focus on "purpose", so that, in addition to an investigation of the psychic element of the part, the interpreter would in fact be led to coin a real disability. Here, in short, the "substantialistic" inspiration would push itself to its maximum.

These settings would be consistently fed by the same supra-ordinary precepts, if it is stated that the process must be "right", one almost has the impression that an invitation to substantial justice is advocated. Of course, maybe only if the rigid observance of the forms leads to irrational results; but, it is well known, the breaking of the legal schemes is able to easily put in crisis the relationship between rule and exception, so that the modules of substantial sign would risk becoming customary, respect of the forms of exception.

In fact, the rigidity of the principle of procedural law is of palpable evidence. While a limit is introduced for the judge, who cannot declare an act invalid when it is in conformity with the law, the failure to comply with the legal precept, sanctioned by invalidity, leads to this simple fact to the declaration of invalidity, without the interpreter having the possibility of verifying its concrete offensive attitude. The investigation on this last element, in any case, would be the essence of abusive behavior. Evidently, if we are faced with the problem of reacting to an abuse, for a behavior that is formally respectful of the law, it is because it causes prejudice (to the efficiency of the system, in this case).

It can be summarized, therefore, by saying that in the face of the element of actual prejudice, the theory of abuse arises in a relationship that in some ways is overturned compared to that which binds it to substantialistic interpretations in terms of disability. In the latter area, the absence of prejudice eliminates the need for invalidating sanctions, even if the behavior is contrary to law; in the other, the presence of injury justifies the identification of another invalidity, although the behavior is formally allowed. We must therefore pay attention to conceptual parallels. If it is true that the abuse of process moves from the above reported settings, it is undeniable that the claim and the stakes on the said side are much higher: the application of the disability is not limited here, but on the contrary, it expands by number and operation.

Given this, it seems that the evocation by the united sections of the concept of abuse is somewhat misleading: two different operational plans are mixed, although they have common features. The applicant, in fact, complained about the nullity deriving from the failure to grant the defense term provided for by the law. The court replies that the refusal of defensive terms or the granting of defensive terms with respect, when no injury, cannot give rise to nullity or impairment derives absolutely from the effective exercise of the right to technical defense. Consequently, court's reply could have been linearly: there is no prejudice, so the complaint is a pretext. It cannot receive protection.

After all, this approach represents in some respects the "limit" of maximum beyond which the internal judge has not gone so far. In the effort to seek a suitable remedy for procedural abuse, we have always moved in the wake of the already known regulatory pathways (for all: that of disability). In other words, the creative effort has tried to reconstruct the notion, even without constructing a general theory and, in particular, with regard to the treatment regime (anchored, it is repeated, to that of disability, based on the containment of their application).

In any case, it would remain a fundamental consideration: is the abuse of process necessary as a procedural category? A discourse is to say that an institution is eccentric in relation to one affair, another is to deduce its practical uselessness for the ordering.

ABUSE OF THE ABUSE OF PROCESS. RISK OF MANIPULATION OF CONSTITUTIONAL PRINCIPLES

Considerations so far carried out lead us directly to a problem in some ways "physiological" to the category of procedural abuse: that of the conceptual manipulation to which it is subject, both on the theoretical and on the practical side. In fact, the problem in question is the consequence of the absence of a systematic classification in the criminal process culture: one could say that there exists, at most, a "culture" of reaction to abusive practices, which takes the form of heterogeneous interpretative modules.

On the other hand, the immediate derivation of the concept from constitutional principles, as the internal jurisprudence seems to have been oriented (both constitutional and legitimacy), if it allows to highlight the (right) relevance of the theme also on procedural ground, then it is capable of leading to dangerous hermeneutical drifts.

What are the risks in question at the end of the day? Those to create a model of invalidity and correlative sanction difficult to control, in consideration of the wide discretion of the union to which it is subject and, as it seems to guess, that of the applicative ubiquity to which the clause elaborated (as declined from the United Sections, it is inferred that the reaction to the abuse is based on a power inherent to the jurisdiction, as an immediate reflection of the need for self-protection of the system). On the other hand, the "nerves" discovered would be many. To be clear: the party that is interested in pleading the abusive conduct of the counterpart, through which the procedural instruments could claim the complaint.

Therefore, it will be worthwhile to dwell briefly on the issue of "constitutional" derivation of the category in question, trying, where possible, to discuss its implications (positive or negative). The result that is obtained, in the end, is to correctly delimit the perimeters of legitimate forecasts, to identify also the values (equally constitutional) with which it should be counterbalanced and, at the limit, when it can prevail or succumb.

Abuse is "measured" through the right of defense with the projection represented by the relationship of trust that the accused establishes with his own defender following the defensive mandate. To affirm that, in certain cases, the exercise of that right can constitute an abuse implies the ingestion in that fiduciary relationship that binds the party and the patron, putting into question the same foundation, when said relationship is based on an "abusive" intent and not on real needs of technical strategy.

It is necessary to identify and delimit the relevant constitutional principles. In order of numerical progression, we can start from the affirmation of the indispensable duties of social solidarity expressed therein. The jurisprudence would have drawn a duty of loyalty and of probity for the parties, at the base of the prohibition of abuse in procedural seat.

Without the need to go too far, it is easy to glimpse in this setting an excess of (so to speak) generality in reconnecting the prohibition of abuse. Regardless of the functions that more or less can be assigned to the precept, one can nevertheless claim to be in the presence of a promising prediction of a general duty of reciprocal probity between the individuals: duty which innervates the social, economic and juridical fabric in its entirety and, therefore, inefficient in principle to connote in a qualifying way the notion of abuse in terms of constitutional foundations.

We have already said the (we might say) heuristic inability of the "fair trial" canon on the side of logical and constitutional foundations of abuse. Besides being misleading and burdened with authoritarian interpretative drifts, it should also be said that the process is "right" regulated by law. It seems, therefore, to be able to sustain a principle that does not crystallize in a body of preconstituted rules. It is the (ordinary) law that progressively implements it, expressing this way a tendency, a "polar star" to which it is essential to look, both in legislation and in interpretation.

The parameter, then, would be the reasonable duration and consequently, in conjunction with the efficiency of the judicial machine which, as stated above, moves from the need to guarantee the rationality of the system and the logical and harmonious use of the process and the relative faculty.

Apparently, we would be facing an endemic, seeming that the efficiency of the process is already included in the nucleus of reasonable duration. However, on closer inspection, they have heterogeneous content. The reasonable duration imposes the containment of process within the temporal, which do not result in a heavy but in useless overload of criminal justice, and to safeguard the position of the accused who, forced to "undergo" the proceedings, is interested in limiting the time of subjection to the procedure.

The efficiency is, otherwise, independent of the reasonable duration. A use of a trial institute can be carried out in a distorted manner regardless of the effect that the process causes in terms of duration. It can stretch it or speed up its course. This is not, however, the point. To exemplify, if the public prosecutor decrees (assuming) a lack of conditions and in order to avoid the adversarial with the defendant, the issuing of a criminal decree, is obviously speeding up the course of proceedings. On the contrary, if it is voluntarily or culpably delayed, the timing of investigations or the registration of the name of the suspect in the register is slowing down. What matters is that it turns against the proper functioning of the judicial machine, or against the correct application of the guarantees of the parties (the accused, in this case) and the interest in the exercise of powers within the purposes dictated by law. It does not seem, therefore, sustainable that the abuse of the public part would harm the reasonable length of the process and, in contrast, that of the accused, the efficiency of the process. From a strictly logical point of view, the idea of abuse is certainly linked to the need for rationality. Rather, it is a concept that is more of a sociological origin, one might say that it requires a legal "specification" in order to remove it from the action of markedly emotional pushes, such as the collective demand for repression or, even, the bending of justice to ethical purposes (to be clear, to prosecute to give strong signals to the public about the morality of the system and institutions).

If this is true, then we can reach a conclusion. Possible norms that lend themselves intolerably to abusive maneuvers, expose themselves to the contrast with some constitutional principles and consequently to the risk of constitutional illegitimacy. Indeed, one could perhaps say, without fear of denial, that the category of procedural abuse assumes the additional function, within the system, of the semantic attribution of the principles of reasonable duration and efficiency of the process, providing it (one would say) a highly practical value.

Constitutional values subject to the aggression of abuse of process were discussed. However, another essential point remains: to ascertain that the forecasts are based on parties' duty to avoid abusive conduct and, at the same time, the limits of this duty that can justify the compression of freedom of action in the process of the same.

MANDATORY PROSECUTION

The notion of procedural abuse, referring to the process in strict sense (here more correctly speaking of abuse of the action) than to the individual procedural acts, spontaneously evokes the problem of relationship with the principle of mandatory prosecution. Recalling the considerations already made but worth summarizing here, the dilemma is given by the stiffness of the axiom. In short, the public prosecutor cannot choose whether to exercise the criminal prosecution; precisely in order to avoid the circumvention of the obligation, the code prepares instruments aimed at safeguarding its rigor (the example of the control carried out by the judge for preliminary inquiries on the filing request is paradigmatic).

It is from here that a possible misunderstanding could arise. If the public part is deprived of evaluations of opportunities for the act of impulsion, this does not mean that the conduct (in a broad sense) of the magistrate's proceedings cannot be distorted.

After all, such reasoning would be in open contradiction with the constant practice shows (which sees the prosecutor attribution of a more than ample freedom of action).

In principle, it is not possible to make a (so to say) syndicate of the purposes underlying the exercise of the prosecution; but this does not mean that there is no prohibition on abuse over it. On the contrary, for the public prosecutor the general prohibition in question would be much more easily obtained than it is with regard to defense. If, in fact, the obligation to exercise the criminal prosecution is imposed, as it is directed to the safeguarding of the purposes dictated by law the functions of the organ in comment are clearly summarized in compliance with the law, in the proper functioning of justice and in repression of crimes, correlatively would sanction a strict obligation to contain the same within the legally predetermined purposes, perhaps even the lemma obligation assumes, with specific regard to the abuse of process, a more meaningful connotation of what would the generic right to act in court to protect one's own interests.

It would be this aspect, therefore, that obligation, which would be properly valued for the purposes of discussion of the abuse to the public works ministry.

As correctly pointed out, in fact, the established principle is placed in the double dimension of the guarantee and the obligation, whereby the latter has already been said and for the former, it is sufficient to note that the guarantee function performed by the law would ensure the external independence of the magistrate from other powers. On closer inspection, the guarantee function is completely neutral for the possible enucleation of a prohibition of abuse; otherwise, the size of obligation would be decisive.

But what could be the operational latitude of this ban on the part of public prosecutor?

On closer inspection, it is also projected into the investigation phase; a fortiori, then, one would say, given that this phase sees the role of absolute prominence of the magistrate in relation to the person under investigation. The room for maneuver, within a procedural moment characterized by secrecy and lack of control not only the defense but also the judge (the judge for preliminary investigations has the function of guarantee, which intervenes only if compulsively), make perhaps even more plausible the possibility of abuse of public part. But not only: can we speak of abusive conduct in the face of activities carried out by the judicial police? An eventual negative answer, based on the formal absence of the qualification of a part of the same, would be short-sighted: the close functional link between the role of police and subsequent determinations by the public prosecutor for the exercise of prosecution make the contrary likely (although in the abstract) the possibility of extending the prohibition area to this body.

At most, here, the problem arises of how and when to assert the defect integrated by the abusive behavior and, where it comes to postpone the detectability of the vice after the beginning of process, if at that point the remedies could be profitable or of the all useless for untimeness.

The problematic relief is perfectly summarized in those cases of failure to exercise criminal proceedings. There is no doubt that this is an abuse, since it would prevent the process from reaching the natural landing (verification of the punitive pretension). But, is it always counterable? The case of requests for extensions to an ad libitum of investigations against an unknown person is hypothesized: there is no particular burden of motivating the request for filing here, nor it would seem of the request for extension as opposed to what happens if the person is identified, hence the danger of abusive maneuvers. Yet, how can this be remedied?

Regardless of the answers to the above questions, it would still seem possible to conclude in this sense: that the prohibition of abuse by the public party, and moreover, that the unfair conduct of magistrate, unlike that established by the defense, has a potential plurilingual attitude. It would not only be at stake, in other words, the need for reasonable duration and efficiency of the process, but also the set of defensive guarantees, which makes the balancing judgment more complex (due to the higher number of interests involved) and also makes the reaction to such distorted practices necessary.

ABUSE OF TRIAL BY THE ACCUSED. THE RIGIDITY OF THE RIGHT OF DEFENSE

As seems to emerge from the previous arguments, it is possible that even an obligation (constitutionally sanctioned) is subject to abuse. It remains to be seen, further, whether a guarantee or, more generally, a right protected by CFREU lends itself to a distorted use.

The issue of susceptibility to abuse of constitutionally protected rights goes back if, in fact, an account is the inviolability of certain rights. The other is their positive regulation, aimed at setting the boundaries of a job within reasonableness.

Thus, if the public prosecutor obtains the premise of a prohibition of abusive conduct, the private parties are subject to (so to say) speculate limitation due to the right of defense. In other words, the right of individual to act in court for the protection of his interests corresponds to the obligation of a coherent and harmonious use of powers that constitute its manifestation. This sits on a general level because, at a closer look, we find the different intensity or, at least, a different way of posing the prohibition of abuse according to the single procedural position taken as a reference. Without delay, logically, the defendant's right to defense is more significant than that granted to other private parties; in the same way, the prohibition in question takes on different contours and connotations in both cases.

In short, with reference to the topic discussed here, it would be a "variable geometry" right.

Leaving aside the considerations due to the fact that the presence in criminal trial of private parties other than the accused is only possible, the reasoning in question is justified in the light of an observation in principle. Every procedural power attributed to the second, in addition to being expression of the right of defense, is a means directly instrumental to the protection of primary good of personal freedom. Consequently, the difficulty of tracing, with regard to the defendant, the limits of "abuse" of the right of defense, also derives from the fact that, on balance, limiting the exercise of a power as an abusive manifestation, means placing an embedding of partisan strategies aimed at protecting personal freedom. In face of the abuses of defense, in essence, the dialectic between the interest of the individual and that of authority takes on very virulent tones. Therefore, from a logical point of view, the possibility of elaborating, with reference to the position of the accused and his defender, a general anti-abusive clause is perhaps more problematic than the operation that would be required on the side of public part, given that a (general) prohibition of surreptitious conduct by the public prosecutor not only summarizes system requirements but, perhaps more meaningfully, to protect personal freedom.

Reduced the speech to the minimum terms, the serious limit with which the criminal process culture has probably traditionally confronted, in the matter of procedural abuse, is to have dealt with it through an exclusive reading key: that of conduct contrary to the reasonable terms and of the right process. It is clear, in fact, that this perspective makes the ground of the right of defense the ideal, if not exclusive for the subject matter, because it seems to be able to say (as noted in the previous paragraph) the abuse of the magistrate assumes a multipurpose valence, backfilling, as well as against the interests of the system, even against those of the individual, that of the counterpart would draw only that of the proper functioning of the system. Beyond any conjecture, if it is not erroneous, the set-up approach is at least strongly limiting, as it is incapable of making sense of the actual dysfunctional abilities of abuse.

With this, be careful, the need to contain the abuses of the right of defense can take second place to that of the limitation of opposite sign. What is suggested is the opportunity to differentiate technically the solutions to the problem of abusive conduct. As we have said, abuse of the public and the accused cannot be placed on the same level, whence the need to diversify the treatment, probably through a reversal of the interpretative approach emerged from the previously analyzed sections. There, the abuse was conceived as a "ubiquitous" clause, which would act as a barrier to the incoherent use of guarantees. Too many dangers of drift, as well as the underlying hermeneutical pitfalls (we will not elaborate on summarizing them). Perhaps, the best way in this last sense, even though aware of the practical difficulties that it generates, is that of a limitation of abuse of defense through legislative intervention, through a progressive work of "perfecting" legislation.

CHAPTER 8

The abuse of process as an internal "citizen"?

Pathological cases of internal system without a specific remedy

Although it has already been the object of consideration, a conceptual premise must be reiterated; the propulsion towards the elaboration of the dogmatic category of the abuse of process arises from a background: the acknowledgment of the inability of law to react to any distortion of the system. The (let's say) physiological inactivity of law to foresee and, therefore, to sanction the distortions, is recreated in practice by the trial actors, compared to the devices abstractly designed by the legislator.

It will come in handy how much punctually with reference to the doctrine of abuse of the reconstructed process within the Anglo-Saxon order. Those that we have defined as symptomatic cases of abusive conduct, apart from the undoubted "representative" and exemplifying value, do not exhaust certainly the list of those behaviors of a part that can configure the application torsion in comment, being able to come to argue that at every procedural faculty corresponds a risk of exploitation. In other words, it is inherent in the faculty or in the power of the trial the danger of a bending of the same for practical purposes of the author of the act.

This is a point, therefore, that we could give for defined. As is to be understood, the judicial practice records an inexhaustible range of party conduct that, apparently conforming to the legal model, are realized in contrast with the ratio of power that had legitimized its completion and, at the same time, without explicit procedural sanctions. On closer inspection, then, the paradigmatic hypotheses that are the subject of prior analysis would constitute manifestations of abuse capable of becoming tangible even within the internal order. Nonetheless, the problematic node is another.

The difficulty, in short, lies upstream: that of understanding when we actually find ourselves within the national criminal process in the face of an abuse of process that, regardless of the "external form" that specifically assumes it, compromises in a sensitive way the overall fairness of the process.

It has already been observed (but on the point we will return more in depth shortly), that the framing of dysfunctionality recreated by the abuse within the frame of the (ir) reasonable duration and efficiency of process integrates a reconstruction for many limited aspects, unable to grasp the real dimension of abusive phenomenology and, consequently, to lead to an appropriate reconstruction of the problem and to elaborate a model of reaction-sanction. In short, as we have observed, the abuse of process involves not only the rational functioning of the judicial machine, but also the rights of the parties in the process and, not least, the fairness of the procedure. That of equity is a notion of supranational matrix principle (conventional, first), hardly "crystallizable" in a preconceived formula or, otherwise, in a predefined apparatus of fundamental guarantees.

We have already tried to point out that the fairness whether one looks at it through the lens of the Anglo-Welsh system, which with that of supranational norms (in particular, of the ECHR), is an essentially practical concept. The attempt to condense the scope (as would the conventional legislator) within a catalog of essential prerogatives is in fact "betrayed" by a practical experience and by a jurisprudence that tends to extend the operational range, as well as the rights that in it would find coverage. At the showdown, viewed as a whole, art. 6 ECHR dictates the basic conditions for which the accused can benefit from an adequate defense, in an (ideally) equal position with the accusation. To play in this sense, reasonably, there is a methodology of assessment and case analysis, proper to the ECtHR, attentive not only to the elements of the individual factual story, but also to the overall stability of the dogma of equity within the procedure. Therefore, a mechanism (so to speak) of counterweights results, where in the end counts that the accused has benefited from a process in which the antagonistic positions were not intolerably unbalanced; id est: the probabilities of conviction were from the beginning consistently superior to those of acquittal, with the consequence that in fact the accused could not prepare an effective defense.

However, the prospect of a direct "transfer" of the Anglo-Saxon doctrine, or of the methodology of assessment applied in supranational, would obviously introduce hermeneutical and syllogistic paths unrelated to the internal tradition, where the measure parameter of a violation and the related instrument of judicial reaction rest on the abstract norm.

Basically, the "concrete case" methodology would be opposed in its internal element.

On closer inspection, the basic problem encountered in the present issue is not the absence in the positive law of a general category such as equity. This is confirmed by the Court of Strasbourg rulings, what counts is the respect by the member state of the obligations resulting from the accession to the international treaty. Independently, then, from the declinations of those guarantees find citizenship in the single state[821]. The one that would detect or, in any case, make the difference is the transposition of the substantial core of the protected guarantees in the supranational headquarters.

This could be translated in the following terms: indifferent is the technique by which such guarantees are implemented in the internal system, provided that this is done and equity is presided.

In any case, what would be the hypothesis of abuse of trial by the public prosecutor without specific remedies in-house? It is an operation, that just mentioned, necessary in order to highlight the usefulness of the prospect "racking" of the reconstructions and of the interpretative methodologies invaded the Anglo-Welsh the conventional system. The positive verification of the existence of manifestations of abuse that they are capable of compromising the overall procedural fairness and, at the same time, without an explicit sanctioning response, would make it possible to appreciate the "added value" of the introjection of those interpretative and applicative paths.

First of all, the same symptomatic cases, which are the object of comparative analysis, are practical examples that, rationally, could well occur also at the domestic level but which, on the contrary, would not be assisted by a precise remedy.

Thus, the conduct of the undercover agent who determines the accused to the commission of a crime that would not otherwise have been committed does not incur any specific sanction from a procedural point of view. However, the logical fact that the criminal process that will follow, concerning the fact committed as a result of instigating the public official, is influenced from the beginning by a sensible disequilibrium of the antagonistic positions, so that the author of that fact will have to face an imputation (to be called in unorthodox terms) "packaged". On the other hand, what could be the hypothetical judicial interventions of rebalancing here? Would be enough to forbid the testimony deposition of the police officer who had operated as an infiltrator?

821 CJEU, C-355/16, Picart od 15 March 2018, ECLI:EU:C:2018:184, published in the electronic Reports of the cases.

Clearly, the answer is negative, given that the evidence (certainly no less relevant), collected in concurrence with the performance of the undercover operations, of unavoidable accusatory sign and difficult to combat by the defense, would still remain. Likewise, the delay in the exercise of criminal prosecution (even if, hypothetically, contained within the period of time necessary to accrue the prescription), due to negligence or operational inefficiency of the prosecutor in carrying out the investigations, could well producing the loss of a fundamental probationary contribution to the defendant, thus substantially compromising the effectiveness of the defensive strategy.

A desire to continue, in a more or less sensitive way, the state of impartiality of the judge and, consequently, the profitability of defense in process.

In any case, it is opportune to insist: the situations evoked, capable of occurring (as the practice, however, would demonstrate) even in the internal and recreating a clear prejudice against the accused, not subject to a sanctioning treatment or to a specific remedy operating within the process itself. The example could be clearer in the face of the phenomenon of delay in the exercise of prosecution. In the domestic system, the only form (generally speaking) of reparation in a generic form that the law provides for the defendant who suffered an impairment due to the length of proceedings is due to the payment of an indemnity. Therefore, we are on a very different level from that in which it was possible a judicial intervention aimed at remedying the malfunctions caused by the delay, eventually (as an extreme solution) putting an end to the established procedure.

But the catalog does not end here, being able to add those cases that we can draw directly from the experience of internal practice.

Reference could be made to those conducted (in a broad sense) of probative "manipulation"; think of the interception of conversations or communications. The public prosecutor attributed to the fact a notitia criminis a legal name among those falling within the category of which proceeds with interceptions; subsequently, during the assessment on merits, that fact will be subject to different legal qualifications. The most intuitive consequence, here, should be that of the uselessness of the results of listening to conversations, as they occurred in violation of a prohibition; nevertheless, the jurisprudence of legitimacy is here granitic in opposing negative answer. The interceptions (better: the results) are fully usable, since the issue of offense is completely of procedural eventuality, and as such, it would not affect an original defect relating to the acquisition of the proof.

The doctrine on abuse of process, elaborated in the Anglo-Saxon system and object of previous analysis, could find citizenship in the national legal system. It is a question that opens up an indefinite series of further problems. We know some of them: how one would be able to reconcile a reconstruction like the one proposed with the legality prevailing in our system.

In any case, the need for a correct reflection setting requires an upstream question. At the basis of any attempt at legal "importation", in fact, attention must be paid to the concrete utility that any implementation of the doctrine in question would have, or said otherwise, about the positive impact of the practical impact that it would have following the introduction. Apparently, we are faced with a question already addressed. Indeed, we have already had the opportunity to discuss around the function that, in general, would cover the category of abuse of process. Nonetheless, the discursive plan here is different. In fact, we no longer speak of the "added value" inherent in the hypothetical judicial power to sanction abuse: in the latter sense, already the logic is at an abstract or principle level, which at a practical level imposes to admit its usefulness. It is good to repeat that a rational legal system must also be able to defend itself from the exercise of rights or faculties deviating from the purpose for which they were recognized. The "price" to be paid, otherwise, would be the implosion of the system itself.

The point is that there is also much else at stake. In fact, it is evident that under the abuse process there is a double ethical guideline. In this respect, the category which, as mentioned, tends to transcend the exclusively technical-legal dimension arriving in the sociological one. It would be divided between a general prevention function and a special prevention function.

From the first point of view, it would operate as a message of an ethical nature towards the Union. It is not possible to abuse the judicial machine; in particular, the use of the same for the achievement of objectives outside the law or its real purposes cannot be allowed. To direct these arguments within the perspective of analysis chosen in the work, the message should result in the "moralization" of the prosecution: the idea of containing the exercise within the scope of the purposes established by law is logically translated into that of not to be able to use the compulsory principle as a "screen" capable of disguising possible abuses of its exercise.

Under the second profile, the abuse of process would act as a "maieutic" tool for the parts of the process. In fact, is inevitable the operation of a procedural sanction resulting from the commission of an abuse (of the trial or of procedural acts). It would have the effect of diverting the parties involved in the dispute from deviant procedural conduct, thus producing an emendation under the behavioral profile also in the continuation of the process.

To considerations just carried out, we would add the findings of a legal nature based on physiological connotations of the process system. As is known, the abstractness and rigidity of positive law cannot be reconciled with an institution that responds, in a subsidiary way, to the inevitable "obsolescence" of regulatory products. This, opportunely reiterated, is true if we look at the legal system not in an "isolated" way, but in the most rational and modern perspective of integration with the supranational scenarios. In short, the progressive expansion of freedoms to a higher regulatory level, together with the internal implementation obligations resulting from it, impose today (perhaps, more than ever) the establishment of flexible tools for self-defense of the system, capable to guarantee the rational conjugation of needs to protect collective interests and subjective guarantees.

Overall, it does not seem that the logical and practical necessity of abuse of process can be put into question, and we may have to discuss the kind of implementation technique of the same (which will merge a specific point of reflection in the following paragraphs).

IS MANDATORY PROSECUTION NECESSARILY AN IMPEDIMENT LIMIT?

It is now right to go back to addressing a point that, although already subject to sparse considerations, needs more clarification and a systematic reflection.

At the end of the day, one of the most important obstacles in which the category of abuse of process could come across was constituted precisely by the principle of mandatory prosecution. The assumption, apparently of immediate intuition, could be summarized as follows. The dogma in question constitutes an indeclinable obligation; therefore, no abuse of the exercise of prosecution would be conceivable, since in relation to it the holder of the power does not have any margin of choice.

Certainly, an analysis of the ideological and cultural background that provided the basis of this option for the constitutional legislator exceeds the aims of the work, just as this cannot be the place to discuss the advisability of a constitutional revision of the principle in question, in consideration of the benefits that would derive and respectively of the systemic inefficiencies that would thus remedied.

More specifically, the purpose of considerations inherent in this principle should be to discern the concrete implications and possible limits that would be able to impose on the (always hypothetical) operation of abuse of process (of the prohibition) in the internal order (in the terms outlined so far), when not even the radical exclusion of the possibility of introducing it.

On the other hand, a decisive aspect, with regard to the analytical objectives set, is that of the substantiation or otherwise of the persistent correlation between the discretionary nature of the criminal action (recognizable in Anglo-Saxon law) and the remedy of the doctrine on procedural abuse. In other words, could this problematic node be tackled in the following terms: supposing that the Italian Constitution foresees the principle of opportunity of criminal persecution, would the abuse of the process be at that point a necessary category? An inescapable tool to protect the individual against possible referees of accusation? The inherent guarantee matrix is widely known, or better, the dual operational direction of the dogma established therein.

On the one hand, the established need for the exercise of punitive pretenses constitutes (ideal) projection of citizens equality before the law, excluding, at least always on a principle level, or in any case contributing to eliminating the risk of arbitrary drifts such as the "targeted" persecutory obstinacy, the "politicization" of the punitive pretension or, in any case, the bending of the same to objectives exceeding the observance of criminal law.

On the other hand, the obligation would have the function of preserving the external independence of public prosecutor with respect to the other powers.

The experience gained under the previous fascist regime had brought to light the dysfunctions recreated by the direct control of the executive magistrate's work by the executive: the solution, therefore, could only be to sanction the obligation to persecute without choice. It is evident, in fact, that the "mandatory" lemma is framed, within the constitutional framework and in consideration of the ideological-cultural references to which it is inspired, in this further dimension: the (abstractly rigid) duty to exercise the action, in the same way that it would not admit any valuation of opportunities on the part of the owner of power, so he would not tolerate external interference, which could eventually lead to its implementation. Essentially, that further connotation inherent in the obligation of prosecution, which would be constituted by the exclusive reserve of ownership of the relative power, would be nothing other than an aspect inherent to the first, a (logical) immanent precipitate.

As is well known, the cultivation of the punitive pretension in an unconditional way, besides not responding to the instances of logic and efficiency of the system, would inevitably collide with the practice that, conversely, shows us how often is necessary to stop the criminal proceedings instituted. If the basic conditions for a verification on the merit of the punitive application are lacking or, in any case, the conditions for proceeding with the procedural procedure are lacking (one can imagine a crime that from the beginning it was totally unfounded and whose registration in the appropriate register, therefore, would appear to be an institutional fulfillment that was completely useless, being obviously destined for archiving). The practice, if we want to express ourselves, would surpass the theory, thus leading the legislator to the introduction of mechanisms that allow the blocking of those criminal proceedings for which the prerequisites for proceeding to the merit phase appear to be non-existent. This would mean in summary that without prejudice to the (original or supervening) lack of conditions of procedure or a cause of extinction of the crime, the prosecutor would not be able to find substantial evidence capable of supporting an accusation in trial.

The institutions set up in this regard are known, materializing in archiving and in the non-place judgment to proceed. However, in order to make effective deference, we need devices to prevent such contingencies from leading to a surreptitious transfiguration of the compulsory nature of criminal prosecution, bringing it back to an operational director of opportunities. The judge constitutes, or at least should constitute, outpost for the protection of the aforementioned principle.

It is not good to argue about the fact that judge's figure, working through these mechanisms, sees an approximation to the position of prosecution. It should be emphasized that the obligation of prosecution is a principle that lives an obvious internal logical contradiction, or rather, a tension between (so to call them) the poles of the exclusivity of the attribution and duty to exercise the action. As mentioned, to ideally separate the contents of the absolute reserve of ownership would serve to remove the public prosecutor from the control of the executive as well as from any external interference, while the obligation (in and of itself) would ensure the equality of individuals ahead of the law, averting the danger of creating "pockets" of privileges. If the action is obligatory, it is necessary for someone who, under certain conditions, is able to impose on the holder of that power not only specific procedural obligations (for example: to carry out an investigative supplement). Even for the same act of impulse, it should be said, if the obligation taken in itself as a denial of discretionary choices at the point of exercising the punitive claim, would be formally respected, the reserve of ownership, a direct emanation of the first, in fact would be compromised.

European Union legislation therefore, although introducing the abovementioned expedients in order to guarantee the observance of constitutional principle, would come to admit what is in any case an inevitable "internal" contradiction.

In the face of abuse of the trial, understood as a possible power-remedy by the judge to the distorted exercise of the prosecution, can one make the same reasoning?

The question could be otherwise put in the following way. For the attribution to the judge, clearly by way of extrema ratio, of a general power-duty to order the non-prosecution of the action, if the presence of an abuse by the public prosecutor is detected, can it coexist with the obligatory nature of the prosecution or, on the contrary, would it be vulnerable?

However, beyond any logical suggestion, the juxtaposition of the terms "duty" and "abuse" only apparently integrate a contradiction. On the contrary, there is a judicial practice that makes it clear how the non-malleable constitutional principle is opposed by the margins of action and operational choices of the prosecuting magistrate who could hardly be traced back to the paradigm of discretion, which, it was not possible to carry out a sort of "trade unions" pursued by the public prosecutor in the exercise of the action, precisely because of the provisions of CFREU. It could well be assumed beyond the apparent theoretical limit given by the rigidity of the principle in the subject-conduct of the public part aimed at bending individual institutions or procedural powers for from non-legal purposes or, using the reconstructive model of common law doctrine, directed at recreating from the beginning an iniquitous process.

The abuse of an obligation, in short, waiting for the wide margins of discretion attributed to the criminal magistrate, is much more than a simple theoretical eventuality. It is a concrete practical possibility, clearly revealing the ease of invoking the obligatory nature of the action as expedient to justify (for example) a "politically" oriented punitive pretension, thus making, perhaps, the elaboration of an anti-abuse clause with reference to the public part most necessary than it is with regard to the accused.

From a different angle, it should also be noted that the possible perplexity that would arise from the fact that, by ordering the arrest of criminal trial and the related blocking of continuation of the action, the judge would come to harm the principle of compulsory moment that would be involved in carrying out the propulsive act of the process. Indeed, through the formulation of the imputation, the public prosecutor has already fulfilled the judicial control. To such an extent, therefore, the garrison in question would intervene precisely in terms of guaranteeing the criminal law itself and, at the same time, the fairness of procedure. On a mere logical level, therefore, one could at least doubt the existence of insurmountable obstacles to the construction of an abuse ban in terms of judicial remedies ex post.

On the other hand, abuse of process doctrine and discretionality (of the prosecutor) would only seem to be an inseparable binomial: on closer inspection, the overall features of Anglo-Saxon reconstruction would show not so much the need to react to the physiological occurrence of a distortion of the discretionary power of the Crown Prosecution Service, as to avoid the continuation of a process contrary to equity or, in any case, to the ethical integrity of the system. In essence, the double dimension of the prohibition of abuse of process in the Anglo-Welsh system, as a form of subjective (unfair trial) and objective (unfair to try) guarantee, would summarize instances of system efficiency and protection of the imputed regardless of whether the prosecutor has concretely remedied the persecutory option or not. Apparently, one would say at most, that the remedy in question is intended to operate when the use of intermediate instruments has been exhausted and without the same were able to "compensate" the prejudice suffered by the defendant.

BETWEEN REQUIREMENTS OF REGULATORY REFORM AND REFLECTION SCENARIOS

Since it seems that the need for elaboration carried out around the category of abuse of process is not revocable, it follows logically the problem concerning the "form" through which it must be introduced into the system.

As can be seen from the regulatory and jurisprudential products, the roads so far traveled seem to be substantially two; therefore, it would be worthwhile to dwell on them, before proceeding to further perspective openings. The hermeneutical line followed insists on the theory of actual prejudice, within which the more specific institution of the abuse of process would be brought back. We will not return to reflect on the critical aspects of pronunciation; however, the relief will be important here for which the abuse of process poses a projection of a broader interpretive direction, which therefore would find its own logic and application paradigm. We are facing a reconstruction from narrow viewpoints: the real problematic aspect that generates the approach adopted in that location, in fact, is constituted by the inability to offer an effective response to the abuse of process as an objective dysfunction of the system and, at the same time, distortion of the ends of a power or of a faculty by the part. In short, the figure outlined is dashed or, so to speak, constructed as a "measure of abuse" by the accused or, in any case, destined not to generally preserve the system from any behavioral manifestation which is an integral part of an abuse.

The actual prejudice could be seen as the negative (implicit) limit of the operation of invalidity (of the nullity, in that case). If an act lacks the requisites required by the law, it is null in principle. Yet, the system suggests that the invalidity should guard concrete, not purely hypothetical, interests, so that the judge would have the power to investigate the existence of an immanent element (prejudice) to the legislative cases concerning invalidity denying protection, in case of a negative outcome, to the request of a party (this, in short, the message launched by the united sections). It is immediately evident, however, that the reconstruction thus carried out is incapable of offering protection to what constitutes the true (and certainly more insidious) manifestation of a procedural abuse.

The intimate essence of the category, in fact, is that of a behavior that is formally respectful of the law or, in any case, not expressly forbidden, but put in place for the achievement of purposes totally unrelated to the logic (normative or social) for which the right-power has been recognized. Evidently, here, the denial of protection for conduct carried out is "improper weapon". It is true that the principle enunciated by the Supreme Court does not explicitly exclude from the scope of its activity any specific procedural part; defendant or public prosecutor (or other private party that is), who exercise a faculty in order to "defend themselves from the trial and not in the process" (to use the well-known slogan evoked by the nomofilattico judge), cannot receive protection.

The defendant and public prosecutor operate on substantially staggered plans. The defendant suffers the trial and, as is logical, there may be situations in which the conduct put in place by the magistrate is formally legitimate, but in fact attacks the interests of the defense, which would be in difficulty to counter a procedural behavior that, under the normative profile, does not go to any censorship.

In summary, the theory of actual prejudice, however suggestive, offers a limited response to the phenomenology of abuse, leaving dangerous (or even more regrettable) discoveries that through the first paradigm would find no contrast. Therefore, it would seem to be difficult to say that it would give the judge the general power-duty to reject a request for a part when, in a deviant behavior (in a broad sense), there is no effective injury to be restored.

The examination of the second path is therefore required. Here, we are under the legislative side. The positive law is fraught with devices designed to avoid or, in any case, to sanction clearly exemplary trial procedures (although not the only ones, the matters of inadmissibility and of the deductibility of the nullities are certainly indicative in this regard). If this is the case, the idea that arises is that of entrusting to the legislator the work of "adjustment" of the system, introducing adequate mechanisms to put the judicial machine safe from procedural abuse.

This guideline would certainly not be unreasonable: it would have, in fact, the undoubted merit not to entrust the resolution of the problems highlighted so far to the jurisprudential work that, however rational, will always suffer from oscillations potentially harbingers of inequalities in terms of treatment. If the perspective in comment is suggestive, the aspect concerning the technique through which the intervention de iure condendo may take place cannot be silenced. The hypothesis closest to reality should be that of a systematic change, aimed at carrying out a general rebalancing of the powers of the parties (in the process and in the process); inevitably, this operation should necessarily be accompanied by another, which would involve the judge.

In essence, it seems logical to assume that the central role within the overall dynamic of abuse is played by the judge who, on the other hand, would see himself handed over in consideration of the characteristics of the category in analysis the function of overseeing not only of the legality and the rights of the trial actors, but also of the efficiency of the system. Let's be clear: the hypothesis of a power-duty of the judge to intervene to sanction the abuse, even blocking the continuation of the procedure if the fairness of the procedure was compromised, would have little to do with the fear of the reintroduction of that " paternalism" so close to the inquisitorial model, where the judge disputed the dispute through penetrating powers of direction and control of the actions of the parties. On the contrary, the work of rebalancing should retain the function of protagonists of the trial, leaving residual jurisdiction over the power-duty to intervene as an exception to punish the abuse eventually committed. With further clarification, a judicial reaction mechanism modulated according to the seriousness of the abusive conduct should correspond to the reorganization of the balances relative to the powers of action of the parties. With greater clarity, we mean that, regardless, the solutions that are actually introduced to react to the subversive behavior of the parties, would require that the remedy was not rigid, but diversified according to the type of abuse, confining to limit situations (possibly) that of the arrest of process.

A basic relief, at most, could be moved to the prospect of a legislative restructuring intervention. As we have already seen, in fact, the abuse of process, in itself, is essentially a refractory category to attempts at rigid classification, as well as hypothetical normative crystallizations. On the contrary, the observations so far carried out would lead towards the diametrically opposite conclusion: the abuse of process is physiologically practical manifestation outside the legal grids which, as such, lends itself to a positivization.

Probably, the most rational conclusion could be summarized in these terms: that if it is not physically possible to offer a complete or even merely exemplary list of the conduct integrating a procedural abuse, it could be more plausible to try to introduce a general clause regarding the power-duty in terms of remedy or sanction. A clause, worth pointing out, that is able to offer the applicative and hermeneutical coordinates to the judge during the sanctioning intervention.

A "WELCOME GUEST"?

Wanting to draw the threads of the speech, it is clear how the problem related to the introduction into the system of abuse of process can probably be summarized in a central question: will we leave the care of public interests to the law or the choice of a group of essays?[822]

822 The dilemma was formerly taken into consideration by ARISTOTELE, Politica, III, 15, 1286 a., who already observed the problematic option between entrusting the care of public interests to the law or the discretionary choice of a circumscribed group of individuals. It is observed how the terms of the just evoked problematic are repeated with the same cadences also in the present times, "striking"-it seems to be able to deduce-singularly every sector of the order.

On closer inspection, the dialectic inherent in the evoked question would be perfectly recreated even within the problem in analysis. Basically, it would be a matter of dissolving a basic alternative: whether to entrust the discipline of the subject matter exclusively to the legislative provisions or if, on the contrary, it is necessary to leave it to the jurisprudential elaboration.

As is well known, the national system is based on a principle of "strong" legality. The idea of introducing an undefined form of invalidity (since, essentially, this would be) by way of interpretation would contradict the same pillars that they support the national criminal process.

At the same time, however, the often outlined characters of the abuse of process, hardly enclosed in a rigid legislative formula, would make at least difficult the hypothesis of a legislative intervention that, at the end of the accounts, in addition to reformulating the balance of power of the parties, would end up inserting into the legal system a clause source of the power-duty of the judge to repress the wrongful conduct of the part. It should also be pointed out that this clause, however sufficiently (hypothetically) described in terms of taxation, would in any case run into the inevitable hermeneutic oscillations, since it is matter, in which the judicial diagnosis is extremely sensitive to the circumstances of individual case, when not even from the same determined. It would therefore be necessary, after all, if the solution to the elaboration of a clause by interpretation is not the most appropriate way and if, at the same time, this reconstructive option can coexist with a system essentially founded on the principle of legality. In short, the speech is reduced to a minimum: to what extent can judicial discretion be pushed? It is an argument that, in fact, cannot be ignored, leading directly to questioning the limits to the exercise of discretionary insistence on the court in matters of procedural invalidity.

The topic has been touched upon in a comparative analysis, but here it is worthwhile to spend a few more words here.

The national procedural order in most of the member states belongs to an inquisitorial cultural tradition. This is contrary to what happens in the Anglo-Saxon order, where the figure of the judge is hypostasis of assurance of the individual against both the potential abuse of the despot, and the excessive rigor of sovereign law. In the internal system, the expression (Anglo-Saxon) judicial discretion would evoke the image of arbitrariness of authority whose limitations must therefore be contained: the judge bouche de la loi is an expression of this requirement and legality, in this sense, is the instrument of elected guarantee for this purpose.

At the basis of every possible prospect of hermeneutical elaboration of a general prohibition of abuse clause in the terms outlined, there is an obstacle of an ideological-cultural nature constituted by preconceived suspicion of jurisprudential reconstructions operating outside the legal grids. Distrust that is intensified, intuitively, when the area invested by the "creator" intervention is that of disability. It is a category in fact (it should be said) that the judge is required to wisely and prudently handle. The effect typically characterizing the same, once the violation has been established and the sanction ex lege ordered, is given by the fall in the (let's call it that) procedural work done. Obviously, then, that the idea of conceiving a model of vice-sanction, capable of stopping the procedural process, dissolved by a minimum even normative abstract reference, generates more than one perplexity when not even a clear opposition. Here, then, that legality operates not only as a guarantor of the individual, but also as an instrument to safeguard the economic process, aiming to contain the demolishing effects of the judicial declaration within strictly determined boundaries.

But, is this an indeclinable principle? Or, under certain conditions, would you also admit some flexibility? In particular, legality is born and operates essentially as a guarantee. Could one consent to an endorsement or a bending of its own direction?

One can certainly not doubt the heaviness of the limits deriving from the historical-cultural heritage, nor the value of protection of the individual who, on the axiomatic level, carries out the principle of legality.

Nonetheless, admitting a bending for the safeguard of needs of no less importance, of a sign however equally guaranteed, perhaps would not necessarily lead to a subversion of the system but, perhaps, to the simple transposition of the needs highlighted by the practice. And, the answer, so it seems, could only go in one direction: if the practice really surpasses the theory, especially in the subject treated, one should take note of the needs expressed by a system that requires, always in order to safeguard the fundamental guarantees of the accused (which, as mentioned, would be compensated in procedural fairness), flexible instruments, without this leading to subversive repercussions.

In any case, a point seems to be confirmed that regardless of whether the emergence of this category in the procedural context is functional to the recovery of maieutic and moralizing instances of justice as a whole, as well as providing the parties with an ethical concerns the procedural conduct, the introduction of an anti-abuse clause would have the double practical function of guaranteeing the accused (as a barrier to the wrong conduct of the prosecution) and of protection of the efficiency of the system (inevitable, in fact, that an abuse, whatever form it takes, draws the correct functioning of the judicial machine). In short, if one cannot doubt the ethical or principle value that the legal system would gain by introducing a general prohibition of abuse, not even could be justified with regard to the side of subjective and objective guarantees. A function (if this is meant) educator, therefore, which would be combined with that of a practical order to safeguard the "health" of the justice system and that, for this reason, would not make the category in question invisible in principle.

In the English system, on the other hand, identifying the usefulness of the abuse would be simpler also considering the function traditionally attributed to the criminal trial: id est, the repression of crimes and the punishment of the guilty (corresponding to the latter aspect then, in a completely specular way, the protection of the innocent from conviction). In this sense, the abuse of process would be a connatural clause for the essential purposes of the Anglo-Saxon process system, aimed at ensuring both the correct convergence of the same, as the concrete possibility for the judge to reach the dissolution of a dry alternative is guilty/not guilty. This, in nuce, would be the meaning of the abuse of process doctrine: marking the judge a barrier to the duty to respond to the punitive pretension.

With regard to the national system, the speech is much more complex; only by way of approximation, but in any case substantially correct, it can be said that the ultimate goal to which the criminal trial naturally tends is to ascertain the validity of the punitive pretension. This means something different than what is seen in the system taken as a model of comparison.

In the Anglo-Saxon order, the hypothetical perspective of an abuse by the accused contradicts the system's postulates (principle of legitimacy), since it would be completely foreign to the very foundations of criminal justice. In the national legal system, however, the reconstruction of a judicial power-duty to sanction the abuse of public prosecutor would essentially clash with the basic approach by which this category was elaborated with the aim of repressing the conduct of public prosecutor, the defendant with whom he wants to escape the process (a guideline, therefore, which would lead directly to look at the proposition by the defendant as an abuse for the sole purpose of obtaining the prescription of the crime, for example). The idea incardinated in the approach established in the internal jurisprudence, is that of a partisan conduct that prevents the process of reaching the prosecution. It would hardly be a remedy to be opposed to the conduct of public prosecutor. To the contrary tending to speed up the timing of the procedure to reach the sentence (of condemnation).

The discourse, evidently changes if the paradigms of reference are changed or, to put it better, if the objectives of the prohibition of abuse are aimed at reach.

The abuse of process put in place by the public prosecutor can undermine the overall fairness of the procedure, creating the risk of an innocent conviction or, in any case, could lead to the celebration of a process where the equilibrium of the dispute is substantially compromised, so that the defendant would not in fact be allowed to perform an adequate defense. It is clear that the amendment of the approach so far elaborated would lead to re-discussing the very tightness of the principle of legality; but the problem is probably in the "sustainability" of the sacrifice that one would accept. In essence, to admit a system that defects a broad clause, to protect both the individual guarantees and the efficiency of the system, in the name of legality and those guarantees that, in any case, would be compromised in the absence of an adequate instrument of reaction to the distorting practices. The latter would probably produce the fall into the void of all the ends that would be under the interest that we would like to preserve, i.e. the legality.

"MORALIZATION" OF CRIMINAL JUSTICE: PROSPECTIVE STRABISMUS AND REAL UNDERLYING PROBLEMS

Trying to close the speech done in the previous paragraph, we conclude with an overall look at the real and suppository reasons that have until now determined an interpretative approach to the topic far from a systematic reconstruction or confined within narrow operational guidelines.

As noted the internal system presents significant profiles of inefficiency, which are reflected in the overall "health" of the jurisdictional machine. The overload of work and the correlative need to ensure a more rational spending of resources have certainly affected the maturation of the interpretative settings on the object of analysis, inducing the jurisprudence to conceive a category of abuse of process according to a deflationary key or, for each way, aimed at stigmatizing the indecorous spectacle of a judgment bent to interests that are antithetical to those institutional.

Logically, within the highlighted scenario, the immediate target of the reaction put in place by the judicial operators (the judges) can only be the defense. It is on the same, in fact, that the reproaches are pointed out (of an ethical nature, first of all) on account of a constant exploitation of forms or, better still, of procedural guarantees. In essence, those who use the same for purposes contrary to those institutional, make fun of the system.

Therefore, it will be clear why the abuse has traditionally been configured as a weapon which, even before the legal-procedural side, would have operated in the "political" or ideological side, when not even as an improper means of pressure de lege ferenda, that is to say, as a real legislative instance for the introduction of corrective instruments of the procedural conduct of the parties, when this was clearly deviant or incorrect.

Reasonable duration of the process and reform of the discipline of prescription, under this aspect, would have represented (and would represent) the sectors in which the anti-abuse line has become more pronounced. However, it would seem even more the gap between the real problems background of the judicial machinery and the interventions concretely made for this purpose, diverting the attention, on the other hand, from what should be the genuine justifying logic of the category commented within the procedural system: convergence of the purposes of criminal justice, as well as safeguarding the fairness of the procedure and the rights of the parties in process.

A few lines, in short, to highlight how at the basis of the "primitive" approach of abuse of law there is a vision of the system and the related apparatus of rights and guarantees of a strictly ethical (or, in any case, pre-juridical) nature. The need to protect these rights not only within their concrete dynamics, but also towards the "outside", that is from their possible retaliation against the state itself, emerging an ideological approach in which the former are not only as subjective positions of advantage, which is aimed at widening the content of the juridical sphere of private individuals, but also as real moral constraints for the latter, which in this way would become the first "custodians" of the coherence and rationality of the legal system.

It has also been observed that in the "ethical" damage or, in any case, in the seriousness and moral integrity of the system the dysfunctions recreated by the abuse do not end.

Here, the abusive conduct would be added to involve the very estate of the legal order and its equilibrium so that it seems to be able to support the need for a "moralization" of criminal justice together with an ethical accountability of the trial actors, one of the analysis keys of the phenomenon of abuse and of the reasons that justify or even impose full introduction into the system.

In short, it is not just an ethical problem. There is much more at stake, since the displacement of the equilibrium of the system itself, assaulted by the abusive dynamic, undermines not only the efficiency of the criminal trial and its reasonable duration, but also the tightness of the subjective guarantees themselves.

This conclusion, on closer inspection, would be in the face of an abuse brought about by the prosecution, aimed at undermining procedural fairness, and compared to that achieved by the defense. In the first case, the aggression and the consequent vacillation of the rights of the defense are immediately evident, in the second one, this aspect is perhaps less intuitive, but still perceptible. The conduct of those who exploit the guarantees, using them for their own profit, generates an (understandable) disapproval by the trial audience (including the judge), instilling (one would say unconsciously) the suggestive but insidious idea that the exercise of a right, for purposes exceeding those underlying the logic of their recognition, cannot receive protection, thus opening the way to a reconstructive address capable of annihilating the minimum contents of the guarantees themselves.

In this case, therefore, the interpretative strabisms that concerned the category under analysis would be summarized, probably preventing it from a complete elaboration and a rational classification. The difficulties of approaching the issue, again, would be appreciated in the face of the attempt to bring back the category, placed as it is halfway between law and sociology (if not also ethics), to a composite legal-technical form. At the bottom of the whole problem on the abuse of process, in fact, leaving aside the limits of interpretation and reconstruction in which the internal practice has occurred, there is a basic difficulty: that of developing tools to combat formally unexceptionable behavior, in respect to legality.

In short, there is also a technical difficulty, certainly not of less weight when you want to translate the idea of a general category into a concrete legal reality. If one wants to put it through a less orthodox but perhaps more effective image, one could say that an anti-abuse clause would lead to a reaction to the prediction gaps physiologically inherent in the principle of legality. This, evidently, is a strong brake to the attempts of systematic reconstruction proposed: the idea of questioning the natural protection of individual guarantees in the intimidating process since it would result in a reaction against the same legality, which in practice one would see herself turning against herself. Fear is not entirely unfounded, of course. Nevertheless, it is perhaps faced with an inadequate view, since it would move from the preconceived equation between "strong" procedural legality and the safeguarding of individual guarantees, so-as a corollary of this reasoning, i.e. a possible decline of the same, would mean a contraction of those guarantees.

Would this really be the key of correct approach?

It has been said that the abuse of process cannot be reduced to a simple deviation from the forms; at least, this reconstructive option would be too narrow. The elaboration of a power-duty of sanction (by legislative or interpretive means) represents only one aspect of the overall problem which, in reality, hides much greater problems. Restricting the application area of an invalidity, according to the theory of the actual prejudice, arises an operation that from a logical point of view is certainly easier. There is no reason to declare invalidity because no one has lost and no one would gain, so the application of the procedural sanction is denied. In essence, the paradigm of the actual prejudice does not undermine the legality at the root, but introduces a temperament by adding to the invalidating cases of an element or a limit of negative operativity.

The abuse of process moves from an opposite direction: a prejudice exists, but it is difficult to oppose it, since the behavior of the part is secundum legis. The whole of the abusive phenomenology attacks all the systemic postulates and its overall equilibrium, so that not admitting a general protection from the abusive manifestations of the parts would, indeed, deny the guarantees on which the system itself is based and the procedural legality that would be the fundamental garrison.

If this is so, then, it would not even be too detached from reality to maintain that a hypothetical introduction of a general prohibition of abuse clause, far from turning back against the law, would rather protect it, since it would constitute the first and (perhaps) maximum deterrent for deviant procedural conduct and, at the same time an incentive to treat forms. Here, in short, the problem of symmetry between forms and substance (better to say: between abstract forms and its ends) has only to do with it, just as the fears about an inquisitorial revivalism due to the introduction into the system of invalidating clauses outside any legislative provision.

The fear (so to call it) underlying the systematic elaboration of the abuse category of the process would be to conceive a procedural legality in fact subservient to the implementation of the substantive one. The corollary of this model of reasoning is more than known: the first should yield if reality shows irrefutable evidence. The abdication of forms is therefore fearing for the benefit of material truth; as can be understood, it is an idea that destabilizes. On the other hand, the conception of a process as a useful tool to reach an upstream interest belongs to the European/national cultural genome: the achievement of the truth, to be understood as the implementation of substantial legality. The image of an ideal watershed between substantive and procedure law, to which the assignment of autonomous purposes would follow, generates in fact the invisible image of a process as a place of fiction, which detaches itself from the reality of facts through a basic approach for which compliance with the "rules of the game" would ensure the goodness of the final result (regardless, therefore, from the fact that the product of the assessment corresponds to what happened historically).

Clearly, within this ideological framework the abuse of process results in an invisible category: prohibition of abuse, recomposing beyond the expressed limits of the system the hiatus between formal and material truth, would lead to the risk to disregard the procedural apparatus. One notices immediately that the function that would be assigned to him is abnormal. Too many hopes and expectations on a category that, in any case, would arise with different claims: the idea of a sanction that affects the attempt of the party to escape the discovery of material truth undoubtedly exceeds that of guarding the correctness of the procedural dialectic, as well as of containing the use of procedural faculties within the proper legal and ethical ends.

Alternatively, it is the same contemporary legal scenarios that exacerbate the fears of those who observe that "the strength of magistrates measures lies less and less in the law", thus postulating the recovery of the primacy of the law. In this perspective, in short, the abuse of process would be the expression of an authoritarian jurisdiction, capable of bending the forms in order not to compromise the achievement of truth.

But, is the feared drift founded? It is repeated: at the basis of the abuse of process there is the need to establish not a symmetry between forms and substance (an objective completely alien to it), but a symmetry between observance of the forms and the achievement of a judicial pronouncement on merit. To better say: the observance of the forms does not become the pretext to escape from an equal final pronouncement.

The difficult task that is assigned to the category should lead to frame it, therefore, in a different light. In short, the need to "do justice" rather than to apply the law, but to adapt the rigor of the forms to the natural end is not at stake of the criminal trial. This would probably be the perspective of analysis of the most correct category, suitable for holding a correct classification of the same: so, therefore, with regard to the behavioral deviations of the defense, as to those of accusation.

In conclusion, it would seem possible to affirm that the "ethical" and at the same time emotional dimension, within which the abuse of process is usually attributed, together with the recall of the deontological duties of the procedural actors that in principle to the category in question that operates, was the easy expedient to resign ourselves to the idea that it is impossible to bring it back to a legal-technical dimension and, consequently, to elaborate a model of procedural sanction tout court.

ABUSE OF THE TRIAL AND PROCEDURAL LEGALITY. PROCEDURAL LEGALITY VS SUBSTANTIAL LEGALITY: THE ORIGINS OF THE DICHOTOMY, THE REASONS FOR THE LEGISLATIVE CHOICE

At the end of the work, a fundamental reflection is required regarding the relationship between the abuse of process and the principle of procedural legality. Indeed, it is a relationship that has been repeatedly highlighted. It is evident, in fact, that attempts of reconstruction of an anti-abuse clause are basically implemented through a "creative" jurisprudential work, which has often found itself intervening not only outside the legal framework, but also as a place in light with the absence of adequate hermeneutical coordinates.

This, as we understand, directly affects the keeping of the aforementioned principle. The object of scrutiny, therefore, will be the conformation of the same, also examining the prospect of a national procedural system that offers, while remaining anchored to a "strong" procedural legality, the possibility of conceiving invalidating clauses (in the broader sense), such as that of the prohibition of abuse of the trial, even if not positivized. At the bottom of the whole question that is addressed, although different in content, there would be a further problematic node: the delicate balance object of never-ending discussions between the substantial legality (which manifests itself in the predisposition of incriminating cases and those that intervene in their application) and the procedural one (which is expressed, instead, in the rules that define the course of the procedure).

This is certainly not the place to deeply explore the just mentioned theme. For completeness of ideas, however, it is worthwhile to carry out some reflection. It is a dialectic that also innervates the present theme.

As evidenced in the course of the work, the temptation to resist (so to speak) to the "charm" (which one would like to define) of abstract norms, bending them to substantialistic logics in the name of interest in the celebration of a "fair" trial in times reasonable, it connects intimately the need to ensure that the procedural law does not become the expedient to avoid the procedure that the former wants to regulate. At the same time, avoiding this "perverse game", thus placing the guarantees in the finalistic frame that would belong to him, the substantial legality would be understood as the implementation of the legal command against the actual violation perpetrated.

In this way, the constant tension that we perceive between (we could call it) the repressive coefficient, inherent in the substantive criminal norm that would base the imputation, and the balance of powers of the trial parties, on which the procedural apparatus would rise, it also reverberates on the abuse of process. More clearly, the public interest in the restoration of (substantial) violated legality is in contrast with the need to ensure a balance of powers between the actors in process. This, in short, translates into individual guarantees which, beyond the specific collocation of context (trial), are obviously resolved in a brake to the overflowing force of the repressive drive. Well, the abuse of process fits within said conflict; abusing the process (of prosecution or prosecution) means interfering with the implementation of the punitive interest. We would escape, avoiding to reach the merit, the possible application of the sentence or, on the contrary, it would reach its imposition in disregard of the "rules (procedural) of the game".

It is a contraposition, therefore, that operates independently from the direction of subjective operation of the procedural abuse. If it is the public prosecutor (hypothesis: in the exercise of the criminal action), the folding of forms with extra-institutional logic manifests itself through a distortion of the punitive pretension, providing what is (probably) the paroxysmal moment of a pathological deviation of the purposes of criminal law. On the diametrically opposite side, the circumvention of the procedural rules or, in any case, the use of a faculty by the defendant for his own profit, is in the invocation by them of the need to comply with the procedural rules for the sole purpose to escape from a sentence. The problem of abuse of process, on closer inspection, also revolves around this tension, even offering an even more singular extrinsecation scenario.

Normally, in fact, the idea that faces the mind of those who imagine the weakening of the rigidity of the forms to the advantage of the "substance" is that of the disregard of a procedural law (for example, concerning an invalidity) when its implementation with what is the reality of the facts or, in any case, with the interest in reaching the truth. In other words, if the application of an invalidity results in the annihilation of a trial activity, therefore in an obstacle (more or less decisive) to the final assessment, it is inevitable that the procedural law, from this visual angle, constitutes an "obstacle" on the path to truth.

The essential core of the problem of the abuse of trial, differently, would not be an excess of disregard of the law (procedural) but, rather the opposite, an excess of invocation of the forms (obligation to exercise the criminal action or a defensive guarantee), to justify the selfish implementation of a partisan interest (punitive or liberation from the prosecution), beyond the institutional limits.

In some respects, therefore, we are in the opposite region with respect to that one derives, often feared in front of the prospect of a reconstruction of a general anti-abuse clause, which would result in the abandonment of "forms for the sake of truth". We are precisely at an antithetical level: abuse is exaggeration of forms, being able to act also as the product of an ideological and cultural process that lasted centuries. The procedure, in fact, is no longer mere praxis iudiciaria, relegated to the margins of the atlas of legal knowledge, but a body of rules whose compliance conditions the goodness of the final result (assessment). Therefore, the requirement that is found, at most, is exactly the opposite: that of not exacerbating the respect of formal rules, when the invocation of these rules is aimed at circumventing the application of the substantive norms.

Clearly, the most relevant aspect of the dilemma is given by the possibility of bending procedural legality. In fact, emblematically, it manifests itself through forms that must be non-malleable, rigid presuppositions. However, the practice constantly shows the limits of a dogma that, besides not being able (physiologically) to include in the bed of its own legal provisions every eventuality of reality, turns against itself: this is what we have defined as abusive act. In short, the distorting practices of the trial actors show what is the most well-known limit of a system which imposes a basic idea, that of a "constantly perfectible" world (normative) through the succession of legislative interventions. A concept of legality in the "strong" sense, in fact, involves a fundamental cultural approach for which the system conforms to the changing nature of reality due to regulatory changes, rather than through the interpretive orthopedics of jurisprudence. A setting that, however, would rationally expose itself to an objection: it is not, at least from the thematic point of view that concerns us, to remedy the possibility of an unjust norm or, in any case, become such an operation that, undoubtedly, could very well bind itself into a skilful legislative draft of correction reacting to the physiological imperfection of positive law: imperfection, on closer inspection, given by the possibility of a misuse of the same or, better still, the powers recognized by it. In this sense (called in simpler terms), one could say that the written law is born in itself "imperfect". Hence the necessity of entrusting the remedy to (as we have called it) intrinsic imperfection of the norms (procedural, in our case).

On the other hand, the idea according to which the gaps of a system based on legality would be accepted as an instrument that, beyond the empty forecasts (for self-inevitable and remediable only ex post), is able to regulate and resolve individual conflicts without the mediation of a "creative" jurisprudence or, in any case, integrator of the first (risk that, indeed, the axiom of law would want to avert). It is an idea, on closer inspection, which clashes with an incontrovertible fact: the reassuring image of a process entirely determined by law, thus far from the danger of a conviction of someone in the absence of a rule that was never issued and (because of) a repression (of exclusive origin) of the judiciary, there is another one in which there are procedural operators to whom the ius ad loquendum is conferred, when not even the function of adapting the application of the abstract rule to the concrete case (function increasingly "delegated" to the judges, in the current times). It is true that the idea of a judicial power without legal basis runs the risk of being the antechamber of arbitrariness; but from this only assumption (which, however, remains in principle correct), it would logically be an error to draw that no bending by the interpretative route of legality is admitted, even coming to affirm that operations of this type would subvert the system.

It could not really take for granted the assertion that procedural law cannot tolerate bending or whatsoever (by hermeneutics), if not for the fact that different dynamics, observable in practice, show how often the tightness of the forms and possible regulatory vulnera is not questioned. A normative complex that, due to distorting practices, would self-contradict itself, favoring the insemination of pushes that are just back against those upstream interests that those forms would protect.

If we are faced with an unavoidable practical necessity, it would perhaps be worthwhile to make an effort in reflection in another sense: how it is possible to guarantee coexistence between formal rigor and inspiration within the domestic "creative" jurisprudential system?

THE NEED TO "INVOKE FORMS": PITFALLS AND DRIFTS (AUTHORITARIAN)

We have already had occasion to highlight both the suggestions and the risks of authoritarian drift inherent in the reference to principles and in the concomitant detachment from legal forms.

One cannot doubt, however, that the exercise of judicial power in the absence of a legal basis and what, in the name of a legal basis and those interests that legality aims to protect, introduce instruments and operational modules aimed at presiding over those interests from destructive violations (equally not provided by positive law), are sensibly different phenomena. At the basis of the conception for which a written law is required, there is an axiomatic co-ordination that is not unrelated to thinkers belonging to the common law ideological cultural context: "when a norm defects (norm legis), everything must assume a suspect"[823]. It is no coincidence, however, that those same intellectuals who have strongly affirmed the need for the primacy of written law, have at the same time highlighted the dangers arising from the lack of a legal basis, but in a specific direction: "it is atrocious to distort the laws, in order to do violence to someone"[824].

The need for a positive right and, likewise, to abide by the dictates of the written law as a guarantee of the individual against the overwhelming power of the sovereign.

Comparatively, the act of binding the ius dicere to a set of uniform rules, written, responds to a necessity of logical and practical order: if the judge, in fact "decides, from time to time on his behalf which rules of justice (are) more suitable, (we would have one) so great uncertainty, that there would be no specific rule of conduct"[825].

It would be strange, at first reading, to note that the thought settings just mentioned come from scholars belonging to what would be the area (perhaps) of the highest expression of a law. What, in fact, could define as legal empiricism would apparently contradict those needs of abstraction and unity of the continental legal area (civil law), where the attempt to settle individual conflicts is accomplished by the legislator.

In all probability, however, not unlike what has been said previously, is a mistake of perspective to believe that the absence of a punctual normative reference, for any verifiable practical eventuality, invariably corresponds to pure arbitrariness: the difference between arbitrariness and discretionality. In fact,

823 F. BACON, De dignitate et augmentis scientiarum, Wirzburg, 1780, VIII, parr. 13, 15, 25 and 96. T. HOBBES, Leviathan, (1651).

824 T. HOBBES, Leviathan, (1651).

825 D. HUME, An enquiry concerning the principles of morals, (1751), III, 2, Hackett Publishing, Indianapolis.

it has already been underlined and the elaboration of unwritten rules, starting from the practical case, would not exaggerate in the first case, if said elaboration still conforms to a basic guideline, aimed at safeguarding precisely that system based on legality.

This suggests a reasoning: if the overall dogma of procedural legality implements a need of guarantee for the individual (defendant), it should provide the minimum conditions to ensure an equitable processing of procedural events and, at the same time, the balance of powers of the parties. Therefore, if the same is incapable of covering the entire area of situations that are likely to occur in the proceeding, the creation of a clause by means of arbitrariness would not properly be the result of arbitrariness.

Interpretation of the praeter legem operation is a fact: the likely result should not be the disruption of axioms or even worse an authoritarian drift, but the exact opposite with the introduction of clauses (so to speak) of rebalancing the system.

If this is so, with the claim to do justice in the individual case, would create his own footing a rule completely divorced from the system, even in order to individual prejudice. On the other hand, if the risk underlying the absence of a legal basis and the need to harness the interpretive flair of the judge is truly linked to the fear of prejudice against the individual, the fact that he is not expressly feared the danger of a "creation" of law by jurisprudential way in bonam partem or, if we want, in a guaranteed sense so, at the same time, safeguarding the same rational estate of the legal system.

Nor, it should be remembered that "the classical mold of the iudex servus legis has itself produced atrocities, immorality, injustice (...) various commendations and enthusiasm for its traditional pillar (the promulgated norms, as "daughters of a general will", in its many variations) are put to the test, hic et nunc. Too often, the law is actually introduced by a small number of "party-leaders", from prevarications, from hidden societies. All this keeps little of that postulated "social will"[826].

826 D. HUME, An enquiry concerning the principles of morals, (1751), III, 2, op. cit.

THE OTHER SIDE OF THE COIN: THE NEED TO TEMPER THE RIGOR OF THE FORMS

Let it be clear: the consequence of reflections should not be that of a scenario of total abandonment of legal forms, to arrive at the complete delivery of the function of "creation" of the right to the jurisdictional body; nor do we want to support a system within which is the practice to provide the interpreter with the rule, that is the basis for the elaboration of a juridical norm, substantially reaching a cultural eradication with the concomitant implantation of reference models unrelated to the internal tradition.

The problematic node is another: highlighted the limits of a procedural system that stands on the principle of legality and admitted the need to proceed to a temperament of the rigor of forms. It is necessary to examine the consequent tightness of the system itself and, equally, to submit to criticize any operations to this effect.

We have already spoken of the dialectic between substantial and procedural legality; one senses that, at the bottom of it, there is a hiatus in some physiological terms, perceptible where only one reflects on the distance that separates the (as it was called) "offered" legality (meaning that which is crystallized in the incriminating cases) and that "reached" (concerning, instead, the one that moves from a crime report that would consolidate in the final assessment). The latter, on closer inspection, follows its own events, within a time frame and a context (the procedural one) determined by contingencies (also random) of individual case.

The criminal trial, as is known, is by its very nature "selective": to determine the judicial assessment is not only the incriminating law that bases the charge, nor the rules governing the unraveling procedure, but all that happens inside it, where the dynamics put in place by the parties concretely shape the material on which the sentence will be based.

In this sense, the alea of the unexpected is a physiological aspect to the procedural legality, since, in fact, the result of what is transfused in the final decision is the result of contingencies that the former is neither able to predict a priori, even if, by hypothesis not believed, you were able to conform them entirely, through the reconstruction made in the sentence, in command of the incriminating offense.

This is not the space for reflections of similar scope; but the logical conclusion to which one would arrive is that of a reversal of the perspective according to which the procedural norm would serve as a servant with respect to substantial legality. This seems to be able to sustain the contrary, in which the correct understanding of the limits of the first and of the adoption of the appropriate corrective measures constitute the direct premise for the keeping and correct implementation of the second.

On the other hand, the expressed fears of that doctrine which for some time have been speaking of a law "without a (abstract) fact" are known. Undoubtedly, a possible drift in a totally anti-legal direction should be viewed with disfavor. But , there would probably be an intermediate perspective: that of conceiving as an intermediate point between the abstract norm and the practical reality of the process (as a single experience and never fully summarized in the formulas of the rite code) the so-called "judicial case".

In other words, this is only the reason with the rules and the practice of the process. Between the purely abstract normative level (given by the cases constructed by the legislator and which we will briefly indicate as those transfused in the procedural code) and that of the single procedure, a sort of median operative and reconstructive module could be placed. Conforming the needs originated by the practice, which requires flexible instruments (also with a view to adapting to supranational indications) to the rigor of an inelastic situation (especially the one established in the matter of procedural invalidity). One could hypothesize a jurisprudence intervention to elaborate adaptation clauses. In any case, it could be said that this expresses the rational need for a temperament of the forms and, at the same time, that the same requirement furnishes the premise of a very unavoidable as well as prudent methodology of elaboration of clauses by jurisprudential way.

AND, THE QUESTION OF METHOD, INDEED, ASSUMES CENTRAL IMPORTANCE

From one side, it would be essential to identify any interpretative parameters through which the elaboration of the aforementioned clauses can take place. With greater clarity, translating the reasoning to the theme of the work, reference is made to the method of detecting vice-abuse. It is necessary to define the constitutive features with the utmost precision and, at the same time, the rigor of the judicial finding at the point of diagnosis.

On the other hand, it is necessary to avoid the risk that, by means of similar exegetical operations, a total erosion of the principle of strict legality is reached, or even to the bending of this option towards the retreating of the punitive interest. It is repeated: the prospect of reconstruction hypothesized would not have the purpose, admitted the need for a temperament of the rigidity of the axiom in word, to subvert the tightness of the system; the logic of jurisprudential intervention, in the name of safeguarding the guarantees of defense and of the efficiency of the system, requires flexible but not uncontrollable instruments. It is in this last sense, then, that it becomes essential, next to the operation aimed at tracing the method of judicial inquiry on the detection of abuse, the profile inherent to the control of the correctness on the technical-legal level of the adopted decision.

These are logically-related aspects: the correct identification of the parameters and elements on which to base both the reconstruction of an anti-abuse clause and the identification of practical manifestations responds to the subsequent need to guarantee an ex post control of the verification on the point. In this sense, if we reserve the right to deal with this aspect in short, who would be the body responsible for carrying out this task?

One point needs to be clarified further. If it really came to materialize, what meaning would the proposed approach from an ideological-cultural point of view have? It is inevitable, in fact, that it should expose itself directly to the objection that by reasoning, in fact, one would surrender to a scenario that sees the overwhelming predominance of jurisprudence on the side of the creation of law, which is shown by a look at daily practice is increasingly forming in the courtrooms that in the texts of the law. Independently, in fact, from the reasons underlying this phenomenon (among which, as we know, are the thrusts coming from supranational law, which tends to introject in the internal system methodologies and operational tools more congenial to the background of common law than to the continental tradition), the one just mentioned is an empirically observable fact.

But if so, would it really be profitable to hold onto a conservative position, really ending up undergoing an epochal transformation instead of trying to govern it?

Rationally, the escalation of the hiatus between conservative instances (basically directed to safeguard the bulwark of strict legality as a form of protection of the individual's needs) and practice (sensitive to the system's efficiency needs) would lead to relegate the academic critique, within which the most advocate settings of maintaining the pillar of strict legality, to a sterile role devoid of concrete "reforming" capacity would be concentrated.

To this point, it is useful to stress again one aspect: if it is true that the practice often surpasses the theory the theoretical solution would be really profitable if, acknowledging the needs expressed by the practice, conforming to it, trying to offer methodologies for the proper governance of the former, in order (at least) to contain those irrational or even potentially subversive pitfalls that lurk in modern interpretative operations.

THE (TOO) ETHICAL AND EMOTIONAL DIMENSION OF THE REASONABLE DURATION AND EFFICIENCY OF THE PROCESS

We can now return to the starting point: what would be the practical benefit that would derive from an organic arrangement of the subject under analysis?

We have already reasoned about the intrinsically metagiuridic and, at the same time, "emotional" nature of the abuse of process. Therefore, the opportunity to criticize the method of elaboration of a general clause (of prediction and set of sanction of the same) should offer at least the merit of not allowing the instrument (prohibition and remedy of the vice) is the vehicle of irrational drives what can be the principles of reasonable duration and efficiency of the process.

With this, the hypothetical reconstructive key does not respond to the need to contain the procedural delays and to ensure the consistent use of procedural tools available to the parties, thereby allowing a rational management of the judiciary workload and good functioning of the justice system in general. It is in fact inevitable that, consequently, even these directions would be summarized by the aforementioned route.

Nonetheless, the danger that we want to highlight here, inherent in the instances of contraction of trial times and efficiency to repressive drives. On the other hand, the difficult verifiability of the rulings regarding procedural abuses, possibly based on the aforementioned parameters.

From the first point of view, it has already been pointed out that the reasonable duration of the process (which would almost seem to form, within this perspective, with the principle of efficiency and proper functioning of the judicial machine, a sort of indissoluble term) has been the most used as a means of justification for the repression of those carried out by the accused aimed at avoiding the ascertainment of merit. In this sense, the need not to leave to the arbitrariness of the same the lengthening of the procedural times (which, as noted, was implemented by denying protection to the request of the party, on the premise of the lack of a concrete prejudice), at least in the interpretation in which it has been customarily placed, makes very close the danger of using such a "weapon" according to persecutory guidelines or, in any case, anti-guarantors.

Regarding the second profile, even if we do not doubt the constitutional "coverage" of the interests in question and their essentiality with regard to the health of the system and the maintenance of individual guarantees, we must remember the difficulty of conceiving a certain and well-conceived form of judicial ex post control on the decisions taken on the basis of the same. It is, as we can see, the (excessively) elastic parameters-principle, subject to the risk of an all-too-wide interpretation, which, on closer inspection, would make the fear of inequality of treatment more than founded. As a general point of view, the evoked instances often constitute, as the daily experience has shown us, the channel of entry, within the process, of emotional pressures that would have little to do with the phenomenon of abuse.

The collective demand for justice (to call it so), together with the need for the state (true or supposed) to provide a strong response to criminal events of serious social alarm, is an "object" by the unpredictable possibility of exploitation, including that used as a pretext to react against the practices of those actors (the defense) that, in order to gain (in the broadest sense possible) impunity, use the laws for their own benefit, exceeding clearly the arguments made in the previous paragraphs for the purposes and the ultimate logic of a general prohibition of abuse.

If, then, we add to this the meta-juridical and emotional "soul" of the abuse itself, which, even before meeting system dysfunctions, unconsciously calls for a push towards the moral accountability of the subjects involved in the process. It is understood that the equally "emotional" exasperation of a category, which, in itself, is permeated by ethical factors, would make it an obscure object, absolutely indecipherable from a juridical point of view and, therefore, unsusceptible to take on a technical form.

POSSIBLE SOLUTIONS: PERSPECTIVES DE IURE SEASONED...

Some reflections are required regarding plausible solutions to the problems generated by the abuse of process. If one excludes a single sentence in which a general classification of the phenomenon and a reaction model has been proposed (reference is made to the well-known ruling of the United Sections, mentioned in the course of the discussion).

Basically, in the difficult scenario of the reflections matured on the subject, we can see a general awareness about the "abuse" problem; one would say that the consequent practical necessities, however, recall types of remedies that clash with a structure of thecriminal process that is refractory to the entry of tools incompressible within the (too) rigid framework of the legal forecast. After all, the reluctance towards the elaboration of system solutions in the aforementioned sense is given by this underlying reason: the difficulty in handling a paradigm that is difficult to combine with strict legality.

However, this does not prevent us from reconstructing a summary picture of the possible emendments of the current scenario. In this sense, the considerations would follow two distinct directions. On one hand, we can try to see a way out of the impasse that is found in the legislative landscape through the tools (normative or interpretative) that the latter offers; on the other hand, one could think about a possible solution in the perspective of future legislation or, in any case, of elaboration of new hermeneutical models or operational modules.

With regard to the first perspective angle, it is useful to return to one aspect: the hypothesis of shifting the "barycentre" of the repressive policies of abuse on the side of disciplinary judgment, which would possibly be initiated against the author of the incorrect procedural conduct, does not provide no satisfactory answer. It would, on closer examination, be yet another (weak, perhaps) attempt to escape from the real problems raised by the phenomenon in question: we are facing a dysfunction from the concrete subversive capabilities of the system, as well as potentially recreating distortions (prejudices) which, through this last option, would never find a remedy within the single proceeding, thus fueling the inefficiency profiles of an already suffering judicial machine.

Reasonably, the solutions should fit in and operate within the criminal process itself in which the violation takes place: endoprocedimental therapeutic intervention, in short, or whatever you want.

In this sense, it would be a matter of working on the actual prejudice, raising this criterion to a real operative paradigm, useful to compose the antinomies generated by the abuse. However, the anguish of perspective of this approach to the issue under analysis has been highlighted: leaving aside the dilemmas caused by a criterion that, even today, in the amplitude of the situations in which it was evoked by jurisprudence, struggling to find an organic arrangement in terms of general theory, this operational guideline does not allow us to offer a complete response to the part's abusive manifestations. It is repeated: the actual prejudice is construction elaborated by the jurisprudence to stem the attempts of the accused to escape the process; therefore, it would be unsuitable for its use in a defensive or, otherwise, as a means of contrasting the "oblique" exercises of prosecution by the public prosecutor.

On the other hand, the premise for the operation of the criterion in question is given by a violation of the law which, however, does not meet the legally established sanction due to lack of specific injury against any party. The abuse of process is the opposite: formally unexceptionable conduct, and yet carried out in contrast with the logic and the institutional ends.

An alternative, perhaps, would be that always omitting, the efforts (however necessary, if you want to insist on such way) directed to supply the hermeneutical module in comment, an organic arrangement to arrive at an amendment of the actual prejudice, changing the same conditions of operation.

In essence, it would be a matter of conceiving the use of such an interpretative construction also with regard to those conducted which, although carried out in accordance with the legal command, actually cause a concrete injury (actual prejudice) to the parts of the process or, in any case, to that objective interest constituted by the efficiency of the system and the achievement of a final merit pronunciation.

We agree, it is not an easy operation at all, but instead perplexing. The criterion of the actual prejudice, in its "classical" declination, although it comes to deny protection to a party request due to the presence of a factual data such as the absence of real injury to the same, relies on a solid basis of reference, given the following legal case. At the end of the accounts, we can "add" to the same an element that assumes implicit (or logical), given the concrete injury (failing which, therefore, the related sanction cannot take place). If, instead, moved to the area of abuse of trial, there would also be lacking the starting substratum constituted by the legal provision of the prohibited conduct: here, in short, the "creative" intervention would be twofold, operating both on the side of the censurable behavior (incorrect conduct, in violation of the ultimate purposes underlying the power that allowed it to be completed in the abstract), and on that of the irrevocable sanction.

At most, if you do not want to follow the interpretative path just proposed, in order not to leave the "nerve" of public prosecutors' abuses in the exercise of criminal prosecution uncovered, an alternative could be found in the acquittal formulas adopted by the internal code system.

The phrases that the prosecution should not be initiated or continued are extensive. There is probably the intention of the legislator to grant the court the possibility of acquitting the accused through a "container" within which may be merged causes not previously sanctioned and, indeed, such as to accommodate possible legislative interpolations or solutions interpretations that emerge in practice; sufficiently extended, then, perhaps, to allow a reading aimed at including also a judicial power of intervention aimed at blocking the surreptitious cultivation of the punitive pretension.

After all, if it is well reflected, the judicial power to stop the trial, because of an abuse of accusation, in practice would be nothing but an acquittal. It would also seem the legal nature that, within this approach, would have the liberating decision adopted: non-merit decision, containing the ascertainment of a limit (not otherwise removable) to the continuation of the procedure. In short, with the basic features of the dogmatic category in analysis: the abuse does not touch in any way the historical event from which the procedural sequence originates. On the contrary, it manifests an evaluation of (in) opportunities regarding the inadequacy of the path towards a judgment of merit, awaiting the intolerable compression of rights of defense and equity.

(FOLLOWS) ...DE LEGE FERENDA

The road to a legislative change, if not necessarily the most appropriate, would certainly be the most congenial to the national criminal process.

If, as it seems, the abuse of process is an anti-systemic phenomenon of immense scope, thus constituting an inescapable problem, the opportunity for legislative intervention in this sense would be appreciated because of the pressures that the legal system receives from the supranational scenarios; this is not due only to the circumstance that the abuse of right (general name with which in the aforementioned normative domains is called the supractical exercise of a faculty or a freedom) is present there, but also to a further and more meaningful one. The path taken through the legal apparatus in comment, aimed at the progressive expansion of the sphere of protection of the fundamental rights of the individual (including undoubtedly the procedural guarantees), logically generates a problem for certain aspects "inherent" to this path: that of fully integrating these prerogatives within states, ensuring their rational use within the guideline of free movement and preventing their use by the destructive potentialities of the system.

We have already introduced the hypothesis of a normative restructuring, aimed at rebalancing in general the powers of the parties and, at the same time, to combine the necessary freedom of action of the same within the dialectic process, with the specular figure a judge who, with a view to suppressing the abuse, would not see a recipient of a properly passive role. On the other hand, it was said of the difficulties that an operation of this type would encounter, as well as of the inadequacy on the technical level (for the physiological "empty" foresight that would in any case remain) and the possible non profit of a similar option.

At most, the entry of the legislator in this field could take the form of the introduction of an upstream clause, regulating the general power of the judge to detect an abuse of the case and, then, to sanction it. To the disadvantages that would have been constituted by having a (hypothetical) necessarily broad rule, which would set only the coordinates of the judicial activity, would certainly oppose the benefits that would be derived from having a flexible instrument, capable of "absorbing" a number of unsuspected behaviors to crystallize into a normative list.

On closer inspection, then, the problems related to the introduction of a clause in this sense would not be exhausted in the sole discipline of a judicial reaction. There would be much more at stake: who would deal with the control of a judicial decision which, by hypothesis, revealed an abuse?

Intuitively, the most immediate answer would be that the body responsible for that task is the judge of the appeal[827]. But which, and how?

If it is well reflected, the abuse of the concrete process in its own right, is different from the traditional patterns that we find in the code of invalidity. So, the questions would be many, only by way of example: would it constitute a real error in proceeding? Or, aware of the difficulty (if not impossibility) of configuring the vice-abuse in the strict terms of a procedural disability, should it be entrusted to the mere critique of the motivational apparatus contained in the sentence?

It is not clearly the goal of the work to hypothesize, at the present time, a complete normative compendium on the subject of abuse of process. At most, the evoked questions are worthy of highlighting the complexity of a possible legislative novelty which, to all intents and purposes, would assume the traits of a real systemic reprogramming[828].

827 D. LIAKOPOULOS, Annäherung der Prozessgesetzgebung Strafverfolgungsmaßnahmen der Mitgliedstaaten: Probleme und Perspektiven, in International and European UnionLegal Matters-working papers, 2018.

828 D. LIAKOPOULOS, Annäherung der Prozessgesetzgebung Strafverfolgungsmaßnahmen der Mitgliedstaaten: Probleme und Perspektiven, op. cit.

CHAPTER 9

The abuse of process doctrine in the Anglo-Saxon system: A reconstruction at the antipodes of the European system.

INTRODUCTION

The so-called functional profile of the abuse of process, as reconstructed in the Anglo-Saxon process system, can perfectly be grasped in the following consideration: "the topic must be taken seriously in order to preserve the welfare of the system"[829].

To be honest, the reflection just mentioned has in this regard the civil trial. In fact, even in the Anglo-Saxon legal system, as in the Italian one, the institute in question originates on the civil procedural ground, as a form of remedy-the distorted use of action or of certain procedural instruments[830]. As equally brought to light, even in the Anglo-Saxon system, like what is found in the domestic

829 N. ANDREWS, Abuse of process in english civil litigation, in A.A.V.V., (ed.), Abuse of procedural rights: Comparative standards of procedural fairness, op. cit., pp. 98 and in the same spirit see also: R. BRAY, Beckford and beyond. Some developments in the doctrine of abuse of process, in Denning Law Journal, 19, 2007, pp. 69ss.

830 R v Forbes, ex p Bevan, [1972], 127 CLR 1, 7, per Menzies J; Taylor v Taylor, [1979], 143 CLR 1, 6, per Gibbs J.; Castro v Murray, [1875], LR 10, Ex 213; Asmore v British Coal Corporation, [1990], 2 QB 338, 348; Bhamjee v Forsdick Practice Note, [2003], EWCA Civ 1113, [2004], 1 WLR 88, 33; Laing v Taylor Walton, [2007], EWCA Civ 1146, [2008], PNLR 11, 303; Jameson v Central Electricity Generating Board, [1998], QB 323, 344. For further details see: I.H. JACOB, The inherent jurisdiction of the Court, in Current Legal Problems, 43, 1990, pp. 43ss. R.G. FOX, Criminal delay as abuse of process, Monash University Law Review, 64, 1990, pp. 74ss. J.A. JOLOWICZ, Abuse of the process of the Court: Handle with care, in Current Legal Problems, 43, 1990, pp. 78ss. K. MASON, The inherent jurisdiction of the Court, in Australian Law Journal, 57, 1983, pp. 449ss. P.H. WINFIELD, The history of conspiracy and abuse of legal procedure, Cambridge University Press, Cambridge, 1921. S. SINE, A practice approach to civil procedure, Oxford University Press, Oxford, 2016. S. BLAKE, J. BROWNE, S. SIME, A practical approach to alternative dispute resolution, Oxford University Press, Oxford, 2012. A. KEANE, P. MCKEOWN, The modern law of evidence, Oxford University Press, Oxford, 2014. P. ROBERTS, Excluding evidence as protecting constitutional rights, in L. ZEDNER ROBERTS JV (eds.), Principles and values in criminal law and criminal justice. Essays in honour of Andrew Ashworts, Oxford University Press, Oxford, 2012, pp. 172ss.

system, we are faced with a notion of origin, matrix of jurisprudence, therefore, outside the positive legal grids.

The words mentioned above, however, are exactly translatable to the criminal trial[831], because of the identity of essence and ratio of the category in both the trial seats.

As will be seen, the essence of the abuse of process (it is given by the discretion), indeed, had specific regard to what is the paradigmatic model of the reaction to the distorted practices put in place by the prosecutor (consistent prosecutor), consistent in the arrest of criminal proceedings by order of the judge, the doctrine in word would also borrow the name: abuse of process discretion (or doctrine). With extreme synthesis, we could say that the lemma discretion assumes a double value on the side of process abuse by operating in two directions.

One can look at it from the perspective of prosecution (prosecutorial discretion): the theoretical object of the analysis that will follow, in fact, originates directly from the need to prevent prosecutor's discretion in the exercise of prosecution can be solved in an intolerable prejudice charged to the accused (up to compromising, as we shall see, the overall fairness of the procedure). But it can be watched from a further angle. The foundation of the power-duty of the judge's intervention, faced with the abuses of the public part, is given by what appears to be an intrinsic element of the jurisdiction: judicial discretion, we can for now define it as (the hyperbole is allowed) the quintessence of the common law: the power to "individualize" justice.

Apparently, we are faced with distinct concepts; one would say: a discourse is the discretionality of the accusation in the exercise of one's functions, another is that which directs the work of jurisprudence. In reality, the overall theoretical abuse of process shows its mutual specularity, so much could be affirmed-that there would be no reason to conceive a judicial discretion in the matter in question, where the prosecutorial discretion was not postulated upstream. Which, in simpler terms, would be like saying: there would be no reason for the jurisprudence to invent a remedy of a discretionary nature, if there was no need to reject an abuse of discretion by the prosecution.

In more detail: in what sense the arrest of the procedure by order of the judge, due to an abuse of the process, is the exercise of a "discretionary" power? The

831 A. CHOO, Abuse of process and judicial stays of criminal proceedings, Oxford University Press, Oxford, 2008, pp. 2.

power to stay is said to be discretionary. In this context, the word "discretionary" indicates that, although there are some clear categories, the circumstances in which proceedings will constitute an abuse of process cannot be exhaustively defined and, in some cases, minds may differ as to whether they do constitute an abuse. It does not indicate that there is a discretion to refuse a stay if proceedings are an abuse of process or to grant one if they are not[832].

We immediately find a fundamental indication, both of a dogmatic (a concept of discretion with regard to the abuse of process), and of a methodological nature. The selection of behaviors that integrate an abuse constitutes a discretionary operation: being inseparable to form a closed number, they will be evaluated case by case (fact-finding approach). Rather, it is the reaction to the established abuse that, if this has irremediably compromised some fundamental interests of the criminal system, it establishes a real duty on the part of the judge[833].

With this, pay attention, it is not to say that the methodological approach just mentioned translates into the impossibility of tracing real paradigmatic cases of abuse of process. Indeed, the guidelines emerged in practice seem to indicate the opposite, showing a progressive effort by the Anglo-Saxon jurisprudence to settle application and interpretation modules characterized by the setting of standards rules and, at the same time, not to rectify the symptoms of abuse cases within a closed number. On the other hand, we are dealing with a highly malleable and magmatic material. This aspect is reflected in the evolutions of a discipline which, on closer inspection, presents itself as an open "container": some prosecution practices, which are at a specific moment in history without specific sanctions, could subsequently-by changing the address jurisprudential-fall within the specter of the abuse of process doctrine.

---

832 R v Carroll, [2002], HCA 55, par Gaudron and Gummow JJ. For further details see: A. ASHWORTH, M. REDMAYNE, The criminal process, Oxford University Press, Oxford, 2010, chapter 1-3. A. SANDERS, R. YOUNG, M. BURTON, Criminal justice, Oxford University Press, Oxford, 2010. M.D. DUBBER, T.H. ÖRNLE (eds), The oxford handbook of criminal law, Oxford University Press, Oxford, 2014. P. ROBERTS, J. HUNTER, Criminal evidence and human rights. Reimagining common law procedural traditions, Hart Publishing, Oxford & Oregon, Portland, 2012, pp. 164ss. C. TAPPER, Cross & Tapper on evidence, Oxford University Press, Oxford, 2010.

833 Hunter v Chief Constable of West Midlands Police, [1982], AC 529, par Diplock J. For further details see: K. PITCHER, Judicial responses to pre-trial procedural violations in international criminal proceedings, ed. Springer, Berlin, 2017, pp. 260ss. I.H. DENNIS, The law of evidence, Sweet & Maxwell, London, 2014.

To summarize, in terms of the abuse of process doctrine, discretion is a qualifying element in a double sense, in the perspective of the accusation and in that of the jurisdiction.

To be sure, if one looks at the side of jurisdiction, one would be tempted to place the remedy in question in the subjective situation of duty[834]. Where the existence of certain premises is verified, the judicial obligation to provide (one could observe) is triggered. In fact, however, the operating procedures that characterize this dogmatic category, in addition to the exceptional nature of the related sanction, which will therefore intervene if another legal instrument is not invokable and only following a balancing of interests in conflict (intrinsically unpredictable evaluation, strictly dependent on the circumstances of the specific factual context[835]), they illuminate the above reported fundamental trait: essentially, discretionary power.

The natural (if we may say so) course of the procedure provides for the duty of the judge to ascertain the merits of the punitive pretension: "the normal course should be that any criminal charge should proceed to full trial, and it is only in the most exceptional circumstances (...) that the court should exercise its undoubted discretion to prevent such a course on the basis that the proceedings amount to an abuse"[836]. This is to say: the accusation has the (discretionary) power to conduct the accused before the court for an examination on the merits of imputation (the latter, which corresponds to an obligation, in principle). In the same way, it is a fundamental public interest to repress crimes and punish the guilty. Nonetheless, the misuse of the prosecution's prosecution (abuse) cannot be tolerated in any way: with the consequence that, in exceptional situations, the interests referred to are "sacrificed" in the face of the moral prejudice that the system of justice would suffer or what the defendant would suffer if the procedure continued (danger of condemnation of an innocent).

834 A. CHOO, Abuse of process and judicial stays of criminal proceedings, op. cit., pp. 2ss. R v. Horseferry Road Magistrates' Court, ex p Bennett, [1994], 1 AC 42, 74, per Lord Lowry. For further analysis see: R. TER HAAR, A. LANEY, M. LEVINE, Construction insurance and UK construction contracts, ed. Routledge, London & New York, 2016.

835 R v Martin, [1998], AC 917, 926; R v Burns, [2002], EWCA Crim 1324, [27]. Jones v Kernott' [2012] Conveyancer & Property Lawyer 159; J Mee 'Jones v Kernott: Inferring and imputing in Essex' [2012] Conveyancer & Property Lawyer 167.Chaudhary v Chaudhary [2013] EWCA Civ 758, [2013] Family Law 1257. For further details see: B. SLOAN, Keeping up with the Jones case: Establishing constructive trusts in "sole legal owner" scenarios, in Legal Studies, 35 (2), 2015, pp. 228ss.

836 In this sense see: CPS v Tweddel, [2001], EWHC Admin 188, [2002], 1 FCR 438, [6].

Where does the recognition in the head of the judge of the power-duty to block the progression of the trial process come from when an abuse of the public prosecutor takes place?

As already anticipated at the beginning of the work, the perspective of framing the Anglo-Saxon doctrine is diametrically antithetical to the European one. Again, with reference to the criminal system, in the European legal system the abuse arises essentially as an instrument of reaction to the obstructionist conduct put in place by the defendant or his defender, when (to repeat a known and representative slogan) the last end of the first becomes the defense "from the" process and not "in" the process. If we want, then, the abuse of the process is conceived in a repressive key: it is necessary to protect the efficiency of the judicial machine, as well as the interest in the celebration of the process in reasonable time, even if this involves the denial of an abstractly legitimate faculty.

On the contrary, as already mentioned in the previous paragraph, the notion of abuse of process is a guarantee: in the Anglo-Saxon justice system, the prosecution is in principle an option of the public prosecutor, to whom the selection is of what is "concretely" worthy of persecution. The need to contain the possible diversions, therefore, could be said to be physiological to a system so conceived: if you want, the doctrine in word arises from an awareness, that is between discretion (in the exercise of criminal action) and arbitrariness passes a very thin border that, if not well subjected to scrutiny, risks resolving itself into an intolerable detriment to the accused and consequently of the system as a whole.

Hence, the first caution to be considered in terms of comparative analysis: we are not dealing with a safeguard clause for objective or systemic needs, such as the efficiency of the procedural machine or the rationality of its functioning (interests that, if anything, they can find protection through the Anglo-Saxon doctrine of abuse in an indirect way, by reflex). Shifts-so we could say-the context of values, the parameters of reference are different. The foundation of the power-duty to punish, here, revolves around two poles that, inevitably, must be in balance: on the one hand, we have the claim to the persecution of the crime-facts. Contrarily, that of ensuring fairness of the process (which, we will deepen it, does not mean other than guaranteeing the starting conditions of the process such that the probabilities of condemnation are equivalent to those of not guilty).

In any case, we continue with the tracing of the basis of power-duty to stop the proceeding.

The leading cases would be many. However, the following can be taken as an example. The R v Connelly, [1964], AC 1254, 1296 case posed the problem-we will see it in more detail later, when we will proceed to the analysis of the symptomatic cases of abuse of process-of the limits and the operational boundaries of the double jeopardy rule. In other words, the prohibition of double judgment (an expression within which the spectrum of contents and discipline of the aforementioned doctrine can be contained) does not provide the defendant with a comprehensive protection. There are situations in which the establishment of a according to the judgment, against the same person for the same fact (or for facts strictly connected to those for which a judgment has taken place) and that emerges from the "coverage" area of the rule referred to. Nevertheless, that which is not expressly forbidden would not become legitimate for this reason. Under certain conditions, the second judgment would be unfair or, in any case, materialize in an injury to the morality of the justice system.

In this specific case, even, the power-duty of the court to react to the wrong behavior by the prosecution would not only stop the progress of the procedure, but also extend to the possibility that the process begins (in short, cutting it on the to be born). Which, beyond any technical consideration inherent in the contents of this power-duty, sounds like a caveat to the public part. Jurisdiction has "inherent (physiological) power", capable not only of questioning the mode of proceed with the accusation, but also and above all the self. In fact, the judge recognizes a basic prerogative: "to prevent a trial from taking place (in the exercise of its) residual discretion (...) are the courts to rely on the Executive to protect their process from the abuse? Have they not themselves an inescapable duty to secure fair treatment for those who come or are brought before them? To questions of this sort there is only one possible answer. The court cannot contemplate for a moment the transference to the Executive of the responsibility for seeing that the process of law is not abused (...)"[837].

This with regard to the legitimacy of this jurisdictional attribution. It should be opportunely highlighted, however, that this is a residual clause, intended to operate in very exceptional circumstances (extraordinary power). It is on this point that, in reality, the greatest difficulties in application are concentrated.

837 R. PATTENDEN, Pre-verdict judicial fact-finding in criminal trials with justice, in Oxford Journal of Legal Studies, 29 (1), 2009, pp. 6ss.

It would therefore be a question of identifying the conditions under which recourse to this power is inevitable.

It has been said that when the accusation is promoted, the court must proceed to verify its validity; in short, there arises the duty to dissolve an alternative: guilty or not guilty. This is true in principle, since there are four fundamental exceptions. In particular, the obligation in question is canceled if the criminal action is impracticable, if it falls in the area of direct operation of the double jeopardy rule (autrefois acquit or autrefois convict), if there is an order not to prosecute the attorney-general (nolle prosequi), or a lack of jurisdiction of the court in question[838].

Now, the anti-abuse clause constitutes the fifth exception, adding to the precedents listed above, which are traditionally accepted by the Anglo-Saxon jurisprudence as true limits to the exercise of the ius dicere.[839]. In any case, the essence of the doctrine in analysis (better: the final sanction in which it is substantiated), also looked at from this visual angle, remains unchanged: it is a remedy for a genetic defect or arising from the action exerted by the public, the jurisdiction is based on a discretionary determination of the prosecutor, who is responsible for choosing to start or not the actual trial, but the impropriety of action can affect the "opportunity" of the action or, more accurately, the fairness of the process. In these cases, it cannot be continued.

At this point, it is necessary to confront a further question: from a technical point of view, what is the arrest of the criminal procedure (stay)?

This is a notion that cannot easily be managed by the Italian jurist (more in general, perhaps, than that of civil law). In fact, in our legal system there is no residual clause by which the judge can order the non-prosecution of the trial (or action). It has a dry alternative, condemnation or acquittal and, it is worth noting, among the causes of acquittal in detail indicated by the law, nothing is found that comes close to the remedy in question.

On the material level, it is not difficult to understand what the arrest of the procedure consists of: the trial ends by express order of the judge. We will not go

838 B. SLOAN, Keeping up with the Jones case: Establishing constructive trusts in "sole legal owner" scenarios, op. cit.

839 R v Chairman, County of London Quarter Sessions, ex p Downes, [1954], 1 QB, 1. R. PATTENDEN, Abuse of process in criminal litigation, in Journal of Criminal Law, 53, 1989, pp. 34ss. R. PATTENDEN, The power of the Courts to stay a criminal prosecution, in Criminal Law Review, 1985, pp. 175ss. A. OWUSU-BEMPAH, Silence in suspicious circumstances, in Criminal Law Review, 2014, pp. 128ss.

further (save, clearly, the possibility for the accusation of proposing an appeal). On the other hand, from a technical point of view, it is inevitable to combine with absolution because, in substance, the effect (better: the benefit) that the defendant draws from both the pronouncements is the same. However, this does not detract from the fact that the stay of the proceeding and acquittal are distinct objects; the first must also be distinguished from another type of judicial decision, with which it would share even more evident affinity margins (verdict of not guilty): " where a defendant arraigned on an indictment or inquisition pleads not guilty and the prosecutor proposes to offer no evidence against him, the court before which the defendant is arraigned may order that a verdict of not guilty shall be recorded without any further steps being taken in the proceedings, and the verdict shall have the same effect as if the defendant had been tried and acquitted on the verdict of a jury or a court (...)"[840]. To simplify, we can say that acquittal and verdict of not guilty are assimilated by the law in terms of the effects resulting from their pronunciation: ne bis in idem. With the second, the arrest of the procedure evidently shares a (if we may say so) methodological aspect. In both cases, in fact, there is no real assessment on the merits of the sub-judicial affair that instead distinguishes the absolution (the defendant is found not guilty following the preliminary investigation and assessment of the fact by the jury).

If so, the real discrete line between the order of non prosecution due to the abuse of trial and the two other rulings can only be constituted by that of the consequential effects: only acquittal or verdict of not guilty follows the prohibition of double judgment (operating for the same, therefore, the aforementioned double jeopardy rule).

Not for the first one: there is something similar, but not the same. Unless there is authorization from the court, the establishment of a second judgment against the same person for the same fact, already arrested for having abused the trial, will also constitute an abuse of the process, with identity of consequences.

However, in this scenario it is not possible to exclude an alternative outcome: that the prosecution does not add any evidence against the defendant,

840 Criminal Justice Act 1967, Section 17. See in argument for further details and analysis: A. OWUSU-BEMPAH, Judging the desirability of a defendant's evidence: An unfortunate approach to s.35(1)(b) of the criminal justice and public order act 1994, in Criminal Law Review, 2011, pp. 692ss. A. GILLESPIE, S. WEARE, The english legal system, Oxford University Press, Oxford, 2017.

with results in no case to answer. In this case, the accused can benefit from a verdict of not guilty, with full operation of the ne bis in idem[841].

JURISDICTION AND EXECUTIVE: THE DOCTRINE OF ABUSE AT THE "TEST BED" OF INTERFERENCE BETWEEN POWERS

It is inevitable that the theory of abuse of process involves the problem of the relationship between jurisdiction and the judiciary magistrature. To better say: in the aforesaid terms, the problem could be faced with the "lens" of Italian law; in the Anglo-Saxon system, we should more correctly speak of: relations between jurisdiction and executive power[842].

Here, of course, the interference that is recreated as a result of the application of the discipline of the abuse takes on significantly greater dimensions and pregnancies: not unjustly, in fact, it has been highlighted that this doctrine resolves into questioning the same discretion inherent in exercise of executive power[843]. In some ways, it was said before that the use of process discretion is the necessary response to the distortions of prosecutorial discretion. The link or, in other words, the interference between the same is a congenital aspect of the overall reconstruction.

In practice, the paralysis of a criminal proceeding on the assumption of the unfair (or, in any case, grossly negligent) conduct of the prosecutor, is substantiated (the expression is allowed) in an invasion of the field: indeed, if the choice inherent to the exercise of the action belongs to the executive (Crown Prosecution Service), the order to block the progression is ingested directly in the same opportunity of the act of impulse (i.e. judgment of inopportunity of continuation).

In order to carry out a reflection of greater theoretical rigor, in the Anglo-Welsh system, the approach of the abuse of process would be at first reading an obvious dystonia with the adversary trial: it is an acquired principle that, following the exercise of criminal action, the relationship between the judge

841 R v Thompson, [2006], EWCA Crim 2849, [2007], 1 WLR 1123. R. PATTENDEN, Abuse of process in criminal litigation, op. cit., p. 353ss. A. CHOO, Abuse of process and judicial stays of criminal proceedings, op. cit., p. 9.

842 A. CHOO, Abuse of Process, and judicial stays of criminal proceedings, cit., p. 9.

843 See the observations of Viscount Dilhorne, in DPP v Humphrys, [1977], AC 1.

and the prosecution is confined to what happens inside the classroom[844]. Thus, it would lose relevance, always on the general level, as materially occurring before or outside (among which, obviously, also those events that would in fact create the conditions of an abuse of the process and, therefore, of the application of the relative sanction). The underlying logic is crystalline, especially for the jurist accustomed to confront the principle of phase separation: the trial is impermeable terrain to what happened extra moenia, coming into play the state of mental neutrality of the judge (of the jury).

In this way, the improper conduct of the prosecutor (prosecutorial misconducts) should be distinguished according to the procedural moment in which they are placed: where they are put in place in court, the judge has full power of intervention (in general, the discipline in question is derived from the police and criminal evidences act of 1984)[845], reporting the dialectic in the correctness path[846]; different discourse would apply to what was done in the phases prior to the trial. From the point of view of the system axioms, it should not even be known by the judge of merit, on pain of an entry of the judge in the field of investigations[847].

Similarly, the speech in question can be done with reference to the police. The traditional Anglo-Welsh setting provided for the responsibility of the said organ both in relation to investigations and to the exercise of the action; the Prosecution of Offenses Act of 1985[848] has significantly changed the following scenario. The Crown Prosecution Service was established, a body of state officials responsible for conducting criminal proceedings following the decision of the police to start (in essence, the latter residual the initial choice to institute criminal proceedings against anyone, being differently attributed to the official of the state the power is to conduct the subsequent investigations, which exercise the prosecution). On closer inspection, if there is no doubt that the referred legislation has visibly changed the relationship between police and prosecutor, we cannot even say that, due to the "new" set-ups introduced, the actions of the

844 Collier v Hicks, [1831], 2 B & Ad 663, 668, 670, 672. See, G. DURSTON, Evidence. Text and materials, Oxford University press, Oxford, 2011.

845 A. GILLESPIE, S. WEARE, The english legal system, op. cit.

846 R v Kalia, [1974], 60 Cr App R 200, 211; R v Maynard, (1979).

847 Cr App R 309, 317-8; R v Olivia, [1965], 49 Cr App R 298; R v Tregear, [1967], 2 QB 574; R v Roberts, [1985], 80 Cr App R 89. For further analysis see: A. CHOO, Evidence, op. cit. R. GLOVER, Murphy on evidence, Oxford University Press, Oxford, 2015, pp. 690ss.

848 A. GILLESPIE, S. WEARE, The english legal system, op. cit.

police are subtracted from the court's abuse, sensing the risk that the choice relating to the establishment of a criminal proceeding is dictated by reasons that exceed the aims of justice or, to be clear, extremely vexatious. We agree, we foresee instruments aimed at putting an embankment to abuse of this type. The director of public prosecutions, in fact, can order at any time of the preliminary stage the interruption of criminal proceedings[849], if you find reasons for inappropriateness of the continuation of the process; however, it does not seem that this mechanism is able to eliminate at the root any potential liability profile for the police in the event of an abuse of process[850].

Returning to the central core of the reflection, we can ask ourselves an essential question: if, as it seems to understand, the assessment of an abuse of the trial by the judge cannot disregard the knowledge of what happened before the trial or, anyway, at the external, are we facing a doctrine in contrast with one of the fundamental axioms of the accusatory process?

Beyond any possible conjecture or attempt to compose the potential conflict of powers, the most appropriate response would seem positive. On the other hand: can the judge rely entirely on the executive, excluding for this reason that the trial is never subject to abuse by the former?

However, there is a different key to reading. The obligation enshrined in constitutional law principally concerns the exercise of the action. The sanctioned reserve, therefore, takes the form of the exclusive attribution to the public prosecutor of the ownership of the act of impulsion which, once it has been put in place, irreversibly rooted the control of the jurisdiction; so-it does not seem entirely irrational to observe-an eventual collocation (assuming: de iure condendo) on the judge of power to stop the criminal trial begun, on the basis of an abuse that makes (so to say) unfair the procedure, it would not really conflict with the obligatory nature of the prosecution, since, in any case, it has already been exercised. A different matter would be in the hypothesis of preventive syndication: a possible mechanism of ex ante control regarding the opportunity of the exercise act would undoubtedly conflict, meeting a pre-announced fate (declaration of illegitimacy). Indeed, probably, the very existence of the obligation

849 Prosecution of Offenses Act (1985), Section 23. For further analysis see: A. GILLESPIE, S. WEARE, The english legal system, op. cit.

850 See in matter the Prosecution of Offenses Act (1985). For more analysis: F. BENNION, The new prosecutorial arrangements: (1) The Crown Prosecution Service, in Criminal Law Review, 1986, pp. 4ss. K.W. LIDSTONE, The reform prosecution process in England: A radical reform?, in Criminal Law Journal, 21,1987, pp. 296ss. A. GILLESPIE, S. WEARE, The english legal system, op. cit.

enshrined therein if, on the one hand, excludes any invasion "from the outside" in relation to the act of impulse, on the other, would make ex-post judicial control necessary.

THE CONCEPT OF JUDICIAL DISCRETION

It will be opportune some clarification in point of judicial discretionality (judicial discretion) that, as already pointed out, constitutes a key element both for the purpose of the understanding as well as in a perspective of framing the essence of the Anglo-Saxon doctrine of the trial abuse. Indeed, one (so to call it) actio finium regundorum of the discretion of the judge in the Anglo-Welsh system should serve to recreate a compromise between the instances of reasonableness (or, as we shall see shortly, of "individualization" of the abstract rule) and those containing the authoritative power.

Reduced the question to the minimum terms, it is a matter of differentiating the discretion from what is its conceptual antipode: the rule of law.

In general, if this last expression identifies a rule-written or not-from the rigid prescriptive content (where the material of the case would follow an exactly predetermined effect), the first lemma would postpone otherwise to the possibility for the judge to orient himself in the individual case in the choice of the concrete solution, through a margin of maneuver (more or less broad) dictated upstream by the law.

This cannot be the place to discuss the philosophical reasons underlying the adoption of operating modules marked by discretion, or the extension that it would be appropriate to recognize within the jurisdictional function[851]. Of course, it is a point that a minimum coefficient of discretion is necessary in judicial activity if, indeed, the rigidity of the abstract rule (rule of law) would guarantee the best of legal certainty, not providing (ideally) any margin in the adoption of viable solutions in the individual case, or the predictability of the effects expected from materializing of a behavior described by the case. on the other hand: " rules without discretion cannot fully take into account the need

851 A.M. GLEESON, Individualised justice-The holy grail, in Australian Law Journal, 20, 1995, pp. 422ss. C.E. SCHNEIDER, Discretion and rules: A lawyer's view, in K. HAWKINS (ed.), The uses of discretion, Oxford University Press, Oxford, 1992. C.R. SUNSTEIN, Problems with rules, in California Law Review, 83, 1995, pp. 953ss. L. GELSTHORPE, N. PADFIELD, Exercising discretion, ed. Routledge, London & New York, 2012, pp. 217ss.

for tailoring results to unique facts and circumstances of particular cases. The justification for discretion is the need for individualized justice (...)"[852].

Therefore, putting aside the main function of judicial discretion, we must dwell on the way to identify its essence.

In other words, what is meant by judicial discretion? The settings substantially matured on the point are two. Like the first, judicial discretion would be a decision-making power totally free from the law (unfettered power). Otherwise speaking: if the law, in a given situation, imposed the behavior A, the judge could deviate from the legal prescription not only not following the legal command, but even independently elaborating a different solution (B)[853]. The setting in question would sound suggestive, but it does not convince: it greatly enhances the moment (so to speak) creative of the rule by the judge. Nevertheless, it is badly suited to the theory of the abuse of the process. As will be better seen in the following paragraphs, the overall construction of the same is based on rigid values, which tend to be incompressible (in terms of the principle of legitimacy and fairness) and, therefore, insane as regards derogation or balancing with interests of an adverse sign. Wanting to exemplify, the adoption of such an approach could entail an eventual fact: there is abuse when the process is unfair. However, if the upstream rule configured by the abuse of process doctrine would impose the arrest of the proceeding in this case, the judge could also deliberately depart from it.

Therefore, the second is better: discretion is the ability attributed to the judge to move within an operating margin or appreciation, prepared by law (open-texturedness) in order to "individualize" the abstract content of a rule in the individual case (but without, as it would be in the context of the first approach, that this entails freedom for the judge to choose whether or not to apply the basic precepts).

To clarify: "a discretion necessarily involves a latitude of individual choice according to the particular circumstances, and differs from a case where the decision follows ex debito iustitiae once facts are ascertained (...)"[854].

852 K.C. DAVIS, Discretionary justice: A preliminary inquiry, op. cit., pp. 17ss.

853 A. CHOO, Abuse of process and judicial stays of criminal proceedings, op. cit., pp. 156ss.

854 Evans v Bartlam, [1937], AC 473, 489 per Lord Wright. For further details see: R. PATTENDEN, The judge, discretion, and the criminal trial, op. cit., pp. 4ss. Y.M. MORISSETTE, The exclusion of evidence under the Canadian Charter of Rights and Freedoms: What to do and what not to do, in McGill Law Journal, 30 (4), 1984, pp. 554ss.

Arguments then (perhaps, but so it would seem) sufficient to anticipate a consideration that will certainly be useful in the continuation, when we will go into the analysis of the doctrine in question. If, as already anticipated, the judicial discretion constitutes a physiological aspect to the theory of abuse, the latter must logically be conceived in the dual dimension of power-duty of the judiciary. With greater clarity, the judge has ample room for maneuver in the reconstruction of situations that legitimize the adoption of remedies established by the doctrine in comment. The diagnosis of such "symptomatic" situations, if it gives positive results, results in an obligation: the application of the sanction (arrest of the procedure).

THE QUALIFYING ELEMENTS OF THE DOCTRINE

It is now a matter of summarizing the hypotheses of application of the doctrine of procedural abuse; better to say: the operational "poles" of the theory. In essence: in which cases can one generally say that an abuse of the process has occurred? Which, on balance, would be tantamount to establishing the qualifying element for the purposes of judicial diagnosis.

The Anglo-Saxon jurisprudence has settled on a double characterization of abusive conduct: "(...) the jurisdiction to stay can be exercised in many different circumstances. Nevertheless, two main strands can be detected in the authorities: -Cases where the court concludes that the defendant cannot receive a fair trial, including cases where the court concludes that it would unfair for the defendant to be tried. In some cases, of course, the two categories may overlap (...)[855].

The reference parameters are therefore two. In the first hypothesis, the process is "falsified" ab origin: contrary to fairness, therefore the defendant is not in a position to exercise full and adequate defense (we will discuss in the next paragraph of the concept of fairness). In the second, although the fairness of the process is not in question and, therefore, the capacity of the accused to elaborate an effective line of action, it would be unfair to prolong the exercise of the punitive pretension, contrary to the moral integrity of the system (moral integrity of justice).

855 R v Beckford, [1996], 1 Cr App R 94, 100-1.

The doctrine in question constitutes the crossroads of two parameters of different nature. Around the first operative pole, the idea of the risk of an unjust conviction rotates: we are therefore faced with a direct intrinsic policy of the system (intrinsic policy), aimed at protecting more than the correct functioning of the judicial machine, that of avoid the condemnation of an innocent. On the second, otherwise, the image of the ethical integrity of the system of justice (extrinsic policy) is thickened: even if there is no risk of reaching the conviction of an innocent subject, the interest in punishing the perpetrators degrades to this a point that can be said to be non-existent (related) to the continuation of the procedural process.

Certainly, the second area of operation is the one most difficult to handle by the Italian jurist: it involves for the judge, when assessing an abusive conduct on the part of the prosecutor, the adoption of metagiuridic reference parameters. We could try to summarize it: "(...) in these cases the question is not so much whether the defendant can be fairly tried, but rather whether for some reason connected with the prosecutors' conduct it would be unfair to him if the court were to permit them to proceed at all. The court's inquiry is directed more to the prosecutors' behaviour than to the fairness of any eventual trial (...) if it is satisfied that it would not be fair to allow the proceedings to continue, the court does not then concern itself with the possibility that any ensuing trial might still be a fair one, because it will have formed the prior view that it would not be fair to the defendant if it were to take place at all (...)"[856]. In essence, rather than

856 R (Ebrahim) v. Feltham Magistrates' Court, [2001], EWHC Admin 130, [2001], 1 WLR 1293, 20. For further analysis and details see: S. FAIRCLOUGH, It doesn't happen...and I've never thought it was necessary for it to happen: Barriers to vulnerable defendants giving evidence by live link in Crown Court trials, in International Journal of Evidence & Proof, 21 (3), 2017, pp. 212ss. S. FAIRCLOUGH, Speaking up for Injustice: Reconsidering the provision of special measures through the lens of equality, in Criminal Law Review, 2018, pp. 7ss. E. HENDERSON, Taking control of cross-examination: Judges, advocates and intermediaries discuss judicial management of the cross-examination of vulnerable people, in Criminal Law Review, 2016, pp. 184ss. J. JACKSON, S. SUMMERS, The internationalisation of criminal evidence: Beyond the common law and civil law traditions, Cambridge University Press, Cambridge, 2012. A. KIRBY, Effectively engaging victims, witnesses and defendants in the Criminal Courts: A question of "court culture"?, in Criminal Law Review, 2017, pp. 950ss. A. LOUGHNAN, Between fairness and "dangerousness": Reforming the law on unfitness to plead, in Criminal Law Review, 2016, pp. 452ss. R.D. MACKAY, Unfitness to plead-Data on formal findings from 2002 to 2014. London: Law Commission, 2016. J. MCEWAN, Vulnerable defendants and the fairness of trials, in Criminal Law Review, 2013, pp. 103ss. L. MULCAHY, Putting the defendant in their place: Why do we still use the dock in criminal proceedings?, in British Journal of Criminology, 53 (6), 2013, pp. 1140ss. A. OWUSU-BEMPAH, Judging the desirability of a defendant's evidence: An unfortunate approach to s.35(1)(b) of the Criminal Justice and Public Order Act 1994, op. cit., pp. 694ss. A. OWUSU-BEMPAH, Defendant participation in the criminal process, ed. Routledge, London, 2017. R. DENYER, Case management in criminal trials, Hart Publishing, Oxford &

focusing on an evaluation of an objective nature (if a fair trial is possible), the judicial assessment would be based on the subjective coefficient of guilt (or bad faith) of the accusation. As it is argued, in this last case the needs of safeguarding the procedural guarantees and those of "moralizing" the system interpenetrate. By comparing categories of principle of legitimacy and fairness, fairness is polysemy: between system requirements, morality and subjective guarantees. We anticipated the question that will merge the subject of this paragraph: what should be understood by fairness of the criminal trial?

A simple semantic transposition would already highlight the problematic nature of the notion: a purely literal meaning would provide us with the term "correctness, loyalty". However, it is not the only one: from a technical-legal point of view, it would correspond to "fairness", which, in any case, would mean a lot. If the first meaning, in fact, evokes a dialectical scenario centered on the obligation of loyalty of the parties, the second aims straight not only to the need to respect the "rules of the game", but also to that of safeguarding the fundamental guarantees of the accused in the criminal proceedings. In essence, the polysemy of the lemma makes it clear of the ethical matrix of a principle that is subsequently placed within a technical framework.

We can also understand another fact: the concept of fairness poses the domestic jurist facing the same difficulties that in general would appear before the common law abuse doctrine. In addition to the deficiency of upstream legality, we are witnessing the merging of instances "moralizing" of the justice system and of the defense of the right of defense, with the inevitable consequences in terms of problematic classification. In any case, to attempt to clarify the content of the concept under analysis, one can move from the call of another fundamental principle in the context of the anti-abuse theory.

In the Anglo-Saxon system, the principle of legitimacy is the first foundation of both the ius dicere and the criminal justice system itself; at the base, there is the idea that jurisdiction derives legitimacy from the duty to protect two essential interests: the protection of the innocent from unjust sentences and the safeguarding of the moral integrity of the system[857]. Wanting to simplify to the maximum, with the first of the interests mentioned, we refer to the need to put the accused in starting conditions in which the probabilities of arriving at

Oregon, Portland, 2012.

857 A.A.S. ZUCKERMAN, Illegally-obtained-evidence-discretion as a guardian of legitimacy, in Current Legal Problems, 40, 1987, pp. 59ss.

a non-guilty pronouncement are equivalent to those of a conviction. In short, a general idea of equality of arms is instilled in the system: it is impossible for it to take place if the criminal trial starts with a clear phase-shift between the accusation and the defendant, where the latter is not in fact able to prepare adequate defense. The nature of this first articulation of the principle of legitimacy is clearly transpired. It has a deliberately broad content, materializing more in an operational direction than in an exactly predetermined technical command. Further, it expresses the need, both from a normative and strictly practical point of view, to guarantee the probable outcome of the equivalent process at the outset, so that always on a plan of principle, any conduct of a part aimed at undermining this ideal equilibrium must be censured.

The second content is different: it reconnects the foundation of the public power (in this case: jurisdiction and repression of crimes) to the collective custody that is placed on justice itself (public confidence). In other words, the idea of a justice system totally dissolved by an "ethical" control of the European Union cannot be in any way confirmed: repressing crimes is certainly of apical interest. However, it is not possible to disregard the need for procedural fair play: this in turn implies that the accusation follows the good faith (to recall the duty of loyalty and probity of the parties), constituting this a real counter, limit to the exercise of punitive power: if exceeded, you would inevitably throw discredit on jurisdiction and justice.

The corollary of what has just been illustrated is summarized as follows.

Between the principle in question and the doctrine of abuse, with specific regard to the two outlined "poles" of operation (unfair trial/unfair to try), there is a close link, which would be summarized in the identity of the base of operations. In the wake of the first articulation of the principle of legitimacy, we find a content that is obviously corresponding to that of fairness: reduced the question to the minimum terms, guarantee initial conditions of the procedure such that the probabilities of condemnation correspond to those of absolution other does not mean if not avert the danger of an unjust conviction, id est: condemnation of an innocent. At the same time, if the process is unfair, there is a lack of legitimacy of the ius dicere; if this is connected to a conduct carried out by the public part, it cannot continue; similarly, a fair trial could also be possible, the conduct of the magistrate could be contrary to the root of correctness. The, the protraction of the punitive pretension is morally unjustifiable. At a practical level, all this translates into a specific technical operation, to which the English judge is called if he considers the opportunity to paralyze the course of the proceedings due to an abuse of process. In particular, he will have to verify the existence of precise conditions: a) the protection of the not guilty by unjust sentences; when the first evaluation gives a positive outcome, b) that the interest in the repression of the guilty continues and, specularly, and that c) such interests do not conflict with the moral integrity of the system.

Summing up: the application of the abuse of process doctrine will be possible if and because, alternatively, there is a real danger when an innocent defendant will be condemned or when the protraction of the procedure constitutes an outrage to the ethical image of justice (more concretely, to the collective trust-public confidence-towards the same)[858].

Based on the considerations made, we would then arrive at a conclusion.

Intercurring an intimate link between the principle of legitimacy and the theoretical abuse of the process (constituting, indeed, the latter a sort of "emanation" of the first practice), we can arrive at the delineation of the content of the process fairness: at the end of the reckoning, it would represent the place of mediation between a teleological projection of criminal process (given in the Anglo-Saxon system, as seen, by the repression of crimes), and that of respect for the defensive guarantees which, in the end, is embodied in the protection of the innocents from unjust sentences.

Consistently with these premises, the innate absoluteness of the rule in comment has been affirmed. It is rigid, unsuitable to found a balancing judgment with opposing values: "rial fairness is an absolute right in that nothing less than fairness to the accused is acceptable"[859].

It would be worth, further, to remove it from any form of balancing test: it would escape compressions of sorts due to possible "counterweights" value[860]. It would be an operation both illogical and juridically unsustainable in such a system: denying fairness is tantamount to denying the fundamentals of criminal jurisdiction.

858 R v Griffin, [2001], 3 NZLR 577, (2001) 19 CRNZ 47 (CA), per Richardson P, Blanchard and Tipping JJ at para 40; R v Forbes, [2001], 1 AC 473, [2001] 2 WLR 1 (HL); Brown v Stott, [2003], 1 AC 681 [2001] 2 WLR 817 (PC); Randall v R, [2002], 1 WLR 2237 (PC) [2002] UKPC 19 at para 28; Montgomery v HM Advocate, [2003], 1 AC 641, [2001] 2 WLR 779(PC). For further details see: M. SPENCER, Concentrate questions and answers evidence, Oxford University Press, Oxford, 2016. B. EMMERSON, A. ASHWORTH, A. MACDONALD, Human rights and criminal justice, op. cit.

859 D. MATHIAS, The duty to prevent an abuse of process by staying criminal proceedings, ed. Robertson, 2004, pp. 6ss.

860 R v Narayan, par Glazebrook J, HC Auckland T 2902: "(...) the balancing of probative value and prejudicial effect (...) is at the heart of the discretion to admit or exclude evidence (...)".

BETWEEN THE ARREST OF PROCEDURE AND "INTERMEDIATE" SOLUTIONS: CRITERIA FOR CHOOSING AN EXTREME REMEDY

As stated above, the arrest of the proceedings due to a procedural abuse constitutes the remedy of last resort. It is not appropriate to dwell on the reasons for the exceptionality: needs linked to the effectiveness of criminal jurisdiction and the repression of crimes lead immediately to this conclusion. The real question is: what are the "intermediate" solutions and, therefore, when it can be said that the same do not provide adequate protection, making appropriate the use of the "extreme" sanction?

The "case-by-case" approach (often highlighted) to the subject matter also precludes the elaboration of a general rule. In the same way in which it is not possible to give an exact definition of the abuse, letting the practice concretize its contents and operating procedures[861] from time to time, so it is not conceivable an abstractization of situations in which the remedy of last resort is imposed[862]. On the other hand, reasoning is not exclusively linked to the physiological pragmatism of the abuse of process, but also to strictly technical considerations related to the changing nature of the concept of fairness over time: concretizing in an (implicit) reference to the operational rules that govern the development of the process, it is clear that the operative modulation (and the correlated eventual prejudice) of the same is affected by the normative or hermeneutical events that directly or indirectly affect it.

Nevertheless, a rough reconstruction can be attempted for which the need to use the arrest of the proceeding was considered in previous case law cases. After all, even in a subject strongly dominated by interpretative and pragmatic oscillations like the one in question, a guideline is present: the prejudice deriving from the accused by the abuse. At the end of the day, this is at the same time the symptomatic element (of the incorrect procedural conduct) and the guiding criterion towards the opportunity of the "therapeutic" intervention of the jurisdiction[863].

861 Watson v Clarke, [1990], 1 NZLR 715, (1988) 3 CRNZ 67.

862 A. PACIOCCO, The stay of proceedings as a remedy in criminal cases: Abusing the abuse of process concept, in Criminal Law Journal, 15, 2001, pp. 315ss.

863 A. PACIOCCO, The stay of proceedings as a remedy in criminal cases: Abusing the abuse of process concept, op. cit.

A further common thread is found: alternative solutions to the arrest of criminal trial are resolved by judicial interventions on the admission or exclusion of the trial. In essence, if-as placed above in light-the interest most heavily guarded by the doctrine in question is constituted by fairness (in its dual articulation of technical operating rule and at the same time "ethics"), it is immediately apparent that the terrain most sensitive to abusive behavior of part, able to compromise (if we want to say) the genuineness of the dialectical process and, therefore, the substantial correctness and equality of weapons in the trial, is that of evidence. Without going too far into a complex area, we can still say that even in the Anglo-Saxon system the judicial "treatment" of the trial follows a diversification of rules for the admission (and acquisition) of the trial and the final evaluation. The consequence is soon said. The alternative remedies to the penalty of maximum rigor are: the possible exclusion of the "contaminated" test (exclusion of tainted evidence), an invitation to caution formulated by the judge to the jury (judicial warning), in the sense of carefully weighing the weight to be attributed to a particular test or the specific meaning to be assigned to the same[864].

In which cases, can we say that the exclusion of a trial is a more appropriate solution than the arrest of the procedure (or vice versa)?

As is known, consistently with the core principles of the adversarial trial of the Anglo-Welsh order, the supporting rule regarding the powers of intervention of the judge on the evidence (requests and/or produced by the parties) is summarized in the general prohibition for the judge of investigation on the method and on the operative modalities adopted by the parts for the obtainment or the finding of the trial during the investigations (lawfully evidence obtained)[865]. Except in exceptional circumstances, the seriousness of the conduct carried out by the public part, aimed at obtaining the proof, imposes its exclusion from the trial field[866].

Now, it is clear that here we are facing a solution of high rigor.

---

864 D. MATHIAS, The duty to prevent an abuse of process by staying criminal proceedings, op. cit., pp. 2ss. See also the next cases: R v Grace, [1989], 1 NZLR 197; R v Sutton, [1988], 4 CRNZ 98 (CA); Mohammed v The State, [1999], 2 AC 111, 123 (PC); R v Buhay, [2003], 225 DLR (4th) 624, 2003 SCC 30.

865 R v Shaheed, [2002], 2 NZLR 377, 2002 19 CRNZ 165 (CA); R v Grayson and Taylor, [1997], 1 NZLR 399; R v Taylor, [1996], 14 CRNZ 426 (CA). J. JACKSON, S. SUMMERS, The internationalisation of criminal evidence: Beyond the common law and civil law traditions, op. cit.

866 R v Dally, [1990], 2 NZLR 184, 1990 5 CRNZ 687. For further analysis see: D. MATHIAS, Discretionary exclusion of evidence, in New Zealand Law Journal, 20, 1990, pp. 25ss.

It is difficult to say which cases are justified in recourse to one rather than the other solution, showing the hermeneutical declinations that emerged in the courtrooms a wide oscillation between the choice to continue with a process vitiated by an improper conduct of the accusation and to recover the "orthodoxy" through the exclusion of the vitiated evidence, or on the contrary to definitively end its course[867].

As you can see, the question revolves around the object of aggression. With greater clarity, we can say that if the overall fairness of the process is at stake, no balancing judgment will be possible as said before, to enucleate the essential features of fairness, on the absoluteness and inelasticity of the same (for that same insuscettibile to bend in front of antithetical interests). Otherwise, if the opposed interest is different, we will have to tend towards the solution of less rigor. The residual doubt always invokes the terms and the degree of reliability of the judicial prognosis. In other words, with what degree of reasonableness can one say that the mere exclusion of proof will preserve the accused from the risk of an unjust conviction and that, for this reason, the impartiality of the jury is sufficiently protected?

Even here, there is no definite answer. Too many allies and factors that can come into play to illustrate the demonstrative "weight" of the evidence that would be excluded from the final decision could play a decisive role. Moreover, the gravity of the offense for which it proceeds and, consequently, the impact (in a broad sense) of emotion that it may have on the soul of the jurors could have little relevance.

The approach to the second problem is different. How to discern cases in which the arrest of the trial is justified by those in which a judicial warning is sufficient. It is opportunely repeated, the invitation made by the judge to the jury can be in a twofold alternative sense: in bringing an appropriate demonstrative "weight" to a test (or, on the contrary, in the invitation not to overemphasize its relevance) in assigning the correct "meaning" or representative content to the test. These are situations, however, more problematic. In cases of this type, in fact, a test has already been admitted and acquired (in the first case, however, the judge could also block the entry of the trial, denying admission). A proof, in short, here is already present in the process: acquired, has already entered the sphere of knowledge of the jury.

867 R v Looseley, [2001], UKHL 53 (25 October 2001), 2001 4 All ER 897 (HL).

It would not be questioned here, at least in appearance, the legality of the proof itself, but the mere evaluative moment of the same. Basically, it is rational to believe that a simple caveat to the jury provides adequate coverage of the process? On the other hand, even the exclusion at the root of the "poisoned fruit" would not elude doubts about the impartiality of the judge of the fact that denying the use of a given evidence for the decision does not mean to erase it from the memory of who learned the contents. In the end, it is a matter of practical sense. From what it seems, we must always have as a point of reference the danger of condemning an innocent person if, therefore, even the exclusion of the proof (and not the simple invitation made by the judge to the jury) should not avert the risk in question, the arrest of the procedure would be an obligatory solution.

THE "CLINICAL" CASES OF THE ANGLO-SAXON SYSTEM

A brief illustration of the "symptomatic" cases of abuse of the process in the Anglo-Welsh system is imposed to such an extent, albeit in a totally summarized manner. The caveat in the premise is the usual: these are practical examples (as well as conceptual), since it cannot be ruled out that the practice will increase the number of cases in the future, as well as a (so to speak) "trial" procedure, usually brought back to the phenomenology of the abuse, in the concrete case then do not configure it (or vice versa, that empirical manifestations traditionally not brought back to the abusive practice subsequently become). In short, the anchoring of the judicial review to parameters of substantial sign, such as the concrete possibility for the accused to benefit from a fair trial or that in the specific case the continuation of the trial results in an outrage to the ethical integrity of justice, in one with the physiological oscillation of the (already reported) fact-finding approach, involves in itself the purely illustrative relevance of the analysis of leading cases in the matter. At the most, this observation serves as a methodological indication for the continuation. We will try not only to shed light on the "specializing" features of symptomatic cases, but also on the type of concrete assessment that the judge is called to play, also trying to clarify with which particular declinations the above mentioned substantialistic parameters are placed within the typical situation.

It is well known that in any modern criminal justice system, the excessive length of procedures is an aspect that is in some ways endemic and unavoidable[868]. This can certainly not be the place to dwell on the reasons behind this systemic inefficiency: if only because the reasons in question are of heterogeneous nature, moving from "physiological" or structural problems of the process itself (from the point of view of the apparatus upstream legislation), to arrive at profiles related to the workload that afflicts the judicial machinery. A consideration, on the other hand, must be immediately carried out: the classification (to use an expression more in keeping with domestic legal terminology) within the Anglo-Saxon order of the reasonable length of the criminal trial within the framework of the fairness of the process. It is a key analysis, in fact, that must be immediately brought to light: in substance, within the Anglo-Welsh criminal process, the defendant's claim to containment within reasonable time of the celebration of the rite answers, first of all, that absolute and incompressible interest that we have seen to be fairness. We will soon have the opportunity to see it in more detail, but it is immediately perceived that the delay in the celebration of the process can be resolved in the risk of an unjust conviction. The course of time alters the capacity reminiscent of the facts of the case, therefore a (so to call it) key-witness to the defense could, as a result of the lapse of time, not be able to clearly re-emerge details that would be essential for the purposes of defensive strategy, alongside for an acquittal. In any case, it must be said that the problem of dilation of the procedural time is able to manifest itself in a double direction, a delay in the exercise of the criminal action (having regard to the interval of time between the beginning of the procedure and the act of impulse of the process), and d delay in carrying out the merit judgment (concerning the excessive length of the trial itself). In the common law system, it detects only-for the purposes of the application of the anti-abuse doctrine-the first form: for the logical reason that, in that case, it is procedural length due to the prosecutor (or, what is the same, to the police in the execution of investigations).

868 In these terms see. D. YOUNG, M. SUMMERS QC, D. CORKER, Abuse of process in criminal proceedings, ed. Bloomsbury, New York, 2014, pp. 2ss. D. BIRCH, C. TAYLOR, "People like us?": Responding to allegations of past abuse in care, in Criminal Law Review, 2003, pp. 824ss. P. LEWIS, Too late to try?, in New Law Journal, 2006, pp. 1458ss. A. CHOO, Abuse of process and judicial stays of criminal proceedings, cit., pp. 71ss.

In general, the answer to the problem of the excessive length of the procedures takes place in modern systems on two fronts. On one side, through the imposition of predetermined duration limits of the procedural stages; while on the other, as a function of closing the system and at the same time to mitigate the rigidity of the phase terms, the jurisprudential processing of discretionary rules on the reasonableness of the duration of the proceedings. One cannot clearly say in a priori way which of the two settings is more efficient. If the introduction of rigid terms makes it possible to identify (at least in principle) with confidence the threshold beyond which the duration of the process must be defined excessive. It is also true that the length of the procedure is (as we said) an endemic problem to justice, so that we cannot even logically rule out that the celebration of a trial, within the maximum times established by the law, does not in any case have an excessive duration or, better to say, implying overall iniquity. It is axiomatic that some delay is inevitable. The question is: at what point does the delay become unreasonable?[869].

In the Anglo-Saxon order, an overview of the terrain of the abuse jurisdiction allows us to deduce the clear favor shown for the second solution.

The story clearly shows how the doctrine in question is "daughter" of jurisprudential elaborations, occurred outside the legal grids and the judicial discretion that underlies it intimately permeates the settings that have emerged on this specific side. If we want to put it in other words, it is a question of cultural heritage: the discretion of the judge constitutes an empirical instrument, intrinsically oscillating; but it is also a critical "tool" which, in the common law's cultural genetic code, protects the rights of the individual, thus ensuring an effective synthesis of individual guarantees and collective interests.

If this is so, it will then be clear why in the system in question the parliament has never introduced a positive discipline in the matter of temporal scans of the phases of the criminal trial. In concrete terms, there is not properly a subjective right of the accused, of legislative matrix, the containment of the times within which the prosecutor can exercise the criminal action[870].

---

869 R v Smith, [1992], 2 SCR 1120, par Sopinka J.

870 D. YOUNG, M. SUMMERS QC, D. CORKER, Abuse of process in criminal proceedings, op. cit., pp. 10ss. A. CHOO, Abuse of process and judicial stays of criminal proceedings, op. cit., pp. 71ss. A clear example of this ideological-cultural guideline can be found in the introduction of the War Crimes Act 1991, aimed at the persecution of war crimes committed in the years 1939-1945 (see, R v Sawoniuk, [2000], 2 Cr App R 220, CA). For further details see: C. SINGH, M. RAMJOHN, Unlocking evidence, ed. Routledge, London & New York, 2016. J. DOAK, M. MCGOURLAY, M. THOMAS, Evidence in context, ed. Routledge, London & New York, 2015. P. ROBERTS, A. ZUCKERMAN,

To this, the "sectoral" provisions given by the Magistrates' Courts Act 1980 are strictly excluded. These are special provisions concerning the summary offences (facts-crime of attenuated gravity, in general): "except as otherwise expressly provided by enactment and subject to subsection (2) below, a magistrates' court shall not try an information or hear a complaint unless the information was laid, or the complaint made, within six months from the time when the offence was committed, or the matter of compliant arose" (Section 127). For the rest, the regulatory framework on this matter is realized, as well as in judicial rulings aimed at establishing precise references in terms of procedural lengths, in what we could define as codes of conduct for practical operators.

Specific reference is made, in the first place, to the Code for Crown Prosecutors, issued by the director of public prosecutions (on the basis of the provisions of the Prosecution of Offenses Act 1985, s.10): in providing a code of guidelines and practices in the prosecution, it is established that a trial will not start if there is a considerable amount of time between the date of commission of the offense and that of the trial, unless: a) the fact- crime is serious; b) the delay has been caused, albeit partially, by the defendant; c) the news of a crime has only recently been learned by the authority; and d) there have been lengthy investigations due to the complexity of the matter.

Secondly, the well-known attorney-general's reference no 1 of 1990[871] should be mentioned. An authentic cornerstone in terms of delay, it is necessary to find the relevance of this "precedent" in having canonized the essential parameters delimiting the threshold beyond which the delay in carrying out the procedure results in an intolerable prejudice against the accused.

Synthetically, the fact is recalled: a police officer was involved in an accident in August 1987. The trial of merit established against him began only in March 1989. The judge (of the Crown Court) accepted the request of the defense to block the continuation of the procedure on the basis of the delay in the exercise of criminal proceedings, included always in a defensive thesis, shared by the judge, an abuse of the trial.

Thus, a problem arose: according to the attorney general's perspective, an interpretation of this guise, which based the opportunity of the exceptional

Criminal evidence, Oxford University Press, Oxford, 2010.

871 A. GILLESPIE, S. WEARE, The english legal system, op. cit. P. ROBERTS, A. ZUCKERMAN, Criminal evidence, op. cit. J. SPRACK, A practical approach to criminal procedure, Oxford University Press, Oxford, 2011.

remedy of the arrest of the proceedings solely on the basis of the objective delay that occurred in the exercise of the action, would have been excessively rigid, since it would not have taken into account both the element of "responsibility" for the redundant length of the procedure, as the fact that (as said at the beginning) the delay is physiological problem to the judicial machine and therefore, to a certain extent, it constitutes an "acceptable systemic risk".

Hence, the question is posed by the attorney general: what is the level of seriousness of the prejudice against the accused in order to justify the appeal of the arrest of the proceeding? That is, if the arrest of the criminal trial could be ordered by the judge only on the basis of the objective delay in the exercise of the prosecution. Regardless of the circumstance, however, the same could be a consequence of a guilty conduct of the prosecutor, in the affirmative answer. In fact, neither the defense in the application for the arrest of the procedure, nor the judge who had ordered it took into consideration two relevant elements. One being the responsibility for the delay in the exercise of the criminal proceedings that occurred; and two being the extent of the prejudice suffered by the accused in consequence of the length of the same and which, in the event of protraction of the court proceedings, would continue to suffer.

The answer to the first question was affirmative. The arrest of the trial is indeed a remedy of an exceptional nature, but the fact that the delay in the exercise of the action does not depend on a behavior guilty of the accusation does not sterilize the resulting injury. Rather, a limit should be imposed (so to say) negative to the operability of the remedy in question: it will not be available where it is established that the delay occurred solely as a consequence of the complexity of the sub-judicial case or, alternatively, if it is chargeable to the defense.

With regard to the second, the determining value of the prejudice that the defense would suffer due to the excessive length of the procedure was affirmed. Basically, in order to operate the doctrine of the abuse of the trial, it is necessary that it derives a concrete compromise of the rights of the accused. The extent of the injury is the usual, settling on the well-known binomial of the theoretical: unfair trial/unfair to try. The burden of proof on this point lies with the defendant: whether it is due to the high probability of not being able to benefit from a fair trial due to the delay (or, alternatively, the ethical reprehension of the protracted trial); both with regard to the seriousness of the damage that would result from the continuation of the process. In this sense, always in consideration of the intrinsic exceptional nature of the remedy in question, the judge will always have to evaluate the alternative viability of intermediate solutions: the non admission of a proof, possibly "spoiled" because of the delay; the indication of guidelines to the jury for the purpose of evaluating the evidential conglomeration.

The following key parameters are then set for the abuse of the process due to delay: a) minimum acceptable injury coefficient. The prejudice that threatens to suffer the defense must be serious. With greater clarity, there must be the risk of an unfair trial (unjust conviction): the course of time significantly alters the demonstrative value of the evidence, making it more concrete the danger of a conviction (we would say) "not beyond reasonable doubt". But, even if a fair trial were possible, there could still be a need to end it: time inevitably soothes the "scuffing" recreated by the crime, leading even to the oblivion of the same in the collective consciousness, thus not justifying itself anymore, in this case, the persecution. Outside this extreme region, the delay must be tolerated as necessary "evil".

Impracticability of intermediate solutions. It was said above. The definitive arrest of the criminal trial passes through a preliminary assessment or, better, a prognosis about the unprofitable experience of intermediate solutions (not admitting a trial, caveat indications to the jury in the decision on the fact).

The "guilt" of the prosecutor. Guideline already highlighted: the charge of the delay to the accusation is not a conditio sine qua non for the arrest of the trial. Rather, it requires special caution when no etiologically relevant conduct of the prosecutor emerges from the available elements. Therefore, the element (so to speak) subjective given by the fault (if not the malice) of the accusation affects a different aspect with reference to the ascertainment of the occurrence of an abuse: the judgment of reproover that the first can be moved into terms of causation of delay and of the procedural inequality that derives from it, whereby causes a delay in the procedure is not part of the abuse. Some hypotheses of "physiological" procedural length are not included in the paradigm of the doctrine in analysis. The objective complexity of the case treated is the most intuitive, and similar to it are the difficulty encountered in investigating by the prosecutor in finding the sources of evidence (imagine the sector of economic crime, notoriously involving very complex and long investigations). In the same way, the delay due to a defense behavior cannot be configured for abuse.

Documentary proof and oral exam. It should be opportunely drawn a line of discrimine between processes mainly based on documentary evidence (the case of crimes in economic matters is referred again) and those based on oral examination (think of sexual crimes). As is well understood, the traditional hermeneutical approach tends to reconnect the opportunity to proceed with the arrest of the procedure due to abuse of the second group of hypotheses (waiting for the "non-usurability" due to the time of a documental contribution)[872].

To summarize: " where delay jeopardises the fairness of a forthcoming trial or where, for any compelling reason, it is not fair to try an accused at all (...) the proceedings must be brought to an end (...)"[873].

The above guidelines have had a large influence on judicial practice to follow, hesitating in setting certain operating points which, on closer inspection, would constitute a "projection" and at the same time a confirmation of the upstream criteria expressed in the leading case analyzed above. It was therefore established that, even if the length of the procedural time is excessive and does not find plausible justification in other reasons (such as the objective complexity of the case), the paralysis of the procedure must be confined to exceptional cases, the sanction of maximum rigor will not take place, unless it is proven that the accused cannot benefit from a fair trial. Alternatively, the protraction of the punitive pretension results in an attack on the moral integrity of justice if the existence of a prejudice against the defendant is proven, the judge must first assess whether the procedural fairness cannot be guaranteed through more attenuated remedies (by extending a trial from the trial or, otherwise instructing the jury on the most suitable criteria for his final evaluation), only when the conditions listed above occur jointly, the criminal trial must be arrested.

At this point, it is worthwhile to make some final considerations regarding the delay in the exercise of the action: in particular, with reference to the concrete relationship between the procedural flaw in question and the two operational "poles" of the abuse doctrine (unfair trial/not fair to try). With regard to the first, it is necessary to move from the premise that, in the Anglo-Welsh system, it constitutes ius receptum the rule by which the exercise of the penal action must necessarily be accompanied by the granting of the concrete possibility of carrying out an adequate defense. This principle makes the assessment of the injury intimately connected to the delay in the process. As lucidly summarized in multiple pronunciations, with the passage of time, memories will tend to vanish; in other words, a re-enactment of the facts will inevitably replace a

872 R v Buzalek and Schiffer, (1991), Crim LR 115, CA; R v Central Criminal Court, ex p Randle and Pottle, (1992), 1 All ER 370, CA.

873 Spiers v Ruddy, (2007), UKPC D2, (2008) E WLR 608, par Lord Bingham of Cornhill.

reconstruction of the same that, as a result of rational workmanship, will still be devoid of that clarity and that genuineness of a memory that resurfaces through the words of a witness[874].

Clearly, the margins of uncertainty in terms of procedural unfairness are not only radically unavoidable; to clarify: the prognosis in point of injury from unjust condemnation is not possible except in probabilistic terms. In short, it would require the judge a perspective look at the reconstruction of the fact that will be made by the jury at the end of the acquisition of evidence. For this reason, instead of the actual impossibility of a fair trial (as for reasons of simplification of soles say), it would be more correct to speak of "substantial risk that the defendant does not benefit from an adequate possibility of defending himself"[875].

Said risk is understandably higher in the processes in which the accusatory construct is based (exclusively or in a determining manner) on the declarative tests[876]. This is generally recognized also in the application area[877], if in fact, the pre-established test, once formed, remains insensitive to the course of time, on the contrary this will produce a physiological alteration of the memories present in the psyche of the witness.

However, the antithetical hypothesis cannot be excluded. The situations could be the most varied, but can be exemplified as follows: expected that the course of time also affects the physical reality (imagine the inevitable changes suffered by the state of the places where, for example, the crime occurred), an unjustifiable delay-either due to operational inefficiency of the requisite office or for any other reason-could lead to a technical assessment, subsequently reversed on a documentary evidence, inevitably characterized by a precarious reliability.

Instead, a different reasoning must be made with reference to the second operative "pole" of the doctrine on the abuse of the process. Because of the time course, the equity of the process may not be in question. Nevertheless, the length of the procedural times would make the protraction of the punitive pretension "morally deplorable". In this specific sense, there is no longer a problem in terms of assessing the probability of unjust conviction. As has been correctly

874 R v S, [2006], EWCA Crim 756, (2006), 2 Cr App R 23, p. 341. For further analysis see: J.R. SPENCER, Evidence of bad character, Bloomsburry, New York, 2016.

875 Cooke v Purcell, [1988], 14 NSWLR 51, 87; Gill v Walton, [1991], 25 NSWLR 190; Herron v McGregor, [1986], 6 NSWLR 246, 254.

876 A. CHOO, Abuse of process and judicial stays of criminal proceedings, op. cit., pp. 92ss. In jurisprudence, see: Doyle v Leroux, [1981], RTR 438.

877 A.L. SCHNEIDER, The right to a speedy trial, in Stanford Law Review, 20, 1968, pp. 499ss.

pointed out, the question here is based not on the "technical" prejudice that the defendant would derive (impossibility of an adequate defense), but on the ethical, sociological or psychological one[878].

Basically, it is a bias operating in two directions: from the public image of prejudice, the (inevitable) negative irradiations of the strepitus fori are well known from a strictly personal point of view, the state of psychological prostration that is ingenious in the defendant, when not even the radical modification of his living conditions (change of residence, loss of work, change of affective relations) is evident. The most problematic aspect, however, of this interpretative operation lies in the identification of the specific conditions under which the interest in the repression of crimes must yield to that of the individual. The general guideline criterion that can be used is the following. If the objective of criminal justice is not exclusively to repress crimes (or to punish the guilty) but, if the person responsible for the fact is repressed, it is also to put the guilty in the condition to become aware of the error committed, in a perspective directly functional to its amendment, it can be said that the time course justifies the arrest of the procedure if the eventual condemnation would not lead to any "maieutic" or socially therapeutic result towards the prevented (in short, it would constitute a further stigma as an end in itself)[879].

PROHIBITION OF DOUBLE JUDGMENT (DOUBLE JEOPARDY)

The rule in question constitutes another paradigmatic hypothesis of application of the anti-abuse doctrine. However, before going into the analysis of the operational declinations of this rule within the matter of the abuse of process, it will be possible to make some preliminary mention of the nature and the connotations of the prohibition of double judgment. In general terms, even in the Anglo-Saxon system it can be summarized in the general prohibition of prosecuting someone twice for the same fact[880].

878 R v Telford JJ, [1991], 2 WLR 866, 876-7; R v Buzalek and Schiffer, [1991]; R v Norwich Crown Court, ex p Belsham, [1992], 95 Cr App R 9, 16-17. For further analysis see: J. HERRING, Criminal law: Text, cases and materials, Oxford University Press, Oxford, 2018.

879 R v Mill, [1986], 52 CR (3d) 1, 91-2.

880 J. JACKSON, J. JOHNSTONE, The reasonable time requirement: An independent and meaningful right?, in Criminal Law Review, 2005, pp. 23ss.

This, so to speak, would be the general brought about by the principle, which is nothing new, one could say, compared to what can be substantially found elsewhere. The rule in comment, however, presents a more multifaceted articulation in the common law; more concretely, it expresses the need to avoid that someone, already condemned or acquitted for a fact, suffers the risk of a second conviction for a story that is substantially the same from a historical point of view (subject to shortly illustrating what should meaning this last expression).

According to a moralizing view of criminal justice, the instrument is designed to stem the repressive zeal of authority in the face of crude criminal manifestations that, by hypothesis, have already gone to an acquittal (in this sense, as will be seen, the rule in. The object also operates with reference to the situation in which a criminal trial began with regard to a fact that acts as a "trailblazer" for a second proceeding concerning a more serious affair closely related to the first).

In any case, the essence of the prohibition could be summarized as follows: "(...) to put a person in double jeopardy may increase the chances of his or her being convicted even though innocent, and will also undermine the moral integrity of the criminal process. The accused may, as a result of having revealed his complete defence at the first trial, be at a greater disadvantage at the second trial and thus less able to defend him or herself effectively. Irrispective of this, it is in any event morally objectionable to subject someone to the embarassment, expense and anxiety of a second prosecution, with the possibility that a verdict might be returned which is ought to be borne in mind when considering stays of proceedings in the double jeopardy context (...)"[881].

As we argue, the intimate logic of the principle is linked to the conceptual core of fairness: there is also a need, strictly practical, to avoid a (second) judgment in which the effectiveness of the defensive strategy is significantly reduced compared to that of antecedent. In any case, it is likely to say what we have generally observed previously: the concrete danger of an unjust conviction, due to a radical "disparity" between weapons of accusation and defense. On the other hand, the rationale of the rule is not found only in a guideline of guarantee. If it is true, as mentioned above, that the upstream need is to avert the "double ordeal" of the proceedings for the same fact, there is also that (certainly no less important) to ensure the rationality and the economic efficiency of the justice system.

881 A. CHOO, Halting criminal prosecutions, in Criminal Law Review, 1995, pp. 866ss.

"(...) the underlying idea, one that is deeply ingrained in at least the Anglo-American system of jurisprudence, is that the state with all its resources and power should not be allowed to make repeated attempts to convict an individual for an alleged offense (...)"[882]. Apart from that, a further point is significant. Economics of the judicial machine regardless, the logical "founding" of the principle in question are exactly corresponding to the above illustrated principle of legitimacy. In the same way that it is necessary to protect the individual from an unjust conviction in a second judgment for the same fact, in the same way it is morally deplorable to subject the "already judged" to a second proceeding for the same affair. In other words, can he ethically justify himself a persecutory obstinacy against someone who has already been subjected to a trial for the same fact? This question, incidentally, places the double jeopardy rule in perfect conceptual linearity even with the dual operational articulation of the process abuse (unfair trial/unfair to try).

In order to complete the reasoning, recalling an approach illustrated at the beginning of this chapter, we could say, that in the first group of hypotheses, we are faced with the opportunity to place the single (potentially innocent) safe from a judgment that, because of a lack of resources (economic, for example), or because of the concrete inactivity to the predisposition of a further defensive strategy, determines a situation of unequivocally starting "unequivocal weapons" (intrinsic policy). This is a risk that, then, would be extremely aggravated in the hypothesis of a second judgment instituted against someone who has been acquitted.

Within the second, it can be said that it is in the public interest not to subject the individual to the psychological prostration of a second judgment for the same fact (extrinsic policy). To provide a concrete dimension to the reasoning carried out, an overview of the casuistry on the subject shows how, more often than not, in the midst of the second judgment, the accused suffers a limitation of personal freedom[883]. More effectively: "(...) a defendant is (...) when invoking the pleas in bar (...) reminding the state-as the community's representative, the community in whose name the business of criminal justice is done-of the limits of its power. The defendant speaks as a member of the political Union and her

882 M. L. FRIEDLAND, Double Jeopardy, Oxford, 1969, p. 4. In jurisprudence see Green v US, [1957], 355 US 184, 187-8. For analysis see: M. S. MOORE, Act and crime: The philosophy of action and its implications for criminal law, Oxford University Press, Oxford, 2010, pp. 313ss.

883 M.L. FRIEDLAND, Double jeopardy, op. cit., pp. 162ss. A. CHOO, Abuse of process and judicial stays of criminal proceedings, op. cit., pp. 23ss.

claim is something like this: "Having once submitted to the process of justice in relation to this offence, and having been duly acquitted (or convicted and punished, as the case may be), your (political, moral) jurisdiction to subject my conduct to examination in criminal proceedings is exhausted. My citizen's duty is done, and I am beyond your reach" (...) this is the special value of finality in criminal proceedings, and the principal rationale underpinning double jeopardy protection (...)"[884].

The illustrated rule receives in Anglo-Welsh practice protection expressed through the institute of autrefois acquit or autrefois convict (plea in bar): respectively, with the first, it protects from the risk of a second judgment for the same fact who is previously been fulfilled, and with the second, specularly, the one who was previously convicted.

Nonetheless (as will be seen shortly), the protection that can be linked to the institute just mentioned is not comprehensive. It is precisely because of this practical emergency that the English jurisprudence has elaborated a form of subsidiary protection: the doctrine on the abuse of the process is a perfect instrument in this regard.

This, in any case, does not mean the identity of institutions or protection: as rightly pointed out, in fact, if the first (plea in bar) becomes a real and absolute right for the accused, this does not apply to the second, i.e. the "specific" protection of the ne bis in idem can be invoked in every state and degree of the procedure. In addition, it cannot be renounced or disputed by the party concerned (an admission of responsibility by the defendant does not remove the power of the judge to proceed according to the rule in question)[885]. The problem therefore arises of delimiting the objective area of (in) applicability of the latter. In essence, which hypotheses come out of its scope of operation?

First of all, it is necessary to illuminate the elements that identify its defining aspects. Attention runs to the meaning of the same offense term.

The interpretative effort of the jurisprudence focused on clarifying the scope of this last phrase. It was not so much questioned-at least, it did not constitute the most relevant aspect of the question-the concept of fact. It is imminent

884 P. ROBERTS, Acquitted misconduct evidence and double jeopardy principles from Sambasivans to Z, in Criminal Law Review, 2000, pp. 954ss. D. BROWN, The judicial role in criminal charging and plea bargaining, in Hofstra Law Review, 46 (1), 2018, pp. 67ss. A. BRUCE, A. GREEN, S.J. LEVINE, Disciplinary regulation of prosecutors as a remedy for abuses of prosecutorial discretion: A descriptive and normative analysis, in Ohio State Journal of Criminal Law, 14, 2016, pp. 144s.

885 Connelly v DPP, [1964], AC 1254, 1305, per Lord Devlin.

principle even in the Anglo-Saxon legal system that the factual nucleus of the sub-novitiate affair must be substantially the same. The interpretative difficulties originate, in fact, from the wider semantic extension of same offense.

The terms of the problem discussed here have been summarized in a well-known leading case on the subject. Connelly refers to DPP[886]: defendant Connelly took part in an armed robbery at a dairy, together with other individuals (all part of a criminal consortium), from which he followed the death of a company employee. Initially tried for murder, he was sentenced in first instance. The sentence was later annulled by the court of appeal for significant procedural violations committed by the judge of the previous grade of proceedings (procedural misdirections). As a result of the failure in the first trial, the prosecution promoted a second trial against the defendant himself, but this time for armed robbery. In this process, both the total factual situation and the evidence support were unchanged compared to those present in the previous procedure. In essence, there was a criminal violation of different species (or nature), matured in the same historical-factual context (the episode of death occurred in the context of a robbery being logically inseparable). The defense, as one guesses, had pleaded the ne bis in idem, on the basis of articulated reasoning. If, as it seems, one cannot doubt that robbery and murder are conceptually distinct and mentally separable episodes; it is also true that for the identity of material context in which they were perpetrated and being both known to the prosecution since the beginning of the criminal proceedings for homicide. It was the obligation of the prosecutor to proceed within the first proceeding jointly for the charges of the same. Differently, by opting according to the defense, one would allow (as in the present case) the accusation of prolonging at will the state of subjection of the prejudice to criminal trial, unduly exacerbating the state of anxiety and moral and psychological prostration already suffering due to previous judgment.

Hence, the origin of the (double) hermeneutic question, submitted to the judge by the defense. First, what should be understood by same offense and, therefore, when this requirement should be considered integrated, necessary for the application of the double jeopardy doctrine? Secondly, whether the protection of the prohibition in question could in this case be applied and, in the event of a negative answer, what remedy was open to action?

In relation to the first question, the preliminarily judge clarified one point: in relation to the concept of same offense, it is not enough that the probative

886 Cooper v New Forest District Council, The Times, 19 March 1992.

material brought by the accusation, in one as in the other process, is the same, even though a useful element for recognizing the violation of the prohibition of dual judgment does not constitute a decisive element. Trial and fact to prove are distinct entities, being clear that (we can hypothesize) the same eyewitness can fully report as much in order to a robbery as to a homicide[887]. To answer the first question further, it would not have been sufficient to focus the attention on the element of the identity of the fact (strictly understood) because, otherwise, the question would have had no reason to be. Although intimately connected from a chronological point of view and material, the offenses subject to separate assessment originated in any case from separate conduct[888]. Evidently, the scope of the expression "same offense" is more extensive. In particular, the question came to be amended in the following terms: if it were possible to start a criminal trial for a fact in relation to which in a previous criminal proceeding the same defendant could have been legitimately convicted (to be understood if the accusation had opportunely raised the charge together with the one that had already founded an assessment). In other words, it can be questioned that: if in the previous criminal proceedings there was no conviction for a fact that, if properly contested, would probably have led to a statement of responsibility, is there a sort of implicit renunciation of the exercise of the action for that affair?

A quicker answer, it was underlined, could be given about the charge that, as an alternative, had been formulated by the prosecutor during the first trial. In fact, Connelly had been primarily accused of murder and, alternatively, of culpable homicide (manslaughter). The fact that the jury had pronounced (with a conviction) on the first accusatory hypothesis inevitably founded an acquittal (so to speak) tacit on the second (which certainly would have founded a plea in bar for autrefois acquitted)[889]. As mentioned before, the defense wanted to go further: the prohibition of new judgment should also be considered operating

887 [1964], AC 1254, 1305, par Lord Devlin.

888 DPP v Humphrys, [1977], AC 1, where the accused, judged and acquitted by the crime of driving without a valid license of a motor vehicle, was subjected to a second judgment for false testimony (perjury) and there condemned, although the defense had submitted a request based on the double jeopardy rule (autrefois acquitted), supporting it on the basis of the consideration that the "decisive" proof in both procedures was the same (testimony of the police officer who would have detected the infraction of the prejudice).

889 N.J. KING, R.F. WRIGHT, The invisible revolution in plea bargaining: Managerial judging and judicial participation in negotiations, in Texas Law Review, 95, 2016, pp. 325, 339ss. D. LIAKOPOULOS, Plea bargaining in international criminal law, in International and European Union Legal Matters, 2013.

in the situation in which the prosecution, perfectly aware of a further fact (robbery), which could be debited already at the time of the first trial, deliberately postponed the persecution.

In order to answer this question, a general criterion was proposed: provided that the offense, challenged in a second judgment, must be the same or substantially the same as that which was the object of a previous assessment, the judge must check whether the evidence, alleged in the context of the second proceeding, could have founded a conviction already within the first. Although not exactly technical, the reasoning evokes the pattern of assessments placed in a relationship of prejudiciality. In short, it means that we are faced with a substantial identity of factual story (and, therefore, to a violation of the rule of ne bis in idem) when the acquittal for the "first" imputation can only lead to the acquittal in sequential way for the "second"[890].

That said, the profile concerning the exceptions to the double jeopardy rule was addressed. The first is in the hypothesis of crime (so we would say, using the domestic legal lexicon) against the administration of justice: in particular, a sentence of acquittal in reference to a crime can be canceled, if it is established that it is achieved at a unlawful pressure against a member of the jury or a witness (for which fact, there has been a criminal proceeding to the same sentence and sentence against the author of the subornation), except that the reopening of the criminal proceedings for the first offense, in reason for the course of a considerable period of time, is not contrary to the interests of justice[891].

The second concerns peculiar criminal categories, characterized by a significant social alarm (intentional or negligent homicide, genocide, kidnapping, sexual violence, to cite a few examples). In this case, where new evidence against a person survives or is discovered acquitted for one or more of the crimes mentioned, the prosecutor, with the written authorization of the director of public prosecutions, if this is not contrary to the interests of criminal justice, may request the revocation of the previous acquittal and the subsequent reopening of the criminal trial against the acquitted.

What, however, arouses the most attention is the fact that the case in analysis had to definitively establish (with an approach that would not be subsequently disavowed) the applicability of the doctrine of the abuse of the trial to

890 Connelly v DPP, [1964], par Lord Hodson.

891 Criminal Procedure and Investigations Act 1996, Section 54. For further details and analysis see: C. MCALHONE, Core statutes on evidence, Macmillan, London, 2013, pp. 182ss.

the violation of the ne bis in idem (better, as you are about to say, to situations placed in a "border" zone with this prohibition).

The answer to the question passed for the enunciation of a general rule, pointing out an opportune fact in the introduction: the top rule of the prohibition of double judgment, as explained above and declined in court, was not applicable to the present case. Heterogeneous situations include exceptions to the separate principle (evidently not conferring with the story in question), where a previous ruling of merit (conviction or acquittal) for a fact, object of new persecution, is not equivalent to the cancellation of procedural defects of a sentence (of condemnation, in this case) for one fact, connected with another for which a second judgment was promoted. The doctrine of the abuse of the trial, therefore, was invoked by the defense against the refusal opposed by the judge at the time of application of the ne bis in idem, as a remedy of extrema ratio to compensate for the protection voids left by the latter.

In any case, it was established that, in principle, the prosecution has the obligation to promote a single criminal trial for all the crimes of which he is aware and has the intent to pursue (for obvious reasons such as procedural economy and the undue protraction of the punitive "ordeal" against the same person). Nevertheless, if such modus procedendi were contrary to the collective interest of the repression of crimes, it would be exceptionally allowed to the magistrate to opt for the separation of the proceedings. In the present case, the conclusion was a negative sign: the ne bis in idem had not been violated, nor could it speak of an abuse of the trial, given that the second trial did not recompense the risk of unjust condemnation against the defendant, nor it constituted an attack on the morality of the system (in that case it was involved in criminal trials involving very serious delinquent forms).

Regardless of the final response, we have a point: the theoretical abuse of the process constitutes a useful tool in limit situations with the prohibition of second judgment, more properly configured as a sort of "completion" or extension of the range of protection projected by the second.

It seems, therefore, to be able to see a further principle "in filigree": the arrest of the procedure (remedy specifically requested by the defense in the case in question) would be abstractly feasible solution, although in progress (reaffirmed by the judge on that occasion) quite exceptional. Secondly, it seems to be able to evoke-perhaps for the first time in a ruling, a configuration of the abuse of the process as an institution beyond the specific legal-factual context (double jeopardy rule), generally valid in terms of subsidiary doctrine, in other words (if we want), it is usable as a true instrument of judicial orthopedics able to fill the gaps left by an express rule.

ENTRAPMENT

Given the premise for any discussion on the subject of entrapment in the Anglo-Welsh legal tradition, it is not the subject of specific discipline and protection[892]. The institute, therefore, or rather, the protection from such distorting practice is exclusively the result of recent jurisprudential elaborations.

The term, in itself, is charged with a negative connotation: it evokes the idea of entrapment, of the trap, providing immediately the image (clearly more exemplary than many other "clinical" manifestations) of the abuse of authority towards the individual.

If you want to give a general definition (albeit subject to subsequent clarification), you can recall that provided in a known court case: "(...) entrapment occurs when an agent of the state-usually a law enforcement officer or a controlled informer-causes someone to commit an offense in order that should be prosecuted (...)"[893].

Otherwise, it is: "the use of deceptive techniques to test if a person is willing to commit an offense"[894]. The pragmatic origin of the institute mentioned above, however, immediately highlights a further characterizing aspect (which, therefore, places it in perfect continuity with the overall theoretical abuse of the process): this is the approach eminently practical to the topic. This implies that the judicial investigation, aimed at reconstructing an eventual or abusive conduct, will be determined by the individual circumstances of the specific case. For this reason, it could be justified to say that, on the one hand, we are dealing with a figure (if we want it) malleable, where the discretion of the judge has (more than ample) ample room for maneuver, on the other, we have significant difficulty in reconstructing the general outlines of a rule that physiologically

892 R v Looseley, [2001], 1 WLR 2060, HL, par Lord Hoffman. A. CHOO, Evidence, op. cit.

893 A. ASHWORTH, Re-drawing the boundaries of entrapment, in Criminal Law Review, 2002, pp. 161ss. A.P. SIMESTER, J.R. SPENCER, G.R. SULLIVAN, Simester and Sullivan's criminal law: Theory and doctrine, Hart Publishing, Oxford & Oregon, Portland, 2014.

894 A.P. SIMESTER, J.R. SPENCER, G.R. SULLIVAN, Simester and Sullivan's criminal law: Theory and doctrine, op. cit.

escapes conceptual generalizations; or to put it more effectively: "each case turns on its own facts"[895].

On the other hand, it is an issue-as has been rightly stressed[896], which has received increasing attention in recent years, because of the "all-out" war not only in the area of drug trafficking, but also in that of terrorism which has as we know, involved the whole Western world. In essence, the number of court cases where the problem of the entrapment has been specifically dealt with has increased significantly over the last fifteen years, bringing to the center of attention (both the doctrine and the jurisprudence) the profile concerning the delimitation of boundaries of operation of the theoretical matured on the point.

Let's start with some upstream observations. It was said that entrapment is not supported by any legal provision expressed or, in any case, by any discipline (not even of jurisprudential origin) that establishes elements and protection. This would be enough (to want to offer some terms of comparison with another common law system), to differentiate the treatment regime concerning the matter that is in the Anglo-Saxon system with respect to the United States (where, on the contrary, the criminal law specifically provides for the institution)[897].

In any case, the evolution of the jurisprudential analyzes on the subject, found in the field of the Anglo-Welsh practice, shows a clear progression with regard to the desire to recognize protection for the accused from the serious conduct of authority. The oppositional limitations that were found in responding to the (broadly speaking) demands of justice of defense were of a twofold order. From the point of view of the fight against crime, the explicit and radical stigmatization of this practice (by hypothesis: to be sanctioned with the paralysis of the criminal proceeding concerning a fact followed by an incitement by the police during investigations) would have resulted in a substantial decrease in the effectiveness of the fight against very serious delinquent forms (see, for example, drug dealing, where- as known, extensive use is made of covert transactions). From the side of judicial practice, then, one understands the difficulty in conceiving a form of protection which, if brought to the radical consequence (abuse of the process, ergo arrest of the procedure), would have actually involved

895 D. CORKER-M. SUMMERS QB, D. YOUNG, Abuse of process in criminal proceedings, op. cit., p. 204.

896 D. CORKER-M. SUMMERS QB, D. YOUNG, Abuse of process in criminal proceedings, op. cit., p. 204.

897 T. ELLIS, S. SAVAGE (eds), Debates in criminal justice: Key themes and issues, ed. Routledge, London & New York, 2012.

the (so to say) lapsed of practically all the judgments where the charge raised by the accusation materialized in an action or omission "caused" by an undercover agent (for the obvious reason that the determining, if not exclusive, proof of the offense was constituted by the following statements of the witness-agent)[898].

To make the abovementioned problems appear to be hand held, the call of a well-known court case is sufficient.

In R v Sang[899], finding in the introduction the vacuum of specific protection in terms of entrapment, as well as of more than three decades of consequent inability to react jurisprudential to the problem (which, of course, was anything but infrequent), were different options taken considerations. Far removed even from the hypothesis of the extreme remedy of the arrest of the procedure, the use of the evidence obtained through the undercover operation of the police officer or, alternatively, the mitigation of the rigor of the penalty eventually imposed. The first solution was discarded not only (as mentioned above)[900] because the exclusion from the probationary material of the exclusive (or even conclusive) proof of the prosecutor would inevitably have led to the collapse of the accusatory castle, but also because this would have building-for the first time-a substantial defense from the factual entrapment, as we said, lacking in the Anglo-Saxon system (both in positive law and in previous jurisprudential elaborations). It was a reasoning, to think well, somewhat labile, if only because it would not leave alternatives: the viable solution that remained was the mitigation of the sentence applied with the sentence, which, clearly, exposes the argumentative construct to strong perplexities. It would soon be countered, in fact,

898 See in particular: Sherman v US, [1958], 356 US 369; Matthew v US, [1988], 108 S Ct 883; Jacobson v US, [1992], 112 S Ct 1535. In argument see the considerations of: R.J. ALLEN, M. LUTTRELL, A. KREEGER, Clarifying entrapment, in International Commentary of Evidence, 1998. A. CARLON, Entrapment, punishment and the sadistic State, in Virginia Law Review, 93, 2007, pp. 1081ss. K.A. SMITH, Psychology fact-finding and entrapment, in Michigan Law Review, 103, 2005, pp. 760ss. P. MARCUS, The entrapment defense, LexisNexis, New York, 2018. H. LAI HO, State entrapment, in Legal Studies, 31 (1), 2011, pp. 74ss.

899 For the investigation methodology see: M. MAGUIRE, T. JOHN, Covert and deceptive policing in England and Wales: Issues in regulation and practice, in European Journal of Crime, Criminal Law and Criminal Justice, 1996, pp. 316ss. A. CHOO, M. MELLORS, Undercover police operations and what the suspect said (or didn't say), in Web Journal of Current Legal Issues Yearbook 1995, 1996. P. GILL, Rounding up the usual suspects? Developments in contemporary law enforcement intelligence, Ashgate Publishing, London, 2000. A. CHOO, Evidence, op. cit., H. QUIRK, The rise and fall of the right of silence. Principle, politics and policy, Taylor & Francis, New York, 2016. A. ASWORTH, M. REDMAYNE, The criminal process, Oxford University Press, Oxford, 2010, pp. 86ss.

900 [1980], AC 402. and in the same spirit see also: R v Tonnessen, [1998], 2 Cr App R, 328; R v Springer, [1999], 1 Cr App R, 217; R v Shannon, [2001], 1 WLR 51, 73. For further details see: J. HERRING, Criminal law: Text, cases and materials, op. cit.

that the mitigation of the quantum poenae does not constitute a remedy, capable to cancel or to put in nothing the conduct of the police officer. It is evident, in fact, that without the interference of the latter in the criminal dynamics, the fact object of subsequent charge would not have been committed by the accused (at least, it is highly probable that the prejudice would not have committed it, lacking a free and wise volitional self-determination). This makes the process, in a certain sense, "sought" or "constructed" by the authority, with the undoubted consequence that-at least in the case in which the proof obtained by the entrapment is exclusive or determining for the condemnation-defense and accusation do not play from the beginning on equal terms.

In any case, if the Anglo-Saxon judicial practice witnessed a stasis, a real propulsive propulsive to the juridical recognition of a specific protection from the distortive practice in question came with a ruling by the European Court of Human Rights (ECtHR)[901].

In short, two agents "in plain clothes" make contact with a narco-trafficker, that VS, who would have acted as intermediary in the story in question, for the purchase of a given amount of heroin; the latter accepts the proposal, making contact with another subject (FO), which takes care to directly conduct the first, together with the two police officers (in the guise of buyers), from the future applicant to the European Court: Texeira de Castro. He, in turn, accepts the purchase proposal from the agents (twenty grams of heroin), accompanying them from that would be the material supplier of the narcotic (this JPO) who, having procured the substance, provides for payment to give it to Texeira, therefore, he definitively gave it to the two police officers; hence his arrest "(...) the use of undercover agents must be restricted and safeguards put in place even in cases concerning the fight against drug-trafficking (...) the right to a fair administration of justice holds such a prominent place that it cannot be sacrificed for the sake of expedience (...) the public interest (see: persecution of offences) cannot justify the use of evidence obtained as a result of police incitement (...)"[902].

---

901 ECtHR, Texeira de Castro v Portugal of 9 June 1998. For further details see: B. RAINEY, W. WICKS, C. OVEY, Jacbos, White and Ovey: The European Convention on Human Rights, op. cit., J.P. COSTA, La Cour europèenne des droits de l'homme. Des juges pour la libertè, op. cit., F. TIMMERMANS, Fundamental rights protection in Europe before and after accession of the European Union to the European Convention on Human Rights, in Liber amicorum Pieter Van Dijk, M. Van Roosmalen and others (eds.), op. cit., pp. 225ss. D. HARRIS, M. O'BOYLE, C. WARBRICK, Law of the European Convention on Human rights, op. cit., pp. 372ss.

902 ECtHR, Texeira de Castro v Portugal of 9 June 1998.

On closer inspection, this is a decisive premise: the established essentiality and, at the same time, the indispensability of the principle of procedural fairness would immediately highlight a line of continuity between the European Convention on Human Rights and the Anglo-Welsh order where, as we have seen, fairness constitutes a rigid, insurmountable balancing or temperament value due to opposing interests. At the end of the reckoning (but the theme will be dealt with in greater detail in the following chapter), it would not seem wrong to say that we are faced with different nomenclatures but, at the same time, with the same conceptual substance. Putting moral integrity aside of the system, if fairness (in the conceptual declination offered in the Anglo-Welsh system) becomes concrete in the need to ensure a process played on equal terms (or, otherwise, where there is no risk of an unjust condemnation due to obvious imbalance in terms of initial probabilities of conviction), it is equally true that art. 6 ECHR by enclosing an indispensable core of guarantees that must be recognized to the accused, to be applied as a minimum standard in national justice systems, would prefigure the basic conditions of a criminal proceeding where the defendant has the real possibility of carrying out an adequate defense. In short, regardless of the declination of the parameters of equity in the specific (which, in the case of the European Convention, are given by a summary of the legal traditions of member states), the conceptual symmetry is palpable.

Given this, the focus shifts to the conduct of police officers. The starting point for establishing the legitimacy of the undercover operation is identified in the "upstream" control by a magistrate (prosecutor or adjudicator) as a key figure not only in terms of impartiality, but also to ensure that the investigations are directed towards someone burdened by clues.

However, the requirement in question lacked in the present case: neither the supervision of a magistrate nor an indicative compendium against the applicant was apparent in the present case before the intervention of the officials in the anti-drug operation (the applicant was subject uncensored, unknown to the officers themselves, who came into contact with the same only through the work of intermediation carried out by third party traffickers). The interference by police officers, therefore, would have already been for this reason illegitimate.

But it is not this or, better, this is not only the aspect that was relevant in this case, in order to be able to state that the conduct kept by police officers constituted undue determination to the crime, such as to encroach on a prohibited practice as disrupting the overall fairness of the criminal trial (article 6 ECHR).

In the specific sense of the entrapment, the reasoning of the court is affixed to the causal element. In other words, the judges of Strasbourg had to assess whether Texseira was concretely recognizable as an autonomous volition in relation to the crime or if, rather, it were the result of an induction of the applicant to the commission of the same, surreptitiously realized by the agents-instigators, whose intromission, therefore, would have constituted in this case, with respect to the cession of narcotic, condicio sine qua non. The answer is precisely in this last sense: no element in the proceedings led to the opposite reconstructive hypothesis, playing in opposite directions or contrary elements, such as the finding of drugs by a third person (not directly by the applicant), a circumstance that no substances were found in possession of the biased besides those explicitly requested by the agents. In short, the work of the undercover officers was not limited, as it would have been necessary, to the conduct of investigations, but exorbitated from these boundaries, to arrive at a real incitement[903].

The ruling, in addition to the content value of the reconstructed prohibition on the subject of entrapment, signaled the fundamental need to contain the operations under cover within certain limits.

The "response" of the Anglo-Saxon order did not wait: the approval of the regulation of Investigatory Powers Act (2000)[904] introduced a composite body of forecasts aimed at circumscribing the conditions of legitimacy of undercover police interventions[905].

---

903 ECtHR, Vanyan v Russia od 15 December 2005; Khudobin v Russia of 26 October 2006; Ramanuskas v Latvia of 5 February 2008. For further details see: O. JOHAN SETTEM, Applications of the fair hearing norm in ECHR art. 6 (1) to civil proceedings, ed. Springer, Berlin, 2016, pp. 486ss. A. SEIBERT-FOHR, M.E. VILLIGER, Judgments of the European Convention of Human Rights. Effects and implementation, ed. Nomos, Baden-Baden, 2017. C. GRABENWARTER. European Convention on human rights: ECHR, C.H. Beck, München, 2014. K.S. ZIEGLER, E. WIKS, L. HODSON, The UK and European human rights. A strained relationship, Hart Publishing, Oxford & Oregon, Portland, 2015. K. PITCHER, Judicial responses to pre-trial procedural violations in international criminal proceedings, op. cit., pp. 46ss.

904 A. SANDERS, R. YOUNG, M. BURTON, Criminal justice, op. cit.

905 S. MCKAY, The definition of the covert human intelligence source, in Archbold News, 2004, pp. 5. Briefly, an undercover operation may be authorized if it is deemed to be well founded that: a) the adoption of such investigative means is proportionate to the outcome of the expected investigation; b) it is necessary for the interests of national security, or c) it is necessary for the prevention or repression of the crime or to prevent unrest; d) it is necessary for the protection of national economy's interests, or e) for the protection of public health or for the repression of tax evasion or, lastly, f) when recourse to such means is requested by order of the Secretary of State.

But not only. The influence of the supra-national "precedent" was manifested in the fundamental change in the jurisprudential direction matured up to that moment within the English classrooms (see R v Sang approach).

If we want to retrace, albeit briefly, the interpretative itinerary that would have led to the today's scenario on the subject, we should mention the first "step" constituted by the opportunity to create a real exclusionary rule regarding entrapment. We started to put in to highlight the necessity, in order to guarantee fair trial, to exclude evidence obtained in the context of undercover operations (although it was possible, it must be said, also due to the launching of the Police and Criminal Evidences Act of 1984, the average tempore, where it was expressly acknowledged-Section 78-the power of the judge to oust the evidence obtained illegally from the trial court)[906]. Clearly, it was an intermediate solution to the arrest of the procedure and that only potentially would have been able to lead to the total fall of the accusatory claim (where, by hypothesis, the evidence of the excluded accusatory sign had been the only one or the determining one, in fact it would have reached the acquittal).

But the real turning point came with R v Latif and R v Shahzad[907]. The pronunciation represents, in fact, the decisive step for the application of the doctrine of the abuse of the process to the entrapment, also coinciding chronologically with a period in which the doctrine in question lived a consistent expansion. For the first time, the power to block the continuation of the procedural procedure was sanctioned, if the work carried out during the police investigation had compromised the overall fairness of the trial or, alternatively, created the premises of a judgment contrary to the morality of the justice.

The details of the factual story at the basis of the dictum can be omitted; we will go straight to the problematic "nucleus" from which the final affirmation moves: we allude to the already-in some way previously emerged-balancing of two opposing instances.

If, in fact, the prospect of a (so to speak) automatism such that the criminal trial, founded exclusively (or in a determining way) from the evidence provided by the agent-instigator, should be arrested, would intolerably compromise the protection of the community from alarming forms of crime (in this case: drug trafficking). On the other hand, the exclusion at the root of this possibility would

906 R v Smurthwaite, [1994], 1 All ER 898.

907 A. ASHWORTH, Should the police be allowed to use deceptive practices?, in Law Quarterly Review, 114, 1998, pp. 120ss.

have supported the view of the public conscience that justice tolerated bad practices and police abuse. For this reason, neither one nor the other would have been concretely practicable. The solution was found in mediam rem: we already know it, that of judicial discretion. The process is unfair, so it goes to the end. Or, as had been hypothesized by the defense in the present case (but with a negative final response from the judge), the trial constitutes an attack on the ethical "status" of the judicial machinery. In the latter case: "(...) it is for the judge in the exercise of his discretion to decide whether there has been an abuse of process, which amounts to an affront to the public conscience and requires the criminal proceedings to be stayed (...) in a case such as the present, the judge must weigh in the balance the public interest in ensuring that those that are charged with grave crimes should be tried and the competing public interest in not conveying the impression that the court will adopt the approach that the end justified any means (...)"[908].

The theoretical subject receives final consecration with R v Looseley; A-G's Reference (no 3 of 2000)[909] which, further, would represent the fulfillment of that interpretative evolution, registered in the Anglo-Saxon courtrooms, aimed at the implementation of the principles established by the European Court in the subject matter (Texeira de Castro v Portugal)[910]. In particular, the key factors analyzed were identified for the applicability of the doctrine on abuse to entrapment: a) the nature of the crime and the complexity of the investigation; b) the reasons for the undercover operation; c) the nature and the concrete causal contribution made by the police in carrying out the crime; and d) the criminal record of the accused. Substantially unaltered, starting from this pronunciation, the hermeneutical scenario related to the theme remained.

908 A. ASHWORTH, Should the police be allowed to use deceptive practices? op. cit. A. SANDERS, R. YOUNG, M. BURTON, Criminal justice, op. cit. S. PICERING, J. MCCULLOCH, Borders and crime. Pre-crime, mobility and serious harm in an age of globalization, ed. Springer, Berlin, 2012.

909 [2001], UKHL 53, 1 WLR 2060.

910 A. ASHWORTH, Entrapment and criminal justice (R v Looseley and Attorney General's Reference (No 3 of 2000)), in Oxford University Commonwealth Law Journal, 18, 2002, pp. 125ss. B. LEWIN, Test purchasing-The impact and the regulation of investigatory powers act 2000, in Justice of the Peace, 2001, pp. 956ss. S. MCKAY, Entrapment: Competing views on the effect of the Human Rights Act on english criminal law, in European Human Rights Law Review, 9 (4), 2002, pp. 764ss. S. O'DOHERTY, Entrapment: From mitigation to abuse, in Justice of the Peace, 2002, pp. 984ss. R.R. JERRARD, Entrapment: Abuse of legal process for police to incite crime, in Police Journal, 2002, pp. 245ss. A. CHOO, evidence, op. cit., M. AMOS, Human rights law, Hart Publishing, Oxford & Oregon, Portland, 2014, pp. 365ss. C. HARFIELD, K. HARFIELD, Covert investigation, Oxford University Press, Oxford, 2012, pp. 145ss. D. OMEROD, J. CYRIL SMITH, B. HOGAN, Smith and Hogan's criminal law, Oxford University Press, Oxford, 2011, pp. 400ss.

(FOLLOWS) DISPERSION OF EVIDENCE (LOST OR DESTROYED EVIDENCE) IS ANOTHER "HOT" TERRAIN OF THE DISPERSION OF EVIDENCE

Its strict bond with the theory of abuse of process is of immediate intuition. Regardless of who the part to which the loss is chargeable, a test to discharge is able to determine the fate of a process or, if we want to comply with the methodology adopted in this matter by the English courts, to significantly compromise fairness. As correctly observed, the issue is a perfect summary of the principle of equality of arms between prosecution and defense[911]. More specifically, it translates into the opportunity to balance the (be allowed) omnipotence of the police in the investigative phase with (although ex post) protection of defensive strategies during actual judgment. It is argued that the stakes are high. Here, too, is a problem intimately connected with the principle of legitimacy that, if on the one hand imposes the repression of crimes and the persecution of the guilty, on the other stigmatizes to the highest degree the "evil" (ethical and juridical) given by the risk of condemnation of an innocent person. Clearly, the claim is not that of a radical elimination of risk (only theoretical), but that of minimization. In essence, the natural tension towards it (so to call it) "optimal" Pareto is implemented through a dual instrument: law and judicial discretion, which, as already mentioned, finds the maximum expression in the theory of the abuse of the process; the law devises mechanisms informed by this principle, to which in hypothesis of inadequacy in the individual case the jurisprudence would be added, which would intervene in order to bring within the confines of the equity a situation resulting from an abuse of authority.

In any case, the fundamental "precedent" on the subject, which established the essential parameters of the discipline, is R (Ebrahim) v Feltham Magistrates' Court[912].

Logically, it was said at the beginning, the dispersion of a trial to discharge is able to question the overall fairness of the proceedings, leading directly to the danger of an unjust sentence. The arrest of the proceeding on account of iniquity, even in this case, will be a strictly exceptional remedy, given the natural

911 D. CORKER-M. SUMMERS QB-D. YOUNG, Abuse of process in criminal proceedings, op. cit., p. 73.

912 M. DODDS, Arguing abuse of process in relation to loss or destruction of CCTV evidence, in Justice of the Peace, 2001, pp. 316ss. S. MARTIN, Lost and destroyed evidence: The search for a principled approach to abuse of process, in International Journal of Evidence and Proof, 9, 2005, pp. 158ss. V. SMITH, Lost, altered or destroyed evidence, in Justice of the Peace, 2007, pp. 556ss.

"self-sterilization" capacity of the criminal trial (emblematic, in this sense, is the prediction of the Police and Criminal Evidence Act 1984, Section 78, which regulates the judicial power of admitting evidence in court, as well as their eventual ouster, conceived as a mechanism of equitative orthopedics). Basically, if it is true that in some cases it is necessary to adopt the penalty of maximum rigor, it will be up to the judge to assess in advance whether the procedural fairness can be sufficiently preserved through the median solution, constituted by the exclusion of a proof of indictment of a sign directly contrary to the one that was lost.

Less direct, perhaps, is the logical link with the second pole of operation abuse (unfair to try). The qualifying element in this direction is given by the prosecutor's bad faith: it requires the accusation of sticking to the general duty of loyalty. We are outside, as we know, procedural rules in the strict sense. Furthermore, the high probability of an unjust conviction is not even questioned: it is the improper conduct of the magistrate who, because of its seriousness, is intolerable, thus not only diminishing the interest in the persecution, but also making it compliant with the public interest in the cessation of criminal persecution. In this case, therefore, unlike the first hypothesis (unfair trial), where there is the objective lack of evidence that jeopardizes (we would say) "beyond reasonable doubt", there is an assessment based on a coefficient of subjective nature: bad faith or the serious fault of the prosecutor or the police in the loss of the evidentiary contribution.

This is the paradigm of the application of the anti-abuse doctrine to the matter in comment. Generally, the case law solutions have been for the rejection of the defense's request to stop the trial due to unfairness of the process. The reasoning, in short, would have based on the fact that the loss of a probative contribution did not undermine the overall fairness of the procedure, which, therefore, had to be considered safeguarded by the presence of further probative data for which the jury would have taken into account[913].

913 R v Beckford, [1996], 1 Cr App R 94, 103; R v Taylor, [2001], EWCA Crim 1106; R v Elliott, [2002], EWCA Crim 1199. For further details see: H. WELCH, Criminal procedure and sentencing, ed. Routledge, London & New York, 2014. R. HUXLEY-BINN, Criminal law concentrate, Oxford University Press, Oxford, 2014.

THE "MEDIA" PROCESS: ADVERSE PUBLICITY

Adverse publicity is a problematic dating: the strepitus fori, especially in the face of incidents of alarming cruelty, can constitute a potential double prejudice for the accused. On the one hand, as can be guessed, we risk submitting the same to the media "pillory", almost as though we are hyperbole apart-the actual criminal trial is flanked by a further procedure (that of the mass media, precisely). We are here, it is inferred, to an "irradiation" of the effects (nefarious for the accused) of the criminal proceedings in public opinion. On the other hand, one can also come across the phenomenon of the opposite direction: the public opinion that, due to the widespread dissemination of the news related to the trial, comes to "pollute" the impartiality of the judge. And it is this last aspect to be noted for the purposes of this part of the discussion.

The relationship between the criminal trial and the media world is too complex and delicate to be analyzed here in great detail. Here, an observation is sufficient: that-as common sense induces us to believe-in certain situations, the influence in the courtrooms exercised by the debate promoted by the mass media is such as to seriously question the state of mental neutrality that he should keep the criminal judge. In other words, under certain conditions, the "polluting" influence of the media debate can go so far as to endanger the fairness of the procedure itself. Inaccurated guilt, a risk of unfair conviction: in substance, a process would take place where the image of a defendant replaces ab initio that of the guilty party. The premises and the rationale of the anti-abuse doctrine do not allow it: hence its application to abstractly evoked scenarios.

Also in this case, it is impossible to say in an a priori manner what exactly are the conditions that justify the recourse to the extreme remedy of the arrest of the proceeding. To this end, it is not enough to put in mind the (already well known) "casuistic" approach that characterizes the subject of the abuse of the process. In reality, the problem concerning the identification of cases in which the media influence has reached intolerable levels, so as to jeopardize the process fairness, is intertwined with a further profile. This type of assessment would be concretized, for all purposes, in a psychological investigation by the judge against the members of the jury. In other words, stating that the criminal trial is hopelessly "distorted", for having come to create the premises of a real (using a terminology more congenial to us) iudex suspectus, it means to make a negative opinion on the third party and impartiality of the judges (an aspect which, it is repeated, inevitably involves the psychic coefficient). What may be the factors object of weighting for this purpose, then, it is difficult to establish, since they will be intertwined so much indices of an objective nature (think of the capillarity and the diffusion of the news related to the case, or the territorial location of the each other and the place where the media debate has predominantly centered), as much as of a subjective nature (constituted, in a broad sense, by the complex of information pertaining to the person of the jurors).

The "precedents" known in this context make these known difficulties[914]. Clearly, the (repeated) exceptionality of the remedy typical of the anti-abuse doctrine also imposes in this case the unavoidability of recourse to the same, with the known prior negative judgment on the inadequacy of possible intermediate solutions (such as, for example, the appropriate caveats or indications that the judge can provide to the jury). Intermediate remedies that, however, to reflect well, would not be able to have the desired effect (avoid the arrest of the procedure), configuring the opposite - one would say - a vicious circle. If the judge invites the jury (hypothesize) not to take into account any public opinion, manifested in relation to the fact-offense being judged, the other effect does not (does not seem wrong to believe) confirm or even sharpen the conditioning explained by the first on impartiality of the jurors. A problem that, although latent, already exists, would thus be virulently brought to the surface.

There was a danger of unjust condemnation. In this case, therefore, the application of the theory of abuse would be limited to the operational pole of the risk of unfair trial. This is what emerges from the analysis of the cases found on this specific area. However, it cannot be ruled out that even the second of the operational articulations of the abuse of the process can be applied here, as it does not seem logical to assume that the media hype, provoked by a criminal affair, from which a profound state of frustration and anxiety for the accused, may constitute an attack on the moral integrity of justice, to the extent that the media "ordeal" is translated into subjecting the person concerned to a real extra-judicial penalty.

914 R v Mc Cann, [1991], 92 Cr App R 239, 253; R v Taylor, [1994], 98 Cr App R 361, 368; R v Abu Hamza, [2006], EWCA Crim 2918, [2007], QB 659. See also: J. GRIFFITHS, P. MCKEOWN, Evidence, Oxford University Press, Oxford, 2012. N. MONAGHAN, Criminal law, Oxford University Press, Oxford, 2018, pp. 91ss. T. STOREY, A. LIDBURY, Criminal law, ed. Routledge, London & New York, 2012.

This is probably the least frequent symptomatic case (in quantitative terms), but certainly the most paradigmatic with regard to the "ethical" foundation underlying the doctrine under examination.

Someone, subjected to criminal proceedings (we assume to be in the investigation phase), makes an agreement with the authority (with the prosecutor or with the police): the latter promises not to promote the prosecution; the "counter-claims" could be different (generally, it is that of the commitment to collaborate with justice). But, if the authority does not comply with the pacts, promoting a criminal trial against the beneficiary of the promise? There is no need to dwell on the prejudice that the beneficiary of the promise of non-persecution would derive.

The violation of the commitment not to prosecute constitutes a distortion-it would seem to be physiologically inherent in the structure of the Anglo-Welsh criminal system. As already mentioned, the prosecution is in principle subject to the discretionary evaluation of the Crown Prosecution Service, without the need to dwell on the reasons that support this systemic option (which would certainly exceed the scope of this analysis), suffice it to note that no other misconduct of authority perhaps, like the present, materializes an abuse (in the literal sense of the term) of the criminal trial, being crystal clear evidence that the breach of the agreement by unilateral choice made by the authority. This simultaneously affects the fundamental interests underlying the two operational articulations of the anti-abuse doctrine. It is of immediate intuition that the one who receives a commitment (assumed) of the prosecutor, independently of the promised "counterpart", renounces to cultivate any defensive strategy for a future trial. The establishment of a trial, therefore, against it, would see these in a physiologically worse position than that of the accusation, inevitably voted towards the risk of an iniquitous sentence, or the authority could renounce the origin of itineris to cultivate the punitive pretension, thus neglecting the collection in investigation of all possible evidence: the subsequent sentence would therefore undoubtedly be undermined by doubt (wrongful conviction). "(...) It is not likely to constitute an abuse of process to proceed with a prosecution unless: a) there has been an unequivocal representation by those with the conduct of the investigation or prosecution of a case that the defendant will not be prosecuted and b) (...) the defendant has acted on the representation to his detriment. Even then, if facts come to light which were not known when the representation was made, these may justify proceeding with the prosecution despite the representation (...)"[915].

THEORETICAL PARADIGM

But, is bad faith necessary? Furthermore, it has been said that the prosecution is attributed to prosecutor, as can a promise of non-persecution coming from the police, where breached (with consequent prosecution of the trial by the prosecution) constitute an abuse of the trial (being, it would be said, of ultra vires act)?

With reference to the first question, we answer immediately negatively. The objective datum is more specific: that, on the basis of the promise received, the prejudice has adopted determinations such as to abandon any self-defense perspective in relation to a setting up of a trial (whence the prejudice)[916], it being understood that the any relief of bad faith at the head of the authority can only exacerbate the judgment of disapproval by the judge, with particular regard to the profile of the injured moral integrity of justice (evidently, a process started with such premises deviates from its institutional goals, also entailing the loss of that fundamental collective interest in the persecution of the guilty).

On the basis of the indices offered by the case studies, it seems therefore that the central element for the detection of a procedural abuse is that of the prejudice suffered by the interested party (detriment). What exactly does it mean?

The applicative declinations have shown different manifestations: the authority refuses to pursue in exchange for the collaboration of the prevented as potential witness (prosecution witness)[917], or the indication to the same of possible competitors in the crime. In any case, there would be an (implicit or not) renunciation of the interested party to any further self-defense active in the criminal trial. This can be translated into the terms of a causal prognosis: the commitment of the authority must have led to the conviction, not guilty, of the definitive closure of the criminal affair; moreover, it will have to occur if the lack of a promise in this sense would have led to totally different determinations of the prejudice (e.g., no collaboration with the authority would have been established by the same).

915 R v Abu Hamza, [2006], EWCA Crim 524.

916 R v Croydon JJ, ex p Dean, [1993], QB 769; A-G of Trinidad and Tobago v Phillip, [1995], 1 AC 396.

917 R v Croydon JJ, ex p Dean, [1993], QB 769.

Between rational opening of system and future scenarios.

The stage of the question to which we can probably assume that we have reached the end of the work revolves around the following question: is it plausible that a criminal system, such as the Italian one, adopts an organic discipline on the subject of the prohibition of abuse?

We will leave the lemma "discipline" intentionally unspecified (without, therefore, re-entering the opportunity to conceive its implementation by legislative or interpretive means).

The need to acquire greater awareness of the dogmatic category under analysis and the actual terms of the problem in which it manifests itself would be, rationally, incontrovertible data. Of this, on closer inspection, one would have demonstrated in a singular circumstance. Tendentially (it is almost constant to say, if one does not run the risk of unbalancing), every attempt to discuss the issue ends up in a look at the unreasonable duration of the criminal trials in Italy, on the urgency of a reform of the statute of limitations and on the need to stigmatize the indecorousness offered by the defense in the court proceedings.

The aforementioned problems are not ineffective with the abuse of the process; nevertheless, they represent one (if it is allowed) tiny exemplifying portion that, if not appropriately "embedded" in the larger mosaic of which it is part, would not only be excessively limited (in terms of correct understanding of the phenomenon), but also misleading and source of strabismus (hermeneutics and perspective). The option to solve the problem by means of a "delegation" to the disciplinary jurisdiction is equivalent, all in all, to a resignation in the face of the inability of the system, as designed, to offer a real and effective response to the phenomenon in question. The limits of a procedural legality[918] have been highlighted, albeit in a synthetic way, which, if we continue to understand it in the traditional declination of a rigid principle, would not allow the way out of the impasse. Probably, this is the real underlying error: pretending to face the issue of abuse with the "lens" of strict legality would be solved in practice in the use of an unsuitable instrument. So, if the same should be invoked (a function that certainly cannot be challenged at the same) as a barrier to arbitrary or authoritarian

918 M. MCCONVILLE, L. MARSH, Adversarialism goes west: Case management in criminal courts, in International Journal of Evidence and Proof, 19 (1), 2015, pp. 172ss. J. MCEWAN, From adversarialism to managerialism: Criminal justice in transition, in Legal Studies, 31 (4), 2011, pp. 519ss. A EDWARDS, The other Leveson report-The review of efficiency in criminal proceedings, in Criminal Law Review, 2015, pp. 400ss. L. MARSH, Leveson's narrow pursuit of justice: Efficiency and outcomes in the criminal process, in Common Law World Review, 46, 2015, pp. 51ss.

drifts, a downturn in the name of those guarantees that would want to preside would certainly not result in an eversion.

If we do not go too far, the arrogance of those conservative settings of a "strong" legality, in an irreducibly legis centric vision, would perhaps show more a fundamental illusion than a genuine will to safeguard the pillars of the system. It is true that the idea of a practice that produces acts that conform perfectly to the ideal abstract-archetypal model of legality-is powerful in its political implications.

It generates the reassuring image of automatic legal operations, where everything is predetermined by a device (the law) that-so looked at-would seem omnipotent. It is useful to repeat: the practice (or, if you want, the daily experience) surpasses the theory. The product of a "reached" legality shows how it is the precipitate of something that never corresponds (entirely) to the legal type. Of course, this does not mean to come to disavow the role of an axiom, such as the one in comment, so as to supplant its natural instrument of expression (legislative activity) with another (the interpretative one).

What would, at most, be to adjust its rigidity to an ever-changing legal, social and cultural context, even admitting-where necessary-an issue.

In short, if what has been said is true, that is to say the difficulties that loyalty to the paradigm are known, linked to the physiological lack of information on all the constitutive elements (of the case), and that the postulate of necessity must not be contested either of a tendential conformity of the practical result to the basic norm, the practice, on the other hand, often shows the contrary need for a temperament of the starting dogma, in order to offer to the system those self-protection instruments that could not be placed in the written law.

It is reiterated: the abuse of the process, conceived in the proposed key of reflection, should not be a weapon capable of disintegrating the law and the principle of respect for forms; on the contrary, it would be (if we want to define it) a silent (unwritten) garrison, directed at opposing those procedural distortions of the genuine logic of the first, as well as the individual guarantees that the same would protect. We agree. The proposed operational and interpretative paradigm is likely to be influenced by (excessive) audacity: the juridical-cultural path in which the internal legal system is inserted (civil law) would not, in principle, show openings in the illustrated direction.

The point, on closer inspection, would perhaps be right here: if it is worthwhile to insist with a line that, as it seems, has already abundantly shown the profiles of inefficiency towards certain dysfunctions highlighted by the practice and, at the same time, the material limits of a legislative activity that, although technically unexceptionable or sensitive to concrete experience, cannot but constitute an approximation, therefore destined to leave gaps that end up sharpening the basic problems of the system. Or else, always with the prudence imposed by an interpretative and operative model that, if hypothesis were introduced, would require a substantial amount of time to settle and become (so to say) ius receptum, take note of the current historical and cultural contingencies, to be ready not to a clumsy as unpopulated tabula rasa of the "old" to enter the "new", but to let everything change, because (the whole itself) remains as it is[919]. Within this perspective dimension, the role of a careful doctrine, in which one believes it can sustain, would be to contribute to a rational and wise control of this change.

CONCLUDING REMARKS

The paragraph will end with some general consideration on the Anglo-Welsh doctrine of the trial abuse. As we have tried to point out immediately, the origin and the cause of the institution's elaboration has an undoubted common feature with the reconstruction matured in the European system: the gaps in the system (in our: from the law) are filled through a jurisprudential substitute work.

Clearly, the Anglo-Saxon is certainly a more fertile ground for the cultivation of the theoretical subject: to the connotations of an order where a written law is structurally lacking, there is the discretionary nature of the prosecution, which would imply-at least theoretically-a greater thus) degree of "abusability" of the procedural instruments in general, if not properly of the process itself.

Attempting to simplify the terms of the discussion as much as possible, one can rationally say that the central element of all the jurisprudential reconstruction so far analyzed is the discretion: as we have seen, recourse to the anti-abuse doctrine is subject to discretionary evaluation by of the judge who, within a broad disciplinary dosimetric spectrum, has more options, reaching the adoption of the extreme solution when the principle of legitimacy is irreparably compromised. At the same time, what we have called "abusability" of the trial (or of the trial institutes) depends directly on the margins of maneuver that the

919 J. JACKSON, S. SUMMERS, The internationalisation of criminal evidence. Beyond the common law and civil law traditions, op. cit.

procedural parties have in the conduct of the dispute. The criminal trial, being the accusation part actress, is at the same time the one that is most able to pollute the overall fairness of the procedure (intuitively, then, if the exercise of the voluntas persecutionis is even remitted to it; one understands the imbalance that is recreated among the necessary parts of the process with regard to the ability to abuse it)[920].

It has also been seen that the arrest of trial constitutes an entirely exceptional remedy: for the most understandable reasons that the paralyzing of the punitive pretension places a sensitive barrier on the collective interest in the repression of crimes, while we are witnessing a cultural scenario in which we generally trust in the "thaumaturgical" capacities of the criminal trial. It is a machine that already has enough tools to guarantee the overall fairness, possibly (if so we want to say) cars-making up during the course. In short, there is generalized trust in a procedural system which, ideally, would represent a correct compendium of needs for the discovery of the truth (repression of crimes) and the protection of guarantees.

On the other hand, the whole theory of abuse of process seems to stand on the dialectic just reported, leading to the adoption of a fundamental system caution: the degree of heuristic penetrance of the process must be modulated. Truth always has a price and, in certain cases, it can become unbearable. In conclusion, it would not seem risky to state that the doctrine of abuse of process can only be citizenship within an accusatory system.

There will be no judgments about the limits or correctness of the reconstruction made in the Anglo-Saxon order (it does not even fall within the scope of the present comparative research). In fact, it interests something else if the instruments offered there are likely, in some way, to import into the internal procedural system. In short, all the meaning of the analysis carried out here should be turned into a final question: if and what in concrete can be borrowed from the Anglo-Saxon system regarding the abuse of process?

920 J. JACKSON, S. SUMMERS, The internationalisation of criminal evidence. Beyond the common law and civil law traditions, op. cit.

ACIERNO, S., The Carpenter judgement: fundamental rights and the limits of the European Union legal order, in European Law Review, 28, 2003, pp. 398ss.

ADAMS, Z., DEAKIN, S., Freedom of establishment and regulatory competition, in A. ARNULL, D. CHALMERS (a cura di), The Oxford Handbook of European Union Law, Oxford University Press, Oxford, 2015, pp. 545ss.

AIRS G., and others, Abuse of tax law across Europe (part I and part II), in EC Tax Review, 19, 2010, pp. 85ss.

AKMAM, O., The concept of abuse in EU competition law: law and economic approaches, Hart Publishing, Oxford & Oregon, Portland, 2012.

ALLEN, R.J., LUTTRELL, M., KREEGER, A., Clarifying entrapment, in International Commentary of Evidence, 1998.

AMBOS, K., Treatise on international criminal law. Foundations and general part, Oxford University Press, Oxford, 2013.

AMOS, M., Human rights law, Hart Publishing, Oxford & Oregon, Portland, 2014, pp. 365ss.

AMSTRONG, K., Mutual recognition, in C. BARNARD, J. SCOTT, The law of the single European market: Unpacking the premises, Hart Publishing, Oxford & Oregon, Portland, 2002, pp. 225.

ANAGNOSTOPOULOU, D., Do Francovich and the principle of proportionality weaken Simmenthal (II) and confirm abuse of rights?, in Common Market Law Review, 38, 2001, pp. 772-774.

ANDENAS, M., BEKKEDAL, T., PANTALEO, L., The reach of free movement, Asser Press & Springer, The Hague, 2017, pp. 135ss.

ANDERSON, D., Abuse of rights, in Judicial Review, 11, 2006, pp. 348ss.

ANSEN, N., ZIMMERMANN, R., Commentaries on European contract laws, Oxford University Press, Oxford, 2018.

ARANGÜENA FANEGO, C., El derecho a la asistencia letrada en la directiva 2013/48/UE, in Revista General de Derecho Europeo, 32, 2014, pp. 8ss.

AREEDA, P.E., HOVENKAMP, H., Antitrust law: An analysis of antitrust principles and their application, Wolters Kluwer, New York, 2018, pp. 146ss

ASHIAGBOR, D., COUNTOURIS, N., LIANOS, I., The European Union after the Treaty of Lisbon, Cambridge University Press, Cambridge, 2012, pp. 109-135.

ASHWORTH, A., Entrapment and criminal justice (R v Looseley and Attorney General's Reference (No 3 of 2000)), in Oxford University Commonwealth Law Journal, 18, 2002, pp. 125ss.

ASHWORTH, A., Re-drawing the boundaries of entrapment, in Criminal Law Review, 2002, pp. 161ss.

ASHWORTH, A., REDMAYNE, M., The criminal process, Oxford University Press, Oxford, 2010, chapter 1-3.

ASHWORTH, A., Should the police be allowed to use deceptive practices?, in Law Quarterly Review, 114, 1998, pp. 120ss.

ATIENZA, M., RUIZ MANERO, J., A theory of legal sentences, ed. Springer, New York, 1998.,

BAKARDJIEVA ENGELBREKT, A., BREMBER, N., MICHALSKI, A., Trust in the European Union in challenges time. Interdisciplinary European studies, Palgrave Macmillan, London, 2018, pp. 179ss

BAMMENS, N., The principle of non-discrimination in international and European tax law, IBFD, Leidend, 2012.

BARAV, A., Judicial of enforcement and implementation of European Union law, ed. Bruylant, Bruxelles, 2017.

BARNARD, C., ODUDU, O., The outer limits of European Union law, Hart Publishing, Oxford & Oregon, Portland, 2009.

BARNARD, C., PEERS, S., European Union law, Oxford University Press, Oxford, 2017, pp. 586ss.

BÄRSCH, S.E., Taxation of hybrid financial instruments and the remuneration derived therefrom in and international cross-border context: Issues and options for reform, ed. Springer, Berlin, 2012.

BECHT, M., MAYERAND, C., WAGNER, H., Where do firms incorporate? Deregulation and the cost of entry, in Journal of Corporate Finance, 14, 2008, pp. 241ss.

BECK, G., The legal reasoning of the Court of justice of the European Union, Hart Publishing, Oxford & Oregon, Portland, 2013.

BEHRENS, P., Centros and the proper law of companies, in J. FERRARINI, K.J. HOPT, E. WYEMMERSCH, Capital markets in the age of the euro, Kluwer Law International, The Hague, 2002, pp. 503ss.

BENNION, F., The new prosecutorial arrangements: (1) The Crown Prosecution Service, in Criminal Law Review, 1986, pp. 4ss.

BERNARD, N., La libre circulation des marchandises, des personnes et des services dans le Traité CE sous l'angle de la competence, in Cahiers de Droit Européen, 34, 1998, pp. 11ss.

BERRY, C., HOMEWOOD, M.J., BOGUSZ, B., Complete European Union law: Text, cases and materials, Oxford University Press, Oxford, 2013.

BERTRAND, B., Que reste-t-il des exigences impératives d'intérêt général?, in Europe, janvier 2012.

BESSELINK, L., CLAES, M., REESTMAN, J.H., A Constitutional moment: Acceding to the ECHR (or not), in European Constitutional Law Review, 11, 2015, pp. 2ss.

BIEZCZAT, S., First amendment protection for unfair labor practices. Reexaming the Noerr-Pennington doctine, in University of Illinois Law Review, 2017, n. 4, pp. 1586ss.

BILLING, F.M.W., The right to silence in transnational criminal proceedings. Comparative law perspectives, ed. Springer, Berlin, 2016, pp. 323ss.

BIRCH, D., TAYLOR, C., "People like us?": Responding to allegations of past abuse in care, in Criminal Law Review, 2003, pp. 824ss.

BLAKE, S., BROWNE, J., SIME, S., A practical approach to alternative dispute resolution, Oxford University Press, Oxford, 2012.

BLUMANN C., (a cura di) Politique agricole commune, ed. Litec, Paris, 1996.

BORG-BARTHET, J., The governing law of companies in European Union law, Hart Publishing, Oxford & Oregon, Portland, 2012, pp. 136, 143ss.

BOURGEOIS, J., WAELBROECK D., (eds), Ten years of effects-based approach in EU competition law: State of play and perspectives, ed. Bruylant, Bruxelles, 2012.

BRATTON, W., MCCAHERY, J., VERMEULEN, E., How does corporate mobility affect lawmaking? A comparative analysis, in American Journal of Comparative Law, 57, 2009, pp. 347ss.

BRAUN, R., EIDENMÜLLER, H., ENGERT, A., HORNUF, L., Does Charter competition foster entrepreneurship? A difference-in-difference approach to European company law reforms, in Journal of Common Market Studies, 50, 2013, pp. 400ss.

BRAY, R., Beckford and beyond. Some developments in the doctrine of abuse of process, in Denning Law Journal, 19, 2007, pp. 69ss.

BREMS, E., ERARDS J., (eds.), Shaping rights in the ECHR. The role of the European Court of Human Rights in determining the scope of human rights, Cambridge University Press, Cambridge, 2014, pp. 188ss.

BROBERG, M., FENGER, N., Preliminary references to the European Court of Justice, Oxford University Press, Oxford, 2014.

BROBERG, M., HOLST-CHRISTENSEN, N., Free movement in the European Union, ed. Djøf Forlag, Copenaghen, 2007, pp. 776ss.

BRODE, D.F., U.S. Antitrust law and enforcement. A practice introduction, Oxford University Press, Oxford, 2010.

BROWN, D., The judicial role in criminal charging and plea bargaining, in Hofstra Law Review, 46 (1), 2018, pp. 67ss.

BROWN, L.N., Is there a general principle of abuse of rights in European European Union law?, in D. CURTIN, T. HEUKELS (eds.), Institutional dynamics of European integration: Essays in Honor of Henry G. Schermers, Martinus Nijhoff Publishers, Leiden, 1994.

BRUCE, A., GREEN, A., LEVINE, S.J., Disciplinary regulation of prosecutors as a remedy for abuses of prosecutorial discretion: A descriptive and normative analysis, in Ohio State Journal of Criminal Law, 14, 2016, pp. 144s.

BUYSE, A., HAMILTON M., (eds.), Transitional jurisprudence and the European Convention on Human Rights. Justice, politics and rights, Cambridge University Press, Cambridge, 2011, pp. 155-156.

CABRAL, P., CUNHA, P., "Presumed innocent": Companies and the exercise of the right of establishment under European Union law, in European Law Review, 25, 2000, pp. 158ss.

CAHN, A., DONALD, D.C., Comparative company law: Text and cases on the laws governing corporations in Germany, the UK and the USA, Cambridge University Press, Cambridge, 2010, pp. 93ss.

CANNIE, H., VOORHOOF, D., The abuse clause and freedom of expression in the European Human Rights Convention: An added value for democracy and human rights protection?, in Netherlands Quarterly of Human Rights, 29 (1), 2011, pp. 59ss.

CANNIZZARO, E., EMILIOU, N., The principle of proportionality in European law, Kluwer Law International, London, The Hague, Boston, 1996.

CARLIER, J.Y., Case C-200/02, Kunqian Catherine Zhu, Man Lavette Chen v. Secretary of State for the Home Department, Judgement of the CJEU of 19 October 2004, in Common Market Law Review, 42 (4), 2005, pp. 1121ss.

CARLON, A., Entrapment, punishment and the sadistic State, in Virginia Law Review, 93, 2007, pp. 1081ss.

CARO DE SOUZA, P., The European fundamentral freedoms: A contextual approach, Oxford University Press, Oxford, 2015.

CARRUTHERS, J., VILLIERS, C., Company Law in Europe, condoning the continental drift?, in European Business Law Review, 11, 2000, pp. 91ss.

CAVALLINI, J., Reconnaissance sur reconnaissance ne vaut, in La Semaine Juridique Social, n. 13, 24 March 2009, pp. 1134ss.

CAVALLINI, V.J., Homologation sur homologation peut valoir, in La Semaine Juridique, 12, 2011, pp. 13-14.

CERIONI, L., The "abuse of rights" in EU company law and EU tax law: A re-reading of the ECJ case law and the quest for a unitary notion, in European Business Law Review, 21 (4), 2010 pp. 783ss.

CHALMERS, D., DAVIES, G., MONTI, G., European Union law, Cambridge University Press, Cambridge, 2014.

CHARNY, D., Competition among jurisdictions in formulating corporate law rules: an American perspective on the "race to the bottom" in the European Communities, in Harvard International Law Journal, 32, 1991, pp. 422ss.

CHOO, A., Abuse of process and judicial stays of criminal proceedings, Oxford University Press, Oxford, 2008, pp. 2.

CHOO, A., Halting criminal prosecutions, in Criminal Law Review, 1995, pp. 866ss.

CHOO, A., MELLORS, M., Undercover police operations and what the suspect said (or didn't say), in Web Journal of Current Legal Issues Yearbook 1995, 1996.

CLOOTS, E., National identity in European Union law, Oxford University Press, Oxford, 2015.

Common Market Law Review, 52, 2015 (2), pp. 363ss.

CONANT, L.J., Justice contained: Law and politics in the European Union, Cornell University Press, U.S, 2018, pp. 46ss.

CONWAY, G., European Union law, ed. Routledge, London & New York, 2015, pp. 464ss.

COPPEL, P., Information rights: Law and practice, Hart Publishing, Oxford & Oregon, Portland, 2014.
CORCHO, R.A., Can we finally say farewell to the "special responsibility" of dominant companies?, in C.D. EHLERMANN, M. MARQUIS, European Competition Law Annual: 2007-A reformed approach to article 82 EC, Hart Publishing, Oxford & Oregon, Portland, 2008, pp. 320-324.
CORNELOUP, S., Citoyenneté européenne: la Cour de justice apporte une nouvelle pierre à son édifice, in Recueil Le Dalloz, 2011, pp. 1325ss.
CORTHAUT, T., EU ordre public, Kluwer Law International, The Hague, 2012.
COSTA, J.P., La Cour europèenne des droits de l'homme. Des juges pour la libertè, ed. Dalloz, Paris, 2017.
COSTELLO, C., Metock: Free movement and "normal family life" in the Union, in Common Market Law Review, 46, 2009, pp. 587ss.
CURRIE, S., Migration, work and citizenship in the enlarged European Union, ed. Routledge, London & New York, 2016.
DA CRUZ VILAÇA, J.L., European Union law and integration. Twenty years of judicial application of European Union law, Hart Publishing, Oxford & Oregon, Portland, 2014.
DABBAH, M.M., International and comparative competition law, Cambridge University Press, Cambridge, 2010.
DAVIES, G., The highwater point of free movement of persons: Ending benefit tourism and rescuing welfare, in Journal of Social Welfare and Family Law, 26, 2004, pp. 211-222.
DE BROE, L., International tax planning and prevention and prevention of abuse. A study under domestic tax law, tax Treaties and EC law in relation to conduit and base company, in IBFD, Leidend, 2007, pp. 765ss.
DE GRAAF, A., EVERS, M., Limiting benefit shopping: Use and abuse of EC law, in EC Tax Review, 18, 2009, pp. 4ss.
DE LA FERIA, R., "Game over" for aggressive VAT planning?: RAL v. Commissioners of customs & excise, in British Tax Review, 55, 2005, pp. 394ss.
DE LA FERIA, R., VOGENAUER, S., Prohibition of abuse of law: a new general principle of EU law?, Oxford University Press, Oxford, 2011.
DE LA FERIA, R., Prohibition of abuse of (European Union law): The creation of a new general principle of EC law through Tax, in Common Market Law Review, 45, 2008, pp. 396ss.
DE LA ROSA, S., La citoyenneté européenne à la mesure des intérêts nationaux. A propos de l'arrêt Förster (aff. C-158/07 du 18 novembre 2008), in Cahiers de Droit Européen, 45, 2009.
DE LONDRAS, F., DZECHTSIAROV, K., Great debates on the European Convention on Human Rights, ed. Macmillan, London, 2018.
DE LUCA, N., European company law: Text, cases and materials, Cambridge University Press, Cambridge, 2017, pp. 302ss.
DE VAREILLES-SOMMIÉRES, P., Forum shopping in the European judicial area, Hart Publishing, Oxford & Oregon, Portland, 2007, pp. 58ss.

DE VOCHT, D.L.F., PANZAVOLTA, M., VAN OOSTERHOUT, M., VAN & VANDERHALLEN, M., Procedural safeguards for juvenile suspects in interrogations: A look at the Commission proposal in light of an EU comparative study, in New Journal of European Criminal Law, 2014, 5 (4), pp. 486ss.

DE VRIES, S., IORATTI, E., GUARDA, O., European Union citizens economic rights in action: Re-thinking legal and actual barriers in the internal market, Edward Elgar Publishers, Cheltenahm, 2018, pp. 253ss.

DE WITTE, B., Article 53, in S. PEERS et al. (eds.), The EU Charter of Fundamental Rights, A Commentary, Hart Publishing, Oxford & Oregon, Portland, 2014, pp. 1523-1538.

DEAKIN, S., Legal diversity and regulatory competition, which model for Europe?, in European Law Journal, 12, 2006, pp. 440ss.

DEAKIN, S., Regulatory competition in European company law, in D. C. ESTY, D. GERADIN (a cura di), Regulatory competition and economic integration, Oxford University Press, Oxford, 2001, pp. 198ss.

DECHEVA, M., Recht der europäischen Union, ed. Nomos, Baden-Baden, 2018.

DENNIS, I.H., The law of evidence, Sweet & Maxwell, London, 2014.

DENUIT, R., Politique culturelle europèenne, ed. Bruylant, Bruxelles, 2017.

DENYER, R., Case management in criminal trials, Hart Publishing, Oxford & Oregon, Portland, 2012.

DENYS, C., Affaire no C-19/92, Dieter Kraus et Land Baden- Württemberg, in Cahiers de Droit Européen, 32, 1994, pp. 638ss.

DEROUIN, P., Fiscalité des fusions de sociétés et échanges d'actions, in Droit Fiscal, 46, 1997, pp. 1100ss.

DITTERT, D., Les droits des citoyens de l'Union: vers un statut détaché de tout élément transfrontalier?, in Revue des Affaires Européennes, 2, 2011, pp. 223ss.

DOAK, J., MCGOURLAY, M., THOMAS, M., Evidence in context, ed. Routledge, London & New York, 2015.

DODDS, M., Arguing abuse of process in relation to loss or destruction of CCTV evidence, in Justice of the Peace, 2001, pp. 316ss.

DORSSEMONT, F., LÖRCHER, K., SCHÖMANN, I., The European Convention on Human Rights and the employment relation, Hart Publishing, Oxford & Oregon, Portland, 2013.

DOUGAN, M., The bubble that burst, in M. ADAMS (a cura di), Judging Europe's Judges, Oxford University Press, Oxford, 2013, pp. 127ss.

DOUMA, S., ENGELEN, F., Halifax Plc and others v. Commissioners of customs & excise: The ECJ applies the abuse of rights doctrine in VAT cases, in British Tax Review, 51, 2006, pp. 429ss.

DREXL, J., KERBER, W., PODSZUN R., (eds), Competition policy and the economic approach: Foundations and limitations, Edward Elgar Publishers, Cheltenham, 2011.

DRIGUEZ, L., Reconnaissance des diplômes: réaction a minima contre

une pratique abusive, in Europe, 126, mars 2009, pp. 15-16.
DRIJBER, B.J., The revised television without frontiers directive: is it fit for the next century?, in Common Market Law Review, 36, 1999, pp. 87ss.
DUBBER, M.D., ÖRNLE T.H., (eds), The oxford handbook of criminal law, Oxford University Press, Oxford, 2014.
DUMONT, V.D., Arrêt Dano: fin du tourisme social ou de la citoyenneté européenne?, in Journal de Droit Européen, 9, 2015, pp. 196ss.
DUNNE, N., Competition law and economic regulation: making and managing markets, Cambridge University Press, Cambridge, 2015.
DURSTON, G., Evidence. Text and materials, Oxford University press, Oxford, 2011.
DWORKIN, R., Taking rights seriously, Harvard University Press, Cambridge, US, 1977.
DZIURDZ, K., MARHGRABER, C., Non discrimination in European and tax treaty law. Open issues and recent challenges, Linde Verlag, Wien, 2015.
EDELMAN, B., Note sur l'arrêt VT4, Recueil Dalloz, 1999, pp. 192ss.
EDWARD, D.A.O., LANE, R., Edward and Lane on European Union law, Edward Elgar Publishers, Cheltenham, 2013.
EDWARDS, A., The other Leveson report-The review of efficiency in criminal proceedings, in Criminal Law Review, 2015, pp. 400ss.
EDWARDS, V., FARMER, P., The concept of abuse in the freedom of establishment of companies: A case of double standards?, in F.G. JACOBS (a cura di), Continuity and change in EU law: Essays in Honour of Sir Francis Jacobs, Oxford University Press, Oxford, 2007, p. 205 ss.
EHLERMANN, C.D., Harmonization versus Competition Between Rules, in European Law Review, 19, 1995, pp. 333ss.
ELLIS, E., WATSON, P., European Union anti-discrimination law, Oxford University Press, Oxford, 2012, pp. 321ss.
ELLIS, T., SAVAGE S., (eds), Debates in criminal justice: Key themes and issues, ed. Routledge, London & New York, 2012.
EMMERSON, B., ASHWORTH, A., MACDONALD, A., Human rights and criminal justice, Sweet & Maxwell, London, 2012.
FAGGIANI, V., Hacia la constitucionalización de los derechos del justiciable en el ELSJ, in Revista General de Derecho Procesal, 36, 2015, pp. 6ss.
FAIRCLOUGH, S., It doesn't happen... and I've never thought it was necessary for it to happen: Barriers to vulnerable defendants giving evidence by live link in Crown Court trials, in International Journal of Evidence & Proof, 21 (3), 2017, pp. 212ss.
FAIRCLOUGH, S., Speaking up for Injustice: Reconsidering the provision of special measures through the lens of equality, in Criminal Law Review, 2018, pp. 7ss.
FALLON Y TELLA, M.J., A three-dimensional theory of law, Martinus Nijhoff Publishers, Leiden, Boston, 2010, pp. 328ss.
FINNIS, J., Revolution and continuity of law, in A.W.B. SIMPSON (a cura

di) Oxford essays in jurisprudence, Second Series, Oxford University Press, Oxford, 1973, pp. 64ss.

FØLLESDAL, A., PETERS, N., ULFSTEIN, G., Constituting Europe: The European Court of Human Rights in a national, European and global context, Cambridge University Press, Cambridge, 2013.

FOLSOM, T.H., Principles of European Union law, including Brexit, West Academic, Minnesota, 2017, pp. 278ss.

FOSTER, N., European Union law directions, Oxford University Press, Oxford, 2016.

FOX, R.G., Criminal delay as abuse of process, Monash University Law Review, 64, 1990, pp. 74ss.

FRONZA, E., Memory and punishment: Historical denialim, free speech and the limits of criminal law, ed. Springer, Berlin, 2018.

GALLASCH, S., Astrazeneca v the Walker process-A Real EU-US Divergence or just an attempt to compare apples to oranges, in European Competition Journal, 2011, pp. 505-526.

GALMOT, Y., BIANCARELLI, J., Les réglementations nationales en matière de prix au regard du droit communautaire, in Revue Trimestrielle de Droit Europèen, 21, 1985, pp. 269ss.

GARRETSON, S.A., The hazards of doing business with the government: Expanding exceptions to Noerr {Eastern R.R. Presidents Conference v. Noerr Motor Freight, Inc., 81 S. Ct. 523}-Pennington {United Mine Workers of Am. v. Pennington, 85 S. Ct. 1585}, in Washington University Journal Urban & Contemporary Law, 26, 1984, pp. 198ss.

GAUTIER, M., Cour de justice, 19 octobre 2004, Kunqian Catherine Zhu et Man Lavette Chen v. Secretary of State for the Home Department, in Revue des Affaires Européennes, 1, 2003-2004, pp. 673ss.

GEIGER, R., KHAN, D.E., KOTZUR, M., EUV/AEUV, C.H. Beck, München, 2016.

GELSTHORPE, L., PADFIELD, N., Exercising discretion, ed. Routledge, London & New York, 2012, pp. 217ss.

GERARD, D., MEROLA, M., MEYRING, B., The notion of restriction of competition: revisiting the foundations of antitrust enforcement in Europe, ed. Bruylant, Bruxelles, 2017.

GILIKER, P., The Europeanisation of english tort law, Hart Publishing, Oxford & Oregon, Portland, 2014.

GILL, P., Rounding up the usual suspects? Developments in contemporary law enforcement intelligence, Ashgate Publishing, London, 2000.

GILLESPIE, A., WEARE, S., The english legal system, Oxford University Press, Oxford, 2017.

GLEESON, A.M., Individualised justice-The holy grail, in Australian Law Journal, 20, 1995, pp. 422ss.

GLOVER, R., Murphy on evidence, Oxford University Press, Oxford, 2015, pp. 690ss.

GOLUB, A.S., The exception of Noerr-Pennington materials from discovery under the petition clause of the first amendment, in St. John's Law Review: 66 (4), 1993, pp. 1099ss.

GOLYNKER, O., Jobseekers' rights in the European Union: challenges of changing the paradigm of social

solidarity, in European Law Review, 30, 2005, pp. 117ss.
GOMIEN, D.I., HARRIS, D., ZWAAK, L., Law and practice of the European Convention on Human Rights and the European Social Charter, Strasbourg, 1996, pp. 52.
GRABENWARTER, C., European Convention on human rights: ECHR, C.H. Beck, München, 2014.
GRAF KERSSENBROCK, O.F., In the wake of Lankhorst-Hohorst, in Intertax, 2004, pp. 306ss.
GRANT, W., The Common Agricultural Policy, ed. MacMillan, London, 1997.
GRIFFITHS, J., MCKEOWN, P., Evidence, Oxford University Press, Oxford, 2012.
GROSSI, P., L'Europa del diritto, ed. Laterza, Roma, 2016.
GROUSSOT, X., PETURSSON, G.T., The EU Charter of the Fundamental Rights five years on. The emergence of a new constitutional framework?, in S. DE VRIES, U. BERNITS, S. WEATHERILL, The EU Charter of Fundamental Rights as a binding instrument. Five years old and growing, Oxford University Press, Oxford, 2015.
GUILD, E., GORTAZAR ROTAECHE, C., KOSTAKOPOULOU, D., The reconceptualization of European Union citizenship, ed. Brill, Martinus Nijhoff Publishers, Leiden, Boston, 2014, pp. 268ss.
GUILD, E., PEERS, S., TOMKIN, J., The European Union citizenship directive. A commentary, Oxford University Press, Oxford, 2014.
GUIMARAES DE LIMA E SILVA, V., Sham litigation in the pharmaceutical sector, in European Competition Journal, 7 (3), 2011, pp. 471-472.
GUTMAN, K.,The constitutional foundations of European contract law: A comparative analysis, Oxford University Press, Oxford, 2014, pp. 332ss.
GUTMANN, D., HINNEKENS, L., The Lankhorst-Hohorst case. The ECJ finds German thin capitalization rules incompatible with freedom of establishment, in EC Tax Review, 3, 2003, pp. 90ss.
HABELSTAM, D., It's autonomy stupid. A modest defense of Opinion 2/13 on EU accession to the ECHR, and a way forward, in Michigan Law Paper 105, 2015.
HAILBRONNER, K., THYM, D., Case C-34/09, Gerardo Ruiz Zambrano v. Office national de l'emploi (ONE), Judgment of the CJEU (Grand Chamber) of 8 March 2011, in Common Market Law Review, 48, 2011, pp. 1253ss.
HALLESKOV STORGAARD, L., European Union law autonomy versus European fundamental rights protection. On opinion 2/13 on EU accession to the ECHR, in Human Rights Law Review, 15 (3), 2015, pp. 487ss.
HANNIGAN, B., Company law, Oxford University Press, Oxford, 2012.
HARFIELD, C., HARFIELD, K., Covert investigation, Oxford University Press, Oxford, 2012, pp. 145ss.
HARRIS, D., O'BOYLE, M., WARBRICK, C., Law of the European Convention on Human rights, Oxford University Press, Oxford, 2014, pp. 372ss.
JOHAN SETTEM, O., Applications of the fair hearing norm in ECHR art. 6 (1)

to civil proceedings, ed. Springer, Berlin, 2016, pp. 486ss.

HARTKAMP, A., SIBURGH, C., DEVROE, W., Cases, materials and text on European Union law and private law, hart Publishing, Oxford & Oregon, Portland, 2017, pp. 282ss.

HATJE, A., TERHECHTE, J.P., MÜLLER-GRAFF, P.C., Europarechtswissenschaft, ed. Nomos, Baden-Baden, 2018.

HATZOPOULOS, V., Exigences essentielles, impératives ou impérieuses; une théorie, des théories ou pas de théorie du tout?, in Revue Trimestrielle de Droit Européen, 34, 1998, pp. 201-202.

HATZOPOULOS, V., Le principe communautaire d'équivalence et de reconnaissance mutuelle dans la libre prestation de services, Sakkoulas/Bruylant, Atene-Bruxelles, 1999, pp. 107ss.

HELMINEM, M., Is there a future for Cfc regimes in EU?, in Intertax, 2005, pp. 117ss.

HELMINEN, M., European Union tax law: Direct taxation, IBFD, Leidend, pp. 102ss.

HENDERSON, E., Taking control of cross-examination: Judges, advocates and intermediaries discuss judicial management of the cross-examination of vulnerable people, in Criminal Law Review, 2016, pp. 184ss.

HEREMANS, T., Professional services in the European Union internal market: Quality regulation and self-regulation, Hart Publishing, Oxford & Oregon, Portland, 2012, pp. 229ss.

HERLIN-KARNELL, E., The constitutional dimension of European criminal law, Hart Publishing, Oxford & Oregon, Portland, 2012, pp. 17ss.

HERRING, J., Criminal law: Text, cases and materials, Oxford University Press, Oxford, 2018.

HILL, J., CHONG, A., International commercial disputes: Commercial conflict of laws in english courts, Hart Publishing, Oxford & Oregon, Portland, 2014.

HINGHOFER-SZALKAY, S.G., Extreme Meinungen und Meinungsäußerungsfreiheit: Die Schranke des Artikel 17 EMRK. Die Straßburger Rechtsprechung und ihre Struktur, in Journal für Rechtspolitik, 20 (2), 2012, pp. 106-114.

HINS, W., Case C-148/91, Vereniging Veronica Omroep Organisatie v. Commissariaat voor de Media, Judgement of 3 February 1993, in Common Market Law Review, 31, 1994, pp. 901ss.

HOENJET, F., The Leur-Bloem judgement: the jurisdiction of the European CJEU and the interpretation of the anti-abuse clause in the Merger Directive, in EC Tax Review, 6, 1997, pp. 206ss.

HOFFMEISTER, F., Enforcing the EU Charter of Fundamental Rights in member States: How far are Rome, Budapest and Bucharest from Brussels, in A. VON BOGDANDY, P. SONNEVAND, Constitutional crisis in the European constitutional area, theory, law and politics in Hungary and Romania, Hart Publishing/Nomos, Oxford, Baden-Baden, 2015, pp. 126ss.

HOFSTOFFER, B., A cascade of rights, or who shall care for little Catherine?, in European Law Review, 34, 2009, pp. 548.

HOFSTÖTTER, B., A cascade of rights, or who shall care for little Catherine? Some reflections on the Chen case, in European Law Review, 30 (4), 2005, pp. 548ss.
HOLST, C., European company law after Centros: is the EU on the road to Delaware?, in The Columbia Journal of European Law, 8, 2002, pp. 323ss.
HORN, N., Einführung in die Rechtswissenshaft und Rechtsphilosophie, C.F. Müller, Heidelberg, 2011, pp. 106ss.
HORNLE, J., Country of origin regulation in cross-border media: One step beyond the freedom to provide services?, in International and Comparative law Quarterly, 55, 2005, pp. 115-118.
HORSPOOL, M., HUMPHREYS, M., European Union law, Oxford University Press, Oxford, 2012, pp. 552ss.
HUGLO, J.G., Liberté d'établissement et libre prestation des services, in Revue Trimestrielle de Droit Européen, 32 (4), 1996, pp. 742ss.
HUXLEY-BINN, R., Criminal law concentrate, Oxford University Press, Oxford, 2014.
HYLTON, K.N., Antitrust law: economic theory and common law evolution, Cambridge University Press, Cambridge, 2010, pp. 370ss.
IDOT, L., Un régime différencié pour l'octroi du credit d'impôt en matière d'impôt sur les sociétés est contraire à l'article 43 CE, in Europe, 55, février 2003, pp. 17ss.
ILIOPOULOU-PENOT, A., Liberté de circulation et abus de droit, in E. DUBOUT, A. MAITROT DE LA MOTTE (a cura di), L'unité des libertés de circulation: in varietate concordia?, ed. Bruylant, Bruxelles, 2013, pp. 185ss.
IONESCU, R., Abus de droit en droit de l'Union européenne: nouvelles applications, notamment en matière de transport, in Journal de Droit Européen, 221 (1), 2015, pp. 100ss.
IONESCU, R., L'abus de droit en droit de l'Union européenne, in C. KESSEDJIAN, Autonomie en droit européen Stratégie des citoyens, des entreprises et des Etats, LGDG, Paris, 2013, pp. 210ss.
JAAP, C., VON DER PFORDTEN, D., Concepts in law, ed. Springer, New York, 2009, pp. 17ss.
JACKSON, J., JOHNSTONE, J., The reasonable time requirement: An independent and meaningful right?, in Criminal Law Review, 2005, pp. 23ss.
JACKSON, J., SUMMERS, S., The internationalisation of criminal evidence: Beyond the common law and civil law traditions, Cambridge University Press, Cambridge, 2012.
JACOB, I.H., The inherent jurisdiction of the Court, in Current Legal Problems, 43, 1990, pp. 43ss.
JACQUÉ, J.P., CJUE-CEDH: 2-0, in Revue Trimestrielle de Droit Européen, 40 (4), 2014 pp. 823ss.
JACQUÉ, J.P., La Cour de Justice de !'Union et !'application de la Charte dans les Etats membres: "Mehr Licht", in European Yearbook on Human Rights, 14, 2014 pp. 125-147.
JACQUÉ, J.P., The accession of the European Union to the European Convention on Human Rights and Fundamental Freedoms, in Common

Market Law Review, 48 (4), 2011, pp. 995, 1005.

JAKAB, A., KOCHENOV, D., The enforcement of EU laws and values. Ensuring member States compliance, Oxford University Press, Oxford, 2017.

JANSSENS, C., The principle of mutual recognition in European Union law, Oxford University Press, Oxford, 2013, pp. 208ss.

JERRARD, R.R., Entrapment: Abuse of legal process for police to incite crime, in Police Journal, 2002, pp. 245ss.

JHERING, R., Der geist des römischen Rechts lauf den verschiedenen Stufen seiner Entwicklung, II, Leipzig, 1869.

JIMENO BULNES, M., Towards common standards on rights of suspected and accused persons in criminal proceedings in the EU, in Centre for European Policy Studies, 2010, pp. 1-20.

JOHNSTON, A., SYRPIS, P., Regulatory competition in European company law after Cartesio, in European Law Review, 6, 2009, pp. 386ss.

JOLOWICZ, J.A., Abuse of the process of the Court: Handle with care, in Current Legal Problems, 43, 1990, pp. 78ss.

JONES, A., SUFRIN, B., EU competition law. Text, cases and materials, Oxford University Press, Oxford, 2016.

JONGEN, F., STROWEL, A., Droit des mèdias et de la communication: Presse, audiovisuel et internet, ed. Larcier, Bruxelles, 2017.

JOSSERAND, C., Essais de téléologie juridique, I,-De l'esprit des droits et de leur relativité, Théorie dite de l'abus de droit, ed. Dalloz, Paris, 1939, pp. 245ss.

KACZOROWSKA-IRELAND, A., European Union Law, Routledge, London & New York, 2016.

KARAYANNIS, V., L'abus de droits découlant de l'ordre juridique communautaire. A propos de l'arret C-367/96 Alexandros Kefalas e.a./ Elliniko Dimosio (Etat hellenique), in Cahiers de Droit Européen, 36, 1999, pp. 521ss.

KARIMERI, R., A critical review of the definition of tax avoidance in the case law of the European Court of Justice, in Intertax, 2009, pp. 315-316.

KÄSEBERG, T., Intellectual property, antitrust and cumulative innovation in the EU and the US, Hart Publishing, Oxford & Oregon, Portland, 2012.

KATSIREA, I., The circumvention principle: An effective defence of national Broadcasting system against abuse?, in Communications Law & Policy, 23, 2005, pp. 130ss.

KATSIREA, I., The television without frontiers directive, in K. DONDERS, C. PAUWELS, J. LOISEN (eds.), The Palgrave handbook of European media policy, Palgrave Macmillan, London, 2014.

KATSIREA, I., The transmission State principle: The end of the broadcasting sovereignty of the member States?, in Cambridge Yearbook of European Legal Studies, 2003-2004, pp. 105ss.

KAUFF-GAZIN, F., Droit de séjour de l'ascendant à charge, membre de la famille du ressortissant communautaire, in Europe, 86, 2007, Comm. n. 86, pp. 14-15.

KEANE, A., MCKEOWN, P., The modern law of evidence, Oxford University Press, Oxford, 2014.
KERIKMÄE, T., Protecting human rights in the EU. Controversies and challenges of the Charter of Fundamental Rights, ed. Springer, Berlin/Heidelberg, 2014, pp. 80ss.
KILPONEN, J., Sovereign risk European crisis-resolution policies and bond spreads, in International Journal of Central Banking, 11 (2), 2015, pp. 287ss.
KING, N.J., WRIGHT, R.F., The invisible revolution in plea bargaining: Managerial judging and judicial participation in negotiations, in Texas Law Review, 95, 2016, pp. 325, 339ss.
KIRBY, A., Effectively engaging victims, witnesses and defendants in the Criminal Courts: A question of "court culture"?, in Criminal Law Review, 2017, pp. 950ss.
KJELLGREN, A., On the border of abuse: The jurisprudence of the European CJEU on circumvention, fraud and other misuses of European Union law, in European Business Law Review, 11 (1), 2000, pp. 180ss.
KLAMMERT, C., The principle of loyalty in European Union law, Oxford University Press, Oxford, 2014.
KLIP, A., European criminal law. An Integrative approach, ed. Intersentia, Cambridge-Antwerp-Portland, 2012, pp. 24ss.
KODANIS, S., French exit tax incompatible with the freedom of establishment, in European Taxation, 4, 2004, pp. 375ss.
KORENICA, F., The EU accession to the ECHR: Between Luxembourg's search for autonomy and Strasbourg's credibility on human rights protection, ed. Springer, Berlin, 2015, pp. 282ss.
KOWALCZYK, W., Dano: A right to freedom of movement or protection against an unreasonable burden imposed upon member State's social security systems?, in European Law Reporter, 2014, pp. 248ss.
KRENN, C., Autonomy and effectiveness as common concerns: A path to ECHR accession after Opinion 2/13, in German Law Journal, 16 (1), 2015, pp. 147ss.
KROMMENDIJK, J., Principled silence or mere silence on principles? The role of the EU Charter's principles in the case law of the court of Justice, in European Constitutional Law Review, 11 (2), 2015, pp. 322ss.
KUIJER, M., The accession of the European Union to the ECHR: A gift for ECHR's 60th anniversary or an unwelcome intruder at the party?, in Amsterdam Law Forum, 4 (3), 2011, pp. 17-32.
KUNOY, B., A Union of National Citizens: The origins of the CJEU's lack of avant-gardisme in the Chen case, in Common Market Law Review, 43 (1), 2006, pp. 179ss.
KUYPER, P.J., Case 229/83, Association des Centres Distributeurs Edouard Leclerc, Paris and Thouars Distribution & Autres S.A., Sainte Verge, v. Au Blé Vert S.a.r.l., in Common Market Law Review, 22, 1985, pp. 808ss.
LADENBURGER, C., Vers l'adhésion de l'Union européenne à la Convention européenne des droits de l'homme, in Revue Trimestrielle de Droit Européen, 47 (1), 2011, pp. 20-26.

LAGONDET, F., L'abus de droit dans la jurisprudence communautaire, in Journal des Tribunaux Droit Européen, 95, 2003, pp. 9ss.
LAI HO, H., State entrapment, in Legal Studies, 31 (1), 2011, pp. 74ss.
LAMBRECHT, S., The sting is in the Tail: CJEU Opinion 2/13 objects to draft agreement on accession of the EU to the European Convention on Human Rights, in European Human Rights Law Review, 15 (1), 2015, pp. 185ss.
LANG, M., PISTONE, M., SCHUCH, J., Introduction to European tax law on direct taxation, Linde Verlag, Wien, 2015. M. HELMINEN, EU tax law: Direct taxation, IBFD, Leidend, 2011, pp. 21ss.
LANG, M., The Marks & Spencer case-The open issues following the ECJ's final word, in European Taxation, 6, 2006, pp. 54ss.
LANG, N., Procedural rules in tax law in the context of European Union and domestic law, Wolters Kluwer, The Hague, 2010, pp. 359ss.
LAROOUCHE, P., SCHINKEL, M.P., The Oxford Handbook of international antitrust economics, Oxford University Press, Oxford, 2015, pp. 164ss.
LAUTERFELD, M., Centros and the EC regulation on insolvency proceedings: The end of the real seat approach towards pseudo-foreign companies in german international company and insolvency law?, in European Business Law Review, 12, 2001, pp. 79ss.
LAZZERINI, N., (Some of) the fundamental rights granted by the Charter may be a source of obligations for private parties: AMS, in Common Market Law Review, 51 (4), 2014, pp. 908ss.
LEBRUN, G., De l'utilitè de l'article 47 de la Charte des droits fondamentaux de l'union europèenne, in Revue Trimestrielle des Droits de l'Homme, 106, 2016, pp. 433ss.
LENAERTS, A., The general principle of the prohibition of abuse of rights: a critical position on its role in a codified European contract law, in European Review of Private Law, 18, 2010, pp. 1122ss.
LENAERTS, K., Exploring the limits of the EU Charter of Fundamental Rights, in European Constitutional Law Review, 2012, pp. 375ss.
LENAERTS, K., MASELIS, I., GUTMAN, K., European Union procedural law, Oxford University Press, Oxford, 2014, pp. 133ss.
LENAERTS, K., The concept of "abuse of law" in the case law of the European Court of Justice on direct taxation, in Maastricht Journal of European and Comparative Law, 22, 2015, pp. 336ss.
LESLIE, C.R., Antitrust law and intellectual property rights. Cases and materials, Oxford University Press, Oxford, 2011.
LEWIN, B., Test purchasing-The impact and the regulation of investigatory powers act 2000, in Justice of the Peace, 2001, pp. 956ss.
LEWIS, P., Too late to try?, in New Law Journal, 2006, pp. 1458ss.
LIAKOPOULOS, D., A comparative analysis of EU and US transnational mergers regulation, Grin Verlag, II edition, München, 2017.
LIAKOPOULOS, D., Annäherung der Prozessgesetzgebung Strafverfolgungsmaßnahmen der

Mitgliedstaaten: Probleme und Perspektiven, in International and European Union Legal Matters-working papers, 2018.
LIAKOPOULOS, D., Die Rechte des Verurteilten Strafrecht: Kritische und vergleichende, in International and European Union Legal Matters-working paper series, 2015.
LIAKOPOULOS, D., European integration and its relation with the jurisprudence of European Court of Human Rights and private international law of European Union, in Homa Publica. Revista Internacional de Direitos Humanos e Impresa, 2 (2), 2018.
LIAKOPOULOS, D., Parità di armi nella giustizia penale internazionale, vol. 1, ed. Libellula, Puglia, 2018.
LIAKOPOULOS, D., Plea bargaining in international criminal law, in International and European Union Legal Matters, 2013.
LIAKOPOULOS, D., Services publics dans le droit communautaire après le traité de Lisbonne, in International and European Union Legal Matters-working paper series, 2011.
LIAKOPOULOS, D., The regulation of transnational mergers in international and European law, ed. Brill/Nijhoff, Leiden, Boston, 2010.
LIEBERT, U., GATTIG, A., Democratizing the European Union law below? Citizenship, civil society and the public sphere, ed. Routledge, London & New York, 2016.
LIMBACH, K., Uniformity of customs administration in the European Union, Hart Publishing, Oxford & Oregon, Portland, 2015.
LOCK, T., The ECJ and the ECtHR: The Future Relationship between the Two European Courts, in The Law and Practice of International Courts and Tribunals, 8, 2010, pp. 375-398.
LOCK, T., The future of EU accession to the ECHR after Opinion 2/13: Is it still possible and is it still desirable?, in Edinburgh School of Law Research Paper Series, 2015.
LONBAY, J., Picking over the bones: Rights of establishment reviewed, in European Law Review, 2, 1991, pp. 510ss.
LOOIJENSTIJN-CLEARIE, A., Centros ltd, a complete U-turn in the right of establishment for companies?, in International and Comparative Law Quarterly, 49, 2000, pp. 636ss.
LOOIJETIJN-CLEARIE, A., RUSU, C.S., VEENBRINK, M., Boosting the enforcement of E competition law at the domestic level, Cambridge Scholar Publishers, London, 2017.
LOUGHNAN, A., Between fairness and "dangerousness": Reforming the law on unfitness to plead, in Criminal Law Review, 2016, pp. 452ss.
LOUSSOUARN, Y., Le droit d'établissement des sociétés, in Revue Trimestrielle de Droit Européen, 27, 1990, pp. 229ss.
LOUTRAKOS, P., NIC SHUIBHNE, M., SYRPIS, P., Exceptions from European Union free movement law. Derogation justification and proportionality, Hart Publishing, Oxford & Oregon, Portland, 2016.
LOVDAHL GORMSEN, L., A principled approach to abuse of dominance in European competition law, Cambridge University Press, Cambridge, 2010.

LOVDAHL GORMSEN, L., Are anti-competitive effects necessary for an analysis under article 102 TFEU?, in World Competition, 36, 2013, pp. 224ss.
LOWRY, J., Eliminating obstacles to freedom of establishment: the competitive edge of UK company law, in The Cambridge Law Journal, 63 (2), 2004, pp. 342ss.
LOYTOMAKI, S., Law and the politics of memory: confronting the past, ed. Routledge, London & New York, 2014.
LUNEL, A., L'abus de droit et la redèfinition des rapports juridiques entre patrons et ouvries en droit français, in Revue Historique de Droit Français et Étranger, 87 (4), 2009, pp. 580ss.
LYONS, T., European Union customs, Oxford University Press, Oxford, 2018.
MACKAY, R.D., Unfitness to plead-Data on formal findings from 2002 to 2014. London: Law Commission, 2016.
MAGGIOLINO, M., MONTAGNANI, L., Astrazeneca's abuse of IPR-related procedures: A hypothesis of ant-trust offense, Abuse of Rights, and IPR Misuse, in World Competition, 34, 2011, pp. 257ss.
MAGUIRE, M., JOHN, T., Covert and deceptive policing in England and Wales: Issues in regulation and practice, in European Journal of Crime, Criminal Law and Criminal Justice, 1996, pp. 316ss.
MAK, C., Rights and remedies: Article 47 EUCFR and effective judicial protection in European private law matters, in Amsterdam Law School Research Paper No. 2012-88. Centre for the Study of European Contract Law Working Paper Series No. 2012-11.
MANGAS MARTÍN, A., Tratado de la Uniòn Europea, Tratado de Funcionamiento ed. Marcial Pons, Madrid, 2018.
MÄNTYSAARI, P., The law of corporate finance: General principles and European Union law, ed. Springer, Berlin, 2010, pp. 254ss.
MARCUS, P., The entrapment defense, LexisNexis, New York, 2018.
MARIATTE, F., Taxe sur la valeur ajoutée et abus de droit, in Europe, 128, 2006, pp. 27-28.
MARSH, L., Leveson's narrow pursuit of justice: Efficiency and outcomes in the criminal process, in Common Law World Review, 46, 2015, pp. 51ss.
MARTIN, D., Comments on Förster (case C-158/07 of 18 November 2008), Metock and others (case C-127/08 of 25 July 2008) and Huber (case C-524/06 of 16 December 2008), in European Journal of Migration and Law, 11, 2009, pp. 95ss.
MARTIN, S., Lost and destroyed evidence: The search for a principled approach to abuse of process, in International Journal of Evidence and Proof, 9, 2005, pp. 158ss.
MARTUCCI, F., Droit de l'Union europèenne, LGDG, Paris, 2017.
MASON, K., The inherent jurisdiction of the Court, in Australian Law Journal, 57, 1983, pp. 449ss.
MATHIAS, D., Discretionary exclusion of evidence, in New Zealand Law Journal, 20, 1990, pp. 25ss.
MATTHEWS, A., The CAP and development in M. CARDWELL, J. MCMAHON (eds.), Research handbook on the Common

Agricultural Policy, Edward Elgar Publishers, Cheltenham, 2014.
MAUBLANC, J.P., Liberté d'établissement- Incompatibilité aves les traités communautaires de la taxation à la sortie par l'article 167 bis du CGI CJCE 11 mars 2004 no 9/02 de Lasteyrie du Saillant, in Revue du Marché Commun et de l'Union Européenne, 444, 2004, pp. 684ss.
MC KENDRICK, E., Force majeure and frustration of contract, ed. Routledge, London & New York, 2013.
MCCONVILLE, M., MARSH, L., Adversarialism goes west: Case management in criminal courts, in International Journal of Evidence and Proof, 19 (1), 2015, pp. 172ss.
MCEWAN, J., Vulnerable defendants and the fairness of trials, in Criminal Law Review, 2013, pp. 103ss.
MCEWAN, J., From adversarialism to managerialism: Criminal justice in transition, in Legal Studies, 31 (4), 2011, pp. 519ss.
MCKAY, S., Entrapment: Competing views on the effect of the Human Rights Act on english criminal law, in European Human Rights Law Review, 9 (4), 2002, pp. 764ss.
MCKENDRICK, E., Force majeure and frustation of contract, ed. Routledge, London & New York, 2013.
MCMAHON, K., Interoperability: "indispensability" and "special responsibility", in high technology markets, in Tulane Journal of Technology & Intellectual Property, 9, 2007.
MEISSE, E., Modalités d'inscription des avocats citoyens communautaires à un barreau d'un État membre, in Europe, 315, novembre 2006, pp. 20-21.
MENDOZ, M., The legal effects of European Union agreement, Oxford University Press, Oxford, 2013, pp. 130ss.
MEUSSEN, G.T.K., Cadbury Schweppes: The ECG significantly limits the application of CFC rules in the member States, in European Taxation, 47, 2007, pp. 13ss.
MEYER J., (ed.), Charta der Grundrechte der Europäischen Union, ed. Nomos, Baden-Baden, 2014, pp. 813-826.
MEYER-HEINE, A., Les apports de la nouvelle directive Television sans frontiéres du 30 juin 1997 entrée en viguer le 31 décember 1998, in Revue Trimestrielle du Droit Européen, 35, 1999, pp. 95ss.
MICHEL, V., Détermination du diplôme pertinent pour l'accès à la profession d'avocat, in Europe, février 2011, pp. 25ss.
MINDA, G., Interest groups, political freedom, and antitrust: A modern reassessment of the Noerr-Pennington doctrine, in Hastings Law Journal, 41, 1990, pp. 908ss.
MINGAM, C., DUVAL, A., L'abus de droit, ètat du droit positif, in Revue Juridique de l'Quest, 4, 1998, pp. 547ss.
MONAGHAN, N., Criminal law, Oxford University Press, Oxford, 2018, pp. 91ss.
MOORE, M.S., Act and crime: The philosophy of action and its implications for criminal law, Oxford University Press, Oxford, 2010, pp. 313ss.

MORANO-FOADI, S., NELLER, J., Fairhurst's law of the European Union, ed. Pearson, London, 2018.
MORANO-FOADI, S., VICKERS L., (eds.), Fundamental Rights in the EU-A matter for two Courts, Oxford University Press, Oxford, 2015.
MORISSETTE, Y.M., The exclusion of evidence under the Canadian Charter of Rights and Freedoms: What to do and what not to do, in McGill Law Journal, 30 (4), 1984, pp. 554ss.
MORRIS, R., European citizenship and the right to move freely: Internal situations, reverse discrimination and fundamental rights, in Maastricht Journal of European and Comparative Law, 18, 2011, pp. 179ss.
MORRISS, A.P., MOBERG, L., Cartelizing taxes: Understanding the OECD's campaign against harmful tax competition, in Columbia Journal of Tax Law, 4 (1), 2012, pp. 12ss.
MUIR, E., Statut et droits du demandeur d'emploi-travailleur-citoyen: confusion ou rationalisation?, in Revue du Droit de l'Union Européenne, 2004, p. 249ss.
MULCAHY, L., Putting the defendant in their place: Why do we still use the dock in criminal proceedings?, in British Journal of Criminology, 53 (6), 2013, pp. 1140ss.
MULLENIX, L.S., Discovery in disarray: The pervasive myth of pervasive discovery abuse and the consequences for unfounded rule making, in Stanford Law Review, 46, 1994, pp. 1393ss.
MURPHY, F., LIBERATORE, F., Abuse of regulatory procedures-the AstraZeneca case, in European Competition Law Review, 2009, pp. 322-323.
NARD, C.A., MADISON, M.J., MCKENNA, M.P., The law of intellectual property, Wolters Kluwer, New York, 2017.
NAZZINI, R., The foundations of European Union competition law: The objective and principles of article 102, Oxford University Press, Oxford, 2011.
NEUVONEN, P.J., In search of (even) more substance for the "real link" test: comment on Prinz and Seeberger, in European Law Review, 39, 2014, pp. 134ss.
NEVILLE BROWN, L., Is there a general principle of abuse of rights in European European Union law?, in D. CURTIN et al. (a cura di), Institutional dynamics of European integration: Essays in Honour of Henry G. Schermers, Martinus Nijhoff Publishers, Leiden, 1994, pp. 512ss.
NIC SCHUIBHNE, N., The coherence of European Union free movement law: Constitutional responsibility and the Court of Justice, Oxford University Press, Oxford, 2013, pp. 88ss.
NICOLA, F., DAVIES, B., European Union law stories, Cambridge University Press, Cambridge, 2017.
NIHOUL, P., The ruling of the General Court in intel: Towards the end of an effect-based approach in European competition law?, in Journal of European Competition Law & Practice, 5, 2014, pp. 52ss.
NOWAK, C., Europarecht nach Lissabon, ed. Nomos, Baden-Baden, 2011.
O'MEARA, N., A more secure Europe of rights? The European Court of

Human Rights, the Court of Justice of the European Union and EU Accession to the ECHR, in German Law Journal, 12, 2011, pp. 1813-1832.

O'SHEA, T., CFC reforms in the UK-Some EU law comments, in The EC Tax Journal, 13, 2012-2013, pp. 65ss.

O'BRIEN, C., Real links, abstract rights and false alarms: the relationship between the ECJ's real link case law and national solidarity, in European Law Review, 33, 2008, pp. 643ss.

O'DOHERTY, S., Entrapment: From mitigation to abuse, in Justice of the Peace, 2002, pp. 984ss.

O'DONOGHUE, R., PADILLA, J., The law and economics of article 102 TFEU, Hart Publishing, Oxford & Oregon, Portland, 2013.

O'SHEA, T., CFC Reforms in the UK-Some EU Law Comments, in EC Tax Journal, 13, 2012-2013, pp. 65ss.

O'SHEA, T., Marks and Spencer v. Halsey (HM Inspector of Taxes): Restriction, justification and proportionality, in EC Tax Review, 6, 2006, pp. 66ss.

O'SHEA, T., The UK's CFC rules and the freedom of establishment: Cadbury Schweppes plc and its IFSC subsidiaries-tax avoidance or tax mitigation?, in EC Tax Review, 7, 2007, pp. 13ss.

ÖBERG, J., Limits to European Union powers: A case study of European Union regulatory criminal law, Hart Publishing, Oxford & Oregon, Portland, 2017, pp. 124ss.

OLIVER, P., ROTH, W.H., The internal market and the four freedoms, in Common Market Law Review, 41 (4), 2004, pp. 407ss.

OLIVER, P.J., Oliver on Free Movement of Goods in the European Union, Hart Publishing, Oxford & Oregon, Portland, 2010, pp. 135ss.

OMAR, J.P., Centros, Überseering and beyond: A European recipe for corporate migration: Part 1, in International Company and Commercial Law Review, 15 (4), 2004, pp. 404ss.

OMAR, P., Centros, Überseering and beyond: A European recipe for corporate migration: Part 2, in International Company and Commercial Law Review, 13, 2005, pp. 23ss.

OMEROD, D., CYRIL SMITH, J., HOGAN, B., Smith and Hogan's criminal law, Oxford University Press, Oxford, 2011, pp. 400ss.

OPPERMANN, T., CLASSEN, C.D., NETTESHEIM, M., Europarecht, C.H. Beck, München, 2016.

ØSTERUD, E., Identifying exclusionary abuses by dominant undertakings under EU, Kluwer Law International, The Hague, 2010.

OWUSU-BEMPAH, A., Defendant participation in the criminal process, ed. Routledge, London, 2017.

OWUSU-BEMPAH, A., Judging the desirability of a defendant's evidence: An unfortunate approach to s.35(1)(b) of the criminal justice and public order act 1994, in Criminal Law Review, 2011, pp. 692ss.

OWUSU-BEMPAH, A., Silence in suspicious circumstances, in Criminal Law Review, 2014, pp. 128ss.

PACIOCCO, A., The stay of proceedings as a remedy in criminal cases: Abusing the abuse of process concept, in Criminal Law Journal, 15, 2001, pp. 315ss.

PAPADOPOULOU, R.E., Situations purement internes en droit communautaire: un instrument jurisprudentiel à double fonction ou une arme à double tranchant?, in Cahiers de Droit Europeén, 38 (1), 2002, pp. 95ss.

PATTENDEN, R., Pre-verdict judicial fact-finding in criminal trials with justice, in Oxford Journal of Legal Studies, 29 (1), 2009, pp. 6ss.

PATTENDEN, R., The power of the Courts to stay a criminal prosecution, in Criminal Law Review, 1985, pp. 175ss.

PATTERSON, D., SÖDERSTEN, A., A companion to European Union law and international law, ed. John Wiley & Sons, New York, 2016.

PECI, B., MORINA, F., The legal framework for harmonization of Value Added Tax (VAT) in European Union, in Acta Universitatis Danubius. Juridica, 13 (1), 2017.

PEERS S., et al. (eds.), The EU Charter of Fundamental Rights, A Commentary, Hart Publishing, Oxford & Oregon, Portland, 2014, pp. 1523-1538.

PEERS, S., The EU's Accession to the ECHR: The dream becomes a nightmare, in German Law Journal, 16, 2015, pp. 213, 222.

PEMSTEIN, M., The basis for Noerr-Pennington immunity: An argument that federal antitrust law, not the first amendment, defines the boundaries of Noerr-Pennington, in Thuergood Marshall Law Review, 40, 2014, pp. 80ss.

PENNINGS, F., SEELEIB-KAISER, M., European Union citizenship and social rights: Entitlements and impediments to accessing welfare, Edward Elgar Publishers, Cheltenham, 2018.

PETEVA, J., Abuse under EC tax law and the standard of review of the European Court of Justice, in M. LANG, P. MELZ, Value added tax and direct taxation: Similarities and Differences, IMFD, Amsterdam, 2009, pp. 498ss.

PETITE, M., The battle over Strasbourg: The protection of human rights across Europe has suffered a setback, thanks to the Court of Justice of the European Union, in Competition Law Insight, 2015, pp. 10ss.

PIANTAVIGNA, D., Tax abuse in European Union law: A theory, in EC Tax Review, 20, 2011, pp. 135.

PICERING, S., MCCULLOCH, J., Borders and crime. Pre-crime, mobility and serious harm in an age of globalization, ed. Springer, Berlin, 2012.

PICOD, F., La Cour de justice a dit non à l'adhésion de l'Union européenne à la Convention EDH, in La Semaine Juridique, Édition Générale, 2015, pp. 230, 234.

PITCHER, K., Judicial responses to pre-trial procedural violations in international criminal proceedings, ed. Springer, Berlin, 2017, pp. 260ss.

PLANIOL, M., Traité Élémentaire de Droit Civil-Tome II, LGDJ, Paris, 1939, par. 871.

POIARES MADURO, M., We the CJEU-The European Court of Justice and the European Economic Constitution, Hart Publishing, Oxford & Portland, Oregon, 1997, pp. 104ss.

POIARES MADURO, M., WIND, M., The transformation of Europe: Twenty-

five years on, Cambridge University Press, Cambridge, 2017, pp. 321ss.
POLAKIEWICZ, J., EU law and the ECHR: Will the European Union's accession square the circle?, in European Human Rights Law Review, 6, 2013, pp. 592-605.
POTTEAU, A., Quelle adhésion de l'Union Européenne à la CEDH pour quel niveau de protection des droits et de l'autonomie de l'ordre juridique de l'UE?, in Revue Générale Droit International Public, 115, 2011, pp. 77-111.
PUCHTA, F.G., Pandekten, Leipzig, 1838, par. 21.
QUIRK, H., The rise and fall of the right of silence. Principle, politics and policy, Taylor & Francis, New York, 2016.
RAINEY, B., WICKS, W., OVEY, C., Jacbos, White and Ovey: The European Convention on Human Rights, Oxford University Press, Oxford, 2017.
RAMMELOO, S., Cross-border company migration in the EU: transfer of registered office (conversion)-the last piece of the puzzle? Case C-106/16 Polbub, in Maastricht Journal of European and Comparative Law, 25 (1), 2018, pp. 89ss.
REESTMAN, J.H., No legal residence requirements for the admission of family members with a third-country nationality of migrated Union citizens, in European Constitutional Law Review, 3, 2007, pp. 463ss.
REICH, N., Competition between legal orders, in Common Market Law Review, 29, 1992, pp. 861ss.
RINGE, V.W.G., Corporate mobility in the European Union-a flash in the pan? An empirical study of the success of lawmaking and regulatory competition, in European Company and Financial Law Review, 10, 2013, pp. 230ss.
ROBERTS, P., Acquitted misconduct evidence and double jeopardy principles from Sambasivans to Z, in Criminal Law Review, 2000, pp. 954ss.
ROBERTS, P., Excluding evidence as protecting constitutional rights, in L. ZEDNER ROBERTS JV (eds.), Principles and values in criminal law and criminal justice. Essays in honour of Andrew Ashworts, Oxford University Press, Oxford, 2012, pp. 172ss.
ROBERTS, P., HUNTER, J., Criminal evidence and human rights. Reimagining common law procedural traditions, Hart Publishing, Oxford & Oregon, Portland, 2012, pp. 164ss.
ROBERTS, P., ZUCKERMAN, A., Criminal evidence, Oxford University Press, Oxford, 2010.
ROBINSON, G., Optimize European Union law, ed. Routledge, London & New York, 2014, pp. 137ss.
ROGERS, N., SCANNEL, R., ROBINSON, W., Free movement of persons in the enlarged European Union, Sweet & Maxwell, London, 2012, pp. 190ss.
ROGERS, N., SCANNELL, R., WALSH, J., Free movement of persons in the enlarged European Union, Sweet & Maxwell, London, 2012.
RONFELDT, T., WERLAUFF, E., Cfc rules go up in smoke-With retroactive effect, in Intertax, 2007, pp. 45ss.
ROSAS, A., ARMATI, L., European Union constitutional law. An introduction, Hart Publishing, Oxford & Oregon, Portland, 2018.

ROTH, W.H., Case C-19/92, Dieter Kraus v. Land Baden-Württemberg, Judgement of 31 March 1993, in Common Market Law Review, 30, 1993, pp. 1251ss.

ROTH, W.H., From Centros to Überseering: Free movement of companies, private international law, and European Union law, in International and Comparative Law Quarterly, 52, 2003, pp. 177-178.

ROUSSELLE, O., LIEBMAN, H.M., The doctrine of the abuse of European Union law: The sword of damocles hanging over the Head of EC corporate tax law?, in European Taxation, 46, 2006, pp. 559ss.

ROUSSEVA, E., Rethinking exclusionary abuses in EU competition law, Hart Publishing, Oxford & Oregon, Portland, 2010.

SAFFIAN, M., DÜSTERHAU, AD., Union of effective judicial protection: Addressing a multi-level challenge through the lens of article 47 CFREU, in Yearbook of European Law, 33 (1), 2014, pp. 3ss.

ŞAHIN, E., Collective redress and European Union competition law, ed. Routledge, London & New York, 2018.

SALEILLES, R., Etude sur la théorie générale de l'obligation dans la second rédaction du projet de code civil allemand, Paris, 1895.

SÁNCHEZ, S.I., The Court and the Charter: The impact of the entry into force of the Lisbon Treaty on the ECJ's approach to fundamental Right, in Common Market Law Review, 49 (5), 2012, pp. 1566ss.

SANDERS, A., YOUNG, R., BURTON, M., Criminal justice, Oxford University Press, Oxford, 2010.

SAVIGNY, F.C., System des heutigen Römischen Rechts (new edition of the Berlin Deit, 1840-1856), Aalen, Berlin, 1981, pp. 331ss.

SAYDÉ, A., Abuse of EU law and regulation of the internal market, Oxford University Press, Oxford, 2014.

SAYDÉ, A., Abuses of European law, regulatory mobility and the law of the internal market, CELS paper, 2011, pp. 2ss,

SAYDÉ, A., Defining the concept of abuse of Union law, in Yearbook of European Law, 33, 2014, pp. 149ss.

SAYDÉ, S., One law, two competitions: An enquiry into the contradictions of free movement law, in Cambridge Yearbook of European Legal Studies, 2010-2011, pp. 395ss.

SCHABAS, W.A., The European Convention on Human Rights: A commentary, Oxford University Press, Oxford, 2015, pp. 1755ss.

SCHAMMO, P., Arbitrage and abuse of rights in the EC legal system, in European Law Journal, 14, 2008, pp. 352ss.

SCHMIDT-KESSEL, M., Rechtsmissbrauch im Gemeinschaftsprivatrecht. Folgerungen aus den Rechtssachen Kefalas und Diamantis, in Prinzipien des Privatrechts und Rechtsvereinheitlichung, Jahrbuch Junger Zivilrechtswissenschaftler, 2000, pp. 75ss.

SCHNEIDER, A.L., The right to a speedy trial, in Stanford Law Review, 20, 1968, pp. 499ss.

SCHNEIDER, C.E., Discretion and rules: A lawyer's view, in K. HAWKINS (ed.), The uses of discretion, Oxford University Press, Oxford, 1992.

SCHÖN, W., Abuse of rights and European tax law, in J.A. JONES, P. HARRIS, D. OLIVER (a cura di) Comparative perspectives on revenue law-Essays in honour of John Tiley, Cambridge University Press, Cambridge, 2008, pp. 78ss.

SCHON, W., CFC legislations and European European Union law, in the British Tax Review, 51, 2001, pp. 250ss.

SCHÜTZE, R., TRIDIMAS, T., Oxford principles of European Union Law, Oxford University Press, Oxford, 2018.

SCHWARZE, J., BECKER, U., HATJE, A., SCHOO, J., EU-Kommentar, ed. Nomos, Baden Baden, 2019.

SEIBERT-FOHR, A., VILLIGER, M.E., Judgments of the European Convention of Human Rights. Effects and implementation, ed. Nomos, Baden-Baden, 2017.

SENATOR, S.N., SERGI, G.M., Noerr-Pennington: Safeguarding the first amendment right to petition the government, in Competition Journal of Antitrust & Unfair Competition Law, 23, 2014, pp. 86ss.

SHUIBHNE, N., Free movement of persons and the wholly internal rule; time to move on?, in Common Market Law Review, 39 (4), 2002, pp. 731ss.

SHUIBHNE, N.N., The coherence of EU free movement law, constitutional responsibility and the Court of Justice, Oxford University Press, Oxford 2013, pp. 85ss.

SIEMS, M., Convergence, competition, Centros and conflicts of law: European company law in the 21st century, in European Law Review, 27, 2002, pp. 47ss.

SIMESTER, A.P., SPENCER, J.R., SULLIVAN, G.R., Simester and Sullivan's criminal law: Theory and doctrine, Hart Publishing, Oxford & Oregon, Portland, 2014.

SIMON, D., RIGAUX, A., La technique de la consécration d'un nouveau principe général du droit communautaire: l'exemple de l'abus de droit, in M. BLANQUET (a cura di) Mélanges en hommage à Guy Isaac: 50 ans de droit communautaire, Presse de l'università de Toulouse, Toulouse, 2004, pp. 560ss.

SIMPSONS, P., Cadbury Schweppes Plc v. Commissioners of Ireland Revenue: the ECJ sets strict test for CFC legislation, in British Tax Review, 56, 2006, pp. 678ss.

SINE, S., A practice approach to civil procedure, Oxford University Press, Oxford, 2016.

SINGH, C., RAMJOHN, M., Unlocking evidence, ed. Routledge, London & New York, 2016.

SLOAN, B., Keeping up with the Jones case: Establishing constructive trusts in "sole legal owner" scenarios, in Legal Studies, 35 (2), 2015, pp. 228ss.

SMITH, K.A., Psychology fact-finding and entrapment, in Michigan Law Review, 103, 2005, pp. 760ss.

SMITH, L.J., Postgraduate degrees, vocational training and reverse discrimination: the narrow divide, in European Law Review, 19, 1994, pp. 67ss.

SMITH, V., Lost, altered or destroyed evidence, in Justice of the Peace, 2007, pp. 556ss.

SNELL, J., And then there were two: Products and citizens in European Union law, in T. TRIDIMAS, P. NEBBIA (a cura di), European Union Law for the twenty-first century, vol. II, Oxford University Press, Oxford, 2004, pp. 62ss.
SØRENSEN, K., Abuse of rights in European Union law: A principle of substance or merely rhetoric?, in Common Market Law Review, 43, 2006, pp. 423ss.
SØRENSEN, V.K., The fight against letterbox companies in the internal market, in Common Market Law Review, 52, 2015, pp. 94ss.
SPAVENTA, E., A very fearful Court? The protection of fundamental rights in the European Union after Opinion 2/13, in Maastricht Journal of European and Comparative Law, 22, 2015, pp. 51ss.
SPAVENTA, E., Family rights for circular migrants and frontier workers: O and B, and S and G, in the Common Market Law Review, 52, 2015, pp. 763, 776ss.
SPENCER, J.R., Evidence of bad character, Bloomsburry, New York, 2016.
SPENCER, M., Concentrate questions and answers evidence, Oxford University Press, Oxford, 2016.
SPRACK, J., A practical approach to criminal procedure, Oxford University Press, Oxford, 2011.
STERN, K., SACHS, M., Europäische Grundrecht Charta, ed. C.H. Beck, München, 2016, pp. 756ss.
STOREY, T., LIDBURY, A., Criminal law, ed. Routledge, London & New York, 2012.
STOREY, T., PIMOR, A., Unlocking European Union law, ed. Routledge, London & New York, 2018, pp. 296ss.
STRAEMANS, G., GOEMANS, C., TV10, in Columbia Journal of European Law, 2, 1995, pp. 319ss.
SUN, J.M., PELKMANS, J., Regulatory competition in the single market, in Journal of Common Market Studies, 33, 1995, pp. 67ss.
SUNSTEIN, C.R., Problems with rules, in California Law Review, 83, 1995, pp. 953ss.
SYRPIS, P., NIC SHVIBHNE, N., SYRPIS, P., Exceptions from European Union free movement law: Derogation, justification and proportionality, Hart Publishing, Oxford & Oregon, Portland, 2016.
SZABADOS, T., National courts in the frontline. Abuse of rights under the citizens rights directive, in Utrecht Journal of International and European Law, 33, 2017, pp. 89ss.
TAPPER, C., Cross & Tapper on evidence, Oxford University Press, Oxford, 2010.
TARUFFO M., (a cura di), Abuse of procedural rights: Comparative standards of procedural fairness, Kluwer, London, Boston, 1999.
TARUFFO, M., General report, in A.A.V.V., Abuse of procedural right: Comparative standards of procedural fairness, Kluwer Law International, Hague-Boston-London, 1999, pp. 23ss.
TEITGEN-COLLY, C., La Convention europèenne des droits de l'homme: 60 ans et après?, ed. LGDJ, Paris, 2013.
TER HAAR, R., LANEY, A., LEVINE, M., Construction insurance and UK

construction contracts, ed. Routledge, London & New York, 2016.
THIES, A., International trade disputes and European Union liability, Cambridge University press, Cambridge, 2013.
THORSON, B., Individual rights in European Union law, ed. Springer, Berlin, 2016, pp. 22ss.
THYM, D., When Union citizens turn into illegal migrants: The Dano case, in European Law Review, 2015, pp. 535ss.
TIETJE, C., The status of international in the European legal order: the case of international Treaties and non-binding international instrument, in J. TILLOTSON, J., FOSTER, N., Text, cases and materials on European Union law, Cavedish Publishing, New York, 2013.
TIMMERMANS, F., Fundamental rights protection in Europe before and after accession of the European Union to the European Convention on Human Rights, in Liber amicorum Pieter Van Dijk, M. Van Roosmalen and others (eds.), Intersentia, Antwerp, Oxford, 2013, pp. 225ss.
TOMLJENOVIĆ, V., BODIROG-VUKOBRAT, N., BUTORAC MALNAR, V., European Union competition and State aid rules: Public and private enforcement, ed. Springer, Berlin, 2017.
TORRES PEREZ, A., Too many voices? The prior involvement of the Court of Justice of the European Union? in European Journal of Human Rights, 40, 2013, pp. 565-583.
TRAVERS, N., The right of establishment of companies which are economically inactive in their member State of registration, in Commercial Law Practitioner, June 1999, pp. 162ss.
TRIANTAFYLLOU, D., L'interdiction des abus de droit en tant que principe général du droit communautaire, in Cahiers de Droit Européen, 38, 2002 pp. 612ss.
TRIDIMAS, T., Fundamental rights, general principles of EU law and the Charter, in Cambridge Yearbook of European Legal Studies, 16 (3), 2014, pp. 364ss.
TRYFONIDOU, A., Case C-200/02, Kunqian Catherine Zhu, Man Lavette Chen v. Secretary of State for the Home Department: futher cracks in the 'great wall' of the European Union?, in European Public Law, 11 (4), 2005, pp. 528ss.
TRYFONIDOU, A., Further steps on the road to convergence among the market freedoms, in European Law Review, 16, 2010, pp. 36ss.
TRYFONIDOU, A., Jia or "Carpenter II": the edge of reason, in European Law Review, 32, 2007 pp. 909ss.
TÜRK, A.H., Judicial review in European Union law, Edward Elgar Publishers, Cheltenham, 2010.
USHERWOOD, J., PINDER, S., The European Union. A very short introduction, Oxford University Press, Oxford, 2018.
VALDESALICI, A., PALERMO, F., Comparing fiscal federalism, ed. Brill, The Hague, 2018.
VAN DER WALT, J., The horizontal effect revolution and the question of sovereignthy, De Gruyter, Hamburg, 2014.
VAN DROOGHENBROECK, S., La proportionnalité dans le droit de la Convention européenne des droits

de l'homme, Facultè St Louis, 2001, pp. 396ss.
VAN DROOGHENBROECK, S., Le droit international et europèen des droits de l'homme devant le juge national, ed. Larcier, Bruxelles, 2014.
VAN ELSUWEGE, P., Shifting the Boundaries? European Union Citizenship and the Scope of Application of EU Law-Case No. C-34/09, Gerardo Ruiz Zambrano v. Office national de l'emploi, in Legal Issues of Economic Integration, 38, 2011, pp. 263ss.
VANISTENDAEL, F., Halifax and Cadbury Schweppes: One single European theory of abuse in tax law?, in EC Tax Review, 15, 2006, pp. 193ss.
VERLOREN VAN THEMAAT, W., REUDER, B., European competition law: A case commentary, Edward Elgar Publishers, Cheltenham, 2018.
VERSCHUEREN, H., Free Movement or Benefit Tourism: the Unreasonable Burden of Brey, in European Journal of Migration and Law, 2014, pp. 147ss.
VERSCHUEREN, H., Preventing "benefit tourism" in the EU: A narrow or broad interpretation of the possibilities offered by the ECJ in Dano?, inVINTHER, N., WERLAUFF, E., Tax motives are legal motives-The borderline between the use and abuse of the freedom of establishment with reference to the Cadbury Schweppes Case, in European Taxation, 6, 2006, pp. 385ss.
VINTHER, N., WERLAUFF, E., Tax motives are legal motives, in the European Taxation, 46, 2006, pp. 385ss.
VINTHER, N., WERLAUFF, E., The need for fresh thinking about tax rules on thin capitalization: the consequences of the judgment of the ECJ in Lankhorst- Hohorst, in EC Tax Review, 3, 2003, pp. 97ss.
VOGENAUER, S., The prohibition of abuse of law: An emerging general principle of EU law, in R. DE LA FERIA, S. VOGENAUER (eds), Prohibition of abuse of law. A new general principle of EU law?, Oxford University Press, Oxford 2011, pp. 520ss.
VON BOGDANDY, A., IOANNIDIS, M., Systemic deficiency in the rule of law: What is this, what has been done, what can we done, in Common Market Law Review, 51, 2014, pp. 64ss.
VON DER GROEBEN, H., SCHWARZE, J., HATJE, A., Europäisches Unionsrecht, ed. Nomos, Baden-Baden, 2015, pp. 820ss.
VRELLIS, S., Abus et fraude dans la jurisprudence de la Cour de Justice des Communautés Européennes, in H. GAUDEMET-TALLON, J.P. LANCET (a cura di), Vers de nouveaux equilibres entre ordres juridiques: Liber Amicorum H. Gaudemet-Tallon, ed. Dalloz, Paris, 2008, pp. 634ss.
WAELBROECK, D., La notion d'abus de droit dans l'ordre juridique communautaire, in Mélanges en hommages à J.V. Louis, ed. Bruylant, Bruxelles, 2003, vol. I, p. 595 ss.
WARD, D., The European Union and the culture industries. Regulation and the public interest, ed. Routledge, London & New York, 2016.
WARD, P.C., Federal Trade Commission. Law, practice and procedure, Law Journal Press, New York, 2018.

WATTEL, P., Case C-23/93, TV10 SA v. Commissariaat voor de Media, Judgement of 5 October 1994; Circumvention of national law; Abuse of European Union law?, in Common Market Law Review, 32, 1995, pp. 1257ss.

WEATHERILL, S., Law and values in the European Union, Oxford University Press, Oxford, 2016.

WELCH, H., Criminal procedure and sentencing, ed. Routledge, London & New York, 2014.

WELLER, M., Mutual trust in search of the future of European Union private international law, in Journal of Private International Law, 11 (1), 2015, pp. 66ss.

WESSEL, R.A., ŁAZOWSKI, A., When Caveats Turn into Locks: Opinion 2/13 on Accession of the European Union to the ECHR, in German Law Journal, 16, 2015, pp. 179ss.

WHISH, R., BAILEY, D., Competition law, Oxford University Press, Oxford, 2015.

WIERZBOWSKI, M., GUBRYNOWICZ, A., International investment law for the 21st century, Oxford University Press, Oxford, 2015.

WILLIS, P., Introduction to EU competition law, CRC Press, New York, 2013.

WILMAN, F., Private enforcement of European Union law before national courts. The European Union legislative framework, Edward Elgar Publishers, Cheltenham, 2015.

WINFIELD, P.H., The history of conspiracy and abuse of legal procedure, Cambridge University Press, Cambridge, 1921.

WINTGENS, L.G., Legisprudence: Practical reason in legislation, Ashgate Publishing, London, 2013, pp. 341ss.

WISHMEYER, T., Generating trust through law? Judicial cooperation in the European Union and the "principle of mutual trust", in German Law Journal, 17, 2016, pp. 342ss.

WOODS, L., WATSON, P., COSTA, M., Steiner & Woods European Union law, Oxford University Press, Oxford, 2017, pp. 494ss.

WOUTERS, A. NOLLKAEMPER, E. DE WET (eds.), The Europeanization of international law: The status of international law in the EU and its member States, Cambridge University Press, Cambridge, 2008.

WYMEERSCH, E., Centros: A landmark decision in European company law, in T. BAUMS, K.J. HOPT, N. HORN (a cura di), Corporations, capital markets and business in the law. Liber Amicorum Richard M. Buxbaum, Wolters Kluwer, London, 2000, pp. 629ss.

XENOS D., (ed.), The positive obligations of the State under the European Convention on Human Rights, ed. Routledge, London & New York, 2012.

YOUNG, D., SUMMERS QC, M., CORKER, D., Abuse of process in criminal proceedings, ed. Bloomsbury, New York, 2014, pp. 2ss.

ZALASINSKI, A., Some basic aspects of the concept of abuse in the tax case law of the European CJEU of Justice, in Intertax, 2008, pp. 160ss.

ZAND, J., The concept of democracy and the European Convention on Human Rights, in University of Baltimore

Journal of International Law, 5 (2) 2017.
ZIEGLER, K.S., WIKS, E., HODSON, L., The UK and European human rights. A strained relationship, Hart Publishing, Oxford & Oregon, Portland, 2015.
ZILINSKY, M., Mutual trust and cross-border enforcement of judgments in civil matters in the European Union. Does the step-by-step approach work?, in Netherlands International Law Review, 64 (1), 2017, pp. 117ss.
ZRVANDYAN, A., Casebook on European fair trial standards in administrative justice, Council of Europe, Strasbourg, 2016, pp. 108ss.
ZUCKERMAN, A.A.S., Illegally-obtained-evidence-discretion as a guardian of legitimacy, in Current Legal Problems, 40, 1987, pp. 59ss.

9 781600 423086

Printed at Repro India Ltd.